■ THE POLITICAL ORDER

THE
POLITICAL
ORDER

A Reader in Political Science

Edited by
HENRY S. KARIEL

Basic Books, Inc., Publishers · *New York* · *London*

Library of Congress Catalog Card Number: 70–94298

SBN 465–05933–3

Manufactured in the United States of America

Designed by Sophie Adler

For Rachel, who would expect no less

■ PREFACE

Those who find themselves enrolled in introductory courses in political science are generally aware of having but one problem: how to negotiate the introductory course successfully. The student's immediate job, it would seem, is to pass the course, somehow to get over it. The course hardly presents him with a *political* problem. After all, there are no authentic choices to be made; there is no need for active participation. And although the course will surely acquaint him with political problems—about choices men must make—he will not necessarily perceive them to be his. On the whole, society has already given him a fairly clear image of his practical options. He more or less knows how to respond to the major demands society will make on him. That is, he will serve his country in time of crisis, pay his taxes, even vote. Or, failing to respond, he will emerge as "alienated" in the accounts of social scientists. What he is aware of is a political order as it in fact impinges on him, not as it ideally might be, not as it may be brought into being.

This volume seeks to compel the student to acknowledge that the dimensions of the political realm may be larger than he suspects. Throughout, it is assumed that the devices men have adopted for ordering their common lives are far from final, not being secured by nature, God, tradition, or history. None of our institutions can be regarded as fully developed; none of our ideologies, organizations, and methods of study are quite adequate. More than that, all are designed (and can be redesigned) by men to serve their needs—above all, the need to promote political growth. In other words, this volume assumes that we can conceive of new political possibilities and, by making greater demands on our political environment, remain a developing community.

The material assembled here, in sum, is expected to open up political possibilities, to present practical and theoretical alternatives revealing the amplitude of political space that is still open for maneuver, and to enlarge

vii

the analytical power of prospective citizens. It is to help them become self-directed, self-conscious actors.

This book aims at these objectives by providing a conception of politics as the pre-eminent activity for reconciling conflicting interests and allocating scarce goods—in particular the goods inherent in personal political participation. This explicitly postulated ideal should serve to make us sensitive to the actual qualities of our political environment. Insofar as we shall then be disturbed by what we perceive—namely, the tension between experienced reality and stipulated ideal—we may feel impelled to learn how man has attempted to civilize power by constructing ideological and political systems. We may furthermore feel moved to consider how the discipline of political science helps order and illuminate reality, how the different methods used by political scientists necessarily focus on different aspects of political life. It should thus become clear that the conceptual system one decides to employ determines which facts one will perceive.

The point of the behavioral sciences, we should learn, is not only to make some pre-existing truth known but also to involve social scientists in a common activity. This activity consists of creatively hypothesizing, experimenting when possible, and finally noting why some order of facts emerges as telling, some set of statistics as striking, or some form of behavior as deviant. Experiments, conducted to put reality to the test, are thus understood as an inseparable part of the very "truth" discovered, their designers *imposing* meaning on reality. It should ultimately become apparent how experimental designs establish the very structure of facts, developing an order in society which society may not actually possess. As scientific truth is thus seen to develop, the facts of political life can be recognized as pliable—as anything but cold and hard, although they may remain stubborn.

It should accordingly become evident that to grasp the facts to which our conceptual systems refer, it is not enough to remain contemplative and absorb the available body of knowledge (as most textbooks still imply); it becomes essential to enlarge one's understanding as well as one's arena of action by making the polity respond to postulated models.

In view of this orientation, the point of an introductory course cannot be to "cover a subject," "fill a gap," "provide background," or "survey an area." It must be—as the following selections argue by implication—to free the student of political life to welcome alternative analytical models, ultimately to encourage him in the design of new ones in the light of which his political world may be given new significance and dignity—not by having him accept "the facts," but by having him act on them from a variety of angles with a variety of strategies. The course, in other words, must provide a basis enabling him to expose the received systems as dated, to create new relationships, and thereby to appropriate more of our political life for himself.

The very structure of this volume is designed to induce students to become critical of whatever ideologies, institutions, and methods of study have become established. Observing these established orthodoxies critically from the outside, we cannot help but become somewhat detached from them.

This detachment alone should suffice to make us aware of the man-made (and hence necessarily limited) character of present political life and its rationalizations. It should make obvious that no definitive solutions are to be found in politics; that, indeed, all we can finally agree on is keeping the procedures for discourse and discovery open.

What remains *durably* relevant for mature citizens, it should become apparent, is not matters of substance but matters of form, not the right answers but the array of methods—parliamentary, discursive, dialectical, scientific—for framing provisional answers. In the end, we should have learned that style is the substance of politics.

To be sure, it may be hard for us to accept this if we in fact care deeply about the triumph of specific policies, having a commitment not to procedures but to results whether the result is the college degree or enacted legislation. Yet it is becoming increasingly possible, as this volume may help testify, to embrace an approach to public affairs that makes political science significantly analogous to the kind of serious play no longer heretical in other academic disciplines, in math no less than art. It thus follows the lead of science courses less concerned with the student's knowledge of rock strata, organisms, or molecules than with his understanding of the way scientists do science. Similarly, it imitates literature courses that acquaint students with styles and modes of writing by ignoring the "messages" of poets and novelists or by assigning only works that have no messages.

Introducing the reader to diverse styles for making sense of one's life, the course laid out by this volume will not *directly* introduce him to the operations of government and the obligations of citizenship. It should, however, impel him to become a self-conscious role player—or at least vicariously to appreciate the combination of detachment and concern which has enabled others to play their roles.

While the stress on form will generate a skepticism toward conclusions, we are hardly without a criterion for judgment: we may well proceed to test how closely diverse ideologies, institutions, and research orientation conform to an ideal political reality by inquiring how much of public life they enable him to manage. In possession of such a criterion, we are induced to recognize the existence of problems: we shall be bound to perceive that the prevailing ideas, institutions, and methodologies, whatever these may be, are conceivably less than perfect.

The approach adopted by this volume may not yet reflect the mood of the present generation of undergraduates. Yet to the extent that teaching can be oriented by (1) a commitment to an ideal political order, (2) skepticism toward all conclusions, and (3) the treatment of form as substance, we may be able to advance what is literally self-government: the mastery of one's own various interest. This orientation should make it possible to assess our political environment. Though an "ideal," it constitutes no predefined order of things: only a commitment to procedures which keep the future open, which enable us to design and redesign the world of politics.

The problem for the instructor of the introductory course is by no means diminished by the orientation here supported. He no longer is free simply "to teach." True, he may still have to amplify, illustrate, and clarify connections. But more fundamentally, he will have to reject the distinction between teaching and research, converting the classroom into a stage on which to dramatize the research process, exposing his own preoccupations in their inconclusive form. He will have to regard the findings resulting from research as properly stored in teaching machines, as belonging in libraries—in encyclopedias, on tape, microfilms, IBM cards. His major problem may well become psychological, for he will have to pursue his professional interests in the open, revealing his false starts, his trials, and his defeats, becoming involved with students who, at least in some establishments, have already conceded that their education suffers from the rigidities entailed by a system of annually repeated lectures, preset class hours, and letter grading.

Such blending of teaching and research is not without risk. It may undermine confidence in both the instructor and the research process. Furthermore, role playing and cynicism are easily confused. Finally, a concern for form may breed a snobbish contempt for substance—the gritty, awesome problems which give rise to political life. Still, it may be possible to bear these risks, especially if students are permitted to learn that one of the results of research is the personal satisfaction derived from participating in an ongoing process. So far the only places such participation is openly supported are in art, math, sport, drama, and wherever the focus is on doing rather than appreciating. Nevertheless, the instructor of political science should find it increasingly possible to engage in his inconclusive quest in plain view of others. This volume should help to sustain him and his academic discipline, as well as his students.

Among the many who permitted themselves to be drawn into designing the approach to politics represented by this book of readings, I should like to mention especially Theodore L. Becker, Richard McCleery, Michael J. Shapiro, Anne Feraru, and Norman Meller. They have criticized and troubled me, thus putting me in their debt. As research assistants, Sheila Kato and Eleanore Chong added a dimension to my work even while lightening it. Three groups of students energetically put both the following material and its editor to the test; I am no less grateful to them.

H.S.K.

Honolulu, Hawaii
November, 1969

■ CONTENTS

PROLOGUE

    1   Collage Theater   *Richard Schechner*   **3**

PART ONE   **The Norm of Politics**

    INTRODUCTION   **5**

    2   The City and Its Citizens   *Norton E. Long*   **8**

    3   The Pleasures of Politics   *Hannah Arendt*   **12**

    4   Political Man   *Harold D. Lasswell*   **15**

PART TWO   **Challenges to Politics**

    INTRODUCTION   **25**

The Problems of Democracy

    5   Mass Democracy   *E. H. Carr*   **28**

    6   The Overdeveloped Society   *C. Wright Mills*   **34**

The Predicaments of Industrial Society

    7   The Omnivorous Organization   *Nathan Glazer*   **37**

    8   The Troubled Metropolis   *John W. Dyckman*   **40**

    9   The Derangement of Human Relations   *Glenn E. Tinder*   **52**

10 The Gross National Product Per Capita—1950–1975
    Bruce M. Russett et al.   57

11 The Imbalance of Wealth   *Barbara Ward*   58

International Disorganization

12 The Spotted Reality   *Kenneth E. Boulding*   59

13 The Precariousness of Politics in the New States
    Rupert Emerson   68

14 The Problems of Abundance   *Robert C. Wood*   73

15 The Pathological State of the International System
    Kenneth E. Boulding   78

PART THREE   **The Ideological Response**

INTRODUCTION   85

16 Nationalism   *Maurice Barrès*   89

17 Communism   *Karl Marx, Friedrich Engels,*
    V. I. Lenin, Mao Tse-tung   92

18 Corporatism   *John K. Jessup*   119

19 Democratic Socialism   *Lewis Coser and Irving Howe*   122

20 Black Power   *Stokely Carmichael*   136

21 Participatory Democracy   *Richard Flacks*   144

PART FOUR   **The American Response**

INTRODUCTION   151

The Governors

22 The Structure of Power in American Society
    C. Wright Mills   155

23 Oligarchical Rule   *David B. Truman*   166

The Governed

24 The Governed Constituents   *Henry S. Kariel*   171

25 Power over Interests   *Robert Paul Wolff*   184

26 The Limits of the Political System
    E. E. Schattschneider   190

27 The Dispossessed   *Daniel Bell*   200

Public Government

28 The National Parties   *Stephen K. Bailey*   204

29 The Congressional Check   *Ronald Steel*   214

30 The Presidency   *Richard E. Neustadt*   221

31 Administration as Politics   *V. O. Key, Jr.*   235

32 The Government Commission   *Daniel Bell*   244

33 The Supreme Court in the System of Alliances
    Robert A. Dahl   247

34 State Government and Private Power
    Grant McConnell   256

35 The Governmental Response to Urbanization
    Scott Greer   271

36 Power, Politics, and Policy Making   *Roger Hilsman* 296

The Public-Private Complex

37 The New Feudalism   *Hans J. Morgenthau*   317

38 The Marbled Mixture   *Michael D. Reagan*   327

39 The Contract State   *H. L. Nieburg*   339

PART FIVE   The Response of Political Science

INTRODUCTION   353

40 Games of Scholarship   *James N. Rosenau*   356

41 Traditionalism as Guide to Knowledge
    Richard B. Wilson   359

42 The Prevailing Paradigm   *Gabriel A. Almond*   362

43 Political Science as Science   *Arthur S. Goldberg* 366

44 The Historical Imagination   *C. Wright Mills*   380

EPILOGUE

45 Children Playing   *Learned Hand*   385

FOR FURTHER STUDY   387

INDEX   391

■ THE POLITICAL ORDER

■ PROLOGUE

1 COLLAGE THEATER

■ *Richard Schechner*

... Cage, that Johnny Appleseed of the arts, first planted the idea of multifocus and collage theater in my head. ... The idea did not start then; it was everywhere: in Happenings, Events, and Activities, in music and dance, in Op Art—all mixtures of camp and virility, fad and authentic impulse. The "static arts" were beginning to exist actively in time; and as they were becoming theatricalized, theater was sure to reciprocate. ...

I was standing in an intersection, and the conflicting traffic was everywhere, and yet my art was going nowhere. And I thought of "radical" in its original, literal sense: what was the "root" of theater and how could I (at least theoretically) redirect it? The roots of theater are the audience and the play. Everything else—actors, directors, stage—serves these two things. If theater was to be changed, the audience and the plays would have to be altered. But change meant more than simply getting new audiences and new plays which, after all, would be very much like the old. And since people do not change (light-footed biology is slow-moving), the task was to make people use faculties they do not now use in theatergoing: a perceptual re-education. As for plays, they had to be thought of as something other than they had been. But before that "other" could emerge, the theater literature that was there had to be removed. The great classics no longer refreshed me; instead they were formidable obstacles. ...

One changes the audience's perception by removing that central focus which has had their attention from the beginning. No seats, no single action,

Used by permission of the author.

3

no inert buildings, no attempt to direct their eyes and ears. Leave the work of selection and focus to them. Shock them not by offering cruel, singular images, but by sending such a multiplicity of visual and aural messages that the basic experience-structuring is forced on them. Go beyond medieval and circus theater. Duplicate the number and approximate the kind of messages sent on Piccadilly at rush hour. Analyze and disintegrate sight and sound somewhat as the first cubists did to two-dimensional vision. Destroy theater's melody line which is the story; but do it more effectively than Ionesco ever did in his "planned chaos" of *The Bald Prima Donna.* Make it all not a sentimental cry against a complex world, but a celebration of the world's complexity.

For example. Take a large, nearly square room. Examine its architecture and plan whatever follows in relation to it. Choose a room that even when empty is visually interesting. Bring a crowd in. Begin in one corner to play a scene from *Hamlet.* The people press close to see and hear. When their attention is focused, play Beethoven's Seventh Symphony over fifteen or twenty loud-speakers: *Hamlet* becomes pantomime, though the actors are still speaking. Then, somewhere else in the room, do a scene from *The Importance of Being Earnest.* In comes the chorus from *The Oresteia,* usurping space for its chants and dances. Moving among audience and performers are several jugglers. Overhead, projected on large screens, are movies of this very scene as it occurred the night before, or the week before: a canopy which is a mirror. The sounds and sights modulate, increase in tempo, vary in intensity; spatial figurations also change—performances impinge upon each other and the spectators. The spectators impinge back. We make a classic collage—we treat the old texts as material, not as model. And we introduce into the interior of the building some approximation of the busyness that fills the outside.

This classic collage is, of course, only one example. There could be modern collages or mixtures. Performances would be unstructured or structured, but always the individual spectator would be asked to choose his own perspective, assemble his own images. Shows would be rehearsed (for there is a difference between an unstructured performance and happenstance). When we have destroyed the silly awe which a literary culture attaches to its books, we could again begin to make plays.

What they would be like I have no idea. But the destructive process itself, like abstract expressionism in painting, would be a most constructive phase in theater history.

PART ONE

■ THE NORM
OF POLITICS

INTRODUCTION

A speech, a labor contract, a sewage disposal system, an athletic association, even a murder—all these emerge in a different light the moment they are regarded as political. Simple at first, they suddenly appear complex. They do not quite mean what they appear to mean. The speaker giving a "political" speech does not simply say what is on his mind. He controls himself and equivocates. He seems to be less than fully committed, and, seeking to engage everyone in his mixed audience, he hedges. His remarks, designed to appeal to men who hold different views, are open to alternative interpretations.

To those who have some clearly defined objective about which the politician remains vague, he will appear to be not flexible and accommodating but spineless and unprincipled. We who are committed to some cause of our own become suspicious of him. His implying that there is at least one other side disconcerts us. Because his ambiguous language impels us to become aware of the views of others, we resent his complicating our lives.

He makes us uneasy insofar as he displays his capacity for entertaining what are in the final analysis contradictory and irreconcilable interests. After all, he succeeds (as we rarely do) in giving expression to a mixture of possibilities, never letting any one of them triumph over the others. He manages (unlike us) to keep a host of diverse interests in mind, to remain sensitive to disparate concerns. His sympathy (unlike ours) is not with any one cause, but with a whole number of causes. Clearly, he personifies an ideal; for who would *not* wish to enrich his life by entertaining all kinds of causes and by coming to terms with all manner of true believers? Yet at the same time he makes us uncomfortable: his very posture reminds us of our shortcomings; that is, of our reluctance to probe alternatives, to welcome an ever widening

5

range of interests and thereby promote our personal development. In short, the authentic political man makes us resentful even while he embodies an ideal we share.

What, specifically, is the nature of this ideal? What, ideally, is *political* man? What is a *political* act? What is a *political* community?

To respond to these questions is to formulate a normative conception of political life, one which should enable us to take account of our common achievements and specify to what degree we are politically developed. Such a conception of politics should constitute a criterion for assessing competing ideologies, competing governmental institutions, and competing analytical designs elucidating the political world.

The chapters which follow are selected to provide a clearer understanding of the ideal of politics, not as struggle for power, not as goal-oriented behavior, but as action which balances the greatest diversity of manageable interests. They should lead us to define an ideal political order in purely formal terms as one which properly (1) aims at the most comprehensive good by successfully integrating partial goods, (2) fosters individual growth by providing the ground for encounters with others, and (3) promotes self-esteem by enabling individuals to govern their conflicting interests.

Political institutions, the selections show, are ideally capable of eliciting and ordering the infinite variety of possible human concerns. Political machinery, when in good repair, will succeed in bringing the various schemes of individuals out into the open and into a state of balance. Ideally, the rules governing public deliberation will keep special interests in check insofar as they make each of their advocates conscious of the partisan character of their claims. Inducing men to see themselves as others see them, political machinery will ideally facilitate participation, thereby heightening individual consciousness and extending the range of human sympathy. The procedures for debating and deciding will compel men to recognize the needs of others and to deny themselves the security of final victory. An ideal political order will accordingly not conform to some positive ideology, being content to inspire participation while keeping the variety of participants in a state of unresolved conflict.

Accepting this perspective, we should see the politically mature individual as capable of *remaining* in a state of conflict, as capable of so ordering his various concerns that none will get the best of him. He will realize that he must treat none of them as exclusively valid. Moreover, he will progressively increase his concerns by embracing those of others. If he cannot ever regard himself as conclusively mature, this is because he is truly a citizen not to the extent that he is "balanced" and "politically stable" but to the extent that he has incorporated a maximum of manageable concerns. This is in fact our norm not only for the individual person but also for the political order: like the individual, it will also incorporate a maximum of manageable concerns. And finally, a scientific discipline may similarly be seen as one which leads to theories meaningfully relating the greatest variety of relevant facts.

In other words, we can apply this formal criterion to all prevailing systems: to the individual, to the political system, to explanatory theories. Moreover, we can note that personal as well as social growth has been explicitly viewed in these terms by thinkers as diverse as Rousseau, John Dewey, Gordon Allport, and Karl Deutsch. Deutsch has provided a concise formulation:

> Growth should mean not merely the highest degree of unity and self-determination within the existing limits of a system . . . ; nor should growth mean a mere enlargement of the system with no change in its characteristics of performance. . . . Rather, growth also should mean an application of learning capacity toward an increase in openness, that is, an increase in the range, diversity, and effectiveness of an organization's channels of intake of information from the outside world. . . . Still further, growth should mean an increase in an organization's ability to make effective responses to its environment and to change this environment in accordance with its need. . . . And, finally, growth should mean an increase in the range and diversity of goals the organization is able to follow, including the power to change goals and to add new ones.[1]

In the light of this formulation, the mature citizen is not committed to some specific creed, but to a certain posture. He must be identified as pre-eminently an innovating being, favoring whatever policies are apt to *keep* him innovating without causing him to lose his balance in the process. He will be sensitive to new possible experiences and seek to make room for the most challenging ones among them. He will continuously test his capacity for incorporating unfamiliar roles and new styles. He will be curious about alternative possibilities, ferret them out, and integrate them in the prevailing equilibrium of interests.

Such activity is distinctively political. The rules which govern it are simply rules of order; they are the civil procedures which facilitate participation in public life. Such activity is carried on in the public sphere in plain view of others, wherever men openly express their interests.[2] In this sphere men who have learned to recognize one another will communicate and realize how much they can bear. Within it our private passions are publicly mediated.

This state, as Aristotle was the first to argue, is wholly natural to us. Its creation and maintenance is the only interest we have in common. When we are not enslaved by nature or by one another, we can acknowledge no higher good.

▪ *Notes*

1. Karl W. Deutsch, *The Nerves of Government* (New York: The Free Press, 1963), p. 140.
2. The political sphere may be seen as analogous to several others, whether it be one within which the scientist structures perceptions, the artist relates experiences, or the individual person orders his desires. Within all of these spheres, relationships between events are established in accordance with accepted rules. The rules are as much subject to debate as the boundaries of the respective spheres. In Aristotle's analysis, the most comprehensive sphere, the one properly including all others, is the political one.

2 THE CITY AND ITS CITIZENS

■ *Norton E. Long*

The key to Aristotle's political philosophy lies in his identification of politics with ethics—his conception of the state as being most significantly a medium for the realization of some conception of the good life, and indeed as being the master institution for this purpose, to which all others are teleologically subservient. Aristotle's exclusive preoccupation with the city-state as the chosen vehicle for man's optimal self-realization has given his work a deceptive appearance of irrelevance to later and widely different forms of political life. . . .

For Aristotle the structure of politics is a structure of institutions, running from the family through the village and the town to the state, each subordinate institution contributing its appropriate part to the final end embodied in the polis state. The state is characterized by its regime, which exemplifies a particular conception of the good life, be it the wealth of oligarchy, the freedom of democracy, or the martial spirit of a timocracy. The ethical principle embodied in the constitution sets the standard for distributive justice in the state; determines the nature and composition of the politeuma, the ruling class, whose members in one sense are or personify the constitution; and informs the subordinate institutions with their appropriate roles in each particular type of constitution.

The Aristotelian conception of autarchy or self-sufficiency sets the limit to the progression of social institutions. The final unit, the state, is self-sufficient and therefore inclusive of all the others. Self-sufficiency depends in part on military and economic considerations, but most significantly on ethical. . . .

The nature of the state, as opposed to its lesser political subdivisions, is that it is ethically "sovereign." Its end is the highest, to which all other associations contribute or should contribute and are subordinate. Aristotle was well aware that not all actual governments were of such a character. The governments of the barbarians, and indeed many of the Greek governments, exemplified no ethically satisfying end in which citizens as opposed to mere subjects could

From Norton E. Long, *The Polity* (Chicago: Rand McNally & Company, 1962), pp. 224–227, 179–181, 183. Reprinted by permission of the publisher.

participate. An ethically satisfying state was for Aristotle a requirement for the fullest development of man. It is not merely a metaphysical requirement, but one that human nature will strive for, however imperfectly, in particular and adverse circumstances. It is thus an empirical fact of human behavior, not just a moral postulate.

The simple scheme of Book I of the *Politics* describes an ethically graded series of associations rising from the household to the polis, with each step in the ascent characterized by an ethically more inclusive and higher end. On the basis of this analysis, local government is differentiated from the higher levels of government as ethically insufficient to stand by itself and as merely minis-terial to an end more adequately realized in a higher level. Thus for Aristotle and Plato the village is, if not a "city of pigs," still too uncivilized for the highest human self-realization. It is inadequate to provide the scope necessary to the fullest self-realization of man and is therefore lacking in self-sufficiency.

If, on one end of the ethical scale of associations, the village is inadequate and the household even more so, the polis itself is characterized by ethical self-sufficiency and a degree of economic and military competence. Aristotle is not talking about an isolated state in an international vacuum. There will be treaties and alliances, economic, military, and for other purposes; there may be Pan Hellenic Festivals and Olympic Games—and thus there are more broadly inclusive associations than the polis (the state). But these broader associations are characterized by partial and less inclusive purposes. They do not contem-plate "the whole end of man."

If one puts the Aristotelian schema aside for the moment and considers the ordering of associations, and especially governmental associations, in accord-ance with the value—and perhaps one should say the felt value—of their ethical ends, it is clear that the Aristotelian picture of a neatly ascending hierarchy, though logically attractive, may or may not be the case from one situation to another. Just as the Austinean schema would give us a neatly ascending order to the final sovereign, so the Aristotelian would give us a hierarchy mounting to the ethically sovereign association. The polemics on sovereignty have frequently led to metaphysical debates between monists and pluralists. A similar logomachy could develop from any conception of an ethically sovereign state. What is important is to investigate the ethical char-acter of governmental associations as significant empirical data of political life. . . .

Governments, local and state, may range from a tight oligarchy of wealth to a demagogic mass dictatorship. For the most part, pure forms are rare. As Aristotle pointed out, there are many claims to political power: wealth, free birth, numbers, noble birth, military prowess, and the like. All of these have a real but limited justice. A stable constitution requires that no single claim prevail and that at least wealth be tempered by numbers. In fact, this mixed government or polity is best achieved through the predominance of the middle-class. Where the rich confront the poor with little or no middle class between them, the city is divided into irreconcilable armed camps. A sociological and economic substructure is necessary to support a given constitution, and that constitution will be radically altered by economic change, as from a peasant democracy to an urban proletariat. Thus Aristotle recognizes that ruling class, legal constitution, ethical order, and economy are interdependent. Changes in one aspect have significant consequences for all others in the dynamic equilibrium of the constitution. . . .

The appeal of the Greek view of citizenship lies in its recognition that political institutions are not mere instruments for the achieving of results but institutions infused with value. The process of politics in this view is valued for its own sake as providing significant roles for the realization of man's ethical potential. While the efficiency of the governmental process in coping with problems common to all political orders is an inevitable and major consideration, the Greek view of citizenship regards the capacity of a political order to provide significant roles for the realization of the citizens' moral potential as a major criterion of its value. In this sense the political order is valued not just for what it produces but for the keen sense of citizen participation in the enterprise. As socialists like DeMann have argued for the workers' sense of dignity and meaning in the productive process as a value independent of and even above his pay, so one may argue that the citizen needs the opportunity of meaningful civic action beyond the mere enjoyment of good government.

This line of argument would lead to an evaluation of local, state, and national governments in terms of their capacity to provide ethically significant roles for citizens. Local and state governments would have worth, not simply as devices to prevent centralization, but as valuable means to widen the possibility of active civic life. A major purpose of these governments would be to attract and hold the active participation of citizens who might well be lost in the undifferentiated, apathetic mass of a centralized nation-state.

A principal obstacle to applying the Greek concept of citizenship to the modern state has been sheer size at the national level and sheer lack of significance at the local level. Can the affairs of a city or a state be given sufficient meaning to provide anything like the challenge to human potentiality the Periclean ideal demands? Some pride of citizenship remained in the cities of the Hellenistic monarchs, and even in those of the Empire, but the older vitality was gone. Possibly any such vibrant vitality as Thucydides depicts would be incompatible with superior national allegiance. When war and foreign policy are no longer part of the stakes of power, some of its tragic significance is lost to politics.

Yet the Greek ideal of functioning at the top of one's bent along some line of excellence in a significant field of action is surely applicable to our thinking about all levels of government. It is especially applicable if we are to call successfully into play the resources of generous ambition that are squandered in commercialism and escape. The stakes here are much more than the education of the lower orders in the responsibilities of municipal housekeeping that Mill saw as a chief value of local self-government.

As the United States becomes more and more a nation living in a few tens of metropolitan areas, the quality of its local citizenships may well become of critical importance. Will the inhabitants of these faceless and form-less aggregates be citizens or resident or even transient aliens with no commitments to the local area beyond the friendships of commerce and pleas-ure it affords? One wonders whether resident aliens of New York are likely to prove active citizens of state or nation. Local citizenship is enervated by a sense of political inefficacy in vitally influencing its neighborhood affairs. Remote municipal bureaucracies are unresponsive, and where, as in Kansas City, an enlightened city manager has attempted to give vitality to neighbor-hood citizenship, it has required tender care of an anemic growth, and in its critics' view has been little more than the manager's machine. The patent need for restoration of neighborhood vitality in cities like New York and Chicago is matched by the need of a more readily workable political system for local problem solving at the metropolitan level. In one sense our cities are so big, with populations so lacking in locality roots, that they provide no meaningful activity where the citizens live. In another, our metropolitan areas are divided among so many jurisdictions that they present well-nigh insuperable difficulties to the active citizens concerned with the responsible government of the metropolitan area.

While it is doubtful if the average man thirsts to be a Greek—he has been taught to be a consumer of politics, a client rather than a self-directed prin-cipal—there are still some who find a merely private and Epicurean free ride on the body politic a painful frustration of their personal potential and ethical need. For these the escape to the garden suburb seems to split the personality and confess defeat, even when, conscience-driven, they return to the cave to man the board of directors of the community chest, the hospital, or the settlement house. Absentee political landlordism is productive not only of a bad conscience but, even more, of a sense of the failure to develop to the full the potentiality of one's personality in the ethical medium of politics. . . .

While the frustrations of the mixed-up mess of metropolis and the anony-mous mass of the great city present a kind of formless futility, they have another and encouraging side. Whatever else they may be, they are not trivial. The issues of metropolitan life are momentous. The resources of the emerging metropolis are such as to challenge the imagination. The possibility, even the necessity, of a great age of cities confronts us. Either these cities will be the theaters of a cultural and political renaissance or their promise will be lost in a shapeless, mindless mass of metics whose best hope is to be well administered and only moderately plucked for the pains. . . .

If this estimate of the situation is correct, one favorable answer can be given to the question as to whether the Greek view of citizenship can be given operational reality in the context of American affairs. The emerging metropolitan areas in which the bulk of our people will live can be structured to create governments whose resources and problems would be such as to provide the kind of scope needed for the type of citizenship envisioned in classical theory. The possibilities of a richly pluralist culture which a galaxy of great American cities might sustain could capture the imagination of the spiritually underemployed now lacking a significant medium for creative action. As we move into an era of greater and greater public consumption, the sustenance of the arts and the refinement of life, as well as the presently burning questions of housing and the conditions of mere existence, will be more and more major functions of urban government. The new city in the terms of Burke may well become a partnership in all art, all science, all culture with a significant concept of the good life as a vital common aspiration. The apostles of metropolitanism are coming to realize that the vision they are seeking is something more than a better means of moving traffic, an improvement in the plumbing, or even an increase in the competitive position of the local economy. It is the possibility of attaining a shared common goal of a better life. The recreated city of the metropolitan area offers the hope of a significant manageable field of civic action in which a warmer sense of fraternity can be realized than in state or nation. . . .

3   THE PLEASURES OF POLITICS

▪ *Hannah Arendt*

. . . Americans knew that public freedom consisted in having a share in public business and that the activities connected with this business by no means constituted a burden, but gave those who discharged them in public a feeling of happiness they could acquire nowhere else. They knew very well (and John Adams was bold enough to formulate this knowledge time and again) that the people went to town assemblies, as their representatives later were to go to the famous conventions, neither exclusively because of duty nor, and even less, to serve their own interests, but most of all because they enjoyed the discussions, the deliberations, and the making of decisions. What brought them together was "the world and the public interest of liberty" (Harrington), and what moved them was "the passion for distinction" which John Adams held to be "more essential and remarkable" than any other human faculty: "Wherever men, women, or children, are to be found, whether they be old or young, rich or poor, high or low, wise or foolish, ignorant or learned, every individual is seen to be strongly actuated by a desire to be seen, heard, talked of, approved and respected by the people about him, and within his knowledge." The virtue of this passion he called "emulation," the "desire to excel another," and its vice he called "ambition" because it "aims at power as a means of distinction."[1] . . .

Jefferson himself—in a paper for the Virginia Convention of 1774 which in many respects anticipated the Declaration of Independence—had declared that "our ancestors" when they left the "British dominions in Europe" exercised "a right which nature has given all men, . . . of establishing new societies, under such laws and regulations as to them shall seem most likely to promote public happiness."[2] If Jefferson was right and it was in quest of "public happiness" that the "free inhabitants of the British dominions" had emigrated to America, then the colonies in the New World must have been breeding grounds of revolutionaries from the beginning. And, by the same token, they must have been prompted even then by some sort of dissatisfaction with the rights and liberties of Englishmen—prompted by a desire for some kind of freedom which the "free inhabitants" of the mother country did not enjoy. This freedom they called later, when they had come to taste it, "public happiness," and it consisted in the citizen's right of access to the public realm, in his share in public power—to be "a participator in the government of affairs," in Jefferson's telling phrase[3]—as distinct from the generally recognized rights of subjects to be protected by the government in the pursuit of private happiness even against public power; that is, distinct from rights which only tyrannical power would abolish. The very fact that the word "happiness" was chosen in laying claim to a share in public power indicates strongly that there existed in the country, prior to the Revolution, such a thing as "public happiness" and that men knew they could not be altogether "happy" if their happiness was located and enjoyed only in private life. . . .

If the ultimate end of revolution was freedom and the constitution of a public space where freedom could appear, the *constitutio libertatis,* then the Jeffersonian system of wards, the only tangible place where everyone could be free, actually was the end of the great republic whose chief purpose in domestic affairs should have been to provide the people with such places of freedom and to protect them. The basic assumption of the ward system, whether Jefferson knew it or not, was that no one could be called happy without his share in public happiness, that no one could be called free without his experience in public freedom, and that no one could be called either happy or free without participating, and having a share, in public power. . . .

Jefferson's true notion of happiness comes out very clearly (without any of the distortions through a traditional, conventional framework of concepts which, it turned out, was much harder to break than the structure of the traditional form of government) when he lets himself go in a mood of playful and sovereign irony and concludes one of his letters to Adams as follows: "May we meet there again, in Congress, with our ancient Colleagues, and receive with them the seal of approbation 'Well done, good and faithful servants.' "[4] Here, behind the irony, we have the candid admission that life in Congress, the joys of discourse, of legislation, of transacting business, of persuading and being persuaded, were to Jefferson no less conclusively a foretaste of an eternal bliss to come than the delights of contemplation had been for medieval piety. For even "the seal of approbation" is not at all the common reward for virtue in a future state; it is the applause, the demonstration of acclaim, "the esteem of the world" of which Jefferson in another context says that there had been a time when it "was of higher value in my eye than everything in it."[5] . . .

The performing arts . . . have indeed a strong affinity with politics. Performing artists—dancers, play-actors, musicians, and the like—need an audience to show their virtuosity, just as acting men need the presence of others before whom they can appear; both need a publicly organized space for their "work," and both depend on others for the performance itself. Such a space of appearances is not to be taken for granted wherever men live together in a community. The Greek polis once was precisely that "form of government" which provided men with a space of appearances where they could act, with a kind of theater where freedom could appear.

To use the word "political" in the sense of the Greek polis is neither arbitrary nor far-fetched. Not only etymologically and not only for the learned does the very word, which in all European languages still derives from the historically unique organization of the Greek city-state, echo the experiences of the community which first discovered the essence and the realm of the political. . . . Only ancient political communities were founded for the express purpose of serving the free—those who were neither slaves, subject to coercion by others, nor laborers, driven and urged on by the necessities of life. If, then, we understand the political in the sense of the polis, its end or *raison d'être* would be to establish and keep in existence a space where freedom as virtuosity can appear. This is the realm where freedom is a wordly reality, tangible in words which can be heard, in deeds which can be seen, and in events which are talked about, remembered, and turned into stories before they are finally incorporated into the great storybook of human history. Whatever occurs in this space of appearances is political by definition, even when it is not a direct product of action. What remains outside it, such as the great feats of barbarian empires, may be impressive and noteworthy, but it is not political, strictly speaking.

▪ Notes

1. John Adams, *Discourses on Davila, Works* (Boston, 1851), VI, 232–233.
2. See Thomas Jefferson, *A Summary View of the Rights of British America, 1774*, in *The Life and Selected Writings* (New York: Random House, 1944), pp. 293 ff.
3. In the important letter on the "republics of the wards" to Joseph C. Cabell, February 2, 1816. *Ibid.*, p. 661.
4. *The Adams-Jefferson Letters*, ed. by L. J. Cappon (Chapel Hill: University of North Carolina Press, 1959), letter of April 11, 1823, p. 594.
5. See the letter to Madison, June 9, 1793.

4 POLITICAL MAN

- *Harold D. Lasswell*

The Self-System in Democratic Character: The Open Ego

. . . Let us take as the outstanding characteristic of democratic character, in reference to identifications, *the maintenance of an open as against a closed ego*. By this expression our intention is to convey the idea that the democratic attitude toward other human beings is warm rather than frigid, inclusive and expanding rather than exclusive and constricting. We are speaking of an underlying personality structure which is capable of "friendship," as Aristotle put it, and which is unalienated from humanity. Such a person transcends most of the cultural categories that divide human beings from one another and senses the common humanity across class and even caste lines within the culture and in the world beyond the local culture. In the extreme case we have "saints" who have undergone the deprivations of a concentration camp without losing the serenity of outlook that reaches out hopefully and tolerantly toward other human beings.

The conception of the open ego is something other than the capacity to enter into an intense and all-embracing sentimental bond with another person. Often such passionate attachments represent a socialization of fears and hostilities directed against other human beings. It operates as a preventive of the degree of detachment which enables the individual to sense the feelings and viewpoints of others in the life of an entire group, such as appears to be characteristic of those persons who are well equipped to function in a democratic manner.[1]

It is apparent that the prototypes of many later experiences are undergone in the early years of life, and especially in early infancy. So far as we can tell, the "primary ego" evolved during the early weeks of life is a fusion of experiences which are not capable of being sorted into a sharply delimited "out there" and "me." Experiences connected with nursing (the intake of food and body contact) are divisible into those which are gratifying (the indulgences) and nongratifying (the deprivations). Harry Stack Sullivan has suggested that the first or gratifying experiences become structured around the image of the "good mother" and that the second or nongratifying experiences are attributed to the "bad mother," even though the boundaries of the ego

From Harold D. Lasswell, *The Political Writings of Harold D. Lasswell* (New York: The Macmillan Company, 1951), pp. 495–509. © Copyright 1951 by The Free Press, a corporation. Reprinted with the permission of The Macmillan Company.

15

are lacking in focus. Soon the limits of the "me" and the "not me" gain in precision, and this in turn redefines the possibilities for symbolizing and localizing the recurring patterns of indulgence and deprivation. When there is a "me," there is also a stream of characterizations emanating from the environment in terms of "good" and "naughty," which are usually integrated with a variety of comforts and discomforts on the physical level. The recurring sources of gratification become stably symbolized as "my mother," "my body," and the like, and the identification system begins to include and exclude according to the prevailing stratifications of the social system into which the infant is becoming integrated.[2]

There is reason to believe that in some cultures the possibility of developing an outgoing democratic character is excluded at an early period. The prevailing patterns of child care appear to induce early despair that profound gratifications can emanate from other human beings; yet they prevent this despair from putting a stop to all externalized activity. Indulgences are wrested from the hostile, reluctant universe by a variety of sly maneuvers.[3]

The Self-System in Democratic Character: Values Multiple and Shared

Our characterization of the democratic community has provided a frame in which the demand system of the democratic character can be rather clearly set forth. Let us speak of the democratic character as *multivalued, rather than single-valued, and as disposed to share rather than to hoard or to monopolize.* In particular, little significance is attached to the exercise of power as a scope value.

The characteristics of democratic character have often been cast into relief by the study of individuals who are infatuated with the pursuit of one value to such a point that the integrity of the common life is imperiled thereby. This is perhaps most obvious in studies that have been made of the *homo politicus,* the man who, when compared with others similarly situated in culture and class, relies with relish on the "pursuit of power by the use of power." Since we understand that power relationships have, or are assumed by the participants to possess, the element of severe deprivation, it is apparent that the human being who is fascinated by power is out of harmony with our basic concept of human dignity.[4] The psychiatrist feels at home in the study of ardent seekers after power in the arena of politics because the physician recognizes the extreme egocentricity and sly ruthlessness of some of the paranoid patients with whom he has come in contact in the clinic. To the power-centered person all human beings and all contacts with others are opportunities for imposing his will, or for enlisting the other person in some manner that contributes to the imposition of his own will in some future situation. Hence he imposes a wall of insulation and isolation between himself and others, with the result that a growing sense of alienation from mankind becomes one of the recurring complaints of those who attain power or only aspire with all the intensity of their being to acquire it.

When the demand for respect is the consuming passion, other values are sacrificed for the sake of receiving symbolic acknowledgments of eminence. The vain man has a special position of dependence on the human beings by whom he is surrounded, seeking to elicit a continuing flow of those reassuring postures, gestures, and symbolic expressions which sustain the inflated image of the ego.[5] We are speaking of the individual who is so sensitized to the admiration of others that he may react with wounded pride to fancied slights and burn with fierce jealousies and resentments against those who receive the plaudits to which he fancies himself entitled, or against those from whom he believes that the plaudits ought to come. The respect-centered character is often disposed to poison human relations "by taking everything personally" and by needing a perpetual stream of reassurance about "how am I doing." The clinician is accustomed to see in the oversensitive neurotic, or in the grandiose delusions of the paranoid, the extreme manifestation of what is known to common sense as abnormal pride. The secret image is not necessarily connected with power, since coercive intentions are not always the cherished means of obtaining boundless admiration.

The excessive demand for affection carries with it a distortion of capacity for full participation in the life of a democratic community. The most extreme examples in our culture turn every human contact into a sexual invitation or assault and are absorbed in the active indulgence or the fantasying of success in sexuality. Many of those who are preoccupied with sexual conquest have no conscious interest in affection, but gloat over sexual achievements as a demonstration of virility (well-being) or as a means to fame (respect).[6] At the moment we are referring only to those whose lives are filled with sex as a mode of giving and receiving affection, or who are absorbed in giving and receiving love. The affection-centered person may not be promiscuous in the choice of love objects, but may, on the contrary, develop an intense and all-absorbing bond with one individual. As we have already intimated in connection with the identification system, these exclusive couplings may represent a withdrawal from fuller functioning in the community. In Western civilization, at least, the woman is expected to specialize on affection much more than the man and to stay within the primary circle of the home. The distorting effect of this cultural pressure on the personality of the woman, and of many with whom she comes in touch, has been described by many observers.[7] An additional source of difficulty rises from the fact that our civilization is in a transitional stage regarding its conception of women, who are gradually being relieved of the disabilities from which they have suffered in theory and in fact. But the "lag" effects are among the sources of distress in modern life.

Hyperspecialization on rectitude produces another set of character deformations. We are speaking of those who are continually beset with questions of right and wrong so that the entire career is transformed in perpetual judgments of the self and others in reference to such standards. These persons may wrap themselves in an impenetrable cloak of self-righteousness and speak censoriously of the imperfections of their fellow men. They may, however, view themselves in a wholly different light and engage in private and public confessions of sin and guilt. Human relations are transformed into occasions for the repetitive application of a limited set of rigid categories, a process that squeezes from sight the richness and variety of values which are essential to the democratic community. Physicians are accustomed to meet symptoms of the kind here described in their patients, whom they recognize as suffering from obsessional or compulsive difficulties.[8]

Some characters are taken up with goods (with wealth). When the fixation on wealth is so intense that other values are almost deprived of meaning, we have miserly, greedy types who are eager to accumulate and to retain goods and services. Such acquisitive and retentive personalities are referred to in the folklore of many cultures with utter disdain, since public service, affection, or other values are all rejected in order to get hold of impersonal and tangible resources.

Overpreoccupation with well-being may take the form of anxious concern for health, which can reach the dimensions of hypochondria, or of disturbing interference in the lives of others in the name of their physical welfare.[9] Or the cult of the body, and of virility as an end in itself, can exclude other values.

Devotion to the exercise of skill may become so complete that an absolute exemption may be demanded from all considerations of rectitude, affection, or any other value. "Art for art's sake" is a slogan which in our civilization is often matched by similar demands in the name of other skills. Scientists, for example, may resent any restraint on the direction or timing of their activities, even when the destiny of mankind is at stake.

Enlightenment, too, can become a "vice" when "being in on the know" becomes an end in itself.

The Self-System of the Democratic Character: Confidence in Human Potentialities

When we turn from the demand structure of the democratic character to the consideration of the pattern of expectation, we note at once that it is essential to have *deep confidence in the benevolent potentialities of man*. This affirmative trust is very different from the apathetic endurance of life in the manner of the apathetic orphan.[10]

Unless there is some early basis for trust in the benevolence of the surrounding world, we can hardly expect that the individual will develop predispositions capable of carrying him through adverse experiences. This is the deep significance of the "good mother" image in contributing to the formation of a perspective that fosters inclusive identifications with other people. It has become amply apparent in the course of research on the infant that the expectation of benevolence is a factor enabling the infant to put forth the energy to live.[11]

Such rigid specializations as those which have been reviewed in relation to each of the eight values fly in the face of the needs of a democratic community and prevent the consolidation of a democratic character.

The Energy System of the Democratic Character: Freedom from Anxiety

The ideal conception of democratic character *includes the specification that the self-system shall have at its disposal the energies of the unconscious part of the personality.* The deviations from this standard are in several directions. The energies may be so divided and opposed to one another that little is available to the ego, which may be relatively immobilized into the performing of an impoverished social role. The superego system of restriction and compulsion may remain at war with the recurring initiatives of the id system, resulting in immobilization through physical incapacitation. The genesis of the "conversion" response is being traced in detail by modern specialists in psychosomatic medicine. A recent statement of the field by Franz Alexander, for example, reviews the research which confirms the psychogenetic factor in gastrointestinal disturbances, bronchial asthma, cardiovascular disturbances, skin diseases, metabolic and endocrine disturbances, disturbances of the joints and skeletal muscles (including rheumatoid arthritis and the accident-prone individual), and of the sexual apparatus.[12]

The basis for ineffectual participation in society may lie in the sphere of fantasy (or autistic reverie) rather than organic malfunctioning. We observe "autistic withdrawal" in forms of psychic suffering experienced by some persons who limit their human relationships more and more. Sometimes these disturbances are sufficiently light to be called "neuroses." But there are many kinds of grave, psychotic processes that carry the individual out of touch with other human beings. However, all internal conflicts do not result in such conspicuous restrictions of overt social activity. In varying degree the person who is suffering from a somatic disturbance with a psychological basis may be able to carry on a regular professional and sociable life. It may even be that the function of the somatic symptom is to dispose of energies that might otherwise interfere with the self-system of the democratic character.[13]

However, the self-system of the democrat may be betrayed chronically or occasionally by eruptions of conduct in flat contradiction to democratic perspectives. In many instances the person is fully conscious of occasional seizures that contradict his conscious demands upon himself. Some men "can't control their temper" on all occasions. Others go in for jags of alcoholism or sexual debauchery, or for athleticism of a type that does serious damage to the body and endangers others. The deviation may be so pronounced that one can only speak of psychopathic distortion of character.[14]

Often the self-system of the democrat is betrayed by *conduct* whose incompatibility with the perspectives of the system are invisible to the man himself, although clear to nearly anyone who observes him. I am not speaking of "hypocrisy," but of the "self-deluded." One familiar example is the humorless, sincere individual who unconsciously persecutes everyone with whom he comes in touch. He may be an extreme advocate of order and puts everything on a timetable. His unfortunate wife, children, and employees suffer the despotism of a man whose purity of motive is beyond self-dispute.

The energies of the unconscious system may also express themselves in deformations of *perspective* which the individual does not recognize. Although he considers himself to possess a democratic character, the person may cling to beliefs that stand in flagrant contradiction of his professed regard for human dignity. It is not a question in these cases of subtle distinctions, but of gross distortions, as when convictions about the equality of all members of the human race are contradicted by statements of belief about specific ethnic groups. Such contradictions within the self-system are screened from self-inspection by the automatic operation of unconscious channels and forces. These individuals differ from the persons cited above in that the distortion is within the belief system and not between beliefs and conduct.[15]

There appears to be a common element in the organization of energies that distort or betray the self-system of an otherwise democratic character. The element is human destructiveness. We have noted that destructive drives may be *externalized* against other human beings or *internalized* against the body of the person. In the former cases, the drives may be directed against groups who have never been included within the self-system. However, the targets may be selected from within the identification pattern of the self, ranging all the way from peripheral individuals and groups to nuclear groups and individuals. When destructiveness is directed against the primary ego, as in psychosomatic illness, the inner core of the ego system becomes the target. As indicated in the previous analysis, any given course of conduct can express a two-edged aggression, as when the value positions of the individual and of other persons are simultaneously reduced. Partial incapacitation may reduce not only the well-being of the sufferer and cut down income and capital, political power and other advantages; the reduction in influence may hamper the family, in this way gratifying grudges of which the individual is quite unaware.

May not destructive tendencies contribute positively to the formation of a self-system and to the effective energies available to the democratic character? To take the latter part of the question first, it is apparent that the destructive energies of a person may be directed against enemies of the democratic community. Indeed, any other behavior would betray the opportunities and responsibilities of democratic citizenship. The reply to the first part of the question is less categorical. Modern studies of human development repeatedly show that democratic responses often arise from motives which are incompatible with it and signify that the individual has achieved part of his democratic outlook by "reaction formation" against tendencies of an opposite kind. Many democrats appear to develop in opposition to antidemocratic parents, for example. And yet, [in] modern personality research, the characters, which are achieved by a complex process of balanced defense are viewed as constituting less enduring formations than those which evolve more directly.

A significant insight into the dynamics of nondemocratic character is contained in the studies of prejudice alluded to above. Prejudice was defined in several ways, ranging from denials of respect (as defined in our list of values) to denials of access to all values, irrespective of common humanity or individual merit. The intensity of the prejudice might range from mildly derogatory reveries and remarks to militant activism designed to exclude target groups from the community (or from effective participation therein according to democratic norms). The research succeeded in demonstrating that prejudiced attitudes not only were connected with immediate, situational factors but represented a carry-over from early experiences in which a certain pattern of character had been formed during early years of life. In our culture, at least, the emerging picture of interconnection was summed up as follows:

The most crucial result of the present study, as it seems to the authors, is the demonstration of close correspondence in the type of approach and outlook a subject is likely to have in a great variety of areas, ranging from the most intimate features of family and sex adjustment through relationships to other people in general, to religion and to social and political philosophy. Thus a basically hierarchical, authoritarian, exploitive parent-child relationship is apt to carry over into a power-oriented, exploitively dependent attitude toward one's sex partner and one's God and may culminate in a political philosophy and social outlook which has no room for anything but a desperate clinging to what appears to be strong and a disdainful rejection of whatever is relegated to the bottom. The inherent dramatization likewise extends from the parent-child dichotomy to the dichotomous conception of sex roles and of moral values, as well as to a dichotomous handling of social ingroup-outgroup cleavages. Conventionality, rigidity, repressive denial, and the ensuing break-through of one's weakness, fear and dependency are but other aspects of the same fundamental personality pattern, and they can be observed in personal life as well as in attitudes toward religion and social issues.

On the other hand, there is a pattern characterized chiefly by affectionate, basically equalitarian, and permissive interpersonal relationships. This pattern encompasses attitudes within the family and toward the opposite sex, as well as an internalization of religious and social values. Greater flexibility and the potentiality for more genuine satisfactions appear as results of this basic attitude.[16]

We know that repetitiveness is one of the most frequent "defense mechanisms" by the use of which the ego prevents itself from being swamped in a flood of anxieties and hostilities. The rigidification goes so far that the perceiving processes of the ego system are affected, and relevant features of a novel situation are pressed into established molds, thus preserving the older categories from the changes that rise from new knowledge. Hence the self-system, even when it conforms to democratic requirements, has at its command only some of the energy of the personality as a whole, much of which is tied down to the task of nullifying the hyperaggressive, destructive drives. The inner stability of the rigid person is imperiled in any situation which is comprehended with difficulty. Hence there is low tolerance for ambiguity, which may be one of the most diagnostic traits of such individuals, as Else Frenkel-Brunswik has pointed out. . . .

▪ Notes

1. Helen Hall Jennings, *A Study of Personality in Inter-Personal Relations,* 2d ed. (New York: Longmans, Green, 1950). "The universal characteristics of the leaders

in this study may be a 'logical' carrying out of their larger insight into the needs of persons generally and at least partially a reflection of greater emotional maturity on their part than appears to characterize the average member," p. 201. This is a report of an investigation conducted by sociometric techniques of the 400 individuals in the New York State Training School for Girls.

2. See especially "The Meaning of Anxiety in Psychiatry and Life," *Psychiatry*, XI (1948), 1ff.

3. Ruth Benedict and Margaret Mead have been the most energetic explorers of the impact of child-rearing practices on the other features of culture. I refer here to the interpretation of the Hobbesan life of Dobu.

4. In the Salmon Lectures at the New York Academy of Medicine the present writer developed some hypotheses concerning the power-centered man. . . . See *Power and Personality* (New York: Norton, 1948).

5. See the examples of how the denial of respect can be used as a base value designed to influence power in Charles E. Merriam, "Political Power" (1934), reprinted in Lasswell, Merriam, and Smith, *A Study of Power* (Glencoe: The Free Press, 1950), Chapter 7.

6. The "old-fashioned" literature on sexology was usually limited to an account of the conscious perspectives of the subjects who were described. Hence the reclassification of the material according to conscious interest in affection (or some other value) is not difficult. Much of the work of Magnus Hirschfeld and Havelock Ellis belongs in this category. See also George W. Henry, *Sex Variants: A Study of Homosexual Patterns* (New York: Hoeber, 1948) (One-volume edition).

7. Notably Karen Horney, Clara Thompson, Helene Deutsch, among psychoanalysts. See also Margaret Mead, *Male and Female* (New York: Morrow, 1949).

8. Described in any textbook that includes the psychoneuroses, such as D. K. Henderson and R. D. Gillespie, *A Text-book of Psychiatry for Students and Practitioners*, 6th ed. (New York: Oxford University Press, 1944).

9. See David M. Levy, "Maternal Over-protection," *Psychiatry*, I (1938), 561–591; II (1939), 99–128, 563–597; IV (1941), 393–438, 567–626.

10. Even though this response may enable the individual to survive under such drastically adverse conditions as a concentration camp in later life. See Ralph R. Greenson, "The Psychology of Apathy," *Psychoanalytic Quarterly*, XVIII (1949), 290–302.

11. Consult Margarethe Ribble, "The Significance of Infantile Sucking for the Psychic Development of the Individual," and "Disorganizing Factors of Infant Personality," reprinted in S. S. Tomkins, ed., *Contemporary Psychopathology: A Source Book* (Cambridge: Harvard University Press, 1947), pp. 1–15. The importance of recognizing the *potential* benevolence of human beings is emphasized, for example, in analyses of democracy by C. E. Merriam, T. V. Smith, A. D. Lindsay, R. M. MacIver, James Bryce, Hugo Krabbe, Hans Kelsen, and many others.

12. Franz Alexander, *Psychosomatic Medicine: Its Principles and Applications*, with a chapter on "The Functions of the Sexual Apparatus and Their Disturbances" by Therese Benedek (New York: Norton, 1950).

13. It should not be supposed that the psychosomatic emphasis is altogether new to physicians. Ralph Waldo Emerson remarked in his essay on the poet that he knew "a witty physician who found the creed in the biliary duct, and used to affirm that if there was disease in the liver, the man became a Calvinist, and if that organ was sound, he became a Unitarian."

14. On the history of this difficult conception see Karl A. Menninger, "Recognizing and Renaming 'Psychopathic Personalities,' " *Bulletin of the Menninger Clinic*, V (1941), 150–156. See Hervey Cleckley, *The Mask of Sanity: An Attempt to Clarify Some Issues about the So-called Psychopathic Personality*, 2d ed. (St. Louis: Mosby, 1950).

15. Numerous examples of the combinations referred to in the foregoing can be found in the volumes of the "Studies in Prejudice" published in 1950 by Harper, New York, and conducted under the auspices of the American Jewish Committee. See especially

The Authoritarian Personality, by T. W. Adorno *et al.*; *Dynamics of Prejudice: A Psychological and Sociological Study of Veterans*, by Bruno Bettelheim and Morris Janowitz; and *Anti-Semitism and Emotional Disorder: A Psychoanalytic Interpretation*, by Nathan W. Ackermann and Marie Jahoda.

16. Adorno *et al., op. cit.*, p. 971. The essential conclusion is confirmed in many respects by the Bettelheim-Janowitz and the Ackermann-Jahoda investigations.

PART TWO

■ CHALLENGES TO POLITICS

INTRODUCTION

When threatened by natural catastrophes—epidemics, famines, hurricanes, or floods—we are ill advised to turn to political institutions for support. The reason is obvious enough: there is nothing to debate when our common interest is self-evident. Disasters compel us to band together, to cease debating alternatives, and to call an end to politics. Ideally, there can be no bargaining about matters of life and death.

Similarly, when an alien oppressor enslaves us, our interests converge and politics becomes irrelevant. To free ourselves, we must make common cause. True, we may in fact be too apathetic or brutalized to act, thus failing to recover the political institutions which might again allow us to pursue alternative goals. We therefore may have to be mobilized. Yet our immediate objective—to regain freedom—should really not be debatable; it is not subject to negotiation and politics. In other words, the brute force of nature or of other men will dissolve the political order.

Extreme threats to the political order are easy to bring to light—at least after the event. They turn out to have been situations in which no one was bluffing, in which we were given no quarter and had no room to compromise. Such total threats to our very existence are more readily defined than those inherent in our ordinary environment. Our day-to-day problem therefore is posed by the need to define the less extreme threats to the political order. Precisely what is it in our present environment (and in ourselves) which leads to the shrinkage of political space, our alienation from politics, the privatization of our lives?

Although political institutions have always been under pressure, the pressures today, as the following chapters make clear, have assumed new forms. Increasingly, the threats to political institutions are posed not by our natural

25

environment but by the environment we have artificially created. Arising from our unprecedented capacity for mastering nature and, indeed, for governing ourselves, bureaucratic establishments, for example, are difficult to recognize as threats. Since they enable us to gain in independence, they can scarcely be regarded as wholly evil. To be sure, they may undermine our ability to develop. But they also make our development possible. If they are threats, they are radically ambiguous, and we had best remain ambivalent toward them.

It is perhaps easiest to understand contemporary challenges to politics by tracing them to the great Western revolutions of the eighteenth century: the Industrial Revolution and the French Revolution. The first of these has brought about a thoroughgoing reorganization of human life, and the second has opened the political order to all classes of society.

It is evident that the mechanization of production determines the arrangement of people as well as their physical environment. Men are variously grouped by an industrial plant, an oil refinery, a fish cannery, and airline terminal, a supermarket, or a communication grid. Each of these relates men to one another in distinctive ways. Accordingly, as men move from village to city, from agrarian pursuits to industrial ones, their social relations are inexorably transformed. Their lives will be geared to the industrial system, and whatever arrangements conform to the system will be considered rational. To ensure low-cost production of standardized goods, it becomes necessary (hence rational) to divide human labor and co-ordinate the separate tasks performed. The individual will be solely concerned with his own small part in the work process and will not need to make sense of the whole. He will be attached to his job—and detached from the completed product, from others in the productive process, from the system as a whole. Though he may have other "nonproductive" interests, he will not be able to devote the best hours of his day to them. Kept from developing his potential capacities, he will be detached from what he might become. Thus he will be alienated, as Marx was to point out, from the products of his work, his fellow workers, and his potential self.

It is understandable that men whose lives are thus fragmented should search for a reintegrated community and respond to whoever promises to give coherence to their existence. Alienated men are ripe for manipulation by demagogues who offer what is so manifestly wanted. Speculating about the American democratic experiment, Tocqueville anticipated in 1840 how a new leadership would gently cater to the mass of men. The governing elite, he said, will take it upon itself to secure the gratification of the masses:

> It would resemble parental authority if, fatherlike, it tried to prepare its charges for a man's life, but on the contrary, it only tries to keep them in perpetual childhood. It likes to see the citizens enjoy themselves, provided that they think of nothing but enjoyment. It gladly works for their happiness but wants to be sole agent and judge thereof. It provides for their security, foresees and supplies their necessities, facilitates their pleasures, manages their principal concerns, directs their industry. . . .

It does not break men's will, but softens, bends, and guides it; it seldom enjoins, but often inhibits, action; it does not destroy anything, but prevents much being born; it is not at all tyrannical, but it hinders, restrains, enervates, stifles, and stultifies. . . .[1]

Yet such a benign leadership need not be as deliberate as Tocqueville implied. We need not think of it as a self-conscious power elite shrewdly making the decisions that determine our work and leisure. We may in fact agree with Michael Harrington that ours is an "accidental century" through which we drift without subjecting our technology to rational control. Thus television, as Charles Frankel has observed,

has affected education and home life, changed the patterns of congressional behavior and political discussion, and fundamentally altered, for better or worse, the operating conditions and purposes of traditional political institutions like legislative investigations and political conventions. But the decisions on how to use television and how not to use it, have been made almost entirely by men whose area of responsibility is very narrow, and who have to think about only a very few, selected values. . . . The traditional liberal mechanisms of public consultation and consent, on which the authority for such basic decisions has been supposed to rest, have next to no influence here. From the point of view of most of us these decisions just seem to happen. . . .[2]

Because this uncontrolled drifting is not incompatible with the doctrine of popular sovereignty, it has been easy to see how the democratic revolutions of the eighteenth and nineteenth centuries, reinforcing industrial tendencies, lead to the erosion of politics. Various writers, tracing the course of this development, have noted that men were freed from the restraints of church, guild, and estate, from religious, economic, and political establishments. The individual emerged as independent from the groups that had given him a sense of belonging. But as he was alone and insecure, he longed, in Erich Fromm's phrase, to escape from freedom. Disoriented and anxious, he was prepared to submit to extremists who offered relief from the burden of politics. When he did not turn to fascism, he became the victim of "public opinion." The destruction of the old order by the democratic revolutions of the modern age is thus seen to have engendered mass conformity. As men became prey to exploitation by a tyrannical minority, civility and politics were effectively destroyed.

Thus industrialism and democracy, each reinforcing the other, could be perceived quite simply as dehumanizing forces, as threats to the political order. Indeed, several generations of writers committed to the preservation of individual choice focused on the negative aspect of democracy and industrialism, disregarding their constructive potential. Max Weber, a fierce individualist, perceived only the dark side of bureaucracy. Robert Michels saw only elite rule in modern organizations. Karl Mannheim painstakingly described the standardization of modern life; Hannah Arendt noted that the political arena had to remain the preserve of the few; Walter Lippmann argued that mass participation in politics could not preserve the public interest. Nietzsche, Burckhardt, Ortega y Gasset, Mumford, Goodman—all became suspicious of equalitarian tendencies.[3] They feared the triumph of public opinion, the destruction of culture, the rise of a new barbarism.

What they failed to note was that the process of modernization not only threatened the institution of politics but also served to enhance it. Reacting against the emergence of the mass society, they assailed the city and ignored the opportunities it opens for exploring alternatives; they assailed the complex organization and ignored the way it enhances individual rationality; they assailed mass society and ignored the way it extends the horizon of individuals; they assailed bureaucracy and ignored its preference for individual merit rather than good social connections. They were more likely to observe how the impersonal university bewilders the student than to realize how its very size enables him to enroll in an incredible variety of courses, to assume various kinds of identity, and to test a multiplicity of roles.

In short, it is necessary to remember both aspects of the trends toward modernization, even though the following chapters focus on the negative one—the one that necessarily concerns us since we wish ultimately to determine how adequately our ideologies, institutions, and research methods meet the challenges that confront us.

■ *Notes*

1. Alexis de Tocqueville, *Democracy in America*, George Lawrence, tr. (New York: Harper and Row, 1966), p. 667.
2. Charles Frankel, *The Case for Modern Man* (New York: Harper, 1955), pp. 198–199.
3. See the works recommended in For Further Study section at end of book.

☐ *The Problems of Democracy*

5 MASS DEMOCRACY

■ *E. H. Carr*

. . . Much has been written in recent years of the decline of reason, and of respect for reason, in human affairs, when sometimes what has really hap-

From E. H. Carr, *The New Society* (New York: St. Martin's Press and Macmillan & Co., Ltd., 1951), pp. 68–76. Reprinted by permission.

pened has been the abandonment of the highly simplified eighteenth-century view of reason in favor of a subtler and more sophisticated analysis. But it is nonetheless true that the epoch-making changes in our attitude toward reason provide a key to some of the profoundest problems of contemporary democracy.

First of all, the notion that men of intelligence and good will were likely by process of rational discussion to reach a correct opinion on controversial political questions could be valid only in an age when such questions were comparatively few and simple enough to be accessible to the educated layman. It implicitly denied that any specialized knowledge was required to solve political problems. This hypothesis was perhaps tenable so long as the state was not required to intervene in economic issues, and the questions on which decisions had to be taken turned on matters of practical detail or general political principles. In the first half of the twentieth century these conditions had everywhere ceased to exist. In Great Britain major issues of a highly controversial character, like the return to the gold standard in 1925 or the acceptance of the American loan in 1946, were of a kind in which no opinion seriously counted except that of the trained expert in possession of a vast array of facts and figures, some of them probably not available to the public. In such matters the ordinary citizen could not even have an intelligent opinion on the question who were the best experts to consult. The only role he could hope to play was to exercise his hunch at the election by choosing the right leader to consult the right experts about vital, though probably still unformulated, issues of policy which would ultimately affect his daily life.

At this initial stage of the argument, reason itself is not dethroned from its supreme role in the decision of political issues. The citizen is merely asked to surrender his right of decision to the superior reason of the expert. At the second stage of the argument, reason itself is used to dethrone reason. The social psychologist, employing rational methods of investigation, discovers that men in the mass are often most effectively moved by nonrational emotions such as admiration, envy, hatred, and can be most effectively reached not by rational argument, but by emotional appeals to eye and ear, or by sheer repetition. Propaganda is as essential a function of mass democracy as advertising of mass production. The political organizer takes a leaf out of the book of the commercial advertiser and sells the leader or the candidate to the voter by the same methods used to sell patent medicines or refrigerators. The appeal is no longer to the reason of the citizen, but to his gullibility. A more recent phenomenon has been the emergence of what Max Weber called the "charismatic leader" as the expression of the general will. The retreat from individualism seemed to issue at last—and not alone in the so-called totalitarian countries—in the exaltation of a single individual leader who personified and resumed within himself the qualities and aspirations of the "little man," of the ordinary individual lost and bewildered in the new mass society. But the principal qualification of the leader is no longer his capacity to reason correctly on political or economic issues, or even his capacity to choose the best experts to reason for him, but a good public face, a convincing voice, a sympathetic fireside manner on the radio; and these qualities are deliberately built up for him by his publicity agents. In this picture of the techniques of contemporary democracy, the party headquarters, the directing brain at the center, still operates rationally, but uses irrational rather than rational means to achieve its ends—means which are, moreover, not merely irrational but largely irrelevant to the purposes to be pursued or to the decisions to be taken.

The third stage of the argument reaches deeper levels. Hegel, drawing out the philosophical implications of Rousseau's doctrine, had identified the course of history with universal reason, to which the individual reason stood in the same relation as the individual will to Rousseau's general will. Individual reason had been the cornerstone of individualist democracy. Marx took Hegel's collective reason to make it the cornerstone of the new mass democracy. Marx purported to reject the metaphysical character of Hegel's thought. But, equally with Hegel, he conceived of history pursuing a rational course, which could be analyzed and even predicted in terms of reason. Hegel had spoken of the cunning of reason in history, using individuals to achieve purposes of which they themselves were unconscious. Marx would have rejected the turn of phrase as metaphysical. But his conception of history as a continuous process of class struggle contained elements of determinism which revealed its Hegelian ancestry, at any rate on one side. Marx remained a thoroughgoing rationalist. But the reason whose validity he accepted was collective rather than individual.

Marx played, however, a far more important part in what has been called "the flight from reason" than by the mere exaltation of the collective over the individual. By his vigorous assertion that "being determines consciousness, not consciousness being," that thinking is conditioned by the social environment of the thinker, and that ideas are the superstructure of a totality whose foundation is formed by the material conditions of life, Marx presented a clear challenge to what had hitherto been regarded as the sovereign or autonomous human reason. The actors who played significant parts in the historical drama were playing parts already written for them: this, indeed, was what made them significant. The function of individual reason was to identify itself with the universal reason which determined the course of history and to make itself the agent and executor of this universal reason. Some such view is, indeed, involved in any attempt to trace back historical events to underlying social causes; and Marx—and still more Engels—hedged a little in later years about the role of the individual in history. But the extraordinary vigor and conviction with which he drove home his main argument, and the political theory which he founded on it, give him a leading place among those nineteenth-century thinkers who shattered the comfortable belief of the Age of Enlightenment in the decisive power of individual reason in shaping the course of history.

Marx's keenest polemics were those directed to prove the "conditioned" character of the thinking of his opponents and particularly of the capitalist ruling class of the most advanced countries of his day. If they thought as they did it was because, as members of a class, "being" determined their "consciousness," and their ideas necessarily lacked any independent objectivity and validity. Hegel, as a good conservative, had exempted the current reality of the Prussian from the operation of the dialectic which had destroyed successively so many earlier historical forms. Marx, as a revolutionary, admitted no such absolute in the present, but only in the future. The proletariat, whose victory would automatically abolish classes, was alone the basis of absolute value; and collective proletarian thinking had thus an objectivity which was denied to the thinking of other classes. Marx's willingness, like that of Hegel, to admit an absolute as the culminating point of his dialectical process was, however, an element of inconsistency in his system; and, just as Marx was far more concerned to dissect capitalism than to provide a blueprint for socialism, so his use of the dialectic to lay bare the conditioned thinking of his opponents lay far nearer to his heart, and was far more effective, than his enunciation of the objective and absolute values of the proletariat. Marx's writings gave a powerful impetus to all forms of relativism. It seemed less important, at a time when the proletarian revolution was as yet nowhere in sight, to note his admission of absolute truth as a prerogative of the proletariat. The proletariat was for Marx the collective repository of Rousseau's infallible general will.

Another thinker of the later nineteenth century also helped to mold the climate of political opinion. Like Darwin, Freud was a scientist without pretensions to be a philosopher or, still less, a political thinker. But in the flight from reason at the end of the nineteenth century, he played the same popular role as Darwin had played a generation earlier in the philosophy of *laissez faire*. Freud demonstrated that the fundamental attitudes of human beings in action and thought are largely determined at levels beneath that of consciousness and that the supposedly rational explanations of those attitudes which we offer to ourselves and others are artificial and erroneous "rationalizations" of processes which we have failed to understand. Reason is given to us, Freud seems to say, not to direct our thought and action, but to camouflage the hidden forces which do direct it. This is a still more devastating version of the Marxist thesis of substructure and superstructure. The substructure of reality resides in the unconscious: what appears above the surface is no more than the reflection, seen in a distorting ideological mirror, of what goes on underneath. The political conclusion from all this—Freud himself drew none—is that any attempt to appeal to the reason of the ordinary man is waste of time, or is useful merely as camouflage to conceal the real nature of the process of persuasion; the appeal must be made to those subconscious strata which are decisive for thought and action. The debunking of ideology undertaken by the political science of Marx is repeated in a far more drastic and far-reaching way by the psychological science of Freud and his successors.

By the middle of the nineteenth century, therefore, the propositions of Locke on which the theory of liberal democracy were founded had all been subjected to fundamental attack, and the attack broadened and deepened as the century went on. Individualism began to give way to collectivism both in economic organization and in the forms and practice of mass democracy: the age of mass civilization had begun. The alleged harmony of interests between individuals was replaced by the naked struggle between powerful classes and organized interest groups. The belief in the settlement of issues by rational discussion was undermined, first, by recognition of the complex and technical character of the issues involved; later and more seriously, by recognition that rational arguments were merely the conditioned reflection of the class interests of those who put them forward; and, last and most seriously of all, by the discovery that the democratic voter, like other human beings, is most effectively reached, not by arguments directed to his reason, but by appeal directed to his irrational, subconscious prejudices. The picture of democracy which emerged from these criticisms was the picture of an arena where powerful interest groups struggled for the mastery. The leaders themselves were often the spokesmen and instruments of historical processes which they did not fully understand; their followers consisted of voters recruited and marshaled for purposes of which they were wholly unconscious by all the subtle techniques of modern psychological science and modern commercial advertising.

The picture is overdrawn. But we shall not begin to understand the problems of mass democracy unless we recognize the serious elements of truth in it, unless we recognize how far we have moved away from the conceptions and from the conditions out of which the democratic tradition was born. From the conception of democracy as a select society of free individuals, enjoying equal rights and periodically electing to manage the affairs of the society, a small number of their peers, who deliberate together and decide by rational argument on the course to pursue (the assumption being that the course which appeals to the majority is likely to be the most rational), we have passed to the current reality of mass democracy. The typical mass democracy of today is a vast society of individuals, stratified by widely different social and economic backgrounds into a series of groups or classes, enjoying equal political rights the exercise of which is organized through two or more closely integrated political machines called parties. Between the parties and individual citizens stands an indeterminate number of entities variously known as unions, associations, lobbies, or pressure groups devoted to the promotion of some economic interest, or of some social or humanitarian cause in which keen critics usually detect a latent and perhaps unconscious interest. At the first stage of the democratic process, these associations and groups form a sort of exchange and mart where votes are traded for support of particular policies; the more votes such a group controls, the better its chance of having its views incorporated in the party platform. At the second stage, when these bargains have been made, the party as a united entity "goes to the country" and endeavors by every form of political propaganda to win the support of the unattached voter. At the third stage, when the election has been decided, the parties once more dispute or bargain together, in the light of the votes cast, on the policies to be put into effect; the details of procedure at this third stage differ considerably in different democratic countries in accordance with varying constitutional requirements and party structures. What is important to note is that the first and third stages are fierce matters of bargaining. At the second stage, where the mass persuasion of the electorate is at issue, the methods employed now commonly approximate more and more closely to those of commercial advertisers, who, on the advice of modern psychologists, find the appeal to fear, envy, or self-aggrandizement more effective than the appeal to reason. Certainly in the United States, where contemporary large-scale democracy has worked most successfully and where the strongest confidence is felt in its survival, experienced practitioners of politics would give little encouragement to the idea that rational argument exercises a major influence on the democratic process. We have returned to a barely disguised struggle of interest groups in which the arguments used are for the most part no more than a rationalization of the interests concerned, and the role of persuasion is played by carefully calculated appeals to the irrational subconscious.

This discussion is intended to show not that mass democracy is more corrupt or less efficient than other forms of government (this I do not believe), but that mass democracy is a new phenomenon—a creation of the last half-century—which it is inappropriate and misleading to consider in terms of the philosophy of Locke or of the liberal democracy of the nineteenth century. It is new, because the new democratic society consists no longer of a homogeneous closed society of equal and economically secure individuals mutually recognizing one another's rights, but of ill co-ordinated, highly stratified masses of people of whom a large majority are primarily occupied with the daily struggle for existence. It is new, because the new democratic state can no longer be content to hold the ring in the strife of private economic interests, but must enter the arena at every moment and take the initiative in urgent issues of economic policy which affect the daily life of all the citizens, and especially of the least secure. It is new, because the old rationalist assumptions of Locke and of liberal democracy have broken down under the weight both of changed material conditions and of new scientific insights and inventions, and the leaders of the new democracy are concerned no longer primarily with the reflection of opinion, but with the molding and manipulation of opinion. To speak today of the defense of democracy as if we were defending something which we knew and had possessed for many decades or many centuries is self-deception and sham.

It is no answer to point to institutions that have survived from earlier forms of democracy. The survival of kingship in Great Britain does not prove that the British system of government is a monarchy; and democratic institutions survive in many countries today—some survived even in Hitler's Germany—which have little or no claim to be called democracies. The criterion must be sought, not in the survival of traditional institutions, but in the question where power resides and how it is exercised. In this respect democracy is a matter of degree. Some countries today are more democratic than others. But none is perhaps very democratic, if any high standard of democracy is applied. Mass democracy is a difficult and hitherto largely uncharted territory; and we should be nearer the mark, and should have a far more convincing slogan, if we spoke of the need, not to defend democracy, but to create it.

6 THE OVERDEVELOPED SOCIETY

■   *C. Wright Mills*

We are at the ending of what is called The Modern Age. Just as Antiquity was followed by several centuries of Oriental ascendancy which Westerners provincially call The Dark Ages, so now The Modern Age is being succeeded by a postmodern period. Perhaps we may call it: The Fourth Epoch. . . . The ideological mark of The Fourth Epoch—that which sets it off from The Modern Age—is that the ideas of freedom and of reason have become moot; that increased rationality may not be assumed to make for increased freedom.

The underlying trends are well known. Great and rational organizations—in brief, bureaucracies—have indeed increased, but the substantive reason of the individual at large has not. Caught in the limited milieus of their everyday lives, ordinary men often cannot reason about the great structures—rational and irrational—of which their *milieus* are subordinate parts. Accordingly, they often carry out series of apparently rational actions without any ideas of the ends they serve, and there is the increasing suspicion that those at the top as well—like Tolstoy's generals—only pretend they know. That the techniques and the rationality of science are given a central place in a society does not mean that men live reasonably and without myth, fraud, and superstition. Science, it turns out, is not a technological Second Coming. Universal education may lead to technological idiocy and nationalist provinciality, rather than to the informed and independent intelligence. Rationally organized social arrangements are not necesarily a means of increased freedom—for the individual or for the society. In fact, often they are a means of tyranny and manipulation, a means of expropriating the very chance to reason, the very capacity to act as a free man.

The atrocities of The Fourth Epoch are committed by men as "functions" of a rational social machinery—men possessed by an abstracted view that hides from them the humanity of their victims and as well their own humanity. The moral insensibility of our times was made dramatic by the Nazis, but is not the same lack of human morality revealed by the atomic bombing of the peoples

From C. Wright Mills, "Culture and Politics," in *Power, Politics and People: The Collected Essays of C. Wright Mills,* ed. by Irving Louis Horowitz (New York: Ballantine, 1963), pp. 236–242. © Copyright 1963 by the Estate of C. Wright Mills. Reprinted by permission of Oxford University Press, Inc.

of Hiroshima and Nagasaki? And did it not prevail, too, among fighter pilots in Korea, with their petroleum-jelly broiling of children and women and men? Auschwitz and Hiroshima—are they not equally features of the highly rational moral insensibility of The Fourth Epoch? And is not this lack of moral sensibility raised to a higher and technically more adequate level among the brisk generals and gentle scientists who are now rationally—and absurdly—planning the weapons and the strategy of the third world war? These actions are not necessarily sadistic; they are merely businesslike; they are not emotional at all; they are efficient, rational, technically clean-cut. They are inhuman acts because they are impersonal.

In the meantime, ideology and sensibility quite apart, the compromises and exploitations by which the nineteenth-century world was balanced have collapsed. In this sixth decade of the twentieth century the structure of a new world is, indeed, coming into view.

The ascendancy of the USA, along with that of the USSR, has relegated the scatter of European nations to subsidiary status. The world of The Fourth Epoch is divided. On either side, a superpower now spends its most massive and co-ordinated effort in the highly scientific preparation of a third world war.

Yet, for the first time in history, the very idea of victory in war has become idiotic. As war becomes total, it becomes absurd. Yet in both the superstates, virtually all policies and actions fall within the perspective of war; in both, elites and spokesmen—in particular, I must say, those of the United States—are possessed by the military metaphysic, according to which all world reality is defined in military terms. By both, the most decisive features of reality are held to be the state of violence and the balance of fright. . . .

What kind of society is the USA turning out to be in the middle of the twentieth century? Perhaps it is possible to characterize it as a prototype of at least "The West." To locate it within its world context in The Fourth Epoch, perhaps we may call it The Overdeveloped Society.

The *Underdeveloped Country*, as you know, is one in which the focus of life is necessarily on economic subsistence; its industrial equipment is not sufficient to meet Western standards of minimum comfort. Its style of life and its system of power are dominated by the struggle to accumulate the primary means of industrial production.

In a *Properly Developing Society*, one might suppose that deliberately cultivated styles of life would be central; decisions about standards of living would be made in terms of debated choices among such styles; the industrial equipment of such a society would be maintained as an instrument to increase the range of choice among styles of life.

But in *The Overdeveloped Nation*, the standard of living dominates the style of life; its inhabitants are possessed, as it were, by its industrial and commercial apparatus: collectively, by the maintenance of conspicuous production; individually, by the frenzied pursuit and maintenance of commodities. Around these fetishes, life, labor, and leisure are increasingly organized. Focused on these, the struggle for status supplements the struggle for survival; a panic for status replaces the proddings of poverty.

In underdeveloped countries, industrialization, however harsh, may be seen as man conquering nature and so freeing himself from want. But in the overdeveloped nation, as industrialization proceeds, the economic emphasis moves from production to merchandising, and the economic system which makes a fetish of efficiency becomes highly inefficient and systematically wasteful. The pivotal decade for this shift in the United States was the twenties, but it is since the ending of World War II that the overdeveloped economy has truly come to flourish.

Surely there is no need to elaborate this theme in detail; since Thorstein Veblen formulated it, it has been several times "affluently" rediscovered. Society in brief has become a great salesroom—and a network of rackets: the gimmick of success becomes the yearly change of model, as in the mass society fashion becomes universal. The marketing apparatus transforms the human being into the ultimately saturated man—the cheerful robot—and makes "anxious obsolescence" the American way of life.

But all this—although enormously important to the quality of life—is, I suppose, merely the obvious surface. Beneath it there are institutions which in the United States today are as far removed from the images of Tocqueville as is Russia today from the classic expectations of Marx. . . .

I should like to put this matter in terms of certain parallel developments in the USA and the USSR. The very terms of their world antagonism are furthering their similarities. Geographically and ethnically both are supersocieties; unlike the nations of Europe, each has amalgamated on a continental domain great varieties of peoples and cultures. The power of both is based on technological development. In both, this development is made into a cultural and a social fetish, rather than an instrument under continual public appraisal and control. In neither is there significant craftsmanship in work or significant leisure in the nonworking life. In both, men at leisure and at work are subjected to impersonal bureaucracies. In neither do workers control the process of production or consumers truly shape the process of consumption. Workers' control is as far removed from both as is consumers' sovereignty.

In both the United States and the Soviet Union, as the political order is enlarged and centralized, it becomes less political and more bureaucratic; less the locale of a struggle than an object to be managed. . . .

In neither of these superpowers are there, as central facts of power, voluntary associations linking individuals, smaller communities, and publics, on the one hand, with the state, the military establishment, the economic apparatus on the other. Accordingly, in neither are there readily available vehicles for reasoned opinions and instruments for the national exertion of public will. Such voluntary associations are no longer a dominant feature of the political structure of the overdeveloped society.

The classic conditions of democracy, in summary, do not exactly flourish in the overdeveloped society; democratic formations are not now ascendant in the power structure of the United States or of the Soviet Union. Within both, history-making decisions and lack of decisions are virtually monopolized by elites who have access to the material and cultural means by which history is now powerfully being made. . . .

☐ The Predicaments of Industrial Society

7 THE OMNIVOROUS ORGANIZATION

■ *Nathan Glazer*

Paul Goodman, in *Growing Up Absurd,* compiles a list of revolutions that have failed in the last hundred years—changes that were set into motion but were never quite consummated: political revolutions, economic revolutions, ethical and moral revolutions. A failed revolution is itself an ambiguous notion. Did it fail because the forces of evil and reaction were too strong? Or did it fail because there was no way for it to succeed, because its vision of "success" contained contradictory elements that could not, in history, be brought together in a stable compound? Did it fail because those attempting to carry it out realized at some point that the good to be attained was disproportionate to the effort required? Did it fail, in other words, because what it attempted to achieve, while undoubtedly good, did not after a while seem good enough?

The latter set of questions, I think, points to the pattern that is characteristic of our own day. For two revolutions which have become closely linked unfortunately *did* succeed—the organizational revolution and the scientific revolution—and their success makes any others infinitely difficult to bring off. The technology of science permits the organization to become ever larger and more effective. And the steady rationality of scientific thinking applied to organizational problems seems to overcome some of the chief characteristics and perhaps weaknesses of organizations in the past—their rigidity, their lack of dynamism, their stubbornness. Perhaps these characteristics once permitted

From Nathan Glazer, "The Good Society," *Commentary,* XXXVI (September, 1963), 226–228. © Copyright 1963 by the American Jewish Committee. Reprinted by permission of the author and the publisher.

us, like primitive mammals around a dinosaur, to outwit the organization, to achieve changes without the exhausting investment of unlimited energy that is now required. But we have suddenly arrived at a point when even the biggest organizations we have—such as the defense forces—can, by the power of a rational analysis, be made flexible. With the help of a newly developed technology for analysis, those great giants, the Army, the Navy, and the Air Force, have by now, we are told, been bent together to common ends, despite their traditions, their organizational character, even their alliances with Congress.

Compare the present situation with one that many of us can recall from only twenty-five years ago. In those days, we—some of us, at any rate—attacked the threat of a $1 billion budget for national defense. There were no intellectuals in the armed forces then; if there were, intellectuals outside the armed forces did not know them. Or think back to the State Department of those days. Perhaps radical and liberal critics of the twenties and thirties, in their ignorance, caricatured professional military men and professional diplomats. Perhaps these men were not as inadequate and self-seeking as we imagined. But the gap between them and us was so great that we could in good conscience denounce and caricature them and honestly believe that we would do much better if we only had the chance. To intellectual critics, men of affairs in the twenties and thirties clearly stood in the way of the obvious steps to a much better society. And I am convinced this was no illusion, just as the contempt the men of affairs had for their "impractical" critics was based on no illusion either. Military men, diplomats, corporation presidents, disinherited radical intellectuals—all stood far apart from each other and distinct; each could see the limitations, stupidity, inadequacies of the other. The system permitted those of us who stood outside it to hate it; and in contrast to that system, it was easy to imagine something better. When we looked at limited people and bound institutions, it was easy to believe that, when the limits and bonds were burst, something newer and cleaner and fresher would emerge.

The bonds were never burst. Rather, they were loosened. The tension between inside and outside relaxed, and as it relaxed, as more interchange between those inside the system and those outside began taking place, it became harder and harder for the outsiders to hate with such healthy directness. It is not only that the critics began to understand the problems of those who ran the organizations; the organizations themselves loosened up to the point where the critics were put into a position of being able to see what those problems were and what the representatives of the status quo were actually like. Indeed, the representatives began even to include some of the critics.

The critics were included or listened to for a number of reasons. One, perhaps, was that the authorities decided that this would be a good way to draw the claws of the critics: weakening the opposition by enfolding it. Another, perhaps, was that the authorities had lost some of their old self-confidence. But more important than either of these reasons was the rise of the new techniques for making organizations more efficient. These techniques—computerization, operations research, management education, "buzz sessions," and so on—exert a far stronger pressure on the organization to include its critics than the old Machiavellian notion of buying them off by bringing them in. The pressure now comes from the principle that everything, or almost everything, is relevant, or may be relevant, to the solution of a problem or the heightening of efficiency.

It is because so many factors are relevant that techniques and technologies have been developed for considering the joint impact of a host of diverse forces in a given area of activity, the effect each of these forces has on every other, and how they can be expected to operate, both jointly and singly, at every stage in a long-run process. The application of science to social problems thus means that many "inputs," many different kinds of knowledge, are required. The inputs required, for example, in national defense now include, in addition to the special expertise of military men, that of economists, industrial managers, political analysts, psychologists, sociologists, town planners, psychiatrists— not that I would exaggerate the influence of these latter three or four categories. Indeed, a properly developed national defense policy would even have to take into account the information and insights of pacifists and those who oppose the current military establishment. . . .

I have suggested that one of the things that has happened to our conception of the good is that the effort to achieve it seems, in many spheres, to be disproportionate to what we might conceivably accomplish. The disproportion is created by a number of factors, of which the first is the process we have just been talking about: the sophistication of the existing organizations under the pressure of new scientific and rational techniques. The "lead time," so to speak, of intellectual and radical critics is growing ever shorter. Their ideas are taken up; they are taken up. Paul Goodman, when he wrote about the movies in the early 1940's, was probably not read by a single person who "counted" in Hollywood. When he writes about television today, Newton Minow, I assume, reads him and David Brinkley writes letters to the *New Republic* to argue with him. I doubt that this is because he is not as radical today as he was then. The explanation is rather that the organizations are more sophisticated, more in touch with advanced ideas, than they used to be. Yet the paradoxical consequence is not that such ideas exert more influence than they once did, but that they are often robbed of their bite and of their influence on the general opinion by being fought against in a highly sophisticated manner.

But even where the organizations are not sophisticated so far as ideas are concerned, the organizational revolution has at least proceeded to the point where they are more efficient than they used to be so far as their own ends are concerned. They cannot easily be gotten around. And if they cannot be gotten around, the critics are forced to work with them at *their* pace and on *their* terms: who, then, is influencing whom? . . .

8 THE TROUBLED METROPOLIS

■ *John W. Dyckman*

Modern cities and the notion of a social order based on freedom grew up together. Towns developed into cities with the rise of bourgeois institutions—standardized weights and measures, uniform codes of law, and freedom from governmental restrictions. In the new society of North America, men entered the cities free of the feudal restrictions of medieval times. Self-interest was the cement of this union. The Enlightenment, in its optimism, was confident that even the constituent atoms of chemical compounds could be held together by mutual affinity. With the French Revolution, the modern urban order was founded, and the way was cleared for commercial and industrial growth in cities.

By the nineteenth century, with the maturation of what Geddes and Mumford have called the paleotechnic age, the optimism of the eighteenth century yielded to doubt, both about the city and about the stable social order based on self-interest. Now, halfway through the twentieth century, it is apparent that the transition from village to town to city has become a runaway movement in which urbanization, a powerful organizing system which merges small cities with large ones, threatens to destroy the distinctions between small and large places within metropolitan areas.

Imperfect order is a necessary companion of rapid growth. Disequilibrium is the father of change. As a group of French scholars observed recently,[1] men have paid for the advantages of larger cities with a certain number of inconveniences, which, at each succeeding level of growth, have been stanchly protested by adherents of traditional civilization. In this chapter, I shall examine several characteristic forms of contemporary urban growth which are capable of upsetting the established social and political order and are likely to impede orderly transition from existing institutions to new ones.

From John W. Dyckman, "Some Conditions of Civic Order in an Urbanized World," *Daedalus,* XCV, "Tradition and Change" (Summer, 1966), 797–812. Reprinted with permission of *Daedalus,* Journal of the American Academy of Arts and Sciences, Boston, Massachusetts.

Runaway Urbanization

The first threat is that of scale. The modern city came to maturity in the late nineteenth century, when the population of Europe increased from 180 to 450 millions, and that of America grew from 5 to 76 millions. This was a century in which mass politics was born, major military confrontations emerged, and the supercities of our era began to take form. Yet none of the cities we have known has prepared us for the scale of the urban complexes which we shall soon experience. It is likely that during the next three generations the cities will have to accommodate populations at least ten times larger than those currently living in urban areas. If present agglomerative tendencies continue, they will lead to integrated metropolitan areas several times larger than contemporary New York. Harvey Wheeler expresses a common fear of this development with the observation that "soon each of the country's ten metropolitan areas may have from 30 to 50 million people compacted into them. Traditional interventionist devices simply cannot cope with demographic dis-equilibrium on such a scale."[2]

This disequilibrium could take several forms. First, by overspilling old community, state, and national boundaries, metropolitan growth could require political reordering, threaten existing social arrangements, and upset the psychological stability of city dwellers. The elaborate technical arrangements necessary to maintain communications and the movement of persons and goods in these large service areas could become exceedingly vulnerable to sabotage or to unforeseen accidents and breakdowns. In addition, such urban growth may lead to population densities which could in time impair biological functioning.

Second, the juxtaposition of high urbanization rates and low per capita economic growth threatens to plunge certain developing nations into financial chaos or to retard their planned national development. In the Chilean economy, for example, costs directly attributable to urbanization claim half the investment funds of the nation. In countries closer to subsistence, the drain may be felt even more keenly.

Third, urban culture, by feeding the revolutionary growth of expectations, is capable of stoking fires of rebellion and unrest. According to those who hold this view, the dense city is a source of mass discontent which may explode against almost any incidental target. In addition, mass urbanization increases the possibility of sudden floods of disquieting communication, including all kinds of inciteful rumors. Where the populations of these urban centers are compartmentalized, the danger of epidemic outbreak, including those of social pathology, is likely to be increased.

Scale and Density

According to Wheeler, the population of the future city of 30 million might be "compacted" into dense masses. If humans living in the cities interacted like gas molecules in a closed container or like rats in cages, increased densities could conceivably lead to overheating, or to a volume of contact which would overload the individual's capacity for response, and result in behavior breakdown. Studies on lower animals, such as rats, suggest that this outcome is a serious possibility.[3] However, there are a number of reasons for believing that this outcome cannot be extended to humans by simple analogy.

In the first place, the metropolitan area is not strictly "closed." Though sizable regions of agricultural and village occupancy are "emptying out" and the populations are pouring into cities, the density of inhabitants in urban areas is not increasing markedly. Density is a function of the technology of transportation and of spatial organization as well as the number of persons per acre. No large residential sector of any city in the United States has population densities equal to those of the lower east side of Manhattan at the turn of the century.

Second, and even more important, humans have a capacity for creating internal order behind the protective wall of privacy. Some of the highest densities in our present urban scene are accompanied by a high degree of privacy, particularly in the areas of luxury living. It must be recognized, however, that the personal defenses which secure this internal order may at times become pathological and lead to social disorder. Privacy may be secured by depersonalization, or by withdrawing entirely into oneself. While the anomie observed by nineteenth-century sociologists is one pathological form, a kind of involuntary privacy, the self-concern of bystanders who watch murder and mayhem in a subway without intervening is another form. A degree of insulation from social concerns may be a price which must be paid for this defense in conditions of extreme overcrowding. Thus, high densities without good transport and communication, without amenities and a means of self-protection, are capable of producing dangerous frictions. Where there are means to overcome these, high densities appear quite tolerable. Modern techniques of transportation and communication have made possible cities in the style of Los Angeles. (The Los Angeles trouble spot of Watts, contrary to the impression created by the mass media, is not a high-density area by conventional urban standards.)

The American urban pattern, in which cities merge in great metropolitan belts, developed as a consequence of the efforts of economically free agents to maximize profits and amenities. In North America, therefore, the city is especially an economic entity. The American city is free, in an economic if not a political sense, to push its boundaries outward. It can preserve a kind of density balance in which individuals' preferences for space are accommodated and technology is used both to concentrate a high intensity of activities and to disperse places of residence. Given the extraordinary heterogeneity of the American population, it is possible that the sprawling development of American cities has actually relieved tension and reduced intergroup conflict by substituting a stratified spatial order for a genuine social accommodation. (The dangers which result from an overly rigid territorial stratification are discussed below.)

In world terms, the new metropolitan growth, with its increasing organization of economic and political life, may be temporarily disequilibrating in a number of ways. First, for poor countries or those in early stages of economic development, the rapid transfer of energies from country to city may appear to be "overurbanization." Second, the shift from rural to urban values and styles of life may, in the absence of appropriate urban opportunities, appear as "premature" cultural transformation or result in an overcommunication of expectations. Third, the specialization of place, occupation, and roles required by urban society may lead to wasteful and dysfunctional competition. Fourth, but not least important, the communications technology of urban agglomerations in the poorer countries may not match the demands placed on it. An organizing vacuum may be created when upward and downward communications are blocked—particularly when traditional communications channels are eliminated.

Urban Costs and Economic Development

The first friction, that of overurbanization, is found in countries where rapid population growth outstrips economic development in the pretake-off period. Overurbanization is a threat to social order because (1) the demand for the minimum urban capital necessary to accommodate the population at tolerable health and efficiency levels cannot be met by scarce national resources, (2) the growth in economic and political expectations of the new urbanites rises more rapidly than their contribution to economic or political life, and (3) concentration in urban centers gives revolutionary cadres a position strategically closer to the management of the society and the conduct of its political life. A principal symptom of overurbanization is the growth of squatter communities on the fringes of the established cities, sometimes accommodating as large a total population as the old cities. In the underdeveloped countries with high rural birth rates, modest growth in productivity, and a low rate of accumulation of capital, population has been moving to the city at rates comparable to those of the Industrial Revolution. This has happened without a corresponding growth in economic development and in a period of improved public hygiene and higher urban birth rates. In areas having high population growth, such as Latin America and the Middle East, the swelling city populations are inadequately housed. In the words of Kingsley Davis:

> By whatever name they are called, the squatters are to be found in all the major cities in the poorer countries. . . . They tend to occupy with implacable determination parks, school grounds and vacant lots; . . . these areas account for about 45% of the housing in the entire city [in greater Baghdad] and are devoid of amenities, including even latrines.[4]

Though employment in cities lags behind the growth of the urban labor force, it is in the cities that the new opportunities are to be found. Success in the city is communicated to the rural areas and towns, and an overresponse results. Because the rural population is increasing much more rapidly than are the corresponding employment opportunities in the villages and the country, squatters occupy land to which they have dubious legal claim, often with the tacit consent of state and municipal authorities. These squatter communities often lack even the most rudimentary water supply and sewage systems, though the public health menace is sometimes no worse than in the corresponding slums of the established cities.

Urban Institutions under Pressure

The real difficulties are institutional and political: the squatter settlements are private governments which have set up their own administrative enclaves within the governmental process, but without benefit of the usual legitimation. They are frequently antigovernment (at least as far as the formal constituted government is concerned) and become centers of resistance, occasionally of rebellion. Governmental communication with the squatters is difficult; they may be outside the machinery of mobilization which can help to match people with opportunities.

Urbanization reduces the traditional violence of "feuds," but increases the chance of epidemic violence. The increasing probability of epidemic violence is not an aspect of mass urban society as such, but is a function of the character of communication in a mass society. In the past, when communication was less reliable and available channels were fewer, outbreaks of disorder were by no means uncommon. The Renaissance cities of northern Italy were, on many counts, riotous and disorderly beyond the tolerable limits of contemporary urban life. Today we have come to depend on reliable communication, such as air-raid warnings, weather reports, and notices of school closings, for the regulation of daily city life. The possibility of manufacturing disorder through unreliable communication has increased with this new dependence. The battle for the radio station is a key feature of any contemporary *coup d'état* from Iraq to Cuba, for the radio is cheap and ubiquitous and does not depend on literacy for its effectiveness.

Expectations of the New Urbanites

A second effect is observable where urbanization raises expectations more rapidly than it improves the means of achieving them. This is a common obstacle to developing countries striving to conserve capital for development schemes. The city is a powerful educative force in the matter of tastes because of its concentrated buying power, the diversity of consumer goods, and the highly cultivated and conspicuous forms of consumption which are evident. Migrants to the city from rural areas swiftly acquire a taste for urban consumer goods. In some countries, as the Yugoslav experience has shown, the demands of the new urbanites place heavy pressure on the supply of scarce credit. In other countries, pressure is placed on the balance of payments by the high propensity to import foreign consumer goods. The more the values of a country are organized around consumption and its growth, the more dangerous these pressures may be.

The Watts uprising in Los Angeles in the summer of 1965 may be viewed, at least partially, in this light. Pent-up resentment against deprivation of the right to participate in the urban consumption orgy exploded into attacks on stores, particularly those which practiced the lure of consumer credit and then repossessed the treasured symbols of urban dignity. In part, the residents of Watts were protesting against their inability to participate in the consumer society; in part, too, they were protesting against the terms on which participation was offered.

The social standards of urban life set these expectations. These standards are not the same in all places—for example, the acceptable or expected behavior in Berkeley, California, and Birmingham, Alabama, would be dramatically different. But in almost every case, differences between urban and rural standards within regions of the same country are greater than the differences between those regions. Until these differences are accommodated, the movement of rural people to the cities will create tension.

Segregation and Conflict

In almost every part of the world where rural-urban migration is large, behavioral and social value differentials are accommodated by detaining the migrants in segregated sectors of the city. In the poorer countries, these enclaves are virtually villages within the city boundaries.[5] In the United States, for example, racial segregation emerged as a permanent feature of urban life only after 1900, when Negroes came to the cities in large numbers.[6]

The historic occupational stratification of cities was once economically functional. The medieval city found it advantageous, even necessary, to cluster guilds in recognizable quarters and to keep villages intact. In contemporary cities, the spatial stratification is frequently less functional. It serves the purposes of social distinction better than it does the efficient use of land, though the latter may be an element in the segregation of industrial and other nonresidential uses.

Segregation is a form of order—a spatial ordering of social relations in the city. The highly developed ancient cities of the Indus Valley assigned residential quarters by occupation, an early expression of the caste system. The medieval city, of which New York is an atavistic reminder, segregated economic activities of the respective guilds. The economic and social order secured by the segregation of social groups by residence has become a source of new forms of disorder.

Rigid territorial allocations lead to fixed boundaries which are difficult to maintain. The boundaries, moreover, become the scenes at which sharply differentiated groups meet, and conflict arises. In this sense, neighborhood borders serve to promote conflict in much the way that badly defined but closed boundaries are the cause of disputes between national states. The gangs of city neighborhoods fight fiercely to protect the home "turf." The ghettos which hold populations in become barriers to movement within the city.

Segregation also leaves an area vulnerable to epidemic invasion, whether of physical or social pathology. The flow of information is accelerated by the narrowness of the channel, the homogeneity of the medium, and the absence of conflicting messages. A rumor can sweep Harlem or Watts in a fraction of the time required for it to circulate through mid-town Manhattan. It is significant that segregation has become the symbol of political and social inequality, the mark of a subject population within the larger political community. Racial segregation has bred separatist movements and has fostered the rise of conflicting nationalisms, of which the Black Muslims are a conspicuous example.

Finally, the segregation of the poor and the withdrawal of the rich to small, semiprivate political enclaves have prevented the formation of integral political units at the metropolitan level. During periods of rapid urban growth, a major source of in-migration to cities is the rural poor. Thus, at a time when cities are growing large, usually by suburban accretion, they are marked by political fragmentation which combines the existing inequality in income and private consumption with a corresponding inequality in public goods provided by the respective local governments. This process hinders the acculturation and development of the in-migrants.

The Integrative City

The city is an integrating organization form. The politics, economics, religion, and instruments of social organization and control of a society can be based on the ecology of the city, since communications are conveniently centered there. One would expect, therefore, that the city would mirror the social and political institutions of the society in which it is situated. But the process of urbanization is so widespread, and the world's economy so increasingly integrated, that cities in many parts of the world reflect this international organizational growth in their structure and ecological adjustments more than they do the national traits of the society of which they are a part. India, for example, is beginning to show the suburbanization of industry characteristic of the United States and of industrially developed societies.[7] At the jet ports of the world, an international, cosmopolitan society can meet and carry on business without regard for historic differences. This is not to say that the physical or social problems of Calcutta are the same as those of New York. The former are infinitely more severe because the level of wealth, income, and technology is so much lower in India than in the United States. What can be concluded, however, is that the city intensifies the contradictions and conflicts which have been developing within the national society. Cairo is a city of villages in which the inhabitants often have lower literacy than would be found in corresponding villages of the countryside precisely because Egypt has not developed the level of economic activity required by the degree of urbanization which events have thrust upon it.

The growth of this interdependent system, in which cities are increasingly integrated into continental and world systems, responds to, and places new demands upon, technological skill. If, as Seymour Mandelbaum has maintained, a ward and precinct organization was a necessary communication channel to link the business decision makers with the immigrant workers in Boss Tweed's New York,[8] television, extended by satellite relay, and jet planes with termini connected by expressways are technical devices for coping with the contemporary world metropolitan system. With growth in scale there is an increase in interdependence, and interdependence in turn requires an increase in discipline. In the mature metropolitan centers, this discipline has come to be ingrained and virtually taken for granted; the behavior of New Yorkers during the power blackout and transit strike showed this conclusively.

The Casualties of Efficiency

The discipline of the city dweller, moreover, is accompanied by a real loss of individual power. The forces that affect the metropolitan resident are largely beyond his control. He is a prisoner of the location of freeway interchanges, the scheduling (or abandonment) of public transportation, and the accident of hundreds of historical, social, and political boundaries. In its struggle to attain a certain measure of efficiency, metropolitan organization throws off more and more individual casualties. Remedial public policy, in turn, tends to add new casualties, as is the case of urban renewal. The old and the unskilled, and particularly the Negro, are hard hit by the selective, exacting requirements of a highly competitive efficiency system, moderated as it is by social status barriers. Even compulsory military service has had its greatest impact on the urban Negro—in this case, the young men who have minimal literacy and are most likely to be unemployed or underemployed because of the efficiency tests of metropolitan society.

The exclusion of the Negroes, the unskilled, the old, and the ideologically anachronistic small-business types (who provide the recruits of the right wing) from full participation in the postindustrial metropolitan society is matched by the growing distance between the advanced industrial nations and the aspiring nations of Asia and Africa in terms of power, wealth, and influence. Not only is the gap between rich and poor nations widening but the latter have, in the last five years, suffered some slippage in annual rates of economic growth, portending an increasing disparity between rich and poor. Indeed, the more effectively the economy is organized and rationalized, the more disadvantaged are the weaker competitors, whether they are firms, regions of a federal system, or nations in a world economy. Pockets of lagging growth find it almost impossible to catch up so long as an explicit equalization mechanism, based on other than efficiency, is not introduced. The programs of Appalachia and Mezzogiorno, not to mention the persistent problems of the southwestern and northern areas in Britain, are evidence of the difficulty encountered by disadvantaged elements of a large, thriving nation integrated into a competitive international economy. Without an industrial complex of a critical scale, investment programs poured into underdeveloped regions may suffer very heavy "leakages." The multiplier on federal investments in Alaska, for example, may be less than one. The interest payment for debt service on foreign aid returns almost half the aid of the United States. In addition to the superior returns to industrial and financial complexes, the very organization of the market for contemporary industry requires a scale of demand well beyond that provided by the poorer countries.

Antiurbanism on the Power Fringes

The planning and rationalization of the world and national economies on efficiency (and often profit) lines have deepened social and political divisions. The Afro-Asian bloc, and particularly China, wishes to lead an ideological foray against the increasing rationalization of the world economy by the industrial powers. In Asia, the friction between the insurgent villages of the countryside and the internationally oriented capital cities is expressed in open conflict. Rural guerrillas are besieging the urban power centers.

In the industrially advanced countries, such as the United States, a strong "antiorganization," "antiestablishment" sentiment is to be found in almost all the dissident groups from the nonideological left to the ideological right. The student movement, with its protests against machine education and IBM-controlled progress, but also the civil rights movement and an appreciable proportion of the so-called activist youth are seeking some way of uniting private and public issues. They feel strongly that the urban industrial scientific planning activities of the "power structure" are separating public canons of conduct from those of morality, at the expense of both. In particular, they rebel against the one-way character of communications and civic control. The message of televised political speeches is rejected in favor of the atavistic public forum of the mass meeting, the debate, and the bull session. With C. Wright Mills, whom they admire, they are seeking for "media of genuine communication . . . with the aid of which they can translate the private troubles of individuals into public issues, and public issues and events into their meanings for the private life." [9]

Control by Communication

The failure of our urban industrial society to communicate effectively with certain groups whose contribution to the control of the society and the management of its technical system is minimal leads to various types of "crises." Effective communication is essential to crisis management. Misinformation, for example, spread rapidly by rumor and other informal channels has long been recognized as an immediate occasion of many forms of civil disorder. In the long range, the most effective form of social control is control by "communication of influential messages." From one standpoint, much of the jockeying for position in foreign policy and other forms of power politics proceeds in this manner. Mobilization, displays of force, exchange of messages, and a variety of other actions can be taken as efforts to communicate strength and intentions to a rival and to influence his behavior. As David Schwartz has observed, the "strength, range, clarity and credibility of messages" [10] are decisive aspects of communication.

The argument has been made that the management of many crises and potential revolts of the working-class population in New York City at the turn of the century was achieved by the effectiveness of the communication of the ward machine organized on Tammany lines.[11] According to this view, political organization maintained effective social control at the local level through its elaborate personal communication system. On certain issues, that control appears to be less effective in the Negro ghettos of American cities today. The most frustrating aspect of Watts from the standpoint of city officials was their inability to find local leadership through whom they could communicate with the masses of the people. One should scarcely expect to find such control in a situation in which the potential local leaders had long been excluded from the inner councils of political leadership in the city (Los Angeles) and in which the rebellious citizens had little or no confidence in or communication with their nominal leaders.

Considerable attention has been given to the failure of communications media to keep pace with the great demands placed on them in our urban industrial society. When it is simply a matter of a lag in recording stock-market changes or communicating with motorists in traffic jams, the cost of the loss of control has been tolerable. In the case of social discontent, it is much more serious. The citizens of Watts challenged the major American principle of the sanctity of private property and the civil order built on it. When the disturbances arose, there was little time for making decisions. The main decision makers had, moreover, failed to anticipate the situation. In the resulting crisis, they displayed a fatal inability to communicate with the aggrieved citizens. By contrast, it was possible for order to be maintained during the power blackout in New York City even with the breakdown of much of the formal communication machinery (only transistor radios were working).

These cases suggest, at least superficially, that processes of social control and social influence depend on the subjective state of those who receive information, as well as on many other factors, including trust. But they may also suggest that there is considerable risk in excluding a major segment of the population from participation in the social and political communication processes in a society which depends so heavily on predictable individual responses in order to preserve the smooth workings of its technology. In a very real sense, our urban centers are becoming more vulnerable to civil disobedience. People can be excluded from the technical decisions, but their ability to sabotage the workings of the system suggests that communication with these citizens is lost at great peril.

The Urban Outsiders

If the city is a powerful integrating device for a society undergoing rapid social and economic change, and if the characteristic modern urban culture is rationalized, pluralistic, and dependent on highly developed communications media, those who are not "integrated" into the urban system will be more completely alienated from participating in the society than were marginal groups in premetropolitan areas. The degree of this alienation and its consequences for social order are functions of the rate and amount of change, the preurban cohesiveness of the societal values, the homogeneity of the population, and the wealth of the society. In rich societies, the "unintegrated" can be bribed not to upset the smooth functioning of the urban machinery, and their dysfunctional behavior can be made the basis of folk art, as is the case with Negro-based popular music in the United States and the expressive "mod" fashions of Britain.

Nevertheless, explosive residues of discontent are found everywhere in the world urban order. In the poor countries, it is the students, whose training has outrun the growth of opportunity in the society and whose break with the folk culture has freed them for protest actions, who form the core of the marginal society and shoulder the burden of social upheaval. The unskilled workers transported to the urban setting are, in the absence of ethnic or tribal animosities, less likely participants in these outbursts. In the rich countries, social protest explodes into mass disorder only where the marginal groups have been completely excluded from participation and communication as well as from sharing in the material benefits of their society. Yet there is evidence that a more subtle and pervasive discontent with the rationalized economic and social organization of the metropolis has penetrated many ranks of life in the most advanced industrial nations.

Traditionally, the pull of the city for small-town and village dwellers lay in social freedom, cultural variety, and economic opportunity. These pulls exist today, but appear to be diminishing in force—being replaced in part by the drive to be in the *main stream,* rather than in an exotic culture. The city is so successfully integrative that it is drying up the regional sources of cultural difference. The outsiders are fighting a rear-guard action against the very success of the city in the postindustrial Western world; they distrust the goals of the processes of integration which it represents. Their "new humanism," which is touched with Renaissance romance, insists upon an assertion of the ends of mankind, upon a release from indirect relations, from organizational discipline, and from the requirements of instrumental efficiency. Unlike their youthful counterparts in the developing countries, the Western outsiders distrust efficiency in the service of material progress.

Material progress, based on mastering the techniques of an industrial civilization, is the professed goal of almost every society in the world. Where ultimate ends diverge, material progress is accepted as a necessary means.[12] The United States has not only succeeded in achieving extraordinary material progress and storing great quantities of goods but also successfully vulgarized the idea of progress. Presumably, this notion of ever spiraling progress in material well-being should carry with it the optimism of the Enlightenment which spawned it. A sizable segment of the American community, including, a preponderance of Negro members, has been imperfectly infected with that optimism. For Negroes, the promise appears hollow; for certain segments of the right, the instrumental costs in terms of other goals have been too high; for a portion of the youth, exclusion from the decision-making processes, bureaucratic control, and depoliticalized decisions by the disciplined industrial command have bred a new kind of distrust.

The city as an artifact of our cultural development may be criticized on aesthetic grounds, may be damned for its unexpected frictions and unwelcome costs, and may be deplored for its heedlessness; but, as an instrument for the accommodation of more and more of the world's population in a single economic efficiency system, it has been effective. Dissatisfaction with urban life in the richer countries of the world stems from the fact that urban trappings are symbolic of ideals which are chimerical to the excluded minorities and with which others have become disenchanted. To the rebels of the poorer nations, the progressive organization of the world in an urban system for economic efficiency is a symbol of the dominance of the capital-rich nations, with their monopoly of modern arms. For both groups, the technological adaptation of of metropolitan life is the heraldry of triumphant, and sometimes inhuman, materialism.

The very technological dependence of the city makes it vulnerable to the resistance of dissidents within it, as events in Saigon have demonstrated. The city, moreover, is the historic incubator of ideas—the richness of its communications milieu produces change. If the city proves to be a force for the disorganization of our present world industrial order, we may expect that the forces will emanate from the ideological unrest of the unassimilated groups in the city, and not from the technical breakdown of the urban apparatus as a result of increased scale, runaway growth, or indigestible communications demands. The city is a threat to our economic-technological order mainly because the inhabitants of the metropolis resist the functional demands and the personal costs of its drive for efficiency.

■ *Notes*

1. "L'Urbanisation," *Prospective,* Vol. XI (Paris, 1964).
2. Harvey Wheeler, *The Restoration of Politics,* an occasional paper (Santa Barbara: Center for the Study of Democratic Institutions, 1965), p. 20.
3. John B. Calhoun, "The Social Use of Space," unpublished manuscript (Bethesda, Md.: National Institutes of Health, 1962).
4. Kingsley Davis, "The Urbanization of the Human Population," *Scientific American,* CCXIII, No. 3 (September, 1965), 40–53, reprinted in *Cities* (New York, 1965), pp. 3–24.
5. Janet Abu-Lughod, "Urbanization in Egypt: Present State and Future Prospects," *Economic Development and Cultural Change,* Vol. XIII, No. 3 (April, 1965).
6. Meyer Weinberg, "Aspects of Southern Urbanization and School Segregation," *A Report for Equal Educational Opportunities Program,* U.S. Office of Education (August, 1965), mimeograph.
7. C. K. Jayarajan, "What Is Happening to the Fringe Areas of Our Cities?" *Civic Affairs* (Kanpur, India, October, 1965).
8. Seymour J. Mandelbaum, *Boss Tweed's New York* (New York: John Wiley, 1965).

9. C. Wright Mills, *The Causes of World War III* (New York: Simon & Schuster, 1960) p. 158.

10. David C. Schwartz, "Crisis Management: On the Influence of Strategic Factors in Crisis Decision-Making," Meeting of the Association for the Advancement of Science (Berkeley, Calif., December, 1965).

11. Mandelbaum, *op. cit.*

12. See, for example, Stanley Hoffmann's "Report of the Conference on Conditions of World Order—June 12–19, 1965, Villa Serbelloni, Bellagio, Italy," *Daedalus* (Spring, 1966), p. 466.

9   THE DERANGEMENT OF HUMAN RELATIONS

▪ *Glenn E. Tinder*

. . . Th[e] new derangement of human relations—*mass* disintegration—can be more fully explored by noting the degree to which most of the principal relationships which man can enter have been attenuated and broken.

Man and Nature

Men in ancient times lived in a companionship with nature which was so continuous and effortless that apparently it seldom occurred to them to mention it. The first great democratic assembly in history, that in Athens, met on an open hillside; drama, trading, judicial proceedings, and conversation were, in ancient Greece, normally carried on out of doors. The Romans, too, although to a lesser degree than the Greeks, lived and worked under the open sky.[1] And not only the masters of classical culture, but the originators of Christianity as well, did much of their work in the sunlight and air. Jesus' teaching was heard mainly on the shores of lakes and in other outdoor places; Paul preached to the Athenians from a great rock. It is hardly an exaggeration to say that Western civilization originated in the presence of nature.

Nor is it an exaggeration to say that today our civilization has broken most of its contacts with nature. There is considerable interest in outdoor activities such as camping and gardening; but the fascinated yet merely occasional attention these activities receive is evidence that they bring satisfactions

From Glenn E. Tinder, *The Crisis of Political Imagination* (New York: Scribner's, 1964), pp. 12–18. © Copyright 1964 by Glenn E. Tinder. Reprinted with the permission of Charles Scribner's Sons.

denied in the daily order of life. Several barriers between man and the natural world have been raised. One of these is made up of the walls of office buildings and factories. Vocational life has had to shift indoors, not only because of the movement of the centers of civilization away from the warm Mediterranean but also because of the development of forms of industry and organization which, with their dependence on machines and paperwork, require shelter.

A second barrier separating man from nature is the city itself. Areas of nature, of course, may be preserved within cities; but this has not generally been done very effectively. Hence the vast process of urbanization, which threatens eventually to make almost everyone a city dweller, is a process for destroying and excluding nature. The ancient city, due to its relative smallness and to the agricultural pursuits of many of its inhabitants, did not shut out the natural world. "The breezes of the open country," as A. E. Zimmern wrote of ancient Athens, "blow through the Parliament and the market-place." [2] But the modern city, with its unending suburbs and its swift and uncontrolled development, is destructive of nature and of man's ancient companionship with sun and sky. Finally, a third barrier between man and nature is constituted by the spoilage of much that is ostensibly still natural. Billboard advertising, roadside commercial enterprises, and large numbers of people often prevent one who has crossed the barriers of vocation and city from entering fully the presence of nature. The immense silence and the innocent magnificence of a great natural scene are rare in the experience of modern man.

Man and Place

The possession of roots depends primarily not on the charm and beauty of a place, but rather on time. When one has been for many years in a single place—particularly if those are the years of childhood—he is united with his surroundings by countless threads of familiarity. The feeling of unity which they effect is so spontaneous that one is unaware of most of them until they are broken. Such rootedness is beautifully described in a passage where Alfred Zimmern attempts to evoke the feeling an ancient Athenian boy held for his city:

> He loved every rock and spring in the folds of her mountains, every shrine and haunt within the circuit of her walls. He had watched every day from his childhood the shadow creeping slowly across the market-place and the old men shifting their seats when the sun grew too hot. He could tell the voice of the town-crier from the other end of the city, and had made a special study, for private performance, of his favorite butt of the comedian in his last year's play. . . . He never forgot the festival of a god or a hero. . . . He was never tired of listening to his father and his uncles telling stories of raids and battles against the men beyond the range. . . . And when his city brought forth not merely fighters and bards, but architects and sculptors, and all the resources of art reinforced the influence of early association and natural beauty, small wonder that the Greek citizen, as Pericles said, needed but to look at his city to fall in love with her. [3]

In all ages uprootedness has been experienced by a certain number of people; but it can never before have been so normal and relentless a phenomenon as it is today. An industrial society, with its master criterion of rationality, cannot pay much respect to merely sentimental and traditional connections. In the industrial mind, men are as movable as material. And while perhaps there is no pure industrial mind, and human beings cannot actually be moved like commodities, industrialism has demanded the thorough and methodic decimation of man's roots. Few people today spend all of their lives in one place or remain as adults where they have spent their childhood. And even those who remain for a long time in the same geographical location are likely to find their environment changing about them. The ceaseless rebuilding which goes with industrial advancement erodes places as remorselessly as the sea does the shore, and far more swiftly. Thus mobility among men and instability of environment co-operate to the same end; relatively few can any longer feel fully at home. One need not dream of a return to the fixities of agricultural society in order to be given pause by the thought that through the experience of whole populations there now runs the uneasiness of the newcomer.

Man and Property

It may seem that, although divided from nature and place, people today at least are joined with reality through their possessions; ownership has never had greater prestige, scope, or security. But what does possession mean? If it is something more concrete and experiential than a mere legal arrangement, it can be asked whether we are really as deeply involved in ownership as our insistent praises of private property suggest. The conception repeatedly found in modern speculation about property—in Locke, in Hegel, in Marx—is that true ownership rests on the embodiment of one's personality in the article possessed. This personalization of physical entities can come about in more ways than one. If a person has created something, he has, as Locke put it, "mixed his labor with it"; further, simply to use an article for many years is to make it a part of one's personality and, to some extent, an image of one's self.

But if possession rests on a personal bond, it is not at all apparent that industrial peoples have really taken possession of the wealth they have produced. To begin with, most possessions have been depersonalized through the standardization of mass manufacture. It is not sufficient merely to remark that the average person makes very few of the things he uses; in a sense it must be said that no one makes them. They have come from an impersonal organization, and no human being has "mixed his labor" in them. Moreover, not many possessions are used in a way which imbues them with personality. The very quantity of goods which most people possess makes personal bonds with any but a few of them difficult; and the fact that many of these goods are intentionally made to be used only briefly and then discarded sets them apart even further from the personality of the user. Finally, men are divided from their possession by the fact that they have little understanding of those which are mechanical. They do not know how they are made, how they operate, or how they are repaired; they are, in a way, the property of specialists. Considering the extent to which pride of ownership today is centered in mechanical devices, such as automobiles and household appliances, the fact that people generally cannot master the technology embodied in even the simpler machines is more than a minor source of estrangement. For all of these reasons it is somewhat inaccurate to say of people today that they have great possessions. It would be more accurate to say that they have the use of many things.

Man and Man

Mass disintegration is manifest in the relations of men with one another as well as in their relations with nature, place, and possessions. The increasing instability of marriage, the decay of the fraternal aspects of trade-unions, the mobility which often attenuates family bonds and disrupts friendships, and the enfeeblement of lodges and neighborhoods are familiar signs of a decomposition which does not eventuate in class warfare, but nevertheless makes men strangers to one another.[4] Many circumstances which are commonly discussed as forces bringing people together actually divide them. Pressures toward conformity, for example, although superficially uniting people by removing their differences, really alienate them from one another by impelling them to forsake the personal fullness and integrity which is the indispensable basis of community; this truth was skillfully crystallized in the title of David Riesman's famous book *The Lonely Crowd*. The great public and private bureaucracies are, in appearance, imposing unities, but insofar as they force their members into specialization and routine they are monuments to disintegration. The market is still, and not always unjustly, celebrated as the most efficient and least tyrannical way of organizing economic transactions; but, as socialist criticism has effectively brought out, the kind of integration which the market produces is outward and mechanical, and the market's reduction of men and all other realities to the status of commodities destroys true unity among persons.

It cannot, of course, be asserted that there are no integral human relationships whatever in modern societies; and it is difficult in this matter confidently to compare the present with earlier times. Obviously there still are enclaves of community; and it can be argued that these always have been rare and insecure. But most of the phenomena mentioned above, such as mobility, bureaucracy, and the market, are in their present power and extension relatively recent. And it is difficult to perceive in previous ages comparably effective causes of disintegration. There was war, but there still is, more devastatingly than ever before; and we have added to it these other more peaceful, but no less penetrating, acids of community. Modern man may fail to notice his loneliness, because he is so accustomed to it and because he is preoccupied with the complex order and the self-conscious "togetherness" which is all about him. But it is reasonable to think that authentic contact among persons is more rare and difficult now than it has generally been in the past.

Man within Himself

There could be no more basic misunderstanding of social disintegration than that of supposing that it leaves intact the individual personality. Every failure of contact results in distortion and fragmentation of personality; a self barred from the other is not wholly a self. Bureaucratic routine, specialization, conformity, and other such forms of behavior separate one from himself as well as from others. Further, there is another aspect of social disintegration which tends to produce personal breakdown; this is what might be referred to as the "unrelatedness" of the environment. Man today is presented with an immense range of realities, because science has penetrated more deeply into nature than ever before, scholarly knowledge has attained unparalleled breadth, and contemporary means of communication and travel have greatly widened the possible scope of personal experience. Yet the various available realities do not readily fit together to form a single world. For example, one who attempts to follow the history of his own time has access to a far greater mass of news each day than he can possibly study; at the same time it is very difficult for him to define, simply, the central developments of the week or the month. Likewise, on the level of formal learning, a student stands before almost numberless fields of knowledge; but he cannot know and integrate more than two or three of these fields. Most people experience the unrelatedness of the environment on a less sophisticated plane, in the rain of impressions which fall on them daily from picture magazines, television, and films, and also in the perplexing variety of opportunities and instruments which a very productive and highly commercialized society ceaselessly puts in their way. An immense task of synthesis is placed before each one. Most people are bound to fail in this task and to reflect in themselves the scattered and purposeless character of their social surroundings. . . .

▪ *Notes*

1. See Alfred Zimmern, *The Greek Commonwealth* (London, 1911; 5th ed., New York: Oxford University Press, 1931), and Jérôme Carcopino, *Daily Life in Ancient Rome*, E. O. Lorimer, tr. (New Haven: Yale University Press, 1940). Both show the degree to which ancient city life was carried on out of doors.
2. Zimmern, *op. cit.*, p. 230.
3. *Ibid.*, pp. 67–68.
4. In *Middletown* (New York: Harcourt, Brace & World, 1937), Robert and Helen Lynd focus on many of these estrangements. See Maurice R. Stein, *The Eclipse of Community* (Princeton: Princeton University Press, 1960), for a review of sociological studies bearing on this matter.

10 THE GROSS NATIONAL PRODUCT PER CAPITA—1950–1975

■ *Bruce M. Russett et al.*

1950		1975	
United States	$2,300	United States	$3,550
Canada	1,750	West Germany	2,900
Britain	1,200	Canada	2,600
Belgium	1,000	Czechoslovakia	1,950
France	750	Belgium	1,875
Netherlands	675	Britain	1,800
West Germany	600	France	1,750
Argentina	500	USSR	1,625
Venezuela	480	Netherlands	1,475
Czechoslovakia	450	Venezuela	1,400
USSR	400	Italy	1,330
Italy	350	Poland	1,300
Chile	340	Japan	1,140
Poland	320	Yugoslavia	925
Spain	290	Spain	700
Brazil	235	Brazil	500
Mexico	225	Chile	480
Colombia	220	Argentina	455
Turkey	200	Mexico	395
Japan	190	Colombia	390
Philippines	185	Philippines	335
Yugoslavia	165	Turkey	305
Egypt	135	Egypt	285
Indonesia	120	China	190
Thailand	85	Indonesia	170

Nigeria	70	Thailand	130
Pakistan	70	Burma	115
India	70	Nigeria	95
China	50	India	85
Burma	45	Pakistan	75

From Bruce M. Russett *et al., World Handbook of Political and Social Indicators* (New Haven: Yale University Press, 1964), pp. 354–355. Reprinted by permission.

11 THE IMBALANCE OF WEALTH

■ *Barbara Ward*

. . . Today the world suffers from contrasts between riches and poverty—internationally, regionally, and locally—which seem enough to incite the sufferers to the most violent protest.

We are becoming familiar with the facts about these contrasts. Indeed, we are in some danger of making truisms of them before we have fully realized them to be true. In the "North" of our planet—above the Tropic of Cancer—about a quarter of the human race enjoys some 75 per cent of its trade, investment, and resources. The minority is largely white and European in origin and lives in market economies. But the exceptions show that this concentration is probably temporary. Russia is only three-quarters white and three-quarters European and, before long, may only be three-quarters planned. Japan belongs to the club only as a market economy—in spite of being counted an "honorary European" in South Africa, a community which, in common with some other stratified societies, often permits wealth to determine acceptability. And perhaps wealth *is* the chief hallmark of this northern "club" which includes white and colored, European and Asian, planned and free. . . .

If there is a long scale of power in the world from the superpowers down to the microstates, so, too, there is a ladder of wealth which in many ways coincides with the scale of wealth, above all, at the top where no state can carry a full nuclear armament without vast resources and skills mobilized to meet the cost. And the instability inherent in unbalanced power is repeated and reinforced by unbalanced wealth. The poor states are under pressure from the hopes and expectations of their own people. If pressure turns to revolt, the temptation to ask for outside help is only equaled, in these ideological days, by the temptation to give it. Either way, we are back with the risks of escalation and nuclear war.

From Barbara Ward, *Spaceship Earth* (New York: Columbia University Press, 1966), pp. 52–54. Reprinted by permission.

At present, the gaps are actually tending to widen. The countries at the bottom of the scale are about holding their present levels of poverty. They grow by about 2 to 3 per cent a year. But so do their birth rates. About half-way up the ladder a few countries—in the $200 to $300 per capita income range—are bounding ahead. Mexico, Greece, Israel, Taiwan have been growing by over 6 per cent a year in terms of per capita Gross National Product—the sum of all the community's goods and services. Then, in the upper reaches, countries which are rich already have been adding 3 to 4 per cent a year to their per capita GNP. With stable populations, steady employment, and rising productivity they have encountered few obstacles to sustained growth. This steady surge has, in the case of the United States, brought the Gross National Product up to some $630,000 millions in 1964 and allowed, in the same year, an increase of over $30,000 millions. Thus, in a single year, America *added* to its GNP the equivalent of the whole of Africa's current wealth or 50 per cent of Latin America's—both continents with a higher population. Such in our day are the gigantic differences in resources between the high and the low on the scale of wealth. . . .

☐ *International Disorganization*

12 THE SPOTTED REALITY

■ *Kenneth E. Boulding*

We are all aware that we are living in an extraordinary time, that in many ways the twentieth century is unique. There has never been anything like it before. There may never be anything like it again. It is a time which is both enormously hopeful and enormously dangerous. The hope and the danger both arise from the fact that we are in the middle of an extraordinary explosion in human knowledge, an acceleration which began perhaps three or four hundred years ago.

From Kenneth E. Boulding, *Current Issues in Higher Education, 1966* (Washington, D.C.: American Association for Higher Education, 1966), pp. 7–15. Reprinted by permission of the author and the publisher.

As one reads the record of evolution, it is clear that there are times when man's evolution goes into a "higher gear" and accelerates rapidly. The development of man himself was a great evolutionary transition. In man's own development we can detect three great periods of transition. The first was the invention of agriculture and the movement from the paleolithic to the neolithic. The second was the development of cities and civilization. We are now in the middle of what I call the third great transition, perhaps even greater than the other two, in which civilization is passing away and something else is taking its place. I used to call this something else postcivilization; but I find that this term scares everybody, because, for some strange reason, civilization has an extraordinarily good press, especially among college types. Actually, civilization has been a rather disagreeable state of man. I suspect that man was happier in the neolithic, because civilization has been characterized by war, slavery, exploitation, and other disagreeable institutions.

Whatever civilization is, it is clear that it is passing away. The advanced countries even today are fantastically different from a hundred years ago and are now moving toward what I call a developed society. This is still quite a long way off, for there are no signs that the process of this transition is slowing down. It will eventually slow down, I am sure, but not perhaps for a hundred, or even four hundred, years; and in the meantime we are undergoing the most rapid social change of any human generation. One sees this especially in Japan, which has achieved the world's record for economic development—about 8 per cent per annum per capita increase in real income for the last twenty years. If they keep this up three or four generations, they will be very rich. Even at more modest rates of economic growth, the developed world at the end of two hundred years is very hard to visualize.

Actually, when I try to think about what the developed society might look like, the principal image that comes into my mind is that of earth as a spaceship, destination unknown; and the politics and the ethics of the spaceship are extraordinarily different from those of the past. Up to now, man has always lived on a great plane. He has never really believed the earth was round. I believed that the earth was round when I went around it and did not fall off, and certainly the astronauts believe it is round; but most of the societies of the past, even civilized societies, did not.

The economic life of a spaceship society is very different from that of the great plane. We shall have to lay a great deal more stress on conservation and the economizing of consumption. We have had, and still have, an economy in which we have extracted materials from the ground and eventually flushed them down the sewers, from which they go into pollutable reservoirs. Now we are beginning to run out of pollutable reservoirs. When I flew across the Great Lakes today, I wondered how long it would take to pollute them completely. As you know, we have already lost Lake Erie and will lose Lake Michigan very soon. It may take only twenty-five years before mankind faces a major crisis in the atmosphere, which is becoming polluted almost to the point where irreversible changes are taking place that are still imperfectly understood.

At any rate, it is obvious that our existing society is fundamentally suicidal; we cannot go on indefinitely, historically speaking, extracting things out of the earth and flushing them into the seas and lakes and atmosphere. Certainly, then, within five hundred years we shall have to develop an economy and society in which we recycle almost everything, with meticulous conservation of all materials, so that we get everything back from the sea and the atmosphere that we flush into it. We still do not have the technology for this, but that perhaps is just over the horizon. A society like this could still be affluent. But as someone has said, "Today we are not so much an affluent society as an effluent society."

Thus, the spaceship society will be a queer kind of mixture of affluence and extreme parsimony. It will have to be parsimonious not only with materials but also in other things. Thus, there is no space in the spaceship for cowboys, even Texas cowboys. You can't play cowboys and Indians in a spaceship; you can't have horses or men on horseback in a spaceship. There isn't room. You have to develop a much more modest society. Greatness is out, as far as I am concerned. It is corrupted inevitably into delusions of grandeur. Man is going to have to learn to live modestly, decently, politely, quietly; and the delusions of today we have to show up as delusions, and very dangerous delusions at that.

The spaceship earth may seem a long way off, but it may be closer than we think. We have to look at the present period as man's last chance to achieve this transition; that is, he will never again have a planet with fossil fuels and an unpolluted atmosphere, and in X years these resources will be gone. I sometimes think gloomily of economic development as the process which brings the the evil day ever closer when everything will be gone. If we raise the standards of consumption of the rest of the world to American levels today, we won't have any fuels or ores left in one or two hundred years.

In a very real sense, this is man's only chance; we have a chance to convert our fossil fuels and oils into enough knowledge to enable us to do without them, and this is possible. I am a long-run optimist.

I think we have a fair chance of making it. The present period is like the bridge of San Luis Rey; we are walking a very narrow tightrope over a very deep chasm, with some kind of promised land on the other side, and we could very easily fall off. That is why this is both a dangerous and very exciting time.

The most obvious danger, certainly, over the next hundred years is a nuclear war or worse; and we must take this seriously, although no one does any more. But certainly it is still a possibility, and no matter what the probability is, it is too much for me. I think even if we suppose it to be only 1 per cent per annum (which I do not think is unreasonable in view of the nature of the international system), if we accumulate this over a hundred years, it looks very alarming. Certainly we have to regard the existing international system as fundamentally unstable and unviable. Stable deterrence, I think, is a delusion. The demonstration is very simple; deterrents would not deter if there were not a probability of the thing's going off. If there is a probability of its going off, accumulate this for long enough, and it goes off; there is no mathematical possibility of deterrence being really stable in the long run. We can only regard ourselves as pretty lucky that it has not gone off already, and we just have to take the chance that it is not going off and regard this as a period in which we can produce the changes in the international system that are necessary for true stability.

The present international system, I think, is not stable; if we add chemical and biological warfare, with their explosive possibilities, we have even a more frightening prospect than we have now. The longer we look into the future, with the existing system, the worse it gets. On the other hand, of course, there are changes going on in the international system. I am not sure it is always changing for the better; but there is, at any rate, a real possibility of developing an international system that does not have this positive probability of almost total disaster built into it.

There are other dangers besides nuclear. I suppose there is a real danger of enormous epidemics, especially with the development of biological knowledge and the conquest of space. I suppose this sounds like science fiction; but, as you know, you have to read science fiction nowadays to keep up with the news. There is real science fiction about this; remember, for instance, how measles killed the American Indian after 1600. That is why in 1620 the Pilgrims were able to establish a settlement on that implausible, rockbound coast. Just as it happened before, it could happen again. Something could get out of the labs. I think we are almost certainly on the edge of an enormous increase in biological knowledge. Even the last ten years in biology have been fantastic; today we stand in biology about where we did in nuclear science when I was born.

Now we know the code of life; we just do not know yet how to write it, but we shall probably be writing it soon. We may have the artificial viruses and enormous changes within the genetic process. We may have coffee-flavored algae, artificial organisms; and perhaps in a hundred years artificial horses will replace these awful things that come out of Detroit. On the other hand, there is a great chance of these things' going wrong; the earth is a terribly delicate system.

Another problem is, of course, our complete inability up to now to control the expansion of population. In fact, I am witness to this. I have five children myself, and this always makes my Malthusian speeches sound a little hollow. Still, we cannot go on expanding population exponentially at any rate whatsoever. This does not just mean planned parenthood; this means population control. How we are going to do this, I don't know. This does not mean just having a certain number of children; this means being prevented from having children. Nobody now is achieving this; not even the Japanese, who are closest to it. The population of Japan is increasing at 1 per cent per annum, which means doubling every seventy years. When you do this for a thousand years—which isn't very much—Japan becomes awfully full!

Perhaps one of the most critical questions that we face in the next hundred years is what is the carrier capacity of the Spaceship Earth? How many can the Spaceship Earth carry; how big is the crew?

I do not know even the order of magnitude. I do not know whether this is a hundred million or a billion or ten billion or a hundred billion. If it is ten billion, we have a little time. If it is one billion, we are in trouble, because I do not know any way of reducing the human population except by disaster. If we have to reduce the population to even a billion, which is one-third of what we have now, and a fifth of what we are going to have in a few years, this is going to be tough. It means a hundred years or two of sheer agony for the human race ahead.

So I am not optimistic about this. I have my own scheme, which I call a green stamp plan for population control. Each person, on reaching adolescence, receives a hundred and ten green stamps, a hundred of which entitles the owner to have one legal child. Then we would set up a market so that the rich could buy them from the poor, and the philoprogenitive could buy them from the monks and nuns and people who do not want to have children. It is also a device for redistributing income, because the rich will have a lot of children and get poor, and the poor will have few children and get rich. I am afraid that no one takes this very seriously as yet.

Even more remote things worry me. We have examples in history of failure of nerve on the part of cultures, and this could happen to the whole human race, perhaps as a result of success. The thing that worries me more than anything else is success, because there is a very fundamental principle that nothing fails like success, because you do not learn anything from it. If, then, you have a success that is only partially understood, this can be very dangerous from the point of view of survival. To survive, you have to have a fair amount of failure and a good deal of inefficiency. As a matter of fact, that is one reason why universities are important; they constitute a kind of human liquid reserve for the society. Universities are a device for institutionalizing what the organization theory people call "slack." We might, however, develop a culture which would paralyze the learning capacity of man; and all this tremendous knowledge explosion that we take for granted would come to an end, or even retreat. There have been societies which have lost knowledge.

Now we come to the cheerful part. As far as I can see, all the means of avoiding the dangers of this extraordinary transition period and bringing it to a successful conclusion revolve around a conscious development of what I call the integrative system. In my private ideology, there are really three great organizers of the great dynamic processes of society. One I call the threat system, where someone says, "You do something nice to me or I will do something nasty to you." Another is the exchange system, where someone says, "You do something nice to me, and I will do something nice for you." This is economics. This does not really cover the water front. There is something left over, which is sort of a ragbag, and I am not sure it isn't a system. This is the whole can of worms that includes things like status, legitimacy, community, affection, trust, love, hate, and all these things that bind us together, whereby someone says, "Well, do something because of what you are and what I am and what we both are, because we are all in the same boat together, because we are all Americans, or all Michiganders, or all human beings." It is the sense of identity, of community.

The very identity of the individual depends on the integrative system that he is integrated into; for if an individual is not integrated into an integrative system, he does not have much identity. People lack identity because they do not have a community. We do not know much about the dynamics of the integrative system as an element in the total, all-around dynamics of society, and yet it is enormously important. I think this is the main key to social dynamics.

Suppose we look at just one aspect of this, which is legitimacy. If you lose legitimacy, you have lost everything. It then really does not matter how much threat capability or purchasing power you have. You can be rich and powerful and still be rejected; and even though threat capability and exchange capability both at times and places create legitimacy, at other times and places they also destroy it. There are some peculiar nonlinear relationships here! A very interesting example of this is what happens in a monarchy. After all, the legitimacy of Queen Elizabeth depends on the fact that William the Conqueror was a bastard. Authority often begins by the exercise of the threat system, and then it becomes legitimized in some way. There came a period in history, however, when, if a monarchy was going to be retained, it had to give up power— threat capability—in order to retain legitimacy. Sometimes survival requires the abandonment of power.

We have had somewhat the same thing happen in the case of empire. In some way that we still don't understand, empire lost legitimacy and the old threat system couldn't put it together again. Similarly, the United States has enormous threat capability in southeast Asia, and yet we seem to be quite incapable of creating any legitimacy. As a result, we are helpless to do anything good. All we can do is evil, and this puts us in an unfortunate position. I don't really understand how communities, nations, or religions are created. These, however, are the most interesting phenomena of the integrative system. Who would have thought that an almost illiterate camel driver would establish the great civilization of Islam? Who would have thought that an old gentleman with a beard in the British Museum in the mid-nineteenth century would have caused so much trouble and would have created an integrative system which now commands the allegiance of a rather large portion of the human race? For all I know, the most important events of this year may be happening in some obscure valley in Ethiopia that nobody is going to hear from for fifty years. Some great prophet may be creating a great integrative system for the twenty-first century.

What it boils down to is that the basic dynamics of society depends on the human learning process. I do not know much about learning; I am just a teacher. And quite frankly, the more I teach, the less I know about it. I find it a baffling phenomenon. I am sure there are things like imprinting in the psyche. The psychologists say that if you catch the growing mind at the right moment with the right experience, you can imprint something into it which will profoundly affect its development. But we don't know much about the over-all internal development of the image or knowledge structure, or how the teacher co-operates with this internal principle of growth of knowledge which can be called the "inward teacher." The main business of the outward teacher is to create an environment which enables the inward teacher to produce knowledge. As yet, we understand this process very little.

The total dynamic process and the whole problem of the transition, as I see it, is how to write a scenario for mankind which can enable us to get across the gulf and to walk the tightrope—that is, how to develop and distribute knowledge and values that will produce the "noosphere," as Teilhard de Chardin calls it, which will permit human survival. We must work on this for a long time.

One of the crucial problems is the lack of any clear image of what we might call integrative development. There is such a concept, certainly; man can and does move toward wider and better communities, more realistic decision making, and a smaller probability of making disastrous mistakes. It is hard to measure even the direction, however, of integrative development. We have nothing in the integrative system like the Gross National Product in economics. In economics we know when something is happening, whereas in the case of integrative development we are not sure. We do not have the information. In the integrative system it is hard to test the realism of our images or the consequences of our decisions.

I don't think the State Department or the people who run the international system, for instance, have any clear idea of integrative development. They tend to see the present international system as going on forever; they have no real sense of growth of the world integrative system, even though there is the beginning of a conscious effort toward this by cultural exchange and that kind of thing.

Partly, I think, this is a problem of historians. I have a great deal of prejudice against historians, because I cannot get them interested in history. Really, I suppose I want them to rewrite history in the light of integrative development. For example, [when] the University of Michigan celebrates its 150th anniversary, [it] is also the 150th anniversary of the Rush-Bagot Agreement which disarmed the Great Lakes. It is also the 100th anniversary of Canada. So it looks like a good opportunity to put on a pageant, or build a monument, or do something to celebrate the Rush-Bagot Agreement. I cannot get the history department interested in this. Yet the Rush-Bagot Agreement of 1817 was the beginning of 150 years of development of an integrative system, even though at first it was precarious. We almost went over the edge several times. We did not get "54–40," and we did not fight. Peace, however, eventually became a habit, and we developed a security community between Canada and the larger British complex and the United States. This didn't have to happen; events might have located the first world war in Oregon.

There is an enormous bias among intellectuals in favor of what is. In fact, however, what is not is much more interesting than what is; and what is, is only a very small example of what might be; in other words, existing systems are an imperfect and inadequate sample of the total possible range of systems. Integrative systems may be hard to perceive. Yet they do develop communities of various kinds, new legitimacies, loyalties, and disloyalties; and these processes are not wholly random, even though all historical systems have strong random elements in them. Because of these random elements almost all actual images of society are tinged with superstition. Superstition is a perceived order in a random system. Even pigeons order random systems, as B. F. Skinner has demonstrated; and politicians and intellectuals do it all the time. They have this infernal rage for order when there is none and find it extremely uncomfortable to live with randomness. Human history is a mixed system with great elements both of order and of randomness in it, but it is hard to perceive the order in the midst of so much randomness.

In the case of the integrative system, we do not really know what exactly are the values that we want to increase—the values of man for human survival. We can be pretty sure that things like love and benevolence are enormously good things and lead to the positive improvements, increasing returns and external economies. If I am happy when you are happy, you are happy when I am happy. This is obviously a system with increasing returns which generates high levels of mutual well-being. These are important elements of the dynamics of the integrative system. Anything that extends the individual beyond himself and creates a satisfactory role and a personal identity, that gives him some sort of satisfactory relationship with other persons in a community, produces integrative development.

What we do not know is the role of consensus, dissensus, alienation, or what we might call creative conflict; that is, of creative dissent or of different and competing subsystems in the development of integrative structures. What, for instance, is the value of variety and of the coexistence of different subcultures? What is the real role of coercion, of exchange processes, of legitimization?

I am deeply involved in conflict resolution. Nevertheless, I am not at all sure that all conflicts should be resolved. Some conflicts are too much fun to resolve. Some conflicts are very creative. I am not going to argue that conflict is necessarily a bad thing. The obvious position is that there is an optimum degree of conflict in any social situation. I became extremely aware of this when a student of mine produced a paper on conflict in the community in the school system in downtown Detroit. She was puzzled because she could not find any. There was none, because there was nothing. The picture of sheer apathy and nothingness in this transplanted Appalachian community was one of the most horrifying things I have read in a long time. Here is a subculture which has been losing content for ten generations. At the end of that time, you have an amount of nothing that can hardly be believed. Conflict would be a sign of something, some stirring of life.

In many situations, we have too little conflict. I suspect that until recently we had too little conflict in race relations, and the intensification of conflict is a sign of development. On the other hand, there is a profound tendency for conflict to get out of hand. The dynamics of conflict always tend to go into perverse dynamics; that is, the sort of dynamic process in which everybody makes everybody else worse off. We see this in the family very often, we certainly see it in international relations in things like arms races, and we see it in childhood problems. I often use my own children as an example of this. I have two little boys and two big boys, and the two little boys behave very much like an international system. They are always making each other worse off, always having verbal arms races, or worse, and they often have to be separated by the United Nations in the shape of parents. The two big boys, who used to be like the two little boys, now manage their conflicts better. They are nasty to each other in creative ways. I do not think they like each other any more, really, but as they have grown up they have learned how to live out their conflicts creatively.

We have the same problems at the university. One of the problems of university administration is that university administrators want to minimize trouble rather than maximize its utility, and they often want to play down conflict when actually there is, often, too little conflict in the university situation. On the other hand, I know universities where there is too much and the university is torn apart by factional strife.

One of the things to beware of is a certain oversimplification. We are all prone to oversimplify in things as complex as social dynamics and the social system. We find people who say, "All we need is that everyone love one another," or "All we need is world government," or "All we need is to hate the Communists," or something of this sort. None of this is satisfactory, simply because the world is a subtle and enormously complex dynamic process in which everything depends on everything else and in which it is extraordinarily hard to tell even the direction in which you are going.

In conclusion, I should like to argue that in this process of integrative development, whichever way it is going, the institutions of higher learning have a very important role. They represent the transmission element of the superculture. The superculture is the developing society. We see it most vividly in the airports, for all airports the world over are the same airport, except the Moscow airport, which has the Victorian charm so characteristic of the socialist countries. All superhighways are the same superhighway; all chemistry departments are the same chemistry department, almost; and in a very real sense, all universities are the same university. Any university person can go into a university anywhere in the world and be immediately at home, especially if he is in his own department. A chemist can go into a chemistry department in Tokyo, Peking, Moscow, Madrid, no matter where it is, no matter what the ideology is, and it is still chemistry. There is no such thing as Communist chemistry or Christian chemistry; there is just chemistry.

Every discipline has a world-wide community. Insofar as the superculture is an integrative system, the universities are its church. Even though they have no pope, they have a solid ecumenical unity.

On the other hand, we all live in many local and national folk cultures which we rightfully cherish. One of the critical problems is how to reconcile the world superculture with the parochial, provincial, and special subcultures, the folk cultures in which we have all grown up and in which we find a great many things of value which we want, quite rightfully, to preserve. I do not want a world purely of universities and superhighways. I want a world of variety, and I want the Japanese to go on having the tea ceremony and the Kabuki, and I want us to go on having Lincoln's Birthday and the Fourth of July. The danger of a superculture is that it is fundamentally rather drab, and the things that give color and variety are precisely these elements of the folk culture with which it often comes into conflict. The management of the conflict between the innumerable folk cultures of the world and the developing world superculture is one of the most critical problems that we face today. . . .

13 THE PRECARIOUSNESS OF POLITICS IN THE NEW STATES

■ *Rupert Emerson*

Of the many democracies which have been born in the past century and a half, only a handful has survived. In the past years the casualties have been peculiarly heavy among the former dependencies of the West for the simple reason that these were the countries which were currently embarking on democratic experiments. The fragile mechanism of representative democracy which almost all of them adopted proved shortly to be unfitted to the needs and capabilities of most of them. In thus at least temporarily abandoning their democratic institutions the ex-colonies were demonstrating no singular weakness or instability, but were following in what has been by far the more common experience of mankind.

Simon Bolivar, liberating Venezuela, was prophetic of the way the world has generally gone: "It is a terrible truth that it costs more strength to maintain freedom than to endure the weight of tyranny. Many nations, past and present, have borne that yoke; few have made use of the happy moments of freedom and have preferred to relapse with all speed into their errors."[1] And when he spoke of the people of the American hemisphere as having been purely passive for centuries with no political existence—"absent from the universe in all that related to the science of government"—he spoke for many other peoples around the globe as well.

The story which has repeated itself over and over is that peoples have set out on the democratic path with revolutionary enthusiasm, but before long they have lost their way and settled back into authoritarian or dictatorial regimes. The real success of democracy has been confined to some of the peoples living in or stemming from western Europe: the British, the Irish, the Belgians and Dutch, the Scandinavians, the Swiss, more dubiously the

From Rupert Emerson, *From Empire to Nation* (Cambridge: Harvard University Press, 1960), pp. 272–273, 277–281. © Copyright 1960 by the President and Fellows of Harvard College. Reprinted by permission of Harvard University Press.

French, and overseas, the peoples of the United States and the older British Dominions. With these central exceptions each of the successive waves of democratic experimentation has ended in over-all failure. The revolt against European rule in Latin America in the nineteenth century brought into being an array of democracies whose record has been spotty and untrustworthy at best. The drive for self-determination which followed the defeat of the autocracies in World War I stimulated the emergence of democratic institutions in central and eastern Europe, but after a few years Czechoslovakia was the sole democratic survivor. Among the noncolonial Asian and African countries which tried out new political forms, only Japan, China, and Turkey could at any time have been seriously counted in the democratic ranks, and none of these three could be cited as a model of democratic behavior. The statistical odds against the survival of democracy outside the small circle of western European peoples and their descendants overseas seem overwhelming. . . .

The reasons for the erosion of democracy are not far to seek. Basically they are common to the new states even though the turn of events in each of them derives from a special set of circumstances which has produced distinctive results. The position of Ne Win in Burma cannot be equated with that of Mohammed Ayub Khan in Pakistan, nor can either of these two be identified with Abdul Karim Kassem in Iraq. Chief of Staff Nasution has not seized power in Indonesia, although he has a large say in the governing of the country, and in Ghana the army has played no political role—its loyalty to the new regime, it has been said, being guaranteed by the fact that its officer corps remains largely British. Yet, when all the differences are taken into account, many common elements stand out.

One among them is the lack of national unity which in virtually all the new countries threatens disruption and is met by enforced centralization. Nationalism is the dominant creed, but the nations are still far from being consolidated. Of Pakistan it has been written that "no recollection of history and concord" binds the two wings, separated by a thousand miles of India;[2] in Burma inchoate civil wars have challenged the hold of the government since independence; and in Indonesia great stretches of territory remain under the control of Darul Islam, the revolutionary government which proclaimed its existence in 1958, and other dissident groups. . . .

In addition to the lack of national unity, the most basic explanation for the failure of democracy in so many of the new states is the almost universal absence of what have been assumed to be the preconditions for its success. Although argument still rages as to precisely what these may be, the usually accepted list includes such items as mass literacy, relatively high living standards, a sizable and stable middle class, a sense of social equality, and a tradition both of tolerance and of individual self-reliance.[3] In virtually no instance are these conditions met in the colonial countries whose independence had led them into democracy. Instead, these countries are characterized by peasant masses living at the subsistence level, overwhelmingly illiterate, unacquainted not only with the great world but even with their own country, accustomed to a high degree of social stratification, and with slight middle classes often strongly alien in composition. The representative government which emerges can be no stronger than the society which it represents.

Furthermore, the democratic institutions which were adopted were the work of the relatively small group which had come to significant acquaintance with the West. They were the product neither of the mass of the people, who inevitably had little understanding of them, nor of the evolutionary development of the society as a whole. Although social mobilization has been in full swing, the sudden universal enfranchisement of the peoples of Asian and African states differed sharply from the gradual adaptation to changing circumstances in the West where there was often a rough coincidence between the rise of new elements to economic and social consequence and their access to the ballot box. It is an immense added complication that while the democracies which came into being in the nineteenth and earlier twentieth centuries were concerned with the management of relatively simple political and economic systems in a still spacious world, the newly rising peoples seek full-scale social welfare states with most complicated mechanisms, plus the extra complexity of the drive for social and economic development, in a terrifying world of population explosion, superpowers, and nuclear weapons.

The increase in the numbers of those who were drawn into some measure of political participation did not necessarily enhance the prospects of democratic achievement. Poverty-ridden people in a climate of rising expectations are not likely to make their first concern the preservation of political forms and liberties whose meaning is obscure to them and whose promise may appear of less significance than other prospects held out to them. If democracy fails to produce results with adequate speed and if the politicians who manipulate the machinery come to be seen as self-interested and corrupt, the masses cannot be counted on to rise to the defense of unfamiliar political machineries.

The people at large lack not only the democratic tradition but also the more basic tradition of standing up to do battle for their rights against the remote and superior authorities which have through the ages pushed them around. Government, save at the local level where it was usually interwoven with old-established ties of family and status, has almost always been something imposed from above. What Gertrude Bell wrote of the Ottoman Empire half a century ago holds true for many other peoples:

> The government was still, to the bulk of the population, a higher power, discon-
> nected from those upon whom it exercised its will. You might complain of its lack
> of understanding just as you cursed the hailstorm that destroyed your crops, but
> you were in no way answerable for it, nor would you attempt to control or advise
> it, any more than you would offer advice to the hail cloud.[4]

Sporadically the people have risen in revolt against abuses felt to be intolerable or at the urging of some popular leader, but little has come their way to imbue them with the sense that they are possessors of human rights and fundamental freedoms which they are entitled and able to defend. The democratic constitutions of the postindependence period have been almost as much imposed on them from above as any of the previous regimes, and in many instances it is probable that the people would feel more at home with a government which tells them what to do than one in which they must exercise freedom of choice.[5] Nasser, writing of the philosophy of the Egyptian revolution, has spoken of the pain and bitterness which tore his heart when he found that the leaders must continue to command because the "majestic masses" which should have joined in the hallowed march to the great end actually brought sloth and inertia and not the needed zeal and ardor.

If the newly enfranchised masses are uncertain defenders of the democratic institutions with which they have been endowed, what of the nationalist elites to whom the institutions owe their being? These elites are composed of men for the most part committed to the proposition that a radical democratization of their societies is in order, but their ability to live up to their proclaimed creed has already been demonstrated to be highly dubious. Even assuming that they or reasonably like-minded successors retain their hold, with what confidence can it be predicted that they will survive the temptation, baited by the insidious corruptions of power, to see themselves as a distinctive corps with closed ranks? A Burmese newspaper editor wrote of the leaders of the dominant political party in Burma that they have "a 'Messiah' complex by which they can justify deviations from democracy with the excuse that they must remain in power for the good of the country."[6]

The tendency of the nationalist parties and movements to be built around dominant personalities rather than on programs or ideologies has often been noted. The emergence of Fascism, the virtual deification of Stalin in the USSR, the return of de Gaulle to supreme power in France, the abundant Latin American experience, and even the wartime pre-eminence of Churchill and Roosevelt, among many other examples, make it absurd to regard this emphasis on personal leadership as in any way a peculiarly oriental or African aberration. Its occurrence elsewhere, however, does not obscure the apparent need of the newly rising peoples to have a single personal focus of loyalty, symbolic of national unity; Gandhi and then Nehru in India, Jinnah in Pakiston, Quezon and Magsaysay in the Philippines, Ngo Dinh Diem in Vietnam, Nasser in Egypt, Nkrumah in Ghana, and Sékou Touré in Guinea, to suggest only a few.

This personalization of loyalties and movements must be attributed in large part to the lack of political experience and sophistication of the mass of the people, who require the personal figure of a leader to bring political abstractions down to the level of comprehensible reality. Another part may perhaps be linked to the general phenomenon of centralization of power in time of national crisis, as in the growth in stature of the American presidency in wartime. On such grounds it is not difficult to explain why the role of the leader should have expanded in Asian and African countries as they came to the critical struggles for independence, national consolidation, and economic development. It remains to be established, however, that leaders who have felt the intoxication of embodying the national will can be trusted to surrender its formulation to the people at large when the critical years are passed. The record of other parts of the world does not encourage the belief that the proclaimed adherence of such leaders to democratic principles is any guarantee that these principles will not be abandoned as the revolutionary tide ebbs and the attractions of power and privilege become greater. . . .

The democratic tides still run strongly in the world, but it would be folly to ignore the fact that they have often been turned aside, as in the Communist version which combines the name of democracy with the reality of totalitarian control. How much credence may be given the pessimistic tone of Guy Wint in his survey of British territories in Asia? "Easy come, easy go. The liberal civilization came more or less by chance from the association of the ancient world with Great Britain, and as easily it may go. It is perhaps simpler to turn Oriental man into an imitation Bolshevik, competent and ruthless, than into an imitation Western liberal."[7]

Save for a chosen few, democratic institutions have not been able to establish the conditions under which democracy could survive the buffeting of the world. It remains to be seen whether authoritarian rule can do better. Dynamic forces are in motion to bring the precondition of democracy into being, and the drive toward social and economic development has its inescapable democratic implications. Even authoritarian regimes will have to take the people at large more into account than in the past and make use of plebiscitary symbols—the familiar frauds of an age which so frequently can neither take democracy nor leave it alone—but with no certainty that they will progress beyond symbolism. . . .

■ *Notes*

1. Cited by C. Northcote Parkinson, *The Evolution of Political Thought* (Boston: Houghton Mifflin, 1958), p. 253. For the succeeding quotation, see A. C. Wilgus, ed., *South American Dictators* (Washington: George Washington University Press, 1937), p. 24.
2. Charles Burton Marshall, "Reflections on a Revolution in Pakistan," *Foreign Affairs,* XXXVII, No. 2 (January, 1959), 253.
3. See Seymour Martin Lipset, "Some Social Requisites of Democracy: Economic Development and Political Legitimacy," *American Political Science Review,* LIII, No. 1 (March, 1959), 69–105.
4. Cited by Zeine N. Zeine, *Arab-Turkish Relations and the Emergence of Arab Nationalism* (Beirut: Khayat's, 1958), p. 91, n. 3.
5. O. Mannoni came to the conclusion that the majority of Madagascans, if left to themselves, would spontaneously recreate a feudal type of society: "They would lack the courage to face the terrors of a genuine liberation of the individual." *Prospero and Caliban: The Psychology of Colonization* (New York: Frederick A. Praeger, 1956), p. 65.
6. U Law Yone, "Burma's Socialist Democracy," *Atlantic Monthly,* CCI, No. 2 (February, 1958), 158.
7. Guy Wint, *The British in Asia* (London: Faber and Faber, Ltd., 1947), p. 131.

14 THE PROBLEMS OF ABUNDANCE

■ *Robert C. Wood*

The Cornucopia of Technology

Underlying the exponential growth in material resources, freedom from disease, increase in education, personal convenience, and career choice is a steadily changing base of science and technology. The modern society builds its stock pile of resources and expands its supply of usable materials in ways undreamed of a generation ago. What sustains the apparent insatiable material appetite for a large number of people is not the abundance of land, water, minerals, and chemicals their country may possess. The critical element is the range and quality of the scientific knowledge and technical skills ready to unlock new sources of energy and extract new materials from the earth's crust and the atmosphere. The future of every modern nation relies on the substantial scientific enterprise—the organization of highly skilled scientists and engineers in a research and development process—that constantly alters materials available to a people and expands the base of a *usable* resource.

In the United States, the national government alone invests $15 billion a year in research—60 per cent of the total the nation spends annually for new products and innovation. Each year, the fruits of progress ripen, replacing old resources or expensive ones and increasing productivity. Microwave stations perform more cheaply the old function of cross-country cables. Skin banks, artery banks, blood banks, mechanical hearts, mechanical kidneys, support and sustain the human body. Insecticides, fungicides, chemical fertilizers, new varieties of seeds, and new breeds of livestock multiply the yield of lands. Electronic controls, computers, synthetic materials, and plastics undergird new industry.

In short, the problems a modern nation has largely left behind are those of mastering nature to secure the necessities of physical existence. The capac-

From Robert C. Wood, "The Future of Modernization," in Myron Weiner, ed., *Modernization* (New York: Basic Books, 1966), pp. 44–51. © Copyright 1966 by Basic Books, Inc., Publishers, New York. Reprinted by permission.

ity to command the energy and matter required to sustain life exceeds the increase in population. Thus the amount of resources available to each person steadily increases.

The Challenge of Modernization: Living with Continual Change

Yet, solving the problem of abundance generates further riddles. Vexing issues of public and private behavior arise: how to ensure that the steadily expanding supply of material is most effectively used and how to cope with the task of accepting new science, new technology, and innovation as a way of life. The fundamental and continuing condition of modernization is the capability of a people to adjust to changed circumstances not once or twice in a lifetime, but every year. This process of adjustment requires social and political institutions, processes and ways of behavior, that permit a constant introduction of new products, new processes, new careers, and new standards of conduct into a society without too great a disruption in personal lives and careers. The development of these institutions, processes, and life styles— as every modern nation has discovered—is not a simple matter.

A number of surface signs attest to this constant tension of adjustment in absorbing innovation while maintaining a sense of individual and national direction.

One is the continual pressure of obsolescence in occupations, professions, and industries that lose their utility in the space of a few short years. During the last generation, the United States and western Europe have witnessed an absolute decline in the number of people in agriculture and the forced evacuation of farm families through occupational displacement. They have seen the relative decline of manufacturing and productive enterprises and a lessening demand for semiskilled and unskilled workers. Currently the requirements for clerical and salesworkers, scientists, engineers, and technicians have risen rapidly, as has the demand for so-called service occupations: workers in finance, insurance, wholesale and retail distribution, transportation, and utilities.

Transitions among these occupations are not easy, unless the individual brings to the task a broad-based education and a considerable feeling of personal confidence. To many American or European workers innovations that increase national productivity are personal disasters. When coal is replaced by atomic power as a basic source of energy, miners find that their services are no longer required. Railroad workers lose their jobs when the volume of air traffic expands. Factory mechanics find that they are no longer needed when automation replaces men on assembly lines. In a very real sense, an individual in a modern society discovers that human energy and diligence are no longer very valuable commodities. Willingness to work, when not associated with possession of a skill, no longer guarantees a job. There is, in short, "no room at the bottom" in a modern society. Only those whose talents fit the needs of the moment seem capable of prosperity and advancement.

The sharp, sudden dislocations that affect groups of workers and families and blight personal careers are often accompanied by uncertainty as to how the new material well-being shall be directed by the majority. Critics of modern life have come to emphasize the so-called materialism of advanced cultures: the conspicuous display of prosperity in long vacations, fancy cars, high living, and a reliance on gadgets. To many philosophers, matters of the spirit, religion, and moral purpose are lost sight of in a consumption-oriented economy. Modern nations have been held to be inferior in the attention they pay to culture, customs, manners, and the human element in their societies. They are called deficient in national purpose and sense of communality. Their citizens are said to know how to live comfortably, but not well.

Root Problems: The Tasks of a Modern Society

Yet, basically these criticisms of sudden dislocations and excessive preoccupation with getting and spending are not the genuine problems of a modern culture. Indeed, systematic explorations reveal that the desires for security and material well-being are common elements in human nature. Modernity simply brings these characteristics to the fore. The unsolved task of modern life is not the deterioration of a nation's character by virtue of becoming "soft"; rather, it is the task of coping with life on a vastly expanded size and scale and of dealing with great complexity in social, economic, and political patterns.

Put another way, developing nations are often said to have a task of stimulating entrepreneurship; advanced societies often have the need to provide a countervailing force to the aggressive, atomistic, and individualistic actions set loose by the drive for productivity. They require new arrangements—or more precisely, systems—to assure intercourse, encounters, and a sense of mutual concern among their members.

In this context, four needs particularly stand out. How does a modern nation shape cities—reconcile itself to becoming an urban culture, rather than a rural one? Second, how does a modern nation provide support for the individual personality in a world in which ties of family, friendship, neighborhood, and community rapidly decline? Third, how does a modern nation assure that all its members participate in the new abundance? Finally, how does a modern nation maintain its innovative processes—its energy and drive and its capacity for continuing to want and to accept change?

City Building

The steady flow of people from country to city is the most striking physical manifestation of modernization. One out of six western Europeans lives today in a city of a half-million people. In the Netherlands, portions of England, and the Ruhr, parts of cities run together in giant "megalopolises." The same trends are discernible in Japan, where Tokyo regained its prewar population of 11 million from a 1945 low of 3 million in less than a decade and now spreads steadily into the countryside. In the United States, urban areas increase in population at the rate of 3 million each year. By 1975, four out of every five Americans are expected to be living in urban areas. The European pattern of interurban blending is also apparent in the United States: thirty-nine major metropolises now merge almost imperceptibly into one another. The acceleration of the widespread use of the automobile and the continued construction of single-family residences heralds the arrival of "the spread city," replacing the more congested cities of the past.

This continuing process of urban development raises a host of problems. Some are simply those of finance and engineering: how to secure the investment for continued construction necessary to house the urban population; how to provide public utilities, water, and sanitary facilities; how to build roads, subway lines, and commuter railroads. More basic ones hinge on the form and size of modern urban areas. Questions of planning for the effective use of space, assigning appropriate functions to old central cities and to new suburbs, grow increasingly persistent.

Here, Europe has clearly led the way. In rebuilding its cities after World War II, conscious plans, imaginative use of public power, and the carefully calculated intermeshing of transportation facilities, homes, and places of work characterize the rebuilt urban complexes of the Low Countries, Scandinavia, Germany, and England. Only slowly have the United States and Japan arrived at a position where consistent and workable public policies guiding the process of city building are appearing. But every modern nation now grapples with the job of checking massive urban concentration, whether in Tokyo, Paris, London, or New York. And every modern nation has begun the process of building entirely new communities to provide for the regional dispersal of its people.

Identity in an Urban World

As urbanization proceeds apace, a second problem appears. Millions of immigrants from farms and small towns no longer required in agricultural pursuits pour into the cities unprepared for the urban way of life. City living, dependent as it is on the specialization of jobs and the development of large business and governmental organizations, tends to be depersonalized living. The daily process of commuting from home to job, the sheer number of individuals active in small spaces, and the complex set of facilities and services required for organized urban existence all tend to undercut ties of neighborhood, friendship, and family which are so strong in small towns and rural life. Symbolic rituals and folk experiences decline, and a sense of personal identity becomes more difficult. So life today becomes increasingly a lonely existence to many residents, untutored in coping with its complexity and lacking the social skills for adjustment.

A wave of social commentary has interpreted these conditions of modern urban living as a result of overorganization: the rise of the gigantic corporations and bureaucracies that direct each aspect of an individual's life. Yet these analyses seem misdirected in two ways. First, they overlook the decline of autonomous, hierarchical, tightly directed institutions: the replacement of the business firm and government agency by interdependent systems of relationships that shape human activity more in terms of voluntary co-option than authoritative fiat and decree. Modern nations are less likely to be organizational societies than persuasive societies. Second, these complex new systems for the competent participant are not destructive of individual choice. On the contrary, they provide more choices, more options, fewer working hours, shorter work weeks, and more time for leisure than ever before. In a very real sense, men and women are freed from the daily routines and grinding labor that characterized poverty-stricken farm areas.

It is probably nearer the truth to say that the difficulty of many people in modern circumstances is not that they are overdirected or overcontrolled, but rather that they lack the resources to find meaningful personal lives. Institutions, customs, habits, and clearly identified appropriate roles and styles are hard to find. Consequently, all the awesome stresses, strains, and pressures of the urban world come to play on the individual personality structure. These must be coped with, handled, and absorbed by whatever defenses the individual psyche may possess. Clear guidelines of professional and organizational behavior tend to disappear.

Increasingly, modern people become preoccupied with job and immediate family circles and find it difficult to engage in meaningful encounters with other classes and groups. It is probably symptomatic of these pressures that the United States' most prevalent disabling ailment is mental illness. Half the beds in nonfederal hospitals are occupied by mental patients. In 1960, more than three-quarters of a million patients were in institutions, suffering from some type of mental illness.

The Nonparticipants

If all members of a modern society find adjustment a continuing and exacting exercise, some are unable to adapt at all to the special roles that fit the needs of the technologically based economy. The constant shift in the composition of the job market and the emphasis on new skills become overwhelming—not in a psychological sense so much as in terms of innate physical and mental capabilities.

Alongside the challenge to ease the tension of change for the majority, every modern nation faces the need to provide employment, purpose, and meaning for a hard-core minority of so-called marginal men. In the United States, almost one-fifth of the population falls in this category—displaced workers and the increasing proportion of old people. Our attention turns to the ways and means for making sure that all people share in the general well-being: special educational programs, neighborhood centers, and new systems to prepare rural immigrants for urban life.

Maintaining Abundance

Finally, as population grows, expectations reach higher, life becomes more complicated, and the need arises for a continuing flood of innovations, research, and development to provide a firm base for an expanding economy. Productivity rates for the most advanced societies tend to become sluggish, and the capacity so to direct innovation becomes more difficult. In the natural sciences and engineering, which now include a vast community of three million Americans alone, the process of making, communicating, and applying innovation is an increasingly complex affair. Major questions of the appropriate level of finance and of the right methods for the organization and management of scientific enterprise rise in importance. For instance, how much should society invest in fundamental physics compared to frontier research in biology? Should we explore the ocean floor or outer space, and, if so, with how much money and man power? What are the best techniques for sustained scientific collaboration among government, business, and university? And how rapidly can we expand our new knowledge in social science in order to design the great urban complexes so that we pay more attention to human needs, improve the learning capacity of the disprivileged, and provide psychological supports to the lonely? All these questions are high on the agenda of advancing nations today.

Thus, the future of modernization is not without its problems. How to live in the cities, how to offer rich, full, individual lives in complex circumstances, how to assure that all participate in a society of ample resources, and how to push that society ahead in the future are persisting and perplexing questions.

But it is important to re-emphasize that these are not the issues that many commentators have identified in their criticisms of modernity. Modern society does not oppress the individual by great organizations so much as it perplexes him in the array of choices it spreads before him. Modern society does not emphasize materialism and sensate experience at the expense of the reflective, the critical, and the contemplative. In the use of expanded leisure time in most modern societies, philosophy, music, and the arts grow as rapidly as mass sports and spectacles. There is no documentation to prove that there is more violence or disorder in modern life than in earlier eras or that the modern character is less moral, less strong, and less ethically oriented.

The genuine issue of modern life is the capacity to mix quality and quantity: to handle new masses of people and new and complex systems of social, economic, and political behavior purposefully with respect for the individual. . . .

15   THE PATHOLOGICAL STATE OF THE INTERNATIONAL SYSTEM

▪ *Kenneth E. Boulding*

. . . The international system is by far the most pathological and costly segment of the total social system, or sociosphere, as it is sometimes called. If we look at the various elements of the social system that are ordinarily regarded as pathological, such as crime, mental and physical disease, and economic stag-

From Kenneth E. Boulding, "The Learning and Reality-Testing Process in the International System," *Journal of International Affairs,* XXI (1967), 5–10, 14–15. Reprinted by permission.

nation, the international system probably costs about as much as all these put together, with the possible exception of economic stagnation, which is itself in part a function of the nature of the international system.

The direct cost of the international system must now amount to something like $150 billion a year. This would include the total spent by all the nations on their military establishments, information systems, foreign offices, diplomatic corps, and so on. In addition, some estimate of the present value of possible future destruction should be included. Any figure placed on this is at best a wild guess. To be pessimistic, let us suppose that the destruction of a third world war would amount to half the present physical capital of the world, or about two thousand billion dollars, and that the chance of this happening is about 5 per cent in any one year; in this case we should add a kind of depreciation or discounting factor to existing world wealth of about $100 billion a year. This would represent, as it were, an insurance premium for war destruction. A more optimistic assumption of, say, a 1 per cent chance of a major world war would reduce this to $20 billion annually. It is interesting to note, incidentally, that the size of the current expenditure on the war industry is almost certainly much larger than any reasonable insurance premium for war destruction would be. This points up a general principle that the cost of the war industry for any country in terms of resources withdrawn from the civilian economy is much larger than any insurance premium that might be conceived for a policy covering destruction by enemy forces. This is often true even in time of war. A study of the impact of the war industry on the Japanese economy[1] suggests that even during World War II the cost of the Japanese war industry to the Japanese economy was of the same order of magnitude as the destruction by the American war machine. One's friends, in other words, generally do more damage than one's enemies.

If we suppose that the gross world product is roughly $1,500 billion, the international system and the war industry account for about 10 per cent of this. It would be extremely surprising if all the other pathological elements in the social system taken together account for more than this. Crime and disease are likely to account for no more than 5 per cent of it, or $75 billion. Even if we include the potential loss resulting from the failure of economic development, and if we suppose that a projected annual growth rate of 2 per cent is not realized, this would only amount to a loss of $30 billion a year, as a measure of what might be called the pathology of the world economy. Even if we raised this projection to an optimistic 4 per cent, the loss would only be $60 billion, far below the cost of the international system.

One may object, of course, that it is unfair to regard the cost of the international system as if it were not offset by benefits, even if is very hard to put a dollar value on them. We get the benefits of nationality: tangible ones like protection when we go abroad, and intangible ones like the sense of identity that thrills to the flag, that expands beyond the narrow limits of family and locality, and that responds gladly to the call for self-sacrifice. The sense of satisfaction that comes from being American or German or British or whatever is certainly an important benefit, however hard it is to evaluate. It must be recognized, however, that such advantages of nationality are virtually the only advantages of the nation-state system. There are no economic pay-offs to the present system; indeed, in addition to the loss of resources we should also add the cost of tariffs and trade restrictions and of the almost universally deleterious effects on the rate of development caused by high military expenditures. There was a time, perhaps, when the international system paid off for its principal beneficiaries, the great powers, in terms of the economic exploitation of their colonial empires. Even if the international system produced little gain for the world as a whole, it could be argued that it redistributed the world product in favor of those who played the international game successfully and became great powers. Today even this argument has little validity. Empire in the last hundred years has turned out to be a burden rather than an asset. And in terms of the rate of economic growth, being a great power has not paid off. The British and French growth rates, for instance, from 1860 on were considerably less than those of many less ambitious countries, such as Sweden or even Japan. The German and Japanese attempts to become great powers were enormously costly; but their ultimate failure provides an even more striking insight into the realities of the present international system. After total military defeat and a complete loss of their great-power status, they have both achieved absolutely unprecedented rates of economic growth, far exceeding the growth rates of the victors.

This is, indeed, a strange world, in which nothing fails like success and nothing succeeds like defeat, in which great powers find that their greatness impoverishes them, and in which the way to get rich is to stay home and mind one's own business well and to participate as little as possible in the international system. Of course, there are also historical examples of countries for whom defeat has been disastrous, though such examples are rather scarce since Carthage, or perhaps Byzantium. It is also possible to find examples of countries that stayed home and minded their own business badly. Such examples, however, do not affect the fundamental proposition that at least since 1860, when the impact of the scientific revolution on economic life really began to be felt, we have been living in a world that is qualitatively different from that of the past—a world in which, as I have said elsewhere, one can extract ten dollars from nature for every dollar one can exploit out of man. The scientific revolution, therefore, has completely eliminated any economic pay-offs that might have been available through the international system in the past. And while diminishing the system's returns, the scientific revolution has at the same time enormously increased the cost of the system. In order to justify the continuation of this costly and precarious system, we have to put an enormous value on the nation-state as such and on the national identity it confers on the individual. It should at least be asked whether the value of these things is commensurate with the risks and costs of maintaining the system.

What, then, are the sources of this pathological state of the international system? A number of answers can be given. Most significantly, a system of unilateral national defense, which still characterizes the international system in spite of the small beginnings of world political organization, is a "prisoner's dilemma" system:[2] the dynamics of the system produce an equilibrium in which everybody is much worse off than in some alternative state of the system. In the two-country version of this system, let us suppose that each country has two choices: disarm or arm. They will clearly be better off economically and more secure politically if they both disarm. If both are disarmed, however, it pays one to arm—at least it may in terms of his image of the system. And if one is armed, the other will have a powerful incentive to follow suit. Both will probably end up by being armed, in which case both will be worse off than they would have been had they remained disarmed.

Whether there is an equilibrium in the world's war industry depends largely on the reactions of the parties concerned. The fundamental parameter here is the "reactivity coefficient"; that is, the extent to which one country will increase its arms expenditures for each additional dollar that it perceives being spent on arms in another country. I have shown in another paper[3] that in a two-country system the product of the reactivity coefficients must be less than one if there is to be an equilibrium; otherwise the war industry will expand explosively until the system breaks down as the result of war or of some sort of parametric change. It can also be shown that the more parties there are in the system, the smaller the reactivity coefficient must be if an equilibrium is to be attained. It must certainly average less than one. As a reactivity coefficient of one might be regarded as normal, it is clear that a system of this kind must be abnormally unreactive if it is to achieve an equilibrium. It is not surprising, therefore, in the light of existing reactivity coefficients, which are certainly close to one if not above it, that the world's war industry maintains an uneasy and continually upward-groping equilibrium at about $140 billion per year. Furthermore, this equilibrium, even if it exists, is inherently precarious in that a very slight change in the reactivity coefficients even on the part of a single country can destroy the equilibrium altogether.

The reactivity coefficients are themselves functions of the value systems of the decision makers and of their general image of the international system, or perhaps of their images of other people's reactivity. And all these in turn are related to the gathering and processing of the information on which the decision makers depend. The pathology of the international system, therefore, is closely related to the method by which it generates and processes information and the way in which these information inputs influence the decision makers' images of the world. The question as to what is meant by the "reality" of these images in the international system is a very difficult one. In the first place, insofar as the system itself is determined by the decisions of a relatively small number of decision makers, it inevitably contains a considerable random element. The image of the system, therefore, should always be an image of probabilities rather than certainties. There is no very good way, however, of finding out what the probabilities of the system are. We do not have enough cases to compute frequencies like the life tables of insurance companies, and whenever one hears the expression "a calculated risk" in international politics one tends to interpret this as meaning "I really don't have the slightest notion." The epistemological problem itself, in the case of international systems, is very difficult; and one certainly cannot come up with any perfect solution for the problem of producing truth in the image of the system, for the system itself consists in considerable part of the images about it.

Even if the truth in an absolute sense may elude us, this still does not prevent us from discussing health, or at least disease, and there are certain diseases of the information system (and the images it produces) in the international system that can be diagnosed. The basic problem . . . is that adequate images of the international system cannot be derived from folk learning, because the simple feedbacks of the folk-learning process are quite inadequate to deal with the enormous complexities of the international system. At the present time, however, the role of science is extremely limited, indeed, almost nonexistent. We do not apply scientific techniques of information gathering and processing, even those available in the social sciences, to the image-creating processes of the international system. Social science, indeed, is regarded with considerable suspicion by most of the professional practitioners in the international system, perhaps rightly so, for it represents a certain threat to their status and power. On the whole, therefore, the images of the international system in the minds of its decision makers are . . . a mélange of narrative history, memories of past events, stories and conversations, and the like, plus an enormous amount of usually ill-digested and carelessly collected current information. When we add to this the fact that the system produces strong hates, loves, loyalties, disloyalties, and so on, it would be surprising if any images were formed that even remotely resembled the most loosely defined realities of the case.

Almost every principle we have learned about scientific information gathering, processing, and reality-testing is violated by the processes of the international system. Indeed, the conflict of values between the subculture of science and the subculture of the international system may well turn out to be one of the most fundamental conflicts of our age. In science secrecy is abhorrent and veracity is the highest virtue. In science there is only one mortal sin: telling a deliberate lie. In the international system, on the other hand, secrecy is paramount and veracity is subordinated to the national interest. The national interest can, indeed, be said to legitimate almost every conceivable form of evil: there is not one of the seven deadly sins that is not made into a virtue by the international system. Another fundamental characteristic of the scientific community is that it is basically a community of equals, for the very good reason that hierarchy always corrupts communication. A dialogue can exist only between equals. In a hierarchy there is an inescapable tendency toward pleasing the superior and hence confirming his own ideas. Hierarchy in organizations, therefore, produces a condition akin to paranoia in individuals. The information-gathering apparatus always tends to confirm the existing image of the top decision makers, no matter what it is. This organizational "mental illness" is nowhere better illustrated than in the international system, which is composed of numerous foreign-office and military-establishment hierarchies that thrive on self-justifying images.

Finally, in the scientific community, power is supposed to have a low value and truth the highest value, whereas in the international system the reverse is the case. It is not surprising that under these circumstances the international system is so spectacularly pathological in an organizational sense. Indeed, if one were designing an organization to produce pathological results, one could hardly do better than an information system dependent mainly on spies and diplomats. This is not to say, of course, that the individuals who occupy these roles in the international system are themselves necessarily crazy, although they do suffer from certain occupational diseases. On the whole, the people who run the international system are well above average in intelligence and education and even in personal morality, for they would probably not be content to serve in a system so absurd if they did not possess high moral ideals. Economic man does not go into the international system. He can live a better life outside it. It is the moral, patriotic, and self-sacrificing individuals who are most likely to be the active participants in the international system. It is the organization, not the individuals, which is pathological, by reason of the corruption of both the information and the values that have produced it. . . .

The one possible cause for optimism about the international system is that there exists what might be called a "macrolearning" process, which seems to be cumulative in much the same way as science. It is only in the last two hundred years, for instance, that we have achieved something that could be called a security community or stable peace in segments of the international system. During that period, we can trace something that looks like a progression from stable war into unstable war into unstable peace and finally into stable peace. As experience accumulates and as the memory of disastrous feedbacks affects present images of the system, these more mature images become a kind of folk wisdom that is transmitted from generation to generation, however precariously; and with the rise of genuinely scientific images of the international system we may expect this cumulative learning process to accelerate. It is reasonable to hope, therefore, that we may be fairly close to that key watershed in which the international system passes from a condition of unstable peace, albeit with enclaves of stable peace, into one in which stable peace becomes a property of the general system, which still, however, may have enclaves of unstable peace within it. At the moment, it must be admitted, the enclaves of stable peace appear as figures on a ground of unstable peace. However, a little expansion of the figures to include, let us say, all of Europe, the United States, the Soviet Union, and Japan, and the ground will become the figure and the figure the ground. Quantitatively this change may be very small; yet it will be a watershed, and the system will never be the same again. One may then expect the enclaves of unstable peace to diminish as the learning process continues, until finally the vision of a world in stable peace, which has haunted mankind so elusively for so long, will be realized. When it is realized it will be the result of a long process of learning, in which cheap methods of learning, such as science and perhaps even accumulated folk wisdom, are substituted for the expensive methods of learning, such as war.

▪ *Notes*

1. Kenneth E. Boulding (with Alan Gleason), "War as an Investment: The Strange Case of Japan," *Peace Research Society (International) Papers*, III (1965), 1–17.

2. Anatol Rapoport and Albert M. Chammah, *Prisoner's Dilemma: A Study in Conflict and Cooperation* (Ann Arbor: University of Michigan Press, 1965).
3. Kenneth E. Boulding, "The Parameters of Politics," *University of Illinois Bulletin* (July 15, 1966), pp. 1–21.

PART THREE

■ THE IDEOLOGICAL RESPONSE

INTRODUCTION

Only man characterizes experienced difficulties as crisis situations. He alone employs symbols to make a troublesome world meaningful and clear to himself. His language enables him to detach himself from his immediate experiences, to recapture the past as well as to outline the future in an orderly fashion. He is capable of anticipating his future by imagining it, and thus he again and again turns out to be disappointed. Events occur which are in effect *critical* of his image of the future simply by not fitting it. The unimagined happens. Floods, epidemics, massacres, shipwrecks, invasions, bankruptcies—all these hardships come to be seen as critical situations.

This does not mean that we feel continuously beset by crisis. We usually move monotonously through the span of our life, expecting and finding our future to resemble our past. Inevitably, however, emergencies do upset our routine. Health is replaced by illness, premarried life by marriage, employment by unemployment, a handicraft economy by the assembly line, an agrarian existence by an urban one, a familiar authority (a father, a king, a president) by an unfamiliar successor.

If we are to keep our balance in the face of the recurrent shocks to our expectations, our new experiences must be somehow comprehended. They must be brought under control, whether by religious myths, common-sense explanations, or scientific laws. More than that, the gulf between the old and the new must be bridged. We must be initiated to the newly impending

85

order of existence lest, uninitiated and anxious, we find ourselves either incapable of moving ahead or else driven to act in a state of mindless frenzy. Unavoidably, the transition—often soothingly characterized as "growth" or "progress" or "development"—demands sacrifices.

During periods of crisis, the foremost problem for the community is to prevent its own disintegration. It must maintain social solidarity even while its individual members find life so agonizing and so meaningless that they threaten to drop out. Society is faced by the need to provide meaning where none would seem evident; its problem is how to make the prevailing frustrations legitimate and therefore acceptable.

The problem may be solved by a leadership determined to exercise coercive power. Individuals who fail to move in a disciplined fashion, refusing to suffer the shocks of transition, may be physically coerced by those in power. But this is no easy matter when large masses must be mobilized. To maintain a coercive system requires a far-flung control apparatus: a large-scale party, a secret police, a military establishment. It is considerably more economical if a population undergoing hardships can be induced to *believe* in the need to work and fight together. It is simply more efficient to have everyone believe it is in his own interest to bear up.

Moreover, we are more likely to keep our balance when we believe our difficulties to be justified by some higher rationality. For some higher end, we will gladly suffer. In fact, when no transcending goal spontaneously reveals itself to us, we are apt to become inventive. There *must* be some point to it all. Our suffering cannot be for nothing. We may be the victim of an accident, —but it cannot *really* be accidental. Behind one's personal disaster, there must be some rational order. Thus our accidents may be perceived as providential, determined by a reasonable deity, by the cause-and-effect sequence of history, by statistical probability. The promise of eternal bliss in the next world can appear to justify our suffering in this one. The biological law of survival of the fittest can be invoked to adjust the victims of the Irish potato famine to their fate. The economic law of laissez faire can be invoked to reconcile parents to having their children labor in cotton mills. The law of dialectical materialism can be invoked to induce the victims of Stalin's terror to testify against themselves. We can be led to tax ourselves, contribute our blood, our very lives, for some alleged transcending purpose— the purity of the race, the grandeur of the nation, the inner meaning of history, the victory of the proletariat. For the sake of states' rights, free enterprise, five-year plans, or puritan virtue, we can be moved to surrender our individual interests.

The ideologies, myths, rituals, and slogans which serve to galvanize the mass of men are not always successful. Ideologies are not equally adequate responses to the predicaments which were outlined in Part Two of this volume. They serve with varying degrees of success in moving men through periods of transition. Men still hesitate before entering the industrial society or any other unexpected world. When an ideology functions well, however, it will inspire men to move uncomplainingly from one order of existence to another, from home to school, school to office, civilian to military life, self-indulgence to self-sacrifice, a rural, preindustrial to an urban, industrial society. Ideologies not only make each transition palatable but, when truly effective, make men enthusiastic about the new order of things. They make it seem rational, or at least necessary.

No doubt, some transitions *are* necessary and rational; to avoid them is to remain arrested in one's development. Not all commencement exercises are pointless. All manner of initiation rites (and the elaborate intellectual defenses supporting them) do in fact facilitate growth, enabling us to integrate progressively more interests and thereby achieve our measure of political maturity. There is a sound case for rituals which *in fact* introduce us to progressively higher stages of development. Thus marriage rites, presidential succession rites, and funeral rites, all of which confer legitimacy on a new order of things, might well be regarded as rational. When natural impulses are so ungovernable and destructive that they block continued development, it may be sensible to subject men to an exhausting ritual at the precise moment they are tempted to abandon themselves to nature. It may therefore be altogether rational to keep men from doing what comes naturally, whether they crave fulfillment through sex, food, property, or power. When a public official succeeds his predecessor in office, it may be desirable, for example, to burden him with the observance of elaborate rites which frustrate him and make him maintain his balance. They function to make him reflective, for they induce him to consider other interests as he is tempted to seek merely his own.

Our myths, rituals, and ideologies, it should be evident, serve not only to move men but also to arrest their movement. Unlike scientific theories, they serve less to enlarge understanding than to influence human conduct. Whether or not such influence is justified is finally always an empirical question. The test of their rationality is their capacity for making us civil, the likelihood of their serving not some special interest, but a variety of interests—ultimately the public interest. The question is whether they support the institution of politics, which is the only concern (as was pointed out in Part One) that all men share. It is thus possible to determine the adequacy of competing ideologies, and this in terms of their capacity not only for moving people but also for moving them toward political maturity. They are desirable to the extent that they satisfy the greatest variety of manageable interests, that they reject special interests—whether these be the interests of race, nation, economic class, religious creed, or scientific establishment. A belief system accordingly merits support if it energizes individuals (this being indispensable, but not sufficient) *and* if it succeeds in incorporating the widest manageable variety of interests.

In the light of this criterion, none of the political doctrines we are offered can be deemed adequate, though some clearly are more adequate than others. None can ever *fully* reflect the public interest. They tend to be professed by special interests, by spokesmen for groups struggling against opposing groups for social or economic power. Rationalizing special interests, they are designed to conceal unpleasant facts—the miseries of urbanization (allegedly necessary for economic growth), the repression of charitable feelings of the ruling class (allegedly in the interest of the development of the poor), the liquidation of an obstinate opposition (allegedly for the sake of political progress).

This does not mean that groups seeking to get or keep power realize that their doctrines are actually self-serving. They are far more likely to regard their beliefs as objectively just and in the public interest. Marx surely did not believe that his interpretation of history was a self-serving ideology, one designed merely to ease *his* conscience or to enable a Communist elite to rule in *its* interest. Similarly, those American thinkers who espouse the doctrine of a new corporation believe their views to be generally valid, not contrived to protect a plurality of economic establishments against the interests of popular majorities.

Yet, whatever the self-image of the proponents of specific doctrines, the relevant question for us is to what extent their belief systems really are ideological, verbal façades behind which power is won and consolidated. Committed to the integrity of the political order, we must inquire to what extent a belief system does justice to *all* interests in society. Does it recognize all the facts we can bear to perceive? Could we tolerate a larger measure of truth without jeopardizing our political development? Is it true, as the advocates of corporatism claim, that even those at the bottom of the various hierarchies in society are represented at the top? Is it true, as the equalitarians claim, that fraternity enables us to overcome the frustrations of modern life? Do the offered ideologies provide us with pictures of reality more distorted than necessary? What *of interest* do they leave out?

It should finally be noted that the commitments we associate with democratic constitutionalism—with a political order generally—remain undiscussed in this section, their desirability having been explicitly postulated and defended in Part One. Unlike the ideologies which challenge it, democratic constitutionalism defends no *fixed* set of political arrangements. Not committed to any institutions as irrevocably sound, it claims no goal for either man or the state as absolutely valid. To defend it is therefore merely to defend political and scientific procedures which can be shown to provide the individual with options, which are apt to enlarge the range of his experience, and which may consequently free him to move toward unspecified, self-determined ends.

16 NATIONALISM

- *Maurice Barrès*

I was asked to deliver the third lecture of the League of the French Nation. I undertook to define nationalism, that is to say, to seek its basic principles and implications.

We must begin, I said, by understanding the causes of our weakness. . . . When a wound fails to heal, the physician thinks of diabetes. Beneath the accident let us seek out the underlying condition.

Our deeply ingrained disease is that we are divided, disturbed by a thousand individual wills, by a thousand individual imaginations. We have fallen apart; we have no common awareness of our aim, of our resources, of our core.

Happy are those nations where movements are linked together, where efforts harmonize as if a plan had been developed by a superior mind!

There are many ways in which a country can have this moral unity. A sense of loyalty may rally a nation about its sovereign. In the absence of a dynasty, traditional institutions can provide a center. But a century ago, our France suddenly cursed and destroyed its dynasty and its institutions. Lastly, some races succeed in becoming aware of themselves organically. Such is the case with the Anglo-Saxon and Teutonic groups which are developing more and more into races. Alas! There is no French race, but a French people, a French nation, that is to say, an entity consisting of a political grouping. Yes, unfortunately, as compared with rival, and, in the struggle for existence, necessarily enemy groups, ours has not achieved a conscious awareness of itself. We implicitly admit this in the way in which our publicists, writers, and artists call us sometimes Latins, sometimes Gauls, sometimes "the soldier of the Church," and then again the great nation, "the emancipator of peoples," depending on the needs of the moment.

In the absence of a moral unity, of a common understanding of what France is, we have contradictory words, varied banners beneath which men

From Maurice Barrès, *Scènes et Doctrines du Nationalisme* (1902), reprinted in *Introduction to Contemporary Civilization in the West* (New York: Columbia University Press, 1946), II, 795–799; 1961 ed., II, 1041–1044.

eager to exercise leadership can gather their following. Each of these groups understands in its own way the internal law of the development of this country.

Nationalism means the resolution of all questions by reference to France. But how are we to do this when we have no common understanding and idea of France?

Should an incident occur, it is interpreted by each party according to the particular meaning the party gives to the concept of France. Hence we can understand the real importance of this Dreyfus Affair: instead of being handled, in a common spirit, by Frenchmen who had the same idea of their country and of what is good for it, it has been considered by doctrinaires who are guided by the precepts of their own taste.

Given this lack of moral unity in a country which has neither dynasty nor traditional institutions, and which is not a race, it is quite natural that dangerous metaphysicians should gain authority over our imaginations, provided that they are eloquent, persuasive, *kindly*. By offering us an ideal, they undertake to give us moral unity. But far from delivering us from confusion, they only increase it by their contradictory assertions.

This is what must be remedied. Only a lazy heart and a mind thoroughly corrupted by anarchy could be content in this France torn and leaderless in thought.

But how can this lacking national consciousness be developed?

First let us repudiate philosophic systems and the political parties to which they give rise. Let us all join our efforts, not behind a vision of our own mind, but behind realities.

We are men of good will: whatever be the opinions which our family, education, environment, and many little personal events have given us, we are decided to take as our starting point that which is, and not our own intellectual ideal. One among us may find that the Revolution has turned us from the most prosperous and happy paths; another may regret that the First Consul, by the Concordat, returned France to the influence of Rome; a third is convinced that the destinies of our country are closely linked to those of Catholicism. Each rewrites the history of France. Let us cast aside these fictions. Why mire ourselves in these hypothetical roads which France might have followed? We shall derive a more certain profit from delving into all the moments of French history, living in our thoughts with all her dead, with every one of her experiences. What moral problems we shall face if our own preference must choose among all these seemingly contradictory revolutions which have occurred in France over a century! After all, the France of the Consulate, the France of the Restoration, the France of 1830, the France of 1848, the France of the authoritarian Empire—all these Frances which go to contradictory extremes with such astonishing agility, all come from the same root and tend toward the same end; they are the fruits of different seasons from the same seed on the same tree. . . .

If the League of the French Nation could succeed in giving its followers this sense of the real and the relative, if it could convince those honest and devoted professors (who at times have done us so much harm) to judge things as historians rather than as metaphysicians, it would transform the abominable political spirit of our nation; it would restore our moral unity; it would, indeed, create what we have lacked: a national consciousness.

To have this national, realistic view of the Fatherland accepted, we must develop sentiments which already exist naturally in the country. Union cannot be built on ideas, so long as they are only processes of reason; they must be bulwarked with emotional strength. At the root of all things is feeling. One would try in vain to establish truth by reason alone, for intelligence can always find a new motive for reopening the question.

To create a national consciousness, we must combine with this dominant intellectualism, whose methods the historians teach, a less conscious, less deliberate element.

Misled by a university training that spoke only of man and humanity, I feel that like so many others I should have embroiled myself in anarchical agitation had not certain feelings of veneration warned me and strengthened my heart. . . . [*Here follows an account of Barrès' emotional reactions to a visit to the military cemetery at Metz.*]

Nothing is more valuable in forming a people's soul than this voice of our ancestors, than this lesson of the soil which Metz teaches so well. Our soil gives us a discipline, for we are the continuation of our dead. That is the reality on which we should build. . . .

The dead! What would a man mean to himself if he stood only by himself? When each of us looks backward he sees an endless train of mysteries, whose recent embodiment is called France. We are the product of a collective being which speaks in us. Let the influence of the ancestors be enduring and the sons will be vigorous and upright, and the nation one. . . . In vain does the foreigner, on naturalization, swear that he will think and live as a Frenchman; in vain has he bound his interests with ours; blood persists in following the order of nature against all vows, against all laws. He is our guest, this son from beyond the Rhine, or English Channel, and we offer him safety and our generous friendship, but we do not owe him a share in the government of the country. Let him first feel our pulse, and, from roots that will grow, nourish himself from our soil and our dead. His grandchildren, indeed, will be French, genuinely, and not merely through a legal fiction.

17 COMMUNISM

■ *Karl Marx, Friedrich Engels,*
V. I. Lenin, Mao Tse-tung

Karl Marx: Economic Determinism

In the social production which men carry on they enter into definite relations that are indispensable and independent of their will; these relations of production correspond to a definite stage of development of their material powers of production. The sum total of these relations of production constitutes the economic structure of society—the real foundation, on which rise legal and political superstructures and to which correspond definite forms of social consciousness. The mode of production in material life determines the general characters of the social, political, and spiritual processes of life. It is not the consciousness of men that determines their existence, but, on the contrary, their social existence determines their consciousness. At a certain stage of their development the material forces of production in society come into conflict with the existing relations of production, or—what is but a legal expression for the same thing—with the property relations within which they had been at work before. From forms of development of the forces of production these relations turn into their fetters. Then comes the period of social revolution. With the change of the economic foundation the entire immense superstructure is more or less rapidly transformed. In considering such transformations the distinction should always be made between the material transformation of the economic conditions of production, which can be determined with the precision of natural science, and the legal, political, religious, aesthetic, or philosophic—in short, ideological—forms in which men become conscious of this conflict

From Karl Marx, *A Contribution to the Critique of Political Economy* (1850) (New York: International Library Publishing Co., 1904), pp. 11–13; Karl Marx and Friedrich Engels, *The Manifesto of the Communist Party* (1848) (Moscow: Foreign Languages Publishing House); V. I. Lenin, *The State and Revolution* (1917), from *Selected Works* (Moscow: Foreign Languages Publishing House, 1950), Vol. II, Book 1; Mao Tse-tung, "Rectify the Party's Style of Work" (1942), *Selected Works* (Peking: Foreign Languages Press, 1965), III, 35–51.

and fight it out. Just as our opinion of an individual is not based on what he thinks of himself, so can we not judge such a period of transformation by its own consciousness; on the contrary, this consciousness must rather be explained from the contradictions of material life, from the existing conflict between the social forces of production and the relations of production. No social order ever disappears before all the productive forces for which there is room in it have been developed, and new, higher relations of production never appear before the material conditions of their existence have matured in the womb of the old society. Therefore mankind always takes up only such problems as it can solve, since, looking at the matter more closely, we will always find that the problem itself arises only when the material conditions necessary for its solution already exist or are at least in the process of formation. . . .

Karl Marx and Friedrich Engels: The Manifesto

A specter is haunting Europe—the specter of Communism. All the powers of old Europe have entered into a holy alliance to exorcise this specter: Pope and Czar, Metternich and Guizot, French Radicals and German police-spies.

Where is the party in opposition that has not been decried as Communistic by its opponents in power? Where the Opposition that has not hurled back the branding reproach of Communism, against the more advanced opposition parties, as well as against its reactionary adversaries?

Two things result from this fact.

I. Communism is already acknowledged by all European powers to be itself a power.

II. It is high time that Communists should openly, in the face of the whole world publish their views, their aims, their tendencies, and meet this nursery tale of the specter of Communism with a Manifesto of the party itself.

To this end, Communists of various nationalities have assembled in London and sketched the following Manifesto, to be published in the English, French, German, Italian, Flemish, and Danish languages.

Bourgeois and Proletarians

The history of all hitherto existing society is the history of class struggles.

Freeman and slave, patrician and plebeian, lord and serf, guildmaster and journeyman, in a word, oppressor and oppressed, stood in constant opposition to one another, carried on an uninterrupted, now hidden, now open fight, a fight that each time ended, either in a revolutionary reconstitution of society at large or in the common ruin of the contending classes.

In the earlier epochs of history, we find almost everywhere a complicated arrangement of society into various orders, a manifold gradation of social rank. In ancient Rome we have patricians, knights, plebeians, slaves; in the Middle Ages, feudal lords, vassals, guildmasters, journeymen, apprentices, serfs; in in almost all of these classes, again, subordinate gradations.

The modern bourgeois society that has sprouted from the ruins of feudal society has not done away with class antagonisms. It has but established new classes, new conditions of oppression, new forms of struggle in place of the old ones.

Our epoch, the epoch of the bourgeoisie, possesses, however, this distinctive feature: it has simplified the class antagonisms. Society as a whole is more and more splitting up into two great hostile camps, into two great classes directly facing each other: bourgeoisie and proletariat.

From the serfs of the Middle Ages sprang the chartered burghers of the earliest towns. From these burgesses the first elements of the bourgeoisie were developed.

The discovery of America, the rounding of the Cape, opened up fresh ground for the rising bourgeoisie. The East Indian and Chinese markets, the colonization of America, trade with the colonies, the increase in the means of exchange and in commodities generally, gave to commerce, to navigation, to industry, an impulse never before known, and thereby, to the revolutionary element in the tottering feudal society, a rapid development.

The feudal system of industry, under which industrial production was monopolized by closed guilds, now no longer sufficed for the growing wants of the new markets. The manufacturing system took its place. The guildmasters were pushed on one side by the manufacturing middle class; division of labor between the different corporate guilds vanished in the face of division of labor in each single workshop.

Meantime the markets kept ever growing, the demand ever rising. Even manufacture no longer sufficed. Thereupon, steam and machinery revolutionized industrial production. The place of manufacture was taken by the giant, modern industry; the place of the industrial middle class by industrial millionaires, the leaders of whole industrial armies, the modern bourgeois.

Modern industry has established the world market, for which the discovery of America paved the way. This market has given an immense development to commerce, to navigation, to communication by land. This development has, in its turn, reacted on the extension of industry; and in proportion as industry, commerce, navigation, railways, extended, in the same proportion the bourgeoisie developed, increased its capital, and pushed into the background every class handed down from the Middle Ages.

We see, therefore, how the modern bourgeoisie is itself the product of a long course of development, of a series of revolutions in the modes of production and of exchange.

Each step in the development of the bourgeoisie was accompanied by a corresponding political advance of that class. An oppressed class under the sway of the feudal nobility, an armed and self-governing association in the medieval commune, here independent urban republic (as in Italy and Germany), there taxable "third estate" of the monarchy (as in France), afterward, in the period of manufacture proper, serving either the semifeudal or the absolute monarchy as a counterpoise against the nobility and, in fact, cornerstone of the great monarchies in general—the bourgeoisie has at last, since the establishment of modern industry and of the world market, conquered for itself, in the modern representative state, exclusive political sway. The executive of the modern state is but a committee for managing the common affairs of the whole bourgeoisie.

The bourgeoisie, historically, has played a most revolutionary part.

The bourgeoisie, wherever it has got the upper hand, has put an end to all feudal, patriarchal, idyllic relations. It has pitilessly torn asunder the motley feudal ties that bound man to his "natural superiors" and has left remaining no other nexus between man and man than naked self-interest, than callous "cash payment." It has drowned the most heavenly ecstasies of religious fervor, of chivalrous enthusiasm, of philistine sentimentalism, in the icy water of egotistical calculation. It has resolved personal worth into exchange value, and in place of the numberless indefeasible chartered freedoms, has set up that single, unconscionable freedom—Free Trade. In one word, for exploitation, veiled by religious and political illusions, it has substituted naked, shameless, direct, brutal exploitation.

The bourgeoisie has stripped of its halo every occupation hitherto honored and looked up to with reverent awe. It has converted the physician, the lawyer, the priest, the poet, the man of science, into its paid wage-laborers.

The bourgeoisie has torn away from the family its sentimental veil and has reduced the family relation to a mere money relation.

The bourgeoisie has disclosed how it came to pass that the brutal display of vigor in the Middle Ages, which reactionaries so much admire, found its fitting complement in the most slothful indolence. It has been the first to show what man's activity can bring about. It has accomplished wonders far surpassing Egyptian pyramids, Roman aqueducts, and Gothic cathedrals; it has conducted expeditions that put in the shade all former exoduses of nations and crusades.

The bourgeoisie cannot exist without constantly revolutionizing the instruments of production, and thereby the relations of production, and with them the whole relations of society. Conservation of the old modes of production in unaltered form was, on the contrary, the first condition of existence for all earlier industrial classes. Constant revolutionizing of production, uninterrupted disturbance of all social conditions, everlasting uncertainty and agitation distinguish the bourgeois epoch from all earlier ones. All fixed, fast-frozen relations, with their train of ancient and venerable prejudices and opinions, are swept away; all new-formed ones become antiquated before they can ossify. All that is solid melts into air, all that is holy is profaned, and man is at last compelled to face with sober senses his real conditions of life and his relations with his kind.

The need of a constantly expanding market for its products chases the bourgeoisie over the whole surface of the globe. It must nestle everywhere, settle everywhere, establish connections everywhere.

The bourgeoisie has through its exploitation of the world market given a cosmopolitan character to production and consumption in every country. To the great chagrin of reactionaries, it has drawn from under the feet of industry the national ground on which it stood. All old-established national industries have been destroyed or are daily being destroyed. They are dislodged by new industries, whose introduction becomes a life-and-death question for all civilized nations, by industries that no longer work up indigenous raw material, but raw material drawn from the remotest zones; industries whose products are consumed, not only at home, but in every quarter of the globe. In place of the old wants, satisfied by the productions of the country, we find new wants, requiring for their satisfaction the products of distant lands and climes. In place of the old local and national seclusion and self-sufficiency, we have intercourse in every direction, universal interdependence of nations. And as in material, so also in intellectual production. The intellectual creations of individual nations become common property. National onesidedness and narrow-mindedness become more and more impossible, and from the numerous national and local literatures, there arises a world literature.

The bourgeoisie, by the rapid improvement of all instruments of production, by the immensely facilitated means of communication, draws all, even the most barbarian, nations into civilization. The cheap prices of its commodities are the heavy artillery with which it batters down all Chinese walls, with which it forces the barbarians' intensely obstinate hatred of foreigners to capitulate. It compels all nations, on pain of extinction, to adopt the bourgeois mode of production; it compels them to introduce what it calls civilization into their midst, i.e., to become bourgeois themselves. In one word, it creates a world after its own image.

The bourgeoisie has subjected the country to the rule of the towns. It has created enormous cities, has greatly increased the urban population as compared with the rural, and has thus rescued a considerable part of the population from the idiocy of rural life. Just as it has made the country dependent on the towns, so it has made barbarian and semibarbarian countries dependent on the civilized ones, nations of peasants on nations of bourgeois, the East on the West.

The bourgeoisie keeps more and more doing away with the scattered state of the population, of the means of production, and of property. It has agglomerated population, centralized means of production, and concentrated property in a few hands. The necessary consequence of this was political centralization. Independent, or but loosely connected, provinces with separate interests, laws, governments, and systems of taxation became lumped together into one nation, with one government, one code of laws, one national class interest, one frontier, and one customs tariff.

The bourgeoisie, during its rule of scarce one hundred years, has created more massive and more colossal productive forces than have all preceding generations together. Subjection of nature's forces to man, machinery, application of chemistry to industry and agriculture, steam navigation, railways, electric telegraphs, clearing of whole continents for cultivation, canalization of rivers, whole populations conjured out of the ground—what earlier century had even a presentiment that such productive forces slumbered in the lap of social labor?

We see then that the means of production and of exchange, on whose foundation the bourgeoisie built itself up, were generated in feudal society. At a certain stage in the development of these means of production and of exchange, the conditions under which feudal society produced and exchanged, the feudal organization of agriculture and manufacturing industry, in one word, the feudal relations of property, became no longer compatible with the already developed productive forces; they became so many fetters. They had to be burst asunder; they were burst asunder.

Into their place stepped free competition, accompanied by a social and political constitution adapted to it and by the economical and political sway of the bourgeois class.

A similar movement is going on before our own eyes. Modern bourgeois society with its relations of production, of exchange, and of property, a society that has conjured up such gigantic means of production and of exchange is like the sorcerer, who is no longer able to control the powers of the nether world whom he has called up by his spells. For many a decade past the history of industry and commerce is but the history of the revolt of modern productive forces against modern conditions of production, against the property relations that are the conditions for the existence of the bourgeoisie and of its rule. It is enough to mention the commercial crises that by their periodical return put on its trial, each time more threateningly, the existence of the entire bourgeois society. In these crises a great part not only of the existing products, but also of the previously created productive forces, are periodically destroyed. In these crises there breaks out an epidemic that, in all earlier epochs, would have seemed an absurdity—the epidemic of over-production. Society suddenly finds itself put back into a state of momentary barbarism; it appears as if a famine, a universal war of devastation, had cut off the supply of every means of subsistence; industry and commerce seem to be destroyed; and why? Because there is too much civilization, too much means of subsistence, too much industry, too much commerce. The productive forces at the disposal of society no longer tend to further the development of the conditions of bourgeois property; on the contrary, they have become too powerful for these conditions, by which they are fettered, and so soon as they overcome these fetters, they bring disorder into the whole of bourgeois society, endanger the existence of bourgeois property. The conditions of bourgeois society are too narrow to comprise the wealth created by them. And how does the bourgeoisie get over these crises? On the one hand by enforced destruction of a mass of productive forces; on the other, by the conquest of new markets and by the more thorough exploitation of the old ones. That is to say, by paving the way for more extensive and more destructive crises and by diminishing the means whereby crises are prevented.

The weapons with which the bourgeoisie felled feudalism to the ground are now turned against the bourgeoisie itself.

But not only has the bourgeoisie forged the weapons that bring death to itself; it has also called into existence the men who are to wield those weapons—the modern working class—the proletarians.

In proportion as the bourgeoisie, i.e., capital, is developed, in the same proportion is the proletariat, the modern working class, developed—a class of laborers, who live only so long as they find work and who find work only so long as their labor increases capital. These laborers, who must sell themselves piecemeal, are a commodity, like every other article of commerce, and are consequently exposed to all the vicissitudes of competition, to all the fluctuations of the market.

Owing to the extensive use of machinery and to division of labor, the work of the proletarians has lost all individual character, and, consequently, all charm for the workman. He becomes an appendage of the machine, and it is only the most simple, most monotonous, and most easily acquired knack that is required of him. Hence, the cost of production of a workman is restricted, almost entirely, to the means of subsistence that he requires for his maintenance and for the propagation of his race. But the price of a commodity, and therefore also of labor, is equal to its cost of production. In proportion, therefore, as the repulsiveness of the work increases, the wage decreases. Nay more, in proportion as the use of machinery and division of labor increases, in the same proportion the burden of toil also increases, whether by prolongation of the working hours, by increase of the work exacted in a given time, or by increased speed of the machinery, and so on.

Modern industry has converted the little workshop of the patriarchal master into the great factory of the industrial capitalist. Masses of laborers, crowded into the factory, are organized like soldiers. As privates of the industrial army they are placed under the command of a perfect hierarchy of officers and sergeants. Not only are they slaves of the bourgeois class and of the bourgeois state; they are daily and hourly enslaved by the machine, by the overseer, and above all, by the individual bourgeois manufacturer himself. The more openly this despotism proclaims gain to be its end and aim, the more petty, the more hateful, and the more embittering it is.

The less the skill and exertion of strength implied in manual labor—in other words, the more modern industry becomes developed—the more is the labor of men superseded by that of women. Differences of age and sex have no longer any distinctive social validity for the working class. All are instruments of labor, more or less expensive to use, according to their age and sex.

No sooner is the exploitation of the laborer by the manufacturer so far at an end that he receives his wages in cash, than he is set upon by the other portions of the bourgeoisie, the landlord, the shopkeeper, the pawnbroker and others.

The lower strata of the middle class—the small tradespeople, shopkeepers, and retired tradesmen generally, the handicraftsmen and peasants—all these sink gradually into the proletariat, partly because their diminutive capital does not suffice for the scale on which modern industry is carried on and is swamped in the competition with the large capitalists, partly because their specialized skill is rendered worthless by new methods of production. Thus the proletariat is recruited from all classes of the population.

The proletariat goes through various stages of development. With its birth begins its struggle with the bourgeoisie. At first the contest is carried on by individual laborers, then by the workpeople of a factory, then by the operatives of one trade, in one locality, against the individual bourgeois who directly exploits them. They direct their attacks not against the bourgeois conditions of production, but against the instruments of production themselves; they destroy imported wares that compete with their labor; they smash to pieces machinery, they set factories ablaze, they seek to restore by force the vanished status of the workman of the Middle Ages.

At this stage the laborers still form an incoherent mass scattered over the whole country and broken up by their mutual competition. If anywhere they unite to form more compact bodies, this is not yet the consequence of their own active union, but of the union of the bourgeoisie, which class, in order to attain its own political ends, is compelled to set the whole proletariat in motion and is moreover yet, for a time, able to do so. At this stage, therefore, the proletarians do not fight their enemies, but the enemies of their enemies, the remnants of absolute monarchy, the landowners, the nonindustrial bourgeois, the petty bourgeoisie. Thus the whole historical movement is concentrated in the hands of the bourgeoisie; every victory so obtained is a victory for the bourgeoisie.

But with the development of industry the proletariat not only increases in number; it becomes concentrated in greater masses, its strength grows, and it feels that strength more. The various interests and conditions of life within the ranks of the proletariat are more and more equalized, in proportion as machinery obliterates all distinctions of labor and nearly everywhere reduces wages to the same low level. The growing competition among the bourgeois, and the resulting commercial crises, make the wages of the workers ever more fluctuating. The unceasing improvement of machinery, ever more rapidly developing, makes their livelihood more and more precarious; the collisions between individual workmen and individual bourgeois take more and more the character of collisions between two classes. Thereupon the workers begin to form combinations (trade-unions) against the bourgeois; they club together in order to keep up the rate of wages; they found permanent associations in order to make provision beforehand for these occasional revolts. Here and there the contest breaks out into riots.

Now and then the workers are victorious, but only for a time. The real fruit of their battles lies, not in the immediate result, but in the ever expanding union of the workers. This union is helped on by the improved means of communication that are created by modern industry and that place the workers of different localities in contact with one another. It was just this contact that was needed to centralize the numerous local struggles, all of the same character, into one national struggle between classes. But every class struggle is a political struggle. And that union, to attain which the burghers of the Middle Ages, with their miserable highways, required centuries, the modern proletarians, thanks to railways, achieve in a few years.

This organization of the proletarians into a class, and consequently into a political party, is continually being upset again by the competition between the workers themselves. But it ever rises up again, stronger, firmer, mightier. It compels legislative recognition of particular interests of the workers, by taking advantage of the divisions among the bourgeoisie itself. Thus the ten-hours' bill in England was carried.

Altogether, these collisions between the classes of the old society further, in many ways, the course of development of the proletariat. The bourgeoisie finds itself involved in a constant battle: at first with the aristocracy; later on, with those portions of the bourgeoisie itself, whose interests have become antagonistic to the progress of industry; at all times, with the bourgeoisie of foreign countries. In all these battles it sees itself compelled to appeal to the proletariat, to ask for its help, and thus to drag it into the political arena. The bourgeoisie itself, therefore, supplies the proletariat with its own elements of political and general education; in other words, it furnishes the proletariat with weapons for fighting the bourgeoisie.

Further, as we have already seen, entire sections of the ruling classes are, by the advance of industry, precipitated into the proletariat, or are at least threatened in their conditions of existence. These also supply the proletariat with fresh elements of enlightenment and progress.

Finally, in times when the class struggle nears the decisive hour, the process of dissolution going on within the ruling class, in fact within the whole range of old society, assumes such a violent, glaring character that a small section of the ruling class cuts itself adrift and joins the revolutionary class, the class that holds the future in its hands. Just as, therefore, at an earlier period, a section of the nobility went over to the bourgeoisie, so now a portion of the bourgeoisie goes over to the proletariat, and in particular, a portion of the bourgeois ideologists, who have raised themselves to the level of comprehending theoretically the historical movement as a whole.

Of all the classes that stand face to face with the bourgeoisie today, the proletariat alone is a really revolutionary class. The other classes decay and finally disappear in the face of modern industry; the proletariat is its special and essential product.

The lower middle class, the small manufacturer, the shopkeeper, the artisan, the peasant—all these fight against the bourgeoisie, to save from extinction their existence as fractions of the middle class. They are therefore not revolutionary, but conservative. Nay more, they are reactionary, for they try to roll back the wheel of history. If by chance they are revolutionary, they are so only in view of their impending transfer into the proletariat; they thus defend not their present, but their future interests; they desert their own standpoint to place themselves at that of the proletariat.

The "dangerous class," the social scum, that passively rotting mass thrown off by the lowest layers of old society, may, here and there, be swept into the movement by a proletarian revolution; its conditions of life, however, prepare it far more for the part of a bribed tool of a reactionary intrigue.

The social conditions of the old society no longer exist for the proletariat. The proletarian is without property; his relation to his wife and children has no longer anything in common with the bourgeois family relations; modern industrial labor, modern subjection to capital, the same in England as in France, in America as in Germany, has stripped him of every trace of national character. Law, morality, religion, are to him so many bourgeois prejudices, behind which lurk in ambush just as many bourgeois interests.

All the preceding classes that got the upper hand sought to fortify their already acquired status by subjecting society at large to their conditions of appropriation. The proletarians cannot become masters of the productive forces of society, except by abolishing their own previous mode of appropriation and thereby also every other previous mode of appropriation. They have nothing of their own to secure and to fortify; their mission is to destroy all previous securities for, and insurances of, individual property.

All previous historical movements were movements of minorities, or in the interest of minorities. The proletarian movement is the self-conscious, independent movement of the immense majority, in the interest of the immense majority. The proletariat, the lowest stratum of our present society, cannot stir, cannot raise itself up, without the whole superincumbent strata of official society being sprung into the air.

Though not in substance, yet in form, the struggle of the proletariat with the bourgeoisie is at first a national struggle. The protelariat of each country must, of course, first of all settle matters with its own bourgeoisie.

In depicting the most general phases of the development of the proletariat, we traced the more or less veiled civil war, raging within existing society, up to the point where that war breaks out into open revolution and where the violent overthrow of the bourgeoisie lays the foundation for the sway of the proletariat.

Hitherto, every form of society has been based, as we have already seen, on the antagonism of oppressing and oppressed classes. But in order to oppress a class, certain conditions must be assured to it under which it can, at least, continue its slavish existence. The serf, in the period of serfdom, raised himself to membership in the commune, just as the petty bourgeois, under the yoke of feudal absolutisim, managed to develop into a bourgeois. The modern laborer, on the contrary, instead of rising with the progress of industry, sinks deeper and deeper below the conditions of existence of his own class. He becomes a pauper, and pauperism develops more rapidly than population and wealth. And here it becomes evident that the bourgeoisie is unfit any longer to be the ruling class in society and to impose its conditions of existence upon society as an overriding law. It is unfit to rule because it is incompetent to assure an existence to its slave within his slavery, because it cannot help letting him sink into such a state that it has to feed him, instead of being fed by him. Society can no longer live under this bourgeoisie; in other words, its existence is no longer compatible with society.

The essential condition for the existence and for the sway of the bourgeois class is the formation and augmentation of capital; the condition for capital is wage labor. Wage labor rests exclusively on competition between the laborers. The advance of industry, whose involuntary promoter is the bourgeoisie, replaces the isolation of the laborers, due to competition, by their revolutionary combination, due to association. The development of modern industry, therefore, cuts from under its feet the very foundation on which the bourgeoisie produces and appropriates products. What the bourgeoisie, therefore, produces, above all, is its own gravediggers. Its fall and the victory of the proletariat are equally inevitable.

Proletarians and Communists

In what relation do the Communists stand to the proletarians as a whole?

The Communists do not form a separate party opposed to other working-class parties.

They have no interests separate and apart from those of the proletariat as a whole.

They do not set up any sectarian principles of their own, by which to shape and mold the proletarian movement.

The Communists are distinguished from the other working-class parties by this only: (1) In the national struggles of the proletarians of the different countries, they point out and bring to the front the common interests of the entire proletariat, independently of all nationality. (2) In the various stages of development which the struggle of the working class against the bourgeoisie has to pass through, they always and everywhere represent the interests of the movement as a whole.

The Communists, therefore, are on the one hand, practically, the most advanced and resolute section of the working-class parties of every country, that section which pushes forward all others; on the other hand, theoretically, they have over the great mass of the proletariat the advantage of clearly understanding the line of march, the conditions, and the ultimate general results of the proletarian movements.

The immediate aim of the Communists is the same as that of all the other proletarian parties: formation of the proletariat into a class, overthrow of the bourgeois supremacy, conquest of political power by the proletariat.

The theoretical conclusions of the Communists are in no way based on ideas or principles that have been invented, or discovered, by this or that would-be universal reformer.

They merely express, in general terms, actual relations springing from an existing class struggle, from a historical movement going on under our very eyes. The abolition of existing property relations is not at all a distinctive feature of Communism.

All property relations in the past have continually been subject to historical change consequent upon the change in historical conditions.

The French Revolution, for example, abolished feudal property in favor of bourgeois property.

The distinguishing feature of Communism is not the abolition of property generally, but the abolition of bourgeois property. But modern bourgeois private property is the final and most complete expression of the system of producing and appropriating products, that is based on class antagonisms, on the exploitation of the many by the few.

In this sense, the theory of the Communists may be summed up in the single sentence: Abolition of private property.

We Communists have been reproached with the desire of abolishing the right of personally acquiring property as the fruit of a man's own labor, which property is alleged to be the groundwork of all personal freedom, activity, and independence.

Hard-won, self-acquired, self-earned property! Do you mean the property of the petty artisan and of the small peasant, a form of property that preceded the bourgeois form? There is no need to abolish that; the development of industry has to a great extent already destroyed it and is still destroying it daily.

Or do you mean modern bourgeois private property?

But does wage labor create any property for the laborer? Not a bit. It creates capital, i.e., that kind of property which exploits wage labor and which cannot increase except upon condition of begetting a new supply of wage labor for fresh exploitation. Property, in its present form, is based on the antagonism of capital and wage labor. Let us examine both sides of this antagonism.

To be a capitalist is to have not only a purely personal but a social *status* in production. Capital is a collective product, and only by the united action of many members, nay, in the last resort, only by the united action of all members of society can it be set in motion.

Capital is, therefore, not a personal, but a social power.

When, therefore, capital is converted into common property, into the property of all members of society, personal property is not thereby transformed into social property. It is only the social character of the property that is changed. It loses its class character.

Let us now take wage labor.

The average price of wage labor is the minimum wage, i.e., that quantum of the means of subsistence which is absolutely requisite to keep the laborer in bare existence as a laborer. What, therefore, the wage-laborer appropriates by means of his labor merely suffices to prolong and reproduce a bare existence. We by no means intend to abolish this personal appropriation of the products of labor—an appropriation that is made for the maintenance and reproduction of human life, and that leaves no surplus wherewith to command the labor of others. All that we want to do away with is the miserable character of this appropriation, under which the laborer lives merely to increase capital and is allowed to live only insofar as the interest of the ruling class requires it.

In bourgeois society, living labor is but a means to increase accumulated labor. In Communist society, accumulated labor is but a means to widen, to enrich, to promote the existence of the laborer.

In bourgeois society, therefore, the past dominates the present; in Communist society, the present dominates the past. In bourgeois society capital is independent and has individuality, while the living person is dependent and has no individuality.

And the abolition of this state of things is called, by the bourgeois, abolition of individuality and freedom! And rightly so. The abolition of bourgeois individuality, bourgeois independence, and bourgeois freedom is undoubtedly aimed at.

By freedom is meant, under the present bourgeois conditions of production, free trade, free selling and buying.

But if selling and buying disappears, free selling and buying disappears also. This talk about free selling and buying, and all the other "brave words" of our bourgeoisie about freedom in general, have a meaning, if any, only in contrast with restricted selling and buying, with the fettered traders of the Middle Ages, but have no meaning when opposed to the Communistic abolition of buying and selling, of the bourgeois conditions of production, and of the bourgeoisie itself.

You are horrified at our intending to do away with private property. But in your existing society, private property is already done away with for nine-tenths of the population; its existence for the few is solely due to its nonexistence in the hands of those nine-tenths. You reproach us, therefore, with intending to do away with a form of property, the necessary condition for whose existence is the nonexistence of any property for the immense majority of society.

In one word, you reproach us with intending to do away with your property. Precisely so; that is just what we intend.

From the moment when labor can no longer be converted into capital, money, or rent, into a social power capable of being monopolized—i.e., from the moment when individual property can no longer be transformed into bourgeois property, into capital—from that moment, you say, individuality vanishes.

You must, therefore, confess that by "individual" you mean no other person than the bourgeois, than the middle-class owner of property. This person must, indeed, be swept out of the way and made impossible.

Communism deprives no man of the power to appropriate the products of society; all that it does is to deprive him of the power to subjugate the labor of others by means of such appropriation.

It has been objected that upon the abolition of private property all work will cease and universal laziness will overtake us.

According to this, bourgeois society ought long ago to have gone to the dogs through sheer idleness; for those of its members who work acquire nothing, and those who acquire anything do not work. The whole of this objection is but another expression of the tautology: that there can no longer be any wage labor when there is no longer any capital.

All objection urged against the Communistic mode of producing and appropriating material products have, in the same way, been urged against the Communistic modes of producing and appropriating intellectual products. Just as, to the bourgeois, the disappearance of class property is the disappearance of production itself, so the disappearance of class culture is to him identical with the disappearance of all culture.

That culture, the loss of which he laments, is, for the enormous majority, a mere training to act as a machine.

But don't wrangle with us so long as you apply, to our intended abolition of bourgeois property, the standard of your bourgeois notions of freedom, culture, law, and the like. Your very ideas are but the outgrowth of the conditions of your bourgeois production and bourgeois property, just as your jurisprudence is but the will of your class made into a law for all—a will whose essential character and direction are determined by the economical conditions of existence of your class.

The selfish misconception that induces you to transform into eternal laws of nature and of reason the social forms springing from your present mode of production and form of property—historical relations that rise and disappear in the progress of production—this misconception you share with every ruling class that has preceded you. What you see clearly in the case of ancient property, what you admit in the case of feudal property, you are of course forbidden to admit in the case of your own bourgeois form of property.

Abolition of the family! Even the most radical flare up at this infamous proposal of the Communists.

On what foundation is the present family, the bourgeois family, based? On capital, on private gain. In its completely developed form this family exists only among the bourgeoisie. But this state of things finds its complement in the practical absence of the family among the proletarians and in public prostitution.

The bourgeois family will vanish as a matter of course when its complement vanishes, and both will vanish with the vanishing of capital.

Do you charge us with wanting to stop the exploitation of children by their parents? To this crime we plead guilty.

But, you will say, we destroy the most hallowed of relations, when we replace home education by social.

And your education! Is not that also social and determined by the social conditions under which you educate, by the intervention, direct or indirect, of society, by means of schools, and so on? The Communists have not invented the intervention of society in education; they do but seek to alter the character of that intervention and to rescue education from the influence of the ruling class.

The bourgeois claptrap about the family and education, about the hallowed co-relation of parent and child, becomes all the more disgusting, the more, by the action of modern industry, all family ties among the proletarians are torn asunder, and their children transformed into simple articles of commerce and instruments of labor.

But you Communists would introduce community of women, screams the whole bourgeoisie in chorus.

The bourgeois sees in his wife a mere instrument of production. He hears that the instruments of production are to be exploited in common, and, naturally, can come to no other conclusion than that the lot of being common to all will likewise fall to the women.

He has not even a suspicion that the real point aimed at is to do away with the status of women as mere instruments of production.

For the rest, nothing is more ridiculous than the virtuous indignation of our bourgeois at the community of women which, they pretend, is to be openly and officially established by the Communists. The Communists have no need to introduce community of women; it has existed almost from time immemorial.

Our bourgeois, not content with having the wives and daughters of their proletarians at their disposal, not to speak of common prostitutes, take the greatest pleasure in seducing each other's wives.

Bourgeois marriage is in reality a system of wives in common, and thus, at the most, what the Communists might possibly be reproached with is that they desire to introduce, in substitution for a hypocritically concealed, an openly legalized community of women. For the rest, it is self-evident that the abolition of the present system of production must bring with it the abolition of the community of women springing from that system, i.e., of prostitution both public and private.

The Communists are further reproached with desiring to abolish countries and nationality.

The working men have no country. We cannot take from them what they have not got. Since the proletariat must first of all acquire political supremacy, must rise to be the leading class of the nation, must constitute itself *the* nation, it is, so far, itself national, though not in the bourgeois sense of the word.

National differences and antagonisms between peoples are daily more and more vanishing, owing to the development of the bourgeoisie, to freedom of commerce, to the world market, to uniformity in the mode of production and in the conditions of life corresponding thereto.

The supremacy of the proletariat will cause them to vanish still faster. United action, of the leading civilized countries at least, is one of the first conditions for the emancipation of the proletariat.

In proportion as the exploitation of one individual by another is put an end to, the exploitation of one nation by another will also be put an end to. In proportion as the antagonism between classes within the nation vanishes, the hostility of one nation to another will come to an end.

The charges against Communism made from a religious, a philosophical, and, generally, from an ideological standpoint are not deserving of serious examination.

Does it require deep intuition to comprehend that man's ideas, views, and conceptions—in one word, man's consciousness—changes with every change in the conditions of his material existence, in his social relations, and in his social life?

What else does the history of ideas prove than that intellectual production changes its character in proportion as material production is changed? The ruling ideas of each age have ever been the ideas of its ruling class.

When people speak of ideas that revolutionize society, they do but express the fact that, within the old society, the elements of a new one have been created and that the dissolution of the old ideas keeps even pace with the dissolution of the old conditions of existence.

When the ancient world was in its last throes, the ancient religions were overcome by Christianity. When Christian ideas succumbed in the eighteenth century to rationalist ideas, feudal society fought its death battle with the then revolutionary bourgeoisie. The ideas of religious liberty and freedom of conscience merely gave expression to the sway of free competition within the domain of knowledge.

"Undoubtedly," it will be said, "religious, moral, philosophical, and juridical ideas have been modified in the course of historical development. But religion, morality, philosophy, political science, and law constantly survived this change.

"There are, besides, eternal truths, such as Freedom, Justice, and so forth, that are common to all states of society. But Communism abolishes eternal truths; it abolishes all religion and all morality, instead of constituting them on a new basis; it therefore acts in contradiction to all past historical experience."

What does this accusation reduce itself to? The history of all past society has consisted in the development of class antagonisms—antagonisms that assumed different forms at different epochs.

But whatever form they may have taken, one fact is common to all past ages, viz., the exploitation of one part of society by the other. No wonder, then, that the social consciousness of past ages, despite all the multiplicity and variety it displays, moves within certain common forms, or general ideas, which cannot completely vanish except with the total disappearance of class antagonisms.

The Communist revolution is the most radical rupture with traditional property relations; no wonder that its development involves the most radical rupture with traditional ideas.

But let us have done with the bourgeois objections to Communism.

We have seen above that the first step in the revolution by the working class is to raise the proletariat to the position of ruling class, to win the battle of democracy.

The proletariat will use its political supremacy to wrest, by degrees, all capital from the bourgeoisie, to centralize all instruments of production in the hands of the state, i.e., of the proletariat organized as the ruling class, and to increase the total of productive forces as rapidly as possible.

Of course, in the beginning, this cannot be effected except by means of despotic inroads on the rights of property and on the conditions of bourgeois production by means of measures, therefore, which appear economically insufficient and untenable, but which, in the course of the movement, outstrip themselves, necessitate further inroads upon the old social order, and are unavoidable as a means of entirely revolutionizing the mode of production.

These measures will, of course, be different in different countries.

Nevertheless, in the most advanced countries, the following will be pretty generally applicable.

1. Abolition of property in land and application of all rents of land to public purposes.

2. A heavy progressive or graduated income tax.

3. Abolition of all right of inheritance.

4. Confiscation of the property of all emigrants and rebels.

5. Centralization of credit in the hands of the state, by means of a national bank with state capital and an exclusive monopoly.

6. Centralization of the means of communication and transport in the hands of the state.

7. Extension of factories and instruments of production owned by the state; the bringing into cultivation of wastelands and the improvement of the soil generally in accordance with a common plan.

8. Equal liability of all to labor. Establishment of industrial armies, especially for agriculture.

9. Combination of agriculture with manufacturing industries; gradual abolition of the distinction between town and country by a more equable distribution of the population over the country.

10. Free education for all children in public schools. Abolition of children's factory labor in its present form. Combination of education with industrial production and so on.

When in the course of development, class distinctions have disappeared and all production has been concentrated in the hands of a vast association of the whole nation, the public power will lose its political character. Political power, properly so called, is merely the organized power of one class for oppressing another. If the proletariat during its contest with the bourgeoisie is compelled by the force of circumstances, to organize itself as a class—if, by means of a revolution, it makes itself the ruling class and, as such, sweeps away by force the old conditions of production—then it will, along with these conditions, have swept away the conditions for the existence of class antagonisms and of classes generally and will thereby have abolished its own supremacy as a class.

In place of the old bourgeois society, with its classes and class antagonisms, we shall have an association in which the free development of each is the condition for the free development of all. . . .

Position of the Communists

. . . The Communists everywhere support every revolutionary movement against the existing social and political order of things.

In all these movements they bring to the front, as the leading question in each, the property question, no matter what its degree of development at the time.

Finally, they labor everywhere for the union and agreement of the democratic parties of all countries.

The Communists disdain to conceal their views and aims. They openly declare that their ends can be attained only by the forcible overthrow of all existing social conditions. Let the ruling classes tremble at a Communistic revolution. The proletarians have nothing to lose but their chains. They have a world to win.

Workingmen of all countries, unite!

V. I. Lenin: The State and Revolution

The State as the Product of the Irreconcilability of Class Antagonisms

What is now happening to Marx's doctrine has, in the course of history, often happened to the doctrines of other revolutionary thinkers and leaders of oppressed classes struggling for emancipation. During the lifetime of great revolutionaries, the oppressing classes have visited relentless persecution on them and received their teaching with the most savage hostility, the most furious hatred, the most ruthless campaign of lies and slanders. After their death, attempts are made to turn them into harmless icons, canonize them, and surround their *names* with a certain halo for the "consolation" of the oppressed classes and with the object of duping them, while at the same time emasculating and vulgarizing the *real essence* of their revolutionary theories and blunting their revolutionary edge. At the present time, the bourgeoisie and the opportunists within the labor movement are co-operating in this work of adulterating Marxism. They omit, obliterate, and distort the revolutionary side of its teaching, its revolutionary soul. They push to the foreground and extol what is, or seems, acceptable to the bourgeoisie. All the social-chauvinists are now "Marxists"—joking aside! And more and more do German bourgeois professors, erstwhile specialists in the demolition of Marx, speak now of the "national-German" Marx, who, they aver, has educated the labor unions which are so splendidly organized for conducting the present predatory war!

In such circumstances, the distortion of Marxism being so widespread, it is our first task to *resuscitate* the real teachings of Marx on the state. . . .

Let us begin with the most popular of Engels' works, *The Origin of the Family, Private Property, and the State.* . . . Summarizing his historical analysis, Engels says:

> The state is therefore by no means a power imposed on society from the outside; just as little is it "the reality of the moral idea," "the image and reality of reason," as Hegel asserted. Rather, it is a product of society at a certain stage of development; it is the admission that this society has become entangled in an insoluble contradiction with itself, that it is cleft into irreconcilable antagonisms which it is powerless to dispel. But in order that these antagonisms, classes with conflicting economic interests, may not consume themselves and society in sterile struggle, a power apparently standing above society becomes necessary, whose purpose is to moderate the conflict and keep it within the bounds of "order"; and this power arising out of society, but placing itself above it, and increasingly separating itself from it, is the state.

Here we have, expressed in all its clearness, the basic idea of Marxism on the question of the historical role and meaning of the state. The state is the product and the manifestation of the *irreconcilability* of class antagonisms. The state arises when, where, and to the extent that the class antagonisms *cannot* be objectively reconciled. And, conversely, the existence of the state proves that the class antagonisms *are* irreconcilable. . . .

The "Withering Away" of the State and Violent Revolution

Engels' words regarding the "withering away" of the state enjoy such popularity, they are so often quoted, and they show so clearly the essence of the usual adulteration by means of which Marxism is made to look like opportunism that we must dwell on them in detail. Let us quote the whole passage from which they are taken.

> The proletariat seizes state power, and then transforms the means of production into state property. But in doing this, it puts an end to itself as the proletariat, it puts an end to all class differences and class antagonisms, it puts an end also to the state as the state. Former society, moving in class antagonisms, had need of the state, that is, an organisation of the exploiting class at each period for the maintenance of its external conditions of production; therefore, in particular, for the forcible holding down of the exploited class in the conditions of oppression (slavery, bondage or serfdom, wage-labour) determined by the existing mode of production. The state was the official representative of society as a whole, its embodiment in a visible corporate body; but it was this only in so far as it was the state of that class which itself, in its epoch, represented society as a whole: in ancient times, the state of the slave-owning citizens; in the Middle Ages, of the feudal nobility; in our epoch, of the bourgeoisie. When ultimately it becomes really representative of society as a whole, it makes itself superfluous. As soon as there is no longer any class of society to be held in subjection; as soon as, along with class domination and the struggle for individual existence based on the former anarchy of production, the collisions and excesses arising from these have also been abolished, there is nothing more to be repressed, and a special repressive force, a state, is no longer necessary. The first act in which the state really comes forward as the representative of society as a whole—the seizure of the means of production in the name of society—is at the same time its last independent act as a state. The interference of a state power in social relations becomes superfluous in one sphere after another, and then becomes dormant of itself. Government over persons is replaced by the administration of things and the direction of the process of production. The state is not "abolished," *it withers away*. It is from this standpoint that we must appraise the phrase "people's free state"—both its justification at times for agitational purposes, and its ultimate scientific inadequacy—and also the demand of the so-called Anarchists that the state should be abolished overnight. [Engels, *Anti-Dühring*.]

Without fear of committing an error, it may be said that of this argument by Engels, so singularly rich in ideas, only one point has become an integral part of socialist thought among modern socialist parties, namely, that, unlike the anarchist doctrine of the "abolition" of the state, according to Marx the state "withers away." To emasculate Marxism in such a manner is to reduce it to opportunism, for such an "interpretation" only leaves the hazy conception of a slow, even, gradual change, free from leaps and storms, free from revolution. The current popular conception, if one may say so, of the "withering away" of the state undoubtedly means a slurring over, if not a negation, of revolution.

Yet, such an "interpretation" is the crudest distortion of Marxism, which is advantageous only to the bourgeoisie; in point of theory, it is based on a disregard for the most important circumstances and considerations pointed out in the very passage summarizing Engels' ideas, which we have just quoted in full.

In the first place, Engels at the very outset of his argument says that, in assuming state power, the proletariat by that very act "puts an end to the state as the state." One is "not accustomed" to reflect on what this really means. Generally, it is either ignored altogether or it is considered as a piece of "Hegelian weakness" on Engels' part. As a matter of fact, however, these words express succinctly the experience of one of the greatest proletarian revolutions—the Paris Commune of 1871, of which we shall speak in greater detail in its proper place. As a matter of fact, Engels speaks here of the destruction of the bourgeois state by the proletarian revolution, while the words about its withering away refer to the remains of *proletarian* statehood *after* the socialist revolution. The bourgeois state does not "wither away," according to Engels, but is "put an end to" by the proletariat in the course of the revolution. What withers away after the revolution is the proletarian state or semistate.

Secondly, the state is a "special repressive force." This splendid and extremely profound definition of Engels' is given by him here with complete lucidity. It follows from this that the "special repressive force" of the bourgeoisie for the suppression of the proletariat, of the millions of workers by a handful of the rich, must be replaced by a "special repressive force" of the proletariat for the suppression of the bourgeoisie (the dictatorship of the proletariat). It is just this that constitutes the destruction of "the state as the state." It is just this that constitutes the "act" of "the seizure of the means of production in the name of society." And it is obvious that such a substitution of one (proletarian) "special repressive force" for another (bourgeois) "special repressive force" can in no way take place in the form of a "withering away."

Thirdly, as to the "withering away" or, more expressively and colorfully, as to the state's "becoming dormant," Engels refers quite clearly and definitely to the period *after* "the seizure of the means of production [by the state] in the name of society," that is, *after* the socialist revolution. We all know that the political form of the "state" at that time is complete democracy. But it never enters the head of any of the opportunists who shamelessly distort Marx that when Engels speaks here of the state's "withering away," or becoming dormant," he speaks of *democracy*. At first sight this seems very strange. But it is "unintelligible" only to one who has not reflected on the fact that democracy is *also* a state and that, consequently, democracy will *also* disappear when the state disappears. The bourgeois state can only be "put an end to" by a revolution. The state in general, i.e., most complete democracy, can only "wither away." ...

The Experience of the Paris Commune of 1871. Marx's Analysis

WHAT WILL REPLACE THE SMASHED STATE MACHINE?

It is still necessary to suppress the bourgeoisie and crush its resistance. This was particularly necessary for the Commune; and one of the reasons of its defeat was that it did not do this with sufficient determination. But the organ of suppression is now the majority of the population, and not a minority, as was always the case under slavery, serfdom, and wage labor. And, once the majority of the people *itself* suppresses its oppressors, a "special force" for suppression is *no longer necessary*. In this sense the state *begins to wither away*. Instead of the special institutions of a privileged minority (privileged officialdom, heads of a standing army), the majority can itself directly fulfill all these functions; and the more the discharge of the functions of state power devolves upon the people generally, the less need is there for the existence of this power.

In this connection the Commune's measure emphasized by Marx, particularly worthy of note, is: the abolition of all representation allowances, and of all money privileges in the case of officials, the reduction of the remuneration of *all* servants of the state to *"workingmen's wages."* Here is shown, more clearly than anywhere else, the *break* from a bourgeois democracy to a proletarian democracy, from the democracy of the oppressors to the democracy of the oppressed classes, from the state as a "special force for suppression" of a given class to the suppression of the oppressors by the *whole force* of the majority of the people—the workers and the peasants. And it is precisely on this most striking point, perhaps the most important as far as the problem of the state is concerned, that the teachings of Marx have been entirely forgotten! In popular commentaries, whose number is legion, this is not mentioned. It is "proper" to keep silent about it as if it were a piece of old-fashioned "naïveté," just as the Christians, after Christianity had attained the position of a state religion, "forgot" the "naïvetés" of primitive Christianity with its democratic-revolutionary spirit. . . .

We are not utopians; we do not indulge in "dreams" of how best to do away *immediately* with all administration, with all subordination; these anarchist dreams, based upon a lack of understanding of the task of proletarian dictatorship, are basically foreign to Marxism, and, as a matter of fact, they serve but to put off the socialist revolution until human nature is different. No, we want the socialist revolution with human nature as it is now, with human nature that cannot do without subordination, control, and "managers."

But if there be subordination, it must be to the armed vanguard of all the exploited and the laboring—to the proletariat. The specific "commanding" methods of the state officials can and must begin to be replaced—immediately, within twenty-four hours—by the simple functions of "managers" and bookkeepers, functions which are now already within the capacity of the average city dweller and can well be performed for "workingmen's wages."

We organize large-scale production, starting from what capitalism has already created; we workers *ourselves,* relying on our own experience as workers, establishing a strict, an iron discipline, supported by the state power of the armed workers, shall reduce the role of the state officials to that of simply carrying out our instructions as responsible, moderately paid "managers" (of course, with technical knowledge of all sorts, types, and degrees). This is *our* proletarian task; with this we can and must *begin* when carrying through a proletarian revolution. Such a beginning, on the basis of large-scale production, of itself leads to the gradual "withering away" of all bureaucracy, to the gradual creation of a new order, an order without quotation marks, an order which has nothing to do with wage slavery, an order in which the more and more simplified functions of control and accounting will be performed by each in turn, will then become a habit, and will finally die out as *special* functions of a special stratum of the population. . . .

The Economic Basis of the Withering Away of the State

THE TRANSITION FROM CAPITALISM TO COMMUNISM

. . . Only in Communist society, when the resistance of the capitalists has been completely broken, when the capitalists have disappeared, when there are no classes (i.e., there is no difference between the members of society in their relation to the social means of production), *only then* "the state ceases to exist," and *"it becomes possible to speak of freedom."* Only then a really full democracy, a democracy without any exceptions, will be possible and will be realized. And only then will democracy itself begin to *wither away* due to the simple fact that, freed from capitalist slavery, from the untold horrors, savagery, absurdities, and infamies of capitalist exploitation, people will gradually *become accustomed* to the observance of the elementary rules of social life that have been known for centuries and repeated for thousands of years in all schoolbooks; they will become accustomed to observing them without force, without compulsion, without subordination, without the *special apparatus* for compulsion which is called the state.

The expression "the state *withers away*" is very well chosen, for it indicates both the gradual and the elemental nature of the process. Only habit can, and undoubtedly will, have such an effect; for we see around us millions of times how readily people get accustomed to observe the necessary rules of life in common, if there is no exploitation, if there is nothing that causes indignation, that calls forth protest and revolt and has to be *suppressed*.

Thus, in capitalist society, we have a democracy that is curtailed, poor, false; a democracy only for the rich, for the minority. The dictatorship of the proletariat, the period of transition to Communism, will, for the first time, produce democracy for the people, for the majority, side by side with the necessary suppression of the minority—the exploiters. Communism alone is capable of giving a really complete democracy, and the more complete it is the more quickly will it become unnecessary and wither away of itself.

In other words: under capitalism we have a state in the proper sense of the word; that is, special machinery for the suppression of one class by another and of the majority by the minority, at that. Naturally, for the successful discharge of such a task as the systematic suppression by the exploiting minority of the exploited majority, the greatest ferocity and savagery of suppression are required, seas of blood are required, through which mankind is marching in slavery, serfdom, and wage labor.

Again, during the *transition* from capitalism to Communism, suppression is *still* necessary; but it is the suppression of the minority of exploiters by the majority of exploited. A special apparatus, special machinery for suppression, the "state," is *still* necessary, but this is now a transitional state, no longer a state in the usual sense, for the suppression of the minority of exploiters, by the majority of the wage slaves *of yesterday,* is a matter comparatively so easy, simple, and natural that it will cost far less bloodshed than the suppression of the risings of slaves, serfs, or wage-laborers and will cost mankind far less. This is compatible with the diffusion of democracy among such an overwhelming majority of the population that the need for *special machinery* of suppression will begin to disappear. The exploiters are, naturally, unable to suppress the people without a most complex machinery for performing this task; but *the people* can suppress the exploiters even with very simple "machinery," almost without any "machinery," without any special apparatus, by the simple *organization of the armed masses* (such as the Soviets of Workers' and Soldiers' Deputies, we may remark, anticipating a little).

Finally, only Communism renders the state absolutely unnecessary, for there is *no one* to be suppressed—"no one" in the sense of a *class,* in the sense of a systematic struggle with a definite section of the population. We are not utopians, and we do not in the least deny the possibility and inevitability of excesses on the part of *individual persons,* nor the need to suppress *such* excesses. But, in the first place, no special machinery, no special apparatus of repression is needed for this; this will be done by the armed people itself, as simply and as readily as any crowd of civilized people, even in modern society, parts a pair of combatants or does not allow a woman to be outraged. And, secondly, we know that the fundamental social cause of excesses which consist in violating the rules of social life is the exploitation of the masses, their want, and their poverty. With the removal of this chief cause, excesses will inevitably begin to *"wither away."* We do not know how quickly and in what succession, but we know that they will wither away. With their withering away, the state will also *wither away. . . .*

THE HIGHER PHASE OF COMMUNIST SOCIETY

. . . The economic basis for the complete withering away of the state is that high stage of development of Communism when the antagonism between mental and physical labor disappears, that is to say, when one of the principal sources of modern *social* inequality disappears—a source, moreover, which it is impossible to remove immediately by the mere conversion of the means of production into public property, by the mere expropriation of the capitalists.

This expropriation will make a gigantic development of the productive forces *possible.* And seeing how incredibly, even now, capitalism *retards* this development, how much progress could be made even on the basis of modern technique at the level it has reached, we have a right to say, with the fullest confidence, that the expropriation of the capitalists will inevitably result in a gigantic development of the productive forces of human society. But how rapidly this development will go forward, how soon it will reach the point of breaking away from the division of labor, of removing the antagonism between mental and physical labor, of transforming work into the "first necessity of life"—this we do not and *cannot* know.

Consequently, we have a right to speak solely of the inevitable withering away of the state, emphasizing the protracted nature of this process and its dependence upon the rapidity of development of the *higher phase* of Communism; leaving quite open the question of lengths of time, or the concrete forms of withering away, since material for the solution of such questions is *not available.*

The state will be able to wither away completely when society has realized the rule: "From each according to his ability; to each according to his needs," i.e., when people have become accustomed to observe the fundamental rules of social life, and their labor is so productive that they voluntarily work *according to their ability.* "The narrow horizon of bourgeois rights," which compels one to calculate, with the hardheartedness of a Shylock, whether he has not worked half an hour more than another, whether he is not getting less pay than another—this narrow horizon will then be left behind. There will then be no need for any exact calculation by society of the quantity of products to be distributed to each of its members; each will take freely "according to his needs." . . .

Mao Tse-tung: Theory and Practice

The Party School opens today, and I wish it every success.

I would like to say something about the problem of our Party's style of work. . . .

What is the problem? It is the fact that there is something in the minds of a number of our comrades which strikes one as not quite right, not quite proper.

In other words, there is still something wrong with our style of study, with our style in the Party's internal and external relations, and with our style of writing. . . .

Certain muddled ideas find currency among many people. There are, for instance, muddled ideas about what is a theorist, what is an intellectual, and what is meant by linking theory and practice.

Let us first ask, is the theoretical level of our Party high or low? Recently more Marxist-Leninist works have been translated, and more people have been reading them. That is a very good thing. But can we therefore say that the theoretical level of our Party has been greatly raised? True, the level is now somewhat higher than before. But our theoretical front is very much out of harmony with the rich content of the Chinese revolutionary movement, and a comparison of the two shows that the theoretical side is lagging far behind. Generally speaking, our theory cannot as yet keep pace with our revolutionary practice, let alone lead the way as it should. We have not yet raised our rich and varied practice to the proper theoretical plane. We have not yet examined all the problems of revolutionary practice—or even the important ones—and raised them to a theoretical plane. Just think, how many of us have created theories worthy of the name on China's economics, politics, military affairs, or culture, theories which can be regarded as scientific and comprehensive, and not crude and sketchy? Especially in the field of economic theory: Chinese capitalism has had a century of development since the Opium War, and yet not a single theoretical work has been produced which accords with the realities of China's economic development and is genuinely scientific. Can we say that in the study of China's economic problems, for instance, the theoretical level is already high? Can we say that our Party already has economic theorists worthy of the name? Certainly not. We have read a great many Marxist-Leninist books, but can we claim, then, that we have theorists? We cannot. For Marxism-Leninism is the theory created by Marx, Engels, Lenin, and Stalin on the basis of practice, their general conclusion drawn from historical and revolutionary reality. If we merely read their works, but do not proceed to study the realities of China's history and revolution in the light of their theory or do not make any effort to think through China's revolutionary practice carefully in terms of theory, we should not be so presumptuous as to call ourselves Marxist theorists. Our achievements on the theoretical front will be very poor indeed if, as members of the Communist Party of China, we close our eyes to China's problems and can only memorize isolated conclusions or principles from Marxist writings. If all a person can do is to commit Marxist economics or philosophy to memory. reciting glibly from Chapter 1 to Chapter 10, but is utterly unable to apply them, can he be considered a Marxist theorist? No! He cannot. What kind of theorists do we want? We want theorists who can, in accordance with the Marxist-Leninist stand, viewpoint, and method, correctly interpret the practical problems arising in the course of history and revolution and give scientific explanations and theoretical elucidations of China's economic, political, military, cultural, and other problems. Such are the theorists we want. To be a theorist of this kind, a person must have a true grasp of the essence of Marxism-Leninism, of the Marxist-Leninist stand, viewpoint, and method, and of the theories of Lenin and Stalin on the colonial revolution and the Chinese revolution, and he must be able to apply them in a penetrating and scientific analysis of China's practical problems and discover the laws of development of these problems. Such are the theorists we really need. . . .

Our comrades in the Party School should not regard Marxist theory as lifeless dogma. It is necessary to master Marxist theory and apply it, master it for the sole purpose of applying it. If you can apply the Marxist-Leninist viewpoint in elucidating one or two practical problems, you should be commended and credited with some achievement. The more problems you elucidate and the more comprehensively and profoundly you do so, the greater will be your achievement. Our Party School should also lay down the rule to grade students good or poor according to how they look at China's problems after they have studied Marxism-Leninism, according to whether or not they see the problems clearly and whether or not they see them at all. . . .

What is knowledge? Ever since class society came into being the world has had only two kinds of knowledge: knowledge of the struggle for production and knowledge of the class struggle. Natural science and social science are the crystallizations of these two kinds of knowledge, and philosophy is the generalization and summation of the knowledge of nature and the knowledge of society. Is there any other kind of knowledge? No. Now let us take a look at certain students, those brought up in schools that are completely cut off from the practical activities of society. What about them? A person goes from a primary school of this kind all the way through to a university of the same kind, graduates, and is reckoned to have a stock of learning. But all he has is book learning; he has not yet taken part in any practical activities or applied what he has learned to any field of life. Can such a person be regarded as a completely developed intellectual? Hardly so, in my opinion, because his knowledge is still incomplete. What, then, is relatively complete knowledge? All relatively complete knowledge is formed in two stages: the first stage is perceptual knowledge; the second is rational knowledge, the latter being the development of the former to a higher stage. What sort of knowledge is the students' book learning? Even supposing all their knowledge is truth, it is still not knowledge acquired through their own personal experience, but consists of theories set down by their predecessors in summarizing experience of the struggle for production and of the class struggle. It is entirely necessary that students should acquire this kind of knowledge, but it must be understood that as far as they are concerned such knowledge is in a sense still one-sided, something which has been verified by others but not yet by themselves. What is most important is to be good at applying this knowledge in life and in practice. Therefore, I advise those who have only book learning but as yet no contact with reality, and also those with little practical experience, to realize their own shortcomings. . . .

There is only one kind of true theory in this world: theory that is drawn from objective reality and then verified by objective reality; nothing else is worthy of the name of theory in our sense. Stalin said that theory becomes aimless when it is not connected with practice. Aimless theory is useless and false and should be discarded. We should point the finger of scorn at those who are fond of aimless theorizing. Marxism-Leninism is the most correct, scientific, and revolutionary truth, born out of and verified by objective reality, but many who study Marxism-Leninism take it as lifeless dogma, thus impeding the development of theory and harming themselves as well as other comrades.

On the other hand, our comrades who are engaged in practical work will also come to grief if they misuse their experience. True, these people are often rich in experience, which is very valuable, but it is very dangerous if they rest content with their own experience. They must realize that their knowledge is mostly perceptual and partial and that they lack rational and comprehensive knowledge; in other words, they lack theory, and their knowledge, too, is relatively incomplete. Without comparatively complete knowledge it is impossible to do revolutionary work well.

Thus, there are two kinds of incomplete knowledge: one is ready-made knowledge found in books, and the other is knowledge that is mostly perceptual and partial; both are one-sided. Only an integration of the two can yield knowledge that is sound and relatively complete. . . .

It follows that to combat subjectivism we must enable people of each of these two types to develop in whichever direction they are deficient and to merge with the other type. Those with book learning must develop in the direction of practice; it is only in this way that they will stop being content with books and avoid committing dogmatic errors. Those experienced in work must take up the study of theory and must read seriously; only then will they be able to systematize and synthesize their experience and raise it to the level of theory; only then will they not mistake their partial experience for universal truth and not commit empiricist errors. Dogmatism and empiricism alike are subjectivism, each originating from an opposite pole.

Hence there are two kinds of subjectivism in our Party: dogmatism and empiricism. Each sees only a part and not the whole. If people are not on guard, do not realize that such one-sidedness is a shortcoming, and do not strive to overcome it, they are liable to go astray.

However, of the two kinds of subjectivism, dogmatism is still the greater danger in our Party. For dogmatists can easily assume a Marxist guise to bluff, capture, and make servitors of cadres of working-class and peasant origin who cannot easily see through them; they can also bluff and ensnare the naïve youth. If we overcome dogmatism, cadres with book learning will readily join with those who have experience and will take to the study of practical things, and then many good cadres who integrate theory with experience, as well as some real theorists, will emerge. If we overcome dogmatism, the comrades with practical experience will have good teachers to help them raise their experience to the level of theory and so avoid empiricist errors.

Besides muddled ideas about the "theorist" and the "intellectual," there is a muddled idea among many comrades about "linking theory and practice," a phrase they have on their lips every day. They talk constantly about "linking," but actually they mean "separating," because they make no effort at linking. How is Marxist-Leninist theory to be linked with the practice of the Chinese revolution? To use a common expression, it is by "shooting the arrow at the target." As the arrow is to the target, so is Marxism-Leninism to the Chinese revolution. Some comrades, however, are "shooting without a target," shooting at random, and such people are liable to harm the revolution. Others merely stroke the arrow fondly, exclaiming, "What a fine arrow! What a fine arrow!" but never want to shoot it. These people are only connoisseurs of curios and have virtually nothing to do with the revolution. The arrow of Marxism-Leninism must be used to shoot at the target of the Chinese revolution. Unless this point is made clear, the theoretical level of our Party can never be raised, and the Chinese revolution can never be victorious.

Our comrades must understand that we study Marxism-Leninism not for display, nor because there is any mystery about it, but solely because it is the science which leads the revolutionary cause of the proletariat to victory. Even now, there are not a few people who still regard odd quotations from Marxist-Leninist works as a ready-made panacea which, once acquired, can easily cure all maladies. These people show childish ignorance, and we should enlighten them. It is precisely such ignorant people who take Marxism-Leninism as a religious dogma. To them we should say bluntly, "Your dogma is worthless." Marx, Engels, Lenin, and Stalin have repeatedly stated that our theory is not a dogma, but a guide to action. But such people prefer to forget this statement, which is of the greatest, indeed the utmost, importance. Chinese Communists can be regarded as linking theory with practice only when they become good at applying the Marxist-Leninist stand, viewpoint, and method and the teachings of Lenin and Stalin concerning the Chinese revolution and when, furthermore, through serious research into the realities of China's history and revolution, they do creative theoretical work to meet China's needs in different spheres. Merely talking about linking theory and practice without actually doing anything about it is of no use, even if one goes on talking for a hundred years. To oppose the subjectivist, one-sided approach to problems, we must demolish dogmatist subjectiveness and one-sidedness. . . .

18 CORPORATISM

■ *John K. Jessup*

The basic right now called in question by the world crisis is the right of self-government. Within the United States, that right needs a newly defined economic base. I suggest that many of the present vague fears and psychic uncertainties of the American people would vanish if they had a good economic reason to believe that theirs is still a limited state, a federal republic. People differ greatly as to when and whether their rights have been transgressed. But these differences are minor compared with the question of whether they have, as a people, some assurance that the federal government will not itself be the final arbiter of those rights. Neither states' rights nor the laws of property can adequately supply this assurance any longer.

To give this assurance, to fill this economic vacuum in our federal republic, I nominate the modern corporation. To make the case fully, and with all the

From John K. Jessup, "The U.S. Corporation: A New Form of Government," in Edward C. Bursk, ed., *Getting Things Done in Business* (Cambridge: Harvard University Press, 1953), pp. 23–27. © Copyright, 1953, by the President and Fellows of Harvard College. Reprinted by permission of the publisher.

necessary hedging, would require a very long nominating speech indeed. I will confine myself to three salient characteristics of the corporation which seem to qualify it for this important political office.

In the first place, the corporation is today our chief source of national wealth. It is our most characteristic way of mobilizing men and resources and organizing work. In this respect its "inherent" powers are less disputable than those of the Presidency. Any President who wants to run a prosperous country depends on the corporation at least as much as, and probably more than, the corporation depends on him. His dependence is not unlike that of King John on the landed Barons of Runnymede where Magna Charta was born. The corporation is a focus of real economic power. It should therefore be capable of limiting and offsetting what has been called the federal government's increasing "efficiency of coercion." This is one political asset of the corporation.

In the second place, the corporation and the business system in which it lives are friendly to certain homely virtues which not only are good in themselves but are thought good by most Americans. Kenneth Boulding's article in the April–May, 1952, *Harvard Business Review* describes the "ethic of capitalism." Among its more obvious virtues are efficiency, thrift, and honesty —virtues which the voters do not always find in their government, but which the business world harbors and perpetuates because they are the laws of its being. Among our institutions which a strong government is most inclined to tamper with and to politicize are the value of the dollar and the predictability of the law. Business has a strong interest in both a predictable dollar and predictable laws. So have the people in the long run. The fact that business stands for these social virtues and valued institutions may on some near occasion make business their political champion, which could be a popular cause.

In the third place, without any sacrifice of its strong economic base, the corporation is fast taking on many new social responsibilities. The practicing businessman knows what these new responsibilities are and how far they may be expected to go. The fact that the corporation promises to become a sort of welfare community is the best guarantee that we need not have a national welfare state.

The intellectuals used to make one very serious charge against private capitalism—namely, that it makes for an atomized society, replacing genuine communities with a mere "cash nexus." The corporation, as Peter Drucker has pointed out, is repairing this damage and making the charge obsolete. Corporation members are not economic atoms; they are part of at least a very large molecule.

The internal life of the corporation is a new frontier, and like the old physical frontier, it can be a fresh fountain of democracy. The chief social tensions of our industrial age, including even the fear of unemployment, are those which arise from the new relation of man to his work. The corporation therefore harbors and confronts practically all these tensions; and the more it resolves them for the sake of its own survival, the more it will have resolved them for society as well.

Thus the corporation has a major and growing role in the political economy of a free nation. It is not an exclusive role. There are many other results of the "organizational revolution," from labor unions to the WCTU, and many of these, like the states and cities, are vital organs of American self-government. Moreover, our politics are ultimately ruled not by economic but by ethical considerations, and these will limit, although they need not disparage, the corporation's role in our civilization. But its chief business after all is business. So long as it succeeds at that, it will fill the American need for a focus of self-government with an economic base.

In its early days the corporation needed no extra social sanction for the permission to exist which the law gave it. It was adequately sanctioned, and so were its profits, by being subject to a competitive market.

More recently the labor movement has placed an additional check on corporate management's freedom of maneuver. Both these checks will continue. In taking on new responsibilities, management should not expect to win any new managerial freedoms. The more responsibility it undertakes, the more society will ask of it. In short, the more nearly impossible will the corporate manager's job become.

But one annoyance, at least, he can count on leaving behind. This is the harassing criticism of those who have hitherto doubted management's very title to manage. This title may still be legally clouded, but the political cloud on it is lifting.

For evidence of this, consider some basic opinions which most American business managers have long held in common. One is that rising productivity is the key to prosperity. This is now a commonplace of general opinion as well. Another is that labor and capital, consumers and vendors, big business and small, all share an interest in rising productivity and that our industrial society is therefore founded on a harmony of classes, not a conflict. This view, too, commands general assent.

The public is also aware that the torch for these hopeful truths has been carried in recent years not by labor, and not by government, and not by intellectuals, but by American business management. The public opinion I speak of is, therefore, just about ready to admit an additional proposition: namely, that of all the interest groups that influence business decisions, management on its recent record has the best claim to disinterestedness and intelligence and hence the best claim to the last word in these decisions. Management is earning the title Colby Chester gives it: "the court of fair rewards."

Public opinion is fickle. The right to manage is not only a severely limited right but one that must be earned afresh with every political generation. Moreover, if my thesis is correct, this right to manage may begin to carry an extra political charge, as people come to acknowledge the corporation's political role.

Just what does all this imply for business managers? Their role does sound portentous. In addition to all they do now, must they become professional politicians as well? No, not in any unpleasant sense of the word. The manager's political function, as I see it, is simply to keep proving in the future what he has already begun to prove; namely, that the corporation is a new, vital kind of commonwealth within which individual citizens can work to produce wealth in harmony and to share it in a spirit of practical justice. As chief of this little commonwealth, the manager has the political job of keeping all his constituents reasonably happy in that part of their lives which relates to their work. Success in that objective makes the corporation successful.

To "get people to do what you want them to do"—at least in a free country—you must, of course, want them to do what is in their own real interest. Modern management has shown that it understands this. It knows how to find a genuine identity between the interest of the corporation as a whole and the interests of its members as individuals. That is quite an achievement. And all I am saying is that this achievement may be even more important than you think. For there is a further identity of interest between a well-run corporation and a well-organized nation.

Let me summarize as follows. In doing its economic job so well, American business has shown how certain economic conflicts, which were getting dangerously and unnecessarily involved in national politics, can be solved by the older methods of private self-government and can therefore be legitimately kept out of the federal orbit. In doing this job, business is erecting a new basis of economic power which is beyond the reach of government, thus helping to preserve freedom.

A nation whose structure includes a multiplicity of healthy self-governing economic units will still have plenty of big national political worries. But they will be more consistent with freedom and more manageable by democratic means.

19 DEMOCRATIC SOCIALISM

■ *Lewis Coser and Irving Howe*

"God," said Tolstoy, "is the name of my desire." This remarkable sentence could haunt one a lifetime, it reverberates in so many directions. Tolstoy may have intended partial assent to the idea that, life being insupportable without some straining toward "transcendence," a belief in God is a psychological necessity. But he must also have wanted to turn this rationalist criticism into a definition of his faith. He must have meant that precisely because his holiest desires met in the vision of God he was enabled to cope with the quite unholy

From Lewis Coser and Irving Howe, "Images of Socialism," *Dissent*, I (Spring, 1954), 122–138. Reprinted by permission.

realities of human existence. That God should be seen as the symbolic objectification of his desire thus became both a glorification of God and a strengthening of man, a stake in the future and a radical criticism of the present.

Without sanctioning the facile identification that is frequently made between religion and socialist politics, we should like to twist Tolstoy's remark to our own ends: *socialism is the name of our desire.* And not merely in the sense that it is a vision which, for many people throughout the world, provides moral sustenance but also in the sense that it is a vision which objectifies and gives urgency to their criticism of the human condition in our time. It is the name of our desire because the desire arises from a conflict with, and an extension from, the world that is; nor could the desire survive in any meaningful way were it not for this complex relationship to the world that is.

At so late and unhappy a moment, however, can one still specify what the vision of socialism means or should mean? Is the idea of utopia itself still a tolerable one?

I

The impulse to imagine "the good society" probably coincides with human history, and the manner of constructing it—to invert what exists—is an element binding together all pre-Marxist utopias. These dreamers and system makers have one thing in common: their desire to storm history.

The growth of the modern utopian idea accompanies the slow formation of the centralized state in Europe. Its imagery is rationalistic, far removed from the ecstatic visions that accompany the religiously inspired rebellions agitating feudal society in its last moments. As the traditional patchwork of autonomous social institutions in western Europe was replaced, in the interests of efficiency, by an increasingly centralized system of rule, men began to conceive of a society that would drive this tendency to its conclusion and be governed completely by rationality. But not only the increasing rationality of political power inspired the thinking of social philosophers; they were stirred by the growth of a new, bourgeois style of life that emphasized calculation, foresight, and efficiency and made regularity of work an almost religious obligation.

As soon as men began to look at the state as "a work of art," as "an artificial man, created for the protection and salvation of the natural man" (Hobbes, *Leviathan*), it took but one more step to imagine that this "work of art" could be rendered perfect through foresight and will. Thomas Campanella, a rebellious Calabrian monk of the seventeenth century, conceived in his *City of the Sun* of such a perfect work of art. In Campanella's utopia, unquestionably designed from the most idealistic of motives, one sees the traits of many pre-Marxist utopias. Salvation is *imposed,* delivered from above; there is an all-powerful ruler called the Great Metaphysicus (surely no more absurd than the Beloved Leader); only one book exists in the *City ol the Sun,* which may be taken as an economical image of modern practice: naturally, a book called *Wisdom.* Sexual relations are organized by state administrators "according to philosophical rules," the race being "managed for the good of the commonwealth and not of private individuals. . . ." Education is conceived along entirely rationalistic lines, and indeed it must be, for Campanella felt that the Great Metaphysicus, as he forces perfection upon history, has to deal with recalcitrant materials: the people, he writes in a sentence that betrays both his bias and his pathos, is "a beast with a muddy brain."

And here we come upon a key to utopian thought: the galling sense of a chasm between the scheme and the subjects, between the plan, ready and perfect, and the people, mute and indifferent. (Poor Fourier, the salesman with phalanxes in his belfry, comes home daily at noon, to wait for the one capitalist—he needs no more than one—who will finance utopia.) Intellectuals who cannot shape history try to rape it, through either actual violence, like the Russian terrorists, or imagined violence, the sudden seizure of history by a utopian claw. In his *City of the Sun,* Campanella decrees—the utopian never hesitates to decree—that those sentenced to death for crimes against the Godhead, liberty and the higher magistrates are to be rationally enlightened, before execution, by special functionaries, so that in the end they will acquiesce in their own condemnation. Let no one say history is unforeseen.

Two centuries after Campanella, Etienne Cabot, a disciple of Robert Owen and Saint-Simon, envisaged the revolutionary dictatorship of Icar, an enlightened ruler who refuses to stay in power longer than necessary for establishing the new society; he no doubt means it to wither away. Meanwhile Icaria has only one newspaper, and the republic has "revised all useful books which showed imperfections and it has burned all those which we judged dangerous and useless."

The point need not be overstressed. The utopians were not—or not merely —the unconscious authoritarians that malicious critics have made them out to be. No doubt some did harbor strong streaks of authoritarian feeling which they vicariously released through utopian images; but this is far from the whole story. Robert Owen wanted a free co-operative society. Decentralization is stressed in Morelly's utopia, "Floating Islands." The phalanxes of Fourier are to function without any central authority, and if there must be one it should be located as far from France as possible, certainly no nearer than Constantinople.

The authoritarian element we find in the utopians is due far less to psychological malaise or power hunger (most of them were genuinely good people) than to the sense of desperation that frequently lies beneath the surface of their fantasying. All pre-Marxist utopian thinking tends to be ahistorical, to see neither possibility nor need for relating the image of the good society to the actual workings of society as it is. For Fourier it is simply a matter of discovering the "plan" of God, the ordained social order that in realizing God's will ensures man's happiness. (Socialism for Fourier is indeed the name of his desire—but in a very different sense from that which we urge!) The imagined construction of utopia occurs *outside* the order or flux of history: it comes through fiat. Once utopia is established, history grinds to a standstill and the rule of rationality replaces the conflict of class or, as the utopians might have preferred to say, the conflict of passions. Friedrich Engels describes this process with both sympathy and shrewdness:

Society presented nothing but wrongs; to remove these was the task of reason. It was necessary, then, to *impose this upon society from without* by propaganda and, whenever possible, by the example of model experiments. These new social systems were foredoomed as utopian; the more completely they were worked out in detail, the more they could not avoid drifting off into pure phantasies. . . .

We can leave it to the literary small fry to solemnly quibble over these phantasies, which today only make us smile, and to crow over the superiority of their own bald reasoning, as compared with such "insanity." As for us, we delight in the stupendously great thoughts and germs of thought that everywhere break out through their phantastic covering. . . . [Italics added.]

Given the desire to impose utopia upon an indifferent history, a desire which derives, in the main, from a deep sense of alienation from the flow of history, it follows logically enough that the utopians should for the most part think in terms of elite politics. Auguste Comte specifies that in the "State of Positive Science" society is to be ruled by an elite of intellectuals. The utopia to be inaugurated by the sudden triumph of reason over the vagaries and twists of history—what other recourse could a lonely, isolated utopian have but the elite, the small core of intellect that, like himself, controls and guides? Saint-Simon, living in the afterglow of the French Revolution, begins to perceive the mechanics of class relations and the appearance for the first time in modern history of the masses as a decisive force. But in the main our generalization holds: reformers who lack some organic relationship with major historical movements must almost always be tempted into a more or less benevolent theory of a ruling elite.

II

Utopia without egalitarianism, utopia dominated by an aristocracy of mind, must quickly degenerate into a vision of useful slavery. Hence the importance of Marx's idea that socialism is to be brought about, in the first instance, by the activities of a major segment of the population, the workers. Having placed the drive toward utopia not beyond, but squarely—perhaps a little too squarely —within the course of history, and having found in the proletariat that active "realizing" force which the utopians could nowhere discern on the social horizon, Marx was enabled to avoid the two major difficulties of his predecessors: ahistoricism and the elite theory. He had, to be sure, difficulties of his own, but not these.

Marx was the first of the major socialist figures who saw the possibility of linking the utopian desire with the actual development of social life. By studying capitalism both as an "ideal" structure and a "real" dynamic, Marx found the sources of revolt within the self-expanding and self-destroying rhythms of the economy itself. The utopians had desired a revolt against history, but they could conduct it, so to speak, only from the space platform of the imaginary future; Marx gave new power to the revolt against history by locating it, "scientifically," within history.

The development of technology, he concluded, made possible a society in which men could "realize" their humanity, if only because the brutalizing burden of fatigue, that sheer physical exhaustion from which the great masses of men had never been free, could now for the first time be removed. This was the historic option offered mankind by the Industrial Revolution, as it is now being offered again by the Atomic Revolution. Conceivably, though only conceivably, a society might have been established at any point in historical time which practiced an equalitarian distribution of goods; but there would have been neither goods nor leisure enough to dispense with the need for a struggle over their distribution; which means bureaucracy, police, an oppressive state, and in sum the destruction of equalitarianism. Now, after the Industrial Revolution, the machine might do for all humanity what the slaves had done for the Greek patriciate.

Marx was one of the first political thinkers to see that both industrialism and "the mass society" were here to stay, that all social schemes which ignored or tried to controvert this fact were not merely irrelevant; they weren't even interesting. It is true, of course, that he did not foresee—he could not—a good many consequences of this tremendous historical fact. He did not foresee that "mass culture" together with social atomization (Durkheim's anomie) would set off strong tendencies of demoralization acting in opposition to those tendencies that made for disciplined cohesion in the working class. He did not foresee that the rise of totalitarianism might present mankind with choices and problems that went beyond the capitalist/socialist formulation. He did not foresee that the nature of leisure would become, even under capitalism, as great a social and cultural problem as the nature of work. He did not foresee that industrialism would create problems which, while not necessarily insoluble, are likely to survive the span of capitalism. But what he did foresee was crucial: that the great decisions of history would now be made in a mass society, that the "stage" on which this struggle would take place had suddenly, dramatically been widened far beyond its previous dimensions.

And when Marx declared the proletariat to be the active social force that could lead the transition to socialism, he was neither sentimentalizing the lowly nor smuggling in a theory of the elite, as many of his critics have suggested. Anyone who has read the chapter in *Capital* on the working day or Engels' book on the conditions of the English workers knows that they measured the degradation of the workers to an extent precluding sentimentality. As for the idea of the proletariat as an elite, Marx made no special claim for its virtue or intelligence, which is the traditional mode of justifying an elite; he merely analyzed its peculiar *position* in society, as the class most driven by the workings of capitalism to both discipline and rebellion, the class that, come what may, utopia or barbarism, would always remain propertyless.

There is another indication that Marx did not mean to favor an elite theory by his special "placing" of the proletariat. His theory of "increasing misery"—be it right, wrong, or vulgarized—implied that the proletariat would soon include the overwhelming bulk of the population. The transition to socialism, far from being assigned to a "natural" elite or a power group, was seen by Marx as the task of the vast "proletarianized" majority. Correct or not, this was a fundamentally democratic point of view.

Concerned as he was with the mechanics of class power, the "laws of motion" of the existing society, and the strategy of social change, Marx paid very little attention to the description of socialism. The few remarks to be found in his early work and in such a later book as *The Critique of the Gotha Program* are mainly teasers, formulations so brief as to be cryptic, which did not prevent his disciples from making them into dogmas. An interesting division of labor took place. Marx's predecessors, those whom he called the "utopian socialists," had devoted themselves to summoning pictures of the ideal future, perhaps in lieu of activity in the detested present; Marx, partly as a reaction to their brilliant daydreaming, decided to focus on an analysis of those elements in the present that made possible a strategy for reaching the ideal future. And in the meantime, why worry about the face of the future, why create absurd blueprints? As a response to Fourier, Saint-Simon, and Owen there was much good sense in this attitude; given the state of the European labor movements in the mid-nineteenth century, it was indispensable to turn toward practical problems of national life (Germany) and class organization (England). But the Marxist movement, perhaps unavoidably, paid a price for this emphasis.

As the movement grew, the image of socialism kept becoming hazier and hazier, and soon the haziness came to seem a condition of perfection. The "revisionist" social democrat Eduard Bernstein could write that the goal is nothing, the movement everything; as if a means could be intelligently chosen without an end in view! In his *State and Revolution* Lenin, with far greater fullness than Marx, sketched a vision of socialism profoundly democratic, in which the mass of humanity would break out of its dumbness, so that cooks could become cabinet ministers, and even the "bourgeois principle of equality" would give way to the true freedom of nonmeasurement: "from each according to his ability and to each according to his need." But this democratic vision did not sufficiently affect his immediate views of political activity, so that in his crucial pamphlet "Will the Bolsheviks Retain State Power?" written in 1917, Lenin, as if to brush aside the traditional Marxist view that the socialist transformation requires a far greater popular base than any previous social change, could say, "After the 1905 Revolution Russia was ruled by 130,000 landowners. . . . And yet we are told that Russia will not be able to be governed by the 240,000 members of the Bolshevik Party—governing in the interests of the poor and against the rich."

What happened was that the vision of socialism—would it not be better to say the *problem* of socialism?—grew blurred in the minds of many Marxists because they were too ready to entrust it to history. The fetishistic use of the word "scientific," than which nothing could provide a greater sense of assurance, gave the Marxist movement a feeling that it had finally penetrated to the essence of history and found there once and for all its true meaning. The result was often a deification of history: what God had been to Fourier, history became to many Marxists—a certain force leading to a certain goal, And if indeed the goal was certain, or likely enough to be taken as certain, there was no need to draw up fanciful blueprints; the future would take care of itself and require no advice from us. True enough, in a way. But the point that soon came to be forgotten was that it is we, in the present, who need the image of the future, not those who may live in it. And the consequence of failing to imagine creatively the face of socialism—which is not at all the same as an absurd effort to paint it in detail—was that it tended to lapse into a conventional and lifeless "perfection."

III

Perfection, in that the image of socialism held by many Marxists—the image which emerged at the level of implicit belief—was a society in which tension, conflict, and failure had largely disappeared. It would be easy enough to comb the works of the major Marxists in order to prove this statement, but we prefer to appeal to common experience, to our own knowledge and memories as well as to the knowledge and memories of others. In the socialist movement one did not worry about the society one wanted: innumerable and, indeed, inconceivable subjects were discussed, but almost never the idea of socialism itself, for history, strategy, and the Party (how easily the three melted into one!) had eliminated that need. Socialism was the future—and sometimes a future made curiously respectable, the middle-class values that the radicals had violently rejected now being reinstated, unwittingly, in their vision of the good society. There could hardly be a need to reply to those critics who wondered how some of the perennial human problems could be solved under socialism: one *knew* they would be. In effect, the vision of socialism had a way of declining into a regressive infantile fantasy—a fantasy of protection.

Our criticism is not that the Marxist movement held to a vision of utopia: that it did so was entirely to its credit, a life without some glimmer of a redeeming future being a life cut off from the distinctively human. Our complaint is rather that the vision of utopia grew slack and static. Sometimes it degenerated into what William Morris called "the cockney dream" by which efficiency becomes a universal solvent for all human problems; sometimes it slipped off, beyond human reach, to the equally repulsive vision of a society in which men become rational titans as well behaved and tedious as Swift's Houyhnhnms. Only occasionally was socialism envisaged as a society with its own rhythm of growth and tension, change and conflict.

Marx's contribution to human thought is immense, but except for some cryptic if pregnant phrases, neither he nor his disciples have told us very much about the society in behalf of which they called men into battle. This is not quite so fatal a criticism as it might seem, since what probably mattered most was that Marxism stirred millions of previously dormant people into historical action, gave expression to their claims and yearnings, and lent a certain form to their desire for a better life. But if we want sustained speculations on the shape of this better life we have to turn to radical mavericks, to the anarchists and libertarians, to the Guild Socialists. And to such a writer as Oscar Wilde, whose *The Soul of Man under Socialism* is a small masterpiece. In his paradoxical and unsystematic way Wilde quickly comes to a sense of what the desirable society might be like. The great advantage of socialism, he writes, is that it "would relieve us from that sordid necessity of living for others which, in the present condition of things, presses so hard upon almost everybody." By focusing on "the unhealthy and exaggerated altruism" which capitalist society demands from people, and by showing how it saps individuality, Wilde arrives at the distinctive virtue of socialism: that it will make possible what he calls individualism.

IV

We do not wish to succumb to that which we criticize. Blueprints, elaborate schemes, do not interest us. But we think it may be useful to suggest some of the qualities that can make the image of socialism a serious and mature goal, as well as some of the difficulties in that goal.

Socialism is not the end of human history, as the deeply held identification of it with perfection must mean. There is no total fulfillment, nor is there an "end to time." History is a process which throws up new problems, new conflicts, new questions; and socialism, being within history, cannot be expected to solve all these problems or, for that matter, to raise humanity at every point above the level of achievement of previous societies. As Engels remarked, there is no final synthesis, only continued clash. What socialists want is simply to do away with those sources of conflict which are the cause of material deprivation and which, in turn, help create psychological and moral suffering. Freedom may then mean that we can devote ourselves to the pursuit of more worth-while causes of conflict. The hope for a conflictless society is reactionary, as is a reliance on some abstract "historical force" that will conciliate all human strife.

The aim of socialism is to create a society of co-operation, but not necessarily, or at least not universally, of harmony. Co-operation is compatible with conflict, is indeed inconceivable without conflict, while harmony implies a stasis.

Even the "total abolition" of social classes, no small or easy matter, would not or need not mean the total abolition of social problems.

In a socialist society there would remain a whole variety of human difficulties that could not easily be categorized as social or nonsocial; difficulties that might well result from the sheer friction between the human being and society, *any* society— from, say, the process of "socializing" those recalcitrant creatures known as children. The mere existence of man is a difficulty, a problem, with birth, marriage, pain, and death being only among the more spectacular of his crises. To be sure, no intelligent radical has ever denied that *such* crises would last into a socialist society, but the point to be stressed is that, with the elimination of our major material troubles, these other problems might rise to a new urgency, so much so as to become *social* problems leading to new conflicts.

V

But social problems as we conceive of them today would also be present in a socialist society.

Traditionally, Marxists have lumped all the difficulties posed by critics and reality into that "transitional" state that is to guide, or bump, us from capitalism to socialism, while socialism itself they have seen as the society that would transcend these difficulties. This has made it a little too easy to justify some of the doings of the "transitional" society, while making it easier still to avoid considering—not what socialism *will* be like—but what our image of it should be. Without pretending to "solve" these social problems as they might exist under socialism, but intending to suggest a bias or predisposition, we list here a few of them.

Bureaucracy

Marxists have generally related the phenomenon of bureaucratism to social inequality and economic scarcity. Thus they have seen the rise of bureaucracy in Leninist Russia as a consequence of trying to establish a workers' state in an isolated and backward country which lacked the economic prerequisites for building socialism. Given scarcity, there arises a policeman to supervise the distribution of goods; given the policeman, there will be an unjust distribution. Similarly, bureaucratic formations of a more limited kind are seen as parasitic elites which batten upon a social class, yet, in some sense, "represent" it in political and economic conflicts. Thus bureaucratism signifies a deformation, though not necessarily a destruction, of democratic processes.

This view of bureaucratism seems to us invaluable. Yet it would be an error to suppose that because a class society is fertile ground for bureaucracy, a classless society would automatically be free of bureaucracy. There are other causes for this social deformation; and while in a socialist society these other causes might not be aggravated by economic inequality and the ethos of accumulation as they are under capitalism, they would very likely continue to operate. One need not accept Robert Michels' "Iron Law of Oligarchy" in order to see this. (Michels' theory is powerful, but it tends to boomerang: anyone convinced by it that socialism is impossible will have a hard time resisting the idea that democracy is impossible.) Thus the mere presence of equality of wealth in a society does not necessarily mean an equality of power or status: if Citizen A were more interested in the politics of his town or the functioning of his factory than Citizen B, he would probably accumulate more power and status; hence, the *possibility* of misusing them. (Socialists have often replied, But why should Citizen A want to misuse his power and status when there is no pressing economic motive for doing so? No one can answer this question definitely except by positing some theory of "human nature," which we do not propose to do; all we can urge is a certain wariness with regard to any theory which discounts in advance the possibility that noneconomic motives lead to human troubles.) Then again, the problem of sheer size in economic and political units is likely to burden a socialist society as much as it burdens any other society; and large political or economic units, because they require an ever increasing delegation of authority, often to "experts," obviously provide a setting in which bureaucracy can flourish. But most important of all is the sheer problem of representation: the fact that as soon as authority is delegated to a "representative" there must follow a loss of control and autonomy.

Certain institutional checks can, of course, be suggested for containing bureaucracy. The idea of a division of governmental powers, which many Marxists have dismissed as a bourgeois device for thwarting the popular will, would deserve careful attention in planning a socialist society, though one need not suppose that it would have to perpetuate those elements of present-day parliamentary structure which do in fact thwart the popular will. Similarly, the distinction made in English political theory, but neglected by Marxists, between democracy as an expression of popular sovereignty and democracy as a pattern of government in which the rights of minority groups are especially defended, needs to be taken seriously. In general, a society that is pluralist rather than unitary in emphasis, that recognizes the need for diversification of function rather than concentration of authority—this is the desired goal.

And here we have a good deal to learn from a neglected branch of the socialist movement, the Guild Socialists of England, who have given careful thought to these problems. G. D. H. Cole, for example, envisages the socialist society as one in which government policy is a resultant of an interplay among socioeconomic units that simultaneously co-operate and conflict. Cole also puts forward the provocative idea of "functional representation," somewhat similar to the original image of the Soviets. Because, he writes, "a human being, as an individual, is fundamentally incapable of being represented," a man should have "as many distinct, and separately exercised, votes, as he has distinct social purposes or interests," voting, that is, in his capacity of worker, consumer, artist, resident, and so on.

But such proposals can hardly be expected to bulk very large unless they are made in a culture where the motives for private accumulation and the values sanctioning it have significantly diminished. If, as we believe, the goal of socialism is to create the kind of man who, to a measurable degree, ceases to be a manipulated object and becomes a motivated subject, then the growth of socialist consciousness must prove an important bulwark against bureaucracy. A society that stresses co-operation can undercut those prestige factors that make for bureaucracy; a society that accepts conflict, and provides a means for modulating it, will encourage those who combat bureaucracy.

Planning and Decentralization

Unavoidably, a great deal of traditional socialist thought has stressed economic centralization as a prerequisite for planning, especially in the "transitional" state between capitalism and socialism. Partly, this was an inheritance from the bourgeois revolution, which needed a centralized state; partly, it reflected the condition of technology in the nineteenth century, which required centralized units of production; partly, it is a consequence of the recent power of Leninism, which stressed centralism as a means of confronting the primitive chaos of the Russian economy, but allowed it to become a dogma in countries where it had no necessary relevance. Whatever the historical validity of these emphases on centralism, they must now be abandoned. According to the economist Colin Clark, the new forms of energy permit an economical employment of small decentralized industrial units. Certainly, every impulse of democratic socialism favors such a tendency. For if mass participation—by the workers, the citizens, the people as a whole—in the economic life of the society is to be meaningful, it must find its most immediate expression in relatively small economic units. Only in such small units is it possible for the nonexpert to exercise any real control.

From what we can learn about Stalinist "planning," we see that an economic plan does not work, but quickly breaks down, if arbitrarily imposed from above and hedged in with rigid specifications which allow for none of the flexibility, none of the economic *play,* that a democratic society requires. Social planning, if understood in democratic terms—and can there really be social planning, as distinct from economic regulation, without a democratic context?—requires only a loose guiding direction, a general pointer from above. The rest, the actual working out of variables, the arithmetic fullfillment of algebraic possibilities, must come from below, from the interaction, co-operation, and conflict of economic units participating in a democratic community.

All of this implies a considerable modification of the familiar socialist emphasis on nationalization of the means of production, increase of productivity, a master economic plan, and so on—a modification, but not a total rejection. To be sure, socialism still presupposes the abolition of private property in the basic industries, but there is hardly a branch of the socialist movement, except the more petrified forms of Trotskyism, which places any high valuation on nationalization of industry per se. Almost all socialists now feel impelled to add that what matters is the use to which nationalization is put and the degree of democratic control present in the nationalized industries. But more important, the idea of nationalization requires still greater modification: there is no reason to envisage, even in a "transitional" society, that all basic industries need be owned by the state. The emphasis of the Guild Socialists on separate guilds of workers, each owning and managing their own industries, summons no doubt a picture of possible struggles within and between industries; all the better! Guilds, co-operatives, call them what you will—these provide possible bulwarks against the monster Leviathan, the all-consuming state, which it is the sheerest fatuity to suppose would immediately cease being a threat to human liberty simply because "we" took it over. The presence of numerous political and economic units living together in a tension of co-operation-and-conflict, seems the best "guarantee" that power will not accumulate in the hands of a managerial oligarchy—namely, that the process already far advanced in capitalist society will not continue into socialism. Such autonomous units, serving as buffers between government and people, would allow for various, even contradictory, kinds of expression in social life. The conflicts that might break out among them would be a healthy social regulator; for while the suppression of conflict makes for an explosive accumulation of hostility, its normalization means that a society can be "sewn together" by noncumulative struggles between component groups. And even in terms of "efficiency," this may prove far more satisfactory than the bureaucratic state regulation of Communist Russia.

Only if an attempt is made to encompass the total personality of the individual into one or another group is conflict likely to lead to social breakdown. Only then would conflicts over relatively minor issues be elevated into "affairs of state." So long as the dogma of "total allegiance"—a dogma that has proven harmful in both its social democratic and Leninist versions—is not enforced, so long as the individual is able to participate in a variety of groupings without having to commit himself totally to any of them, society will be able to absorb a constant series of conflicts.

Nor would the criterion of efficiency be of decisive importance in such a society. At the beginning of the construction of socialism, efficiency is urgently required in order to provide the material possibility for a life of security and freedom. But efficiency is needed in order, so to speak, to transcend efficiency.

Between the abstract norms of efficiency and the living needs of human beings there may always be a clash. To speak in grandiose terms, as some anarchists do, of Efficiency vs. Democracy is not very valuable, since living experience always requires compromise and complication. All one can probably say is that socialists are not concerned with efficiency as such, but with that type of efficiency which does not go counter to key socialist values. Under socialism there are likely to be many situations in which efficiency will be consciously sacrificed, and indeed one of the measures of the success of a socialist society would be precisely how far it could afford to discard the criterion of efficiency. This might be one of the more glorious ideas latent in Engels' description of socialism as a "reign of freedom."

These remarks are, of course, scrappy and incomplete, as we intend them to be, for their usefulness has a certain correlation with their incompleteness; but part of what we have been trying to say has been so well put by R. H. S. Crossman that we feel impelled to quote him:

> The planned economy and the centralization of power are no longer socialist objectives. They are developing all over the world as the Political Revolution [the concentration of state powers] and the process is accelerated by the prevalence of war economy. The main task of socialism today is to prevent the concentration of power in the hands of *either* industrial management *or* the state bureaucracy—in brief, to distribute responsibility and so to enlarge freedom of choice. This task was not even begun by the Labour Government. On the contrary, in the nationalized industries old managements were preserved almost untouched. . . .
>
> In a world organized in ever larger and more inhuman units, the task of socialism is to prevent managerial responsibility degenerating into privilege. This can only be achieved by increasing, even at the cost of "efficiency," the citizen's right to participate in the control not only of government and industry, but of the party for which he voted. . . . After all, it is not the pursuit of happiness but the enlargement of freedom which is socialism's highest aim.

Work and Leisure

No Marxist concept has been more fruitful than that of "alienation." As used by Marx, it suggests the psychic price of living in a society where the worker's "deed becomes an alien power." The division of labor, he writes, makes the worker "a cripple . . . forcing him to develop some highly specialized dexterity at the cost of a world of productive impulses. . . ." The worker becomes estranged from his work, both as process and product; his major energies must be expended on tasks that have no organic or creative function within his life; the impersonality of the social relationships enforced by capitalism, together with the sense of incoherence and discontinuity induced by the modern factory, goes far toward making the worker a dehumanized part of the productive process rather than an autonomous human being. It is not, of course, to be supposed that this is a description of a given factory; it is a "lead" by which to examine a given factory. This theory is the starting point of much speculation on the nature of modern work, as well as on the social and psychological significance of the industrial city; and almost all the theorizing on "mass culture," not to mention many of the efforts to "engineer" human relations in the factory, implicitly acknowledges the relevance and power of Marx's idea.

But when Marx speaks of alienation and thereby implies the possibility of nonalienation, it is not always clear whether he has in mind some precapitalist society in which men were presumably not alienated or whether he employs it as a useful fiction derived by a process of abstraction from the observable state of society. If he means the former, he may occasionally be guilty of romanticizing, in common with many of his contemporaries, the life of pre-capitalist society; for most historians of feudalism and of that difficult-to-label era which spans the gap between feudalism and capitalism strongly imply that the peasant and even the artisan was not quite the unalienated man that some intellectuals like to suppose. Nonetheless, as an analytical tool and a reference to future possibilities, the concept of alienation remains indispensable.

So long as capitalism, in one form or another, continues to exist, it will be difficult to determine to what degree it is the social setting and to what degree the industrial process that makes so much of factory work dehumanizing. That a great deal of this dehumanization is the result of a social structure which deprives many men of an active sense of participation or decision making and tends to reduce them to the level of controlled objects can hardly be doubted at so late a moment.

We may consequently suppose that in a society where democratic ethos had been reinforced politically and had made a significant seepage into economic life, the problem of alienation would be alleviated. But not solved.

In his *Critique of the Gotha Program* Marx speaks of the highest stage of the new society as one in which "the enslaving subordination of individuals in the division of labor has disappeared, and with it also the antagonism between mental and physical labor; labor has become not only a means of living, but itself the first necessity of life. . . ." Remembering that Marx set this as a *limit* toward which to strive and not as a condition likely to be present even during the beginning of socialism, let us then suppose that a society resembling this unit has beeℓ reached. The crippling effects of the division of labor are now largely eliminated because people are capable of doing a large variety of social tasks; the division between physical and mental labor has been largely eliminated because the level of education has been very much raised; and— we confess here to being uncertain as to Marx's meaning—labor has become "the first necessity of life." But even now the problem of *the nature of work* remains. Given every conceivable improvement in the social context of work; given a free and healthy society; given, in short, all the desiderata Marx lists—even then there remains the uncreativeness, the tedium, what frequently must seem the meaninglessness, of the jobs many people have to perform in the modern factory.

It may be said that in a socialist society people could live creatively in their leisure; no doubt. Or that people would have to do very little work because new forms of energy would be developed; quite likely. But then the problem would be for men to find an outlet for their "productive impulses" not in the way Marx envisioned but in another way, not in work but in leisure. Except for certain obviously satisfying occupations—and by this we do *not* mean only intellectual occupations—work might now become a minor part of human life. The problem is whether in any society it would now be possible to create—given our irrevocable commitment to industrialism—the kind of "whole man" Marx envisaged, the man, that is, who realizes himself through and by his work.

It is not as a speculation about factory life in a socialist society that this problem intrigues us, but rather as an entry into another problem about which Marx wrote very little: what we now call "mass culture." Socialists have traditionally assumed that a solution to economic problems would be followed by a tremendous flowering of culture, and this may happen; we do not know. But another possible outcome might be a population of which large parts were complacent and self-satisfied, so that if hell is now conceived as a drawing room, utopia might soften into a suburb. In any case, we are hardly likely to feel as certain about the cultural consequences of social equality as Trotsky did when he wrote in *Literature and Revolution* that under socialism men might reach the level of Beethoven and Goethe. This seems implausibly romantic, since it is doubtful that the scarcity of Beethovens and Goethes can be related solely to social inequality; and what is more, it does not even seem very desirable to have a society of Beethovens and Goethes.

Between the two extreme forecasts there is the more likely possibility that under socialism a great many people would inevitably engage in work which could not release "a world of productive impulses," but would be brief and light enough to allow them a great deal of leisure. The true problem of socialism might then be to determine the nature, quality, and variety of leisure. Men, that is, would face the full and terrifying burden of human freedom, but they would be more prepared to shoulder it than ever before.

VI

"The past and present," wrote Pascal, "are our means; the future alone our end." Taken with the elasticity that Pascal intended—he surely did not mean to undervalue the immediacy of experience—this is a useful motto for what we have called utopian thinking, the imaginative capacity for conceiving of a society that is qualitatively better than our own, yet no mere fantasy of static perfection.

Today, in an age of curdled realism, it is necessary to assert the utopian image. But this can be done meaningfully only if it is an image of social striving, tension, conflict; an image of a problem-creating and problem-solving society.

In his "Essay on Man" Ernst Cassirer has written almost all that remains to be said:

A Utopia is not a portrait of the real world, or of the actual political or social order. It exists at no moment of time and at no point in space; it is a "nowhere." But just such a conception of a nowhere has stood the test and proved its strength in the development of the modern world. It follows from the nature and character of ethical thought that it can never condescend to accept the "given." The ethical world is never given; it is forever in the making.

Some time ago one could understandably make of socialism a consoling daydream. Now, when we live in the shadow of defeat, to retain, to will the image of socialism is a constant struggle for definition, almost an act of pain. But it is the kind of pain that makes creation possible.

20 BLACK POWER

▪ *Stokely Carmichael*

One of the most pointed illustrations of the need for black power, as a positive and redemptive force in a society degenerating into a form of totalitarianism, is to be made by examining the history of distortion that the concept has received in national media of publicity. In this "debate," as in everything else that affects our lives, Negroes are dependent on, and at the discretion of, forces and institutions in the white society which have little interest in representing us honestly. Our experience with the national press

From Stokely Carmichael, "Toward Black Liberation," *Massachusetts Review,* VII (Autumn, 1966), 639–651. © Copyright Student Non-Violent Coordinating Committee. Reprinted by permission.

has been that where they have managed to escape a meretricious special interest in "Git Whitey" sensationalism and race-warmongering, individual reporters and commentators have been conditioned by the enveloping racism of the society to the point where they are incapable even of objective observation and reporting of racial *incidents,* much less the analysis of *ideas.* But this limitation of vision and perceptions is an inevitable consequence of the dictatorship of definition, interpretation, and consciousness, along with the censorship of history that the society has inflicted upon the Negro— and itself.

Our concern for Black Power addresses itself directly to this problem: the necessity to reclaim our history and our identity from the cultural terrorism and depredation of self-justifying white guilt.

To do this we shall have to struggle for the right to create our own terms through which to define ourselves and our relationship to the society and to have these terms recognized. This is the first necessity of a free people and the first right that any oppressor must suspend. The white fathers of American racism knew this—instinctively it seems—as is indicated by the continuous record of the distortion and omission in their dealings with the red and black men. In the same way that southern apologists for the "Jim Crow" society have so obscured, muddied, and misrepresented the record of the reconstruction period, until it is almost impossible to tell what really happened, their contemporary counterparts are busy doing the same thing with the recent history of the civil rights movement. . . .

The "Black Power" program and concept which is being articulated by SNCC, CORE, and a host of community organizations in the ghettos of the North and South has not escaped that process. . . . A national committee of influential Negro churchmen affiliated with the National Council of Churches, despite their obvious respectability and responsibility, had to resort to a paid advertisement to articulate their position, while anyone shouting the hysterical yappings of "Black Racism" got ample space. Thus the American people have gotten at best a superficial and misleading account of the very terms and tenor of this debate. I wish to quote briefly from the statement by the national committee of churchmen which I suspect that the majority of Americans will not have seen. This statement appeared in the *New York Times* of July 31, 1966.

We an informal group of Negro Churchmen in America are deeply disturbed about the crisis brought upon our country by historic distortions of important human realities in the controversy about "black power." What we see shining through the variety of rhetoric is not anything new but the same old problem of power and race which has faced our beloved country since 1619.

. . . The conscience of black men is corrupted because, having no power to implement the demands of conscience, the concern for justice in the absence of justice becomes a chaotic self-surrender. Powerlessness breeds a race of beggars. We are faced now with a situation where powerless conscience meets conscience-less power, threatening the very foundations of our Nation.

. . . We deplore the overt violence of riots, but we feel it is more important to focus on the real sources of these eruptions. These sources may be abetted inside the Ghetto, but their basic cause lies in the silent and covert violence which white middleclass America inflicts upon the victims of the inner city.

. . . In short; the failure of American leaders to use American power to create equal opportunity *in life* as well as *law*, this is the real problem and not the anguished cry for black power.

. . . Without the capacity to *participate with power, i.e.,* to have some organized political and economic strength to really influence people with whom one interacts—integration is not meaningful.

. . . America has asked its Negro citizens to fight for opportunity as individuals, whereas at certain points in our history what we have needed most has been opportunity for the *whole group*, not just for selected and approved Negroes.

. . . We must not apologize for the existence of this form of group power, for we have been oppressed as a group and not as individuals. We will not find our way out of that oppression until both we and America accept the need for Negro Americans, as well as for Jews, Italians, Poles, and white Anglosaxon Protestants, among others to have and to wield group power.

Traditionally, for each new ethnic group, the route to social and political integration into America's pluralistic society has been through the organization of their own institutions with which to represent their communal needs within the larger society. This is simply stating what the advocates of black power are saying. The strident outcry, *particularly* from the liberal community, that has been evoked by this proposal can only be understood by examining the historic relationship between Negro and white power in this country.

Negroes are defined by two forces: their blackness and their powerlessness. There have been traditionally two communities in America: the white community, which controlled and defined the forms that all institutions within the society would take, and the Negro community which has been excluded from participation in the power decisions that shaped the society and has traditionally been dependent on, and subservient to, the white community.

This has not been accidental. The history of every institution of this society indicates that a major concern in the ordering and structuring of the society has been the maintaining of the Negro community in its condition of dependence and oppression. This has not been on the level of individual acts of discrimination between individual whites against individual Negroes, but as total acts by the white community against the Negro community. This fact cannot be too strongly emphasized—that racist assumptions of white superiority have been so deeply ingrained in the structure of the society that it infuses its entire functioning and is so much a part of the national subconscious that it is taken for granted and is frequently not even recognized.

Let me give an example of the difference between individual racism and institutionalized racism, and the society's response to both. When unidentified white terrorists bomb a Negro church and kill five children, that is an act of individual racism, widely deplored by most segments of the society. But when in that same city, Birmingham, Alabama, not five but five hundred Negro babies die each year because of a lack of proper food, shelter, and medical facilities, and thousands more are destroyed and maimed physically, emotionally, and intellectually because of conditions of poverty and deprivation in the ghetto, that is a function of institutionalized racism. But the society either pretends it doesn't know of this situation or is incapable of doing anything meaningful about it. And this resistance to doing anything meaningful about conditions in that ghetto comes from the fact that the ghetto is itself a product of a combination of forces and special interests in the white community, and the groups that have access to the resources and power to change that situation benefit, politically and economically, from the existence of that ghetto.

It is more than a figure of speech to say that the Negro community in America is the victim of white imperialism and colonial exploitation. This is in practical economic and political terms true. There are over twenty million black people comprising 10 per cent of this nation. They live for the most part in well-defined areas of the country—in the shanty towns and rural black-belt areas of the South and increasingly in the slums of northern and western industrial cities. If one goes into any Negro community, whether it be in Jackson, Mississippi, Cambridge, Maryland, or Harlem, New York, one will find that the same combination of political, economic, and social forces is at work. The people in the Negro community do not control the resources of that community, its political decisions, its law enforcement, its housing standards; and even the physical ownership of the land, houses, and stores *lies outside that community.*

It is white power that makes the laws, and it is violent white power in the form of armed white cops that enforces those laws with guns and night sticks. The vast majority of Negroes in this country live in these captive communities and must endure these conditions of oppression because, and only because, *they are black and powerless.* I do not suppose that at any point the men who control the power and resources of this country ever sat down and designed these black enclaves and formally articulated the terms of their colonial and dependent status, as was done, for example, by the Apartheid government of South Africa. Yet, one cannot distinguish between one ghetto and another. As one moves from city to city, it is as though some malignant racist planning unit had done precisely this—designed each one from the same master blueprint. And indeed, if the ghetto had been formally and deliberately planned, instead of growing spontaneously and inevitably from the racist functioning of the various institutions that combine to make the society, it would be somehow less frightening. The situation would be less frightening because, if these ghettos were the result of design and conspiracy, one could understand their similarity as being artificial and consciously imposed, rather than the result of identical patterns of white racism which repeat themselves in cities as distant as Boston and Birmingham. Without bothering to list the historic factors which contribute to this pattern

—economic exploitation, political impotence, discrimination in employment and education—one can see that to correct this pattern will require far-reaching changes in the basic power relationships and the ingrained social patterns in the society. The question is, of course, what kinds of changes are necessary, and how is it possible to bring them about?

In recent years the answer to these questions which has been given by most articulate groups of Negroes and their white allies, the "liberals" of all stripes, has been in terms of something called "integration." According to the advocates of integration, social justice will be accomplished by "integrating the Negro into the mainstream institutions of the society from which he has been traditionally excluded." It is very significant that each time I have heard this formulation it has been in terms of "the Negro," the individual Negro, rather than in terms of the community.

This concept of integration had to be based on the assumption that there was nothing of value in the Negro community and that little of value could be created among Negroes, so the thing to do was to siphon off the "acceptable" Negroes into the surrounding middle-class white community. Thus the goal of the movement for integration was simply to loosen up the restrictions barring the entry of Negroes into the white community. Goals around which the struggle took place, such as public accommodation, open housing, job opportunity on the executive level (which is easier to deal with than the problem of semiskilled and blue-collar jobs which involve more far-reaching economic adjustments), are quite simply middle-class goals, articulated by a tiny group of Negroes who had middle-class aspirations. It is true that the student demonstrations in the South during the early sixties, out of which SNCC came, had a similar orientation. But while it is hardly a concern of a black sharecropper, dishwasher, or welfare recipient whether a certain fifteen-dollar-a-day motel offers accommodations to Negroes, the overt symbols of white superiority and the imposed limitations on the Negro community had to be destroyed. Now, black people must look beyond these goals to the issue of collective power.

Such a limited class orientation was reflected not only in the program and goals of the civil rights movement but in its tactics and organization. It is very significant that the two oldest and most "respectable" civil rights organizations have constitutions which *specifically* prohibit partisan political activity. CORE once did, but changed that clause when it changed its orientation toward black power. But this is perfectly understandable in terms of the strategy and goals of the older organizations. The civil rights movement saw its role as a kind of liaison between the powerful white community and the dependent Negro one. The dependent status of the black community apparently was unimportant since—if the movement were successful—it was going to blend into the white community anyway. We made no pretense of organizing and developing institutions of community power in the Negro community, but appealed to the conscience of white institutions of power. The posture of the civil rights movement was that of the dependents, the suppliant. The theory was that without attempting to create any organized base of political strength itself, the civil rights movement could, by forming coalitions with various "liberal" pressure organizations in the white community—liberal reform clubs, labor unions, church groups, progressive civic groups, and at times one or other of the major political parties—influence national legislation and national social patterns.

I think we all have seen the limitations of this approach. We have repeatedly seen that political alliances based on appeals to conscience and decency are chancy things, simply because institutions and political organizations have no consciences outside their own special interests. The political and social rights of Negroes have been and always will be negotiable and expendable the moment they conflict with the interests of our "allies." If we do not learn from history, we are doomed to repeat it, and that is precisely the lesson of the reconstruction. Black people were allowed to register, vote, and participate in politics because it was to the advantage of powerful white allies to promote this. But this was the result of white decision, and it was ended by other white men's decision before any political base powerful enough to challenge that decision could be established in the southern Negro community. . . .

The major limitation of this approach was that it tended to maintain the traditional dependence of Negroes and of the movement. We depended on the good will and support of various groups in the white community whose interests were not always compatible with ours. To the extent that we depended on the financial support of other groups, we were vulnerable to their influence and domination.

Also the program that evolved out of this coalition was really limited and inadequate in the long term and one which affected only a small, select group of Negroes. Its goal was to make the white community accessible to "qualified" Negroes, and presumably each year a few more Negroes armed with their passport—a couple of university degrees—would escape into middle-class America and adopt the attitudes and life styles of that group; and one day the Harlems and the Watts would stand empty, a tribute to the success of integration. This is simply neither realistic nor particularly desirable. You can integrate communities, but you assimilate individuals. Even if such a program were possible its result would be, not to develop the black community as a functional and honorable segment of the total society, with its own cultural identity, life patterns, and institutions, but to abolish it—the final solution to the Negro problem. Marx said that the working class is the first class in history that ever wanted to abolish itself. If one listens to some of our "moderate" Negro leaders, it appears that the American Negro is the first race that ever wished to abolish itself. The fact is that what must be abolished is not the black community, but the dependent colonial status that has been inflicted upon it. The racial and cultural personality of the black community must be preserved, and the community must win its freedom while preserving its cultural integrity. This is the essential difference between integration as it is currently practiced and the concept of black power.

What has the movement for integration accomplished to date? The Negro graduating from MIT with a doctorate will have better job opportunities available to him than to Lynda Bird Johnson. But the rate of unemployment in the Negro community is steadily increasing, while that in the white community decreases. More educated Negroes hold executive jobs in major corporations and federal agencies than ever before, but the gap between white income and Negro income has almost doubled in the last twenty years. More suburban housing is available to Negroes, but housing conditions in the ghetto are steadily declining. While the infant mortality rate of New York City is at its lowest point ever in the city's history, the infant mortality rate of Harlem is steadily climbing. There has been an organized national resistance to the Supreme Court's order to integrate the schools, and the federal government has not acted to enforce that order. Less than 15 per cent of black children in the South attend integrated schools; and Negro schools, which the vast majority of black children still attend, are increasingly decrepit, overcrowded, understaffed, inadequately equipped and funded.

This explains why the rate of school dropouts is increasing among Negro teenagers, who then express their bitterness, hopelessness, and alienation by the only means they have: rebellion. As long as people in the ghettos of our large cities feel that they are victims of the misuse of white power without any way to have their needs met—to get the welfare inspectors to stop kicking down your doors in the middle of the night, the cops from beating your children, the landlord to exterminate the vermin in your home, the city to collect your garbage—we will continue to have riots. These are not the products of "black power," but of the absence of any organization capable of giving the community the power, the black power, to deal with its problems.

SNCC proposes that it is now time for the black freedom movement to stop pandering to the fears and anxieties of the white middle class in the attempt to earn its "good will," and to return to the ghetto to organize these communities to control themselves. This organization must be attempted in northern and southern urban areas as well as in the rural black-belt counties of the South. The chief antagonist to this organization is, in the South, the overtly racist Democratic party, and in the North the equally corrupt big city machines.

The standard argument presented against independent political organization is "But you are only 10 per cent." I cannot see the relevance of this observation, since no one is talking about taking over the country, but taking control over our own communities.

The fact is that the Negro population, 10 per cent or not, is very strategically placed because—ironically—of segregation. What is also true is that Negroes have never been able to utilize the full voting potential of our numbers. Where we could vote, the case has always been that the white political machine stacked and gerrymandered the political subdivisions in Negro neighborhoods so the true voting strength was never reflected in political strength. Would anyone looking at the distribution of political power in Manhattan ever think that Negroes represented 60 per cent of the population there?

Just as often the effective political organization in Negro communities is absorbed by tokenism and patronage—the time-honored practice of "giving" certain offices to selected Negroes. The machine thus creates a "little machine," which is subordinate and responsive to it, in the Negro community. These Negro political "leaders" are really vote deliverers, more responsible to the white machine and the white power structure than to the community they allegedly represent. Thus the white community is able to substitute patronage control for audacious black power in the Negro community. . . .

We must organize black community power to end these abuses and to give the Negro community a chance to have its needs expressed. A leadership which is truly "responsible"—not to the white press and power structure, but to the community—must be developed. Such leadership will recognize that its power lies in the unified and collective strength of that community. This will make it difficult for the white leadership group to conduct its dialogue with individuals in terms of patronage and prestige and will force them to talk to the community's representatives in terms of real power.

The single aspect of the black power program that has encountered most criticism is this concept of independent organization. This is presented as third-partyism which has never worked, or a withdrawal into black nationalism and isolationism. If such a program is developed it will not have the effect of isolating the Negro community, but the reverse. When the Negro community is able to control local office, and negotiate with other groups from a position of organized strength, the possibility of meaningful political alliances on specific issues will be increased. That is a rule of politics, and there is no reason why it should not operate here. The only difference is that we will have the power to define the terms of these alliances.

The next question usually is, "So—can it work, can the ghettos in fact be organized?" The answer is that this organization must be successful, because there are no viable alternatives—not the War on Poverty, which was at its inception limited to dealing with effects rather than causes and has become simply another source of machine patronage. And "integration" is meaningful only to a small chosen class in the community.

The revolution in agricultural technology in the South is displacing the rural Negro community into northern urban areas. Both Washington, D.C., and Newark, New Jersey, have Negro majorities. One-third of Philadelphia's population of two million people is black. "Inner city" in most major urban areas is already predominantly Negro, and with the white rush to suburbia, Negroes will in the next three decades control the heart of our great cities. These areas can become either concentration camps with a bitter and volatile population whose only power is the power to destroy, or organized and powerful communities, able to make constructive contributions to the total society. Without the power to control their lives and their communities, without effective political institutions through which to relate to the total society, these communities will exist in a constant state of insurrection. This is a choice that the country will have to make.

21 PARTICIPATORY DEMOCRACY

■ *Richard Flacks*

I

The most frequently heard phrase used for defining participatory democracy is that "men must share in the decisions which affect their lives." In other words, participatory democrats take very seriously a vision of man as citizen; and by taking seriously such a vision, they seek to extend the conception of citizenship beyond the conventional political sphere to all institutions. Other ways of stating the core values are to assert the following: each man has responsibility for the action of the institutions in which he is embedded; all authority ought to be responsible to those "under" it; each man can and should be a center of power and initiative in society.

II

The first priority for the achievement of a democracy of participation is to win full political rights and representation for all sectors of the population. Democracy, in fact, is an issue for this generation of radicals largely because their political experience has been shaped by the Negroes' elemental struggle for a political voice in the United States. This struggle has not been simply for the right to vote—though even this right has not yet been guaranteed—but, more broadly, it has been an effort to win a share of political power by poor Negroes. It has been the experience of Negroes in the North, where voting rights have been formally guaranteed, that Negroes as a group have remained systematically underrepresented in the political process and that, where Negro representation exists, it operates in behalf of Negro middle-class interests and is highly dependent on the beneficence of white-dominated political machines. The results of this situation are plain to see in every northern city. Thus the

From Richard Flacks, "On the Uses of Participatory Democracy," *Dissent*, XIII (November–December, 1966), 701–708. Reprinted by permission.

main thrust of radicals in the civil rights movement has to do less with breaking the barriers of legal segregation and formal exclusion than with attempting
to build viable grass-roots organizations of poor Negroes, which would actually
represent the needs of the poor and remain independent of white and middle-
class domination. The ideology of "participatory democracy" has been useful
in this effort, since it provides a rationale for avoiding premature "coalition"
of grass-roots groups with more powerful white or middle-class organizations,
for effectively criticizing "charismatic" styles of leadership which prevent rank-
and-file people from learning political skills, for criticizing tendencies toward
bureaucratism, demagoguery, and elitism which are predictable in mass movements. Moreover, "participatory democracy," unlike black nationalist ideology,
which also helps to mobilize grass-roots Negroes, offers a possible bridge
between Negroes and other groups of poor or voiceless people. Thus we find
much of the same rhetoric and organizing technique being used by SNCC
workers in southern Negro communities, SDS organizers among poor whites
in Chicago and Cleveland, and farm labor organizers among the multinational
grape workers in California.

Just how is participatory democracy being applied to the organization of
economically disadvantaged groups? It has influenced the analysis of the
problem of poverty in an affluent society by stressing political voicelessness
and lack of organization as a root cause of deprivation. This analysis leads to
an emphasis on grass-roots organization and mobilization of the poor as the
main way of ending poverty. Since the people involved lack political skill,
organization requires a full-time staff, initially composed of students and
ex-students, but soon involving "indigenous" leadership. This staff has the
problem of allaying the fear, suspicion, and sense of inadequacy of the
community—hence there has been a strong emphasis on building a sense of
community between staff and rank and file and of finding techniques which will
facilitate self-expression, enable new leadership to emerge, enable people to
gain dignity by participation and the organization to become self-sustaining.
Such techniques include: rotation of leadership, eschewing by staff of opportunities to "speak for" the organization, the use of "consensus" to foster
expression by the less articulate.

More important than such procedural techniques has been the attempt to
generate institutions which help to bind people to the organization, to see
immediate benefits from participation. . . . Although these new institutions are
sometimes viewed as alternatives to participation in "organized society" (*vide*
Staughton Lynd in *Dissent*, Summer, 1965), in practice, they are a very important way of sustaining a developing organization. They enable people to participate in an organization in a continuing fashion, help develop organizational
resources, train people for leadership, and give people a sense of the possibilities
for social change. But they are in no sense a *substitute* for political activity,
direct action, and the development of a program. These, and not the development of "parallel institutions," constitute the main functions of the local
political parties, community unions, and so on which are developing in many
urban slum and rural areas.

The emphasis on participary democracy has helped these developing grass-roots organizations formulate and articulate *issues and programs*. Although the constituencies of these organizations include the most impoverished sectors of society, it is remarkable that—particularly in the northern cities—the main activity of these organizations has not been focused on economic issues. They have rather, been struggling over issues of *control, self-determination,* and *independence*: Shall the poor have a voice in the allocation of War on Poverty funds? Shall urban renewal be shaped by the people whose neighborhood is being renewed? Shall the police be held accountable by the community? Who is to decide the dispensation of welfare payments? Who makes the rules in the welfare bureaucracies? Who controls the ghetto?

The outcome of these grass-roots organizing efforts, of course, cannot be predicted. The civil rights movement, in its direct action phase, began the process of bringing Negroes and the poor into the political arena—and the results, in terms of political alignments and issues, have already been substantial. The more recent efforts of political organization initiated by the participatory democrats will certainly increase the degree of Negro representation in the political process. These efforts are now being emulated by more established and less insurgent agencies—Martin Luther King's Southern Christian Leadership Conference, for example, in the massive organizing campaign in Chicago, used many of the techniques and rhetorical devices developed by SNCC and SDS.

It seems clear, then, that the poor are being organized and mobilized. But such mobilization can lead in two directions. On the one hand, there is the strong probability that the newly developed constituencies will take their place alongside other ethnic and interest groups, bargaining for benefits within the framework of the Democratic party. An alternative to this path is embodied in the vision of participatory democracy—the development of community-based, self-determining organizations, having the following functions:

Achieving community control over previously centralized functions, through local election of school and police administrators; by forming community-run co-operatives in housing, social services, retail distribution, and the like; by establishing community-run foundations and corporations.

Maintaining close control over elected representatives; running and electing poor people to public office; ensuring direct participation of the community in framing political platforms and in shaping the behavior of representatives.

Acting like a trade-union in protecting the poor against exploitative and callous practices of public and private bureaucracies, landlords, businessmen, and others.

III

The values underlying participatory democracy have, so far, achieved their fullest expression in efforts to organize and mobilize communities of disenfranchised people, but such democratizing trends and potentialities also exist in other sectors of society. The most obvious example is the nationwide effort by university students to change the authority structure in American higher education. For the most part, this activity has been directed at protest against arbitrary restrictions of student political expression and against paternalistic regulations limiting students' rights to privacy and self-expression. The most dramatic and widely known instance of this activity was that of the civil disobedience and student strikes at Berkeley in the fall of 1964. But the Berkeley situation has been repeated in less intense form on scores of campuses across the country. Student reform efforts have increasingly shifted from protest and direct action to demands for a continuing voice in the shaping of university policy. Some students now have demanded representation on administrative committees. Others have looked to the formation of organizations along the trade-union model—organizations which would be independent of and could bargain with university administrators, rather than becoming participants in administration. Thus far, the impact of the student protest has been to generate a considerable degree of ferment, of re-examination and experimentation among college faculties and administrators, as well as efforts coercively to repress the protest.

Student protest has spread from the elite, liberal campuses to Catholic schools and from there to other clerical bodies. The talk at Catholic seminaries now prominently includes "participatory democracy," and "New Left" clergymen have gone so far as to propose the establishment of a trade-union for priests. But the university and the church are not the only institutions witnessing challenges to existing authority structures. In recent years, there has been an enormous growth of unionization among schoolteachers and other white-collar workers, particularly among employees in the welfare bureaucracies. Now one can also observe ferment in the professions: young doctors and young lawyers are developing organizations dedicated to challenging the authority of the highly conservative professional societies and to bringing an active sense of social responsibility to their professions.

It is not farfetched to predict that the idea of "workers' control" will soon become a highly relevant issue in American life. American industrial unions have largely had to sacrifice the struggle for control in the workplace for higher wages and fringe benefits; but at union conventions, control over working conditions is repeatedly urged as a high-priority bargaining demand. The impetus for making such a demand paramount, however, may first come from the ranks of white-collar and professional employees. The authority structure of the modern bureaucratic organization is plainly unsuited for a work force which is highly educated and fully aware of its competence to participate in decision making. The first impulse of modern managers faced with threats to authority has been to make small concessions ("improve channels of communications"). But the exciting time will come when such insurgency turns from protest over small grievances to a full-fledged realization of the possibilities for first-class citizenship in public bureaucracies and private corporations. The forms of such democratization could include further unionization of the unorganized, worker representation in management, young-turk overthrows of entrenched leaderships in the professions, and, ultimately, demands for elections and recall of managers and administrators and for employee participation in the shaping of policies and regulations.

IV

The most authoritarian sector of public decision making in the United States is in the area of foreign policy. The American Constitution gives enormous power to the President to make foreign policy without substantial built-in checks from Congress. The scope of Presidential power has, of course, been greatly expanded by the technology of modern war; the unchecked power of the government to mobilize support for its policies has been greatly enhanced by the invention of conscription, by the mass media and their centralization, by covert intelligence operations, and so forth. It is not surprising that foreign policy has been the special province of elites in America and, since World War II, has been carried on within a framework of almost total popular acquiescence.

The simultaneous occurrence of the Vietnam War and the emergence of a New Left in America may generate change in this situation. Due largely to student initiative, we are witnessing more protest during time of war than in any other comparable period in United States history. Not only does this protest begin to shatter the foreign policy consensus but it also shows signs of bringing about more permanent change in the structure of foreign policy decision making.

First, the teach-ins and similar initiatives mark the emergence of an *independent public* in the foreign policy area—a body of people, satisfied neither with official policy nor with official justifications of policy, determined to formulate alternatives, stimulate debate and criticism, and obtain independent sources of information. This public is to be found largely in universities, but now spills over to include much of the intellectual community in the country. Moreover, the teach-in, as a technique for disseminating information suggests, at least symbolically, a significant breakthrough in the effort to find alternatives to the propaganda media controlled or manipulated by the state.

Second, the emerging foreign policy public has plainly had an at least transitory impact on Congress. The revival of congressional independence with respect to foreign policy would be a signal advance of democracy in America.

Third, the attempts to find a nonreligious moral ground for conscientious objection in time of war has led to a rediscovery of the Allied case at the Nuremberg Trials—a case which argued in essence that individuals were responsible for the actions of institutions taken in their name. This principle, taken seriously, is revolutionary in its implications for individual-state relations; and it converges, interestingly enough, with "participatory democracy." The Nuremberg principle is now being used as a basis for legal defense of draft refusal and civil disobedience at draft boards; it inspires professors to refuse to grade their students and become thereby accomplices to Selective

Service; it inspires intellectuals and artists to acts of public defiance and witness. In fact, it is possible that one positive outcome of the war in Vietnam will have been its impact on the moral sensibility of many members of the intellectual and religious communities—forcing them to rethink their relationship to the state and to the institutions of war.

It is possible, then, that an unforeseen by-product of the highly developed society is the emergence of potential publics that are (1) competent to evaluate the propaganda of elites and (2) impatient with chauvinistic definitions of loyalty. The organization of such publics in the United States may be a significant outcome of the war in Vietnam. These publics do not have the power to change the course of this war, but the spread of their influence may be a factor in transforming the issues and alignments of American politics in the coming period. Moreover, the strength of these publics on the campus is now being reflected in the growing conflict over the role of the universities in national mobilization. The current campaign to prevent university participation in the Selective Service induction process may portend a more profound effort to make universities centers of resistance to encroaching militarization. The outcome of this particular struggle could be important in democratizing the structure of foreign policy decision making.

V

The development of democratic consciousness in communities, organizations, and foreign policy decision making will mean little if the national distribution of power remains undisturbed. This means that the social theory of the New Left must be centrally concerned with the development of relevant models for democratic control over public decisions at the national level.

It is clear that implicit in the New Left's vision is the notion that participatory democracy is not possible without some version of public control over the allocation of resources, economic planning, and the operation of large corporations. Such control is, of course, not missing in the United States. The federal government has taken responsibility for national planning to avoid slump, to control wages and prices, and to avoid inflation. Moreover, the postwar period has seen a tremendous increase in public subsidy of the corporate economy—through the defense budget, urban redevelopment, investment in research and education, transportation and communication, and so on. In many ways the "two governments"—political and corporate—are merged, and this merger approximates an elitist corporatist model (hence breaking down even the modest pluralism which once characterized the system). The further development of this trend will foreclose any possibility for the achievement of democratic participation.

The demand for more national planning, once the major plank of American socialism, is now decidedly on the agenda of American political and corporate elites. The question for the Left has become how to *democratize* that planning. There are as yet no answers to this or to the question of how to bring the large corporations under democratic control.

VI

Thus the main intellectual problem for the new radicals is to suggest how patterns of decentralized decision making in city administrations, and democratized authority structures in bureaucracies, can be meshed with a situation of greatly broadened national planning and co-ordination in the economy.

That no such programs and models now exist is, of course, a consequence of the disintegration of the socialist tradition in America and of the continuing fragmentation of American intellectual life. Unless the New Left consciously accepts the task of restoring that tradition and of establishing a new political community, the democratizing revolts which it now catalyzes are likely to be abortive.

VII

These tasks were, less than a generation ago, declared by many American intellectuals to be no longer relevant. Ideology, it was argued, had no place in highly developed societies where problems of resource allocation had become technical matters. But the reverse may be true: that ideological questions—that is, questions about the structure and distribution of power—are *especially* pertinent when societies have the capacity to solve the merely technical problems.

It seems clear that the issue in a highly developed society is not simply economic exploitation; it is the question of the relationship of the individual to institutional and state authority which assumes paramount importance. In America, today, the familiar mechanisms of social control—money, status, patriotic and religious symbols—are losing their force for a population (particularly the new generation) which has learned to be intensely self-conscious and simultaneously worldly; to expect love and self-fulfillment; to quest for freedom and autonomy. All this learning is a consequence of increasingly sophisticated educational opportunities, of increasingly liberated standards in family and interpersonal relations, of affluence itself. Against this learning, the classic patterns of elite rule, bureaucratic authority, managerial manipulation, and class domination will have a difficult time sustaining themselves.

The virtue of "participatory democracy," as a basis for a new politics, is that it enables these new sources of social tension to achieve political expression. Participatory democracy symbolizes the restoration of personal freedom and interpersonal community as central political and social issues. It is not the end of ideology; it is a new beginning.

PART FOUR

■ THE AMERICAN
RESPONSE

INTRODUCTION

We keep our balance in the face of challenges not only by upholding ideological positions but also by designing political institutions. Institutions, too, may be seen as resulting from human inventiveness. True, they are so much the consequence of trivial decisions and minute adjustments, of muddling through by trial and error, that we scarcely think of them as having been fashioned by men at all. As we have built pyramids, constructed dams, defended cities, or maintained communications in a complex society, we have considered the political arrangements supporting these activities as so natural that it has been hard to realize how much rational deliberation (and cunning) went into their design. The fact is, of course, that they have not grown spontaneously. The medieval university, the modern nation-state, the structure of the Teamsters Union, the two party system, the United Nations, the Bureau of the Budget—none of these intricate contrivances was simply given by nature. All of them may be seen as political inventions, more or less successfully satisfying desires and meeting needs. All of them are more or less adequate responses to what men have perceived as crises.

To test how successfully various political systems have responded to crisis situations, we would ideally collect data about them and engage in systematic comparative analysis. This is, of course, no easy matter. If, for example, we wanted to identify the elements which failed to preserve the Weimar Republic in 1933, we should have to find a political system identical to it in all significant respects but one. (The one different element might be its social system,

151

its level of affluence, prior political experience, or the nature of its leadership.) And we should then have to note how effectively the system we use for purposes of experimental control responded to the same kind of pressure. Like Aristotle, we should have to collect constitutions; and unlike Aristotle, who had no computers to serve him, we should have to proceed with quantitative scientific analysis. We should thus learn about the capacity of different types of political systems for meeting challenges of varying degrees of intensity. Having knowledge of their survival capacity, we should know how stable they are.

Our analysis would not, however, enable us to know how just they are. Which one conforms most closely to our conception of a sound political order? To answer, we should have to apply the kind of norm which was stipulated in Part One and proceed somehow to measure the gap between stipulated ideal and observable reality.

Given the inordinate difficulties inherent in any effort to determine the stability *and* the merits of alternative regimes, it may be useful to turn to the American system of government. Here, at least, the issue of the stability of its central political institutions is not in doubt. It has succeeded in remaining stable despite the challenges posed by waves of immigrants, industrialization, urbanization, depression, domestic violence, and foreign war. Precisely because of its stability it allows us to raise questions about its merits. Seen from the perspective of a political order which maximizes authentic participation and prevents the imposition of any definitive creed, how successful is our own?

To provide an answer, we shall have to make an effort to see as much of the present system as we can bear without losing either our patience or nerve. Aware of the demands of an ideal political order, we shall have to confront our own and search out the pertinent facts—even such facts as are still labeled nonpolitical. It becomes relevant, accordingly, to inquire not only about the formal structure of government—the party system, the federal system, the three branches—but about the society which the structure was designed to serve. It becomes essential to distinguish between that part of the society which is educated, articulate, organized, and influential and that part which is undereducated, inarticulate, unaffiliated, and powerless. It becomes essential to take cognizance of *all* agencies which govern our lives, to be concerned with *all* public policy, whether it is made by administrative boards, business corporations, labor unions, trade or professional associations, or any combination of these. It becomes essential, furthermore, to take note of that part of society which is effectively integrated within organizations and governed by a self-perpetuating organizational leadership. Thus it should be instructive *first* to consider America's active public; *second,* to review how policy is enacted in the official channels of government; *third,* to note how official agencies have blended with nonofficial ones, creating a new public-private complex; *fourth,* to inquire about the power which organizations exercise over their own members; and *fifth,* to take account of the more or less visible Americans who exist outside the political system altogether.

It is especially appropriate for us to explore the character of the American system because it is extraordinarily complex and yet so evidently the result of rational deliberation. That is, it is elaborate enough to reveal the ramifications of an effort to govern a large-scale, industrialized, modernized society, and it was very obviously designed to achieve well-identified objectives. In fact, its distinctively modern quality is the wholly explicit way in which it was conceived. Those who laid out the Constitution—and it is surely significant that we think of them as draftsmen—went about their business in an extraordinarily self-conscious fashion. They thought of political institutions as mechanisms they could rationally design to satisfy human needs. To be sure, they knew that they were not starting from scratch. They brought with them a tradition of common law, habits of civility, and respect for constitutional order. Nevertheless, they properly thought of their constitutional design as a work quite deliberately created by them.

They created it, above all, to cope with human nature as they conceived it. It was meant to discipline men who, when left merely to their own devices, would be driven to destroy one another in a brutal struggle for power. Because men were not angels, as James Madison put it, a government would have to be empowered to keep them in line and would in turn have to be controlled to keep it from becoming oppressive. Beyond this, it was essential for the state to meet whatever foreign or domestic threats might arise.

Clearly the drafters of the Constitution did not seek to blueprint a utopian society. They were content to plan for one in which no specific group would oppress others. They were not intent on establishing a regime that was in some sense absolutely just, but merely one in which no partisan definition of justice could prevail. They conceived of the Constitution, as John Marshall was to affirm, as "intended to endure for ages to come, and, consequently, to be adapted to the various crises of human affairs." It was to remain a flexible instrument. And so that no special interest might prevail, all fanatics and visionaries were to be checked either by denying them office (and the power to make law) or by opposing them with counterpressures within the government. Ambition, Madison wrote, was to counteract ambition. Contained by this governmental framework, Americans were expected to pursue their diverse ends.

And so they have. Americans—most of them most of the time—have sought to realize a welter of private interests and to enlist their government in doing so. Again and again, as they succeeded in establishing some governmental agency to promote some special interest (usually in the name of the public interest), a countervailing agency would emerge. In the process, no one interest ever appeared to win out conclusively. There was to be not only a Department of Agriculture but also one of Commerce and one of Labor. Such governmental agencies—and, of course, the special policies they were designed to implement—may initially have been really expected to achieve the specific ideals entertained by the private group behind the agency. But in practice, each pressure group managed to compromise and acknowledge the demands of competing ones. It always seemed more important to preserve the constitutional system than to uphold a principle—a Civil War proving to be an exception. No group in America, it would seem, has ever been able to have its way altogether. Some special interest might win out in the House of Representatives, only to be curbed by the Senate, the President, the federal courts, or perhaps administrators who felt free to deflect the impact of the law.

Yet various political analysts have raised the question whether the prevailing constitutional system has not actually worked in an unjustifiably discriminatory fashion. They claim that although no one group has ever prevailed over its competitors, one specific *category* of groups nevertheless did. What is their argument? They concede that we may, indeed, have continuously adapted the Constitution to changing needs, accepting a two party system, new regional governments (such as the Tennessee Valley Authority), new private-public organizations (like the Business Council or the Communications Satellite Corporation), and an entire fourth branch of government ranging from state boards of health to the Interstate Commerce Commission. Furthermore, we may have passed legislation and promulgated administrative rules which satisfied the groups that were active in the American political arena. And yet, so it has been contended, our governmental institutions and our political behavior may still not be an adequate response to the challenges which confront us. The reason is that our institutions—our very political style—are responses, not to all that is needed, but only to that which is believed to be needed by that cluster of groups best categorized as well-established, articulate, active, and influential. To note that these groups (dramatically labeled The Power Elite by C. Wright Mills) make public policy is not to demonstrate that they blatantly intervene in the policy-making process so as to exercise the ultimate power to make the big public decisions of war and peace or tax cuts and tax hikes. But it implies, as least, that they decide on policies which pervasively discipline our work and leisure by limiting the range of alternatives open to us, whether in education, transportation, housing, medical care, or television programming. Accepting the view of the political order offered in Part One, we should see the policies effective in these fields as *public* policies. But if such policies are, in fact, responses to the interests of but *one* category of groups, where does this leave the rest of society? Where does this leave the public interest?

The force of this question is certain to give point to the study of the American political system—*any* political system. Our inquiry should acquire a special meaning as we ask about the adequacy of American political institutions and speculate about alternative mechanisms and conventions might make them more adequate.

Our test of adequacy, it is worth noting, is not only the ideal political order defined in Part One of this volume but also the objectives of those who framed the Constitution. For them, as for us, a political system was desirable if it combined stability with an ongoing commitment to policies that are hospitable to new impulses, new visions, new styles of life—policies that lead to the inclusion of the greatest possible diversity of interests, including barely visible ones at what is literally the frontier.

In the light of this standard, we can persist in asking to what extent the American political system is capable of coping with challenges that arise on its periphery, that grow out of grievances which find no legitimate expression within it, that come from dispossessed, frustrated, immature, and disaffected parts of the population. Regarding ourselves as no less free and inventive than preceding generations, we, too, can adapt the Constitution to the needs of the times, even if our needs are manifest only in underdeveloped areas at the fringe of our political system.

☐ *The Governors*

22 THE STRUCTURE OF POWER IN AMERICAN SOCIETY*

■ *C. Wright Mills*

I

Power has to do with whatever decisions men make about the arrangements under which they live and about the events which make up the history of their times. Events that are beyond human decision do happen; social arrangements do change without benefit of explicit decision. But insofar as such decisions are made, the problem of who is involved in making them is the basic problem of power. Insofar as they could be made, but are not, the problem becomes who fails to make them?

We cannot today merely assume that in the last resort men must always be governed by their own consent. For among the means of power which now prevail is the power to manage and to manipulate the consent of men. That we

*A draft of this lecture was presented at a residential week end at the Beatrice Webb House, Surrey, on March 2, 1957; and at the University of Frankfurt on May 3, 1957. A more detailed exposition of the general argument, as well as documentation, will be found in *The Power Elite* (New York: Oxford University Press, 1956).

From C. Wright Mills, "The Structure of Power in American Society," *British Journal of Sociology,* IX (March, 1958), 29–41. Reprinted by permission of the Estate of C. Wright Mills.

do not know the limits of such power, and that we hope it does have limits, does not remove the fact that much power today is successfully employed without the sanction of the reason or the conscience of the obedient.

Surely nowadays we need not argue that, in the last resort, coercion is the "final" form of power. But then, we are by no means constantly at the last resort. Authority (power that is justified by the beliefs of the voluntary obedient) and manipulation (power that is wielded unbeknown to the powerless) must also be considered, along with coercion. In fact, the three types must be sorted out whenever we think about power.

In the modern world, we must bear in mind, power is often not so authoritative as it seemed to be in the medieval epoch: ideas which justify rulers no longer seem so necessary to their exercise of power. At least for many of the great decisions of our time—especially those of an international sort—mass "persuasion" has not been "necessary"; the fact is simply accomplished. Furthermore, such ideas as are available to the powerful are often neither taken up nor used by them. Such ideologies usually arise as a response to an effective debunking of power; in the United States such opposition has not been effective enough recently to create the felt need for new ideologies of rule.

There has, in fact, come about a situation in which many who have lost faith in prevailing loyalties have not acquired new ones and so pay no attention to politics of any kind. They are not radical, not liberal, not conservative, not reactionary. They are inactionary. They are out of it. If we accept the Greek's definition of the idiot as an altogether private man, we must conclude that many American citizens are now idiots. And I should not be surprised, although I do not know, if there were not some such idiots even in Germany. This—and I use the word with care—this spiritual condition seems to me the key to many modern troubles of political intellectuals, as well as the key to much political bewilderment in modern society. Intellectual "conviction" and moral "belief" are not necessary, in either the rulers or the ruled, for a ruling power to persist and even to flourish. So far as the role of ideologies is concerned, their frequent absences and the prevalence of mass indifference are surely two of the major political facts about the Western societies today.

How large a role any explicit decisions do play in the making of history is itself a historical problem. For how large that role may be depends very much on the means of power that are available at any given time in any given society. In some societies, the innumerable actions of innumerable men modify their milieus and so gradually modify the structure itself. These modifications—the course of history—go on behind the backs of men. History is drift, although in total "men make it." Thus, innumerable entrepreneurs and innumerable consumers by ten thousand decisions per minute may shape and reshape the free-market economy. Perhaps this was the chief kind of limitation Marx had in mind when he wrote, in *The 18th Brumaire,* "Men make their own history, but they do not make it just as they please; they do not make it under circumstances chosen by themselves."

But in other societies—certainly in the United States and in the Soviet Union today—a few men may be so placed in the structure that by their decisions they modify the milieus of many other men and in fact nowadays the structural conditions under which most men live. Such elites of power also make history under circumstances not chosen altogether by themselves; yet, compared with other men, and compared with other periods of world history, these circumstances do, indeed, seem less limiting.

I should contend that "men are free to make history," but that some men are indeed much freer than others. For such freedom requires access to the means of decision and of power by which history can now be made. It has not always been so made; but in the later phases of the modern epoch it is. It is with reference to this epoch that I am contending that if men do not make history, they tend increasingly to become the utensils of history makers as well as the mere objects of history.

The history of modern society may readily be understood as the story of the enlargement and the centralization of the means of power—in economic, in political, and in military institutions. The rise of industrial society has involved these developments in the means of economic production. The rise of the nation-state has involved similar developments in the means of violence and in those of political administration.

In the Western societies, such transformations have generally occurred gradually, and many cultural traditions have restrained and shaped them. In most of the Soviet societies, they are happening very rapidly, indeed, and without the great discourse of Western civilization, without the Renaissance and without the Reformation, which so greatly strengthened and gave political focus to the idea of freedom. In those societies, the enlargement and the co-ordination of all the means of power have occurred more brutally, and from the beginning under tightly centralized authority. But in both types, the means of power have now become international in scope and similar in form. To be sure, each of them has its own ups and downs; neither is as yet absolute; how they are run differs quite sharply.

Yet so great is the reach of the means of violence, and so great the economy required to produce and support them, that we have in the immediate past witnessed the consolidation of these two world centers, either of which dwarfs the power of Ancient Rome. As we pay attention to the awesome means of power now available to quite small groups of men we come to realize that Caesar could do less with Rome than Napoleon with France; Napoleon less with France than Lenin with Russia. But what was Caesar's power at its height compared with the power of the changing inner circles of Soviet Russia and the temporary administrations of the United States? We come to realize—indeed, they continually remind us—how a few men have access to the means by which in a few days continents can be turned into thermonuclear wastelands. That the facilities of power are so enormously enlarged and so decisively centralized surely means that the powers of quite small groups of men, which we may call elites, are now of literally inhuman consequence.

My concern here is not with the international scene, but with the United States in the middle of the twentieth century. I must emphasize "in the middle of the twentieth century" because in our attempt to understand any society we come upon images which have been drawn from its past and which often confuse our attempt to confront its present reality. That is one minor reason why history is the shank of any social science: we must study it if only to rid ourselves of it. In the United States, there are, indeed, many such images, and usually they have to do with the first half of the nineteenth century. At that time the economic facilities of the United States were very widely dispersed and subject to little or to no central authority.

The state watched in the night, but was without decisive voice in the day.

One man meant one rifle, and the militia were without centralized orders.

Any American as old-fashioned as I can only agree with R. H. Tawney that "whatever the future may contain, the past has shown no more excellent social order than that in which the mass of the people were the masters of the holdings which they ploughed and the tools with which they worked, and could boast . . . 'It is a quietness to a man's mind to live upon his own and to know his heir certain.' "

But then we must immediately add: all that is of the past and of little relevance to our understanding of the United States today. In this society three broad levels of power may now be distinguished. I shall begin at the top and move downward.

II

The power to make decisions of national and international consequence is now so clearly seated in political, military, and economic institutions that other areas of society seem off to the side and, on occasion, readily subordinated to these. The scattered institutions of religion, education, and family are increasingly shaped by the big three, in which history-making decisions now regularly occur. Behind this fact there is all the push and drive of a fabulous technology; for these three institutional orders have incorporated this technology and now guide it, even as it shapes and paces their development.

As each has assumed its modern shape, its effects on the other two have become greater, and the traffic between the three has increased. There is no longer, on the one hand, an economy, and, on the other, a political order, containing a military establishment unimportant to politics and to money-making. There is a political economy numerously linked with military order and decision. This triangle of power is now a structural fact, and it is the key to any understanding of the higher circles in America today. For as each of these domains has coincided with the others, as decisions in each have become broader, the leading men of each—the high military, the corporation executives, the political directorate—have tended to come together to form the power elite of America.

The political order, once composed of several dozen states with a weak federal center, has become an executive apparatus which has taken up into itself many powers previously scattered, legislative as well as administrative, and which now reaches into all parts of the social structure. The long-time tendency of business and government to become more closely connected has since World War II reached a new point of explicitness. Neither can now be seen clearly as a distinct world. The growth of executive government does not mean merely the "enlargement of government" as some kind of autonomous bureaucracy: under American conditions, it has meant the ascendency of the corporation man into political eminence. Already during the New Deal, such men had joined the political directorate; as of World War II they came to dominate it. Long involved with government, now they have moved into quite full direction of the economy of the war effort and of the postwar era.

The economy, once a great scatter of small productive units in somewhat automatic balance, has become internally dominated by a few hundred corporations, administratively and politically interrelated, which together hold the keys to economic decision. This economy is at once a permanent war economy and a private corporation economy. The most important relations of the corporation to the state now rest on the coincidence between military and corporate interests, as defined by the military and the corporate rich and accepted by politicians and public. Within the elite as a whole, this coincidence of military domain and corporate realm strengthens both of them and further subordinates the merely political man. Not the party politician, but the corporation executive, is now more likely to sit with the military to answer the question: what is to be done?

The military order, once a slim establishment in a context of civilian distrust, has become the largest and most expensive feature of government; behind smiling public relations, it has all the grim and clumsy efficiency of a great and sprawling bureaucracy. The high military have gained decisive political and economic relevance. The seemingly permanent military threat places a premium on them, and virtually all political and economic actions are now judged in terms of military definitions of reality: the higher military have ascended to a firm position in the power elite of our time.

In part, at least, this is a result of a historical fact, pivotal for the years since 1939: the attention of the elite has shifted from domestic problems—centered in the thirties around slump—to international problems—centered in the forties and fifties around war. By long historical usage, the government of the United States has been shaped by domestic clash and balance; it does not have suitable agencies and traditions for the democratic handling of international affairs. In considerable part, it is in this vacuum that the power elite has grown.

To understand the unity of this power elite, we must pay attention to the psychology of its several members in their respective milieus. Insofar as the power elite is composed of men of similar origin and education, of similar career and style of life, their unity may be said to rest on the fact that they are of similar social type and to lead to the fact of their easy intermingling. This kind of unity reaches its frothier apex in the sharing of that prestige which is to be had in the world of the celebrity. It achieves a more solid culmination in the fact of the interchangeability of positions between the three dominant institutional orders. It is revealed by considerable traffic of personnel within and between these three, as well as by the rise of specialized go-betweens as in the new-style high-level lobbying.

Behind such psychological and social unity are the structure and the mechanics of those institutional hierarchies over which the political directorate, the corporate rich, and the high military now preside. How each of these hierarchies is shaped and what relations it has with the others determine in large part the relations of their rulers. Were these hierarchies scattered and disjointed, then their respective elites might tend to be scattered and disjointed; but if they have many interconnections and points of coinciding interest, then their elites tend to form a coherent kind of grouping. The unity of the elite is not a simple reflection of the unity of institutions, but men and institutions are always related; that is why we must understand the elite today in connection with such institutional trends as the development of a permanent war establishment, alongside a privately incorporated economy, inside a virtual political vacuum. For the men at the top have been selected and formed by such institutional trends.

Their unity, however, does not rest solely on psychological similarity and social intermingling nor entirely on the structural blending of commanding positions and common interests. At times it is the unity of a more explicit co-ordination.

To say that these higher circles are increasingly co-ordinated, that this is *one* basis of their unity, and that at times—as during open war—such co-ordination is quite willful, is not to say that the co-ordination is total or continuous or even that it is very surefooted. Much less is it to say that the power elite has emerged as the realization of a plot. Its rise cannot be adequately explained in any psychological terms.

Yet we must remember that institutional trends may be defined as opportunities by those who occupy the command posts. Once such opportunities are recognized, men may avail themselves of them. Certain types of men from each of these three areas, more farsighted than others, have actively promoted the liaison even before it took its truly modern shape. Now more have come to see that their several interests can more easily be realized if they work together, in informal as well as in formal ways, and accordingly they have done so.

The idea of the power elite is, of course, an interpretation. It rests on and it enables us to make sense of major institutional trends, the social similarities and psychological affinities of the men at the top. But the idea is also based on what has been happening on the middle and lower levels of power, to which I now turn.

III

There are, of course, other interpretations of the American system of power. The most usual is that it is a moving balance of many competing interests. The image of balance, at least in America, is derived from the idea of the economic market: in the nineteenth century, the balance was thought to occur between a great scatter of individuals and enterprises; in the twentieth century, it is thought to occur between great interest blocs. In both views, the politician is the key man of power because he is the broker of many conflicting powers.

I believe that the balance and the compromise in American society—the "countervailing powers" and the "veto groups," of parties and associations, of strata and unions—must now be seen as having mainly to do with the middle levels of power. It is these middle levels that the political journalist and the scholar of politics are most likely to understand and to write about—if only because, being mainly middle class themselves, they are closer to them. Moreover, these levels provide the noisy content of most "political" news and gossip; the images of these levels are more or less in accord with the folklore of how democracy works; and, if the master image of balance is accepted, many intellectuals, especially in their current patrioteering, are readily able to satisfy such political optimism as they wish to feel. Accordingly, liberal interpretations of what is happening in the United States are now virtually the only interpretations that are widely distributed.

But to believe that the power system reflects a balancing society is, I think, to confuse the present era with earlier times and to confuse its top and bottom with its middle levels.

By the top levels, as distinguished from the middle, I intend to refer, first of all, to the scope of the decisions that are made. At the top today, these decisions have to do with all the issues of war and peace. They have also to do with slump and poverty which are now so very much problems of international scope. I intend also to refer to whether or not the groups that struggle politically have a chance to gain the positions from which such top decisions are made and, indeed, whether their members do usually hope for such top national command. Most of the competing interests which make up the clang and clash of American politics are strictly concerned with their slice of the existing pie. Labor unions, for example, certainly have no policies of an international sort other than those which given unions adopt for the strict economic protection of their members. Neither do farm organizations. The actions of such middle-level powers may indeed have consequence for top-level policy; certainly at times they hamper these policies. But they are not truly concerned with them, which means of course, that their influence tends to be quite irresponsible.

The facts of the middle levels may in part be understood in terms of the rise of the power elite. The expanded and centralized and interlocked hierarchies over which the power elite preside have encroached upon the old balance and relegated it to the middle level. But there are also independent developments of the middle levels. These, it seems to me, are better understood as an affair of intrenched and provincial demands than as a center of national decision. As such, the middle level often seems much more of a stalemate than a moving balance.

The middle level of politics is not a forum in which there are debated the big decisions of national and international life. Such debate is not carried on by nationally responsible parties representing and clarifying alternative policies. There are no such parties in the United States. More and more, fundamental issues never come to any point or decision before Congress, much less before the electorate in party campaigns. In the case of Formosa, in the spring of 1955, Congress abdicated all debate concerning events and decisions which surely bordered on war. The same is largely true of the 1957 crisis in the Middle East. Such decisions now regularly by-pass Congress and are never clearly focused issues for public decision.

The American political campaign distracts attention from national and international issues, but that is not to say that there are no issues in these campaigns. In each district and state, issues are set up and watched by organized interests of sovereign local importance. The professional politician is, of course, a party politician, and the two parties are semifeudal organizations: they trade patronage and other favors for votes and for protection. The differences between them, so far as national issues are concerned, are very narrow and very mixed up. Often each seems to be forty-eight parties, one to each state; and accordingly, the politician as campaigner and as congressman is not concerned with national party lines, if any are discernible. Often he is not subject to any effective national party discipline. He speaks for the interests of his own constituency, and he is concerned with national issues only insofar as they affect the interests effectively organized there, and hence his chances of re-election. That is why, when he does speak of national matters, the result is so often such an empty rhetoric. Seated in his sovereign locality, the politician is not at the national summit. He is on and of the middle levels of power.

Politics is not an arena in which free and independent organizations truly connect the lower and middle levels of society with the top levels of decision. Such organizations are not an effective and major part of American life today. As more people are drawn into the political arena, their associations become mass in scale, and the power of the individual becomes dependent on them; to the extent that they are effective, they have become larger, and to that extent they have become less accessible to the influence of the individual. This is a central fact about associations in any mass society: it is of most consequence for political parties and for trade unions.

In the thirties, it often seemed that labor would become an insurgent power independent of corporation and state. Organized labor was then emerging for the first time on an American scale, and the only political sense of direction it needed was the slogan "Organize the unorganized." Now, without the mandate of the slump, labor remains without political direction. Instead of economic and political struggles, it has become deeply entangled in administrative routines with both corporation and state. One of its major functions, as a vested interest of the new society, is the regulation of such irregular tendencies as may occur among the rank and file.

There is nothing, it seems to me, in the make-up of the current labor leadership to allow us to expect that it can or that it will lead, rather than merely react. Insofar as it fights at all, it fights over a share of the goods of a single way of life, and not over that way of life itself. The typical labor leader in the United States today is better understood as an adaptive creature of the main business drift than as an independent actor in a truly national context.

The idea that this society is a balance of powers requires us to assume that the units in balance are of more or less equal power and that they are truly independent of one another. These assumptions have rested, it seems clear, on the historical importance of a large and independent middle class. In the latter nineteenth century and during the Progressive Era, such a class of farmers and small businessmen fought politically—and lost—their last struggle for a paramount role in national decision. Even then, their aspirations seemed bound to their own imagined past.

This old, independent middle class has, of course, declined. On the most generous count, it is now 40 per cent of the total middle class (at most 20 per cent of the total labor force). Moreover, it has become politically as well as economically dependent on the state, most notably in the case of the subsidized farmer.

The *new* middle class of white-collar employees is certainly not the political pivot of any balancing society. It is in no way politically unified. Its unions, such as they are, often serve merely to incorporate it as hanger-on of the labor interest. For a considerable period, the old middle class *was* an independent base of power; the new middle class cannot be. Political freedom and economic security *were* anchored in small and independent properties; they are not anchored in the worlds of the white-collar job. Scattered property holders were economically united by more or less free markets; the jobs of the new middle class are integrated by corporate authority. Economically, the white-collar classes are in the same condition as wage workers; politically, they are in a worse condition, for they are not organized. They are no vanguard of historic change; they are at best a rearguard of the welfare state.

The agrarian revolt of the nineties, the small-business revolt that has been more or less continuous since the eighties, the labor revolt of the thirties— each of these has failed as an independent movement which could countervail against the powers that be; they have failed as politically autonomous third parties. But they have succeeded, in varying degree, as interests vested in the expanded corporation and state; they have succeeded as parochial interests seated in particular districts, in local divisions of the two parties, and in Congress. What they would become, in short, are well-established features of the *middle* levels of balancing power, on which we may now observe all those strata and interests which in the course of American history have been defeated in their bids for top power or which have never made such bids.

Fifty years ago many observers thought of the American state as a mask behind which an invisible government operated. But nowadays, much of what was called the old lobby, visible or invisible, is part of the quite visible government. The "governmentalization of the lobby" has proceeded in both the legislative and the executive domain, as well as between them. The executive bureaucracy becomes not only the center of decision but also the arena in which major conflicts of power are resolved or denied resolution. "Administration" replaces electoral politics; the maneuvering of cliques (which include leading senators as well as civil servants) replaces the open clash of parties.

The shift of corporation men into the political directorate has accelerated the decline of the politicians in Congress to the middle levels of power; the formation of the power elite rests in part on this relegation. It rests also on the semiorganized stalemate of the interests of sovereign localities, into which the legislative function has so largely fallen; on the virtually complete absence of a civil service that is a politically neutral, but politically relevant, depository of brain power and executive skill; and on the increased official secrecy behind which great decisions are made without benefit of public or even of congressional debate.

IV

There is one last belief on which liberal observers everywhere base their interpretations and rest their hopes. That is the idea of the public and the associated idea of public opinion. Conservative thinkers, since the French Revolution, have, of course, Viewed With Alarm the rise of the public, which they have usually called the masses, or something to that effect. "The populace is sovereign," wrote Gustave Le Bon, "and the tide of barbarism mounts." But surely those who have supposed the masses to be well on their way to triumph are mistaken. In our time, the influence of publics or of masses in political life is in fact decreasing, and such influence as on occasion they do have tends, to an unknown but increasing degree, to be guided by the means of mass communication.

In a society of publics, discussion is the ascendant means of communication, and the mass media, if they exist, simply enlarge and animate this discussion, linking one face-to-face public with the discussions of another. In a mass society, the dominant type of communication is the formal media, and publics become mere markets for these media: the "public" of a radio program consists of all those exposed to it. When we try to look upon the United States today as a society of publics, we realize that it has moved a considerable distance along the road to the mass society.

In official circles, the very term "the public" has come to have a phantom meaning, which dramatically reveals its eclipse. The deciding elite can identify some of those who clamor publicly as "Labor," others as "Business," still others as "Farmer." But these are not the public. "The public" consists of the unidentified and the nonpartisan in a world of defined and partisan interests. In this faint echo of the classic notion, the public is composed of these remnants of the old and new middle classes whose interests are not explicitly defined, organized, or clamorous. In a curious adaptation, "the public" often becomes, in administrative fact, "the disengaged expert," who, although ever so well informed, has never taken a clear-cut and public stand on controversial issues. He is the "public" member of the board, the commission, the committee. What "the public" stands for, accordingly, is often a vagueness of policy (called "open-mindedness"), a lack of involvement in public affairs (known as "reasonableness"), and a professional disinterest (known as "tolerance").

All this is, indeed, far removed from the eighteenth-century idea of the public of public opinion. That idea parallels the economic idea of the magical market. Here is the market composed of freely competing entrepreneurs; there is the public composed of circles of people in discussion. As price is the result of anonymous, equally weighted, bargaining individuals, so public opinion is the result of each man's having thought things out for himself and then contributing his voice to the great chorus. To be sure, some may have more influence on the state of opinion than others, but no one group monopolizes the discussion or by itself determines the opinions that prevail.

In this classic image, the people are presented with problems. They discuss them. They formulate viewpoints. These viewpoints are organized, and they compete. One viewpoint "wins out." Then the people act on this view, or their representatives are instructed to act it out, and this they promptly do.

Such are the images of democracy which are still used as working justifications of power in America. We must now recognize this description as more a fairy tale than a useful approximation. The issues that now shape man's fate are neither raised nor decided by any public at large. The idea of a society that is at bottom composed of publics is not a matter of fact; it is the proclamation of an ideal, and as well the assertion of a legitimation masquerading as fact.

I cannot here describe the several great forces in American society as well as elsewhere which have been at work in the debilitation of the public. I want only to remind you that publics, like free associations, can be deliberately and suddenly smashed, or they can more slowly wither away. But whether smashed in a week or withered in a generation, the demise of the public must be seen in connection with the rise of centralized organizations, with all their new means of power, including those of the mass media of distraction. These, we now know, often seem to expropriate the rationality and the will of the terrorized or—as the case may be—the voluntarily indifferent society of masses. In the more democratic process of indifference, the remnants of such publics as remain may only occasionally be intimidated by fanatics in search of "disloyalty." But regardless of that, they lose their will for decision because they do not possess the instruments for decision; they lose their sense of political belonging because they do not belong; they lose their political will because they see no way to realize it.

The political structure of a modern democratic state requires not only that such a public as is projected by democratic theorists exists but that it be the very forum in which a politics of real issues is enacted.

It requires a civil service that is firmly linked with the world of knowledge and sensibility and is composed of skilled men who, in their careers and in their aspirations, are truly independent of any private, which is to say, corporation, interests.

It requires nationally responsible parties which debate openly and clearly the issues which the nation, and indeed the world, now so rigidly confront.

It requires an intelligentsia, inside as well as outside the universities, who carry on the big discourse of the Western world and whose work is relevant to and influential among parties and movements and publics.

And it certainly requires, as a fact of power, that there be free associations standing between families and smaller communities and publics, on the one hand, and the state, the military, the corporation, on the other. For unless these do exist, there are no vehicles for reasoned opinion, no instruments for the rational exertion of public will.

Such democratic formations are not now ascendant in the power structure of the United States, and accordingly the men of decision are not men selected and formed by careers in such associations and by their performance before such publics. The top of modern American society is increasingly unified and often seems willfully co-ordinated: at the top there has emerged an elite whose power probably exceeds that of any small group of men in world history. The middle levels are often a drifting set of stalemated forces: the middle does not link the bottom with the top. The bottom of this society is politically fragmented and, even as a passive fact, increasingly powerless: at the bottom there is emerging a mass society.

These developments, I believe, can be correctly understood in terms of neither the liberal nor the Marxian interpretation of politics and history. Both these ways of thought arose as guidelines to reflection about a type of society which does not now exist in the United States. We confront there a new kind of social structure, which embodies elements and tendencies of all modern society, but in which they have assumed a more naked and flamboyant prominence.

That does not mean that we must give up the ideals of these classic political expectations. I believe that both have been concerned with the problem of rationality and of freedom: liberalism, with freedom and rationality as supreme facts about the individual; Marxism, as supreme facts about man's role in the political making of history. What I have said here, I suppose, may be taken as an attempt to make evident why the ideas of freedom and of rationality now so often seem so ambiguous in the new society of the United States of America.

23 OLIGARCHICAL RULE

■ *David B. Truman*

The effects of occupying managerial positions—whether elective or appointive—may be quite varied. They stem, however, from the specialization, the

From David Truman, *The Governmental Process* (New York: Knopf, 1951), pp. 143–146, 148–149, 154. © Copyright 1951 by Alfred A. Knopf, Inc. Reprinted by permission of the publisher.

"know-how," necessary in key positions in a hierarchy. Anyone who has observed a legislature in action will have noted how important to the effectiveness of a bloc is a knowledge of parliamentary tricks. The newcomer in such a setting is almost powerless unless he, too, learns how to operate the machinery. Tenure of such positions not only permits a tactical manipulative advantage but gives such individuals some control over the flow of ideas to the rank and file.

The effects on the development of an active minority of acquiring managing skills are particularly well illustrated by labor groups. Even at the local union level "the development of a bureaucracy seems almost inevitable irrespective of the philosophy or political outlook of the leadership," and local union leaders enjoy a wide discretion in matters of policy. At the more inclusive level of the international unions, the situation is more striking. As one close observer has put it: "The top executive of a national union exercises tremendous power—and the term 'tremendous' is used advisedly." [1] Such officials and their immediate associates, through their greater familiarity with the organization's affairs, through their power to name the membership of key committees, and through other advantages derived from their position, play a disproportionately large role in determining policy.[2] The situation is similar in a federated national group like the AFL. The Executive Council of that organization determines the major business to come before the annual convention; such business is largely transacted in committees led by members of the active minority. Millis and Montgomery indicate as fairly typical a convention of the AFL in which the chairmen of thirteen out of fourteen convention committees were either AFL vice-presidents or other major officers. They sum the matter up in the following terms: "Thus it is for the most part the voice of labor as interpreted by the Executive Council that becomes articulate in the legislation of the AFL. The policies of the Federation are essentially those of the official class." [3]

In the National Association of Manufacturers the paid staff constitutes only a segment of the active minority, but they are reported to have more than a little to do with molding objectives and formulating policy, owing to such factors as long tenure in office and knowledge of the affairs of the association. A key figure of this sort was the late James A. Emery, who was counsel and chief legislative representative of the NAM for thirty years; the late Walter B. Weisenburger was executive vice-president for nearly fifteen years; Noel Sargent has occupied various administrative positions, including that of manager of the industrial relations department and secretary of the association, since 1920.[4]

In the American Medical Association, as in the NAM, the active minority is made up partly of long-term holders of various elective and appointive positions and partly of its salaried administrators, many of whom have been in the same positions for long periods of time. Dr. Morris Fishbein, who in the eyes of many laymen was the AMA, served as the editor of its principal publication for nearly thirty years. The implications of such arrangements are fairly obvious.

For such men, work for organized medicine is a large part of their life, and for some it is their only career. . . . Secretaries, editors, and technicians develop skills which are useful primarily in "organized medicine" as such. It is natural and not wholly unrealistic that, to some commentators, they should appear themselves to be "organized medicine." [5]

The functions and power of such minorities become most apparent when they are used, not necessarily without reason, to resist either a change in long-established policy or the inclusion of new elements in the minority, or both. For example, a struggle has been carried on in the American Legion since 1945 over the inclusion of veterans of World War II among the major officers. Attempts to make a younger man National Commander have taken place at every postwar convention. One influential legionnaire has been quoted as saying: "After all, this Legion is a billion dollar corporation. You don't just throw something that big over to a bunch of inexperienced boys." [6] Despite the voting strength of the "boys," the elected National Commander is invariably the man groomed and named for the position by the active minority, known in Legion parlance as the kingmakers. . . .

Other examples could be given at length. In his New Jersey study McKean found in all the groups he studied that control lay in the hands of a small group of officers, among whom the paid officials were an important element. About fifteen directors actually governed the New Jersey State Chamber of Commerce; control of the Manufacturers Association of New Jersey was in the hands of its secretary and the other officers; an executive secretary controlled the New Jersey Taxpayers Association, allegedly with support from the railroads.[7] The position of the paid executive in many trade associations has already been alluded to. It is well summarized in a statement by the general manager of one such group to the effect that less than a dozen association secretaries "can very largely control the general thought and action of employers' associations of the country." [8] The board of directors and the paid staff are the principal source of program and policy for the Chamber of Commerce of the United States. Even in the Board of Temperance, Prohibition, and Morals of the Methodist Episcopal Church, Herring noted some years ago: "The pronouncements of a few men in a central office are . . . able to direct the thought and actions of a large church body." [9] . . .

Leadership is time-consuming, and only a few can afford to spend the necessary time without remuneration. Michels found the emergence of paid, professional leadership one of the signs of developing minority control; [10] and in part, this professionalized leadership is a product of the managerial skills, already discussed, that it develops. But these manipulative skills seem to be also a consequence of the professional leader's continuing preoccupation with the affairs of the organization. Even unpaid, nonprofessional leaders acquire such skills as a consequence of spending more time on, and gaining greater familiarity with, the group's activities than can the rank and file. Professionals can give most of their time to the group because they are paid for it. The nonprofessional leader gives the time that he can spare from the activities by which he secures his livelihood.

In many groups only those with personal financial security and success in the institution to which the association is peripheral can afford the time required of unpaid leaders. In many instances the consequence is a highly conservative leadership, since, because of their status, the leaders have most to lose by any change in existing arrangements. Thus in the Chamber of Commerce of the United States and the National Association of Manufacturers the segment of the active minority that is not included among the professional leaders and staff is quite naturally drawn from among men whose jobs permit their devoting considerable time to the activities of these groups. Indeed, major corporation executives, from the very nature of the positions they occupy, may find it desirable to engage in the activities of such associations. The leaders of most large corporations today carry an extensive responsibility for managing the company's relations with various outside groups, of which labor unions are only one example. Remembering the functions of the association in stabilizing such relations for individuals and subgroups similarly situated, we can understand why the heads of large companies can afford time for extensive participation in these associations.

The influence, in the American Medical Association, of the fact that unpaid leaders must be men of some leisure has been spelled out in considerable detail. A study of the principal elective bodies of the AMA over a period of fifteen years, and of several of the state societies, has indicated that specialists from the more urbanized areas have held positions of power in numbers out of all proportion to their numbers in the medical population as a whole. Those with long tenure (eight years or more) in their positions were especially likely to fall into this category. In accounting for this characteristic, Garceau observes:

A man must have some margin of wealth and leisure to leave his practice and attend conventions, to say nothing of serving on active operating committees, with trips to the state capital or to Chicago. Politics and the public office that goes with it take time; less it is true, in associational politics than in the politics of the state, but too much for a man in active general practice where substitutes are rivals and there may often, in fact, be no one to care for the community if the doctor goes off on a junket.[11]

The American Legion provides another illustration. As in the AMA, so in the Legion, membership on key committees tends to fall disproportionately to those who can afford the leisure necessary for frequent participation in group actions. The necessity for such leisure favors city specialists among the doctors; in the veterans' organization it encourages higher military officers, both active and retired. . . .[12]

Concerning the American scene Myrdal . . . observes:

Despite the democratic organization of American society with its emphasis upon liberty, equality of opportunity (with a strong leaning in favor of the underdog), and individualism, the idea of leadership pervades American thought and collective action. The demand for "intelligent leadership" is raised in all political camps, social and professional groups, and, indeed, in every collective activity centered around any interest or purpose—church, school, business, recreation, philanthropy, the campus life of a college, the entertaining of a group of visitors, the selling of patent medicine, the propagation of an idea or of an interest.[13]

To this he adds: "The other side of this picture is, of course, the relative inertia and inarticulateness of the masses in America."[14]

▪ Notes

1. Philip Taft, "Democracy in Trade Unions," *American Economic Review,* XXXVI, No. 2 (May, 1946), 361–363.
2. *Ibid.,* p. 364; cf. Harry A. Millis and Royal E. Montgomery, *Organized Labor* (New York: McGraw-Hill, 1945), p. 256; Arthur M. Ross, *Trade Union Wage Policy* (Berkeley: University of California Press, 1948), p. 41; Robert R. R. Brooks, *When Labor Organizes* (New York: McGraw-Hill, 1945), pp. 257–258.
3. Millis and Montgomery, *op. cit.,* p. 308.
4. Arthur S. Cleveland, "Some Political Aspects of Organized Industry" (unpublished doctoral dissertation, Harvard University, 1946), Chapter 4.
5. Oliver Garceau; *The Political Life of the American Medical Association* (Cambridge: Harvard University Press, 1941), p. 49. See also p. 25.
6. Quoted in Justin Gray, *The Inside Story of the Legion* (New York: Boni and Gaer, 1948), p. 171. For a good account of the line-up at the 1947 meeting, see the *New York Times,* August 27, 1947.
7. Dayton D. McKean, *Pressure on the Legislature of New Jersey* (New York: Columbia University Press, 1938), Chapter 4.
8. U.S. Senate, Subcommittee of the Committee on Education and Labor, *Hearings on Violations of Free Speech and Rights of Labor,* 75th Cong., 3d Sess. (1938), part 17, p. 7431.
9. Pendleton Herring, *Group Representative before Congress* (Baltimore: Johns Hopkins Press, 1929), p. 211.
10. Robert Michels, *Political Parties* (London: Jerrold and Sons, 1915), pp. 40 ff.
11. Garceau, *op. cit.,* p. 54. This mobility and leisure afforded by a favorable financial situation help to define the active minority in the American Library Association also. See Garceau, *The Public Library in the Political Process* (New York: Columbia University Press, 1949), Chapter 4.
12. Marcus Duffield, *King Legion* (New York: Cape and Smith, 1931), pp. 110–111.
13. Gunnar Myrdal, *An American Dilemma* (New York: Harper, 1944), p. 709.
14. *Ibid.,* p. 712.

☐ The Governed

24 THE GOVERNED CONSTITUENTS

- *Henry S. Kariel*

The paramount organizational form in which the processes and imperatives of industrialism define themselves in the United States is unquestionably the large-scale business corporation. What sort of an institution is it? How, within the immense physical, social, and psychological area it spans today, does it affect the rights of individuals to direct their lives? How does it stabilize and centralize the power to pursue diverse ends?

The answers to these questions are difficult not only because the modern business corporation fails to conform to some singular type—General Motors and H. J. Heinz, Sears, Roebuck and Safeway Stores all have different personalities—but also because its various types are always changing. Yet even though it is constantly transforming both itself and its public image, it is now being cast in a mold sufficiently well defined to enable students of society to consider it anew, to contemplate it as Madison contemplated the unratified system of states in a union under a constitution. . . .

By its techniques of government, whether harsh or gentle, the corporation defines not merely its own goals but those of outsiders as well. In so doing, it is gradually and persistently trying to bring under control the environment in which it lives. As its millions of day-to-day decisions take cumulative effect, it manages to reshape the physical foundations, the emotional dispositions, and, ultimately, the political ideology of the American community. The makers of corporate policy, by their *ad hoc* decisions, suggest what is painful and what is pleasurable, attach prestige to some forms of behavior and detach it from

From Harry S. Kariel, *The Decline of American Pluralism* (Stanford: Stanford University Press, 1961), pp. 27, 38–49, 51–55. © Copyright 1961 by the Board of Trustees of the Leland Stanford Junior University. Reprinted by the permission of the publisher.

171

others, and legislate the relative soundness of popular indulgences and deprivations. Above all, they are in the position to use their power to establish and
maintain an attitude of approval in those segments of the public whose interests
are assumed to be the same as the corporation's. From one point of view, first
articulated in 1949 in Harold J. Laski's *The American Democracy,* the various
publics surrounding the great industrial corporations are quite unconscious of
their interests; they are therefore apathetic, easily diverted, and readily directed
by a power elite which they cannot or will not influence. This view, however, is
incomplete. American corporations have obligingly responded to many of the
special interests with which they deal, at times not imposing what the customer
might accept; they have remained sensitive even to latent public opinion, at
times not charging what the market might bear; and they have accommodat-
ingly bent to the will of the national government, at times adjusting their
foreign policies to the dictates of American foreign policy.

To understand this kind of behavior—whether virtuous or merely prudent,
responsible or merely expedient—requires thinking of the corporation in non-
legal terms. It is misleading to think only of the managers on top and the host
of the managed at the bottom, to picture managerial decisions as flowing but
one way—down. More importantly and realistically, the corporation must be
seen as at least one group of economists has seen it right along: a far-flung,
working institution. Approached in this light, its boundaries are not set by
public laws or individual contracts; they range as far as the network of ties
which all involved interests habitually respect. From this expanded point of
view, it is possible to see how public policies privately enacted by the managers
of a few firms can effectively govern a set of major groups in society: owners,
employees, and consumers. Each of these groups might be considered in turn.

The classic exposition of the extent to which corporate management has
become immune to owner interest is still the study by Berle and Means.[1] In
detail, it shows how the evolution of the corporate system—which the authors
in 1932 expected to become "as all-embracing as was the feudal system in its
time"—involved the progressive separation of property ownership and managerial power. Because individual wealth (in the form of stocks and bonds)
tends to be dispersed, minorities can and do exercise corporate power. The
devices by which they retain control with relatively small investments are
familiar enough: pyramiding through holding companies, using nonvoting
stock and voting trusts, exploiting the proxy machinery, or simply exercising
control in those common situations in which no group of owners happens to
have a share large enough to outweigh that of the management.[2] Under
such conditions, the influence of owners on management decisions is negligible,
especially when shareholders are appeased by the steady returns (dividends of
about half of average earnings) they have learned to expect. Their legal rights,
formally guaranteed, become practically meaningless. As Robert Aaron
Gordon understated the facts in 1945,

By the nature of the case, the rank and file of stockholders cannot continuously
initiate or approve leadership decisions, nor can they exercise any continuous

co-ordinating function. Their participation . . . is limited to voting at stock-holders' meetings. The range of decisions open to them at these meetings is very narrow.[3]

Management necessarily initiates decisions, the stockholder "saying yes or no to proposals submitted to him." The obstacles in his way to opposing man-agement, while they can sometimes be overcome, are formidable. The organi-zation of factions, requiring the means to communicate with potentially dissi-dent stockholders, is expensive and difficult. "Viewed in this fashion," Gordon has concluded, "the proxy machinery is not so much a means of depriving the stockholder of his vote as an alternative to his doing nothing with his vote at all. The proxy machinery becomes a partial—and by no means completely satisfactory—substitute for complete disfranchisement." This is confirmed by later observations. As Berle was to attest in 1954, "When an individual invests capital in the large corporation, he grants to the corporate management all power to use that capital to create, produce, and develop, and he abandons all control over the product."[4] Management, favored by every legal presumption, is all the more unencumbered by the wishes of owners because, with the nota-ble exception of utility companies, it generates its own capital to plow back into the enterprise.[5] And when it is able, like Sears, Roebuck and Company, to depend on the trustees of its own pension trust fund to invest voting stock back into the very corporation whose employees make compulsory contribu-tions, there is no need for management to feel intimidated by the latent threat of individuals who might invest or withhold their savings. Berle has written:

A corporation like General Electric or General Motors which steadily builds its own capital does not need to submit itself and its operations to the judgment of the financial market. Power assumed to be brought under the review of banking and investment opinion a generation ago is now reviewed and checked chiefly by the conscience of its directors and managers.[6]

While equity owners tend to be passive and hence marginal to the self-replenishing enterprise, employees in production, maintenance, and manage-ment—including those working for suppliers and distributors—are its integral human material. They are properly the members of what is publicized as the corporate team.[7] They do not merely agree to work for the organization; they model themselves on provided criteria so as to belong to it. They become attached to the corporation by a fealty transcending the rational demands of legal documents or economic necessity. As members of industrial families serving the nation, they voluntarily live within the corporate realm, co-operating for their mutual advantage and united by a common interest. Their attachment as individuals is as free and unforced as that of the 26,000 firms (all with less than 500 employees) that General Motors boasts of supplying with goods and services. There may be occasional resistance, such as an attempt by an automobile dealer to appeal over the heads of his cor-poration to a committee of the United States Congress. Or there may be an occasional revolt by a supplier or a distributor. But to the extent that they are all linked to the corporate order, moving carefully and willingly within it, they come to identify themselves with it, realizing, as one president of Du Pont has calmly noted, that "they have something to conserve." [8] Thus the automobile dealers themselves have seen the wisdom of maintaining intimate relations with the manufacturers. At least the well-established, conservative dealers have sought to strengthen their ties with Detroit. Asking for "equality of competitive opportunity," they urged Congress in 1958 to by-pass the antitrust laws and stabilize their sales territories. Fighting a distribution system one of them likened to an oriental bazaar, they petitioned Congress to permit the manufacturers to penalize the nonprofessional upstart who makes deals and sells outside his own territory.[9] While such distributors may appear to be detached outsiders, they in fact constitute a voluntary fraternity of individuals jointly nourishing what they know to be their enterprise, faithfully and often proudly serving through generations.

At best, the corporation develops its own work force entirely. When it can, it schools its own executives by its own training programs. What is actually "its own" must be understood, however, in the broadest of terms. It employs the output of universities which, by responding not so much to direct business pressure as to diffuse but cumulatively significant student preferences, cannot help but tailor their faculties and curricula to satisfy vaguely anticipated corporate needs. Moreover, the potential members of corporate teams are not caught unaware when confronted by their new jobs. As one survey has made clear, they quite naturally groom themselves to become what the corporation desires, always on the lookout for helpful cues.[10]

When their alertness, displayed perhaps by acceptance of a "career-oriented summer job," has been rewarded by employment, they remain aware of the unspoken demands of the hierarchy of their institution. The institution, it is true, will provide them with genuine opportunities for advancement—indeed, with a surfeit of undefined ones. But an organization's internal looseness does not necessarily enlarge the freedom of the individual determined to move up. The task of orienting himself is merely added to his managerial duties. The very generosity of the organization is likely to make him sensitive to his peers and superiors, slowly turning conditional into compulsive loyalty.

Once adjusted, the executive finds it difficult to detach himself from his firm to join another. Of course, to gauge his value or respond to an itch to move, he may quietly offer himself to competing firms and thereby, in the fashion of automobile industry executives, manage to circulate, entering a seemingly new environment. There is, however, a specific penalty even for specious mobility: promotions tend to be made from within the firm. And long tenure has its rewards. The corporation has come a long way since, in the effort to control labor turnover, it first distributed free tulip bulbs and planting advice to the wives of production workers. Today, organizations captivate their members not only with decent salaries and agreeable working conditions; they also offer that host of schemes which, however hard for the individual to size up, specifically weds him to the corporation—plans for health and welfare, for sharing profits and purchasing stocks, for obtaining pensions and insurance, for supplementing unemployment benefits, for reducing the cost of moving, housing, travel, entertainment, and recreation. And at the higher levels, loyalty may be additionally secured by such emoluments as stock options and elastic accounts for private expenses. Thus as benefits accrue by virtue of membership, privileges are collectivized.

Nor is the rank and file left unadjusted. The reward for labor is fixed by well-synchronized decisions determining wage patterns which workers, for understandable reasons, cannot take part in formulating. It is the fully unionized giant firm which sets the pace in deciding the level and structure of wage rates. Negotiating on an industry-wide basis, its agreements tend to be made "at the expense of the real incomes enjoyed by workers in less favored industries, in less protected mercantile and white-collar employment, and in the low-income industry of agriculture."[11] Favorably situated power blocs, rather than begetting countervailing ones, are thus reinforced. They find themselves in a position to govern the economic standard of living of their memberships.

As an advancing technology makes jobs more demanding, as it requires the upgrading of production employees, and as economic and social distinctions between worker and bureaucrat consequently tend to fade, the opportunity to find fulfillment within the corporation opens up to the career worker no less than to the career bureaucrat. Encouraged to become involved in an expanding community, both are driven to use the corporation as a status-bestowing institution, as a point of reference for their values. Yet at the same time, they exercise no meaningful control over the forces which drive them, especially when they have uncritically permitted those forces to work within themselves. Management employees no less than workers are affected by decisions establishing dovetailed patterns which remain unchallenged and unassessed—patterns of leisure and work, of capital investment and personnel allocation, of education and character. These are legislated by corporate management, which feels impelled to define the expectations of the very individuals who own the enterprise and labor in it.

If owners and workers are engulfed by the corporation, what of the market where it meets the consumer? The free, competitive market in which the sovereign consumer rationally chooses between alternative goods and services is an ideal so remote from reality that deference to it remains only verbal. While the extent of corporate power over the market is certainly debatable, its presence is undeniable.

With their unchallenged power to capitalize on major innovations, to pool patents to exploit unexpected research results, to consign resources, to influence advertising media, and to control retail outlets, corporations are certainly not without power to regulate competition. Furthermore, they can employ the manifold forms of legitimate private or quasi-private price administration which mark especially the steel, textile, oil, and cement industries.

In its more subtle variants, corporate power affects the consumer not by rigging the market but by reaching him directly. The freedom of the large corporation to decide what kind and quality of product or service it will promote gives it a unique power first to confuse and then to straighten out its customers. By the process Schumpeter called "creative destruction," it may supply new products of greater comfort, convenience, or serviceability; but it also manages, as Bernard De Voto once observed, to build worse mouse-traps and then to force the world to beat pathways to its retail outlets. For large sectors of the economy, it imposes positive values on new goods and makes old ones not merely undesirable (which they may or may not be) but undesired. By dramatically portraying esteemed social groups as appalled by the old and gratified by the new, it provides the standards of seemly consumption. With the help of brand names, it plans well-marked routes of escape from the very anxieties it has created. In fact, it forces the adaptation of tastes even when one of its particular sales campaigns fails, even when the consumer moves on to a competitive product. For while he moves, the consumer nevertheless remains within that realm of values upheld by advertisement and consumer education.

What sellers and their advertisers establish is not a specific value standard to be rejected or shared by the purchaser, but a set of speciously alternative standards within a pervasive climate of consumer taste. It is a standard of taste to which, in practice, it is uncomfortable to take exception. More is involved, however, than offering the consumer goods whose values are rationally debatable; he is at the same time encouraged to believe, as he scurries about to register his preference at the retail outlet, that he exercises significant options.

The point here is emphatically not that some corporate elite rules autocratically, but rather that our basic commitment to unceasing productivity induces corporations to spend some twelve billion dollars annually on advertising (not to mention an incalculable amount for consumer education) in order to initiate the productive process. Thus corporations and consumers become thoroughly integrated through their joint commitment to productivity. All talk of the manipulators vs. the manipulated to the contrary, both parts become but complementary functions of a larger whole in which all find peace.

It is the corporation's widely accepted power to create preferences, coupled with its growing skill to appraise what the partially frozen market is likely to yield, which enables it to engage in those diffuse activities the gains and losses of which simply cannot be reflected on annual reports and balance sheets. No wonder, then, that corporate trustees are irresistibly driven to attempt to form a more perfect union, endeavoring to establish justice, to ensure domestic tranquillity, to provide for the common defense, to promote the general welfare, and, ultimately, to secure the blessings of liberty to ourselves and our posterity—endeavoring, in short, to invade, occupy, and govern the realm of human ends. Of course, the effort to secure community benefits and underwrite public virtue (rather than to increase dividends, raise salaries, or expand facilities) may also represent an attempt to maximize long-run profits. But the possibility of taking such an elastic view of profits suggests the need to shift the vocabulary away from economic to broadly political terms, to talk not of "profitable" public relations but of "beneficial" ventures pursued in an "altruistic" spirit so as to achieve what is morally "good" in obedience to right reason and sound ethical dictates.

There are innumerable manifestations of an attempt—still undesigned, fumbling, and reticent—to deal with a social system immeasurably larger than the one acknowledged by the rhetoric of early capitalism. Clarence B. Randall, in one of the less timid of the available pronouncements, has urged that businessmen participate in community affairs, that they lend-lease themselves to the national government (there saving "us more money in two years . . . than they possibly could by staying at their desks in our plants and offices"), that they become active in party politics, and that they vigorously support the higher learning in America.[12] As one report has it:

> Jersey Standard has kept up with the times, and recognized the structure and the obligations of the modern corporation. It is in part a moneymaking machine, but in greater part it is an economic agent of the community, responsible to the community. . . . A recent editorial in *The Lamp* states the company's philosophy: "If today's managers of private enterprise are to justify their positions, they must conceive their duties in broader terms than simply the production of goods. They must have a sense of public responsibility, and must assume active roles." [13]

In 1956 *Time* magazine claimed that "the average top executive spends up to one third of his time on community projects, expects his subordinates to follow his example."[14] A widespread interest in symphonies, art, architecture, community parks, and nontechnological research centers is but another manifestation of the enlarged vision of business.

More weighty, perhaps, is business activity in the field which most intimately and elusively shapes the character of a society: that of education. Rarely taking the crude form exposed by Veblen's *The Higher Learning in America,* rarely appearing as Charles E. Wilson's proposal to have the businessman define "goals of attitude, outlook, and knowledge" and "provide high policy guidance for the action-taking body of the college," it is more commonly concealed by corporation-supported charitable foundations. These, at least according to one student, have become increasingly important "in the determination of educational policy, the goals of research in all spheres, and the direction of thinking in international affairs." And as foundations are "increasingly becoming a by-product of the large business corporation, the latter can, to a significant extent, influence educational and cultural policy." [15] To the extent that industrial research is carried on within the private realm, which is well protected against infringements on its arsenal of patents, the speed and the direction of scientific and technological progress are quietly fixed by those who exercise corporate power.

Co-operating with the major organs of the national government and more or less peaceably disposed toward the leadership of the great labor unions, the corporate giants occupy a strategic economic position. Well-disciplined organizations with control of their material and financial resources, they have the means to promote not only their social but also their economic policies. Generously permitting smaller corporations and public governments at all levels to share a portion of their surplus, they constitute a formidable reservoir of public power. However sensitive to the aspirations of the groups that they govern, however inefficient their rule in practice, and however responsive to a government-endorsed national interest when it is virtually unanimous, they wield power in a stupendously large sector of our economic order. They determine the level and the distribution of national income. They direct the allocation of scare resources, and they decide the extent and the rate of technological and economic developments.[16] They fix the level and the conditions of employment,[17] the structure of wage rates, and the terms, tempo, and season of production not only for themselves but also for those who use their bargaining agreements as models. They decide which labor markets to exploit and which to reject.[18] And they control the quality of goods and services as well as the standards and quantities of consumption.

Insofar as corporate oligarchies effectively control industrial systems, and insofar as the systems manage to bring under their influence vast areas of the public, it is corporate oligarchies that control public life. As their environment remains at peace, they become secure; as the world outside becomes dependent, they become independent. Their law becomes *de facto* constitutional law; their economic behavior becomes statesmanship; their social conduct becomes public morality. The organizations they control emerge as self-maintaining political communities prospering in a social setting made ever more hospitable. Their professional duty becomes to govern well, to operate as self-appointed stewards, responsible but unaccountable, integrating a multitude of interests, not selfishly but for the sake of the enterprises they rule. Their systems are self-centered: once properly primed, they generate, replenish, and purify themselves. Above all, they provide their own validation, their own excuse for being. Ironically, they come to resemble the sovereign, conscience-burdened individuals in whose behalf John Locke vindicated the Glorious Revolution. . . .

The contemporary labor union, whether active in the business corporation or facing it from the outside, places the classical problems of governing men in a modern frame. As one of the most important organizational variants in American political pluralism, unions provide a fertile field in which to examine individual rights and obligations. Extending from the relatively autocratic Federation of Musicians to the relatively democratic Upholsterers Union, they raise problems of governmental centralization and decentralization, of membership participation and apathy of citizenship and subversion. . . .

In reaching their present dimensions, American unions were inevitably forced to develop tactics and organizational arrangements that would assure their survival. Somehow they had to respond to the potent antagonistic forces in their environment: to ideology, public law, and the sheer violence of business. Nor was the worker himself always the friend of organized labor. He could often afford, literally, to be indifferent; he could *feel* that he was free to move from plant to plant and from one social group to another. As unions sought to come to terms with these environmental forces, they naturally discarded practices that proved wasteful, and they became increasingly similar. They began to rationalize their affairs under a leadership which slowly had to become centralized. Labor leaders, unable to accept anything approaching pure democracy, yet encouraged by successes to abandon militancy, gradually lost their roles as heroic fighters. Initially tough and uncompromising, they were impelled to emerge as efficient co-ordinators. As such, it became their major task to keep their vast social machines together, forcing rival interests to work in unison; in attempting to maintain what was typically a conglomeration of power blocs, they were led to create relatively autonomous national offices which, in turn, were eventually to be linked with the AFL-CIO. Although the AFL-CIO can hardly be said to govern 180-odd nationals, it could insist, as George Meany did for the first time in 1957, on the expulsion of unsavory ones.

The obstacles to such internal consolidation have been considerable. The unions have had to absorb a stream of new members whose political education had been European and who, when they did not permit themselves to be infatuated by Horatio Alger, contentiously urged their organizations to fight on a broad front for social justice. Nevertheless, the organizational drift almost invariably obeyed Michels's iron law: what began as a movement to protect individual members from outsiders generally ended as one to protect the leadership from insiders. Not unexpectedly, the power to make decisions has come to reside in well-protected, self-perpetuating incumbents whose prestige and skill—backed by an extensive staff of professional attorneys, economists, statisticians, writers, and administrators—are such that the rank and file, perhaps gratefully unconcerned, only rarely challenges their word.[19]

It was never likely that union leaders would find it expedient to keep their organizations small and voluntary and thereby homogeneous. The advantages of large size and compulsory membership have always been evident, with heterogeneity and the consequent need to impose discipline a small price to pay. The involuntary nature of membership is no secret. "I don't know," James C. Petrillo has mused about the musician expelled from the union, "where he would get a job today. An expulsion is a very serious matter for a man who is making his living with his instrument." [20] What is more, voluntary departure is certainly inhibited when seniority may be lost and the accumulated benefits of unemployment, retirement, medical, and pension plans may be forfeited. The incentive to stick it out is consequently strong. Finally, unions have also become increasingly unwilling (or unable) to discriminate against applicants with unorthodox viewpoints, differing racial backgrounds, or great variations in education, skill, and age. Therefore the kind of homogeneous membership which had characterized the early craft union—and which had made it possible to identify the policy of the leaders with the wishes of the members— has clearly become a thing of the past.

While the large-scale, heterogeneous, and involuntary union has thus emerged, procedures for taking account of the various newly incorporated interests have not been welcomed. Oligarchies remain entrenched; the rank and file is kept in line; and a semblance of policy concensus is achieved either by straightforward coercion or by a more oblique engineering of consent, with slight concessions to voluntarism, parliamentarianism, and politics. These propositions are not hard to document.[21]

Hostility to intraunion politics is widespread and certainly understandable. Factional fights are bitter. And since they make for disunity, members are not likely to take issue with what was forcefully expressed in Philip Murray's address to the 1942 convention of the United Steelworkers:

> I do not want—as a matter of fact, I shall fight any attempt that is made to have little back room caucuses while this convention is going on. There is going to be one convention in the city of Cleveland and it is going to be held in this hall. We are not going to permit sharp practices and petty politics to be played in the Steelworkers. So if any of the boys are thinking right now of midnight sessions in strange places in the city of Cleveland, just begin to forget about it right now. There is going to be one convention. . . . That is the democratic way to do business.[22]

"If we started to divide up and run a Republican set of officers, a Democratic set, a communist set and something else," Harry Bridges frankly told his Longshoremen in 1947, "we would have one hell of a time."[23] What occurred in 1958 at the biennial convention of the Steelworkers is distinguished by its dramatic management not its uniqueness. Without naming his major opponent to presidential office, incumbent David J. McDonald asked 3,522 delegates to "rip this cancer out of your bowels through your own doing and don't leave it up to me." He did not have to point out that he was referring to one of the delegates, Donald Rarick, a local union president who had had enough support the previous year to cut into McDonald's majority. Actually, McDonald need not have worried, for Rarick had no base whatever for effective opposition. Not only did McDonald have an "administration" on his side—some 750 union employees prepared to lobby for him—but more important, as the incumbent he himself had the power to determine how his challenger might get a hearing. What President McDonald did, giving no advance warning, was to summon Delegate Rarick to his side on the speaker's platform. Ostentatiously tolerant, he then stopped the booing from the floor and asked that Rarick be given a chance. Although caught off balance, Rarick made an attempt to state his position. But McDonald had little trouble presenting his rebuttal and obtaining a solid majority to vote for trials to purge the rebel and his lieutenants.[24]

Legally, of course, a national convention ratifying such decisions is the supreme legislative organ. But a president who controls a convention's committees—especially a credentials committee able to screen out delegates unenthusiastic about the machine in power—effectively influences its behavior. He is in a position, not surprisingly, to secure the approval of his policies, to assure his own re-election, and to designate his associates and successors. He is the great allocator of the union's resources—its legal skill, its fighting power, its ability to reward and punish. Funds flow to him from locals which collect per capita taxes, initiation fees, reinstatement dues, and special assessments. Of course, not all locals are equally dependent. Yet wherever the president is empowered to grant or revoke local charters, to funnel the resources of his office to his adherents alone, local autonomy is necessarily a fiction—as was well illustrated by the case of the Teamsters in the 1950's. At best, locals become administrative agencies of the nationals. Paul Jacobs's comments on the relation between the president of the Teamsters and his organization are to the point:

> The president has "authority to interpret the Constitution and laws of the International Union and to decide all questions of law thereunder. . . ." He alone determines whether strike or lockout benefits will be paid. The bylaws of local unions are subject to his approval. He appoints and may remove all the international organizers. And the president appoints the four chairmen of the conferences, the most important informal power bases within the International. . . .
>
> Except to say that vice-presidents are members of the general executive board, the union's constitution is silent on their duties and responsibilities. In practice, an informal, reciprocal relationship of mutual protection and dependence exists between them and [President] Beck.[25]

His extensive appointive power gives the president the opportunity to absorb potential dissidents in his administration; and once absorbed, they are without a base on which to build their own reputations. Thus, even though a union president and his top officers, like those who govern the Amalgamated Meat Cutters and Butcher Workmen, might be legally responsible to both the national convention and an executive board, this means little if the members of the executive board serve without compensation and draw salaries because they fill positions to which the president has power to appoint them. In the United Mine Workers, this control has been even more forthright: the president simply appoints and removes board members. Such arrangements for leadership continuity are merely amplified when a union constitution—for example, that of the Hod Carriers, Building and Common Laborers—permits the membership, by referendum, to postpone holding a convention for as long as thirty years. Add to this the leadership's power to act as accuser as well as judge in disciplinary proceedings, and the union membership remains as little more than a massive organ of assent and affirmation.[26]

Union oligarchies, presuming to take full account of men whose purposes cross, transform these purposes into unified policies. They enforce harmony despite many real conflicts: between old workers and young workers, employed and unemployed members, those in competitive concerns and those in stable ones, those who want pensions and those who want pay increases, those who exercise union power and those who desire to. When the leadership deals with business concerns or addresses the community outside, it has no alternative. Although the interests spoken for are plural, the voice with which the union speaks must be singular. Thus every union policy effectively discriminates against some internal union interest. Every agreement circumscribes the lives of members: it creates and distributes their rights and their duties; it defines the nature and pace of work as well as the duration and locale of strikes.

▪ *Notes*

1. A. A. Berle, Jr., and Gardiner C. Means, *The Modern Corporation and Private Property* (New York: Commerce Clearing House, 1932), p. 9.

2. Less familiar is owner control by the use of foundations: "It is this peculiar circumstance—*retention of control*—which largely explains the emergence of family foundations as the dominant feature on the foundation scene today. Men who have built successful enterprises and seen the value of their equity swell have sought, naturally, to keep control within the family. They have accordingly established charitable family foundations, minimized their tax, enjoyed the satisfaction of promoting good works, and retained practically all but the dividend benefits of ownership. Such persons, it has been said, actually do not give away their property at all, but only the income thereon—though this is perhaps an overstatement." Note, *Virginia Law Review*, XXXIV (February, 1948), 182–201, 188.

3. Robert Aaron Gordon, *Business Leadership in the Large Corporation* (Washington: Brookings Institution, 1945), pp. 160–161. See also Joseph A. Livingston, *The American Stockholder* (Philadelphia: Lippincott, 1958).

4. A. A. Berle, Jr., *The 20th Century Capitalist Revolution* (New York: Harcourt, Brace, 1954), p. 30.

5. Thus in the ten years preceding 1954, retained earnings averaged 54 per cent of corporate profits after taxes. See Report of the President's Council of Economic Advisers, January, 1955, Table D-49; see also S. P. Dobrovolsky, *Corporate Income Retention, 1915–1943* (New York: National Bureau of Economic Research, 1951).

6. Berle, *The 20th Century Capitalist Revolution*, p. 41.

7. There is more specific material on membership in primitive folk societies, Greek city-states, medieval universities, or religious communities than there is on the relations between individuals and the modern corporation. See, however, C. Wright Mills's *White Collar* (New York: Oxford University Press, 1951) and *The Power Elite* (New York: Oxford University Press, 1956), William Whyte's *Is Anybody Listening?* (1952) and *The Organization Man* (New York: Simon and Schuster, 1956), and the work of such novelists as John P. Marquand. No less revealing are the occasional autobiographical works of apostates, such as T. K. Quinn's *Giant Business* (New York: Exposition Press, 1954) and Alan Harrington's *Life in the Crystal Palace* (New York: Knopf, 1959).

8. Quoted in *Time*, November 26, 1956, p. 98.

9. See Senate Committee on Interstate and Foreign Commerce, *Hearings on S. 3865*, June 23 and 24, 1958.

10. "The Crown Princes of Business," *Fortune*, XLVIII (October, 1953), 152 ff. See also "The Nine Hundred," *Fortune*, XLVI (November, 1952), 132 ff.

11. Mordecai Ezekiel, "Distribution of Gains from Rising Technical Efficiency in Progressing Economies," *American Economic Review, Papers and Proceedings*, XLVII (May, 1957), 361–373, 372.

12. See Clarence P. Randall, *A Creed for Free Enterprise* (Boston: Little, Brown, 1952), p. 83. See also "Corporations Make Politics Their Business," *Fortune*, LX (December, 1959), 100 ff.

13. Stuart Chase, *A Generation of Industrial Peace: Thirty Years of Labor Relations at Standard Oil Company (N.J.)* (New Jersey: Standard Oil Co., N.J., 1946), pp. 51–52.

14. "The New Conservatism: A Bold Creed for Modern Capitalism," *Time* (November 26, 1956), p. 98.

15. Wolfgang F. Friedman, "Corporate Power, Government by Private Groups, and the Law," *Columbia Law Review*, LVII (February, 1957), 155.

16. Berle has pointed out that in 1954 General Motors committed over a billion dollars

in new capital development allegedly to counter the possibility of a nationwide depression. See Berle, *The 20th Century Capitalist Revolution*, p. 34.

17. See especially Ralph S. Brown, Jr., *Loyalty and Security* (New Haven: Yale University Press, 1958).

18. The prerogatives of management may "include power to determine that certain towns or areas shall be developed and shall become industrialized, and heretofore has included (the power is now in dispute) capacity to leave a community, taking its operations elsewhere, possibly leaving a broken city behind." Berle, *The 20th Century Capitalist Revolution*, p. 33.

19. This massively documented tendency toward oligarchy is not, of course, confined to to unions. But the union leader finds himself in a peculiar situation. His stake in his office is doubly great since, unlike his counterpart in the business corporation, the loss of his office is likely to be a serious matter for him. There is nowhere else to go, at least in the present stage of the labor movement when his managerial skills are likely to be appreciated only in the more competitive industries. Ironically, the less he is corrupted by business interests beckoning from outside his union, the more unscrupulously he will secure himself within it. Unless he has cultivated nonunion business, he must remain attached. Hence his effort to prevent his displacement may be formidable.

20. House Committee on Education and Labor, *Hearings on Restrictive Union Practices of the American Federation of Musicians*, 80th Cong., 2d Sess. (1948), part 1, p. 343.

21. See especially House Committee on Education and Labor, *Hearings on Union Democracy*, 81st Cong., 1st and 2d Sess. (1950); Senate Committee on Labor and Public Welfare, *Welfare and Pension Plan Investigation, Final Report*, 84th Cong., 2d Sess., (1956); Select Senate Committee on Improper Activities in the Labor Management Field, *Hearings*, Part 8, 85th Cong., 1st Sess. (1957), especially pp. 2800–2801, 2805, 3084–3087; A. L. Gitlow, "Machine Politics in American Trade Unions," *Journal of Politics*, XIV (August, 1952), 370–385.

22. Quoted in Grant McConnell, "The Spirit of Private Government," *American Political Science Review*, LII (September, 1958), 754–770, 760. For an explicit prohibition of factionalism, see the constitution of the International Brotherhood of Electrical Workers, Article 27.

23. ILWU, *Proceedings of the Seventh Biennial Convention* (San Francisco, 1947), p. 178.

24. See the *New York Times*, September 16, 1958, p. 1. On conventions generally, see especially William M. Leiserson, *American Trade Union Democracy* (New York: Columbia University Press, 1959).

25. Paul Jacobs, "The World of Jimmy Hoffa—II," *Reporter* (February 7, 1957), pp. 10–17, 17.

26. In 1955, the National Industrial Conference, having examined the disciplinary provision of 194 national unions, found that in 44 of them a local union executive board was empowered to investigate charges and to impose penalties. In 72 of them, the national president or the executive board had the power to assume original jurisdiction to discipline members—with appeal always possible to the convention. See National Industrial Conference Board, *Handbook of Union Government and Procedures*, 1955, as cited in Sar A. Levitan, *Government Regulation of Internal Union Affairs Affecting the Rights of Members* (Washington: Government Printing Office, 1958). See also Philip Taft, *The Structure and Government of Labor Unions* (Cambridge: Harvard University Press, 1954); Leo Bromwich, *Union Constitutions* (New York: Fund for the Republic, 1959); Clyde Summers, "Disciplinary Powers of Unions," *Industrial and Labor Relations Review*, III (July, 1950), 483–513; and "Disciplinary Procedures of Unions," *Industrial and Labor Relations Review*, IV (October, 1950), 15–31; H. W. Benson, "Labor's Uncertain Trumpet," *Progressive*, XXIII (June, 1959), 41–44.

25 POWER OVER INTERESTS

▪ Robert Paul Wolff

In order to clarify the relationship between the government and the prevailing network of private associations, we must first observe that while some groups perform their function and achieve their goal directly, others are organized as pressure groups to influence the national (or local) government and thus achieve their end indirectly. Needless to say, most associations of the first sort engage in political lobbying as well. Nevertheless, the distinction is useful, for it enables us to identify the two principal "pluralist" theories of the relationship between group and government.

The first, or "referee," theory asserts that the role of the central government is to lay down ground rules for conflict and competition among private associations and to employ its power to make sure that no major interest in the nation abuses its influence or gains an unchecked mastery over some sector of social life. The most obvious instance is in the economic sphere, where firms compete for markets and labor competes with capital. But according to the theory a similar competition takes place among the various religions, between private and public forms of education, among different geographic regions, and even among the arts, sports, and the entertainment world for the attention and interest of the people.

The second theory might be called the "vector-sum" or "give-and-take" theory of government. Congress is seen as the focal point for the pressures which are exerted by interest groups throughout the nation, either by way of the two great parties or directly through lobbies. The laws issuing from the government are shaped by the manifold forces brought to bear upon the legislators. Ideally, Congress merely reflects these forces, combining them—or "resolving" them, as the physicists say—into a single social decision. As the strength and direction of private interests alter, there is a corresponding

From Robert Paul Wolff, *A Critique of Pure Tolerance* (Boston: Beacon Press, 1965), pp. 10–12, 40–52. Reprinted by permission of the Beacon Press. © Copyright 1965 by Robert Paul Wolff.

alteration in the composition and activity of the great interest groups—labor, big business, agriculture. Slowly, the great weather vane of government swings about to meet the shifting winds of opinion. . . .

The application of pluralist theory to American society involves ideological distortion in at least three different ways. The first stems from the vector-sum or balance-of-power interpretation of pluralism; the second arises from the application of the referee version of the theory; and the third is inherent in the abstract theory itself.

According to the vector-sum theory of pluralism, the major groups in society compete through the electoral process for control over the actions of the government. Politicians are forced to accommodate themselves to a number of opposed interests and in so doing achieve a rough distributive justice. What are the major groups which, according to pluralism, comprise American society today? First, there are the hereditary groups which are summarized by that catch phrase of tolerance, "without regard to race, creed, color, or national origin." In addition there are the major economic interest groups among which, so the theory goes, a healthy balance is maintained: labor, business, agriculture, and—a residual category, this—the consumer. Finally, there are a number of voluntary associations whose size, permanence, and influence entitle them to a place in any group analysis of America: groups such as the veterans' organizations and the American Medical Association.

At one time, this may have been an accurate account of American society. But once constructed, the picture becomes frozen, and when changes take place in the patterns of social or economic grouping, they tend not to be acknowledged because they deviate from that picture. So the application of the theory of pluralism always favors the groups in existence against those in process of formation. For example, at any given time the major religious, racial, and ethnic groups are viewed as permanent and exhaustive categories into which every American can conveniently be pigeonholed. Individuals who fall outside any major social group—the nonreligious, say—are treated as exceptions and relegated in practice to a second-class status. Thus agnostic conscientious objectors are required to serve in the armed forces, while those who claim even the most bizarre religious basis for their refusal are treated with ritual tolerance and excused by the courts. Similarly, orphanages in America are so completely dominated by the three major faiths that a nonreligious or religiously mixed couple simply cannot adopt a child in many states. The net effect is to preserve the official three-great-religions image of American society long after it has ceased to correspond to social reality and to discourage individuals from officially breaking their religious ties. A revealing example of the mechanism of tolerance is the ubiquitous joke about "the priest, the minister, and the rabbi." A world of insight into the psychology of tolerance can be had simply from observing the mixture of emotions with which an audience greets such a joke, as told by George Jessel or some other apostle of "interfaith understanding." One senses embarrassment, nervousness, and finally an explosion of self-congratulatory laughter as though everyone were relieved at a difficult moment got through without incident. The gentle ribbing nicely distributed in the story among the three men of the cloth gives each member of the audience a chance to express his hostility safely and acceptably and in the end to reaffirm the principle of tolerance by joining in the applause. Only a bigot, one feels, could refuse to crack a smile!

Rather more serious in its conservative falsifying of social reality is the established image of the major economic groups of American society. The emergence of a rough parity between big industry and organized labor has been paralleled by the rise of a philosophy of moderation and co-operation between them, based on mutual understanding and respect, which is precisely similar to the achievement of interfaith and ethnic tolerance. What has been overlooked or suppressed is the fact that there are tens of millions of Americans—businessmen and workers alike—whose interests are completely ignored by this genial give-and-take. Nonunionized workers are worse off after each price-wage increase, as are the thousands of small businessmen who cannot survive in the competition against great nationwide firms. The theory of pluralism does not espouse the interests of the unionized against the non-unionized, or of large against small business; but by presenting a picture of the American economy in which those disadvantaged elements do not appear, it tends to perpetuate the inequality by ignoring rather than justifying it.

The case here is the same as with much ideological thinking. Once pluralists acknowledge the existence of groups whose interests are not weighed in the labor-business balance, then their own theory requires them to call for an alteration of the system. If migrant workers, or white-collar workers, or small businessmen are genuine *groups,* then they have a legitimate place in the system of group adjustments. Thus, pluralism is not explicitly a philosophy of privilege or injustice; it is a philosophy of equality and justice whose *concrete application* supports inequality by ignoring the existence of certain legitimate social groups.

This ideological function of pluralism helps to explain one of the peculiarities of American politics. There is a very sharp distinction in the public domain between legitimate interests and those which are absolutely beyond the pale. If a group or interest is within the framework of acceptability, it can be sure of winning some measure of what it seeks, for the process of national politics is distributive and compromising. On the other hand, if an interest falls *outside* the circle of the acceptable, it receives no attention whatsoever, and its proponents are treated as crackpots, extremists, or foreign agents. With bewildering speed, an interest can move from "outside" to "inside," and its partisans, who have been scorned by the solid and established in the community, become Presidential advisers and newspaper columnists.

A vivid example from recent political history is the sudden legitimation of the problem of poverty in America. In the postwar years, tens of millions of poor Americans were left behind by the sustained growth of the economy. The facts were known and discussed for years by fringe critics whose attempts to call attention to these forgotten Americans were greeted with either silence or contempt. Suddenly, poverty was "discovered" by Presidents Kennedy and Johnson, and articles were published in *Look* and *Time* which a year earlier would have been more at home in the radical journals which inhabit political limbo in America. A social group whose very existence had long been denied was now the object of a national crusade.

A similar elevation from obscurity to relative prominence was experienced by the peace movement, a "group" of a rather different nature. For years, the partisans of disarmament labored to gain a hearing for their view that nuclear war could not be a reasonable instrument of national policy. Sober politicians and serious columnists treated such ideas as the naïve fantasies of bearded peaceniks, Communist sympathizers, and well-meaning but hopelessly muddled clerics. Then suddenly the Soviet Union achieved the nuclear parity which had been long forecast, the prospect of which had convinced disarmers of the insanity of nuclear war. Sober re-evaluations appeared in the columns of Walter Lippmann, and some even found their way into the speeches of President Kennedy—what had been unthinkable, absurd, naïve, dangerous, even subversive, six months before, was now plausible, sound, thoughtful, and—within another six months—official American policy.

The explanation for these rapid shifts in the political winds lies, I suggest, in the logic of pluralism. According to pluralist theory, every genuine social group has a right to a voice in the making of policy and a share in the benefits. Any policy urged by a group in the system must be given respectful attention, no matter how bizarre. By the same token, a policy or principle which lacks legitimate representation has no place in the society, no matter how reasonable or right it may be. Consequently, the line between acceptable and unacceptable alternatives is very sharp, so that the territory of American politics is like a plateau with steep cliffs on all sides rather than like a pyramid. On the plateau are all the interest groups which are recognized as legitimate; in the deep valley all around lie the outsiders, the fringe groups which are scorned as "extremist." The most important battle waged by any group in American politics is the struggle to climb onto the plateau. Once there, it can count on some measure of what it seeks. No group ever gets all of what it wants, and no *legitimate* group is completely frustrated in its efforts.

Thus, the vector-sum version of pluralist theory functions ideologically by tending to deny new groups or interests access to the political plateau. It does this by ignoring their existence in practice, not by denying their claim in theory. The result is that pluralism has a braking effect on social change; it slows down transformation in the system of group adjustments, but does not set up an absolute barrier to change. For this reason, as well as because of its origins as a fusion of two conflicting social philosophies, it deserves the title "conservative liberalism."

According to the second, or referee, version of pluralism, the role of the government is to oversee and regulate the competition among interest groups in the society. Out of the applications of this theory have grown not only countless laws, such as the antitrust bills, pure food and drug acts, and Taft-Hartley Law, but also the complex system of quasi-judicial regulatory agencies in the executive branch of government. Henry Kariel, in a powerful and convincing book entitled *The Decline of American Pluralism,* has shown that this referee function of government, as it actually works out in practice, systematically favors the interests of the stronger against the weaker party in interest-group conflicts and tends to solidify the power of those who already hold it. The government, therefore, plays a conservative, rather than a neutral, role in the society.

Kariel details the ways in which this discriminatory influence is exercised. In the field of regulation of labor unions, for example, the federal agencies deal with the established leadership of the unions. In such matters as the overseeing of union elections, the settlement of jurisdictional disputes, or the setting up of mediation boards, it is the interests of those leaders rather than the competing interests of rank-and-file dissidents which are favored. In the regulation of agriculture, again, the locally most influential farmers or leaders of farmers' organizations draw up the guidelines for control which are then adopted by the federal inspectors. In each case, ironically, the unwillingness of the government to impose its own standards or rules results not in a free play of competing groups, but in the enforcement of the preferences of the existing predominant interests.

In a sense, these unhappy consequences of government regulation stem from a confusion between a theory of interest conflict and a theory of power conflict. The government quite successfully referees the conflict among competing *powers:* any group which has already managed to accumulate a significant quantum of power will find its claims attended to by the federal agencies. But legitimate *interests* which have been ignored, suppressed, defeated, or which have not yet succeeded in organizing themselves for effective action, will find their disadvantageous position perpetuated through the decisions of the government. It is as though an umpire comes upon a baseball game in progress between big boys and little boys, in which the big boys cheat, break the rules, claim hits that were outs, and make the little boys accept the injustice by brute force. If the umpire undertakes to "regulate" the game by simply enforcing the "rules" actually being practiced, he does not thereby make the game a fair one. Indeed, he may actually make matters worse, because if the little boys get up their courage, band together, and decide to fight it out, the umpire will accuse them of breaking the rules and throw his weight against them! Precisely the same sort of thing happens in pluralist politics. For example, the American Medical Association exercises a strangle hold over American medicine through its influence over the government's licensing regulations. Doctors who are opposed to the AMA's political positions, or even to its medical policies, do not merely have to buck the entrenched authority of the organization's leaders. They must also risk the loss of hospital affiliations, speciality accreditation, and so forth, all of which powers have been placed in the hands of the medical establishment by state and federal laws. Those laws are written by the government in co-operation with the very same AMA leaders; not surprisingly, the interests of dissenting doctors do not receive favorable attention.

The net effect of government action is thus to weaken, rather than strengthen, the play of conflicting interests in the society. The theory of pluralism here has a crippling effect on the government, for it warns against positive federal intervention in the name of independent principles of justice, equality, or fairness. The theory says justice will emerge from the free interplay of opposed groups; the practice tends to destroy that interplay.

Finally, the theory of pluralism in all its forms has the effect in American thought and politics of discriminating not only against certain social groups or interests but also against certain sorts of proposals for the solution of social problems. According to pluralist theory, politics is a contest among social groups for control of the power and decision of the government. Each group is motivated by some interest or cluster of interests and seeks to sway the government toward action in its favor. The typical social problem according to pluralism is therefore some instance of distributive injustice. One group is getting too much, another too little, of the available resources. In accord with its modification of traditional liberalism, pluralism's goal is a rough parity among competing groups rather than among competing individuals. Characteristically, new proposals originate with a group which feels that its legitimate interests have been slighted, and the legislative outcome is a measure which corrects the social imbalance to a degree commensurate with the size and political power of the initiating group.

But there are some social ills in America whose causes do not lie in a maldistribution of wealth and cannot be cured, therefore, by the techniques of pluralist politics. For example, America is growing uglier, more dangerous, and less pleasant to live in, as its citizens grow richer. The reason is that natural beauty, public order, the cultivation of the arts, are not the special interest of any identifiable social group. Consequently, evils and inadequacies in those areas cannot be remedied by shifting the distribution of wealth and power among existing social groups. To be sure, crime and urban slums hurt the poor more than the rich, the Negro more than the white—but fundamentally they are problems of the society as a whole, not of any particular group. That is to say, they concern the general good, not merely the aggregate of private goods. To deal with such problems, there must be some way of constituting the whole society a genuine group with a group purpose and a conception of the common good. Pluralism rules this out in theory by portraying society as an aggregate of human communities rather than as itself a human community; and it equally rules out a concern for the general good in practice by encouraging a politics of interest-group pressures in which there is no mechanism for the discovery and expression of the common good. . . .

By insisting on the group nature of society, it denies the existence of society-wide interests—save the purely procedural interest in preserving the system of group pressures—and the possibility of communal action in pursuit of the general good.

A proof of this charge can be found in the commissions, committees, institutes, and conferences which are convened from time to time to ponder the "national interest." The membership of these assemblies always includes an enlightened business executive, a labor leader, an educator, several clergymen of various faiths, a woman, a literate general or admiral, and a few public figures of unquestioned sobriety and predictable views. The whole is a micro-cosm of the interest groups and hereditary groups which, according to pluralism, constitute American society. Any vision of the national interest which emerges from such a group will inevitably be a standard pluralist pic-ture of a harmonious, co-operative, distributively just, *tolerant* America. One could hardly expect a committee of group representatives to decide that the pluralist system of social groups is an obstacle to the general good! . . .

Pluralism is fatally blind to the evils which afflict the entire body politic, and as a theory of society it obstructs consideration of precisely the sorts of thoroughgoing social revisions which may be needed to remedy those evils. Like all great social theories, pluralism answered a genuine social need during a significant period of history. Now, however, new problems confront America: problems not of distributive injustice, but of the common good. . . .

26   THE LIMITS OF THE POLITICAL SYSTEM

■ *E. E. Schattschneider*

Theoretically, the American political community consists of about one hundred million adult citizens. This assumption is a natural one because the franchise has now been extended to nearly all adult citizens, and the right to vote might reasonably be taken as a mark of membership in the political community. On the other hand, if belonging to the community is thought of as something involving active participation in the political process, the system is much smaller. The difference between fact and theory is shown by a single datum: *about forty million adult citizens do not vote in Presidential elections.* Voting is not a strenuous form of activity, but it is apparently beyond the level of per-formance of four out of every ten adults. In one way or another, factors unknown to the law block out a stupendous segment of the nation from the political system. The distinction between the people who exercise their fran-chise and those who do not deserves to be examined because it may be most important in the political system.

If forty million adult citizens were disfranchised by law, we would consider that fact the first datum about the system. It may be even more important that this result has been accomplished by extralegal means.

From E. E. Schattschneider, *The Semisovereign People* (New York: Holt, Rinehart, and Winston, 1960), pp. 97–113. © Copyright 1960 by E. E. Schattschneider. Reprinted by permission of Holt, Rinehart, and Winston, Inc.

Obviously, no political system could achieve 100 per cent participation in elections. Even when full allowance is made, however, the scale of nonvoting in the United States is so great that it calls for some explanation beyond the various psychological and educational factors usually cited.[1]

The blackout of the forty million or so calls for re-examination of the whole system. Nonvoting on this scale sheds a strange light on American democracy because it points up a profound contradiction between theory and practice. In this chapter, we shall discuss the nonvoting millions as a study in the scope, intensity, and bias of the political system.

With some important exceptions, the most striking fact about the phenomenon is that it seems to be voluntary. Outside of the South, it has not been considered necessary to erect barriers against an invasion of the political system by the nonvoters, and no one seems about to do so. The community is willing to live with the hazards of a situation that places a curtain—a tissue-paper curtain, but still a curtain—between the participants and the nonparticipants. If the abstention of several tens of millions makes a difference, as it almost certainly does, we are forced to conclude that we are governed by invisible forces, for to an astonishing extent the sixty million are at the mercy of the rest of the nation, which could swamp all existing political alignments if it chose to do so. The whole balance of power in the political system could be overturned by a massive invasion of the political system, and nothing tangible protects the system against the flood. All that is necessary to produce the most painless revolution in history, the first revolution ever legalized and legitimatized in advance, is to have a sufficient number of people do something not much more difficult than to walk across the street on election day.

Every regime lives on a body of dogma, self-justification, glorification, and propaganda about itself. In the United States, this body of dogma and tradition centers about democracy. The hero of the system is the voter, who is commonly described as the ultimate source of all authority. The fact that something like forty million adult Americans are so unresponsive to the regime that they do not trouble to vote is the most truly remarkable fact about it. In the past seven presidential elections, the average difference in the votes cast for the winning and the losing candidates was about one-fifth as large as the total number of nonvoters. The unused political potential is sufficient to blow the United States off the face of the earth.

Why should anyone worry about twenty or thirty or forty million American adults who seem to be willing to remain on the outside looking in? What difference do they make? Several things may be said. First, anything that looks like a rejection of the political system by so large a fraction of the population is a matter of great importance. Second, anything that looks like a limitation of the expanding universe of politics is certain to have great practical consequences. Does nonvoting shed light on the bias and the limitations of the political system?

In American history, every change in the scope of the political system has had an impact on the meaning and operation of the system. Broadly speaking, the expansion of the political community has been one of the principal means of producing change in public policy; expansion has been the grand strategy of American politics. Every major change in public policy (the Jefferson, Jackson, Lincoln, and Roosevelt revolutions) has been associated with an enlargement of the electorate. Has something gone wrong with the basic pattern of American politics? Has the political system run out of gas? Have we lost the capacity to use the growth of the electorate to provide a new base for public policy? If we have lost the capacity to involve an expanding public in the political system, it is obvious that American democracy has arrived at a turning point.

What kind of system is this in which only a little more than half of us participate? Is the system actually what we have been brought up to think it is?

One of the easiest victories of the democratic cause in American history has been the struggle for the extension of the suffrage. After a few skirmishes in the first decades of the nineteenth century, the barriers against male suffrage gave way all along the line. A generation ago one distinguished United States Senator was in the habit of saying that rivers of blood have been shed for the right to vote. No greater inversion of the truth is conceivable. The struggle for the ballot was almost bloodless, almost completely peaceful, and astonishingly easy. Indeed, the bulk of the newly enfranchised, including Negroes and nearly all women, won battles they never fought. The whole thing has been deceptively easy. Somewhere along the line the antidemocratic forces simply abandoned the field. It is hard for Americans to believe how easy it was because they have a hopelessly romantic view of the history of democracy which attributes a revolutionary significance to the extension of the legal right to vote.

The expansion of the electorate was largely a by-product of the system of party conflict. The rise of the party system led to a competitive expansion of the market for politics. The newly enfranchised had about as much to do with the extension of the suffrage as the consuming public has had to do with the expanding market for toothpaste. The parties, assisted by some excited minorities, were the entrepreneurs, took the initiative, and got the law of the franchise liberalized. It has always been true that one of the best ways to win a fight is to widen the scope of conflict, and the effort to widen the involvement of more or less innocent bystanders produced universal suffrage. Our understanding of this development has been greatly confused by the compulsion to interpret our past in terms of the classical definition of democracy which inevitably assigns a dramatic place in history to the seizure of power by the people.

The meaning of political competition in the expansion of the electorate is illuminated by the experience of the Solid South. The South is the last remaining area in the United States in which the struggle against democracy is carried on in terms of legal and extralegal restrictions of the right to vote. The southern states were able to exclude the Negro from the political system only by establishing a political monopoly. Once established, the system has been used not only to disfranchise Negroes but also to depress political participation generally.

The socialization of politics as far as the right to vote is concerned has now been nearly complete for a generation, but the *use* of the ballot as an effective instrument of democratic politics is something else altogether. This is the point at which the breach between theory and practice of American democracy appears to be widest. If we do not understand what this breach is about, we simply do not understand American politics. The question is: If the conflict system is responsible for the extension of the legal right to vote, is it also responsible for limiting the practice of voting?

It is reasonable to look for some of the causes of massive self-disfranchisement in the operation of the political system. What is there about the system that depresses participation? Obviously, the relation of the electorate to the government is not as simple as it is commonly supposed to be.

The American political system is less able to use the democratic device of majority rule than almost any other modern democracy. Nearly everyone makes obeisance to the majority, but the idea of majority rule has not been fully legitimatized. The explanation of the ambivalence of the system is well institutionalized and has never been fully legitimatized. The explanation of the ambivalence of the system is historical.

Democracy as we now understand it has been superimposed on an old governmental structure which was inhospitable to the idea. The result is a remarkable makeshift. Resistance to the growth of the political community has taken the form of attacks on all efforts to organize the majority—attacks on politics, politicians, and political parties. The offspring of this mixed parentage is a kind of monstrosity, a nonpolitical antimajoritarian democracy.

Massive nonvoting in the United States makes sense if we think of American government as a political system in which the struggle for democracy is still going on. The struggle is no longer about the *right to vote,* but about the *organization of politics.* Nowadays the fight for democracy takes the form of a struggle over theories of organization, over the right to organize and the right of political organizations; that is, about the kinds of things that make the vote valuable.

Another way of saying the same thing is to say that the vote can be vitiated as effectively by placing obstacles in the way of organizing the electorate as it can be a denial of the right to vote. Nonvoting is related to the contradiction, imbedded in the political system, between (1) the movement to universalize suffrage and (2) the attempt to make the vote meaningless. We get confused because we assume that the fight for democracy was won a long time ago. We would find it easier to understand what is going on if we assumed that the battle for democracy is still going on, but has now assumed a new form.

The success or failure of the political system in involving a substantial fraction of the tens of millions of nonvoters is likely to determine the future of the country. This proposition goes to the heart of the struggle of the American people for democratic self-realization.

In spite of the fact that there have been a number of get-out-the-vote movements, it is obvious that no serious measures have been taken to bring the forty million into the political system; nothing half as serious as the enactment of a uniform national elections law, for example.

Why has so little been done? Perhaps we shall be near to the truth if we say that little has been done because the question is too important, too hot to be handled. It is by a wide margin the most important feature of the whole system, the key to understanding the composition of American politics. Anyone who finds out how to involve the forty million in American politics will run the country for a generation.

Unquestionably, the addition of forty million voters (or any major fraction of them) would make a tremendous difference. The least that the forty million might do to the political system would be to enhance tremendously the authority of the majority.

The fatuous get-out-the-vote movement conducted through the mass media at election time is a classical instance of the ambivalence of American attitudes toward the problem. The mass communications industry is precisely the least effective instrument for changing the voting habits of nonparticipants, probably because the limitations of the mass communications system are much like the limitations of the political system.

An attack on the problem of nonvoting calls for a new kind of thinking about politics. What is required to enlarge the political community? A substantial change in public policy might do it. The inference is that the forty million are not likely to become interested in the political system as it is. What the sixty million quarrel about evidently does not excite the forty million. In other words, the forty million can be made to participate only in a new kind of political system based on new cleavages and *about* something new. It is impossible to involve the forty million or any major fraction of them short of a large-scale change in the agenda of politics. What kind of offer do we have to make to get the abstainers into the system?

The problem is serious because the forty million are the soft underbelly of the system. The segment of the population which is least involved or most convinced that the system is loaded against it is the most likely point of subversion. This is the *sickness* of democracy.

The key to the problem is to be found in the nature of public policy and the organization of public support for policy. To put it another way, political support for a major shift of policy can only be found outside the present political system.

It is profoundly characteristic of the behavior of the more fortunate strata of the community that responsibility for widespread nonparticipation is attributed wholly to the ignorance, indifference, and shiftlessness of the people. This has always been the rationalization used to justify the exclusion of the lower classes from any political system. There is a better explanation. Abstention reflects the suppression of the options and alternatives that reflect the needs of the nonparticipants. It is not necessarily true that the people with the greatest needs participate in politics most actively. *Whoever decides what the game is about decides also who can get into the game.* If the political system is dominated by the cleavage AB, what can the people who want another alignment (CD) do? One thing they may do is to stop voting.

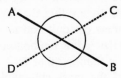

An examination of the social structure of the disfranchised lends support to the foregoing proposition. Who are the forty million? Every study of the subject supports the conclusion that nonvoting is a characteristic of the poorest, least well-established, least educated stratum of the community. Unquestionably, an expansion of the scope of the system would bring a new kind of voter into the community and would change the balance of forces.

The question is: Has the quarrel that underlies American politics been so defined that it excludes a major segment of the nation from the political system.[2]

What is the difference between voters and nonvoters? It is relatively easy to show that the *voters* are more involved in the community than the nonvoters. The voters are better educated, are better off, and belong to more organizations than nonvoters. Voting has something to do with the way in which large areas of need and interest are excluded from the political system.

If the distinction between the forty million and the sixty million is as important as it seems to be, there ought to be some evidence, aside from the voting habits of the people, to support this conclusion. Voting is not an isolated social phenomenon; it is a part of the social condition of the people. There are some general grounds for supposing that the economic community is divided in about the same way the political community is divided.

It is surprising how often magnitudes of the general proportions of sixty million appear in American social and economic statistics.

Scope of the Community

Telephone subscribers (1953)	48,056,308
Newspaper circulation (daily, English language, 1953)	54,472,286
Households (1953)	46,828,000
Employment (1959)	62,700,000
Old Age Survivors (insurance coverage, 1954)	69,200,000
Income Tax Returns (1951)	55,042,597
Homes with radio sets (1954)	50,000,000
Automobile registrations (1953)	56,279,864
Television sets (1954)	33,000,000
Votes cast in 1956 election	61,550,918

Without pressing the argument unduly because the statistics are obviously not consistent, does not the recurrence of these magnitudes suggest that the effective social and economic community may be about as large as the political community?

The data might seem more significant if they were inverted. It is probably not terribly far from the truth to say that the forty million nonvoters can be matched by comparable numbers of adult nonsubscribers to daily newspapers, adult nonowners of automobiles, adult nonhouseholders, and so on. In other words, there is some basis for thinking that the scope of the political system is about the same as that of the mass communications audience, the automobile market, the tax system, the social security system, or the market for toothpaste.

Loosely, perhaps we have a sociopolitical community consisting of about sixty million newspaper readers, jobholders, income-tax payers, automobile owners, householders, and voters. On the other hand, we have about forty million adults in the community who are less likely to possess these tokens of participation and status. Crudely the scope of the political community corresponds to the social facts of life. If the *political* distinction between voters and nonvoters corresponds to a social distinction between broadly the same segments of the community, it is the most important datum about the political system—much more important than the distinction between Republicans and Democrats.

The social system makes a substantial distinction between those who have relatively more and those who have relatively less. This is the bias of the system. Have we misconceived the real cleavage in the community? Perhaps the significant division is not between the rich and the poor, as these terms are commonly understood, but between people who are more strongly motivated by the economic system and those who are less strongly motivated. Thus an underpaid bank clerk may be greatly excited by the prospect of economic advancement, while a scrubwoman working in the same bank may be demoralized and frustrated. The political system is now so preoccupied by *the cleavage within the sixty million* that it has become insensitive to the interests of the largest minority in the world.

Characteristically the processes by which the forty million are excluded from the political system are invisible and imperceptible. Since people are easily overwhelmed or ignored, it takes a special sensitivity to become aware of the needs and experiences of the bottom of the social order. It is one of the great claims of democracy as a moral system that it is able to do this better than any other governmental system, but not all democracies do it equally well.

If politics is thought of as part of the total social experience of people, there must be a great deal about that experience that contradicts the democratic professions of the community.

What is it that people do unconsciously to alienate so large a fraction of the nation? The system operates largely through processes of which people are unaware. Stratification and isolation and segregation are to a great extent the unconscious or semiconscious by-products of the way the social system operates to organize the community. It is not necessary to speak one unkind or ungracious word to keep a poor man out of a rich man's church or college or club or hotel. Anyone familiar with the compulsive standards of dress and play in American schools can understand why the children of the poor drop out of school even when schooling is free.

It is not enough to say that the poor are not hungry and cold. People can suffer from humiliation and degradation as much as from hunger. Poverty is always relative. The point is that *the process is automatic, unconscious, and thoughtless.* People reconcile their democratic faith and their undemocratic behavior by remaining comfortably unaware of the inconsistency of theory and practice.

The sixty million share the same values and play the same game; they participate in politics the way they participate in the life of the community and share in the output of the community. They compete for goods and power. Unfortunately, this is not a game in which the whole nation seems to participate.

It is probably fair to say that the existing party system is simply the political organization of the sixty million.

The situation as a whole looks like a good example of the dominance and subordination of conflicts. Since the Democratic-Republican version of the cleavage between government and business has dominated American politics, the submerged millions have found it difficult to get interested in the game.

In view of the foregoing, we can start to define the political system all over again: It is the largest, most broadly based ruling oligarchy in the world, but it is not as inclusive and as broadly based as some other systems.

The contradictions in the political system have produced a party system that is able to exploit some kinds of issues, but is much less able to exploit other kinds. Whatever the cause, the present boycott of the political system has brought the political system *very near to something like the limit of tolerance of passive abstention.*

All divisions in the community are maintained at a cost. The existence of a large body of dissociated people is part of the price we pay for the dominance of the cleavage between government and business. This cleavage has tended to freeze the stakes of politics at a point that has never involved the whole community.

Obviously, however, the cleavage between the sixty million and the forty million could be exploited by a new kind of political effort devoted to the development of an array of issues now submerged. On the assumption that the raw materials of a revolution are not likely to remain untouched indefinitely, is it not likely that this is where the future of American politics is to be found?

The root of the problem of nonvoting is to be found in the way in which the alternatives in American politics are defined, the way in which issues get referred to the public, the scale of competition and organization, and above all by *what* issues are developed. The existence of a large nonvoting population provides an insight into the nature of the unresolved historic tensions in the system.

The political system *has never assigned to the elective process a role as overwhelmingly important as that played by British elections.* The political system is not well designed to bring great issues to a head in a national election. Until recently the party alignment was so sharply sectional that the bulk of American voters lived in one-party areas where they had little incentive to vote because they had no choices. A national party system based on national cleavages is only now beginning to emerge, and it may be some time before all Americans have a genuine party choice, even in presidential elections.

Whether or not the rate of political participation will ever be developed on a satisfactory scale depends to a great extent *on the evolution of American policy about politics*, political organization, and the rights of political organizations.

A great multitude of causes languish because the forty million or so nonvoters do not support them at the polls. It staggers the imagination to consider what might happen if the forty million suddenly intervened, for we cannot take it for granted that they would be divided in the same proportions as the sixty million. All political equations would be revised.

All classical concepts of democracy have overestimated the strength and universality of the self-generated impulse of people to participate in the life of the political community. It has been assumed that only legal barriers inhibited the disfranchised. We know better now. The exclusion of people by extralegal processes, by social processes, by the way the political system is organized and structured, may be far more effective than the law.

Two major tasks of modern politics suggest that the problem deserves examination. First, politics today must cope with the potentialities and the problems created by annihilation of space. The mobility of modern man makes him a member of more and larger communities than any of his predecessors. Nobody knows what the potentialities of these new communities are. The political process of large-scale society are unlike those of the old, and the balance of forces is inevitably different.

In the second place, modern politics must deal with a kind of shift of emphasis from the politics of the distribution of benefits to the politics of the apportionment of burdens. The traditional concept of politics (once described as who gets what, when, and how) was invented at a time when the stability and survival of the American community could be so fully taken for granted that it was possible to think about the political process almost exclusively in terms of the acquisitive instinct.

Today our view of politics is greatly modified by the fact that the United States is involved in a titanic struggle for survival. Burdens that were inconceivable a few years ago seem to have become a permanent part of the public function. *The primacy of foreign policy* calls for a new kind of politics involving a wholly new calculus. The government now needs above everything else the steady support of the public, and this support cannot be had without a new scale of public involvement in public life.

A greatly expanded popular base of political participation is the essential condition for public support of the government. This is the modern problem of democratic government. The price of support is participation. The choice is between participation and propaganda, between democratic and dictatorial ways of *changing consent into support, because consent is no longer enough.*

Perhaps the calculation that is going to have the greatest influence on the future of the system is based on the estimate that it is easier to bring a new voter into the system than it is to induce an old partisan to change sides. The expansion of the community is related to the nationalization of politics; the larger the community, the more likely it is to be favorable to the admission of new elements, whereas localization has historically been the strategic base for restricting the scope of politics.

The expansion of the participating political community ought to be a major objective of American politics. We ought, therefore, to elicit the support of those people already in the participating political community who are likely to have the greatest interest in its expansion. We ought to look to the new-comers and the less privileged elements of the population to elicit their support for new programs of public action. In other words, *we ought now to use political means to extend the scope of social and political organization.* What we need now is public policy about politics.

▪ Notes

1. It has often been pointed out to us that the turnout in parliamentary elections outside of the United States is apt to be about 80 per cent, approximately 20 per cent higher than it is in the United States. However, American elections are not very much like British elections, to take a European example. An Englishman voting in a general election casts one vote for a single candidate for one office, using a ballot about the size of a government post card. American elections are, on the other hand, extremely complex. Not only do we elect about eight hundred thousand officials but before the elections there are the primaries, and before the primaries, in many jurisdictions, comes periodic personal registration of voters. American voters must cope with fifty systems of election laws. Technical arguments about the exact size of the nonvoting public are not important. It is a large piece of cheese, no matter how one slices it. See Austin Ranney, *The Governing of Men* (New York: Holt, 1958), p. 266, for an analysis of American statistics for the 1956 election. The whole subject is discussed extensively in Robert E. Lane, *Political Life* (New York: The Free Press of Glencoe, 1959).
2. "The apathy toward the parties cuts across every ward and income group, but the highest percentage of unenrolled people is to be found in the low-income Catholic wards where those who do indicate party affiliation are largely Democrats. Political inactivity is also revealed in the failure to register to vote. This tendency is deepest in low-income Democratic, Catholic areas." K. Underwood, *Protestant and Catholic* (Boston: Beacon Press, 1957), pp. 295–296. See also L. Warner and Associates, *Democracy in Jonesville* (New York: Harper, 1949), Chapters 6, 9, 12. See Lane, *op. cit.,* Chapter 16, for a review of the data about the influence of status on political participation.

27 THE DISPOSSESSED

■ *Daniel Bell*

The Sources of Strain

There have been, in the past thirty years, deep changes taking place in the social structure that are reworking the social map of the country, upsetting the established life chances and outlooks of old, privileged groups and creating uncertainties about the future which are deeply unsettling to those whose values were shaped by the "individualist" morality of nineteenth-century America.

The most pervasive changes are those involving the structural relations between class position and power. Clearly, today, political position rather than wealth, and technical skill rather than property, have become the bases from which power is wielded. In the modes of access to privilege, inheritance is no longer all-determining, nor does "individual initiative" in building one's own business exist as a realistic route; in general, education has become the major way to acquire the technical skills necessary for the administrative and power-wielding jobs in society.

In the older mythos, one's achievement was an individual fact—as a doctor, lawyer, professor, businessman; in the reality of today, one's achievement, status, and prestige are rooted in particular *collectivities* (the corporation, being attached to a "name" hospital, teaching at a prestigious university, membership in a good law firm), and the individual's role is necessarily submerged in the achievement of the collectivity. Within each collectivity and profession, the proliferation of tasks calls for narrower and narrower specializations, and this proliferation requires larger collectivities and the consequent growth of hierarchies and bureaucracies.

The new nature of decision making—the larger role of technical decision—also forces a displacement of the older elites. Within a business enterprise, the newer techniques of operations research and linear programing almost

From Daniel Bell, ed., *The Radical Right* (Garden City, N.Y.: Anchor Books, 1964), pp. 21–37. Reprinted by permission of the author.

amount to the "automation" of middle management and its displacement by mathematicians and engineers, working either in the firm or as consultants. In the economy, the businessman finds himself subject to price, wage, and investment criteria laid down by the economists in government. In the polity, the old military elites find themselves challenged in the determination of strategy by scientists, who have the technical knowledge on nuclear capability, missile development, and the like, or by the "military intellectuals" whose conceptions of weapon systems and political warfare seek to guide military allocations.

In the broadest sense, the spread of education, of research, of administration, and of government creates a new constituency, the technical and professional intelligentsia; and while these are not bound by some common ethos to constitute a new class, or even a cohesive social group, they are the products of a new system of recruitment for power (just as property and inheritance represented the old system), and those who are the products of the old system understandably feel a vague and apprehensive disquiet—the disquiet of the dispossessed.

The Generational Dispossessed

. . . In identifying "the dispossessed," it is somewhat misleading to seek their economic location, since it is not economic interest alone that accounts for their anxieties. A small businessman may have made considerable amounts of money in the last decade (in part because he has greater freedom than a large corporation in masking costs for tax purposes) and yet strongly resent regulations in Washington, the high income tax, or more to the point, his own lack of status. To the extent that any such economic location is possible, one can say that the social group most threatened by the structural changes in society is the "old" middle class—the independent physician, farm owner, small-town lawyer, real estate promoter, home builder, automobile dealer, gasoline station owner, small businessman, and the like—and that, regionally, its greatest political concentration is in the South, the Southwest, and California. But a much more telltale indicator of the group that feels most anxious—since life styles and values provide the emotional fuel of beliefs and actions—is the strain of Protestant fundamentalism, of nativist nationalism, of good-and-evil moralism which is the organizing basis for the "world view" of such people. For this is the group whose values predominated in the nineteenth century and which for the past forty years has been fighting a rear-guard action. . . .

The Managerial Dispossessed

To list the managerial executive class as among the dispossessed may seem strange, especially in the light of the argument that a revolution which is undermining property as the basis of power is enfranchising a new class of technical personnel among whom are the business executives. And yet the managerial class has been under immense strain all through this period, a strain arising in part from the status discrepancy between their power in a particular enterprise and their power and prestige in the nation as a whole.

The old family firm was securely rooted in the legal and moral tradition of private property. The enterprise "belonged" to the owner and was sanctioned, depending on one's theological tastes, by God or by natural law. The modern manager lacks the inherited family justifications, for increasingly he is recruited from the amorphous middle class. He receives a salary, bonus, options, expense accounts, and "perks" (use of company planes, memberships in country clubs), but his power is transitory, and he cannot pass on his position to his son. . . .[1]

The Military Dispossessed

The irony for the American military establishment is that at a time when, in the new states, the military has emerged as the ruling force of the country (often because it is the one organized group in an amorphous society),[2] and at a time in American history when the amount of money allocated to military purposes—roughly 50 per cent of the federal budget—is the highest in peacetime history, the military is subject to challenges in its own bailiwick. The problems of national security, like those of the national economy, have become so staggeringly complex that they can no longer be settled simply by common sense or past experience. As a writer in the *Times Literary Supplement* recently put it,

The manner in which weapons systems are likely to develop; the counters which may be found to them; the burdens which they are likely to impose on the national economy; the way in which their possession will affect international relations or their use the nature of war; the technical problems of their control or abolition; all these problems are far beyond the scope of the Joint Planning Staff study or the Civil Service brief.[3]

The fact is that the military establishment, because of its outmoded curriculum, its recruitment and promotion patterns, the vested interests of the different services, and the concentration at the top levels of officers trained in older notions of strategy, is ill equipped to grasp modern conceptions of politics or to use the tools (computer simulation, linear programing, gaming theory) of strategic planning. As Morris Janowitz has pointed out in his comprehensive study of the military:

There is little in the curriculum to prepare the officer for the realities of participating in the management of politico-military affairs. While the case-study and war-games approaches give the officer a direct understanding and "feel" for the logistics and organizational apparatus that must be "moved" for military operations, there is no equivalent training for the political dimensions of international relations. . . .

All evidence indicates that both absolutists and pragmatists—in varying degree—overemphasize the potentials of force. The realistic study of international relations involves an appreciation of the limits of violence. Military education does not continually focus on these issues, as it relates both to nuclear and limited conventional warfare. Paradoxically, military education does not emphasize the potentialities of unconventional warfare and political warfare, since these are at the periphery of professionalization.[4]

In the last decade, most of the thinking on strategic problems, political and economic, has been done in the universities or in government-financed but autonomous bodies like the Rand Corporation. A new profession, that of the "military intellectual," has emerged, and men like Kahn, Wohlstetter, Brodie, Hitch, Kissinger, Bowie, and Schelling "move freely through the corridors of the Pentagon and the State Department" as the *Times Literary Supplement* writer observed, "rather as the Jesuits through the courts of Madrid and Vienna three centuries ago."

In structural terms, the military establishment may be one of the tripods of a "power elite," but in sociological fact the military officers feel dispossessed because they often lack the necessary technical skills or knowledge to answer the new problems confronting them. Since the end of World War II, the military has been involved in a number of battles to defend its elite position, beginning in 1945 with the young physicists and nuclear scientists, down to the present action against the "technipols" (the technicians and political theorists, as the military derisively calls them), whom Secretary McNamara has brought into the Department of Defense. . . .

The point of all this is that such reorganization means more than the introduction of modern management practice into a top-heavy bureaucratic structure. For the reorganization on program and mission lines stemmed from a new conception of the strategic distribution of the armed forces—a political conception of the role of limited wars and nuclear capabilities, most of which came from the "technipols," rather than from the military establishment. . . .

■ Notes

1. On the decline of inherited position and nepotism in the large corporation, see Mabel M. Newcomer, *The Big Business Executive* (New York: Columbia University Press, 1955).
2. One of the factors that has acted to safeguard democracy in England and the United States is that both countries have never had any permanently large standing armies. The insularity of England made it place its protection in the Navy, whose forces were always far from shore, and the continental isolation of the United States made it unnecessary to build up any permanent military force. Where large armies have existed, the military, because it has represented an organized bloc whose control over the means of violence could be decisive, has almost invariably been pulled into politics. Thus the German Army in one crucial situation, in 1920, defended the Weimar Republic (against the Putschists of the right), but in a second crucial instance, in 1932 (the machinations of von Schleicher), contributed to its downfall. In Spain in 1936, in France in 1960, and more recently in Argentina, Turkey, Korea, Pakistan, Burma, and so on, the armed forces have been the decisive political element in the society.

3. "The Military Intellectuals," *Times Literary Supplement* (London), August 25, 1961.
4. Morris Janowitz, *The Professional Soldier* (New York: The Free Press, 1960), p. 429.

☐ *Public Government*

28 THE NATIONAL PARTIES

■ *Stephen K. Bailey*

The Parties and Responsible Power

The American government today suffers from three weaknesses: (1) its difficulty in generating sustained political power; (2) its difficulty in developing a flow of imaginative, informed, consistent, and power-related responses to pressing national and world issues; (3) its difficulty in making policy truly accountable to a national popular majority.

These are serious defects, not only because they interfere with wise and coherent governing in these dangerous days but because they undermine the faith of the citizen in the reality or even the possibility of responsible representative government. . . .

The defects are not new. Occasionally, in the past, they have been masked by brilliant presidential leadership in times of crisis or by the virtuosity of congressional leaders in times of presidential ineptitude. But the underlying defects have not disappeared. . . .

V. O. Key sounds not a hopeful but an ominous note when he writes:

> Representative bodies, the institutional embodiment of democratic ideology, have by the compelling force of events lost both power and prestige. Their role in the initiation of public policy has been diminished by losses to pressure groups and administrative agencies; their authority to decide many issues has, of necessity, been delegated to the administrative services. They have been driven towards a role of futile and uninformed criticism, at its worst motivated either by partisan or picayune considerations.[1]

From Stephen K. Bailey, *The Condition of Our National Parties* (New York: Fund for the Republic, 1959), pp. 3–8, 11, 17–21. Reprinted by permission of the publisher.

Even if we assume that the work of modern government is so technical and complex that enormous discretion must be lodged in the hands of experts, their capacity to act steadily in the public interest depends on the effectiveness of the very institutions whose influence is threatened by the expert mind. This dilemma will continue until we recognize that our representative institutions invite disuse and denigration because their structure is inadequate to perform the functions required of them. It is increasingly obvious that there are innovative, integrative, and perhaps sacrificial tasks ahead for which our government is not institutionally equipped.

To say that we need a new kind of political leadership may be true, but it begs the question. Where and how does political leadership arise in the United States? Who selects Presidential and congressional candidates? How can the process of selection be improved? How can leadership be sustained? How can first-class political executives be found to run our great public departments? Why is their present tenure so ephemeral? By what means can presidential and congressional purposes be brought into a working relationship? And why cannot leadership be held more fully accountable to the desires of popular majorities?

All these questions are related to the structural handicaps under which the American government now operates. At first glance, the problem seems to be constitutional—and in part it is. But the only two structural faults of the Constitution which really get in the way of responsible power in the national government are the Twenty-second Amendment, which limits the President to two terms, and the provisions for staggered elections. . . .

The root of the weakness is that while the two national parties for years have genuinely competed for the Presidency, they have not made a similar effort in the election of United States Senators and Members of the House of Representatives. Nor have they been of sufficient help to the President and Congress in providing candidates of high quality for the grand patronage of departmental and agency direction. So long as we lack strong national parties operating as catalysts in Congress, the executive branch, and the national government as a whole, and between the national government and state and local governments, power will continue to be dangerously diffused or, perhaps what is worse, will whipsaw between diffusion and Presidential dictatorship.[2]

Political reform does not include making the parties any more ideological than they are now. It does include making them competitive across the nation, allowing them to appeal to the natural ideological divisions within the population and within us as individuals. The stumbling block in this task is that neither party has a sufficiently unified structure to enable it to dramatize its program around its ideology; neither has the power, even if it had the right structure, to carry out the program; neither has sufficiently clear and unambiguous lines of political accountability running to the voters.

The structural limitations of the parties have grave consequences. First, they virtually ensure a government by fits and starts. Some historians claim that the United States was wise in having rejected the League of Nations;

but few would claim that the *process* by which the League was rejected was a rational way of arriving at a major foreign policy decision. In more recent times presidential requests for an adequate United States Information Agency budget have been listened to one year and ignored the next by the House Appropriations Committee. As a result, cultural officers abroad have had to spend much of their time hiring and firing—inflating and deflating programs like an accordion. This has made us look ridiculous as a nation and has also made it extremely difficult for a coherent information program to develop as a vital element in our foreign policy. The same has been true of foreign economic aid.

Spasms in domestic policy have been equally obvious and equally unsettling. The executive department and Congress have been unable to agree on any co-ordinated methods of applying the kind of devices needed to stabilize the economy and promote the goals of the Employment Act of 1946. Similar fits and starts have been noticeable in defense policy, atomic energy policy, welfare policy, and conservation policy. They have been quite as apparent when the Presidency and both Houses of Congress have been in one party as when the control of the government has been divided.

The second consequence of the structural limitations of the parties has been the lack of rationality and consistency in the substance of much public policy. In Paul Appleby's phrase, in this day and age someone or something has to "make a mesh of things." In a world in which, for example, the indiscriminate dumping of rice on the world market in order to ease a temporary glut in Louisiana could cost us the friendship of Burma, there are huge dangers in having unlinked centers of power making their own policy for the nation. And yet, parochial groups in Congress (often in league with sections of the executive branch and with outside pressure groups) still carry an inordinate amount of power.

The third consequence of the absence of coherent party machinery truly responsive to popular majorities is that congressional compromise tends to fall with considerable regularity on the side of minority rather than majority interests. Committee chairmen from "safe," and often sparsely populated, one-party states and districts; the minority-weighted bipartisan rules committee; and the myths, rules, and influence structure which enable congressional leaders to ignore demands for greater majority representation in policy decisions—all these combine to inflate the power of minority interests at the expense of the national popular majority. . . .

This is government by tollgate. It leads directly to consequence four: the increasing danger of public cynicism and apathy toward Congress, partly because its power is too diffuse or too subtle to comprehend; partly because when the power *is* clearly identifiable it seems to work more consistently for minorities than for the majority.

The last and by no means the least important consequence stemming from the absence of a unified party structure is that desperately needed criticism of both domestic and foreign policy is dissipated and discouraged. There is no effective vehicle for responsible opposition criticism of programs; there is no machinery for anticipating the implications of social changes and their effects on policy. . . .

In sum, the absence of effective party machinery in each House, and in the government generally, means that policy is frequently developed by an infinitely intricate system of barter and legerdemain.

Some defenders of America's traditional disorder have discounted the dangers to policy making of these intermittencies and irresponsibilities. They argue that our survival suggests that Presidential leadership and a congressional desire to co-operate during periods of crisis can save us in the future as they have in the past; that the thermidor between crises allows the divergences in our society to have their day without being subject to the tyranny of a transient numerical majority; and that the accepted American tradition of government by extraordinary or "concurrent" majorities has not stopped innovation or social criticism; it has only slowed change, and in the process has ensured a healthy unity behind public policy.

In relation to the past, these may be strong arguments. But are they addressed to a world of big bureaucracies, sustained cold wars, and chronic international and domestic crises? Are there any longer identifiable periods between crises? As long as the frontier was open and the spirit of laissez faire encouraged political parties to be barriers against government action, anarchy in program and uncontrolled shifts in power in the national government were of little consequence. For many years the parties were antigovernmental vehicles, so to speak, minimizing public policy and fencing off large sections of the population and of the domain for private exploitation and private dreams. But we are now in a very different world. As E. E. Schattschneider has pointed out:

> The revolution in communications, the dissolution of nationality blocs, the impact of the labor movement, urbanization, the revolution in public policy, the expansion of the practising electorate in recent years, and the new world position of the United States are only a few of the influences likely to give impetus to political reorganization in the present generation. It is obvious that the *purposes* of political organization are not what they once were. There was a time when it might have been said that the purpose of the party system, or large parts of it, was *obstruction*. In an era of perpetual crisis, political organization is reasonably certain to reflect the anxieties that now dominate all public life.[3]

. . . Inexorable forces are now clearly at work preparing the soil for a crop of politics far different from what we have known in the past century. It is time for a stringent look at the national politics we have had, the kind of national politics we want, and the reasons for believing that our traditional party system, like a vast glacier, may now have reached the edge of the sea.

The Parties Today: A Mystic Maze

The closer one gets to our two great national parties, the more difficult it is to find them. If you contend that they exist in their quadrennial national conventions, you must be prepared to answer where they are between conventions. If you identify them with the national committee offices in Washington, or one of them with the White House, you will hear immediate disclaimers from the party leaders on Capitol Hill. If a temporary marriage should be negotiated between the party in Congress and the party's executive wing, the great cellular blocks of the party at the state and local levels might well ask embarrassing questions about the true locus of party power.

Perhaps the shortest route through the maze of national party structure begins with the presidential nominating conventions. These are the formal governing bodies of the parties, the selectors of national candidates and issues for the quadrennial elections. They are composed of delegates chosen in a variety of ways and responsible to a wide variety of power groups within the states and beyond the states; governors, machine leaders, senators, members of Congress, pressure groups, individual presidential candidates and their followers, the incumbent President and so on.

But national conventions generally last less than a week. In order to provide continuity and necessary machinery in the long years between conventions, both parties elect national committees to serve for four years from the adjournment of the conventions. Actually, each state delegation proposes the two national committeemen (one is a woman) who are "elected" by the convention.[4]

The long history of the parties shows that it would be a mistake to suggest that the national committees have been at the power apex of their parties.

Although the party organization can be regarded as . . . capped by the national committee, it may be more accurately described as a system of layers of organization. Each successive layer—county or city, state, national—has an independent concern about elections in its geographical jurisdiction. Yet each higher level of organization, to accomplish its ends, must obtain the collaboration of the lower layer or layers of organization. That collaboration comes about, to the extent that it does come about, through a sense of common cause rather than the exercise of command.[5]

But even this does not tell the whole story. In the case of election campaigns for the Senate and the House, for example, there is no one layer of the party organization clearly responsible for these campaigns.[6] The groups that come closest are the respective party campaign committees in each House, but their power lies merely in the intermittent services and limited financial help they are able to offer; there is no hierarchical power or consistent influence here.

The formal organization of the parties can be described, if at all, then, as a series of pyramids with a common base in the shifting sands of active party membership, and generally with no clear locus of power in or out of the government.

As Key has pointed out, there are a number of reasons why the party system has had more *pluribus* than *unum:*

Both unity and disunity within the national organization have their roots in the diverse social, economic, and political interests in the party following. Yet another foundation of deconcentration of party leadership is the federal form of government. State and local party organizations are built up around the patronage of state and local government; and these organizations, particularly in cities and states dominated by one party, have a continuous life regardless of whether the party is in or out of power nationally. State and local patronage makes the local machine financially independent of the national headquarters and contributes to a spirit of independence. Federalism in our formal government machinery includes a national element independent of the states, but in our party organization the independent national element is missing. Party structure is more confederative than federal in nature. The state and local machines, built on state patronage, are allied with or paralleled by machines built around the patronage controlled by Senators and Representatives; and owing to the method of dispensation of this patronage, the resultant machines are almost as independent of central control as are the purely local organizations. Federalism in government tends to encourage confederation in the party's government.[7] . . .

These, then, are our national parties: unified for presidental contests, otherwise divided in power and lacking in definition; sporadically financed through various channels, subterfuges, and individual candidacies; peculiarly confused as out-parties; weak vehicles for executive-legislative co-operation as in-parties. They have performed valued services of reconciliation and compromise in our history—services which should not be underestimated. But the problem today is how to transcend these services in order to provide the government with sustained and responsible national power. . . .

The Traditional Conflicts

. . . The parties historically have performed a variety of very valuable functions in American society. They have been functions of accommodation, compromise, and the peaceful transmission of power. Only rarely have the parties been concerned with ensuring coherence of program or responsible power in the carrying out of program. Their lack of interest in national policies backed by national political power can be largely explained by the nature of the social conflicts with which they have had to deal. These traditional conflicts merit brief examination before we pass on to the contention of this chapter that the character of the conflicts is changing and that the party system must change with it.

One of the perennial conflicts in American history has been that between new and old settlers. . . . Historically, as one generation became settled and adjusted, it tended to look hostilely at new arrivals, particularly if the newcomers were from a different part of the Old World, spoke a different language, or had a different religion. In the fourteen years before World War I, immigration rose to a peak of a million a year. In contrast to the nineteenth-century immigration, the largest part of this million came from southern and eastern Europe: Italy, Poland, Russia, Hungary, Greece. Their attempts to find a life for themselves, especially in the urban areas of the East and Middle West; the resistances they met; the fears they created and suffered; the help local politicians gave them in exchange for their votes—all this has been and, although greatly modified by now, still is the stuff of American politics. Each group in turn has pursued the American dream; each in turn has found the upward ladder wobbly and at times sticky. Part of the glory of our traditional party system has been that when other ladders were removed the political ladder was almost always open. But many crowded on the ladder at once; and as some of those below overtook those on the higher rungs, conflict was inevitable.

If the new and old have warred, so have sections and classes. In the early days it was the frontier farmer against the commercial and financial interests of the seaboard. How much of our history has been devoted to this struggle!

As the continent expanded, other regional economic interests developed to complicate the conflict: commodity interests—tobacco, cotton, wheat, corn, sheep, minerals, fish, cattle, fruit, dairy products, oil, and an infinite variety of regional manufacturing interests. Some wanted high tariffs, some wanted low; some wanted federal aid, some wanted no federal interference of any kind. For years these regional interests were dominant forces in American politics.

For a brief period during the Jacksonian era, the Whig party forged an uneasy upper-class national alliance which attempted to bind regional interests into a national party. But the localized economic and social pressures were too strong, and the Whigs disintegrated in 1852. It was the parochialism of the economic and social interests of the South before the Civil War that made the irrepressible conflict irrepressible. After the war, a relatively nationwide two-party system came into being, but, as regional pressures erupted, the system became increasingly unstable. By 1896 the "solid Democratic South" had become a fixed political reality, and it was more than matched by a "solid Republican North" which effectively dominated American politics, except in the Wilsonian period, for a generation.

The remnants of these and other regional struggles are still with us, especially in Congress, but they have been complicated—sometimes modified, sometimes egregiously promoted—by far-ranging class conflicts between rich and poor, debtor and creditor, capital and labor, small farmers and big farmers. On a few occasions, these class collisions have got beyond the control of existing political machinery. But this has been rare. In the words of David Potter, we have been a "people of plenty," and for much of our history the frontier has provided a real as well as a psychological safety valve. What it could not provide, democratic politics by and large has provided: a redress of intolerable economic grievances.

In one form or another the Negro problem has always been with us. Like some vast geologic fault, it has rendered the land unstable and created deep moral fissures. It was an issue in colonial days; it had to be compromised in the drafting of our Constitution. It was the emotional core of the Civil War. In the cruel and stupid days of Reconstruction, the social and political inversions imposed by northern occupation terrified both whites and Negroes and left raw scars of fear, hatred, and anti-Republicanism.

The Negro issue has occupied a central place in the development of the national party organizations and in the formation of political alliances. Because the issue seemed until recently a "southern" problem, the Democratic party as the more national of the two parties had to live a precarious existence astride a two-headed donkey. It survived by promising the Presidency to the North and Congress to the South. The Republican party, on the other hand, as a party operating effectively only in the North, was able to strike a bargain with southern Democrats which linked white supremacy and business supremacy in the policy labyrinths of Congress. The bargain clouded the image of each party and put largely irresponsible power over policy in the hands of a southern Democratic–northern Republican coalition, buttressed by seniority and hallowed by carefully designed rules. None of this would have happened if the parties had not had to juggle the Negro issue. It has been the most useful device of the economic conservatives to keep the political parties from becoming coherent instruments of majority rule. . . .

The national parties have become what they are because of these historical conflicts which they have had to settle, hide, or gloss over. In some cases, they have been the master brokers between rich and poor, country and city, butter and oleo, capital and labor, Italian and Irish, new and old. At other times, they have hidden certain conflicts in order to satisfy powerful economic interests which have stood to gain by exploiting conflict locally and disguising it nationally. Each party has been caught in the dilemma, on the one hand, of trying to forge an image of harmony in the interests of the majority in order to win the Presidency and, on the other hand, of being unable to eradicate the very different kind of image which generations of conservative log-rolls and bipartisan "inner-clubism" in Congress have created in the public eye.

But what happens when the conditions of conflict change? For they are changing, and rapidly, in the United States.

Take the struggle between the old and the new. We used to be able to tell the difference between old and new settlers by their accent, or dress or occupational level. But we are fuller of 100 per cent Americans every day and are rapidly reaching the time when nationality politics will be as anachronistic as the trolley car. . . . Matters which once split us and made us fearful are now absorbed almost without question as our population becomes increasingly homogenized.

Or take sectional and class conflict. The heart has been cut out of sectionalism by vast changes in technology and communications which have dispersed industry and revolutionized agriculture. Where are the one-crop "Cotton Ed" Smiths of a few years back? The fact is that there are precious few one-crop areas left in America. And even where there are, as in some of the great agricultural regions of the Great Plains, technology is bringing a revolution of another kind. In the last five years almost four million people have left the farm. The forecast for reapportionment of congressional seats after the 1960 census suggests a dramatic decrease in rural representation in the United States Congress, and this trend will continue as the rise in population throws more and more people into metropolitan areas.

The movement in urban politics tends to be toward class rather than regional politics. But even class politics has changed. It is no longer a kind of rabble vs. gentry rivalry. Rather, among other things, it is a national industry against highly bureaucratized and well-paid national labor. Senator Barry Goldwater of Arizona is not a regional figure. In the congressional elections of 1958, national giants contended in that sparsely populated desert state, and for national stakes.

What bothers the auto worker in Detroit bothers the auto worker in Los Angeles. What worries the businessman in Chicago worries his competitor in Boston. With transcontinental jet planes, the political or labor or industrial leader whose home is in San Francisco is almost more accessible to his counterpart in New York than is a train traveler from Boston; and, in any case, distance has been obliterated by electricity, electronics, and the direct-dial telephone.

And what is happening to the Negro issue? It, too, is becoming nationalized. Today there are more Negroes in New York than in New Orleans; more in Detroit than in Birmingham, Alabama; more in Pittsburgh than in Little Rock; more in Los Angeles than in Richmond; more in Chicago than in Atlanta. The Negroes' locustlike migration to northern metropolitan centers may have brought new problems to city governments, but it has aroused a critical competition between the two major parties in the North and West to capture the Negro vote. In heavily populated, evenly divided states, a bloc shift of a few votes can mean thirty or forty electoral college votes for a Presidential candidate.

Perhaps more than any one other factor, the northern migration of the Negro is working tremendous transformations in our political life. The South no longer can exercise a veto in either Presidential convention. Some diehards may walk out in 1960, but the result will only be that they will risk losing what waning power they have in Congress. For, in more than sixty congressional districts in the North and West, the Negro holds the political balance of power if he decides to bloc-vote; and in the South his political power is likely to increase steadily despite the present tensions. . . .

The shifts in the nature of the conflicts are reflected in the changes that are already taking place in our party system:

1. The number of one-party states and one-party congressional districts is dramatically declining. . . .

2. The permanent staffs of the national party committees and the variety of committee functions have grown greatly during the past decade. Until World War II both national committees were served by skeletal staffs except for the few months before national Presidential elections. Today both of them maintain year-round staffs of between seventy-five and a hundred people. In election years this number doubles or triples. The annual budget of each committee amounts to almost a million dollars—a figure which skyrockets during election years.

3. Both national committees are doing everything in their power to spread their financial base. The evolution has been from fat cats and expensive fund-raising banquets to mass appeals and direct-mail solicitation.

4. Almost unnoticed, a revolution has occurred in the "nationalization" of off-year senatorial and congressional campaigns. As recently as 1938, the press

and the public criticized President Roosevelt for campaigning in an off-year election. But in 1954, when both the President and the titular leader of the Democrats actively campaigned in their parties' congressional elections, both the newspapers and the voters seemed to accept the fact that it was perfectly all right for the executive wings of the parties to interest themselves actively in the outcome of the legislative contests. in 1958, both national committees sent out representatives to help develop party strength in various regions and to give services to local campaigns. . . .

5. Since 1937, the Presidents have met regularly with party leaders in Congress on matters of legislative priority and strategy. This has elevated the prestige and power of these men, particularly on matters of foreign policy and national defense. . . .

6. The creation of the Democratic Advisory Council and the recent appearance of an embryonic Republican counterpart show a new concern in both parties for clarifying the party image.

This far from exhaustive list of the responses of our political system to nationalizing forces represents only the beginnings of adaptation and adjustment. Our basic political institutions, and their relationships to each other and to the public, are in a state of flux. If we want a political system designed to give full play to America's political energies and to hold them within bounds set by a popular majority, we are obligated to modify the system still further.

▪ *Notes*

1. V. O. Key, *Politics, Parties, and Pressure Groups,* 4th ed. (New York: Crowell, 1958), p. 762.
2. See John Fischer, "Unwritten Rules of American Politics," *Harper's* (November, 1948), pp. 27–36; Peter Drucker, "A Key to American Politics: Calhoun's Pluralism," *Review of Politics* (October, 1948), pp. 412–425; Ernest F. Griffith, *Congress: Its Contemporary Role* (New York: New York University Press, 1951); Murray Stedman and Herbert Sonthoff, "Party Responsibility — A Critical Inquiry," *Western Political Quarterly* (September, 1951), pp. 454–486; Julius Turner, "Responsible Politics: A Dissent from the Floor," *American Political Science Review* (March, 1951), pp. 143–152; William Goodman, "How Much Political Party Centralization Do We Want?", *Journal of Politics* (November, 1951), pp. 536–561; and, especially, Austin Ranney, *The Doctrine of Responsible Party Government* (Urbana: University of Illinois Press, 1954).
3. E. E. Schattschneider, "The Struggle for Party Government" (pamphlet) (University of Maryland, 1950), pp. 28–29.
4. In 1952 certain Republican state chairmen were added to the Republican National Committee under a "reward for victory" formula. See Key, *op. cit.,* p. 348, for details.
5. *Ibid.,* p. 347.
6. An exception to this rule is the State of Indiana, in which congressional district organizations are a formal part of the state party machinery.
7. Key, *op. cit.,* p. 368.

29 THE CONGRESSIONAL CHECK

▪ *Ronald Steel*

On entering the House of Representatives at Washington one is struck with the vulgar demeanor of that great assembly. The eye frequently does not discover a man of celebrity within its walls. Its members are almost all obscure individuals, whose names present no associations to the mind; they are mostly village lawyers, men in trade, or even persons belonging to the lower classes of society. In a country in which education is very general, it is said that the representatives of the people do not always know how to write correctly.

—Alexis de Tocqueville, *Democracy in America*

It is comforting to know that some things never change, or at least not very much. One can still drop into that sprawling chamber where the people's representatives meet in solemn session and wonder how anything of the slightest importance could possibly happen there. A handful of men in baggy suits can be seen in various postures of repose—a few reading newspapers, another picking his nose, one sound asleep—while from somewhere in a sea of mahogany desks a voice rises in droning tribute to the milkweed pod or the orthodontist. Even high-school civics teachers know better than to allow their wards to linger in the House gallery on spring vacation trips to the capital. Lest they all turn into cynics, they are hustled off after a few minutes to see the stuffed Indians at the Smithsonian.

But if Tocqueville was right, we have to remember that the public spectacle of the lower chamber has always been mostly for show and a few laughs. The real business, then as now, goes on behind the scenes, in the committee rooms where the feudal barons of the legislative process dispose of the public business at their private discretion. As Woodrow Wilson wrote during his professorial days: "The House sits not for serious discussion, but to sanction the conclusions of its committees as rapidly as possible." If the ratification

From Ronald Steel, "Is Congress Obsolete?" *Commentary*, XXXVII (September, 1964), 59–64. © Copyright 1964 by *Commentary*. Reprinted by permission of Harold Matson Company, Inc.

ceremony has little drama and even less debate, nobody seems to mind very much. To expect rapier wit and probing cross questioning on the floor of the House is to ask of that august body a quality which it does not consider to be a virtue. In the rich heritage of custom the House holds dear, there is little room for question askers or boat rockers. Was it not, after all, the late Sam Rayburn, venerated by friend and foe alike as the living incarnation of everything that is most honorable in the House, who summed up the creed governing the institution over which he presided for so many years in the immortal words: "To get along, go along"?

Going along has always been to the House what economic determinism is to Marxists or predestination to Calvinists: an article of faith and a philosophy of life. Those who vote prudently when the chips are down and don't ask too many questions are drawn into the fold and given the sacraments—assignment to a powerful committee, a new federal highway through their district, speedy action on a private bill for an influential constituent. The few others, who for reasons of temperament or conscience have a hard time going along, find the role of a legislator a mine field of bad intentions. As Senator Paul Douglas, a pioneer of the lonesome road himself, reminded a would-be rebel: "The legislation you favor will not go through. The dam your constituents want will not be built. The river improvements your constituents want will not be built."

Yet a few malcontents invariably appear in the House who ignore Sam Rayburn's advice. Among the most poignant are the idealists who think that all issues are decided on moral principle and resolved by the logic of debate. In his collection of round-table discussions, *The Congressman—His Work As He Sees It,* one of a number of recent books on the House, Charles Clapp quotes such a disappointed idealist as saying:

> I came here thinking this was for real, that this was the only parliament where democratic processes were at work. That is a myth, I find. You can't stand on the floor and inform people; they don't want to listen. If anybody thinks he is going to come down here and legislate, he is crazy. When I first arrived and looked around the Capitol, the White House and the Washington Monument, I had a lump in my throat and I felt pretty humble about being part of this great scene. But now all I see is skullduggery and shenanigans.

There speaks a man who thought he was going to the House of Commons and discovered himself in the House of Representatives, an organization whose leaders have no desire to be informed on the floor by their junior fellows nor any intention of letting them legislate. While newcomers often complain bitterly about the five-minute limitation on debate, they gradually come to realize that it is not so much a tyranny imposed by the leadership as a handy device for dispensing with the irrelevant—that is, a debate that would not make the slightest difference in the way members cast their votes. With the horse trading all wound up before the bill ever reaches the floor, the only thing a debate could accomplish would be to tell the voters what was being done to them in the name of their best interests. But since the House does not consider the enlightenment of the electorate to be one of its primary functions, most congressmen are ardent supporters of the five-minute gag on debate. . . .

To be sure, Congressmen, like everyone else, are subject to persuasion. It is just that the real persuaders are not those who deliver fervent addresses, nor even the President and his various arm-twisting minions, but the handful of venerable figures in the House catbird seat: the Speaker, the minority leader, the chairmen of the half-dozen key committees. Theirs are the hands that guide the strange, and sometimes incomprehensible, workings of the House, that hold out rewards and exact punishments, that allow certain bills to be voted on and consign others to the limbo of the forgotten. These are the men who decide on the assignment of their colleagues to the legislative committees—an act filled with all the darkness and much of the ceremony of the Eleusinian Mysteries. Congressman Bob Wilson, for example, whose political career is mightily helped by a steady flow of defense contracts into his California constituency, told Clapp that he was not exactly sure why he was put on the Armed Services committee, although "one factor of great significance" must have been "that my district has many military installations in it and thus is a logical one to be represented on the committee." Another Congressman, benefiting from Sam Rayburn's dictum that the new Democrats on the Education and Labor Committee must first be cleared by the AFL-CIO, found that his assignment was made "when some labor lobbyists came to me and asked whether I would go on if they could get me on. They went ahead and got me on. I neither asked for it nor lifted a finger for it."

As far as the individual Congressman is concerned, the most awesome seat of power in the House has been the Appropriations Committee. . . .

If the Appropriations Committee has the key to the public purse and the Congressman's heart, another House institution, the Rules Committee, manages to exercise veto power over legislation without having any substantive authority at all. Theoretically empowered only to decide the order in which bills approved by other committees shall be sent to the floor for consideration, it has in reality established itself as the moral overseer of legislation, deciding not merely when the House shall consider bills but whether it should be allowed to consider them at all. An early chairman of this committee was not speaking through his hat when he said, "In me reposes absolute obstructive powers." Similarly, in 1960 the venerable current chairman, Judge Howard Smith, told two members of his committee who were seeking the release of several key bills: "The only legislation I will agree to consider is the minimum-wage bill. You can tell your liberal friends that they will get that— or nothing. If you try to bring up anything else, I'll adjourn the meeting."

Crafty parliamentarian that he is, Judge Smith has adjourned a good many meetings, with the result that he has usually been able to block the bills he didn't like and speed through the ones he admired—such as the Communist control act that bears his name. It is a favorite pastime among liberals to fulminate against the Judge and curse him for having a black heart. Yet the

Rules Committee is the House's creation, not his, and it perfectly reflects the political ethos which dominates that institution. Who would vote to remove Judge Smith from the chairmanship of "his" committee—a position which he acquired and maintains by virtue of having been returned to Congress for sixteen consecutive terms—when to do so would be a direct blow to the seniority system from which every Congressman can expect to benefit? Even Sam Rayburn, cunning fox that he was, was unable to pry key administration bills loose from the Rules Committee; nor was he able to purge William Colmer from his second-ranking position on it despite the fact that Colmer, a Mississippi Democrat, actively campaigned against Kennedy in the 1960 election.

To a foreign observer there must have been something pathetic, if not totally mystifying, in the late President's complaint that much of his program would have been approved had the Rules Committee allowed his bills to come to a vote in the House. After all, the committee had a two-thirds Democratic majority, was headed by a member of the President's own party, and was supposedly acting as an agent of a Democratic-controlled House. But as James MacGregor Burns has told us in his admirable study, *Deadlock of Democracy,* there are two Democratic parties, one controlled by some ninety Congressmen elected by two million voters, and another (when the Democrats are in power) headed by the President and making its appeal to sixty million voters. The congressional Democrats, with Judge Smith as their rock and Adam Smith as their prophet, view themselves as defenders of the republic against its wild-eyed enemies "downtown" in the White House and the government agencies. And in this crusade they have found natural allies in Republicans like Charles Halleck, the pugnacious minority leader, who sees the Rules Committee as a "roadblock to unwise, ill-timed, spendthrift, socialistic measures."

Those critics who are trying to save the House from itself and pump some blood back into its congealed arteries naturally seize upon the Rules Committee as the logical place to begin. . . . The fact, however, is that both the leadership and the majority of the House seem quite content with the conduct of the Rules Committee and have consistently refrained from any serious attempt to discipline it. It is too handy as a graveyard for legislation that the majority does not want, but dares not oppose openly.

But then has not Congress always looked upon the nonpassage of bills as a function at least as important as their passage? As Robert Bendiner says in *Obstacle Course on Capitol Hill,* his informative and witty study of the non-legislative process at work: "A United States Congressman has two principal functions: to make laws and to keep laws from being made. . . . Indeed, if that government is best that governs least, then Congress is designed, by rule and tradition, to be one of the most perfect instruments of government ever devised." Following various bills for federal aid to education on their long and tortuous path to extinction, Bendiner delves into the labyrinth of congressional obstructionism as it has been refined over the years by the best parliamentary minds in the business. The result is a revealing insight into the nonworkings of our legislative system and a fascinating account of how an intelligent minority has been able to impose its will on a disorganized majority.

Considering all the hurdles and pits that Congress has placed in the path of legislation, it is less remarkable that the system performs so badly than that, like the chess-playing dog, it performs so well. One would be hard pressed to think of any other functioning democracy where the chief executive could not even persuade the legislature to consider, let alone pass, one-fifth of the bills he sent to it. Yet somehow or other the system creaks on; the absolutely vital measures get passed in one form or another, while the controversial ones gather dust until there is sufficient popular demand to force them to a vote—or until the Supreme Court does Congress' work for it. Which is no ground for complacency, but none for hysteria either. Looking back on some of the legislation that has been whooped through the House— such as the perennial wire-tap bills, the Smith Act, or the 1950 resolution to cut off Marshall Plan aid to England until the British Parliament ended the partition of Ireland—one might have second thoughts about the desirability of speedy congressional action.

Perhaps, in any case, it is only the political scientists who take Congress' legislative role seriously. If forced to express an opinion, most Congressmen would probably not place legislating very high on their list of public duties. Faithful servant of the people, the average member of the House takes greater pride in his job of representation. He delights in considering himself a liaison between his constituents and the federal government, serving as a conduit for baffled inquiries about overdue social security checks, veterans' benefits, and draft deferments. The size of the country and the impersonality of the bureaucracy make this function important, although only in the United States is it considered to be the main job of the nation's legislators. While he perpetually grumbles about the time it consumes, the Congressman enjoys playing this role—even to the point of acting as a travel agent for his constituents, reserving hotel rooms for them, and finding them choice seats for the selection of Miss Cherry Blossom. It all gives him a sense of service, and it forges ties with the voters that come in handy every second November. . . .

The burden these legislators operate under does not come from the narrow prejudices of their district—a civics-class myth it is time we disposed of— but from a procedural system that prevents a numerical majority from imposing its will on an entrenched minority. To free Representatives from the pressure of their constituents would in no way threaten the power of the oligarchs who have manipulated the rules of the House to their own purposes and are responsible to no one but themselves. A more effective remedy, therefore, would lie in freeing Congress from its own procedural prison. Not that this would necessarily bring Congress wisdom, but it could at least help it to function once again.

Nevertheless, it would be foolish to deny that the Representative is a man subject to intense local pressures—pressures which he cannot ignore without sacrificing his political life. He may find these pressures narrow and ignorant;

he may even defy them if he thinks he can; but he dare not cut too many bridges of support or he will soon find himself with nowhere to turn and his career in Washington collapsing under him. This is one of the reasons why Congressmen feel it essential to reply to every letter that comes into their office, no matter how undeserving or unnecessary of response. Those from marginal districts where two-party politics is a reality live under the constant terror of offending a single voter. Only an iconoclast like Stephen Young has the courage to reply to crackpots: "Dear Sir, Some damned fool sent me a stupid letter and signed your name to it." But then Stephen Young is not only a free spirit and a man of exquisite sense; he is also a Senator; and Senators can do things that no Congressman would dream of in his wildest flights of fantasy. Blessed with a six-year term and supported by the assumption that voters have short memories, Senators can even court temporary unpopularity by favoring the needs of the nation over the feelings of their constituents. To be sure, even a Senator has to keep the fences mended at home, and never for a minute can he forget that he is an elected official with his state's interests to represent; but at least he has more leeway than his colleagues in the House of Representatives.

The Representative, unless he is permanently entrenched in office by a one-party constituency, takes a national view of public affairs only at his own peril. As D. W. Brogan has pointed out:

> An American Congressman who, for the best of reasons, offends local pressure groups, or by not talking for Buncombe, wastes his time on mere national issues of the first order, may be out—and out forever. The history of Congress is full of martyrs to the general welfare, but any given Congress is full of men who have had more sense than to prefer the general welfare to the local interest.

Thus, Congressmen from marginal districts feel that they must work both sides of the political fence if they are to be re-elected. . . .

Because Representatives are constantly running for re-election, the House, it is said, more accurately reflects the national will than the Senate. But here we come upon a paradox, for is it not often the case that the Congressman trails behind public opinion, faithfully waving the banner of last year's slogan? The gap between that vast amorphous entity known as The Country and the incestuous little world of Washington has not developed—as most Congressmen like to think—mainly because of the electorate's backwardness. It is a result of the isolation and caution of legislators who are so enmeshed in congressional gamesmanship that they no longer have any clear idea of what the voters are thinking—and in some cases, they have even ceased to care. Instead of legislating, Congress holds hearings; instead of educating the voters, it bemoans their ignorance; instead of offering leadership, it complains that it is not the President; and instead of drafting its own bills, it merely acts as a receptacle for legislation drawn up by the White House and the federal agencies.

Reflecting on the ways of the House, an institution that fills him with alternating mirth and consternation, Murray Kempton writes:

It is argued that the House of Representatives has damaged the country by its persistence in negation. But the real point is that this habit has damaged the House of Representatives more than it has anything else. Negation, long indulged, renders any institution impotent. The House can no longer offer any alternative to Executive discretion on matters truly critical; its attitude has, in fact, turned government into a series of private compacts to do what has to be done without admitting that it is being done. And what should be serious debate ends as only a saber dance. The Congress is content with gestures; it has surrendered to the President what power there is for substantial action.

ˋ In the paralysis of its procedures and the negativism of its philosophy, the Senate has been just as irresponsible as the House, and with even less reason, since it cannot fall back on the excuse that a two-year term somehow ties its hands. Together the two chambers form a poignant diptych of Tweedledum and Tweedledee, joined in impotent wedlock by the fetters of their own making. As a result, the role of Congress in the American system of government has become basically one of obstruction and harassment. It can block administration bills which have overwhelming public support, such as medicare or federal aid to education, but it is unable to offer any constructive alternatives of its own. It can slash the foreign aid bill to ribbons and hamper the conduct of foreign policy by cutting off aid to countries whose leaders it doesn't like, while shunting off the consequences of its irresponsibility to a frustrated executive branch. It can annoy the administration, of whatever party, by investigations designed more to embarrass public officials than to enlighten the public and by indiscriminate hacking at the budgets of administrative agencies that incur the displeasure of one of the congressional oligarchs. It can drive Cabinet officials to distraction by forcing them to make perpetual appearances before its various committees in hearings which often seem designed more to satisfy congressional vanity than to provide information. In the face of this collapse of legislative responsibility, even Walter Lippmann, a man not given to dramatic generalizations, has found "reason to wonder whether the congressional system as it now operates is not a grave danger to the Republic."

What is most alarming about the inability of Congress to legislate is that it may lead to a breakdown of our peculiarly successful, but not necessarily permanent, democratic system. The checks and balances written into the Constitution are the very fiber of American democracy, and if they are disturbed over too long a period, the system itself must suffer. A self-reliant and responsible legislature is, after all, an anomaly in the world, not a commonplace. For all its sense of drama and lofty standards of debate, the French parliament was so totally incapable of coping with its duties and had fallen to such a level of public contempt that its demise was greeted with indifference or delight. The American Congress, too, could become a purely ceremonial body, providing country lawyers with prestigious titles to cap their careers and offering a source of harmless entertainment for a cynical public.

This is certainly one way of resolving the congressional impasse, but it is one over which liberals should contain their enthusiasm. It is only relatively recently that liberals have found such virtue in a strong-arm executive and a politically motivated Supreme Court—institutions which were both looked upon with considerable suspicion when they were manned by incumbents of different political hue. We have had reactionary Courts and right-wing Presidents before, and we are likely to have them again. . . .

30   THE PRESIDENCY

▪ *Richard E. Neustadt*

There are many ways to look at the American Presidency. It can be done in terms juridical or biographical, political or managerial: the office viewed primarily as a compendium of precedents, a succession of personalities, a fulcrum for party politics, a focus for administrative management. This chapter denies the relevance of none of these approaches and makes use, incidentally, of them all, but aims at observation from a rather different point of view. This is an effort to look at the Presidency *operationally*, in working terms, as an instrument of governance in the middle years of the twentieth century; as man-in-office, that is to say, in a time of continuing "cold war," spiraling atomic discovery (and vulnerability), stabilized "big government," and stalemated partisan alignment—the *policy* environment capsuled by Clinton Rossiter as "new economy" and "new internationalism"; the *political* environment billed by Samuel Lubell as "politics of twilight." . . .[1]

The Presidency in Government

"His is the vital place of action in the system," wrote Woodrow Wilson of the President toward the close of TR's term.[2] And this, a new discovery for Wilson's generation, is now, at mid-century, a matter of course. Presidential leadership is now a matter of routine to a degree quite unknown before World War II. If the President remains at liberty, in Wilson's phrase, "to be as big a man as he can," the obverse holds no longer: he *cannot* be as small as he might choose.

Once, TR daringly assumed the "steward's" role in the emergency created by the great coal strike of 1902; the Railway Labor Act and the Taft-Hartley Act now make such interventions mandatory upon Presidents. Once, FDR dramatically asserted personal responsibility for gauging and guiding the American economy; now, the Employment Act binds his successors to that

From Richard E. Neustadt, "The Presidency at Mid-Century," in a symposium, "The Presidential Office," *Law and Contemporary Problems*, XXI (Autumn, 1966), 609–615, 619–632, published by the Duke University School of Law, Durham, North Carolina. © Copyright 1957 by Duke University. Reprinted with permission.

task. Wilson and FDR became chief spokesmen, leading actors on a world stage at the height of war; now UN membership, far-flung alliances, the facts of power, prescribe that role continuously in times termed "peace." Through both World Wars, our Presidents grappled experimentally with an emergency-created need to "integrate" foreign and military and domestic policies; the National Security Act now takes that need for granted as a constant of our times. FDR and Truman made themselves responsible for the development and first use of atomic weapons; the Atomic Energy Act now puts a comparable burden on the back of every President. In instance after instance, the one-time personal initiatives, innovations of this century's "strong" Presidents, have now been set by statutes as requirements of office. And what has escaped statutory recognition has mostly been absorbed into Presidential "common law," confirmed by custom, no less binding: the unrehearsed press conference, for example, or the personally presented legislative program.

The "vital place of action" has been rendered permanent: the *forms* of leadership fixed in the cumulative image of *ad hoc* assertions under Wilson and the two Roosevelts, past precedents of personality and crisis absorbed into the government's continuing routines. For the executive establishment and for Congress, both, the Presidency has become the regular, accustomed source of all major initiatives: supplier of both general plans and detailed programs; articulator of the forward course in every sphere of policy encompassed by contemporary government. Bold or bland, aggressive or conciliatory, massive or minimal, as the case may be, the lead is his.

Thus, we have made a matter of routine the President's responsibility to take the policy lead. And at the same time, we have institutionalized, in marked degree, the exercise of that responsibility. President and Presidency are synonymous no longer; the office now comprises an officialdom twelve hundred strong. For almost every phase of policy development, there is now institutional machinery engaged in preparations on the President's behalf: for the financial and administrative work plan of the government, the Budget Bureau; for the administration's legislative program, the White House counsel and the Budget's clearance organization; for programing in economic and social spheres, the Council of Economic Advisers (and to some degree the cabinet, Eisenhower style); in foreign and military fields, the National Security Council; in spheres of domestic preparedness, the Office of Defense Mobilization; these pieces of machinery, among others, each built around a program-making task, all lumped together, formally, under the rubric, "The Executive Office of the President," an institutional conception and a statutory entity less than two decades old.

These are significant developments, this rendering routine, this institutionalizing of the initiative. They give the Presidency nowadays a different look than it has worn before, an aspect permanently "positive." But the reality behind that look was not just conjured up by statutes or by staffing. These, rather, are *responses* to the impacts of external circumstances on our form of government; not causes, but effects.

Actually or potentially, the Presidency has always been—at least since Jackson's time—a unique point of intersection for three lines of leadership responsibility: "executive" and partisan and national. The mandates of our Constitution, the structure of our political parties, the nature of the President's electorate, fused long ago to draw these lines together *at that point and there alone:* the Presidency at once the sole nationally elective office,[3] independently responsible to a unique constituency; sole centralizing stake of power, source of control, in each party (as a glance at either party out of power shows); sole organ of foreign relations and military command; sole object of the "take care" clause and of the veto power; and with all this, sole crownlike symbol of the Union.

By Wilson's time, that combination, in the context of world power stakes and status, had brought a fourth line of leadership into play, a line of leadership abroad, its only point of intersection with the other three the White House, once again. Since then, there have been revolutionary changes in the world and in American society and in the character of government's commitments toward both; changes productive of fast-rising expectations and requirements for leadership transmitted toward the Presidency along each line—four streams of action impulses and obligations converging on the President, whoever he may be, their volume and their rate of flow varying with events, a source which never, nowadays, runs dry.

The contemporary President, in short, has *four constituencies,* each with distinctive expectations of him and demands upon him. One of these is his "government" constituency, comprising the great group of public officers—congressional as well as executive—who cannot do their own official jobs without some measure of performance on his part. A second is his "partisan" constituency, comprising at once his own party's congressional delegation and its organization leaders, workers, even voters, all those whose political fortunes, interests, sentiments, are tied, in some degree, to his performance. A third is his "national" constituency, comprising all those individuals and groups among Americans who look to him, especially when crises come, for an embodiment and an expression of government's relationship to its citizenry, for a response to their needs, purposes, endeavors. And fourth, his "overseas" constituency, comprising not alone the officers of foreign governments but the political oppositions, the opinion molders, even the plain citizens to some degree, in every country where our power, policies, or postures have imposed themselves upon domestic politics.

In respect to the first three of these constituencies, membership is not a mutually exclusive matter. A number of American officials—among them Cabinet officers and Congressmen, are members of all three. And most Americans hold membership in two, as at once partisans and citizens. But whatever its effects on individual or group behavior, multiple membership does not preclude distinctly differentiated sets of Presidency-oriented expectations and demands, identifiable with each constituency, arising in the circumstances of mid-century from the pervasive needs of each for governmental action.

In these terms, it appears no accident that at a time when stakes of government are high for all the President's constituents, to him has passed, routinely, the continuing initiative in government. That role is both assured him and required of him by the very uniqueness of his place at the only point of intersection, the sole juncture, of those four lines of leadership responsibility and the constituencies they represent.

Yet, the demands and expectations pressing in upon the President propel him not alone toward enunciation but toward delivery. Executive officials want decisions, Congressmen want proposals, partisans want power, citizens want substance, friends abroad want steadiness and insight and assistance on their terms—all these as shorthand statements of complex material and psychological desires. These things are wanted *done;* given our Constitution and our politics, that means done by, or through, or with assistance from, or acquiescence of, the President. The very factors that contribute to his unique opportunities—and routinized responsibilities—as an initiator make him essential also as protector, energizer, implementor, of initiatives once taken. His special place in government requires of him, indeed, thrusts upon him, a unique responsibility—and opportunity—to oversee and assure execution.

But while responsibility for the initiative has now been routinized and even institutionalized, authority to implement the courses set remains fragmented in our system. In most respects and for most purposes, the President lacks any solid base of assured, institutionalized support to carry through the measures he proposes. His four constituencies are capable of constant pressure, but not of reliable response to downward leads. The "executive" is not a unity with a firm command-and-subordination structure, nor is the government, nor is the political party, in Congress or out, nor is the nation, nor the alliance system overseas. All these are feudalities in power terms; pluralistic structures, every one of them. Our Constitution, our political system, our symbolism, and our history make certain that the President alone assumes, in form, the leadership of each—and guarantee, no less, that he will not have systematic, unified, assured support from any. Indeed, precisely the conditions vesting him alone with leadership responsibility for all prevent the rendering of any one of them into tight-welded followings. The constitutional separation of powers—really, of institutions sharing powers—the federal separations of sovereignty, hence politics, the geographic separations of electorates—these and their consequences at once have helped the Presidency to its special place and hindered the creation of a strong supporting base. And, at a time when the executive establishment has grown too vast for personal surveillance, when Congress is controlled in form by narrow, shifting partisan majorities, in fact by factional coalition, weighted against the President's electorate, the hindrances are bound to be enhanced. Ours is that sort of time.

This does not mean that Presidents are powerless; far from it. Their four-way leadership position gives them vantage points aplenty for exerting strength in government, in party, in the country, and abroad: collectively, by all odds, an array of strong points quite unmatched by any other single power-holder in our system. It does mean, though, that Presidential power must be exercised *ad hoc,* through the employment of whatever sources of support, whatever transient advantages can be found and put together, case by case. It means the President can never choose a policy with certainty that it will be approximated in reality or that he will not have it to unmake or make again. It means he cannot, as he pleases, moderate, adjust, or set aside the rival, overlapping, often contradictory claims of his constituencies. *He has no option but to act, at once, as agent of them all, for their conjunction in his person is the keystone of his potency;* none is dispensable; hence the demands of none are automatically disposable at his convenience. Events, not his free choices, regulate their pressures and condition his response.

Dilemmas, consequently, are the Presidency's daily bread. The President must now initiate specific policies and programs for all fields of federal action; he has become the focus for all forward planning in our system; whatever leads the government and country and his party (and, indeed, the opposition also) are to have will stem from him. Yet, not his preferences only, but events in an inordinately complex world—not his reasoning alone, but his constituencies' felt requirements, contradictory as they may be—mold his determinations, limit his choices, force his hand. What he initiates he must attempt to implement. He must try so to manage the executive establishment, and Congress, and his party oligarchs, and the other party's also, and "public opinion," and overseas support, that the essential things get done—so far at least as government can do them—to keep administration reasonably competent, the country reasonably prosperous, the cold war reasonably cold, and his party in the White House; objectives which will seem to him synonymous (no President in memory, Mr. Eisenhower naturally not excluded, has ever thought his policies could best be carried forward by the other party's men). Yet, none of these agencies of action, of execution, is subject to his management by fiat; not even those closest to home, his own administration, his own party, are constructed to provide him with assured support. Rarely can he order; mostly must he persuade, And even were his controls taut and sharp, there would remain, of course, those agencies beyond his power to command: events.

No doubt, in times of great emergency, sharp crisis seen and felt as such throughout the country, the Presidency's measure of assured support from public, party, and administration tends to increase dramatically, if temporarily, while "politics as usual" abates, at least until the sharpness wanes; witness the situation *circa* 1942. But it is characteristic of our circumstances at midcentury—in all the years since World War II—that while our government's responsibilities retain a trace of every prior crisis, no comparable sense of national emergency pervades our politics. If this is an "era of permanent crisis," it is one in which Presidents must manage without benefit of crisis consensus. . . .

The Freedom to Choose

If Presidents were free to choose the matters they made choices on, their problems of choice making would be relatively simplified; but Presidents are not. The flow of issues they must face cannot be turned off like a water tap; to know that, one has but to note its sources.

Why do men in government and politics (and in the country and the world) bring issues to a President, invoke his act of choice? To amplify the foregoing analysis, it may be said that they do so for one, or another, or all of three reasons. First, there are matters that by law or custom require some sort of personal performance on his part: his signature, his presence, or his voice. Second, there are matters on which others, theoretically competent to act, want the loan of his potency or the cover of his prestige, his impetus behind their preferences, his brand on their performance. Third, there are the matters he himself wants made his own, that on his own initiative he has marked "count me in," matters on which he exercises the discretion we have already discussed. And in the circumstances of mid-century, no President will lack for quantities of matters of each sort.

In the first of these three categories, volume is adjustable, at least to a degree. A President who does not like to sign his name hundreds of times a day can ease that chore somewhat by turning over to department heads his formal exercise of statutory powers; so Eisenhower has done in some routine instances. A President who dislikes handshaking ad infinitum may find excuses for curtailment of big White House social functions, as FDR did with the war and Truman with repairs and Eisenhower with his heart attack. But such adjustments are mere nibbles at the fringes; they may save time or energy but not the mind and heart. No President can delegate the formal exercise of constitutional prerogatives, and it is from those that the greatest number of tough, touchy signatures derive. No President can be excused from all political speechmaking, disaster visiting, fireside chatting, dignitary dealing, least of all from the big ones, sources of greatest strain.

As for the second category, the most a President seriously can hope to do is slow the rate of flow, shut out the marginal case. He may pound tables at associates, demanding that they mind their business on their own responsibility; he may set obstacle courses for them to run, complete with committees, secretariats, and Sherman Adamses—and still there will be persons, plenty of them, spurred by their convictions or their fears, their sense of others' power or of their own insufficiency, who press on him the matters in their bailiwicks, or in their neighbors'. So Secretary Benson took care to get Eisenhower's affirmation (on a partial presentation) of his plan to fire Ladejinsky. So Administrator Stassen took pains, it appears, to gain Presidential sanction for the course of action which then put Ladejinsky back to work. And when matters partake in some degree of both these categories—as oftener than not they do—when his distinct prerogatives become involved, however marginally, in choices his associates are loath to make (or to let others make) themselves, the pressure for a Presidential take-over can push the White House hard; witness the Dixon-Yates affair or the 1947 tankers case immortalized by Louis Koenig.[4]

There remains the third category, where interventions come at *his* initiative. There, he has the option, theoretically, of moving not at all. But this is fatal;

also quite impracticable. No doubt, some Presidents may relish, others shy away from forcing matters into their own hands. No doubt, each will evolve some special preferences according to his particular competences, interests. But every President will find some issues that he wants to seize and ride— Truman on Point Four, Eisenhower on Atoms for Peace—and each will find a plenitude he feels *impelled* to take upon himself: so Truman took the fate of Lamar Caudle out of that worthy's hands and the Attorney-General's, so Eisenhower acted in the Talbot case. When Mrs. Hobby panicked over polio vaccine, when Secretary Stevens got entangled in his own inanities regarding Zwicker and Peress, when Adam Clayton Powell blasted Public Health and Navy on account of segregation, the President moved in. Had he an option? To sense imperatives, one need but scan the "inside" stories Robert Donovan supplies.[5]

Since acts of choice are often negative, there are, of course, more instances of such "enforced" discretion than will appear in current press reports: Eisenhower choosing time and again, as Donovan records, *not* to blast McCarthy; Truman choosing—as he sometimes did—not to leap, guns blazing, into loyalty cases that aroused his ire; so forth, ad infinitum. The "I don't know about that" in press conference is deceptive as a guide to Presidential doings. In most such cases, this would remain the expedient response, assuming he did know. Yet every President, one may suppose, will now go out of office wishing that in some respects he had pushed further still, discretion *un*enforced, toward taking over at times and in places where contemporary happenings did not push him. . . .

But time stands in his way. He cannot afford to do nothing at his own discretion; but neither can he manage to do everything. Priority of place on his choice-making production line belongs of sheer necessity to matters with *deadlines* attached. And in most days of his working week, most seasons of his year, a President has quite enough of these to drain his energy, crowd his attention regardless of all else. It is not "policy" but pressure that determines what comes first.

What makes a "deadline"? For one thing, constitutional or statutory obligations: the President must send his annual messages to Congress, must sign or veto its enactments. Or, for another, items on political agenda all across the country: the nomination and election contests over offices, both partisan and public, the distribution of the patronage, the management of national conventions and campaigns. Or, for a third, turns of events in diplomacy or war: the approach to the "summit" spurring a disarmament departure, "open skies"; the outbreak in Korea forcing a new Formosan policy. Or, for a fourth, "outside" events at home: a sharpened economic trend (whether up or down), a dragged-out strike, a natural disaster, a race riot; not necessarily the great things only, but the small-with-bite, as when a Texas waitress would not serve the Indian Ambassador. Or, finally, for a fifth, such operational disorders in administration, day by day, as dot the preceding pages—plus, of course, their congressional counterparts. Dates-certain make for deadlines; so does heat; dates generated by our laws, our politics, and our diplomacy;

heat generated by events impacting on the needs and expectations of Presidential constituents. Singly or together—though most readily inflammable
combined—dates and heat start the fires burning underneath the White House.

The President, of course, has influence on deadline making and unmaking,
but only to a limited degree. He sets or evades dates when he voluntarily
decides on a message or a meeting or a speech. He turns heat on when he
permits himself to arouse expectations, as Eisenhower did in his press conferences before Geneva. He turns heat aside, if not off, when he finds plausible
grounds, proper-looking means for "further study," as was done so notably
in 1953. But these are marginal endeavors relative to the totality of dates and
heat potentially imposed on him from outside. And even these are usually
reactions or responses to pressures not intrinsically his own. For the most
part, even deadlines self-imposed are only nominally self-engendered. Save
in rare instances, a mid-century President, however talented, simply has not
time to man both ends of the choice-generating process.

The result is to put him in a paradoxical position anent the whole discretionary range of his choice making. To reach out and take over *before*
the dates are nigh or the heat on—publicly at least—can be crucially useful
in his interest; yet, he always has to deal first with deadlines already at his
desk. As has been said above, he cannot count on the initiatives of others to
spur him into interventions timely in *his* terms; yet he is poorly placed to be
his own self-starter. He needs to be an actor; yet he is pre-eminently a reactor,
forced to be so by the nature of his work and its priorities. . . .

Ideally, a President concerned for the efficiency of his own choice making
in furtherance of his own purposes as *he* conceives them should have free
rein in choosing what to choose—and when—within the range of matters
subject to his choice at his discretion. In practice, though, that is precisely
what he *cannot* have. His discretionary range, while not a sham, is nowhere
near as open as the term implies. Only his compulsions are potentially un-
bounded; his opportunities are always limited. Ideals apart, he is in no position
to do more than seek some finite widening of those confines; he has no chance
to break them down. But paradoxically, the only practical direction which
his search can take—given the conditions here described—is toward some
means of putting pressure on himself, *of imposing new deadlines on himself,*
to come to grips with those things he would want to make his own if only
he had time to contemplate the world about him, interfering at his leisure.
And it is ironic that the very measures that a President may take to spare
himself for "bigger things" by staffing out the "small" tend to work in the
opposite direction. Of this, more later.

The limitations on "what" and "when" which so restrict freedom of
choice are reinforced by certain other limits of a different sort: limits on the
substance of alternatives in choices actually made. The President's discretion
is restricted by these limits also; they, too, are features of his landscape subject to some rearrangement, but beyond his power to remove. What are these
limitations on alternatives? Mainly three: limits of presentation, of substantive complexity, and of effectuation, each term loosely descriptive of a

whole array of complications worth a chapter to themselves, though necessarily denied it here.

By "presentation" is meant time, form, and manner in which issues reach a President for his determination. If his desk is where the buck stops, as Truman liked to say, by the same token, it is the *last* stop on the line. Most matters reach him at a late stage of their evolution into issues calling for his choice; and many when they reach him warrant action fast. Wherever they occur, lateness and urgency—singly or combined—are bound to narrow options and to curtail chances for fresh looks or second thoughts. As for the *form* which issues take, the *context* of their presentation to a President, his settling of a budget sum, or phrasing of a speech, or soothing of a legislator, each in its own terms may mean disposal of an issue multifaceted in terms of but one facet, thereby foreclosing options anent others. There is no counting the occasions on which Presidents have backed themselves—or been backed—into corners by this route. Moreover, those who brief a President, who can appeal to him, who can argue before him, have interests of their own which grow remote from his with every increment of organizational distance, institutional independence. Rarely will they see an issue wholly in his terms; oftener in some hybrid of his and theirs, sometimes in theirs alone. And Presidents are no less vulnerable than others (rather more so, in the circumstances) to the lure of wrong answers rightly put.

A tracing out of many of the illustrations posed above would show the workings of these presentation limits; signs of their presence are, of course, no novelty to readers of the *New York Times*. Nothing is intrinsically new about them nowadays, nor anything particularly obscure, though they are none the easier for being old and obvious. But when it comes to limits raised by substantive complexity, the case is rather different. Though not by any means a mid-century invention unknown to earlier times, the magnitude (and durability) of complications in the substance of issues with which Presidents must deal, these days, is greater in degree, to some extent in kind, than we have known before.

Take the question of the military budget which has haunted Eisenhower as it haunted Truman. That budget represents more than half the dollars of federal outlay year by year, four-fifths of the persons on all federal payrolls, half the government's civilian personnel. It represents a mainstay of deterrence and recourse in the cold war, a bedrock stabilizer in the national economy. Its annual determination raises issues of strategy, of economics, politics, administration, and (emphatically) technology; none of which is really manageable in annual or financial terms (the limit of form, again); none of which is really soluble by reference to anybody's certain knowledge, for nothing is certain save uncertainty in these spheres. To estimate what the American economy can "stand" is not to answer what Congress and interest groups will "take" (or what would be required to equate the two). To estimate what new weapons may do is not to answer what may be demanded of them, or opposed to them, years hence. To estimate the Russians' *capabilities* is not to answer what are their *intentions*.

Yet, on some sorts of "answers" to these questions must military budgets now be built. And limited in terms of what is knowable, a President has no recourse but to select among the "guesstimates" of others—or to compound a compromise among them—by way of searching for his answer-substitutes. In such a search, the signs most readily discerned are bound to be those rendered most concrete by visibility, or pressure, or personal proclivities, or "common sense." No doubt a President needs better signposts in times of cold war, technological revolution; but given the uncertainties these generate, whence are such signs to come? . . .

Finally, there is the problem of effectuation, the third of the stated factors limiting alternatives in choice. How is a President to make "no" stick; to translate "yes" into performance, actually? He is not bound to make each choice dependent on his response to these questions, but in the normal course he cannot fail to ask them and to give the answers weight. When Truman chose intervention in Korea, it happened that the necessary military means lay near at hand across the Sea of Japan; a factor, surely, in his choice. The obverse holds, of course, for our passivity in the last days of Dien Bien Phu; the means that were at hand were scarcely suited to the circumstance. But to cite instances of capability in military terms is to belittle the complexity of the how-to-do-it factor; in other terms, there are few choices blessed by aspects so nearly absolute or so readily calculable. Mostly the problem for the President is both more tenuous and more complex in character: how far can he hope to carry matters by persuading those whom he cannot command to do those things he lacks capacity to compel?

"I sit here all day," Truman used to remark, "trying to persuade people to do the things they ought to have sense enough to do without my persuading them." And on each posed alternative, in every act of choice, the question becomes whether to that work load he should add one thing more; with what prospect, at what risk. That question asked and answered may suffice to cancel options of all sorts; the President's choice making ultimately interlocking with his power to persuade.

The Power to Persuade

Concrete acts of choice engender concrete efforts at persuasion. Persuasion of whom? In general, of the President's constituencies, any or all as the case may be. In particular, of those who do the daily chores of governing this country: administrators, Congressmen, and organization politicians. To these one might add certain foreign notables and private persons prominent at home, on whom the government depends for something in particular, a boost, a service, or a sacrifice; but since such dependence is *ad hoc,* intermittent, their case can be ignored for present purposes.

In the main, day by day, it is the public officers and party politicians whom a President must reach to get his choices rendered into government performance. He may move toward them indirectly through public or interest-group opinion, sometimes his only routes, but they remain his objects because they, not the "public," do the close work; his preferences conditioned on their doing. To influence these men at work, he has at his disposal a quantity of

instruments—refined and crude in varying degree—derived from his prerogatives of office as filtered through his personality.

Those instruments of influence, tools of persuasion, are common knowledge,
no mystery about them and none pretended here: There is the aura of his
office, coupled to the impact of his person and prestige, such as they may be.
There are the varied forms of help, concrete and psychological, that Congressmen want from the White House in dealing, as they must, with the executive establishment. There are, in turn, the various assistances desired by
executive officialdom in dealing with Congress. There are also the loyalties,
varying in depth, of administrators to their chief, of party members to the
boss, of Congressmen (and citizens) to the head of state and government. In
party terms, there are, at once, supplies of federal patronage, such as it is,
a Presidential record which no party nowadays can shake, the prospect of a
renewed candidacy (for first-termers, anyway), and—save for Democrats,
perhaps—a constantly replenished campaign chest, centrally controlled. These
things, among others, are available to Presidents for use, reversibly, as carrots and as sticks in aid of their persuasion.

This listing has a formidable ring. In theory, is deserves it. For if a President could bring to bear that whole array effectively and all at once upon a
given point, one may presume he would be irresistible. But practically speaking, such conjunctions are not easily arranged; far from it. Oftener than not,
one or another of these tools will turn out ineffective of itself or in the hands
of its prospective user, unsuited to use, by him, in any combination of resources he contrives. Why should this be so? What dulls their cutting edge
and limits their employment? These questions become our immediate concern.
Full answers would run far beyond the compass of this chapter; no more can
be attempted here than a suggestion of some factors that seem especially
significant in the contemporary setting.

First among these factors—in order of discussion, not importance—is the
uncertainty of a President's own hold upon his instruments of influence. They
may attach to his office, but can slip away from *him*. One doubts that at any
time since 1935, or thereabouts, and not often before, have Presidents got
half the mileage out of patronage the textbooks advertise. . . .

In addition, sources of supplies to aid persuasion on one front may be
endangered by the very effort at persuasion on another. A great share of a
President's potential trading stock with Congress is actually in the hands of
the executive departments: jobs, expertise, publicity, administrative actions
of all sorts. No less a share of his potential leverage with the departments is
actually in the hands of his congressional supporters: protection or defense,
consideration or support, in every sort of legislative situation. Too many
sticks applied too often on the Hill may tend to uproot the supply of carrots
growing there for use downtown, and vice versa.

A second factor is the tendency of certain Presidential tools to cut in opposite directions, thereby impairing their simultaneous employment. It is not
easy for a President to combine partisan approaches with attempts to crystal-
lize support around the symbol of his office. He courts trouble when he tells
his party's Congressmen that his proposals will help them at the polls and

simultaneously exhorts the other party's men to do their patriotic duty by their President. He courts trouble when he tries to draw upon the loyalties of subordinate officials and at the same time offers up their kind as human sacrifices on the altar, say, of adequate appropriations for their work. Such troubles come in infinite varieties; in every instance, they will tend to limit hypothetical effectiveness of each paired instrument. . . .

A third factor complicating the persuasion process can be stated, most simply, as general dissatisfaction with the product to be "sold." It is difficult, in other words, to press a course of action intrinsically lacking much appeal to *any* of the persons whose support is being sought. Instruments of influence, however handled, are poor substitutes for genuine enthusiasm on the part of somebody among the movers and shakers in the case. And if the substitution must be made, as not infrequently occurs, the limits on the efficacy of persuasive tools will tend to be severe. . . .

Alongside these three factors there is need to place a fourth, which looms at least as large under mid-century conditions: the factor of too many things at once. . . .

A President's tools of persuasion are put under great strains when used on many projects simultaneously. Look at the tools themselves, and that becomes quite obvious. Yet, such use is the normal practice, nowadays; often mandatory, always wanted. No more as persuaders than as choice makers are contemporary Presidents at liberty, discretion unconfined, to choose the "what" and "when" of their endeavors to persuade.

Four factors have been named, so far, as limiting the efficacy of persuasive instruments. But there remains a fifth, a factor so important as to dominate the rest, continually affecting the dimensions of all four. This is the element of "setting" in persuasion, a matter not of instruments, as such, but of the *background* against which they are employed. As a rough rule, it may be said that for a fraction of the persons on whom Presidents depend, continuing exposure to the White House and its occupants provides a background favoring—though not, of course, determining—effective exercise of Presidential influence on them. The bigger the "staff system," the smaller the fraction; but even an open door could not enlarge it into a preponderance. For most officials, both public and partisan, a favorable background will be differently derived. Derived from what? To this we may now turn.

In the case of executive officials, all sorts of variables of time, place, situation, substance, tend to affect actual responses to a particular pressure from the President. But there would seem to be one variable always present, always influential: their own instinctive estimate of his prestige with Congress, his potency on Capitol Hill. . . .

This does not mean that there is any one-to-one relationship between a President's congressional prestige and agency compliance with his wishes—though sometimes, certainly, the correlation is that close—but rather that a favorable background for persuasive efforts at his end of Pennsylvania Avenue is markedly dependent, over time, on his prestige at the other end, with Congress. And in precisely the same sense—no more, no less—a favorable background for persuasion of Congress is provided by his prestige with the country. . . .

Woodrow Wilson once wrote, in an academic vein, that a President "may be both the leader of his party and the leader of the nation or he may be one or the other." [6] Whatever the case fifty years ago, no such option is open to him now. He must endeavor to lead "party" (for which read public officers as well), since "nation" does not run the government machine, cannot itself effectuate his choices. But if he is to manage those who make the wheels go round, he needs public opinion at his back, must seek consensus as his context for persuasion. And in that dual compulsion lies the *ultimate dilemma* of the Presidential operation at mid-century.

How describe this dilemma? One may begin by pointing to the sources of that popular prestige which so affects the President's own power to persuade. His general public—in our terms, national and partisan constituencies combined—actually comprises a diversity of Presidential publics, their expectations nurtured variously by claims on him as "government," by respect for his office, by ties to his personality: "interest" publics, "capacity" publics, and "personal" publics, each subdivided many times, all linked by the crisscrossing lines of overlapping membership, collectively encompassing the country, or that part of it which cares about the President.

His national prestige, therefore—which Congressmen and politicians watch and weigh—is simply the net balance of favorable response these many groups, in sum, accord their varied images of him (a matter always to be gauged, not scientifically determined, the result influenced, of course, by the affiliation of the gauger). Those images and the responses to them are not static; they can and do vary over time. And what are the determinants of variation? Happenings, mainly, or the appearance of happenings, ascribable—or anyway ascribed—to him: the reward or frustration of a bread-and-butter want, an ethical attitude, a psychological identification; to such as these his publics will react wherever and in whatever degree they see his office or his person as the cause. Inevitably, every concrete choice he makes, both positive and negative, and every effort at persuasion will set off some reactions of the sort, and not all of one kind; if somebody is pleased, then someone else is bound to be offended.

For the President to give offense is to risk blurring his own image in the eyes of those offended, hence to risk lowering their favorable response to him. But on a maximum of such response, as aggregated all across the country, must he depend for the effectuation of his choices. And on choice making he depends for the impression of his person on the product of his office. But the conduct of office is liable to require policy initiatives in all directions, not as free will, but as constituency pressures and events decree. Hence, acts of choice and of persuasion become mandatory, inescapable. Yet, they are bound to give offense.

This, then, is the ultimate dilemma, the vicious circle Presidents must tread by virtue of their unique placement in our system, the personal equivalent for them, as individuals, of that disparity which haunts their office, routinely responsible for programing without assured support to carry through. . . .

The years since World War II have neither been perceived, widely, as crisis times nor have they been, in fact, peacetimes in any familiar sense. And nowadays, the things that Presidents must do and those they may be called upon to do expose them regularly to the penalties of *both* such times with no assurance that they can gain the rewards of either. These days, both doing and not doing give offense in indeterminate proportion to offsetting approbation; almost all actions now *tend* to produce a negative reaction more concrete than favorable response. Both forms of action are abrasive; from neither can our Presidents now *count* on a bonus of response. Yet, they are constantly impelled to actions of both sorts; and so it has to be, these days, their preferences notwithstanding.

Consider what a President must do in times we now call "peace": keep taxes relatively high, armed forces relatively large, the budget "swollen," the bureaucracy "outsize"; inject himself into labor disputes just when tempers grow highest, into defense of overseas constituents just when they seem, at home, most irritating or unwise. And so the list goes on. Consider, also, what a President now may be called upon to do: intervene with arms in Korea, Indo-China; intervene with counsel in southern school segregation; back the Benson plan for aid to farmers; endorse the Hobby plan for aid to schools; accept the Rockefeller plan for aid abroad; impose the New York Bar committee plan for personnel security; keep Nixon or take Herter; choose silence on McCarthy or attack; these among others. Such "musts" and "mays," as manifested in his acts of doing or not doing, are bound to outrage some among his publics (and anger may last long), to be accepted grudgingly by many as unpleasant facts of life, to warm the hearts of an uncertain number whose warmth may be short-lived. Whichever way he acts, his penalties may outrun his rewards in prestige terms. And rarely can he calculate with certainty, in advance, the net balance either way. Yet act he must. . . .

■ Notes

1. These terms are taken from Clinton Rossiter's *The American Presidency* (New York: Harcourt, Brace, 1956) and from Samuel Lubell's *The Future of American Politics* (New York: Harper, 1952).
2. Woodrow Wilson, *Constitutional Government* (New York: Columbia University Press, 1908), p. 73.
3. Discounting the Vice-Presidency, which I am prepared to do.
4. The reference is to the "Sale of Tankers," a case study included in Harold Stein, *Public Administration and Policy Development* (New York: Harcourt, Brace, 1952).
5. The reference is to Robert J. Donovan, *Eisenhower: The Inside Story* (New York: Harper, 1956).
6. Wilson, *op. cit.,* p. 69.

31 ADMINISTRATION AS POLITICS

- *V. O. Key, Jr.*

Administration consists of more than management of routines. In some respects it is, like the legislative process, between-election politics; it must cope with similar problems, and its practice requires similar skills. Great administrative decisions, like legislative acts, may involve a reconciliation of conflicting interests and must be made with an alertness to their general public acceptability. Nor is the task of the President in the leadership of federal administration simply one of the issuance of directions to subordinates: the arts of compromise, of negotiation, of persuasion, have as great a relevance in the White House as in Congress.

Administrative Agencies: Actors in the Political Process

. . . Administrative agencies are not as clay in the hands of the President and his partisan associates. They tend to have a tradition, an outlook, and a policy inclination of their own. To budge them from their predetermined paths is not always easy. Vast aggregations of public servants, military and civil, organized into well-knit hierarchies and animated by common aims and spirit, have a potency in the political process that is often underestimated or even ignored. Government departments and agencies at times act as spokesmen or representatives before legislative bodies and the public for segments of society that they serve. Through the prosecution of research that reveals public needs and points toward public action, administrative agencies often initiate movements leading to new public policy. In the management of programs of procurement and expenditure, agencies may affect significantly the fortunes of great industries. In the politics of appropriations almost every administrative bureau or department seeks to maintain or enlarge the scope of its operations.

In one respect administrative agencies are like pressure groups: they operate continually, in Republican and Democratic administrations alike, to
advance their interests; indeed, often the closest working relations are maintained between a pressure organization and the governmental agencies in which
it is interested. Pressure groups and administrative departments are elements
in the pattern of politics that may be jarred and realigned by the results of
an election, but are seldom completely thrown from power. The administrative
organization exerts its strength through transient department heads and
Presidents, no matter what party is in power. With close relationships between its headquarters personnel in Washington and Congress it is able to
make its wishes known to Congress either through the department head or
through unofficial channels. Often with a personnel distributed over the nation, it is sometimes able to stir up, by discreet measures, pressure from
home to bear on Congress. With almost a monopoly of information in its
sphere of interest, the administrative organization is able to release or withhold data in such a fashion as to influence the course of legislative action.[1]

A factor that conditions the task of the President in the direction of
administration is the representative role of administrative agencies. Pressure
groups and administrative agencies themselves often contend that the agency
has a duty to act in furtherance of the interests of the group it serves. This
is a doctrine of bureaucratic representation: that the Department of Labor
should speak for and represent the interests of labor in making recommendations for new legislation; that the Department of Agriculture should promote vigorously the interests of the farmer and ignore those of other groups;
and so on. A characteristic statement of this notion is one made in 1943 by
the National Co-operative Milk Producers' Federation:

> Eleven months from now the people will go to the polls. They will decide many
> important issues. One of the greatest issues which farmers will help decide will
> be on the question of who controls the Department of Agriculture. We believe
> that the organized farmers of America will demand of both political parties that
> they will provide a reconstituted Department of Agriculture to serve agriculture.
> Other Departments of Government serve the groups for which they are named.
> The Department of Agriculture today is not being permitted to function for the
> farmers. We call for definite pledges on this great fundamental issue.[2]

With agency after agency attached to the interests of particular groups
and under pressure to promote partial interests, the President as administrative leader has no little difficulty in bringing about the operation of the government in accord with a party program dedicated to the general welfare. The
prevailing practice is that the administrative agencies represent the interests
they serve.[3] Many of them owe their existence to the groups they serve. As
new groups or classes rise to power and influence, they are recognized through
the establishment of governmental departments. The creation of the Department of Agriculture was the first recognition of an economic class in the
administrative structure; later the Departments of Commerce and Labor were
established.

The degree to which an administrative agency becomes an attorney for its constituency varies with circumstances. The Veterans Administration is rarely in a position to oppose the interests of the veterans. On the other hand, when an agency is subjected to pressure from conflicting interests, it may enjoy a greater freedom in formulating and advocating its recommendations. The Department of Agriculture cannot satisfy completely the beet-sugar growers, the beet-sugar refiners, the Louisiana cane-sugar growers, and the seaboard cane-sugar refiners. When different interests play on an administrative agency, it may seek to work out a program of legislative recommendations appeasing divergent demands insofar as practicable.

By their close communion with interests in society, administrative agencies may gain a certain independence of Presidential direction. By the same token they become beholden to those groups on whose support they depend. These group relations often extend over into alliances involving the administrative agency, the pressure group, and Congress. Administrative agencies develop friends in Congress whose policy interests parallel those of the agency. At times a bureau or agency may become virtually independent of the President, so powerful is its support in Congress. These relationships make it difficult to bring the work of such agencies into line with the President's program, and insofar as it is a party program they tend to vitiate party responsibility. To the extent that a President fails as a legislative leader, he is also likely to fail as chief administrator; when Congress has the whip hand in legislation, it also tends to undercut the President as chief executive.

In the objectives they seek, administrative agencies are almost as varied as they are numerous. Yet most agencies seek to maintain, if not to expand, their activities and to assure the retention of administrative arrangements they regard as satisfactory. Every bureau is eager to obtain appropriations to carry out its program on an adequate scale, and few bureau chiefs believe that last year's appropriation was enough. An organization's prestige is measured in part by the size of its appropriations and the number of its employees; aside from such considerations, in seeking appropriations the personnel of an agency is animated by a faith in the worth of the work that is being done and by a belief that the public interest will be advanced by the appropriation of the amount requested. Persons employed by the government, like those employed elsewhere, are likely to have enthusiasm about what they are doing.

The administrative agency usually exerts its strength to defend itself and its program from attack in legislative bodies. Administrators tend to have a vested interest in the law they enforce; and when its enemies attack, the agency is quick to line up its legislative friends in defense. A special type of legislative proposal that arouses intense interest of administrators is a reorganization bill. Comprehensive schemes to reorganize the administration through legislation have invariably been defeated in Congress in large measure through pressure exerted by the bureaucracy. Only with the greatest of difficulty did Franklin D. Roosevelt obtain passage of a reorganization measure delegating to the President the power to shift administrative units from

one department to another; yet certain agencies succeeded in bringing about
the adoption of amendments excepting them from the operation of the act.
The Army Corps of Engineers, for example, which has been one of the
most persistent opponents of administrative reorganization, has succeeded in
maintaining the status quo for itself.[4] Fights on questions of administrative
organization are sometimes battles between two federal agencies for jurisdiction over a particular matter, such as the dispute between the Department
of Agriculture and the Department of the Interior over the Forest Service.
The Forest Service, with its far-flung field service closely knit into the life
of the communities served, has gained strong public support and has successfully resisted efforts to transfer it to the Department of the Interior.[5]

From the public prints it might be supposed that administrative agencies
ceaselessly seek to enlarge their functions and to advance their cause. Such
drives for power exist, but quite as prevalent is an institutional inertia almost
gyroscopic in its effect. The responsibilities of political direction may require
that an agency be jolted from its ancient ruts. Some political heads of agencies impress their views on the organization they direct, but at times the
department as an institution has a momentum and a pattern of action that
escape direction.[6] "The department" over a long period builds up a tradition,
a policy, and, one could almost say, a "personality" of its own. A point of
view comes to permeate the organization; and if new recruits do not have
the departmental attitude, they acquire it in time. These departmental traditions are difficult to bring to life on paper, but they are of enormous importance in the determination of the direction in which the department will exert
its influence in the legislative process. Moreover, departmental policy tends
to harden into a tradition that resists alteration. The institutional pattern of
ideas comes to be set in a certain fashion, and it tends to stay that way.[7] In
consequence, chief executives and legislative bodies often have to seek advice
on public policy from outside existing administrative services to offset the
force of tradition. Under extreme conditions, about the only way to get a
job done may be to establish a new agency.

Partisan control of administration may be regarded as a simple exercise
of command. If it is that and nothing more, it is apt to be both sterile and
futile. Few political heads of departments know enough to tell their staffs
what to do; their task is to use the resources of their departments in the
public interest. From the permanent staffs of government agencies emerge
ideas for action and plans for improving the efficiency of administration. From
the same source may come judgments, informed by experience, on the wisdom
or probable repercussions of contemplated courses of action. The thinking
and planning of the civil servant may approach the intelligent and informed
exercise of a trusteeship of the public welfare. The effective political head of
an agency finds ways to blend the resources of his department with his own
skills in political maneuver and to accommodate the mandates of his party
and the creative capacities of the permanent service.

Politicians cannot think up all the laws; a skillful administrative politician
may be the midwife who brings to fruition the ideas of his staff. In some
spheres administrative officials possess what amounts to a sovereignty of

competence. Since a large proportion of legislation consists of modifications of old policy, those in charge of the administration are in possession of information and experience basic to the formulation of changes. For example, in the application of tax laws the Internal Revenue Service discovers loopholes facilitating evasion and suggests remedies to Congress. A crusading Food and Drug Administration urges changes in the law in order to broaden its coverage to protect the public and to make effective enforcement more feasible. Scientists of the Department of Agriculture discover means to control a pest and recommend suitable measures. The Children's Bureau calls attention to high rates of infant mortality and agitates for a program to bring about a reduction. In every sphere of governmental activity the influence of the knowledge and experience of the administrative official makes itself felt in new legislation.[8]

These remarks pose in general terms the problem of political direction of administration. Scores of administrative entities, if we observe the reality that some departments are units only in name, constitute a vast and cumbersome apparatus the victorious party must bring under its control. Each of the major agencies enjoys the support, and perhaps opposition, of organized interests. Each has its friends in Congress. Each may be of particular concern to some faction or group within the party. A party can meet the requirements of accountability only if it can bring under control those actions of the administrative apparatus most likely to touch party policy or to produce party embarrassment. The nature of that problem of control may be illuminated by an examination of the modes of action of administrative agencies and the techniques of direction by the President.

Administration and Public Policy: Methods

Embedded in the administrative agencies are powerful particularistic drives that at times threaten to fragment the government. The President presides over the unruly assemblage of administrative institutions and attempts to maintain within it a semblance of order and a harmony with party policy on at least the major questions. Hierarchical etiquette makes the President the boss of the administrative apparatus, but by custom, and on occasion by a bit of insubordination, administrative agencies enjoy considerable freedom in the promotion of their objectives.

The techniques of administrative agencies in presenting their case to the public and to the lawmakers are fundamentally similar to those employed by private lobbying groups. Almost every governmental agency conducts some sort of public relations program, but only a small proportion of the publicity issued by administrative agencies is concerned with the promotion of proposed courses of public policy. The objectives of the bulk of governmental publicity are the performance of a function, such as the dissemination of information on improved farming methods by the Department of Agriculture, or the furnishing of information to the public on the course of public affairs, such as the news releases issued by the Department of State.

Administrative agencies are concerned with the creation of a reservoir of good will among the general public that can be drawn on when specific legislative proposals are under consideration by the legislative body. A "good" press and a "good" name are of great value in convincing Congress of the necessity for an increased appropriation or for other legislation requested by the agency. On the other hand, a "bad" press can make the agency's relations with Congress difficult. Sometimes the public relations strategy is to dramatize the agency through publicizing its chief. The Federal Bureau of Investigation furnishes an excellent example of this technique. Other agencies do not build up a single personality, but seek to create a public opinion favorable to the service as an institution. Still other agencies seek to propagate an idea.

None of the types of public relations activities cited involves an appeal for public support for any particular policy advocated by the agency; rather, they are calculated to establish a favorable general attitude toward the personalities, services, and ideas concerned. If this type of generalized publicity is effective, an underlying sentiment is formed that is likely to help when specific legislation is under consideration by Congress.

A different type of publicity—a sort of administrative guerrilla warfare—flows from the informal and often surreptitious relations of the administrators with journalists. Information is fed to these persons, who report it "on high authority" or as from "informed sources." By this means Congress may be needled, the President nudged, a fire lighted under a superior, or officials in another department stirred to action or to anger. The most spectacular examples of this practice occur when the Navy, the Air Force, and the Army engage in psychological warfare through the press. Bitter debates among the bureaucrats tend to spill over into the press.[9] The services, too, engage in extensive publicity calculated to improve their public image. If, by some miracle, all the public relations men of the services could be transformed into militarily useful man power, our striking power would be given an impressive boost.

While there are critics of the public relations activities of administrative agencies, in truth, an agency, if it is to function effectively, must develop support in Congress, from its clientele, and from the public generally. An act of Congress is not enough to establish it firmly, particularly if its operations affect some powerful group adversely. As an agency recruits sufficient support to assure a degree of stability, however, it thereby gains a degree of autonomy which may limit Presidential direction. Agencies may, in rare instances, completely escape Presidential control.

Since a large proportion of the legislative output either originates in administrative experience or affects administrative operations, administrative agencies play an extremely important role in the process of lawmaking as a whole. They originate legislative proposals; they attempt, at times, to defeat proposals originating from other sources; and, at other times, they seek to bring about alterations in proposals pending in the legislative bodies. To carry out these activities, the agency must have facilities for drafting and for responsible consideration of proposals. It must also watch the course of legislation to keep informed on proposals that might affect its work; otherwise, legislation might be enacted that either would be difficult to administer or would tie the agency in knots.[10]

Most legislation is routine and arouses no controversy. It seeks to accomplish objectives that, by common consent, are wise and necessary for the conduct of public business. Congress routinely requests the advice of administrative agencies on legislation. Representatives of agencies appear before the committees of Congress and present information indicative of the need for action or the advisability of inaction. The relation of the agency to Congress is often not so much one of advocacy as of consultation with committeemen who have a responsible concern about the administrative operation in question.

Administration bills that propose a major change in public policy are likely to arouse opposition and to call for a vigorous presentation of the department's case. Under these circumstances the department may call on its allies among the pressure groups for assistance in dealing with Congress. When the objectives of the Department of Agriculture, for example, are coincidental with those of the American Farm Bureau Federation, the lobbyists of the Federation will appear, present testimony, buttonhole members of Congress, and perhaps focus on Congressmen pressure from their constituencies. Or, if the Farmers' Union is with the Department and the Federation against it, the Department may plan its legislative strategy in consultation with Union officials. Connections exist between nearly every administrative unit and private associations, which are of great importance in the promotion of legislation. There is a deep-seated congressional jealousy of "bureaucrats," and the bureaucracy is restricted in the methods that it may use in dealing with Congress. If it seeks to stir up popular pressure on Congress in support of specific legislation, it is likely to arouse criticism and resentment in Congress; but its allied private pressure groups may turn the pressure on Congress more freely.[11]

It is chiefly in political disputes involving questions of high policy that the administration attempts to focus a supporting public sentiment on Congress. And the important figures in these affairs are not petty bureaucrats, but the principal leaders of the administration. On these great questions the President or Cabinet members may appeal to the country for support in coping with Congress.

Fulfillment of party responsibility and achievement of party purpose require that the administrative agencies be brought under party control. In this endeavor the role of the President is crucial. Two broad methods are at his disposal to impress on the machinery of government his party's policies: the power of appointment and removal; the authority to review and superintend operations of administrative agencies.

The relevance of the power of appointment for party policy becomes most evident when control of the Presidency shifts from one party to another. Republican Cabinet officers ordinarily have a different policy orientation from that of Democratic department heads. Appointments and removals of officials of subcabinet rank will also be tinged by policy considerations as well as by patronage factors.[12] The affiliations of appointees often parallel the obligations and commitments of the incoming party and foreshadow the course of its actions.[13] Undoubtedly an incoming party tends to replace a higher proportion of the upper levels of the bureaucracy than is necessary to gain effective control of the administrative apparatus. After the election of 1952 this result came about in part from the demands for patronage from a party long out of power and in part from the unfamiliarity with governmental practice of many of the top-level Republican appointees. Victims of their own propaganda, they believed themselves to be surrounded by New Deal bureaucrats engaged in a conspiracy to sabotage the Eisenhower crusade, a point of view that became less marked as the businessmen learned their way around Washington.

While the power to appoint the heads of agencies is essential, it does not solve the problem of direction of the administrative apparatus. The President has a continuing task of guiding and co-ordinating the work of the administrative agencies, which, left to their own devices, go off in all directions. In this task he has the assistance of the White House staff. The Bureau of the Budget serves as a staff aid to the President in the review of budget requests; it is bad form for an agency head to seek from appropriations committees a greater sum than is recommended in the President's budget. Agency legislative proposals are required to be cleared through the Bureau of the Budget for advice on their conformity with the President's program.[14] The Council of Economic Advisers aids in the co-ordination of economic policies of the government departments, while the President has at his disposal the National Security Council to simplify the task of riding herd on those responsible for diplomatic and military policies.[15]

As the President seeks to maintain control over the unwieldy administrative system, he may act at times as party leader; he also acts as chief executive. Were there no parties or elections, the chief executive would have to be equipped with machinery to aid in co-ordinating and directing the administrative system. Yet in his role as principal administrator the President must look to the achievement of the aims of his party, and he himself makes a substantial proportion of the record on which his party must stand at the next election. . . .

▪ Notes

1. See J. L. Freeman, "The Bureaucracy in Pressure Politics," *Annals*, CCCXIX (September, 1958), 10–19.
2. National Co-operative Milk Producers' Federation, *A Daily Policy for 1944*, p. 7.
3. See Charles Wiltse, "The Representative Function of Bureaucracy," *American Political Science Review*, XXXV (1941), 510–516.
4. See Arthur Maass, *Muddy Waters* (Cambridge: Harvard University Press, 1951). The capacity of administrative agencies, often in association with their pressure-group allies and congressional friends, to resist reorganization suggests the limitations of Presidential control over administration. See Avery Leiserson, "Political Limitations

on Executive Reorganization," *American Political Science Review,* XLI (1947), 68–84.

5. On rivalry among the Forest Service, the Bureau of Land Management, and the National Park Service in the area of recreation policy, see Julius Duscha, "The Undercover Fight over the Wilderness," *Harper's* (April, 1962).

6. Consider the widespread public astonishment generated by President Kennedy's Secretary of Defense, Robert McNamara, when he proceeded to operate on the assumption that it was really his job to run the Department of Defense.

7. Public lands, including forested lands, were at one time in the custody of the General Land Office of the Department of the Interior. After considerable political pyrotechnics, forests were assigned to the Department of Agriculture for protection and management. "The national forest idea ran counter to the whole tradition of the Interior Department," said Gifford Pinchot, who was chief of the Bureau of Forestry of the Department of Agriculture in Theodore Roosevelt's administration. "Bred into its marrow, bone and fiber, was the idea of disposing of the public lands to private owners." "How the National Forests Were Won," *American Forests and Forest Life* (October, 1930).

8. On the administrative origin of reforms of the Progressive Era in California, see C. D. Nash, "Bureaucracy and Economic Reform: The Experience of California, 1899," *Western Political Quarterly,* XIII (1960), 678–691.

9. See S. P. Huntington, "Interservice Competition and the Political Roles of the Armed Services," *American Political Science Review,* LV (1961), 40–52.

10. To be differentiated from legislative proposals by administrative agencies are bills initiated by organizations of public employees. Such groups are prolific sources of bills on retirement, leave, compensation, and related matters. For an analysis of their activities in one congressional session, see R. L. Frischknecht, "Federal Employee Unions and the First Session, Eightieth Congress," *Western Political Quarterly,* I (1948), 183–185.

11. A 1959 investigation disclosed that the Army had induced one of its major contractors to put on an advertising campaign extolling the merits of the Nike missile at a moment when Congress was confronted with the problem of choice among types of missiles sponsored by different military services.

12. Consider the impact of Republican laissez-faire policy on the role of the Bureau of Standards as reported by S. A. Lawrence, *The Battery Additive Controversy* (ICP Case No. 68, 1962).

13. The early Eisenhower appointments included officials who had been strongly on record as opposed to the programs they were to administer: "The new head of the Rural Electrification Administration is regarded in his home state of Minnesota as an opponent of REA projects; the new head of the Housing and Home Finance Administration fought hard and consistently in Congress against the program he is now to administer; an arch protectionist who voted against the Reciprocal Trade Program when he was in the House has been appointed to the Tariff Commission; an Assistant Secretary of Interior appears to oppose conservation and has testified that the public lands should ultimately be turned over to private citizens; the new general counsel of the Department of Health, Education, and Welfare is a former Congressman who voted to restrict social security coverage; the new chairman of the Federal Trade Commission previously made his living representing interests who did battle with the Commission; and the President's original appointee to head the Bureau of Mines was so articulate in his opposition to the Mine Safety Law he was to administer that the congressional committee forced the White House to withdraw his name." H. M. Somers, "The Federal Bureaucracy and the Change of Administration," *American Political Science Review,* XLVIII (1954), 138–139.

14. See R. E. Neustadt, "Presidency and Legislation: The Growth of Central Clearance," *American Political Science Review,* XLVIII (1954), 641–671; Arthur Maass, "In Accord with the Program of the President?" *Public Policy,* IV (1953), 77–93.

15. These remarks give only the faintest notion of the enormity of the President's task in directing administrative agencies, each with its own traditions, its own connections with pressure groups, its peculiar alliances in Congress, its habits and conceptions of the public interest.

32   THE GOVERNMENT COMMISSION

■ *Daniel Bell*

In recent years, the number and variety of government commissions have expanded enormously, and these commissions seem to be developing into a new and unanticipated mechanism of government. Curiously, there is no full record available, in government, of the number of government commissions, statutory and *ad hoc*, created in the last half-dozen years. Inquiry at the Records Office of the White House, the personnel office of the White House, and other government agencies has revealed that no such inventory exists.

One can say, perhaps schematically, that five different kinds of functions are served by government commissions. There are, broadly, the *advisory* kind of commission, such as the President's Science Advisory Committee (PSAC) or the Labor-Management Advisory Committee, which are statutory bodies with fixed-term memberships; the *evaluation* commissions, such as that headed by Dean Woolridge to assess the operations of the National Institutes of Health or the one headed by Emanuel Piore of IBM to assess the work of government science laboratories; the *fact-finding* bodies, the most typical of which are those created to deal with national strikes; the *public relations* groups, such as the White House conference on education to call public attention to various problems; and the *policy recommendation* commissions, such as the DeBakey Commission on Health, which recommended a national policy to focus research and treatment on heart, cancer, and stroke; the Linowitz Commission on Foreign Aid, or the National Commission on Technology, Automation, and Economic Progress.

To some extent such bodies take over, duplicate, or compete with the functions of congressional committees, whose role as watchdog agencies, or as public hearing bodies, has also expanded considerably in the last few decades. But, as mechanisms of the executive branch, they have several new functions:

(1) To provide a means for the direct representation of "functional constituencies" in the advisory process. There is an increasing tendency for the

From Daniel Bell, "Government by Commission," *Public Interest*, I (Spring, 1966), 6–9. Reprinted by permission of the author and the publisher.

American polity to be organized in functional terms, and it is increasingly thought to be useful and proper to seek the "advice and consent" of such groups.

(2) To permit the government informally to explore the "limits" of action by taking soundings within various bodies (such as the Labor-Management Advisory Commission) and to enable the government to exert pressure more directly within such bodies for particular policies.

(3) To serve as a direct public relations device to call attention to certain issues and to generate public sentiment for support of various policies. In the past, it was not unknown for government to encourage the formation of "independent" citizens groups which served as "fronts" for government-desired policies. The White House conferences represent an advance on this procedure; they are less a marked "pressure" device and permit more open scope for discussion and confrontation with government spokesmen.

(4) And finally, the creation of various government bodies on public policy problems fosters what the political scientists call "elite participation" in the formulation of government policy.

All these devices present certain dangers. The evident danger is that they simply become one more means of increased government manipulation of "public opinion." This danger is less real than it might seem, however; for government is not a monolith, shooting out orders from some central source, but a hydra-headed body with diverse interests and looking in different directions. Moreover, the plain fact remains that national commissions often are among the few places where a central debate over specific policy issues can be conducted. In the normal play of politics, the effort to formulate coherent policies, even by such disinterested bodies, say, such as the National Planning Association or Resources for the Future, or the more technical study groups such as the Brookings Institution, necessarily remain partial in their focus. The distinctive virtue of the government commission arrangement is that there is a specific effort to involve the full range of elite or organized opinion in order to see if a real consensus can be achieved. In the National Commission on Technology, Automation, and Economic Progress, for example, the process of debate was, in some ways, as important as the conclusions that were finally reached. The labor people, for example, had to confront the hard, technical data which belied some of their ideological presuppositions; the industry people, in turn, had to grapple with the problems of providing for the "hard-core" unemployed, the failure of the market mechanism to meet various community needs, especially in health, air and water pollution, and various other social deficiencies in the system. The desire to deal with concrete problems, in a nondoctrinaire way, did mean, in part, the surrender of older prejudices and the emergence of some new, imaginative social proposals. Even hard-shell conservative opposition to certain ideas was worn down quickly by the argument that new ideas were at least worth testing in some pilot fashion; while the facile and sometimes doctrinaire argument that "the government" should undertake all kinds of across-the-board programs was whittled away by the demonstration of ineptitude or heavy-handed institutional rigidity on the part of many government agencies. Increasingly, both arguments led to a conviction that more and more public functions had to be taken over by "new social forms"—be they regional authorities, inter-state compacts, decentralized authorities, and other devices which would assure the maximum flexibility, adaptiveness, and responsiveness to the multi-farious nature of social change. And all of this was put within the context of the next ten years. It is true that the commission did not expect any radical rupture in the pace of technological change ("We do not expect output per man-hour . . . to rise during the next decade at a rate substantially faster than the 2.8 percent characteristic of the postwar period. . . . Most major tech-nological discoveries which will have a significant economic impact within the next decade are already . . . in a readily identifiable style of commercial development"). But the relevant point is that the policy recommendations were framed within a series of expectations about the future. In effect, what the National Commission on Technology had become was a "surmising forum."

All of this becomes more important in the face of what is surely the most important change in the character of government today—the attitude of being future-oriented. No government today can be passive in the face of the rapid changes which erode older social forms or indifferent to the linked nature of economic change which now so quickly ties together all parts of the society. The concern of the administration with health, education, poverty, and urban affairs indicates that the government necessarily has to become an active agent to design new policies and to implement them. But as some of the studies of the Commission on the Year 2000 (of the American Academy of Arts and Sciences) have shown, many of these problems have to be looked at in terms of twenty- and thirty-year cycles, and ways have to be found to build these perspectives into some capital budgetary process.

Yet in this respect we are sadly deficient. The government today does not have any single agency which seeks to "forecast" social and technological change (though an individual agency, such as the Census Bureau, may be concerned with population trends, and the Council of Economic Advisers with short-run economic projections). There is no agency which seeks to link up current and possible future changes in a comprehensive way so as to trace out the linked effects on different aspects of government policy. And perhaps most importantly, at a time when we must begin consciously to choose among "alternative futures," to establish priorities about what has to be done—for it is only an illusion that we are affluent enough to take care of all our economic problems at once—we have no "forum" which seeks to articulate different national goals and to clarify the implications and conse-quences of different choices. Congress is not such a forum. As Roscoe Drum-mond pointed out in a review of the legislation passed during the Johnson administration: "Congress does not resolve national controversies; it can only act after most of the controversy has been removed. This is what hap-pened on all of this once controversial legislative program on which the Administration won such comfortable votes."

In his characteristically witty way, Bertrand de Jouvenal has summed up the problem as a choice between "Seraglio and Forum." In the one, decisions are taken in secluded rooms by small groups of men; in the other, decisions take shape by the process of open discussion. The contrast arises most sharply because of the altered nature of government. It is no accident that, throughout the world, political power has passed increasingly to a strong executive and that we have witnessed the decline of parliamentary, legislative, and congressional government. Efforts to "mobilize" a society—for war or for social change—necessarily give the executive an active and interventionist role and reduce the importance of the legislature. Therefore, one of the major problems for the political process in a democracy is the question, as de Jouvenal has put it: *"How can the future become a matter for public opinion?"* This is where the study of the future and a "surmising forum" join hands. And this is where government by commission makes, perhaps, its most useful contribution.

33 THE SUPREME COURT IN THE SYSTEM OF ALLIANCES

- *Robert A. Dahl*

To consider the Supreme Court of the United States strictly as a legal institution is to underestimate its significance in the American political system. For it is also a political institution—an institution, that is to say, for arriving at decisions on controversial questions of national policy. As a political institution, the Court is highly unusual, not least because Americans are not quite willing to accept the fact that it *is* a political institution and not quite capable of denying it; so that frequently we take both positions at once. This is confusing to foreigners, amusing to logicians, and rewarding to ordinary Americans who thus manage to retain the best of both worlds. . . .

I

No one, I imagine, will quarrel with the proposition that the Supreme Court, or indeed any court, must make and does make policy decisions. . . . But such a proposition is not really useful to the question before us. What is critical is the extent to which a court can and does make policy decisions by going outside

From Robert A. Dahl, "Decision-Making in a Democracy: The Supreme Court as a National Policy-Maker," *Journal of Public Law*, VI (1957), 279–286, 291–295. Reprinted by permission of the author and the publisher.

established "legal" criteria found in precedent, statute, and constitution. Now, in this respect the Supreme Court occupies a most peculiar position, for it is an essential characteristic of the institution that from time to time its members decide cases where legal criteria are not in any realistic sense adequate to the task. A distinguished associate justice of the present Court has recently described the business of the Supreme Court in these words:

> It is essentially accurate to say that the Court's preoccupation today is with the application of rather fundamental aspirations and what Judge Learned Hand calls "moods," embodied in provisions like the due process clauses, which were designed not to be precise and positive directions for rules of action. The judicial process in applying them involves a judgment . . . that is, on the views of the direct representatives of the people in meeting the needs of society, on the views of Presidents and Governors, and by their construction of the will of legislatures the Court breathes life, feeble or strong, into the inert pages of the Constitution and the statute books.[1]

Very often, then, the cases before the Court involve alternatives about which there is severe disagreement in the society, as in the case of segregation or economic regulation; that is, the setting of the case is "political." Moreover, they are usually cases where competent students of constitutional law, including the learned justices of the Supreme Court themselves, disagree; where the words of the Constitution are general, vague, ambiguous, or not clearly applicable; where precedent may be found on both sides; and where experts differ in predicting the consequences of the various alternatives or the degree of probability that the possible consequences will actually ensue. . . .

If the Court were assumed to be a "political" institution, no particular problems would arise, for it would be taken for granted that the members of the Court would resolve questions of fact and value by introducing assumptions derived from their own predispositions or those of influential clienteles and constituents. But, since much of the legitimacy of the Court's decisions rests on the fiction that it is not a political institution but exclusively a legal one, to accept the Court as a political institution would solve one set of problems at the price of creating another. Nonetheless, if it is true that the nature of the cases arriving before the Court is sometimes of the kind I have described, then the Court cannot act strictly as a legal institution. It must, that is to say, choose among controversial alternatives of public policy by appealing to at least some criteria of acceptability on questions of fact and value that cannot be found in or deduced from precedent, statute, and Constitution. It is in this sense that the Court is a national policy maker, and it is this role that gives rise to the problem of the Court's existence in a political system ordinarily held to be democratic.

Now, I take it that except for differences in emphasis and presentation, what I have said so far is today widely accepted by almost all American political scientists and by most lawyers. To anyone who believes that the Court is not, in at least some of its activities, a policy-making institution, the discussion that follows may seem irrelevant. But to anyone who holds that at least one role of the Court is as a policy-making institution in cases where strictly legal criteria are inadequate, a serious and much debated question arises, to wit: Who gets what and why? Or in less elegant language: What groups are benefited or handicapped by the Court and how does the allocation by the Court of these rewards and penalties fit into our presumably democratic political system?

II

In determining and appraising the role of the Court, two different and conflicting criteria are sometimes employed. These are the majority criterion and the criterion of right or justice.

Every policy dispute can be tested, at least in principle, by the majority criterion, because (again, in principle) the dispute can be analyzed according to the numbers of people for and against the various alternatives at issue and therefore according to the proportions of the citizens or eligible members who are for and against the alternatives. Logically speaking, except for a trivial case, every conflict in a given society must be a dispute between a majority of those eligible to participate and a minority or minorities; or else it must be a dispute between or among minorities only.[2] Within certain limits, both possibilities are independent of the number of policy alternatives at issue, and since the argument is not significantly affected by the number of alternatives, it is convenient to assume that each policy dispute represents only two alternatives.

If everyone prefers one of two alternatives, no significant problem arises. But a case will hardly come before the Supreme Court unless at least one person prefers an alternative that is opposed by another person. Strictly speaking, then, no matter how the Court acts in determining the legality or constitutionality of one alternative or the other, the outcome of the Court's decision must either (1) accord with the preferences of a minority of citizens and run counter to the preferences of a majority; (2) accord with the preferences of a majority and run counter to the preferences of a minority; or (3) accord with the preferences of one minority and run counter to the preferences of another minority, the rest being indifferent.

In a democratic system with a more or less representative legislature, it is unnecessary to maintain a special court to secure the second class of outcomes. A case might be made out that the Court protects the rights of national majorities against local interests in federal questions, but so far as I am aware, the role of the Court as a policy maker is not usually defended in this fashion; in what follows, therefore, I propose to pass over the ticklish question of federalism and deal only with "national" majorities and minorities. The third kind of outcome, although relevant according to other criteria, is hardly relevant to the majority criterion and may also be passed over for the moment.

One influential view of the Court, however, is that it stands in some special way as a protection of minorities against tyranny by majorities. In the course of its 167 years, in seventy-eight cases, the Court has struck down eighty-six different provisions of federal law as unconstitutional, and by interpretation it has modified a good many more. It might be argued, then, that in all or in a very large number of these cases the Court was, in fact, defending the rights of some minority against a "tyrannical" majority. There are, however, some exceedingly serious difficulties with this interpretation of the Court's activities.

III

... The view of the Court as a protector of the liberties of minorities against the tyranny of majorities is beset with . . . difficulties that are not so much ideological as matters of fact and logic. If one wishes to be at all rigorous about the question, it is probably impossible to demonstrate that any particular Court decisions have or have not been at odds with the preferences of a "national majority." It is clear that unless one makes *some* assumptions as to the kind of evidence one will require for the existence of a set of minority and majority preferences in the general population, the view under consideration is incapable of being proved at all. In any strict sense, no adequate evidence exists, for scientific opinion polls are of relatively recent origin, and national elections are little more than an indication of the first preferences of a number of citizens— in the United States the number ranges between about 40 and 60 per cent of the adult population—for certain candidates for public office. I do not mean to say that there is no relation between preferences among candidates and preferences among alternative public policies; but the connection is a highly tenuous one, and on the basis of an election it is almost never possible to adduce whether a majority does or does not support one of two or more policy alternatives about which members of the political elite are divided. For the greater part of the Court's history, then, there is simply no way of establishing with any high degree of confidence whether a given alternative was or was not supported by a majority or a minority of adults or even of voters.

In the absence of relatively direct information, we are thrown back on indirect tests. The eighty-six provisions of federal law that have been declared unconstitutional were, of course, initially passed by majorities of those voting in the Senate and in the House. They also had the President's formal approval. We could, therefore, speak of a majority of those voting in the House and Senate, together with the President, as a "lawmaking majority." It is not easy to determine whether any such constellation of forces in the political elites actually coincides with the preferences of a majority of American adults or even with the preferences of a majority of that half of the adult population which, on the average, votes in congressional elections. Such evidence as we have from opinion polls suggests that Congress is not markedly out of line with public opinion, or at any rate with such public opinion as there is after one discards the answers of people who fall into the category, often large, labeled "no response" or "don't know." If we may, on these somewhat uncertain grounds, take a "lawmaking majority" as equivalent to a "national majority," it is possible to test the hypothesis that the Supreme Court is shield and buckler for minorities against the national majorities.

Under any reasonable assumptions about the nature of the political process, it would appear to be somewhat naïve to assume that the Supreme Court either would or could play the role of Galahad. Over the whole history of the Court, on the average one new justice has been appointed every twenty-two months. Thus a President can expect to appoint about two new justices during one term of office; and if this were not enough to tip the balance on a normally divided Court, he is almost certain to succeed in two terms. Thus, Hoover had three appointments; Roosevelt, nine; Truman, four; and Eisenhower, four. Presidents are not famous for appointing justices hostile to their own views on public policy nor could they expect to secure confirmation of a man whose stance on key questions was flagrantly at odds with that of the dominant majority in the Senate. Justices are typically men who, prior to appointment, have engaged in public life and have committed themselves publicly on the great questions of the day. As Mr. Justice Frankfurter has recently reminded us, a surprisingly large proportion of the justices, particularly of the great justices who have left their stamp on the decisions of the Court, have had little or no prior judicial experience.[3] Nor have the justices—certainly not the great justices—been timid men with a passion for anonymity. Indeed, it is not too much to say that if justices were appointed primarily for their "judicial" qualities without regard to their basic attitudes on fundamental questions of public policy, the Court could not play the influential role in the American political system that it does in reality play.

The fact is, then, that the policy views dominant on the Court are never for long out of line with the policy views dominant among the lawmaking majorities of the United States. Consequently it would be most unrealistic to suppose that the Court would, for more than a few years at most, stand against any major alternatives sought by a lawmaking majority. The judicial agonies of the New Deal will, of course, quickly come to mind; but Roosevelt's difficulties with the Court were truly exceptional. Generalizing over the whole history of the Court, the chances are about one out of five that a President will make one appointment to the Court in less than a year, better than one out of two that he will make one within two years, and three out of four that he will make one within three years. Roosevelt had unusually bad luck: he had to wait four years for his first appointment; the odds against this long an interval are four to one. With average luck, the battle with the Court would never have occurred; even as it was, although the "court-packing" proposal did formally fail, by the end of his second term Roosevelt had appointed five new justices, and by 1941 Mr. Justice Roberts was the only remaining holdover from the Hoover era.

It is to be expected, then, that the Court is least likely to be successful in blocking a determined and persistent lawmaking majority on a major policy and most likely to succeed against a "weak" majority; for example, a dead one, a transient one, a fragile one, or one weakly united on a policy of subordinate importance.

IV

An examination of the cases in which the Court has held federal legislation unconstitutional confirms, on the whole, our expectations. Over the whole history of the Court, about half the decisions have been rendered more than four years after the legislation was passed.

Of the twenty-four laws held unconstitutional within two years, eleven were measures enacted in the early years of the New Deal. Indeed, New Deal measures comprise nearly a third of all legislation that has ever been declared unconstitutional within four years after enactment. . . .

Application of the majority criterion seems to show the following: First, if the Court did in fact uphold minorities against national majorities, as both its supporters and critics often seem to believe, it would be an extremely anomalous institution from a democratic point of view. Second, the elaborate "democratic" rationalizations of the Court's defenders and the hostility of its "democratic" critics are largely irrelevant, for lawmaking majorities generally have had their way. Third, although the Court seems never to have succeeded in holding out indefinitely, in a very small number of important cases it has delayed the application of policy up to twenty-five years. . . .

V

How can we appraise decisions of the third kind just mentioned? Earlier I referred to the criterion of right or justice as a norm sometimes invoked to describe the role of the Court. In accordance with this norm, it might be argued that the most important policy function of the Court is to protect rights that are in some sense basic or fundamental. Thus (the argument might run) in a country where basic rights are, on the whole, respected, one should not expect more than a small number of cases where the Court has had to plant itself firmly against a lawmaking majority. But majorities may, on rare occasions, become "tyrannical"; and when they do, the Court intervenes; and although the constitutional issue may, strictly speaking, be technically open, the Constitution assumes an underlying fundamental body of rights and liberties which the Court guarantees by its decisions.

Here again, however, even without examining the actual cases, it would appear, on political grounds, somewhat unrealistic to suppose that a Court whose members are recruited in the fashion of Supreme Court justices would long hold to norms of right or justice substantially at odds with the rest of the political elite. Moreover, in an earlier day it was perhaps easier to believe that certain rights are so natural and self-evident that their fundamental validity is as much a matter of definite knowledge, at least to all reasonable creatures, as the color of a ripe apple. To say that this view is unlikely to find many articulate defenders today is, of course, not to disprove it; it is rather to suggest that we do not need to elaborate the case against it [here].

In any event the best rebuttal to the view of the Court suggested above will be found in the record of the Court's decisions. Surely the cases . . .

where the policy consequences of the Court's decisions were overcome only after long battles will not appeal to many contemporary minds as evidence for the proposition under examination. A natural right to employ child labor in mills and mines? To be free of income taxes by the federal government? To employ longshoremen and harbor workers without the protection of workmen's compensation? The Court itself did not rely on such arguments in these cases, and it would be no credit to their opinions to reconstruct them along such lines.

So far, however, our evidence has been drawn from cases in which the Court has held legislation unconstitutional within four years after enactment. What of the other cases? Do we have evidence in these that the Court has protected fundamental or natural rights and liberties against the dead hand of some past tyranny by the lawmakers? The evidence is not impressive. In the entire history of the Court there is not one case arising under the First Amendment in which the Court has held federal legislation unconstitutional. If we turn from these fundamental liberties of religion, speech, press, and assembly, we do find a handful of cases—something less than ten—arising under Amendments Four to Seven in which the Court has declared acts unconstitutional that might properly be regarded as involving rather basic liberties. An inspection of these cases leaves the impression that, in all of them, the lawmakers and the Court were not very far apart; moreover, it is doubtful that the fundamental conditions of liberty in this country have been altered by more than a hair's breadth as a result of these decisions. However, let us give the Court its due; it is little enough.

Over against these decisions we must put the fifteen or so cases in which the Court used the protections of the Fifth, Thirteenth, Fourteenth, and Fifteenth Amendments to preserve the rights and liberties of a relatively privileged group at the expense of the rights and liberties of a submerged group: chiefly slaveholders at the expense of slaves, white people at the expense of colored people, and property holders at the expense of wage earners and other groups. These cases, unlike the relatively innocuous ones of the preceding set, all involved liberties of genuinely fundamental importance, where an opposite policy would have meant thoroughly basic shifts in the distribution of rights, liberties, and opportunities in the United States—where, moreover, the policies sustained by the Court's action have since been repudiated in every civilized nation of the Western world, including our own. Yet, if our earlier argument is correct, it is futile—precisely because the basic distribution of privilege *was* at issue—to suppose that the Court could have possibly acted much differently in these areas of policy from the way in which it did in fact act.

VI

Thus the role of the Court as a policy-making institution is not simple; and it is an error to suppose that its functions can be either described or appraised by means of simple concepts drawn from democratic or moral theory. It is possible, nonetheless, to derive a few general conclusions about the Court's role as a policy making institution.

National politics in the United States, as in other stable democracies, is dominated by relatively cohesive alliances that endure for long periods of time. One recalls the Jeffersonian alliance, the Jacksonian, the extraordinarily long-lived Republican dominance of the post-Civil War years, and the New Deal alliance shaped by Franklin Roosevelt. Each is marked by a break with past policies, a period of intense struggle, followed by consolidation, and finally decay and disintegration of the alliance.

Except for short-lived transitional periods when the old alliance is disintegrating and the new one is struggling to take control of political institutions, the Supreme Court is inevitably a part of the dominant national alliance. As an element in the political leadership of the dominant alliance, the Court, of course, supports the major policies of the alliance. By itself, the Court is almost powerless to affect the course of national policy. In the absence of substantial agreement within the alliance, an attempt by the Court to make national policy is likely to lead to disaster, as the *Dred Scott* decision and the early New Deal cases demonstrate. Conceivably, the cases of the last three decades involving the freedom of Negroes, culminating in the now famous decision on school integration, are exceptions to this generalization; I shall have more to say about them in a moment.

The Supreme Court is not, however, simply an *agent* of the alliance. It is an essential part of the political leadership and possesses some bases of power of its own, the most important of which is the unique legitimacy attributed to its interpretations of the Constitution. This legitimacy the Court jeopardizes if it flagrantly opposes the major policies of the dominant alliance; such a course of action, as we have seen, is one in which the Court will not normally be tempted to engage.

It follows that within the somewhat narrow limits set by the basic policy goals of the dominant alliance, the Court *can* make national policy. Its discretion, then, is not unlike that of a powerful committee chairman in Congress who cannot, generally speaking, nullify the basic policies substantially agreed on by the rest of the dominant leadership, but can, within these limits, often determine important questions of timing, effectiveness, and subordinate policy. Thus the Court is least effective against a current lawmaking majority—and evidently least inclined to act. It is most effective when it sets the bounds of policy for officials, agencies, state governments, or even regions, a task that has come to occupy a very large part of the Court's business.

Few of the Court's policy decisions can be interpreted sensibly in terms of a "majority" versus a "minority." In this respect the Court is no different from the rest of the political leadership. Generally speaking, policy at the national level is the outcome of conflict, bargaining, and agreement among minorities; the process is neither minority rule nor majority rule, but what might better be called *minorities* rule, where one aggregation of minorities achieves policies opposed by another aggregation.

The main objective of Presidential leadership is to build a stable and dominant aggregation of minorities with a high probability of winning the

Presidency and one or both houses of Congress. The main task of the Court is to confer legitimacy on the fundamental policies of the successful coalition. There are times when the coalition is unstable with respect to certain key policies; at very great risk to its legitimacy powers, the Court can intervene in such cases and may even succeed in establishing policy. Probably in such cases it can succeed only if its action conforms to and reinforces a widespread set of explicit or implicit norms held by the political leadership— norms which are not strong enough or are not distributed in such a way as to ensure the existence of an effective lawmaking majority, but are, nonetheless, sufficiently powerful to prevent any successful attack on the legitimacy powers of the Court. This is probably the explanation for the relatively successful work of the Court in enlarging the freedom of Negroes to vote during the past three decades and in its famous school integration decisions.

Yet the Court is more than this. Considered as a political system, democracy is a set of basic procedures for arriving at decisions. The operation of these procedures presupposes the existence of certain rights, obligations, liberties, and restraints; in short, certain patterns of behavior. The existence of these patterns of behavior in turn presupposes widespread agreement (particularly among the politically active and influential segments of the population) on the validity and propriety of the behavior. Although its record is by no means lacking in serious blemishes, at its best the Court operates to confer legitimacy not simply on the particular and parochial policies of the dominant political alliance but on the basic patterns of behavior required for the operation of a democracy.

▪ Notes

1. Felix Frankfurter, "The Supreme Court in the Mirror of Justices," *University of Pennsylvania Law Review,* CV (1957), 781, 793.
2. Provided that the total membership of the society is an even number, it is technically possible for a dispute to occur that divides the membership into two equal parts, neither of which can be said to be either a majority or minority of the total membership. But even in the instances where the number of members is even (which should occur on the average only half the time), the probability of an exactly even split, in any group of more than a few thousand people, is so small that it may be ignored.
3. Frankfurter, *op. cit.,* 782–784.

34 STATE GOVERNMENT AND PRIVATE POWER

- *Grant McConnell*

I

Few conditions of American political life have been more important in the distribution of power than federalism. Its effects have been different at different times, and invariably they have been complex. At the time of the adoption of the Constitution, federalism represented a great movement toward centralization. Moreover, the terms of federal relationships have been sufficiently fluid that considerable change has been possible within its context, much of the change centralizing in character. Over time, nevertheless, federalism has had a strongly decentralizing force. The perpetuation of the states as partially autonomous ("sovereign") units has clearly inhibited much change of a centralizing character that would otherwise have occurred. Considerably more important, however, federalism as an influence for decentralization has served to maintain and enhance a variety of systems of private power in the nation.

The strength of the states in the federal system is occasionally disputed and the supposedly much expanded power of the federal government deplored. This sort of evaluation, like its opposite, rests on a particular concept of the proper degree of centralization or decentralization. Even granting the relative character of such a valuation, however, it has been made abundantly clear in recent years that the states have not been weakened to the point of impotence.[1] Moreover, general belief in the merit of the states as autonomous units of government remains strong. The grounds for this belief are varied. Some (although probably not most) people feel direct loyalty to individual states as though to separate nations. The states, moreover, seem to embody the virtues of decentralization and smallness in an overly complex world. Occasionally, they appear virtuous just because, unlike the federal government, they do not deal with

From Grant McConnell, *Private Power and American Democracy* (New York: Knopf, 1966), pp. 166–168, 170–178, 180–195. © Copyright 1966 by Alfred A. Knopf, Inc. Reprinted by permission of the publisher.

256

foreign policy or foreign aid and because they have almost nothing to do with national defense and cannot formulate or carry out a monetary policy. The most persistent and strongly held belief in the virtue of the states, however, is based on a feeling that they are closer to the people and that power in their hands represents self-government more than does power in the hands of the federal government, a belief supported by virtually all the arguments advanced in favor of decentralization of any kind. Also, the states are perceived as presenting opportunities for experimentation and as sources of innovation in government. Certainly, a number of innovations have come from the states: the unicameral legislature of Nebraska, the initiative and referendum of Oregon, Wisconsin's regulatory commissions, the Georgia unit system, to name some outstanding examples. Yet the total list of such innovations is not long; the states' imitative tendencies are probably much more impressive. Sometimes partisans of decentralization to the states maintain that since state governments are closer to the people in point of geography, the people can know and understand them better. The fact, however, is that the state governments have a "low visibility" and are not well known even to their citizens.[2] Probably the strength of partisanship for the states vis-à-vis the nation is to be explained not so much by the reasons usually advanced as by a simple, unexamined belief that local autonomy *is* democracy—and by the intuitively understood advantages that accrue to local elites from autonomy.

Although there are very great differences in conditions in the fifty states, a common spirit pervades many of their political institutions. This spirit, different from that prevailing in the federal government, is largely the consequence of that decentralization the states represent. The institutions in which it is embodied give very great advantages to structures of private power and to private interests generally. These institutions are by no means unfamiliar; some of them have been under criticism by reformers for a long time. Their greatest significance, however, can be seen if they are regarded as features of a common pattern of power.

One of the first features of state government to emerge in any general survey concerns the quality of state constitutions. The most cursory glance at these documents reveals that almost all of them are entirely different in character from the Constitution of the United States. The difference is most apparent in the length of the state documents, the overwhelming majority of which are very long. . . . In some degree, their length and openness to change are expressions of a general outlook which accords less sanctity to the state constitutions than to the United States Constitution. This suggests that in a very basic sense the spirit of state government may be considerably more majoritarian than its national counterpart. Certainly, many states have been deeply influenced by Progressivism and have incorporated measures such as the initiative, the referendum, the direct primary, and even the recall of judges, all of which bespeak an intention to democratize the processes of government in a highly majoritarian spirit. But the issue is very complex, and if the determination to give effect to the will of the majority is genuine, the reality is an ironic commentary on it.

II

It is largely meaningless to lay claim to majority rule unless the constituency in which a majority prevails is defined. The most obvious illustrations of this proposition have for a long time been the state legislatures. For many years students of government have pointed to the highly unrepresentative character of these bodies when they are regarded as state-wide wholes. Most of the upper houses of state legislatures have been in some way based on area as well as population. Often the constituent boundaries of their representative districts have been related to the counties, that is, subdivisions created by the states themselves; perhaps the most notorious situation of this sort has been the California Senate, which has offered the contrast of one district in the Sierra with less than 15,000 voters electing one senator, and Los Angeles County with more than 6,000,000 voters also electing one senator. But the lower houses have also been seriously unrepresentative. As the United States Advisory Commission on Intergovernmental Relations summarized the condition existing in mid-1961,

> In only 11 States did 35 percent or more of the population elect a majority of the members to both houses of the State Legislature; in only five of these States did the figure exceed 40 percent. On the other hand, there were at least seven states where less than 30 percent of the population elected a majority of the representatives to both houses of the legislature.[3]

This condition seemed impossible to challenge until 1962, when the United States Supreme Court handed down its decision in *Baker v. Carr.*[4] . . . In that decision the Court held that the courts do have a responsibility to see that the equal protection of the laws is extended to each citizen through equal participation in selecting his lawmaker. The Court did not say exactly what "equal protection of the laws" meant as it applied to the problem and left immediate solutions to be passed on by the lower courts. But the issue was at least opened to change. In rapid succession, state after state undertook to adjust the boundaries of legislative districts to forestall court attacks. While it is too early to see what all the consequences will be, it is certain that ultimately a very substantial redistribution of political power will be effected.

Why have the state legislatures been so unrepresentative so long? The most important reason is the very strong American attachment to the value of localism—an attachment which in the legislatures takes several forms. In the lower houses it is common to give each county at least one seat. Where the state has many counties, however, the result is a serious distortion of representation; thus Iowa with 99 counties and 108 seats in the lower house gives its smallest county eighteen times the representation allowed its largest.[5] Limitation on the number of seats one district may have prevents sparsely populated areas from being overbalanced by densely populated areas; by the same token it prevents urban voters from having a voice commensurate with that of rural voters, an effect particularly evident in some of the upper houses. . . .

The other important factor explaining unrepresentative legislatures is that while the United States has become progressively urban, redistricting to take account of this shift occurs, at best, only at ten-year intervals after the taking of the national census. Some states have shown little enthusiasm for making the adjustments so plainly called for by changes in population distribution. Thus Tennessee, the state that occasioned the dispute of *Baker v. Carr*, had not adjusted the boundaries of its legislative districts from 1901 until the Court intervened, despite a provision of the state constitution that required reapportionment every ten years. . . .

Unfortunately, court action in enforcing redistricting by the states can be only the first step in a long process that might lead to equitable apportionment. The efforts of the legislatures at reapportionment all too often fall short of the reformers' ideal of one man, one vote. And there remains the nicely developed American art of the gerrymander, which, while obviously more difficult to practice when the courts require constituencies to be roughly equal in size, is by no means banished. . . .

What is the significance of an inequitable distribution of voting power? Given the form in which the inequity exists, it might be (and frequently is) supposed that rural areas benefit at the expense of cities. Certainly it is evident that in many states representation of the countryside heavily overbalances that of the cities. The picture of a fundamental conflict of interest between town and country is thus easily conjured up. But this conflict may be less important than it seems. Issues that are solely rural or solely urban are not numerous, and there is some evidence that the conflict between city and country is less dramatic than it may have seemed; thus a study of voting in the legislature of Illinois, a state in which this division would seem particularly strong, indicates that urban and rural delegations do not vote solidly against each other.[6] The significance of inequitable representation lies elsewhere.

III

Another potentially important dimension of difference in the established distribution of voting power is that between the two major parties. This dimension very clearly is involved where the two parties exist as vital organizations. In a number of states the exaggerated representation given rural areas seems to have helped maintain the power of a particular party, usually the Republican. In Illinois and New York, for example, it is axiomatic that the Republican party is strongest in the areas outside the major metropolis, while the Democratic party must base itself on the big city.

Nevertheless, the consequences of particular partisan strength, even where they do exist, are not the really important aspects of the patterns of representation in the states. Despite the rather spotty coverage of the fifty states' political systems in scholarly analysis, there is sufficient evidence to indicate that parties are considerably less important than the frequency of reference to them in the press may suggest. Perhaps the basic general fact here is that vital two-party systems are not the rule among the states. The existence of one-party rule in the eleven southern states has long been common knowledge. For the whole nation, different tabulations give different views of the incidence of the one-party phenomenon. A 1955 estimate was that 18 states had single-party systems.[7] A more recent list named 23 states as either one-party states or states with one dominant party. Of the remaining 23 (the officially non-partisan states of Nebraska and Minnesota, as well as Alaska and Hawaii, were not counted), 14 additional states were considered to be two-party states only in a limited sense.[8] . . .

The meaning of these tabulations goes considerably beyond the evident conclusion that effective party competition is not the norm in the states. The figures only suggest the actual degree of weakness of many systems in the two-party category and say nothing about the vitality of those many single-party organizations. And it is just here that their significance lies. In his landmark study *Southern Politics,* V.O. Key demonstrated that one-party politics is no-party politics.[9] . . . The general picture is of a disorganized and atomized politics.

The results achieved by this disorganization must be very troubling to anyone who takes at face value the orthodoxy of small local units as devices for democratic participation. In a memorable discussion Key indicated what these results have been in the southern states:

Not only does a disorganized politics make impossible a competition between recognizable groups for power. It probably has a far-reaching influence on the kinds of individual leaders thrown into power and also on the manner in which they utilize their authority once they are in office. . . . Factional fluidity and discontinuity probably make a government especially disposed toward favoritism. Or to put the obverse of the proposition, the strength of organization reflecting something of a group or class solidarity creates conditions favorable to government according to rule or general principle, although it is readily conceded that such a result does not flow invariably. In a loose, catch-as-catch-can politics highly unstable coalitions must be held together by whatever means is available. This contract goes to that contractor, this distributor is dealt with by the state liquor board, that group of attorneys have an "in" at the state house, this bond house is favored. . . .

The significant question is, who benefits from political disorganization? Its significance is equalled only by the difficulty of arriving at an answer. There probably are several answers, depending on the peculiar circumstances in each case. Politics generally comes down, over the long run, to a conflict between those who have and those who have less. In state politics the crucial issues tend to turn around taxation and expenditure. . . . It follows that the grand objective of the haves is obstruction, at least of the haves who take only a short-term view. Organization is not always necessary to obstruct; it is essential, however, for the promotion of a sustained program in behalf of the have-nots, although not all party or factional organization is dedicated to that purpose. It follows, if these propositions are correct, that over the long-run the have-nots lose in a disorganized politics. They have no mechanism through which to act and their wishes find expression in fitful rebellions led by transient demagogues who gain their confidence but often have neither the technical competence nor the necessary stable base of political power to effectuate a program.[10]

What prevails in the South, then, is a pattern in which most political questions are relegated to the uncertain workings of a near chaos of loosely organized local factions or are not treated within the political framework at all. . . . In other regions, parties are not as weak—or, rather, as nonexistent —as they are in the South, but often they are very weak indeed.

The reasons for this condition, and its consequences, are somewhat different in nonsouthern areas. . . . In state after state would-be reformers have erected legal barriers to the development of parties. . . . They included the direct primary, the initiative, the referendum, and elaborate codes regulating the composition and government of parties. At every point these devices were intended to achieve the frustration of parties, a goal that has been to no small degree accomplished. As Key remarked in his general survey of American state politics, "Within a large proportion of the states only by the most generous characterization may it be said that political parties compete for power." [11]

Although weak-party systems outside the South have not had the same effects of domination over Negroes, they nevertheless substantiate Key's general argument. If they vary from state to state and from locality to locality, it is because the underlying social patterns of power vary. The advantages of disorganized politics accrue quite impartially to whatever groups, interests, or individuals are powerful in any way. Where power is not organized in broadly based parties, lesser power organized in smaller and narrower groups suffices. If there is no formal political organization at all, the social and economic ties that exist everywhere are the most important political reality; in general, however, the individuals and groups that benefit from them are those who have some sort of stake in the maintenance of existing arrangements and, thus, are opposed to change. Such arrangements may, as in the South, be directed against change in the status of submerged groups, but such extremes will not always be found. Often, other influences such as the deeply believed-in egalitarian doctrines of the "American Creed," as Myrdal called it, have produced a social pattern much less bleak, and the political order is accordingly far milder in its discriminations. Nevertheless, the absence of significant party organization anywhere places strong restraints on meaningful participation in politics by those whose economic or social bases of power are relatively weak.

Important differences among the states cannot be overlooked. There are genuine differences of degree in the cohesiveness and solidarity of parties from state to state; thus one study of a group of states has shown that conflict along party lines is more consistent in New Jersey than in Ohio and more consistent in both of these than in California or Tennessee.[12] Without question a comprehensive study would permit a rank order among the two-party states on the score of party conflict. But there are also significant differences among the so-called one-party states, in which factionalism may be more or less well organized, however different the organization from genuine party systems.

Thus Vermont has a bifactional system of some strength and durability. Interestingly, this bifactionalism seems to produce less demagoguery than appears where there are many factions.[13] . . .

Any comparison of the politics of the different American states is false if it subsumes all these diverse systems into a single pattern. It is of the essence of a federal or decentralized politics that various dominant purposes exist among the units making it up. These purposes and the interests to which they belong differ from state to state. Nevertheless, the disorganization of political parties in favor of other and lesser forms of organization does produce a fundamental similarity among the weak-party states. This consists of the heightened degree of power all confer on fairly narrow interest groups. Understandably, these groups vary in character. Some are more extreme than others in their demands, and some are perhaps wiser than others in their concern for public values. Thus a student of Montana politics has argued that the Anaconda Company, the strongest interest group in the state ("the company"), plays a stabilizing role in an economy and government that might otherwise be disorderly.[14] Whether this service and the close co-operation between Anaconda, the Montana Power Company, the state's three large railroads, and the sugar refinery companies are worth the costs so obviously implied may be another matter. Of Maine it has been claimed that "in few American States are the reins of government more openly or completely in the hands of a few leaders of economic interest groups" (a statement with parallels in studies of various other states). In Maine, however, the interests are timber companies, paper manufacturers, and developers of hydroelectric power.[15]

These examples suggest a number of different points. First, the interest groups which are important in the politics of a state are those which are otherwise important in the state; they are different in different states. Second, the interest-group structure of politics is simple to the degree that the state is itself simple and undiversified. In California, where a diversity of significant interest groups exists, the political organization of interest groups is relatively complex; in Maine or Montana, where the important interest groups are relatively few, political organization is relatively uncomplicated. Third, the interest groups are generally strong when parties are weak, and vice versa. This is perhaps most evident in the organization of legislatures, but it is noteworthy that interest groups may also take the place of parties in promoting political careers, particularly in the weaker, less competitive party systems.[16] Fourth, parties are likely to be weak where there is lack of diversity of interests in the state. This is not perfectly borne out by experience, since states like California have had weak parties while containing much diversity; here, however, the element of the antiparty Progressive "reforms" is obviously an added factor.[17] Weak parties and lack of diversity do, however, seem to be related.

It is apparent, then, that in a very large part of the United States, state politics does not provide the coherence of policy that might be expected from competitive party systems. There are strong grounds, moreover, for suspecting that to a serious degree state politics minimizes—or suppresses—the voices of significant elements of the state populations. Probably many issues are settled without controversy simply because the political context permits no ready challenge to the positions taken by entrenched groups. For example, a study of two sessions of the Illinois general assembly showed that 73 per cent of all roll call votes were unanimous. Although many of the measures handled in this fashion were undoubtedly of limited interest, routine, or otherwise unimportant, it is difficult to believe that the treatment given all of them reflected underlying unanimity of interest among the people of Illinois. The result is certainly related to the party reality indicated by the fact that only 3.95 per cent of the votes in one session and 2.5 per cent in the second session were cast along party lines.[18] The appearance of consensus which the lack of division suggests is false and is in part the product of the political machinery itself. Inside the legislatures of states lacking strong party machinery, logrolling, often managed by lobbyists themselves, readily avoids dispute and creates an illusion that there are no grounds for controversy.[19] The stability thus produced may be illusory in the long run.

IV

The character of state political systems is reflected in the pattern of governmental structure shared by most states; reciprocally, this structure has considerable influence in perpetuating the political system. The outlines of this pattern are common knowledge, and it has been the target of reformers for many years. Indeed, there is remarkably little disagreement among students of state government about the nature of the changes needed; for half a century demands have been repeated for fundamentally the same type of reforms—demands which have been collectively dignified as "the state reorganization movement." The subject, however, has been consistently treated as merely structural and technical in character, a very dry matter with little interest for the general public. Indeed, there are grounds for suspecting that tidiness has often been the reformers' highest objective; certainly the presentation of the argument for reform often suggests this value as the most important issue. Much more is at stake, however, as has been clear to the ablest analysts. V. O. Key, for example, has correctly noted the connection between political organization and the problem of state administrative organization.[20] Administration does involve politics, and in the states it is at least arguable that administration is the most important area of politics.

Perhaps the most conspicuous feature of state administration is the multiplicity of elective offices. Although there is considerable variety among the states on this score, most of their ballots have long lists of offices to be filled by direct choice of the electorate. . . .

This feature of state administration is of long standing. In origin it recalls the long and gradual growth of governmental activities in the states. The tendency has been to treat each newly added function as something separate and unrelated to other functions. A majoritarian conception of democracy has, moreover, produced an insistence that the voters have the greatest possible degree of participation. The idea of providing additional checks on executive power by breaking up the administrative machinery has also been used to justify the practice of making administrative offices elective. The process and its justification are still to be seen and heard in many states. And the same process continues at a lively rate in local government, with the multiplication of special districts for single functions where population growth compels the establishment of fire and police protection and other services. In the state the reorganization movement has had some successes in reversing the tendency, but, with a few exceptions, they have not been large. Despite the impetus given by the "little Hoover Commissions," which have studied the problem in some two-thirds of the states since World War II, accomplishment has been meager.

The persistence of this pattern in the face of such widespread and determined crusading for reform is interesting, suggesting the presence of active resistance to change. This resistance can summon up a variety of justifications, but is actually based on the advantages disorganized and ill-co-ordinated administration gives to narrow power-holding groups.[21] To groups that have established preferential positions for themselves in state government, the prospect of a centralization of authority in the governor's office through powers of appointment and removal is a serious threat. The multiplicity of elective offices, whether established by constitutional provision or statute, is a guarantee of the governor's impotence to require conformity with his own policy. Clearly it is also a check on power and limits the capacity for evil in anything the governor might wish. But by the same token, it is an obstacle to co-ordination, and even more important, it is a limitation on the ability of the whole public to influence policy. Given the general absence of strong parties in the states, it is unlikely that all the different elected officers will be of the governor's party or faction. Although these officers are usually selected by the same general electorate which votes for the governor, the obscurity of many of their offices greatly diminishes the public's interest in them. Interested groups, however, pay great attention to some of these posts. Consequently the effective constituencies of some of them (such as directors of education or agriculture, commissioners of highways, and the like) are less than the general public and consist preponderantly of the groups most immediately concerned. The condition of a multiplicity of elective administrative offices thus tends to defeat democratic control of policy, and thus, rather than co-ordination or orderliness of administration, is the main issue.

A second problem of administration that has troubled reformers is the sheer multiplicity of agencies in state government. . . .

Despite the reformers' emphasis on the problems posed by many elective offices and separate agencies, change on both these scores would probably leave the fundamental problem largely unsolved: the widespread pattern of administrative agencies each of which is effectively accountable only to a narrow constituency consisting of the group or groups most directly and intimately affected by the agency's activities. Many different kinds of arrangements lead to this result, including the multiplicity of elective offices and agencies, but the extensive use of boards and other devices to make or advise on policy for administrative agencies is at least as important. Despite the diversity among these boards and commissions, they have one common quality: all to some degree limit the responsiveness of policy to the large constituency most clearly represented by the governor. In the clearest pattern of this situation a board is chosen, usually by statutory requirement, from members of a particular trade or industry—sometimes even *by* recognized units of the trade or industry—to advise or make policy for the state department or agency charged with public policy in the area involved. Often the official description of the board's powers does not correspond to the reality of the situation; thus a given board with policymaking duties may actually be no more than a rubber stamp for a strong professional administrator in the regular civil service. Often, however, a board legally invested with merely advisory powers is able to impose its policies on the line administrators. The latter condition is the more probable, since the board members are likely to have been chosen from the leadership, or on the nomination of the leadership, of well-organized interest groups with strong influence in the fragmented and substantially non-partisan legislatures. In the long run only a strong governor can protect the strong-willed and independent line administrators, and strong governors are not common in the American system.

California has presented a particularly clear example of this problem. This is not a state unusually notorious for bad government. It has great diversity and is even included among the "two-party" states. Until very recently, however, its administration has been fragmented; in 1961 it had more than 350 agencies presumably reporting to the governor. These agencies were highly miscellaneous in structure and placement, but there were in general two main groups: the departments, with their subunits arranged in hierarchical pattern, and a great array of boards and commissions. The position of the departments here was particularly interesting, most of them being attached to one or more boards with policy functions. Thus the Department of Education was linked to the Board of Education, the Curriculum Commission, and several others; the Department of Natural Resources was associated with the State Park Commission, the State Board of Forestry, the Soil Conservation Commission, the District Oil and Gas Commissions (six of them), and the Small Craft Harbors Commission; the Department of Public Works had the Highway Commission. The pattern was almost universal, except for the many boards quite unattached to any departmental structure.[22] There was some variety in the functions of these boards. Thus the State Board of Forestry, in the official language, "prescribes general policies for the operation of the Division of Forestry." Its members were chosen to represent the pine and redwood industries, forest land, livestock and agricultural operators, and water users. The State Mining Board "establishes policies for administration of the division (of Mines). It consists of five members representing the mining industry." In the Oil and Gas Division, "A board of commissioners is elected by oil and gas operators in each of five districts," its duties to include ruling on drilling and conservation. The Department of Agriculture had a number of boards, including the Agricultural Prorate Advisory Commission, a body with considerably more than advisory powers in a field of great economic importance to others than farmers.[23]

A number of things are conspicuous in this pattern. First, the responsibility recognized and generally enforced was strictly to the most interested groups. Second, the governor's powers of supervision and control were minimal. Third, the boards' personnel was chosen by the regulated groups themselves. . . .

Although not all other states have the consistent pattern of board influence and control by particular constituencies that has prevailed in California, many of them have comparable situations. New York, which is exemplary by contrast with other states on many scores, makes extensive use of advisory boards and councils in its various departments. Thus an advisory board consisting of representatives of the various branches of the insurance business exists in the Insurance Department. An advisory board of individuals associated with the supervision of cemeteries "assists" the Cemetery Board in the Department of State. The Advisory Council on Placement and Unemployment Insurance has an active part in administration.[24] But Alabama shows perhaps the extreme situation of this kind. Here, the State Health Officer is appointed by the State Board of Health but this body is ex officio the Medical Association of Alabama.[25]

In regulation of business, particular representation of the groups regulated has been especially prominent. Some years ago a study of state regulatory agencies commented that banking and insurance-regulating agencies have been "to a significant degree creatures of the enterprises they regulate."[26] But the sphere that shows the most nearly universal control of regulation by the regulated through the medium of nearly autonomous boards is the licensing of trades and professions. The practice of giving public authority—sometimes formally, but often in practice—to private associations of professionals is quite old. As early as 1859 the North Carolina legislature enacted that "the association of regularly graduated physicians . . . is hereby declared to be a body politic and corporate," with "power to appoint the body of medical examiners."[27] Other states followed suit, although by the 1920's some recession from this practice had occurred: a bit later, however, it was revived. North Carolina was again a leader with a self-governing bar act requiring all members of the legal profession to belong to the bar association.[28] The parade of other trades and professions in many states toward this ideal of "self-government" was sardonically summarized by one observer with the words, "the gild returns to America." By the 1950's, a study of state licensing legislation involving 927 licensing boards showed that statutory provisions required all members to be practitioners of the given occupation in 567 boards; in 140 of the others a majority of the members had to be practitioners. Appointment of some practitioners was required on most of the others. Moreover, direct selection by the association was required in 17 boards and appointment by the governor from an association list for 246 boards.[29]

The impulses leading to the creation of these agencies are largely the same. On the one hand all are justified by appeal to an ideal of professionalism and protection for the public. . . . Undoubtedly many professional problems are difficult for nonspecialists to understand; undoubtedly also, genuine concern for the public's welfare often exists in the professions. It is quite obvious, however, that the legal restraints exercised by licensing boards operate to the peculiar advantage of established practitioners of the skill involved. All of them administer regulations which limit entry to the vocation. Certainly in some professions, such as medicine and dentistry, such regulations are justified. But the list of activities frequently given state authority to regulate the qualifications of their members also includes barbers, hairdressers ("cosmetologists"), dry cleaners, funeral directors, cemetery salesmen, and many others. Even garage mechanics have attempted to gain such standing. Clearly, protection of the job market, which has been behind much trade-unionism, forms a large part of the motivation to establish under state authority licensing systems effectively controlled by members of a given vocation.[30]

A number of conclusions emerge from this survey. First, the practice of securing special legal status to protect established members of a line of activity is widespread. What is sometimes slurringly referred to as "trade union mentality" is by no means limited to trade unions; its manifestations, indeed, are at least as far-reaching in some professions and businesses as in the trades. Second, the machinery of state administration has made an extensive accommodation to the demands of particular groups. Third, this accommodation has amounted to a parceling out of public authority to private groups. This process is frequently indirect, as through the required appointment to public bodies of representatives of particular groups; it is sometimes, however, quite direct and formal.

This system of protection for favored groups (and it should be clear that only a minority of the people of any state enjoys such status) has struck deep roots in state governmental structures. All the features of government and politics which render the governors weak favor this system of protection. Wherever possible, the various groups have sought to give their own favored public bodies special constitutional status, although such efforts may be self-defeating in that a multiplication of continual provisions on such matters tends to erase the distinction between statutory and constitutional subjects. And other features of established arrangements ensure the perseverance of the pattern. "Earmarking" of public funds, for example, goes far to render some boards and commissions impervious to any requirement of co-ordination of public policy or effective consideration of other than clientele needs. Sometimes the federal requirements contained in grants-in-aid help achieve this result.[31] The most important factor, however, is the presence of informal ties between the administrators and the interests concerned. Where virtual autonomy of boards or agencies is achieved, the supposed antithesis between private and public bodies tends to dissolve. Interest group and regulator develop symbiotically, and under their joint influence, the legislature becomes friendly. The process of government may become quite informal.[32]

V

The spirit of state government and politics which emerges from this discussion is remarkably consistent. At almost every point it inspires a vision of democracy in which the people themselves rule, in which there is no coercion, in which government is servant rather than master. The vision pictures widespread participation in political life and a diffusion of power. It seems to carry the torch of equality high among other values.

In general these ends are sought by the defeat of any tendency which might produce centralization of government or political organization. Weakness of the governor, of central administration, of parties, is at every point the goal. Yet paradoxically this does not mean weak government; the powers state governments exercise are often both strong and far-reaching. The actual target of all the devices surveyed here is not so much power itself as centralized power. The key to the paradox lies in the unstated assumption that power in the hands of particular citizen groups is not power at all. This, in turn, is related to an assumption that the matters on which regulations are enforced through the exercise of state authority affect others than members of the regulated groups to only a minor degree. It also implies that there are no differences of interest among the members of the groups most affected. If these assumptions were correct, it would be reasonable to suppose that no coercion is involved in the regulation of policy areas through public bodies dominated by particular groups. . . . The people would regulate themselves and thus be free, and power would not exist in any important degree. . . .

In what would otherwise be a political vacuum . . . a great number of interest groups and narrowly based factions of different kinds have flourished to provide such political organization as most states have. Some of these are tautly disciplined; others are quite loose. They by no means conjointly include the whole population or the sum of all the interests in any state, for very significant interests and very substantial categories of people are left outside the pattern. Important values are thus excluded from the political process that results. The illusion of unanimity disappears when closer examination reveals the existence of very real and sometimes fundamental conflict of interest. There is no more striking example of this than the long-term exclusion of Negroes from political participation in the South and the monumental façade of unity that has stood before this fact. The absence of controversy is too easily taken as proof of unanimity.

The weakness of parties is closely paralleled by the weakness of governors. Although it is perhaps no longer correct to consider the American governor a figurehead, much distance remains to be traversed before he can be regarded as a genuine leader or, more important, as the central medium for representation of all those interests which are widely shared but not reflected in the vaunted pluralism of interest groups and factions.[33] To an important degree the weakness of parties as the means of organizing the entire community is the basis for the weakness of governors. The governor is consequently reduced almost to the status of a factional leader. He can often wield the influence that derives from substantial patronage, but this power is often almost matched by that of similar patronage in the hands of other elected officials. Where parties are weak, little more than mutual bargaining among the governor and these other officials is available for their co-ordination. The availability of patronage does give the governor a degree of power in legislation, but it is not commensurate with the need. . . .

Government has indeed been fragmented and politics atomized. Yet power has not been abolished. The co-ordination of factions and autonomous bureaus generates important power from which appeal is very difficult. . . .

In an abstract but very real sense, the problem is one of informality. Interpersonal ties, friendships, and relationships take the place of rules and formal procedures by reducing government and politics to small units. In legislatures, for example, logrolling is the product of the great complexities of established and anticipated personal obligations. The resulting web is woven from admirable human traits—friendship and gratitude—but rationality and concern for those not immediately involved are rare and slender threads in it. On another dimension, the problem is the dissolution of the distinction between what is public and what is private. One consequence is often to make the ways of government and politics humane and intimate, but another is to expose government to the play of favoritism and arbitrariness and to make politics the preserve of those who are already economically or socially powerful. It is to surrender the peculiar functions of government to private hands over which many who must feel government power can have no influence. Self-government in this sense may enlarge the freedom of the powerful, but it may also diminish the freedom of the weak. . . .

The particular form of political organization so prevalent among the states has probably contributed to stability. It has provided for the recognition of established power—for the most part, that of functional interest groups and factions formed about individuals. The organization of state politics and government has involved co-opting these scattered centers of power, whose co-operation has been gained on a logrolling basis and has resulted in effective devolution to their hands. Where affairs of minor importance have been involved, such as the licensing of barbers, the cost has been minor; but with matters of greater importance, like the regulation of insurance, the costs have been considerable. By far the greatest problems, however, have been the product of the comprehensive pattern of many fragmentary constituencies controlling parts of government and in effect exercising public authority. The lack of co-ordination has entailed a waste of resources. The failure to encompass in the scheme of politics all the interests and values important to the people of the states may during the years to come diminish the stability the states have enjoyed in the past. Should this prove true, the federal system will come under increasingly serious challenge.

▪ Notes

1. The Commission on Intergovernmental Relations (Kestnbaum Commission) perhaps began with a presumption that the states had become dangerously weakened. As time went on, however, the presumption disappeared and the ultimate report took a very moderate view. The Commission's *Report* is dated June, 1955 (Washington, D.C.).
2. The American Assembly, *The Forty-Eight States* (New York: Columbia University Press, 1955), p. 65.
3. U.S. Advisory Commission on Intergovernmental Relations, *Apportionment of State Legislatures* (Washington, D.C., 1962), p. 15.
4. 369 U.S. 186 (1962).
5. Malcolm E. Jewell, *The State Legislature: Politics and Practice* (New York: Random House, 1963), p. 22.
6. See article by D. R. Derge, "Urban-Rural Conflict: The Case of Illinois," in John C. Wahlke and Heinz Eulau, *Legislative Behavior* (Glencoe: Free Press, 1959). See also discussion in Jewell, *op. cit.,* pp. 60–67.
7. Dayton McKean in American Assembly, *op. cit.,* p. 75. He apparently was following the estimate in Belle Zeller, ed., *American State Legislatures* (New York: Crowell, 1954).
8. Jewell, *op. cit.,* pp. 10, 11.
9. V. O. Key, Jr., *Southern Politics in State and Nation* (New York: Knopf, 1949), p. 299. See Chapter 14 *in toto.*
10. *Ibid.,* pp. 304–307. To this might be added the comment of Karl Bosworth: "Experience in one-party states makes clear that personal politics tends to displace issue-oriented politics." American Assembly, *op. cit.,* p. 87.
11. V. O. Key, Jr., *American State Politics* (New York: Knopf, 1956), p. 120.
12. John C. Wahlke *et al., The Legislative System: Explorations in Legislative Behavior* (New York: John Wiley, 1962), p. 351. See also Key, *American State Politics.*
13. See Duane Lockard, *New England Politics* (Princeton: Princeton University Press, 1959), pp. 14 ff.
14. Roland R. Renne, *The Government and Administration of Montana* (New York: Crowell, 1958), p. 78: "It [Anaconda] works closely with key legislators in getting useful information into their hands, assists them with drafting bills, advances arguments for or against a particular measure, and develops strategy for getting the measure enacted into law."
15. Lockard, *op. cit.,* pp. 79–80.
16. Wahlke, *op. cit.,* p. 100.
17. A comparison of states for conflict along party lines ranked New Jersey, Ohio, California, in that order. See Wahlke, *op. cit.,* p. 351.
18. William J. Keefe, cited in Neil F. Garvey, *The Government and Administration of Illinois* (New York: Crowell, 1958), p. 106. There were 2,324 roll call votes in the first session.
19. See, for example, Gilbert Y. Steiner and Samuel K. Gove, *Legislative Politics in Illinois* (Urbana: University of Illinois Press, 1960), pp. 76–80. Few more remarkable devices for creating an illusion of unanimity exist than the "agreed bill" procedure in Illinois. See Gilbert Y. Steiner, *Legislation by Collective Bargaining: The Agreed Bill in Illinois Unemployment Compensation Legislation* (Urbana: University of Illinois Institute of Labor and Industrial Relations, n.d.).
20. Key, *Southern Politics,* p. 306n: "Comparative analysis of some southern and some northern states suggests the inference that theorists of the state reorganization movement have by and large failed to see the relation of political organization to the problem of state administrative organization. A state such as New York adapts itself to an integrated state administration under the direction of a governor who is

the leader of a relatively cohesive and organized party. A governor in a loose factional system does not have organized about him social elements necessary to produce enough power to control the entire state administration. Nor does he occupy a position as party leader that makes him appear sufficiently accountable to warrant vesting him with broad authority for the direction of administration."

21. For a summary of the usual arguments for and against reform on this score, see Ferrel Heady, *State Constitutions: The Structure of Administration* (New York: National Municipal League, 1961), pp. 2–5.

22. See chart in "The Agency Plan for California," summary prepared by California Department of Finance, April, 1962 (mimeographed).

23. These examples and quotations are from *California State Government, A Guide to Organizations and Functions* (Sacramento: California State Department of Finance, 1951).

24. Lynton K. Caldwell, *The Government and Administration of New York* (New York: Crowell, 1954), pp. 284, 285.

25. Coleman E. Ransome, Jr., *The Office of Governor in the United States* (University: University of Alabama Press, 1956), p. 270.

26. James W. Fesler, *The Independence of State Regulatory Agencies* (Chicago: Public Administration Service, 1942), p. 32.

27. J. A. C. Grant, "The Gild Returns to America," *Journal of Politics*, IV (1942), 303–336, 459–477.

28. *Ibid.*, p. 316.

29. Council of State Governments, *Occupational Licensing Legislation in the States* (1952).

30. For a radical critique of licensure, see Milton Friedman, *Capitalism and Freedom* (Chicago: University of Chicago Press, 1962).

31. Cf. Ransome, *op. cit.*, pp. 381–383.

32. Cf. the comments of Paul Dolan on the informal administrative process in Delaware, *The Government and Administration of Delaware* (New York: Crowell, 1956), pp. 102–103.

33. Leslie Lipson may correctly have seen the long-term development of the office of governor, but the subtitle to his pioneering work was perhaps premature. Leslie Lipson, *The American Governor: From Figurehead to Leader* (Chicago: University of Chicago Press, 1939).

35 THE GOVERNMENTAL RESPONSE TO URBANIZATION

■ *Scott Greer*

The Governmental Mosaic of the Metropolis

Late in the last century a distinguished commentator on American life noted that municipal government was the one conspicuous failure of our

From Scott Greer, *Governing the Metropolis* (New York: John Wiley, 1962), pp. 45–77, 80–81, 83–87. Reprinted by permission of the publisher.

society. Coming from Britain, where local government is administered by the middle class in terms of its understanding of the general welfare, Lord Bryce was shocked.[1] American cities, with elaborate machinery for enforcing democracy, were run by gangs. Tammany Hall shamelessly bribed, corrupted, and sold out the policy of New York City to the highest bidder. The men who ran our governments operated by a moral code whose chief distinction was that between "honest graft" and "dishonest graft." (The immortal phrase is from Plunkitt of Tammany Hall, whose self-designed epitaph was, "He seen his opportunities and he took them.")[2] Enormous contracts were sold for private income; criminals bought hunting licenses from the police; ordinary enterprise paid tribute to the *condottieri* of City Hall.

There is more to this picture, however. Seth Low, Mayor of Brooklyn at the time of Lord Bryce's visit, appends a rebuttal to the last edition of the Englishman's book. Eloquently, he makes a major point. At whatever cost in plunder and crime, the cities of America in the last half of the nineteenth century grew tenfold. Urban population increased from less than four million to more than thirty million. A rapidly growing nation which was 15 per cent urban in 1850 was 40 per cent urban by the turn of the century. It was a true population explosion. And as Low points out, these floods of people were housed, order was maintained, streets were built, transport was established, water was brought in, and wastes were carried away. What wonder that many mistakes were made? More impressive is the over-all achievement. The fantastic expansion of the urban plant in nineteenth-century America is one of the most striking examples of collective achievement.

Lord Bryce, however, might still retort, "Yes, but at what a cost." And most of the unnecessary cost of that development was due to governmental structure inadequate to the burdens of explosive urbanization. To understand this we must look at American definitions of municipal government. These were the rules, inherited from the past, codified in law and the state constitutions, which set the limits within which our urban governments could develop. They were quite inadequate to the floods of history.

American cities ceased to be administered by appointed delegates of the state after the Revolutionary War. Instead, an effort was made to combine dominance by the state legislatures with Jacksonian democracy. At the price of considerable simplification, let us say that Jacksonian ideology was translated into these norms: (1) the city was responsible to the ordinary citizen through universal manhood suffrage; (2) office was open to all and could be managed successfully by any citizen; (3) the citizens had a sacred right to local self-rule. The results were chiefly visible in the incompetence and peculation common to urban government. With massive public works, a flood of culturally illiterate new citizens, and the exposure of all key offices to the electorate, government became a key form of private enterprise to its practitioners. And, because of their interdependence within the urban area, many nonpolitical persons were drawn willy-nilly into the "ring" that ran the city. The basic ambivalence between local self-rule and the doctrine that the legal city was merely a creature of the state led to frequent special and discriminatory acts at the state capitol. The big, wicked city was deemed incapable of governing itself. State legislatures responded with "ripper legislation" aimed at destroying powers of the city. Some major cities, such as Memphis and Mobile, were actually abolished. The police force of St. Louis is still partially controlled from Jefferson City, the little capital city of Missouri.[3]

At the same time, the state constitutions provided easy means of incorporating new municipalities. Under the "right to local self-rule," state constitutions also specified extremely difficult processes for annexation or amalgamation of existing cities. Furthermore, translation of this right into political form meant that the city was required to gain the consent of the citizens for any major change in police power and fiscal capacity. Thus tax rates, bond issues, structural changes, annexations and mergers, were submitted to the voters. *Vox populi* was indeed interpreted as *vox Dei*—the voice of the people was considered to be the only legitimate voice where major change was concerned. Wherever a group of residents saw their common interest demanding it, a municipality could be created. It was extremely difficult to destroy the legal entity once it was created without the consent of the citizens, while formal change was almost impossible except by referendum.

This governmental response to social change was one typical of social organizations. Every effort was made to persist in the earlier patterns of behavior, for such patterns represented commitments for many persons. In the face of the astronomical increase in population, in social functions, in the scale of the total society, every effort was made to carry on local government business as usual. For on the existing scheme of things rested the plans and hopes of political bosses, ward heelers, contractors, private businessmen, ethnic enclaves—all those concerned with the city government as a major factor in their lives and business.

The emphasis during the period of rapid urbanization was on getting the job done. If the city needed a street-car grid, or a rapid transit, and the unwieldy city council objected, bribe the council. If the electoral machinery with its laundry list of elected officers made rational voting impossible, accept the organized machinery of the parties. If a hundred thousand new citizens did not understand Anglo-Saxon traditions of self-rule, let the "pols" teach them the ropes. It was a strategy of opportunism and expediency. In the process, the polity of the city was degraded; it became a necessary tool for the achievement of ends by private enterprise. The great capital investments of the period were largely the creation of private capital, working with franchise, contracts, and permits bought, stolen, or forced from the elected officials of local governments. When, in short, the burdens on government became too much for the legitimate system of government, ways were found to circumvent the system.

Needless to say, there was little concern for long-range planning in such a system. Government followed private enterprise: the labor force surged into a booming city, bringing its families and problems and social costs with it. Willy-nilly, government accepted the consequences—in the maintenance of public safety, the provision of charity, the extension of the city's physical plant, the policing of labor-management relations, the struggle to control organized criminal rings. Rather than planning for the future, urban government was continually struggling with its debts to the past, and it was always in arrears.

There was, after all, little to guide a planner. The forecasting of urban growth is still a primitive science, and in the earlier days of urbanization when there was no precedent for such growth, nobody really understood what was happening. Thus the framework of local government was not radically re-examined in the light of the vast social transformation described earlier. Instead, reformers concentrated on the most obvious abuses in the existing system. They struggled to take the policy away from the political machines (those organizations interested primarily in the monetary rewards of politics) through the institution of nonpartisan government, civil service systems, and eventually the city manager form of government. The reformers were, in short, chiefly concerned with civilizing a governmental jungle where politics was simply a form of private enterprise.

However, the city was already changing under their feet, and with its change new problems emerged. The commuter trains, and later the electric railways, opened many new sites for settlement, some of them far beyond the city limits. Those with the resources in money and time began to move outward from the central city. The suburban dispersal had begun. As they moved outside city boundaries, the resources of the central city were no longer at their disposal. The suburban enclaves were faced with the housekeeping problems of the spatial community; under the permissive constitutional provisions, they solved them through incorporating their residential neighborhoods as villages or towns. Thus the central cities began to be surrounded by a series of satellites, incorporated and protected by governmental walls.

For a time the satellites did not constitute a problem. When the boundaries of the central city nudged those of the suburb, the suburb was annexed with little difficulty. However, such annexation came to a halt in the 1920's. Since that period most metropolitan areas have presented the same picture: a "landlocked" central city, increasingly aged and obsolete, surrounded by a growing patchwork of suburban municipalities. The key question is this: why did the boundaries of the central city cease to expand, following its dispersed population? We cannot answer with certainty; however, a comparison of central city and suburban population may be helpful.

Central City vs. Suburbs

It was in the 1920's that the automobile revolution began to make vast areas on the outskirts of the cities available for residential sites. Country towns became nuclei for white-collar commuter settlements: empty pastures and cornfields became the sites for large-scale housing development. But the people who left the central city for the suburbs were not a random assortment. As we have seen, they were distinguished from those who remained behind by social rank, ethnicity, and life style.

The automobile was at first used mostly by the upper social ranks. Its costs were substantial. Those who could bear these costs were also persons likely to want new residences, and new construction was largely on the periphery of the city. The older central city, with its structures dating back to the Age of Steam, had little space to offer those in search of new sites, but on the outskirts the supply was greater than the demand. There were, thus, powerful economic arguments for the location of new middle-class neighborhoods in the suburbs. With their construction, however, the physical difference between the two parts of the metropolis was augmented. The suburbs were new, middle-class, residential neighborhoods: the inner city was a mixture of workplace, markets, and homes, surrounded by mile upon mile of older neighborhoods.

The new suburbs were also apt to be "exclusive." That is, they exercised formal and informal controls to prevent the "wrong kind of people" from moving in. Ethnic minorities, the foreign-born, Jewish, Catholic, or nonwhite citizens of the metropolis found the governmental walls of the suburbs impossible to scale. They perforce remained behind in the central city. Thus, with continuing in-migration of Negroes, Puerto Ricans, and Mexicans, the central city became ever darker in complexion, while the suburbs looked ever more "lily white" in contrast. The suburbs are, today, overwhelmingly populated by the white (or as Kipling called them, the "pinko grey") urbanites, usually a generation or more removed from the original immigrants. Most identifiable minority groups still live in the older central city.

We have noted earlier the increasing choice in life style available to urban Americans. That kind of life which we have called familism, dedicated to children, home, and neighborhood, is best carried on in areas populated by similar people. In America, those who choose familism have a strong prejudice for the single-family dwelling unit secure in the middle of its fifty-foot lot. Neighborhoods made up of such dwellings demand a great deal of horizontal space—space not to be found in the old central city without expensive demolition and rebuilding. With the automobile revolution, however, enormous new spaces became available on the outskirts. The suburbs attracted a population emphatically biased toward the familistic life style, rather than the more urbane existence of the apartment houses in the densely developed center.

Suburban folk tend to be of higher social rank, of white "old American" heritage, and committed to a familistic way of life. Though much of the city population is similar, much of it is different, indeed. The older dwellings house a working-class population. The ethnic minorities, particularly the nonwhite enclaves, populate broad expanses of the city's housing grid. Those with a more urbane life style remain in the city (and sneer at suburbia), while those committed to familism live in the outer wards of the city or wait for the day when they can afford a suburban ranch house.

Such variation produces a lurid ideology—"the city is old and overrun by Negroes; the suburbs are shallow, jerry-built, cheap." This is reinforced by the government variation between the areas—"central city government is crooked; suburban government is trivial." The central city is one massive governmental unit, while the suburbs contain hundreds of little municipalities, with over 1,400 local units in the New York metropolitan area alone. Government in the city is big government. It represents a great deal of power, money, and technology, and it seems far away and hard to understand. It is also partisan government. In the suburbs the small municipalities are usually nonpartisan, and the white middle class feels that it has solved the problem of local government by taking politics out of government. In short, there are weighty differences between suburbs and central city with respect to physical plant, population types, governmental structure, and the political process. We will discuss the latter items in more detail; it is sufficient for the moment to indicate the very real differences between the two halves of the metropolitan complex.

The suburban municipalities are going concerns. Though they are small and weak, compared to the colossus at the center, most of them provide basic governmental services, collect taxes, and exercise the police power. Most important of all, they exercise a monopoly on the powers of municipal government as defined by the constitutional government of the states. While they hold such powers, no other government can do so. And this is not unrelated to their reason for being.

Many of the early suburbs were collective responses to the problems created by interdependence. Small residential enclaves built their own power plants, sewers, water systems, because they could not share those of the central city and could not interest private enterprise in the job. Many of them were also incorporated to allow for a tighter control over land-use development and population than was possible for unincorporated neighborhoods. But recently, many suburban municipalities have one major purpose for their citizens: incorporation protects the residential community from annexation and governmental control by a larger unit. They are, in effect, governmental game preserves whose citizens are relatively immune to municipal law. Some suburban municipalities are simply industrial sites, freed from municipal smoke control and other nuisances; some are tax-free preserves for industry; some protect their citizens from adequate taxes and from housing codes, allowing them to build shanty towns, to keep chickens and cows, or to carry on home crafts and the like on rutty lanes without fire protection; some are governmental shelters where gambling, prostitution, and other generally illicit activities are permitted.

In short, the Jacksonian ideology, appropriate enough to an agrarian society, produces a paradoxical governmental structure in the metropolis. It is free enterprise in the founding of governments, and every municipality for itself. The ease of incorporation allows for a multiplicity of municipalities, created for the most diverse purposes. (Many towns in Dade County, Florida, were incorporated for the sole purpose of securing liquor licenses; a state law allowed only two to a municipality.) All these municipalities, once in being, constitute the *only* legitimate delegates of municipal powers. With respect to any larger problem or purpose, they are "dog in the manger" governments; they will not act nor allow other governments to do so.

Any governmental entity, once in being, is difficult to disband. This is particularly true of the suburban municipality. The Jacksonian ideology supports rule by friends and neighbors, nurturing suspicion of the Big City.[4] Whatever the truth, it flatters the citizens with an image of their community as a semirural small town, a repository of the rustic virtues. And, translated into the constitution of the state, the Jacksonian ideology requires popular consent for the extermination of any municipality. When campaigns occur to abolish, annex, or amalgamate such governments, however, all who think they benefit from the status quo are vocally opposed. Any existing structure builds up some differentially distributed advantages—somebody prefers it to alternatives. When this is combined with the poetry of rusticity, the staying power of the municipality is clear. Thus the Dade County suburb, originally incorporated for the purpose of securing two liquor licenses, today stands for home, mother, democracy, and virtue. The imaginary boundary lines and the place name become symbols, made to contain the diverse values of the residential neighborhoods.

The Governmental Dichotomy and Some Consequences

Today, a bird's-eye view of the metropolitan governmental structure would typically encompass the great circle of the central city and the dozens or hundreds of small units clustered side by side on the outskirts. More literally, the central city would be marked by higher, denser structures, shelving downward rapidly to the peripheries; the suburbs would be horizontal, dispersed, with perhaps one-fifth the population of the inner central city per square mile. From a bird's-eye view we would also note that the air over suburbia is often filled with fumes and smoke from the center. The whole urban complex lies across one or two great watersheds, and streams flow across governmental boundaries, bearing effluvia from here to there. The flow of traffic also moves momentarily throughout the area, without regard to municipal boundaries, knitting together the scattered sites for human activity in a larger system of action. In short, one would see the governmental division as arbitrary with respect to many of the collective systems of human action which constitute the being of the city.

Indeed, the entire urban complex is in many ways a unity. The scattered thousands are interdependent in each of the ways we have detailed; they man the complex, exclusive work organization we have discussed earlier. The wealthy suburbanites depend on the unskilled ethnic laborers and machine operatives of the central city for the social product that feeds them. The central city banks depend on the suburban investors; the suburban department stores depend on the central city banks. All the residents together are subject to the age-old kinds of interdependence detailed earlier: they require order in intergroup relations, protection of person and property, and the maintenance of a transport system, water and sewage systems, fire protection, and public health. In short, there is a sense in which we can call the metropolitan area a unity.

This unity, however, is not reflected in government. The problems created by contiguity and mutual dependence are not allocated to any government which includes all those affected and affecting others. The central city government does not work in close co-operation with those of suburbia; how could it? Suburban governments are themselves unco-ordinated, with no center of power and information. Yet the co-operation of suburbia is frequently crucial to the programs in the central city: traffic on a freeway system which ends abruptly in the main street of a country town is apt to back up halfway to City Hall, and smoke abatement will be less than complete until the suburban industrial park complies. There is, however, no normative prescription in Jacksonian philosophy for the forced integration of local government. Nor is there a constitutional formula that frees the governmental structure from the heavy hand of the referendum voter. Thus many important problems generated in the metropolitan complex are insoluble within the existing governmental structures. Our political culture lags far behind the emerging problems of the metropolitan world in which we live. It is embedded in the folk thought of the citizen and the phrases of the law.

Meanwhile, massive changes continue. In two decades our cities will grow by more than fifty million people. Most of the net growth will be in suburbia.[5] Even today, 49 per cent of our total metropolitan population lives in the suburban fringe. Thus the one large-scale government in the metropolis, that of the central city, will encompass a dwindling proportion of the land in use and the people in residence. There is little indication that the manufacture of small municipalities in suburbia will cease. While the scale of organization in the United States progressively increases, while work, play, religion, and other major activities are carried out through very large-scale organizational networks, local government moves doggedly in the opposite direction. Our ability to plan and provide for the entire metropolitan complex within the inherited framework of local self-government is declining relative to our ability to exercise over-all control in other segments of our lives.

Yet certain problems are inescapable. We refer, once again, to the minimal needs of human collectives living in cities. These problems are so basic that, should they not be solved, the city would perish. But our cities do not appear to be in such mortal danger, so we must ask: how is the polity maintained so that the resources and order requisite for these millions may indeed be predictably there when they need them? In answering this question, we shall consider first the government of the old central cities. Then we shall turn to the congeries of municipalities on the fringe, that dark and unknown governmental realm called suburbia.

The Governance of the Central City

The aged central city, its structure reflecting the paleotechnic city of the nineteenth century, is the living past of the metropolitan area. Here we find the monuments to earlier technology, leaders, social circles, artistic achievement. Here the visitor feels that he has really discovered the essence of the metropolis. At Times Square in New York, the Loop in Chicago, Penn Center in Philadelphia, or Market Street in San Francisco the metropolis seems to come into focus. However, what was basic and definitive in an earlier city may be very misleading in a metropolis with half or two-thirds of its population living in the suburbs; the focus is far off center. Still, there was a time not long ago when the central city did encompass the totality of the urban complex, and its downtown was the hub of the metropolis. Its governmental boundaries encircled the densely built-up urban area, and its polity was the public decision-making process for the entire urban complex.

Before the automobile the central city included the entire array and variety of the urban worlds. It took the brunt of the rapid urbanization we have discussed; here was the process of increasing scale in concrete form. The soaring skyscrapers represented the "peak organizations" which were melding continental networks of activity. Railroads, banks, insurance companies, petroleum companies, all built their headquarters at the center. One saw also the other aspects of increasing scale—in the polyglot crowds of Sicilians, Poles, Hungarians, and Jews who crowded the streets of the lower East Side of Manhattan, the near North or near South Side of Chicago. Areas of cheap, dense housing lay close to the workplaces of the center and were the typical ports of entry for the immigrants and country boys drawn by economic opportunity and glamour to the city.

As we have noted, the government of the central city faced a congeries of tremendous tasks. Increasing scale produced new problems of intergroup relations. Expanding economic enterprises, based on new energy sources and machinery, were violent and radical departures from an older organization of work. Labor agitation and labor unions arose as a response to a catastrophic change, from a work force still oriented to small-scale family enterprises, shops and farms and crafts.[6] The relationships between organizing labor and management were uneasy, unstable, and frequently bloody from the Civil War to the 1940's (and still are in regions of rapidly increasing scale, such as the South). The government of the city was usually the only agency responsible for maintaining public order among these forces. At the same time, the sheer mixture of populations produced endemic and violent conflict between ethnic enclaves. Negroes and Irish, Italians and Jews, Poles and Negroes, competed for homes, neighborhoods, jobs—living space. Their competition frequently descended into overt conflict, and many of them did not understand the "rules of the road" in an urban place ordered by the inherited laws of the Anglo-Saxon people. Small nuances of expression and tone of voice could turn a policeman's friendly admonition to, for example, a newly arrived Pole into a brawl or a murder.

The variation in cultural background alone produced great areas of anarchy and danger in the organizational interstices. The cities of America have old histories of rioting, lynching, and pillaging. In the streets, alleys, parks, lobbies, terminals, and public transport there were always problems of policing. The need for police always outran the supply, for the consequences of increase in scale to the local community were typically disregarded or underestimated. Weakness of the law enforcement agencies led, in turn, to the organization of effective criminal gangs. The wide array of illegal behavior, the variety of cultural backgrounds, and the poor control system meant that fortunes could be made in gambling, prostitution, and the sale of narcotics. The organizations that carried on such illegal commerce were frequently of different ethnic origins; thus gang warfare was both pecuniary and ethnic in its nature.

The development of the physical plant also lagged behind demand. Only in the twentieth century did most American cities assure themselves of a safe water supply. Streets and street lights, sidewalks and their maintenance, continually demanded new outputs of societal wealth. Sewage disposal was a continual problem. Only extreme failure of the system made most citizens aware of its importance; yet sewage disposal systems had to expand continually because of the mushrooming population. We have not mentioned schools, parks, museums, libraries: all were in short supply as the customers multiplied astronomically.

The solution of these problems had to be found, as we have observed, within the framework of a democratic dogma. Vast and difficult operations were to be commanded by any "common man" who could be elected by the votes of others; important operating decisions were to be made by the voters in referendum elections. The moral and technical control of the government depended in large part on the judgment of the ordinary citizen. But these citizens were frequently unable to understand even the English language, much less the complex system of American local government. Those who did understand were not competent to monitor the unprecedented process of city building and organization forced on them by large-scale society in expansion.

The impasse was resolved by the development of powerful party machines at the local level. The party machine was an organization devoted to the control of the vote and, through the vote, power and the profits of power. Without a guiding ideology (or set of formulated ideals), it operated as an exchange system, a business enterprise. At the lowest level the precinct captains exchanged jobs, bonuses, turkeys on Thanksgiving, coal in wintertime, for the votes of families, friendship cliques, ethnic enclaves. The machine was a vast retail system for trade in votes. Frequently, of course, the actual voting could be made irrelevant, for fraud was another means of affecting the tally (which in turn affected the supply of "Wholesale goods" or authority to be exchanged). Plunkitt describes the hardship of his early days, when his wife stayed up all night ironing out ballots so that they might be inserted through the crack in the bottom of the ballot box. Without extensive discussion of the technology of fraud, let us note that the exchange of favors for votes was the staple technique, with fraud a supplementary device. Together, these allowed the machine to count on a dependable plurality. Of course, there are usually two or more party machines in competition. This fact introduced the note of uncertainty which heated up the campaign and made politics a great spectator sport in the nineteenth-century cities.

The dominant machine was related to the rest of the urban community through an exchange system. At the higher level, the political boss treated with the financial and industrial interests of the city. His trading cards were franchises for the rapidly expanding transportation system, contracts for lucrative public works, permits to operate various businesses, as well as waivers of the public law for favored parties. His price was reciprocal favor or cash. Money, in turn, was reinvested in the machine, trickling down through district and ward to the precinct, where the precinct officers in turn distributed favors. (Of course, the boss took substantial profits from the transaction.)

The importance of the cash nexus, and the relative public irresponsibility of the political boss, meant that money could be translated into political power. Lincoln Steffens described, in some detail, the things that rich and respectable entrepreneurs bought from local government in the nineteenth-century American city.[7] They were worth having. (A slightly fictionalized biography of Yerkes, the "Robber Baron" who bought the right to monopolize public transport in Chicago, is given in Theodore Dreiser's novel, *The Titan.*) Aside from using money, the upper class could also influence the local boss through the crusading daily newspapers (which might expose delicate and secret operations) and through power at the state or national governmental levels. In summary, there were many ways for business interests to determine policy in the city.

It was indeed a society oriented toward business. Businessmen were the first-class citizens, and the chief operations of government were delegated through contracts to business enterprise. The material tasks of local government, apart from such unprofitable enterprises as police and fire protection, were very small operations compared with the developing corporations of nineteenth-century America. Though a majority of the citizens may have been ethnic and working-class (in 1910 a majority of Americans were from minority groups), their interests were not paramount. Those of business were.

Such a system could be imagined as a pyramid, with a power elite at the top. The power elite was made up of the wealthy, whose control of men and money, whose ties with the national and state governments, whose influence with the newspapers, and whose "ownership" of the mayor and council (through the boss) gave them tremendous leverage for the control of both the public and private aspects of the city's development. Such an interpretation was documented in dozens of novels; it was congruent with the stories of the muckrakers, as well as the ideology of the socialists, anarchists, and syndicalists. It was a conspiracy as local government, with politicians seen as merely tools of "the executive committee of the bourgeoisie."

This image of urban government has persisted into our own day. Floyd Hunter has spent a great deal of energy identifying the "thirty men who run Atlanta."[8] Other scholars have studied a number of American cities. In each case they move from expert informants, who know the situation, to a set of nominated power figures. These in turn nominate others until the circle is closed and new persons do not get mentioned; from those most frequently nominated they select the personnel for the power elite.

Their technique has recently been radically questioned. Some have noted that, if there is only a *myth* about a power elite and it is believed by the more informed citizens, then the scholar is only documenting that myth when he asks them how they think the city works. This would explain why we could find a power elite whether it exists or not. Others have more drastic criticisms. They note that when the "Big Mules" of Cleveland or St. Louis try to help reorganize the local government of the metropolis their projects go down in defeat at the polls. When the civic leaders of Chicago want to refurbish the near North Side or locate a new campus for the University of Illinois, their efforts are frustrated and the final decision is made by the mayor—or no decision at all results.[9] In short, the power elite image of control in the central city has lately been exposed to an extremely skeptical group of critics. This leads us to ask: Was the political image of the city equally fictitious in earlier days? Or do the critics of the power elite theory today simply misunderstand the nature of organization in the contemporary central city? It seems more likely that the discrepancy does not just reflect variation in opinion, but instead indicates differences among cities and, more important, the continuing effects of increase in scale which change cities over time. The big-city machine, a response to increase in scale, may also have become a victim of the continuing process. Let us look at urban government in this context.

Social Change and the Machine

Continual increase in scale has had four major consequences for the problems of urban government and their solution. It has produced an increasing bureaucratization of governmental and other functions; it has led to rapid organizational mergers in private enterprise; it has radically changed the general character of the urban population; and it has resulted in a massive multiplication of the population and therefore of the size of the organizational tools of urban government. Let us consider each of these in relation to its implications for the classic big-city machine.

The bureaucratization of governmental services affected the machine in two separate ways. First, with the Great Depression of the 1930's it became apparent that all Americans were part of a nationwide economic system, and when that system failed, the problem of unemployment and poverty was a nationwide problem. As a consequence, what had been charity became the work of the Department of Health, Education, and Welfare, and vast programs were administered through the nationwide bureaucracies of government. Second, the management of local governmental enterprises became increasingly professionalized; the reformers were successful in convincing the people (and later the politicians) that such services as the city provided were better handled by civil servants, selected and trained through nonpolitical methods to do their jobs without favoritism or political counsel. These two changes struck deep at the roots of politics as a simple exchange system. The goods which the precinct captain once traded for votes were disbursed by a federal agency staffed by civil servants. The decisions about street layouts, hospital construction, zoning, and planning, once so profitably controlled by politicians, were increasingly made by professional public personnel—planners, hospital administrators, traffic engineers. At the same time voting became better organized and mechanized, with a bureaucracy (subject to review) in charge of the tallies. Quality control made fraud difficult and dangerous. Both at the lowest and highest levels the exchange system of the machine was mortally damaged.

The rapid and continuous process of organizational merger had other effects on the urban polity. The drawing of major enterprise into national organizations and the further bureaucratization of the corporation, as it separated ownership from management, resulted in a class of professional managers whose first duty was to the nationwide, or international, corporate network. The most powerful economic figure in town was no longer the owner of the major industry; he was a manager. Consequently, the economic dominants (as they are sometimes called in the literature on the power elite) became increasingly withdrawn from concern with the local community. Schulze has documented the steps by which Ypsilanti, Michigan, moved from a classical power elite structure to one in which the branch plant managers were interested in the local community only on rare occasions. Rather than wishing to run the show, they only wanted a veto on certain kinds of governmental act. Otherwise, they did not wish to be involved.[10]

The result of corporate merger has been the freeing of economic organizations from dependence on, and hence interest in, particular cities. This has combined with the increasing geographical mobility of the managerial elite; as they move upward in the corporate hierarchy they move around the country. They become identified with one community only when they have ceased to be occupationally mobile. (One longitudinal study indicated that, even in Red Wing, Minnesota, a town of ten thousand, the personnel change among those nominated as civic leaders was more than 60 per cent in the relatively short period of six years.)[11] Turnover of leadership makes effective organization (the compromising of interests, the assignment of tasks, the integrating of action) extremely difficult. Furthermore, we must remember that the business leadership in a city of any size is apt to be divisible on more issues than those on which it is unitable. (A recent study by Scoble, for example, shows a very low rate of consensus among the dominant leaders in a New England town of less than fifteen thousand persons.)[12] It requires *more* work to achieve coordination when there is high turnover; yet there are fewer people committed to achieving it. In short, the changing nature of exclusive, membership organizations has greatly weakened their machinery for controlling the political decisions of the city. And such change is of particular importance in the metropolis, the headquarters city of the corporation.

Meanwhile, the population of the metropolis has been changing in the directions discussed earlier. Social rank has on the average moved upward; the illiterate, unskilled workman of foreign birth is a vanishing breed. Even in the central city, education, occupation, and real income have risen to once-unimaginable levels in the past sixty years. At the same time, the children and grandchildren of the foreign-born are socialized from the beginning to the American urban milieu. As a result of these changes in combination the definition of the vote has changed; it is no longer simply an expression of ethnic solidarity, but rather a more complex decision, based on a variety of interests. The children of the immigrants live in a different city from that of their parents and have different techniques for managing their urban environment. Their toleration for fraud shrinks as they become more informed and committed to American civic virtues. Their vote is not for sale.

An indirect effect of increasing size, but an important one, is the suburban-central city dichotomy. With increasing population and static boundary lines, the population of the metropolis is almost equally divided between central city and suburbs. But we have also noted the difference between the population in the two areas: those who remain in the central city are predominantly ethnic and working-class social types. In 1950, according to Philip Hauser, "Los Angeles was the only city among the five largest in the United States in which the native white population of native parentage was greater than half, and even there it was only 55 per cent."[13] These populations are the ones most likely to prefer the Democratic party in national elections; when there is a partisan organization of local elections (and this is true of all but one of our very large cities), the working class and the ethnic voters go Democratic. A direct consequence is the collapse of the Republican party in the political arena of the central city. One by one, Republican strongholds are giving way to Democratic majorities, as the nordic white Protestant middle class makes its way to the suburbs. Today, in many of our great cities, two or three Republican councilmen represent the "two-party system" among a host of Democratic officials. As the process of segregation by polity continues, the central city will become, in fact if not in theory, a one-party state.

Finally, we have to consider the increase in the size of urban concentrations. In 1900 two American metropolitan areas had a population of a million or more; in 1960, there were nineteen complexes this large. The sheer aggregation of population had two major effects on the control system of the central city. First, and not to be overlooked, was the sheer increase in the size of the problems that had to be handled in the rounds of urban housekeeping and the consequent size of the organizations which handled them. The City of New York, for example, employs 50,000 persons in its educational system, 26,000 in its police department, and 13,000 in its fire department.[14] The sheer aggregation of numbers and budget results in the proliferation of organizational centers with a degree of autonomy and, hence, power. The number and strength of leadership groups are multiplied with increasing population.

The total effect of these changes has been the destruction of the old-time political machine, and with it the power elite. Increase in scale has destroyed the basis for the political machine *as an exchange system;* in the urban wards of Stackton it is as hard to recruit precinct workers as in the small-town Republican strongholds of Illinois. Whyte reports the visible attrition of the Democratic machine in Boston during the 1930's, while Reichley discusses the steady weakening of Republican power in Philadelphia during the same period.[15] The ability of the political boss to control his "Hessians," and through them the vote of the people, may have been overrated in the past: it is very easy to overrate it today.

The collapse of the exchange system has, in turn, destroyed the ability of the power elite to call the tune. Businessmen have never had a preponderant influence, at the polls, on the city population as a whole. They have relied on the machine as a mechanism for translating money into political power. By bribing the politicians and by contributing to campaign chests, business interests assured themselves a strong voice in the political decisions of the central city. Even with the Republican party's power fading away, they could still exert leverage on the Democratic machine, for the machine was primarily a nonideological exchange system. With its weakening, however, the business-man had literally no way of reaching the voters.

The result is a drastic separation of numbers and wealth in the contemporary metropolis. Businessmen, resident in the suburbs, have great stakes in the central city polity. That polity, however, is controlled by a set of politicians who have a declining need for the businessman and are elected by the votes of the ethnic and working-class constituencies of the center. Such a separation of numbers and wealth is not, of course, contrary to the democratic dogma. It is, however, an anomaly to those who still consider the businessman as the first-class citizen and his interests as paramount for the community.

It is also anomalous to those who explain American government through the theory of the two-party system, with its assumptions of organized control and competition for power. The anomaly leads us to ask: How, then, does the government of today's central city operate? How is it that order is maintained and essential tasks are performed?

The Machine of the Incumbents

The disappearance of party competition in the general elections of the central city does not destroy party organization. Instead, it changes the basis of organi-zation: the old-style exchange system is replaced by a new order. Before discussing the new state of things, however, it is important to note the cause and consequences of one-party government for the dominant Democratic organization.

The central city electorate, with its predisposition to vote Democratic, is (like the southern Democrats) basically a captive electorate. Whoever is designated Democrat on the ballot will usually get a majority of the votes. One might jump to the conclusion that such one-party government could mean only a sort of totalitarianism. Instead, it seems to result in a general loosening of the control mechanism; as V. O. Key demonstrates for the one-party system in the South, the very basis for much of the party's control is weakened by the disappearance of the opposition party.[16] The reduction of threat in the general election eliminates the need for party discipline and ferocious *esprit de corps* for, no matter what happens, the Democratic party will take most of the elective offices.

Under these circumstances, however, the Republican minority is rapidly demoralized. Political organization is postulated on occasional victory; moral victories are sustaining only when there is some eventual possibility of non-moral, tangible victory. In the central city, however, Republican votes continue to decline despite all efforts made by the Republican parties. As this occurs, the Republican party's leadership and its elected local officials in cities like St. Louis and Chicago begin to resemble Republicans of the South. They are either lonely idealists, whose words are purely symbolic since they lack power to implement them, or else a sort of auxiliary of the dominant Democrats. (Chicago's delegation to the state legislature in Springfield includes the "sanitary Republicans," Republican legislators whose chief source of income is office in the Democratic-controlled Chicago Sanitary District.) Such officials may even vote with the Democrats and against their fellow Republicans on crucial issues. Thus, even if the Republicans had a powerful issue, it is doubtful that the existing leadership could mobilize a campaign to exploit it. They stand not so much for an alternative governance as for the existing distribution of electoral strength in the central city; in fact, they depend on it for their working conditions.

The Democratic monopoly of victory in the general election, however, means that the primary election becomes the major arena for gaining office. And at the primary level the party organization is considerably weakened, for nomination to office (tantamount to election) becomes an apple of discord thrown among the Democratic ranks. In some cities the party cannot officially designate a slate in the primary; even when it can, its decisions are basically divisive. There are many deserving party men, and little to prevent one from running his district. If he has been an effective leader at the block and precinct level, he may very well win, for the mobilization of friends and neighbors can easily produce strong opposition to the organization's designated candidate. Since the candidates do not need actual logistic support in the general election (the simple party designation will usually suffice), the field is clear for "mavericks" to compete.

Yet the party organization can usually control most of the offices in the primary election. The reason for this is clear enough; the ordinary voter usually does not know or care enough about the primary to vote. Thus the organization, though it may control only a small percentage of the potential vote, can nevertheless swing the margin of victory to its candidate. This organizational level is considerably augmented in many cities by the organization's control of the electoral machinery. Efforts range from differential requirements for certification as a candidate to the ignoring of irregularities in the campaign and the voting (though the latter practices are becoming increasingly dangerous for reasons noted earlier). We may surmise also that much of the power of the organization results from a simple misapprehension of its effective force by potential dissidents. The machine *was* all-powerful for many years in some of our cities; those interested in politics are differentially exposed to the organization. They may fear official disapproval, not just in the immediate election, but in the future. Even if the party machine's power is now a myth, myths may long outlive their factual base and have consequences.

Thus the organization maintains a continuing control, though not an iron-clad one, over the distribution of offices. However, with the disappearance of effective opposition it no longer needs the money of the businessman to win its campaigns. Being able to win the general election in any event, the power relations between politician and business leader have shifted radically. The politician is clearly in the more advantageous position: he has the trading cards.

There have also been radical changes in the dominant party's organization. With the weakening of the machine, the power relation between the nonelective party boss and the elected officials reverses. First, the elected mayor develops a considerable autonomy from the machine; standing above all other elected figures in the metropolis, his role is visible and his words are news. From the rostrum of office he tends to dominate the mass media and through the media develops a powerful electoral attraction of his own. Then party ceases to be a differentiating label in the one-party central city; the major differentiator becomes incumbency. Those who are in office become *de facto* rulers of the party, for the party needs them more than they need its cohorts. They dispense the patronage and make the decisions.

Thus the central city mayor assumes a major if not dominating role in the dramatis personae of local politics. Other stellar roles include the head of the county government and perhaps the president of the council or board of aldermen. They also are familiar figures in the news, for they are elected officials with city-wide constituencies in image if not in fact. Along with them rise the managers of the great governmental bureaucracies: school superintendents, engineers, police commissioners, and the like. Such men, elected or appointed, stand for the expertise of their office, the legitimacy of the tasks which their bureaucracy performs, and the logistics of money and men. The dominant figures in central city politics tend to be the dominant officials of government; they constitute a "machine of incumbents." No matter how they reached office in the first place, once there they are formidable forces.

The central city mayor can, indeed, become an enemy of his party's organization. Concerned with the entire city, he is sensitive to opinion in the middle-class, familistic, outer wards of the city; his political score in the general elections depends on his ability to carry these "good government" and "newspaper" wards. He responds to the criticism of the daily press and the statements of public leaders representing various interests: welfare, hospital, education, and the like. Though these interests cannot defeat him at the polls, he nevertheless engages in implicit bargaining with them, anticipating the effects of his words and actions on the newspapers, civic leaders, and hence the outer wards. At the same time the central city mayor is the dominant public official for the entire metropolitan area. Insofar as there is a metropolitan community, he is its highest elected official. (In St. Louis, suburbanites and central city voters alike accorded the mayor of the city more trust and confidence than all other leaders combined, and their reasons rested on his office, his expertise, and his character as a civic notable.) As representative of more than the laundry list of special interests in the area, he stands for the general welfare. Businessmen, no longer his employers, return as influentials insofar as they are virtual representatives of many values and aspects of the metropolis.

In fact, the central city mayor tends to believe that good government is good politics. But in the process of pursuing good government he may destroy much of the effectiveness of the Democratic organization.[17] The separation of the offices of precinct captain for the party and precinct captain of police may be good governmental administration: it may also be very demoralizing for the political actors who had counted on the promotion to police captain as a possible reward. Nevertheless, the metropolitan mayor is free to continue his swing toward good government, for the machine cannot control him. And he may look beyond the central city to position in the state government, or the federal government in Washington, where his "good government" policies may count heavily. Furthermore, he is, ironically, strengthened at home by his symbolic separation from the machine. He can have his cake and eat it too. Meanwhile the old-style political machine is further weakened; the rewards of political work disappear right and left. As one consequence, the persons who can be recruited for the hard and tedious work at the block level change in character; the ranks of party workers become disproportionately composed of those who have few alternatives for social distinction and mobility. The over-all picture is one in which old-style machine politics fades away before the new order, the machine of the incumbents.

To repeat the argument: The continual segregation of population by governmental boundaries means an increasing domination of the central city vote by the poor, the ethnics, and therefore the Democratic party label. This, in turn, relaxes the tensions of conflict at a party level, leading to a one-party state. To be sure, the process has gone further in some cities than others; it is still possible for the Republicans to win a battle occasionally if their wards are numerous and the Democrats make a series of catastrophic mistakes.

This will become rarer as the proportion of working-class ethnics increases. It is also true that, in West Coast cities like Los Angeles, Republicans may rule under the guise of nonpartisanship. It is likely, however, that such cities, never having known a machine, have simply skipped a stage and landed directly in the future—the one-party or nonparty polity ruled by the machine of the incumbents.

The Weakening of Positive Government

One-party government, in fact, approaches very closely the condition of nonpartisan government. The weakening of the party organization's hold on the incumbents softens the impact of those who wish to translate wealth and social power garnered in other fields into pressure on the policy of the city. The incumbents are freed from many pressures; however, it is a "freedom from" rather than a freedom to accomplish new and radical enterprises. This is because power becomes basically fractionated and dispersed. The elected officials, the heads of the great bureaucracies, state and federal levels of government, private capital, and the party organization each hold certain resources necessary for massive action. To these must be added the governmental divisions of the metropolis. Multiple municipalities, counties, and special districts are vested with the legitimate power to perform certain tasks and to refuse to co-operate in others. . . .

The mayors of our great cities, symbols and symbolic leaders of the metropolitan community, reign but do not rule. They are brokers, conciliators, who reconcile the people to what they get from their government. They legitimatize the *fait accompli* on the rare occasions when the necessary resources for action result from transitory coalitions among the major contending organizations. For the rest, they preside over routine caretaker governments. And from one point of view, this is what the situation may seem to demand. The pioneer work of building the plant and establishing an order for the central city is long since complete: the population explosion will not rock its foundations, for a vast apparatus is in existence, and new growth will largely settle outside the center, in suburbia. The great bureaucracies which provide necessary governmental goods and services are already in being: they pursue the organizational destiny of expansion, increasing professionalization and multiplying the career opportunities for civil servants. All this they can do within the precedents established in the past and legitimatized through use.

There is, however, no organization capable of mounting a major offensive for innovation. The central city's polity is passive and adaptive before the continuing results of increase in scale; only catastrophe seems capable of creating the opportunity for new development. Meanwhile, the trends continue; the suburban move of industry is added to the differentiation of central city and suburban populations, the increasingly obsolete neighborhoods, and the increasing proportion of colored populations who suffer most from economic depression and expect the most action from their city government. Taken all together, these trends result in a rapid drift of the city away from its older status of centrality and totality. Faced with such changes, most people who consider the central city's destiny agree that massive counteraction, planning and construction, and governmental change are necessary. Such counteraction is difficult to imagine in the governmental structure of our great cities as they operate today.

The Suburbs: "Republics in Miniature"

The concept of suburbia is a hazy one. It is one that changed through time, adding meaning indiscriminately, until today it can mean simply the outer edges, the residential spillover of the city, the little "bedroom community," the home of the organization man, the upper-class municipality, or the dead level of American middle-class society. Through time it has gathered symbolic overtones; it is a fighting word. Those who are still ambivalent about America's urbanization may value suburbs indiscriminately as the representatives of small-town and rural values; those committed to an urban style of life may see them as only a movement backward, a regression to the "nuzzling herd society of the village." Obviously, a term so mixed in its reference must be clarified before it has any utility at all.

We can distinguish four kinds of meaning for the term. First, and clearest, suburbs are urban areas outside the governmental boundaries of the central city; they may or may not be incorporated as municipalities. Second, any outlying district far from the center may be called suburban; this is the ecological or spatial meaning. Third, suburban population is frequently considered to have distinctive attributes: it is more familistic, of higher social rank, and less ethnic. Finally, many persons have imputed a particular kind of social structure to the suburbs; they are regions where the spatially based group, the community, is strong. Neighborliness, friendship among fellow residents, a proliferation of organizations in the area are taken to be attributes of suburbanism as a way of life.

Because this is a book about government, we shall take the first meaning as definitive and relate it to the others. We are concerned with those urban populations that live outside the boundaries of the central city, but are part of the urban whole through interdependence of the kinds discussed earlier. Looking at such populations en masse, we can make some generalizations. First, the central city's boundaries usually include populations nearest the center; suburban populations are apt to be more spatially isolated from the center. Second, suburban buildings, reflecting more recent construction, are apt to be suitable as new residences for population types that are on the increase, and to be inhabited by them. These are households of middle to upper social rank, generally native-born and white, and familistic in their life style.

Their relative isolation from the ambit of the central city means that their daily experience does not center in the typical social groups of the center. Their lives, particularly if they are women and children, are bounded by the immediate residential community, the public schools, playgrounds, streets, and business centers of the peripheral settlement. Even men, though they work in the center, spend a majority of their time, and their freest time, in the home community. The assortment of similar people into given residential areas by social rank, life style, and ethnicity means that the average suburban family lives among its own kind.

The homogeneous and familistic populations of suburbia produce a particular kind of associational structure. Bound together by the interaction of children, the similarity of family norms and family goals, and a common commitment to the neighborhood as the site for home and family living, familistic populations develop intensive neighboring patterns. Out of their common interests in the school, the care of children, the maintenance of the residential values in the area, they develop organizations to defend and promote those interests. The familistic neighborhoods manifest a high density of formal voluntary organizations—PTA, Boy Scouts and other youth-centered groups, fraternal and service organizations, community-oriented organizations, church-centered organizations. From the familistic nature of the population, in contiguity and interaction, results a powerful organizational structure. Based on interdependence, it leads to communication, involvement, and the ordering of behavior. Suburban neighborhoods are more apt to approach the conditions of true "social community." This is what some of their incoming residents seek.

The populations outside the political bounds of the central city, however, manifest considerable variation in all these attributes. Although most suburban areas are farther from the center than most neighborhoods of the center city, there are anomalies. Some incorporated municipalities have been enveloped by the central city, yet retain their independence. They are governmental islands surrounded by the sea of the central city. Here we find the industrial "shelters," governments used only to protect industry from regulation and taxation by the central city. Here also we find such persisting municipalities as Hamtramck in Detroit (a Polish neighborhood) and Culver City in Los Angeles. On the other hand, some central cities have far-flung boundaries and include in their limits residential areas which are fifteen miles or more from the center. Such neighborhoods are ecologically isolated, but integrated into the central city's jurisdiction.

We have already noted the fact that the central city contains many familistic neighborhoods. Suburbia also contains areas where the population is more urban than much of the central city, where ethnic populations are concentrated, and where social rank is very low. A result of historical patterns in land development, these variations indicate we must be careful of loose generalization. In the St. Louis metropolitan area, for example, one suburb (University City), though of higher social rank, is predominantly Jewish and more urbane than the average in its typical life style. Another (Kinloch) is of extremely low social rank, entirely Negro in its population, and more familistic than the average for the central city Negro population. There are working-class suburbs in growing numbers as the automobile becomes a universal possession and new land is opened to settlement. And the older suburban populations nearest the central city boundary become increasingly urban in life style when apartment houses, market centers, and manufacturing plants are located in their boundaries. (Satellite manufacturing cities like Gary, Indiana, are a somewhat different case; their population is seldom of the sort discussed above.)

Thus the governmental definition of suburbia does not exactly coincide with the ecological or the population-type definitions. Nevertheless, the picture that holds true on the average, the best possible summary, is this. Most suburbs are far from the center, separately incorporated settlements of familistic populations. Whether ethnic or not, whether high or low in social rank, their familistic life styles produce the kind of social order sketched above. They are beehives of interaction at the neighborly level, and a large proportion of their households are members of local organizations, are involved in a spatially defined local community. . . .

Political Issues of Suburbia

The rapid spread of suburban settlement is first of all a result of increase in societal scale. Many political issues of suburbia grow out of the various concomitants of increase in scale, developing out of the question: how can we organize to accommodate these changes? We emphasize two aspects of the former: (1) the sheer expansion of suburban settlements in a short period of time and (2) the broader changes in the nature of the American population's way of life.

Rapid increase in population, in suburb after suburb, has automatically produced problems. First, there is the question of controlling new growth.

What kinds of enterprise and population are wanted, and where should they be located? The commitments made in the present are the limits within which the future must work. Furthermore, simple increase in quantity inevitably means an expansion of the services and goods provided by the government. This brings up the entire question of equity: who shall pay for the new plant and its operations, and who shall benefit, and how shall these be related? Sheer expansion of residential numbers thus creates serious issues: equally serious are those created by change in way of life.

We have said that the entire population is experiencing changes, with movement upward in social rank, with increasing familism, with rapid acculturation of many ethnics to the "all-American way of life." In the suburbs each may result in the creation of major public issues. Increasing social rank means a general rise in the level of living of the population; the streetcar rider as he grows older has two cars in his garage, the tenement dweller's children live in a ranch house with three bathrooms, and the grandchildren of the urban poor worry about their income taxes. As these citizens come to expect more and better privately purchased goods and services, they also expect more of their government. Thus, even if the suburban government approximates the consumption norms of yesterday, the rising aspiration of its residents may leave it continually in the red. Those once satisfied with gravel streets today object to paved four-lane roads because they are inadequate to the rush-hour traffic. Septic tanks give way to costly sewage disposal systems; the small schoolhouse becomes a sprawling campus within an educational system, and the pressure is on the superintendent to add classes for "exceptional children," to expand the school's medical program, to add more cultural and community functions. In many suburbs there is continual demand for increased park space, public swimming pools, and playgrounds. All these services cost money, demand taxes, and raise the questions: Can we afford it? How shall we pay for it?

The increasing investment of Americans in home and family also results in issues for suburban communities. With increasing commitment to it as a *home*, the suburban residential area stands for the future of an investment in property—its image, environment, market value. It also stands for the kind of life a person desires for his family. The neighbors are the most important social environment of the wife and children, and the public schools are in many respects the most crucial environment and resource for the children's later careers. The familistic populations are deeply invested in their neighborhoods, and through them their residential community; thus the political structure, which may influence all of these, is of major concern.

Finally, with the increasing acculturation of many ethnic minorities to the middle-class American way of life, some interesting and important issues arise. For the second-generation Italian, Pole, or Jew a move into suburbia may be the most striking signal of success. For those who have arrived, however, it may be a signal that the neighborhood is being "invaded," that cherished values are threatened. And when the second generation has arrived in a suburb, what is it to think about the middle-class Negro family that wishes to move in, or the still swarthy second-generation Mexican-American clan? The acculturation of ethnics raises as many problems as their original encapsulation in the ghettos raised—and raises many of them in suburbia.

Translated into the political issues of suburbia, any of these changes may produce fierce debate and electoral struggle. First, and perhaps prior to any specific decision, is the general question: How shall the political order be drawn, so that it will satisfy the democratic dogma and at the same time create and maintain the kind of community desired? How shall the voters be organized, the key officials chosen, and what kind of power shall they have? Who shall be represented, and in what way? The range of solutions here is wide. Some suburbs operate with a one-party system, the "good government caucus," which hand-picks a slate for office. They may further avoid politics by leaving the day-to-day operation of government in the hands of a manager. Other suburbs, however, tend to divide into political moieties: the "ins" and the "outs," the older residents and the newcomers. They may struggle for office or may even struggle over the basic constitution of the city. (This may be a battle for a new city charter, or it may be focused on changing the municipality's "class" and therefore governing forms according to the state constitution.) Such issues typically arise in periods of rapid change, when the municipality is new or when it has accepted a large number of new residents.

A second and continuing type of issue is that of service provision. What services and what levels of services should the municipal government provide? The possibilities are practically infinite, but the budget is always tight. When the service level is decided, the next question is: How shall we pay for them? How shall benefit and cost be related? Who shall decide? These questions range from the proper method of issuing bonds (what rate of discount, what period of time, renegotiable or not) to the proper method of assessing property for taxation. Such issues become salient whenever the consumption norms of the population have risen or the existing level of services has declined (due to a shrinking tax base, inflation, or a flood of new residents).

A third congeries of issues is generated by commitment to the community. When this is combined with rapid growth in the suburban area, very serious conflict may arise. Planning and zoning issues may become battlegrounds for rival factions. Should Meadowlane become a partially industrial municipality, with many of the characteristics of the central city left behind? What of the increased traffic in trucks, the commuters from elsewhere who work in the plants and warehouses? Or, should the beaches of Winonama be opened to the public? What of the transients who will drop in, unknown and perhaps dangerous to the play of local children? Or, should a bowling alley be allowed on the corner of Elm and Aster? So near the school, and selling beer? (Though this latter sounds ridiculous, it was, in fact, taken seriously by the leaders of one suburban municipality.) In short, what kind of a community are we trying to build (or maintain), and how shall we go about doing it?

Closely related to the last type of issue is any matter having to do with schools. As we have stressed already, the familistic population of suburbia, with its concern for children and their future, is particularly conscious of the school system. (In the St. Louis area the *only* widespread concern for schools was among the higher-rank, extremely familistic suburbs.) For one thing, most people in familistic neighborhoods have children in the public schools; for another, the school tax is ordinarily between half and three-fourths of the total local tax bill in suburbia. Thus a decision on school policy may easily become a major public issue. In one "blue ribbon" suburb, for example, increasing population forced the construction of another high school. However, the existing school was a very famous one, generally agreed to be one of the best in the United States. The outcry over the new school was heart-rending, for, as many parents whose children would attend the new high school said, "We moved here in the first place to give our children the benefit of going to X High School."

Finally, and again connected with the previous issues, we have the question of ethnicity. Who shall be accepted in this community, which contains our treasures, home, family, children, and neighborhood? A recent and vivid example of such an issue was the action of the Village Council in Deerfield, Illinois. The council condemned a large plot of ground for a public park, shortly after the real estate development company that owned it announced that the residential neighborhood it was building would be integrated and one-fifth Negro. This case was lurid enough and was widely publicized. Many other struggles go on "within the family" of the suburban town's population. The Jewish child who is the only one in his schoolroom not invited to a birthday party; the Negro family which quietly sells its house after vandals have broken the windows—such incidents as these, while not overtly political in nature, indicate something about school integration and equal protection under the law in the suburban municipality. At the same time, we must remember that such issues can have opposite resolutions: many of our most exclusive residential suburbs have substantial Jewish and Catholic populations, and even Negroes are eventually accepted in some cases (and in small numbers).

In summary, most of the issues of suburban politics seem to center around a few questions. What is the most common image of the desirable community? How can it be created (or maintained)? What will be the price, and who shall pay that price? In the community image are summarized the aspirations of middle-class, familistic, white citizens of native birth. There is a paucity of information on the political processes by which such decisions are made. In the next section, however, we shall try to learn something about suburban politics by examining some municipal systems.

Suburban Political Orders

A major characteristic of suburban politics is their nonpartisan nature. The national Democratic and Republican party organizations or labels are seldom important factors in the elections of the suburbs. It is tacitly agreed that "there is no Republican or Democratic way of collecting garbage," that the general interests of the community are the proper center of concern and are irrelevant to larger political issues. The politics of suburbia is a friends-and-neighbors politics, largely nonideological in nature. Like the machine, it is little concerned with the long-run character and fate of the nation; its primary concern is with the building of neighborhood communities and the housekeeping tasks of the spatial area.

The disappearance of the party label, however, means that elected officials are largely middle-class Republicans. The basic dominance of business ideology, the businessman as first-class citizen, is sharply evident in suburbia. Thus in St. Louis County, in 1956, the largest occupational category represented in elected municipal offices was that of manager and professional, employed by business firms outside the suburban municipality where office was held. The second most important category was that of local businessman or professional in the electing municipality. A majority of elected officials were from these categories. This reflected, of course, the general composition of the suburban residents—but it was far more than a proportional representation of these categories.

When the electorate is organized on a party basis, it is typically a local, municipal party, concerned only with local affairs. The independents, the Good Government party, the Progressive party appear in many suburbs; they nominate slates and campaign for their election on purely local issues. The personnel of such parties reflects the social structure of suburbia; Community Actors are their basic cadres, and these actors are about equally made up of men (usually absentee-employed) and their wives. Thus suburban local politics has a distinctly heterosexual flavor; women are probably better represented in the political process of suburbia than at any other level, anywhere else in America.

As we have noted earlier, there is considerable variety among suburban municipalities. Though most are familistic, some are working-class and some are blue-ribbon suburbs of the wealthy; a small but growing proportion is urban and hardly distinguishable from the middle wards of the central city; a few are predominantly ethnic. Such variations are important for the political process of the community, but probably the most important variation of all is simply that of stability. Rapid change is typically the ground for the raising of serious questions which, translated into political issues, are fought out in the local arena. It sets clear and ineluctable tasks for the governmental process.

▪ *Notes*

1. James Bryce, *The American Commonwealth* (London and New York: Macmillan, 1889).
2. George Washington Plunkitt, *Plunkitt of Tammany Hall* (as recorded by William Riordan (New York: McClure-Philips, 1905).
3. For an extensive discussion of the underlying political norms and their translation into governmental rules, see Charles R. Adrian, *Governing Urban America,* 2d ed. (New York: McGraw-Hill, 1961).

4. For a lively picture of the changing American picture of the city, see Anselm Strauss, *Images of the American City* (New York: Free Press, 1961).
5. See Philip Hauser, *Population Perspectives* (New Brunswick: Rutgers University Press, 1960), Chapter 4, p. 101.
6. For an organizational analysis of the rise of the labor unions, see Scott Greer, *Social Organization* (New York: Random House, 1955).
7. Lincoln Steffens, *The Autobiography of Lincoln Steffens* (New York: Harcourt, Brace, 1931).
8. Floyd Hunter, *Community Power Structure* (Chapel Hill: University of North Carolina Press, 1953).
9. For a careful study of the way major issues of Chicago were resolved (or, more often, tabled), see Edward C. Banfield, *Political Influence* (New York: Free Press, 1961).
10. Robert O. Schulze, "The Bifurcation of Power in a Satellite City," in Morris Janowitz, ed., *Community Political Systems* (New York: Free Press, 1961).
11. Donald W. Olmsted, "Organizational Leadership and Social Structure in a Small City," *American Sociological Review*, XIX, 273–281.
12. Harry Scoble, "Leadership Hierarchies and Political Issues in a New England Town," in Janowitz, *op. cit.*
13. Hauser, *op. cit.*, p. 125.
14. Wallace S. Sayre and Herbert Kaufman, *Governing New York City* (New York: Russell Sage Foundation, 1960).
15. The political machine in Stackton is described and analyzed by Peter H. Rossi and Phillips Cutright in "The Impact of Party Organization in an Industrial Setting," in Janowitz, *op. cit.* For the Philadelphia case see James Reichley, *The Art of Government* (New York: Fund for the Republic, 1959). William Foote Whyte presents a study, in depth, of the changing relations of the machine to the ethnic neighborhood he studied in Boston, in *Streetcorner Society* (Chicago: University of Chicago Press, 1943).
16. V. O. Key, Jr., *Southern Politics in State and Nation* (New York: Knopf, 1949).
17. Banfield, *op. cit.*, discusses the destructive effect of the "good government mayor" at some length.

36 POWER, POLITICS, AND POLICY MAKING

■ *Roger Hilsman*

The making of foreign policy is a political process. When decisions are made on the big questions—questions requiring sacrifices by the nation or the concentration on one set of objectives at the cost of neglecting others—there is struggle and conflict. At the same time, there is a "strain toward agree-

From Roger Hilsman, *To Move a Nation* (New York: Doubleday, 1967), pp. 542–563. © Copyright 1964, 1967, by Roger Hilsman. Reprinted by permission of Doubleday & Co., Inc., and the Robert Lantz Literary Agency.

ment,"[1] an effort to build a consensus, a push for accommodation, for compromise, for some sort of agreement on the policy decision. There are independent participants in the process who may be able to block a policy, or sabotage it, or at least snipe away at it from the side lines. There may be other men whose active, imaginative support and dedicated efforts are required if the policy is to succeed, and it may take concessions aimed directly at them and their interests to enlist this kind of willing co-operation. And, finally, there is in all participants an intuitive realization that prolonged intransigence, stalemate, and indecision on urgent and fundamental issues might become so intolerable as to threaten the very form and system of governance.

The Concentric Rings of Decision Making

Political scientists in America clung for generations to an ideal of decision making in democracy in which the electorate was to decide among rival policies as well as choosing among rival leaders. The view was most eloquently voiced by Woodrow Wilson, when he was still a professor, in his book *Congressional Government.* Wilson pined for the logic and clearly fixed responsibilities of parliamentary government modeled on what he conceived to be the British system of his day. He admired the party discipline the British displayed and the clear-cut choices their system at least *appeared* to offer the electorate. Congress, on the other hand, appalled him. He was convinced that its noisy and often undignified procedures were an unsurmountable obstacle to good government. Its untidiness outraged his Calvinist soul.

The truth of the matter is that the British system never did work the way Wilson and his intellectual followers thought it did. If it had, the results would undoubtedly have been disastrous. The few examples where the two parties momentarily approximated the ideal and offered grand alternatives which they insisted on following have not been happy ones. The postwar nationalization and denationalization of steel as the Labour and Conservative parties came in and out of office are only suggestive of the wrenches the British economy and society would have been subjected to. Instead of offering grand alternatives, the parliamentary system, like the congressional system, works to find compromises that blur the alternatives rather than sharpen them.

The great fallacy in the Wilsonian ideal was to suppose that all the electorate would be equally interested in all subjects and acquire the specialized information and knowledge to choose intelligently between the alternatives. But when the interests of political scientists turned to empirical work, it quickly became clear that different segments of the public were interested in different things. As Gabriel Almond wrote in *The American People and Foreign Policy,* there is not one public, but many. Within the general public, there is a division of labor—one "attentive public" for agricultural policy, another for Latin American affairs, and perhaps still another for policy toward Asia. Informed and interested groups follow each policy area, but the "general" public becomes involved in a particular policy only rarely. Ending the

Korean War became a major issue in the election of 1952, but war touches all our lives, and examples of foreign policy issues that directly influenced the outcome of elections are rare.[2]

Approached from the other direction—from the Washington end, as this chapter does—the policy-making process presents itself as a series of concentric circles.[3] The innermost circle, of course, is the President and the men in the different departments and agencies who must carry out the decision—staff men in the White House, the Secretaries of State and Defense, the Director of CIA, and the Assistant Secretaries of State and Defense who bear responsibility for whatever the particular problem may be. Some matters never go beyond this circle, but even here the process is political—the "closed politics" of highly secret decision making.[4] The decision in September of 1962 about how many U-2 flights would be made over Cuba and how many around its periphery is an example. There were conflicting interests among the State Department, the Defense Department, and the CIA. The power of those representing different views influenced the decision, and so did the possibility that the result might affect the future power position of the different participants. As it was, there was at least a tentative effort to shift the blame to the Secretary of State by asserting that the Soviet missiles would have been discovered sooner if that decision had gone the other way. If the crisis had turned out badly for the United States, the effort to shift the blame would have been massive.

Beyond this innermost circle lie other departments of the executive branch and other layers within the agencies and departments already involved, including Presidential commissions, scientific advisory panels, and so on. Even though the debate might still remain secret from the press, Congress, and the public, these second layers soon become involved. In the Laos crisis of 1962, for example, the debate over whether or not to send American troops directly into Laos from Thailand continued for weeks. It was all still top secret, but more and more people became involved in the "closed politics" of the decision. Specialists in the State Department's Bureau of Intelligence and Research and in the Policy Planning Staff, similar specialists in CIA and the Defense Department, became aware of the debate and pushed forward additional information in their province of responsibility that bore on the subject or wrote interpretive memoranda that might have an influence one way or another. People in the RAND Corporation . . . learned of the struggle and rushed copies of their study of the logistical capacity of the transportation routes in Laos to people they knew would use it to good advantage. The longer a policy debate goes on, no matter how delicate the issue is, the more people will become involved until eventually the debate spills over into the public domain. It is for this reason that there is sometimes an incentive to avoid "forward thinking" or any other form of contingency planning. For example, Secretary Rusk, in that same Laos crisis of 1962, wished to avoid even asking the President for a decision about whether or not we would order American forces into Laos if the Communists continued their nibbling tactics.

The Public Arena

The next arena is the public one, involving Congress, the press, interest groups, and—inevitably—the "attentive publics." In this arena, a decision on policy may be made in any one of several ways. The Cuban missile crisis became public, but it never did enter the public arena for decision. The decision was made in the arena of "closed politics," and although the President had always to consider the effects and reactions and repercussions in the wider public arena, the crisis moved too fast for a public debate to catch up. Policy toward Indonesia during the confrontation with Malaysia became public in a variety of ways—focused especially through Congress' authority over appropriations—but it remained the province only of those very few in Congress, the press, and so on who had already had a developed interest. Important though reaching an understanding of the emerging nations might be in the long run, for most Americans the problem of Indonesia remained esoteric. Like blue cheese, it was an acquired taste.

In the Congo crisis, in Laos, in China policy, in Vietnam—in all of these a wide variety of people became involved in one way or another. The debate over Vietnam, to cite the most vivid example, took place in the National Security Council, in the halls of Congress, in the press, in academic journals, inside the United States Mission in Vietnam, in each of the departments and agencies of the executive branch in Washington, and so on and on. The battle lines were drawn between the State Department and the Defense Department, but alliances also cut straight across the institutional boundaries. Individual members of the embassy and of CIA shared the views of a segment of the press, represented by Halberstam and Sheehan, while other members of the embassy and CIA were allied with the opposing segment of the press, represented by Alsop and Higgins. Some members of Congress, such as Senator Church, shared the view of a group in the State Department opposed by other members of Congress allied with others in the Executive. And inevitably the activities of a group in one institution supported the activities of its allies in the other—with or without any attempt at connivance. In Saigon, one group leaked to Halberstam and the other to Higgins. In Washington, Senator Church put in his resolution in the hopes of strengthening the hands of those he agreed with in the State Department, although they did not ask for it and even felt obliged to urge him to hold back.

And there was also the "strain toward agreement"—the effort to reach a consensus, to work out a compromise, to enlist the support of others standing at the edge of the debate. Considering the depth of the disagreement in some of the problems we have examined—Laos, Vietnam, China policy, and the Congo, for example—the remarkable thing is not that there was conflict, but that there was sufficient accommodation to make a decision possible. And the extent of accommodation and consensus would probably look even more remarkable if the scope of the inquiry were broadened to include the other great issues of foreign policy since World War II—the Marshall

Plan, NATO and the containment of the Soviet Union, and the bitter inter-service quarrels over weapons and military strategy.

Characteristics and Consequences of the System

The fact that policy is made through a political process of conflict and consensus building accounts for much of the untidiness and turmoil on the Washington scene. The issues are important; there are rival policies for dealing with them; and the rival policies are sponsored by different groups of advocates competing for the approval or support of a variety of different constituencies. Attracting the attention of such varied audiences requires something dramatic. It takes effort, and many comings and goings, to enlist allies and forestall opponents. A high noise level is a natural consequence of the system itself.

The "Leak"

Consider, for example, the seemingly endless leaks of secret information. Many are not leaks at all. Sometimes a leak is really a trial balloon, launched anonymously in a "background" press conference to test the possibility of building a consensus without the penalty of making a full-scale attempt and failing.

Sometimes information leaks, not because the policy makers want it to, but because the press drills a hole. There is a deeply idealistic conviction in the Washington press corps that they have a duty to inform the wider public of what the government is doing.[5] A selfish interest is added by the fact that conflict and disagreement within the government put their stories on the front page. And there are always, as we saw in the case of Vietnam, Laos, and the others, some in the press who are just as passionately committed to a particular policy view as any of the officials inside the government and just as anxious to influence the policy decisions.

All these are high incentives, and many a "leak" is just hard digging by diligent and defeated reporters. My favorite example occurred in the wake of the Cuban missile crisis, when there were so many charges of "managing the news" that both the press and the policy makers were a little touchy. There had been an exchange of cables in which Khrushchev had finally made a concession on withdrawing troops. Just about this time, a reporter from the *New York Times* and one from the *Washington Post* cornered McGeorge Bundy at a reception and pushed him hard about "news management." Irritated, Bundy said that he knew something that would sooner or later be released and that it would make a big headline—but that the press would *not* be told until the government was good and ready. The two reporters were equally irritated, and each went back to his office and called in as many of his colleagues as he could reach. After talking it over, each group developed two or three ideas about what it might be that Bundy was holding back—and the possibility that it might be a cable from Khrushchev about something to do with Cuba was naturally on both lists. Each set of reporters began to make telephone calls—asking officials if it was true that the cable from Khrushchev had said thus and so—trying a different idea each time. "Oh, no, no, no," one or another official would say, falling into the trap, "It wasn't like that at all." By the time several different officials had "corrected" what would have been a damaging story, both sets of reporters had full and accurate accounts of what was in the cable.

Many "leaks" are of this order. Some others are sheer accident. But then there are true leaks, deliberate and knowing. But even these are not really blab-bermouthed irresponsibility, but more often attempts by men who are deeply convinced, rightly or wrongly, that their cause is overwhelmingly just. They believe that they have both the right and the duty, if their inside effort has failed, to use the public channel—to force an issue or policy alternative up to the level of decision, to outflank the proponents of a rival view, or to appeal a decision to a higher tribunal and a wider public. And they will have sympathetic encouragement from allies in both the press and Congress.

The Oversimplification of the Policy Debate

The fact that policy is made in a political process of conflict and consensus building also accounts for some of the other apparent absurdities of the Washington scene. Often the public debate on foreign policy is childishly oversimplified, for example. The problem of Sukarno and Indonesia was far more complicated than Congressman Broomfield pictured it when he called Sukarno a "Hitler," and the problem of Tshombe and the secession of Katanga was not just a question of the "good guys" versus the "bad guys" as Senator Dodd's speeches implied. Both Broomfield and Dodd probably understood this as well as anyone else. But if the debate is taking place in front of a variety of audiences whose attention is easily diverted, the alternatives must be very clear-cut, simple, and dramatic and the arguments painted in colors that are both bold and bright.

Another consequence of the multiplicity of constituencies involved in policy making is that more and more problems are thrown into the White House. It is only the Presidency—the President himself, his immediate aides in the White House, or *his* men in the departments and agencies—that can consider the whole broad range of interconnections between conflicting interests and demands. Judging these interconnections from the point of view of the President requires someone who partakes of the pressures *on* the President—facing Congress, the press, and the demanding interest groups—and who has his own future tied to the President and his administration. It was only the President himself or someone who identified with him rather than the particular department or agency in which he served, for example, who could ask, as President Kennedy so often asked, "How can we justify fighting a war with American troops in Southeast Asia, which is nine thousand miles away, when we can't justify it in Cuba, which is only ninety miles away?"

All this means that competition for attention at the decision-making level of government becomes more intense. Before a new problem or proposal can be raised to the level of decision, it must jostle out hundreds of others. And what might be called the "jurisdictional" effect of bureaucracy tends to increase still more the number of problems that must elbow their way right to the very top. The essence of bureaucracy is specialization of function and a division of labor and responsibility accordingly. This device is indispensable in managing large-scale enterprises. But it presents peculiar difficulties when it comes time to fix responsibility for problems that cut across jurisdictional lines—which foreign policy problems tend to do in any age and especially so in time of external threat when both military and economic instrumentalities are prominent. More often than not, complex problems arising out of interaction, as between military and political considerations, can be "recognized" as problems in an official sense only at the top. The heart of the problem of guerrilla warfare, for example, lies at the intersection of political and military factors. No one department or agency can begin to cope, and the whole problem can be faced only at the level of the Presidency. Since the solution is the same mixture, carrying out the policy in the field requires the same type of over-all authority: presenting a problem in implementation for which the American form of government is ill equipped.

A policy-making system that revolves around developing a consensus among a wide range of participants also puts a high premium on effective communication and an even higher penalty on a failure of communication. In the first round of the Congo crisis, for example, Mennen Williams and the "New Africa" group were defeated mainly because they had neglected to communicate effectively what it was they were trying to do and why to the Washington constituencies that might have been their allies. Achieving sophisticated policies is not just a problem of policy planning by an elite staff but also one of persuading and educating. What is more, there seems to be no one place where these tasks can be accomplished fully, since there are too many participants too widely scattered to be reached by the communications resources available to any one group of participants, except, perhaps, those available to the White House itself.

The need for wide support sometimes leads to overselling a policy proposal in the sense of claiming too much for it. This happened to some extent in the case of Kennedy's policy of neutralizing Laos and even more in the case of Vietnam. But the classic example would be the foreign aid program as a whole. Foreign aid was supposed to create military allies and at the same time ensure democratic regimes as economic development was achieved. But both of these claims created false expectations at home that eventually eroded support for foreign aid not only among conservatives but among the very liberals who were the most ardent backers of the aid program.

Paradoxically, the need for wide support for a foreign policy sometimes creates an incentive *not* to communicate effectively, to be a little fuzzy in articulating policy and its possible outcomes. Different groups climb aboard a particular policy for different reasons, sometimes because of a differing estimate of just what the true outcome of a policy will be. The politician in a President has a need at times to postpone a decision until there is time to build a consensus, or to proceed in painfully slow increments for the same reason. Every President has occasionally been accused of obfuscation and indecisiveness. Some of Lincoln's cabinet members despaired of getting a decision from him, and similar incidents are told of both Roosevelts, Wilson, and the other Presidents with a reputation for strength and decisiveness. As an executive and the leader of a large and complicated organization, the President needs to be articulate and precise; as a politician, he may need to be vague. And inevitably there is tension between the two.

The effort that must go into "selling" a policy that requires wide support, the tension between the need for articulation and the need for fuzziness, the difficulty in getting some kinds of problems "recognized" except at the top, and the competition for the attention of the many constituencies and levels of government all combine to put obstacles in the way of any attempt at systematic policy making. Some issues or proposals are the subject of massive concentration, while others are neglected almost entirely. There is a tendency to bounce from the crest of one crisis to the crest of another and a bias toward postponing final choice among the possible alternatives until the new crisis forces decisions that are mainly reactions, the children of events rather than their master. Because so many different people and so many different constituencies are involved, it takes the urgency of crisis to force attention and point up the necessity for the mutual concessions and accommodation out of which consensus on a policy is reached.

Incrementalism

There is also a tendency to decide as little as possible.[6] Partly this is because of the impossibility, as Charles E. Lindblom has pointed out, of the task of giving rational consideration to the whole wide range of goals and the multiplicity of alternative means for achieving them and calculating the myriad of consequences and interactions.[7] Policy, as Lindblom says, tends to proceed in a series of incremental steps, tentative and easily reversible. But it seems clear that this is true not only because of the impossibility of analyzing the grand alternatives rationally but also because of the political process of consensus building by which policy is made. The acquiescence of a key constituency might be given for what could be regarded as a tentative, reversible experiment when it would be withheld for a grand leap.

All of this—the bouncing from crisis to crisis, the overselling, the incrementalism—leads to what might be called a discontinuity of policy development. There are gaps in both analysis and policy as a result of the working of the system itself. The Sino-Soviet dispute showed that the Communist world was not the monolith it was supposed to be, but policy based on the assumption that it was a monolith continued through the sheer inertia of the process itself. Guerrilla warfare showed the inadequacy of strategic thinking, but a massive conventional military effort continued to dominate strategy in Vietnam long after a more sophisticated concept had been worked out. Americans feel that they have been too often surprised by the turn of international events, and they tend to blame intelligence, on whom, they feel, so much effort has been lavished to what seems so little avail. But the real reason for their being surprised seems more likely to be here, in the discontinuities growing out of the very nature of the policy-making process.

Advantages of the Process

But in spite of the untidiness and turmoil of the politics of policy making in Washington, such an open process of conflict and consensus building, debate, assessment, and mutual adjustment and accommodation can be solidly effective in the assessment of broad policy alternatives if the conditions are right. The conditions are, first, that the subject be one on which the competing groups of advocates are knowledgeable. Second, both the participating constituencies in the government and the "attentive publics" outside must be well informed. Third, all levels of government, those who will carry out the policy as well as those who decide it, must be responsive to the decision and persuaded by it. Under these conditions, the chances are good that the policy will be wise, that the effort and sacrifice required will be forthcoming, and that the work of carrying out the policy will go forward intelligently and energetically. An example is the development of United States policy toward Europe in the years following World War II—the broad policy highlighted by the Truman doctrine, the Marshall Plan, and the establishment of NATO—which successfully halted the slide of western Europe into Soviet domination and eventually helped to bring it to security and prosperity. The advocates of rival policies, the constituencies inside the government, and the attentive publics outside were equipped with a frame of knowledge about Europe and its problems against which to test proposed policies, and the results were good.

An example of the opposite is the story of China policy, which for so long reflected a lack of the necessary frame of knowledge for intelligent debate at every level, within the government and outside it. Even the Assistant Secretary of State for Far Eastern Affairs at the time, Dean Rusk, could argue, as we saw, that the Chinese Communist regime might be a "colonial Russian government," but that it was "not Chinese." China policy also illustrates how a doctrinaire rigidity can take over and substitute for a frame of knowledge. The Committee of One Million and its allies in Congress and the press, for example, were still insisting that Communism was a "passing phase" on the mainland long after an ordinary citizen would have taken the common-sense view that the Communists had been in control too long to be considered merely a "passing phase" even if they were successfully ousted.

Interestingly enough, the point seems to hold even when the needs of secrecy and speed keep the process circumscribed—when the decision is made in a process of "closed politics" rather than open. In the Cuban missile crisis the number of participants was small. But the frame of knowledge was there, the alternative views were expressed, the debate was wide-ranging, and the presence of competing interests and the wider implications were felt even though the representation was limited. One has the impression, for example, that the President decided against an air strike in his own mind almost immediately and that the long discussion of it over the next few days was to try to bring the "hawks" around and, failing that, at least to have the record show that their alternative was given a full and complete hearing. The result was a policy decision that not only was successful but seems as wise under the scrutiny of hindsight as it did at the time.

The obvious example from the Kennedy administration of a decision made in "closed politics" that suffered from an inadequate frame of knowledge was, of course, the Bay of Pigs. But what is worth pondering is that, unlike the case of China policy, the necessary knowledge was in fact available in Washington. The trouble was different. In the Cuban missile crisis the demands for secrecy kept the number of participants small, but all the different viewpoints, constituencies, and centers of expertise were still represented. In the Bay of Pigs decision, however, secrecy resulted in the exclusion not only of rival advocates but also of centers of expertise and prevented debate before the full range of governmental constituencies.

Some Theoretical Implications

This is not intended to be a book of political science theory, but some further comment on theoretical implications may be in order.

One is the similarity between decision making about foreign policy in Washington and decision making on the international scene.[8] We have spoken of policy making in Washington as a political process, one of conflict and consensus building. People tend to think of war as the principal mode of conflict between nations and thus to assume that conflict between nations is fundamentally different from the conflict within a single country or in private lives. Yet even in the "total" wars of recent times, the use of force is limited. Mankind uses force against some natural enemies with the full intention of exterminating them—as the wolves in England were exterminated or the snakes in Ireland. But except for Hitler's maniacal policy toward the Jews, no modern nation has deliberately set about to destroy another people. Physical violence, in fact, is not really a very common state of affairs between nations. In the history of most nations the years of peace far outnumber the years of war. Even when conflict is the dominating theme in a set of relationships, statecraft is not really concerned as much with physical violence, the military art, as it is with threats of physical violence, or still more accurately with manipulating all the varied forms of power—since physical violence is only one of several means that nations use to coerce or influence one another.

It is on the conflict in international affairs that a pure power theory of world politics focuses. Yet for all its utility in explaining the maneuverings of states, a pure power theory has limitations. Without a sizable list of inelegant qualifications, it cannot account for the long periods of peace in international relations, for the stability of certain friendships, and for the not uncommon occasions when nations knowingly relinquish positions of power. For the practical purposes of estimating the consequences of different policies and so of choosing between them, a pure power theory of politics is a cumbersome and uneconomic tool.

The difficulty comes from the multiplicity of values shared by people on both sides of national boundaries—peace, security, prosperity, self-determination, and the sanctity and freedom of the individual. Thus one nation's gain is not always another's loss, and accommodation and concerted action occur almost as frequently in international affairs as conflict.[9]

The obvious example of nations acting in concert are alliances for security against a common enemy. But nations also act in concert for a variety of lesser purposes: to regulate trade, to counter economic depressions, to conserve such natural resources as fisheries, to combat crime, and to provide international postal and other services.

There is accommodation between adversaries, too. Rival nations often agree, formally or tacitly, to respect spheres of exclusive influence, to act together in neutralizing a third country, or to refrain from bringing certain matters into the arena of competition. The bitterest rivals have a stake in restricting their competition to means that are appropriate to the goals at issue and in avoiding measures that will bring about the sacrifice of things more cherished than those to be won. Even nations at war have reached agreements. Gas was outlawed in World War II, although not all the participants had signed the convention on the rules of war. In the Korean War there was a tacit agreement to respect sanctuaries. The United Nations forces refrained from bombing north of the Yalu, and the Communist forces conformed by avoiding Pusan and our bases in Japan. In Vietnam, there was until 1965 a tacit agreement that the United States would refrain from bombing North Vietnam and the North Vietnamese would refrain from infiltrating their regular battalions into the south.

Thus international politics has a mixture of conflict and accommodation similar to that in domestic politics. As a consequence, the business between nations, like the business of reaching decisions within a single nation, requires techniques for persuasion, negotiation, and bargaining as well as for manipulating power.

The practitioners of statecraft, the operators in foreign offices and embassies, do not make a practice of generalizing about the "decision-making procedures of world politics" or the "international decision-making system." Neither do they comment on the resemblance between international politics and a process of consensus building. Yet, faced with the problem of *doing* something in international affairs—whether it is trying to bring about a Geneva conference on Laos or implementing a decision to blockade Cuba—any practitioner, from desk officer to assistant secretary, would unerringly tick off the steps to be taken. Nation A would have to be consulted in advance; Nations B and C would have only to be informed. *This* line of argument should be taken in the UN; *that* line of argument with the press. Moscow should be told *this* at *that* stage; Paris should be handled in a different way. Practitioners may not generalize about the "international decision-making system," but they know how to operate it.

The Nature of Politics

A second theoretical comment that might be made is on the nature of politics. How one defines politics depends very much on what analytical purposes one has in mind. Politics has been defined as the struggle to determine "who gets what, when, and how" for one analytical purpose.[10] It has been defined as a struggle for power, pure and simple, for other purposes.[11] And there are still other definitions.[12] Most of them are reasonably valid and useful for particular purposes, and most of them are not completely satisfactory for all purposes. And it is probably not necessary to strain for the perfect definition. Most people have a common-sense definition that is good enough. People speak of "office politics," for example, and everyone knows what they mean. As a general rule, people assume that politics is concerned with power, that it is more likely than not concerned with matters of government, and that political decisions of the largest moment are concerned with the ordering and regulating of society itself. In its broadest meaning, politics concerns the activities and relationships of groups of people as groups.

Politics as Group Decision Making

For the purpose of analyzing the making of foreign policy, it seems most useful to look at a political process as a device for making group decisions, a procedure by which a group of people can decide what they should do as a group, the goals they should seek and the means for achieving them, or how they should divide among themselves those benefits already available. Politics would be concerned with both the making of such decisions and the maneuvering to acquire the power and influence to affect them.

There are, of course, other devices for the making of group decisions—judicial and administrative procedures, for example, in which decisions are made by the interpretation, guided by precedent, of sets of laws, policies, rules, and regulations, or, perhaps, by tribal customs.

One can conceive of group decisions made in a purely hierarchical way, in which only the head man has a vote. At the other extreme, one could also conceive of a pure type of democratic decision making in which there was no leader at all and decisions were made unanimously or by the majority, with each man really having only one vote and no influence other than his vote. But the real world is more complex. It differs from the pure hierarchical model of decision making in that more than one person has power or influence on decisions and from the pure democratic model in that the participants have differing amounts of power and influence. The active cooperation of some people may be required for a decision, as we have seen, while only the acquiescence of others may be necessary. Some participants might have to give formal approval before some decisions could be made; and on other decisions these same people might be safely ignored.

Also, several different forms of group decision making might be operative at the same time. Within a single department of the government, some decisions are made by hierarchical procedures, some by judicial, and some by political—and perhaps some by a combination of all three. Not infrequently officials are called upon to play roles appropriate to every possible form of decision making in swift and bewildering succession with few cues as to when the scene is changing.[13]

Characteristics of a Political Process

Three characteristics distinguish a political process of decision making from other ways of making group decisions. In the first place, politics implies a diversity of goals and values that must be reconciled before a decision can be reached. It is not just a question of whether this or that value should be pursued, but what mixture of values should be pursued. It also implies alternative means for achieving values whose precise effects may be in dispute. There is never a political debate over the tensile strength required for the truss members of a bridge, which can be determined with great exactitude. But there frequently is a political debate over the economic and social effects of locating the bridge at one place on a river rather than another, which cannot be determined with such exactitude.

Frequently, a debate over the probable effects of alternative means is really a mask for a disagreement about goals that remains unspoken. But in the making of foreign policy, at least, it is noteworthy how often the debate is truly over means and predictions about what a particular means will or will not accomplish. In the Cuban missile crisis, in the Congo crisis, in China policy, in the Laos crisis, in South Vietnam—in all of these there was by and large agreement about the general objective, and the debate was over which means would best accomplish the objective at what risk and at what cost.

Politics, in other words, begins to come to the fore when there is disagreement (1) about the goals the group should seek as a group, or (2) about the effects of alternative means for achieving the goal, or (3) about the rules governing competition between individuals and subgroups, or (4) about the allocation of benefits held or distributed by the group as a whole, or (5) about the sacrifices required by different segments of the group as a whole. It is not competition alone that produces politics. If there is substantial agreement, for example, that unrestrained economic enterprise shall govern the distribution of material benefits, the competition will take place in other than political terms. It is when there is disagreement about the rules for economic competition that politics begins.

A second characteristic of a political process is the presence of competing clusters of people in the main group who are identified with each of these alternative goals and policies. In the policy-making arena, for example, we have found not just the traditional political parties but subgroups of many kinds, including some that lie within the government as well as outside it— frequently entirely informal alliances that cut across departmental or institutional lines, including the line between the Executive and Congress. In the Congo crisis, as we saw, this pattern was particularly sharp. The "New Africa" group had friends and allies in Congress, in the press, and in the "attentive publics," while the "Old Europe" group found an entirely different set of allies in Congress and the press, bolstered by those in the Pentagon. But the same pattern of subgroups and informal alliances ran through each of the other major policy disputes, sometimes more and sometimes less prominently.

In a political process, finally, the relative power of the different groups of people involved is as relevant to the final decision as the appeal of the goals they seek or the cogency and wisdom of their arguments. It was the political power that the China lobby could muster at the height of its influence, to cite the most obvious example, that bound policy so tightly for so long, and not the persuasiveness of the argument. Who advocates a particular policy is as important as what he advocates.

Viewing policy making as a political process in the sense described by these characteristics illuminates the diversity and inconsistency of the goals that national policy must serve . . . and calls attention to the powerful but sometimes hidden forces through which these competing goals are reconciled. It helps explain, as we said, why the push and pull of these cross currents are sometimes dampened or obscured and why they are sometimes so fiercely public. And the roles of such "*un*rational" procedures as bargaining also become more clear.

Political Power

A third, and final, theoretical comment that might be made here is on the nature of political power as illuminated in the making of United States foreign policy. It seems beyond dispute that power is a factor in any political process. Everyone recognizes the obvious fact that some people have more power than others, and all the great social thinkers have devoted their attention to the nature of power. As Robert A. Dahl has pointed out, the existence of so much comment arouses two suspicions.[14] The first is that where there is so much smoke there must be fire, and some "Thing" that can be called power must exist. The second suspicion is that "a Thing to which people attach many labels with subtly or grossly different meanings in many different cultures and times is probably not a Thing at all but many Things." It is in the spirit of this notion that political power is probably many different things and—without attempting any general or systematic essay on power in the United States—that attention might be drawn to a few of the implications of the case studies of foreign policy issues. . . .

The Power of Congress

Consider the power that Congressmen exercise in the making of foreign policy. In their exploration of the policy-making machinery of government, Senator Jackson and his subcommittee forestalled a number of moves toward reorganizing the "machinery" of the government and killed such ideas as creating a "Vice-President for Foreign Affairs." Second, they made an effective case for giving the State Department and the Secretary of State the central role. Even though neither the department nor the Secretary took up the opportunity presented, and the President, aided by McGeorge Bundy and the White House staff, had to fill it himself, it was the Jackson Subcommittee that was mainly responsible for giving them the opportunity. Yet Senator Jackson accomplished this, not by legislation, but by commissioning staff studies and by holding hearings to serve as a platform for people with ideas. It was, in effect, an exercise in semiformal and public consensus building.

Senator Keating in the Cuban missile crisis and Senator Dodd in the Congo crisis played similar roles. The benefit to these particular Senators of picking up a foreign policy issue in just the way they did is obvious. Senator Keating had been a member of the House for many years representing an upstate district. As Senator, he needed to become known in New York City and to build a "statesman" image to overcome his rather parochial, conservative record as an upstate Congressman. Senator Dodd had the problem of representing a state that borders New York City and houses commuters who listen to its radio and TV and read its newspapers. How does a Senator from either Connecticut or upstate New York get on New York City's radio and TV and on the front page of the *New York Times*? Picking up a continuing foreign policy issue and being the focal point for opposition to State Department policy is not only an effective way but . . . politically cheap. Both Cuba and the Congo offered an opportunity for the Senators to take a strong anti-Communist stand, which is always popular, without risk of alienating anyone except the State Department—and, as far as the voters of New York and Connecticut were concerned, this was itself undoubtedly a plus.

But what effect did Keating and Dodd have on the substance of foreign policy? Keating attracted attention to the possibility of the Soviets' putting missiles in Cuba, but the government was already so sensitive to that possibility it was quivering. Actually, Keating and Goldwater between them almost caused the agreement with the Soviets about withdrawing their troops to break down, which was certainly not in either their interest or the nation's. And Dodd was never able to force the government to adopt his policy for the Congo, that of supporting Tshombe and the secession of Katanga. Yet their activities were always a factor to be taken account of in the policy discussions—and policy was at times either adjusted to accommodate some element of their view so as to disarm them or presented in such a way as to forestall them. For even though Keating and Dodd did not become the rallying points for an alternative policy, they had the potential for doing so, especially if the policy the government was actually pursuing failed dramatically.

In Vietnam, during President Kennedy's administration, Congress did not play a large role. There was pressure from the liberals to dissociate the United States from President Diem, but after the Buddhist crisis dissociation also became the general direction of official policy. The conservatives of both parties agreed with the "war hawk" view that advocated bombing North Vietnam and the United States' taking over direction of the struggle from the

Vietnamese, but they did not make a great effort to get the policy adopted. The irony is that one of the main reasons this group did not push harder for stepping up the war was that the Pentagon, their main ally in the executive branch, kept stubbornly insisting that the war was already being won. If the war was already being won, there was no need to bomb the north and take over responsibility from the Vietnamese.

Congressman Broomfield attempted to cut off all aid to Sukarno's Indonesia, even though the aid was mainly designed to strengthen the army's capacity to deal with the Communists when the showdown came. But he could not, in fact, change policy. President Kennedy would have signed the determination that the aid was in the national interest and gone ahead. Although President Johnson refused to sign and, in effect, adopted Broomfield's policy, he did it, not in response to pressure from Broomfield and Congress, but because the policy conformed to his own view. But here again, Broomfield's position had at least to be considered by President Kennedy—if only as a potential rallying point for opposition, should effective opposition really be aroused.

In all these examples, the influence and power of Congress were indirect or limit-setting rather than direct or initiative-taking. In domestic policy, Congress occasionally can take the initiative and force a new policy according to its tastes, but rarely so in foreign policy. In foreign policy, the Executive calls the tune—and there are reasons. In the first place, it is the Executive who controls the detailed flow of information from overseas. There need be no conscious intention to suppress one kind of information and emphasize another to accomplish the same result as deliberate suppression and emphasis. No one deliberately distorted the information on the way the war was going in Vietnam, for example, but it was distorted. The policy position of the Executive will have its effect on the way information is presented, even when passions run less deep than they did over Vietnam. In such a massive flow of information, merely winnowing the raw data down to what one man could conceivably absorb would of itself present a partisan picture of the situation.

The increasing technicality of foreign affairs also robs Congress of its power. Understanding the Buddhists in Vietnam, the nature of the new nationalism, the complexities of the Sino-Soviet dispute, and so on requires expert knowledge; and it is the Executive who has the greater command of experts. As a consequence, it is the Executive who sets the framework in which policies are discussed, who defines the problems we will essay as a government and the alternatives from which we choose the course of action to meet them.

This command of both information and expertise gives to the Executive the intellectual initiative in making foreign policy. Congress as a whole can criticize; it can add to, amend, or block an action by the Executive. But Congress can succeed only occasionally in forcing Executive attention to the need for a change in policy, and rarely can it successfully develop and secure approval from the public for a policy of its own.

The Executive also has an "instrumental" initiative in foreign affairs. It is the Executive who carries out a policy, who deals with problems face to face. In doing so, the Executive must inevitably make a host of secondary decisions that can and do set new lines of policy. Here again, this is especially true in foreign policy. It is the Executive who conducts negotiations with other powers, and in these negotiations it can make promises and commitments that Congress cannot fail to honor. Frequently, indeed, the Executive may proceed without any formal reference to Congress at all. Kennedy concluded the Laos agreements of 1962 without formal reference to Congress. Eisenhower's commitment to South Vietnam in 1954 was not formally referred to Congress; and neither was Kennedy's in 1961. And there is a host of other examples: Roosevelt's destroyers-for-bases deal with Great Britain; the Yalta agreement, which so many Congressmen resented for so long; Truman's decision to meet the blockade of Berlin with an airlift; and his even bolder decision to resist Communist aggression in Korea with troops as well as with material aid.

But this power of the Executive to proceed in some matters without reference to Congress, or even to evade the expressed desires of Congress, is only part of the story. Congress has little direct control over foreign policy, and it can take few initiatives. It participates only fitfully in the actual formulation of foreign policy and takes formal action only in approving or rejecting appropriations, treaties, and resolutions and in confirming the appointments of ambassadors and high officials. Yet it is equally clear that Congress—subtly and indirectly, but nevertheless effectively—plays a decisive role in setting the tone of many policies and the limits on many others.

The most dramatic example of the power of Congress to set the policy tone is the case of China policy. Congress and Congressmen took the lead in solidifying a national consensus on a rigid policy toward Communist China, and the viciousness of the McCarthy era set it in concrete. Once this kind of wide consensus is set, inertia rules. It then takes almost heroic action to overcome even the mildest congressional resistance. President Kennedy wished to bring about a change in China policy, but progress was painfully slow. In the beginning of his administration, he sought to start by recognizing Mongolia, but the Nationalists objected, and their friends in Congress quickly shot the proposal down. Nothing dramatic or specific would have been accomplished by recognizing Mongolia—the effects would have been symbolic and psychological, indicative of a *coming* change in China policy. And this was the trouble; for when the purpose is a change in policy against a massive inertia of the kind surrounding policy toward China, it is essential to have quick results to point to and beat off the counterattacks.

Legally and constitutionally, President Kennedy could have gone ahead and recognized Mongolia. But he would have had to be willing to take the consequences: not just angry speeches and threats of impeachment, but retaliatory action on a whole range of other matters over which Congress has more direct legal and constitutional power. In a very real sense, the peculiarly negative, limit-setting power of Congress over foreign policy is the power of deterrence and the threat of "massive retaliation."

The Sources of Power

We have argued that policy making is a political process, and on the face of it power and politics are intertwined. Yet power is a crude concept, as we have said, and it fails to satisfy as an explanation of the mixture of both conflict and accommodation that is present, of the motives that presumably lie behind the decisions on foreign policy, or of the techniques that are used to achieve agreement or acquiescence on a policy.

If it is correct to say that the peculiar province of politics is matters in which there is disagreement about either group goals and values or the rules of competition and allocation of those individual values and interests that are regulated by the group, then power need not be quite so central in either domestic politics or international. Power need not be the motive force for most participants, nor the cause of politics, nor even a necessary condition, but only one of the more pervasive and perhaps decisive of the several instruments of politics.

At certain times and in certain places, military power, for example, may be starkly central in domestic affairs—civil war is the obvious example. But to the extent that military strength is a *source* of power on the domestic scene, the mechanism is not so crude. In the making of foreign policy in the cases studied here, there was a policy view and position from what President Eisenhower called the "military-industrial complex" on some issues, such as Laos and Vietnam, in both of which there was a large military stake. And in these cases power was clearly exerted in support of that view and position. But as a force the military-industrial complex was loosely organized, amorphous—more potential than structured. Nothing in any of the foreign policy issues examined here, certainly, resembles in the slightest the "power elites" described in Marxist and neo-Marxist literature. The oil companies had a huge investment in Indonesia, for example, but their inclination was not to push the United States into greater involvement but to get themselves out. More than once it was only because of the urgings of the United States government that American businesses were persuaded to stay in Indonesia as long as they did.

In the domestic scene, clearly, power has more varied and subtle sources than in either force and violence or wealth and class. Power grows not only "out of the barrel of a gun," as Mao Tse-tung would have it, but also in legitimacy, in legal authority, in expertise, and in special interest that is recognized as legitimate, such as the interest of the farmer in agricultural policy or the banker in monetary policy. It is so varied and subtle in its sources, indeed, that one wonders whether "power" is the most useful word.

Power can be the negative power that Congress has of making life difficult for the President if one of its treasured views is ignored. It can be the legal and constitutional right to decide in a formal sense, which is usually the President's in foreign affairs, but sometimes belongs to Congress. It can be influence, in the sense of having the ear of the President or the respect of the leaders of Congress without holding any office at all. It can be the ability to have one's views at least taken into account because one represents a special interest group like the farmers, as we said, whose legitimacy is recognized. It can also be the ability to have one's views taken into account simply because one has convinced the world that one speaks for a wider public and that there will be political consequences if one is ignored. An example is Marvin Liebman, who as Executive Secretary of the Committee of One Million could get a hearing because he was accepted as the spokesman for the China lobby and presumably for a wider public that supported the views of Chiang Kai-shek. It can also be the ability to have one's views taken into account because of one's personal expertise. When George Kennan speaks about policy toward the Soviet Union, for example, the government listens even when it abhors the advice offered and refuses to take it. Power can also come simply because one has a "platform" which gives one the opportunity of enlisting a particular constituency. An Adlai Stevenson or a Chester Bowles out of office can influence policy by his ability to command a hearing before "liberals" and the possibility that he might swing the whole constituency with his persuasiveness. A scientist who is completely unknown outside the scientific community might develop such leverage, and if the subject matter concerned a scientific question, the leverage might be overwhelming. No President would lightly go against the consensus of scientists on a matter in the area of their specialty.

In the executive branch itself power comes to some people because they enjoy the confidence of the President. Power also comes from using a "job platform" so that it fills a larger need, which can bring still wider responsibility and more power. The position and title—the "platform"—that McGeorge Bundy occupied in the Kennedy administration existed in Eisenhower's day, but it was Bundy who made it powerful. Power comes from expertise, from representing a particular constituency, whether within or outside the government, from institutional backing, and from statutory or designated authority and responsibility. The mere title of the Secretary of State gives him authority, in addition to what he acquires through statute and custom.

The richness of the sources of power over the making of foreign policy goes back to the nature of the political process of conflict and consensus building by which policy is made. Within the government and outside it, to repeat, there are different constituencies with a stake in the outcome. The State Department may have jurisdiction over the general problem, for example, while the Pentagon must implement one aspect of it and the Agency for International Development another. Even if the President's prestige and position are not involved, his approval may be a legal or a political necessity. This may be true of Congress, also. If so, the outside constituencies are likely to be drawn in— interest groups, newspapermen, academic commentators, and the still wider constituency of the particular "attentive public."

In a major problem of foreign affairs, as we have said, the advocate of a particular policy—even if there is neither a rival advocate nor a rival policy— must build a consensus to support his policy in the different constituencies in the government and frequently outside as well. He needs the active co-operation and support of some, the formal or informal approval of others, and at least the acquiescence of still others. He may prevail over the active opposition of one or another constituency, but rarely if it is from within the government and the enterprise is large. For even passive opposition can bring a large and complicated enterprise to failure, not by sabotage, but simply lack of enthusiasm. When there are rival advocates or rival policies, on the other hand, there is not only debate before the different constituencies but competition for their support. Alliances are formed, and all the techniques of consensus building appear: persuasions, accommodation, and bargaining.

Over some of this at certain times, the President may merely preside, if it is a matter of slight interest to him and has little impact on his position. But if *he* is an advocate or if the outcome affects *his* position and power, the President, too, must engage in the politics of policy making. In the field of foreign affairs, the President's power is immense. His is the constitutional authority as Commander in Chief. His is the monopoly in dealing with other states. But he, too, must build a consensus for his policy if it is to succeed. He must bring along enough of the different factions in Congress to forestall revolt, and he must contend for the support of wider constituencies, the press, interest groups, and "attentive publics." Even in the executive branch itself, his policy will not succeed merely at his command, and he must build co-operation and support, obtain approval from some, acquiescence from others, and enthusiasm from enough to carry it to completion. This is the truth that so amused President Truman when he said that Eisenhower would find that the Presidency was not "a bit like the Army." It is the truth that President Kennedy had in mind when he joked about the "inner club." It is the "half-observed realities," as Neustadt says, underneath our images of "Presidents-in-boots, astride decisions"—the realities of "Presidents-in-sneakers, stirrups in hand, trying to induce particular department heads, or congressmen, or senators to climb aboard."[15]

▪ Notes

1. The phrase is Warner R. Schilling's. See his "The Politics of National Defense: Fiscal 1950," in Schilling, Hammond, and Snyder, *Strategy, Politics, and Defense Budgets* (New York: Columbia University Press, 1962), p. 23.
2. Even if foreign policy *issues* do not seem to play a very important role in elections, the electorate apparently wants its candidates for national office to have qualifications or experience that show *competency* in foreign affairs. See Angus Campbell *et al., The American Voter* (New York: John Wiley, 1960, 1964).
3. The theoretical model of the policy-making process that follows owes much to the work of Gabriel A. Almond, especially his *American People and Foreign Policy* (New York: Frederick A. Praeger, 1960). An earlier attempt at this model—influenced not only by Almond but also by Charles E. Lindblom's article, "The Science of 'Muddling Through,'" and the works of Robert A. Dahl—is contained in my 1958 and 1959 articles, "Congressional-Executive Relations and the Foreign Policy Consensus" and "The Foreign Policy Consensus: An Interim Research Report." The model as presented here draws on the subsequent work of Warner R. Schilling, "The Politics of National Defense: Fiscal 1950," *loc. cit.;* Samuel P. Huntington, *The Common Defense* (New York: Columbia University Press, 1960); and Thomas Schelling, *The Strategy of Conflict* (Cambridge: Harvard University Press, 1960); as well as the later work of Almond, Dahl, and Lindblom.
4. The phrase is C. P. Snow's. See his *Science and Government* (Cambridge: Harvard University Press, 1960, 1961).

5. Bernard C. Cohen, *The Press and Foreign Policy* (Princeton: Princeton University Press, 1963).

6. On this point, see Warner R. Schilling, "The H-Bomb Decision: How to Decide without Actually Choosing," *Political Science Quarterly* (March, 1961).

7. Charles E. Lindblom, *The Intelligence of Democracy* (New York: Macmillan, 1965), Chapter 9.

8. Others who have commented on the parallel between domestic and international politics are: Nicholas John Spykman, *America's Strategy in World Politics* (1942); W. T. R. Fox in his lectures at Yale and Columbia; and Warner R. Schilling, *op. cit.*

9. For descriptions of international politics in which both conflict and accommodation appear, see the following, among others: Nicholas John Spykman, *op. cit.;* W. T. R. Fox, *The Superpowers* (1944); Hans J. Morgenthau, *Politics among Nations* (New York: Knopf, 1962); Arnold Wolfers, "The Pole of Power and the Pole of Indifference," *World Politics* (October, 1951); and Thomas C. Schelling, *op. cit.*

10. Harold Lasswell, *Politics: Who Gets What, When, How* (New York: World, 1958).

11. Charles E. Merriam, *Political Power: Its Composition and Incidence* (1934); Hans J. Morgenthau, *op. cit.*, 3d ed. (1960).

12. Although they by no means exhaust the list, three others might be noted here: first, V. O. Key's definition of politics as the "human relationship of superordination and subordination, of dominance and submission, of the governors and the governed" (*Politics, Parties, and Pressure Groups,* 4th ed. [New York: Crowell, 1958]); David Easton's as the making and executing of the "authoritative," that is, legally binding, decisions in a society (*The Political System: An Inquiry into the State of Political Science* [New York: Knopf, 1953]; and "An Approach to the Analysis of Political Systems," *World Politics* [April, 1957]); and Gabriel A. Almond's and James Coleman's as "that system of interactions to be found in all independent societies which performs the functions of integration and adaption (both internally and vis-à-vis other societies) by means of the employment, or threat of employment, of more or less legitimate physical violence" (*The Politics of the Developing Areas* [1960]).

13. On the overlapping of different forms of decision making and the psychological problems posed for the individual, see Robert A. Dahl, "Hierarchy, Democracy, and Bargaining in Politics and Economics," in *Research Frontiers in Politics and Government* (Washington: Brookings Institution, 1955).

14. Robert A. Dahl, "The Concept of Power," *Behavioral Science* (July, 1957).

15. Richard E. Neustadt, "White House and Whitehall," *Public Interest,* No. 2 (Winter, 1966).

☐ The Public-Private Complex

37 THE NEW FEUDALISM

▪ Hans J. Morgenthau

We have thus far dealt with one of the two paradoxes of contemporary democracy, the paradox of thwarted majority rule: universal democratization goes hand in hand with a drastic shift of power from the people to the government. We turn now to the paradox of thwarted government: that drastic increase in the power of the government in relation to the people goes hand in hand with a drastic decrease in the over-all power that constitutional authorities exercise within the state. In other words, universal democratization and the increase of the power of the government at the expense of the people result in a net loss of governmental power. While more powerful vis-à-vis the people than it has been in living memory, the government governs less than it did when it was weaker. This paradox is the result of the decomposition of governmental power from within and without: through the feudalism of semiautonomous executive departments and through the feudalism of the concentrations of private power.

When we refer to the executive branch of the government, we are really making use of a figure of speech in order to designate a multiplicity of varied and more or less autonomous agencies that have but one quality in common: their authority has been delegated to them either by the President or by Congress. But neither the President nor Congress is able to control them. The

From Hans J. Morgenthau, *The Purpose of American Politics* (New York: Knopf, 1960), pp. 274–291. © Copyright 1960 by Hans J. Morgenthau. Reprinted by permission of Alfred A. Knopf, Inc.

reason must be sought in the inadequacy of the Presidency and of Congress for the control of the executive branch as it has developed in our time. The executive branch of the American government has become an enormous apparatus of the highest quantitative and qualitative complexity. The functions of the executive branch have been divided and subdivided and parceled out to a plethora of agencies. Most of the functions these agencies perform overlap or are at the very least interconnected to such an extent that an agency needs the support of other agencies in order to perform its functions. There can be but few policies of any importance which an agency is able to pursue without regard for the position of other agencies. In the absence of hierarchical direction and control, one agency can act only with the consent of another agency, and how to secure that consent—through co-operation or competition—becomes a vital issue on which the usefulness of the agency depends.

This quantitative proliferation of the executive function is accompanied by its qualitative atomization, which is due to the technological complexity of many of the most important executive functions. This complexity gives the agency that masters it an advantage in policy formation which may well amount in some of the most important areas to a virtual monopoly. Such specialized knowledge, which is a unique source of power, is typically guarded by a wall of secrecy, and excluded from it are not only the general public and Congress but also other—and especially rival—agencies.

Upon this sprawling and unwieldy agglomeration of executive agencies, which are legally speaking but an arm of the Executive and the legislature, the President and Congress try in vain to impose their will. The President as Chief Executive and Commander in Chief has, of course, the constitutional power to impose his conception of policy on the executive departments, with the exception of the independent regulatory commissions, which are supposed to operate according to the statutory standards laid down by Congress. However, reality diverges sharply from the constitutional scheme. Even so strong and astute a President as Franklin D. Roosevelt was incapable of assuming full control even over the State Department, the constitutional executor of his foreign policy. His successors have had to an ever increasing degree to limit themselves to laying down general principles of policy in the hope that they would not suffer too much in the far-flung process of execution. On the other hand, the main weapon at the disposal of Congress, the investigating power, is clumsy; it can at best deal effectively with abuse and violation of the law, but is hardly able to correct an executive policy that is at variance with its own. For the statutory standards by which Congress must judge the executive performance are generally so vague as to leave the executive branch and, more particularly, the regulatory commissions a vast area of discretion.

Thus the constitutional intent to translate the Presidential and congressional will into purposeful action, as the movements of the arm reflect the impulses emanating from the brain, has produced instead the anarchy of a war of all against all, fought among as well as within the executive departments. The objective of the war is the determination—either directly or by influencing the decisions of higher authority—of at least that segment of policy which falls in the jurisdiction of the agency. The proliferation of agencies with overlapping functions and the equal status of many of them make the interagency phase of the war almost inevitable. The absence of clear lines of authority and of an organization appropriate to the functions to be performed invites intra-agency war and in certain departments, such as State and Defense, makes it inevitable. To win these wars, the belligerents enter into alliances with other belligerents, with factions in Congress and in the White House, with business enterprises, and with the mass media of communications. The deliberate leak to a journalist or member of Congress becomes a standard weapon with which one agency tries to embarrass another, or force the hand of higher authority, or establish an accomplished fact.

This process of policy formation and execution resembles the feudal system of government in that the public authority is parceled out among a considerable number of agencies which, while legally subordinated to a higher authority, are in fact autonomous to a greater or lesser degree. The executive agency, competing for the determination of policy with other agencies, more and more resembles a feudal fief that owes its existence to the delegation of powers by higher authority, but becomes in active operation an autonomous center of power, defending itself against other centers of power and trying to increase its power at the expense of others. This system of government resembles the feudal system also in that the fragmentation of public power carries in itself a diminution of the sum total of public power. Fragmented power is weak power, and the sum total of the fragments, each following its own impulse, is of necessity inferior to what the public power would have been had it remained in one piece, harnessed to a single purpose. The government, instead of speaking with one strong and purposeful voice, speaks in many voices, each trying to outshout the others, but all really weak as well as contradictory.

It is worthy of note that this fragmentation and consequent diminution of the public power, which characterizes the executive branch of the government, was erected by the Constitution into a fundamental principle of the American system of government in the form of the separation of powers. The separation of the public power into three separate departments, in good measure independent of one another, seeks to prevent one branch from imposing its will on the whole and thereby becoming too strong for the liberty of the citizens. It seeks to weaken the government by dividing it. What the Constitution sought to achieve for the whole government by intent, the executive branch has achieved for itself through haphazard, fissiparous growth.

The debilitating effect which the separation of powers was intended to exert on the government was innocuous as long as the functions which the government had to perform were limited and exercised in normal circumstances. However, when a crisis required strong action by the government and, more particularly, by the Executive, which alone is capable of direct action in the true sense of the word, it was the President who, through the authority of his office, the strength of his will, and the persuasiveness of his vision, gave the government that unity of purposeful action commensurate with the task to be performed. And the Constitution designed the Presidency to be equal to such a crisis situation by investing the President with the powers of an "uncrowned king."

What the philosophy of the Constitution could conceive only as the extreme and exceptional conditions of crisis have become the normal conditions of American existence. The revolutions of the Civil War, the Square Deal, the New Deal, and the Cold War have established in permanence the dominant role of the government in the affairs of the nation. The quantitative proliferation of executive agencies implements that role. Yet the organization of the Presidency is adequate only to lead and control the weak and but sporadically active federal government of bygone times, but not a federal government which has become in permanence the determining factor in the vital concerns of the nation. No President can perform at the same time the functions of Head of State, Chief Executive, Commander in Chief, and head of his party. He cannot even plan, formulate, co-ordinate, and supervise the execution of policy at the same time. The President has the constitutional authority to do all these things: but he has not necessarily the extraordinary combination of knowledge, judgment, and character required for such a task; and most certainly he does not have the time. In the absence of an effective Cabinet system, the President is separated from the day-by-day operations of the executive branch by a gap which he can but occasionally bridge. Normally, he presides over the executive branch, but he does not govern it.

Congress, on the other hand, is kept from effective control of the executive branch by the constitutional separation of powers, especially as interpreted by the executive branch itself. This impotence, bred in good measure by ignorance of what the executive branch is doing, has engendered in Congress an endemic mood of frustration and irritation which seeks relief in the harassment and persecution of persons rather than in the formulation, supervision, and enforcement of policies. Lack of party discipline and archaic rules of procedure make it difficult for Congress to discover a will of its own and impose it on the executive branch. The disintegration of the executive branch and the debilitation of the public power resulting from it must be cured, on the one hand, by infusing the executive branch with a purpose transcending the feudal interests and loyalties that rent it asunder and, on the other, by superimposing on it a power capable of neutralizing, subduing, and fusing the fragments of feudal power which tend to be a law unto themselves. Both purpose and power can come only from the President's office, for only here do we find the visible authority and the fullness of implied powers necessary to make the national purpose prevail over the parochialism of feudal fiefdoms. As in sixteenth- and seventeenth-century Europe the monarchical authority and power had to be called into being in order to create a nation out of the fragments of a territorial feudalism, so in our age must the Presidential power and authority come forward to save the unity of the national purpose from functional fragmentation.

The debility of the executive power, caused by its inner fragmentation, invites attack from the concentrations of private power, especially in the economic sphere. Throughout history, factions within the state have frequently made common cause with a foreign enemy in order to improve their position in the domestic struggle for power and have thereby delivered the state itself into the hands of its enemies. So the feudal lords in the executive branch ally themselves with the princes of private power, each ally pursuing his particular goal. The former seek to expand their fiefdoms in the executive branch and thereby increase their share in the power of the government. The latter seek to turn the instruments of government control to their own advantage and expand their own power without regard for, and at the expense of, the public power. Thus, the public power is diminished through concerted action from within and without. The economic sphere has lost whatever autonomy it has had in the past: it is subject to political control as it, in turn, tries to control political decisions. We are in the presence of the revival of a truly political economy, and the major economic problems are political in nature.

The interconnectedness of the political and economic spheres is not peculiar to our age. Even in the heyday of nineteenth-century liberalism, the strict separation of the two spheres was in the nature of a political ideal rather than the reflection of observable reality. The monetary, tax, and tariff policies of the government had then, as they have now, a direct bearing on the economic life —and so had the outlawry of associations of workingmen as criminal conspiracies. Yet the ideal of strict separation served the political purpose of protecting the economic forces from political control without impeding their influence in the political sphere.

What is peculiar to our age is not the interconnectedness of politics and economics, but its positive philosophic justification and its all-persuasiveness. The state is no longer looked upon solely as the umpire who sees to it that the rules of the game are observed and intervenes actively only if, as in the case of the railroads, the rules favor one player to excess and thereby threaten to disrupt the game itself. In our age, aside from still being the umpire, the state has also become the most powerful player, who, in order to make sure of the outcome, rewrites the rules of the game as he goes along. No longer does the government or society at large rely exclusively on the mechanisms of the market to ensure that the game keeps going. Both deem it the continuing duty of the government to see to it that it does. . . .

With the government thus exerting an enormous controlling, limiting, and stimulating influence on the economic life, the ability to influence the economic decisions of the government becomes an indispensable element in the competition for economic advantage. Economic competition manifests itself inevitably in competition for political influence. This political influence is exerted through two channels: control of, and pressure on, government personnel.

The most effective political influence is exerted by the direct control of government personnel. The economic organization which has its representatives elected to the legislature or appointed to the relevant administrative and executive positions exerts its political influence as far as the political influence of its representatives reaches. Insofar as the representatives of these economic organizations cannot decide the issue by themselves, the competition for political influence and, through it, economic advantage will be fought out within the collective bodies of the government by the representatives of different economic interests. While this relationship of direct control is typical in Europe, it is by no means unknown in the United States. State legislatures have been controlled by mining companies, public utilities, and railroads, and many individual members of Congress represent specific economic interests. Independent administrative agencies have come under the sway of the economic forces they were intended to control. The large-scale interchange of top personnel between business and the executive branch of the government cannot help but influence, however subtly and intangibly, decisions of the government relevant to the economic sphere.

However, in the United States the most important political influence is exerted through the influence of pressure groups. The decision of the government agent—legislator, independent administrator, member of the executive branch—is here not a foregone conclusion by virtue of the economic control to which he is subject. His decision is in doubt, for he is still open to different economic pressures. The competition for the determination of the decisions of the government takes place, not among the government agents themselves, but between the government agent, on the one hand, and several economic pressure groups, on the other. Only after this competition has been settled will the government agents, provided the issue is still in doubt, compete with one another.

The political struggle, ostensibly fought for victory in periodical elections by political parties, reveals itself in good measure as a contest of economic forces for the control of government action. In consequence, the decision of the government, and more particularly of legislatures, ostensibly rendered "on the merits of the case," tends to reflect the weight of economic influence and, at worst, to give political sanction to decisions that have been taken somewhere else. Legislators and administrators tend to transform themselves into ambassadors of economic forces, defending and promoting the interests of their mandatories in dealing with each other on behalf of them. The result is again a new feudalism which, like that of the Middle Ages, diminishes the authority of the civil government and threatens it with extinction by parceling out its several functions among economic organizations to be appropriated and used as private property. And just like the feudalism of the Middle Ages, these new concentrations of private power tend to command the primary loyalties of the individual citizens who owe them their livelihood and security. In the end, the constitutionally established government tends to become, in the words of Chief Justice Marshall, a "solemn mockery," glossing over the loss of political vitality with the performance of political rites.

If giant concentrations of economic power, in the form of business enterprises and labor unions, had thus become laws unto themselves, deciding with finality the matters vital to them and using the government only for the purpose of ratifying these decisions, they would not only have drained the life blood from the body politic but also have destroyed the vital energies of the economic system. For the vitality of the American economic system has resided in its ability to renew itself from new technological opportunities unfettered by the interests identified with an obsolescent technology. Seen from the vantage point of individual enterprise, this is what we call freedom of competition. This freedom of competition has been a function of the rules of the economic game, as formulated and enforced by the state.

Yet the new feudalism, if it is not controlled and restrained, must inevitably tend to abrogate these rules in order to assure the survival of the economic giants which, in turn, tend to take over the functions of the state. The consummation of this development, possible but not inevitable, would be a state of affairs in which for those giants the rule of life would not be freedom of competition, which might jeopardize their survival, but freedom from competition in order to secure their survival. The dynamics of the capitalistic system, especially in the United States, as continually destructive and creative as life itself, would then give way to a gigantic system of vested interests in which the established giants would use the state to make themselves secure from competitive displacement, only to die a slow death from attrition.

It is the measure of the quandary which modern society faces in this problem that the most obvious cure raises issues as grave as the disease. That cure is a state strong enough to hold its own against the concentrations of private power. Yet such a state, by being strong enough for this task, cannot fail to be also strong enough to control, restrain, and redirect the economic activities of everybody. In other words, as the liberal tradition correctly assumes, a strong government, whatever else it may be able to accomplish, threatens the liberties of the individual, especially in the economic sphere. Thus, modern society is faced with a real dilemma: a government which is too weak to threaten the freedom of the individual is also too weak to hold its own against the new feudalism; and a government which is strong enough to keep the new feudalism in check in order to protect the freedom of the many is also strong enough to destroy the freedom of all.

There can be no doubt as to which horn of the dilemma the government has chosen. It is in full retreat before the onslaught of private power and a passive onlooker at its unbridled exercise. It can no more see to it that the natural monopolies in the fields of transportation, utilities, and mass communications be used in the public interest than it can protect the public interest in its dealings with the suppliers of manufactured goods. The government has become the biggest customer of private industry, but it has also become one of its most hapless customers because it is among the most impecunious ones. In the field of military supplies in particular, the government is at the mercy of its suppliers. Only within very narrow limits can it do what customers in a market are supposed to be capable of doing if they do not like the terms of trade and the quality of the product: take its business elsewhere.

This dependence of the government on the suppliers of its military matériel evokes still another similarity with the feudal system. As the king had to buy military support from the feudal lords with parcels of his land and fragments of his power, so is the government within the terms of a commercial relationship at the mercy of its suppliers who control not only the quality of the product and the terms of trade but in good measure also the very identity of the product.

While the government is thus a weak contractual partner of the concentrations of private power, it is a virtually impotent bystander when it comes to the control over the exercise of private power. The government is incapable of enforcing the laws against a corrupt and tyrannical union. It cannot enforce the criminal laws against its officials, nor can it protect the members of the union against the abuse of power on the part of the union officials. The government of the union has become in good measure an autonomous private government, making and enforcing its own laws and pursuing its own policies, regardless of the public laws, the public policy, and the public interest.

What holds true of unions applies to the legitimate business enterprise, and it applies likewise to the illegitimate business enterprise, the racket. The racket is in our society the most highly developed type of private government in that it operates not within the letter of the public law, as do the private governments of legitimate business, but, by definition, outside it. Its distinctive characteristics are the institution of private criminal justice and methods of commercial competition resembling feudal warfare.

The retreat of the public power before the expansion of private governments has been particularly patent when it has failed to perform its most elemental function: to defend the public interest—and more particularly the public peace—against the war, industrial or physical, of private governments. Both Truman and Eisenhower were unable to prevent or settle industrial warfare between the giants of industry and labor. After Truman's seizure of the steel industry during the strike of 1952 had been invalidated on constitutional grounds, Eisenhower did not even attempt to intervene in the steel strike in 1959.

The issue in industrial wars of this kind is but ostensibly economic; in truth, it concerns the distribution of power between either management and labor or different labor unions or both. The economic settlement by which such a war is finally terminated amounts essentially to a conspiracy between management and labor to shift the economic burden of the settlement to the consumer. Whether or not such a settlement is actually supported and sanctioned by the government and whether or not its effects on consumer prices are postponed for tactical reasons, as was done in the settlement of the steel strike of 1959, does not affect the intrinsic nature of the settlement and the government's impotence in the face of it.

The impotence of the government to assert its authority against the private governments comes nowhere more strikingly to the fore than in its dealings with the rackets. A racket is actually not only a private government but also a countergovernment, complete with all the characteristics of a public government, such as police and military forces, executive organs, courts, taxation; and its similarity with a feudal fiefdom in its organization, functions, and relations to the public power, other rackets, and its outside tributaries is, indeed, most impressive. The racket as an institution has proven invulnerable to the authority of the public power. The best the latter has been able to accomplish has been sporadic harassment of the institution and the elimination of some of its members through criminal, contempt-of-court, and deportation proceedings. The very fact that the public power has found its most effective weapon in the income-tax laws, whose evasion constitutes neither the most serious of the misdeeds of the rackets nor one peculiar to them, demonstrates the weakness of the public power's position.

Harassment by the public power, more or less good-naturedly submitted to by private government, has become the essentially ritualistic method by which the public power asserts, and the private government submits to, its authority, similar in its symbolic function to the feudal obeisance. The arrest of known hoodlums, the indictment of labor racketeers, and the antitrust proceedings against business enterprises perform that function. The general futility of such public measures in terms of the institutional relationship—in contrast to their effects on certain individuals—only serves to underline the weakness of the public power and the semiautonomy of private government. Were it not for the public power's ability to tax the private governments—which has remained effective, albeit impaired—and for the public power's control over the most potent means of physical violence, the autonomy of the private governments would be complete. And it must be said in passing that the public power is weak in meting out justice even to individual wrongdoers; of 2,340,000 persons arrested in 1958 for major crimes only 88,780—that is, less than 4 per cent —were sent to state and federal prisons.

The decline of the public power, revealed by disintegration from within and usurpation from without, can be traced to a paralysis of will in the public power itself. That paralysis, in turn, has been brought on by that perversion of the democratic process which reduces the government to an agent of what is thought to be public opinion. Such a government, as we have seen, cannot be but a weak government. A government which considers itself the agent rather than the molder of public opinion cannot help setting in motion that fatal mechanism through which influence over public opinion is being surrendered by default to the counterelite of the private governments. Public opinion, which in view of its interests ought to be the ally of the public power, then becomes the instrument with which the private governments disarm the public power.

That so enfeebled a government still gives the appearance of governing and actually governs with a modicum of coherence is due to the discipline of the budget, the leadership of the President, and the immanent force of the national purpose.

The budget of the federal government is, as it were, the master plan that assigns missions to all the branches of the government and determines the material resources to be expended for their achievement. However much the quality of the achievement and its faithfulness to the budgetary policy may depend on individual performance, the budget constitutes a detailed charter of policy which ties all agents of the government to its choice of ends and means. It operates as the great centrifugal force that tends to neutralize the feudalism from within. It delineates, as it were, the outer limits which that feudalism cannot overstep without forsaking the sanction of the law.

The degree of firmness of these budgetary ties depends not only on the strict interpretation of the letter of the law but also and most importantly on the will and skill of the President and, to a much lesser extent, of Congress. The members of the executive branch are, legally speaking, merely agents of the President as Chief Executive, from whom they have received by way of delegation whatever authority they possess. The unity and purposefulness of action the federal government is capable of are largely determined by the degree to which the President is capable of making his conception of policy prevail throughout the executive branch and of imbuing with his will the myriad separate steps of which the execution of policy is composed. That task of the President as the initiator, executor, and supervisor of policy is served by the administrative and political measures through which the Presidential presence makes itself felt at all levels of the execution of policy. It is also served more intangibly and perhaps more importantly by the President as the articulator and living symbol of the national purpose.

The public power is weakened and threatened with disintegration from within and without by a new distribution of power, by new private interests, and by the universalism of the democratic processes misunderstanding the nature both of democracy and of executive decision. These threats are of a material and, to a greater or lesser degree, of a tangible nature; they are social facts that are subject to direct empirical observation. Yet the public power is being protected and in a certain measure immunized against disintegration by a factor which is intangible in that its existence can be ascertained only by indirection from certain words, deeds, and conditions pointing to its existence. That factor is the all-persuasiveness of the national purpose. Both the defenders and the opponents of the public power—like the partisans of the other great political controversies of the past—are parties to the purposeful consensus which sets America apart from other nations. They are Americans before they are partisans. The vitality of that consensus stands in inverse relation to the strength of the disintegrating factors threatening the purposeful unity of the nation itself. The disintegration of the public power remains relative so long as the national consensus outweighs in the thoughts and deeds of the people the commitment to parochial interests. That disintegration becomes absolute and, hence, disastrous for the public power when this commitment takes precedence over the consensus. Either the public power will then survive only as a shadow to which autonomous feudal fiefdoms will pay ritual tribute, or else it will be destroyed in one cataclysmic act through revolution and civil war, perhaps to be resurrected by one feudal power prevailing over the others. . . .

38 THE MARBLED MIXTURE

- *Michael D. Reagan*

While public attention has been largely directed to conflicts between government and business, a much more significant development has gone relatively unnoticed: the gradual erasure of long-standing distinctions between private and public economic activities and, as a result, the increased amalgamation of the sectors. The most recent illustration of this trend is the communications satellite system and the peculiar corporate arrangement under which it is to operate—an arrangement which makes American Telephone and Telegraph, the National Aeronautics and Space Administration, and the Federal Communications Commission partners in the communications business. Special legislation created the corporation, which will have three board members appointed by the President and will operate within guidelines specified by Congress, in order to ensure operation in the public interest. Hence, it is not an ordinary private corporation. Yet it is not a public corporation in the sense that TVA is, for half of its capital stock is available for sale to the public in the same manner as the stock of AT&T itself, half to the communications carriers; and the investors rather than the public at large will receive the dividend share of any profits that may be produced.

Government by Contract

Experimental forms of collaboration between industry and government have also developed in the atomic energy program and in the field of missiles and rocketry, where defense agencies not only have placed orders for hardware but have delegated to private, nonprofit corporations the prior jobs of developing the weapons system and even the strategic concepts into which the systems are to be fitted. These programs—communications, missiles, atomic energy—are all notable for being dependent to a considerable extent on ad-

From Michael D. Reagan, *The Managed Economy* (New York: Oxford University Press, 1963), pp. 190–210. © Copyright 1963 by Oxford University Press, Inc. Reprinted by permission.

vanced scientific and technological research. Such research is becoming ever more prominent, but, since it is too expensive and risky for private industry to finance on its own, there is certain to be a continuation and expansion of government aid and participation in these programs. In 1962, the national government allocated 14.7 billion dollars for research and development, of which over 80 per cent goes for work contracted out to private industry.

The "contracting out" system of research and development under which a public agency contracts to have the work done by a nongovernmental organization—which may be an ordinary business firm, a nonprofit corporation, or an educational institution—is advantageous to the government because it provides greater flexibility and ease in shifting resources from one project to another than would be the case within a governmental establishment, and it by-passes the restrictive regulations on the number of employees and their salaries. Because salaries for top-flight scientists, engineers, and other specialists in government laboratories and arsenals are much lower than private pay for equivalent skills, the contracting system may be the only way that government can obtain the services it needs. By contract, public funds are used by the private contractor to pay specialists the higher salaries that government cannot pay them as civil servants under existing law. The government thus obtains needed services indirectly, yet sometimes loses those few men technically qualified to assess the quality of the contractors' work!

The problem of staffing the public service is not the crucial point, though; it is instead the confusion of public and private interest. When a research and development firm does government work on contract, and almost no work for private sector clients or customers, is that firm public or private? Are its employees public servants? In form, the firm and its employees remain private; yet the client is public, the task is public, the salaries are paid out of appropriations. Thus, the firm and its employees are public in crucial respects.

A number of questions have arisen in this area for which there are no ready answers. Since tax money is being used, should the government write into its contracts controls over executive compensation schemes? If government is indirectly exceeding its own salary limits, should the practice of competitive pay without legal limits be followed in the explicitly public sector, too, at least in certain agencies or for certain types of positions? (We have moved in this direction in a small way with special legislation setting higher salaries for selected categories and specified numbers of employees in certain defense and high-technology programs.) When the firm is a profit-seeking producer, paid by government and often using government-owned plant facilities, should the contract include controls over dividends, advertising and promotion expenditures, patent rights, and collective bargaining agreements, since the taxpayers are often the largest investors?

So far, the questions concern how far the government should intervene in the "private" aspects of such firms. An even more important problem arises from the use of private firms as enforcement administrators for a variety of public policies. When a business firm enters into a contract with the government, the contract gives the government a handle for imposing requirements that would be beyond its authority in the absence of the contract. The quasi-public nature of the contracting firm is given implicit recognition by requirements that the firm conduct itself similarly to a government agency in abiding by policies that bind such an agency. The range of policies includes nonsegregation in employment, adherence to prevailing wages in the area of the contractor's plants, determination of security risks among employees, and positive steps to promote maximum use of small businesses in subcontracting of defense orders.

A kind of decentralization by contract ("federalism by contract," Don K. Price has called it) is involved here, with national policies carried to local areas through contracting firms rather than through subordinate layers of government. Each prime contractor, for example, has been required in recent years to maintain a subcontracting office whose public task is to seek out small-business suppliers. This is done in order to counteract the main trend in defense contract awards, which concentrate prime contracts among a very small number of firms; for example, each year approximately two-thirds of such contracts go to one hundred firms. Whether such a program can ever be very effective may be doubted, but that is irrelevant to the fact that private business firms are acting as *de facto* antitrust administrators under this system.

Although a nondiscrimination clause is included in each government contract, producers, especially those with southern plants, have been slow to comply so long as the contracting agencies paid little attention to compliance. Under the present administration, however, the President's Committee on Equal Employment Opportunity has taken vigorous steps to ensure compliance. In at least two instances in the spring of 1962, firms were put on notice that because of their record of noncompliance they would receive no further government business unless and until they had shown compliance in good faith. Contracts thus become sticks as well as carrots, giving the government leverage over the internal policies of corporate managements wherever the contract relationship exists or is contemplated. As the size of the public sector and the purchasing role of the government increase, this leverage becomes more extensive. The relationship is not unilateral, however. By using firms as administrative arms, the government also becomes more dependent on private managers for effectuating public policies.

Most dubious of the delegations of public functions to private managements is the industrial personnel security program, which has required contractors to make determinations of a strictly political nature regarding a man's political beliefs and associations. Managements have no competence in this area and are bound to play it safe at the expense of their employees. . . .

Dual Assignments

Another mode of public-private intermingling, not confined to defense, yet most highly developed there, is the fusion of public and private roles in the same persons. Because of the technical complexity of governmental programs today, government must have expert advice on whom to hire, what firms to ask to do certain jobs, and the feasibility of desired projects. To supply this knowledge, literally thousands of advisory committees have sprouted up all over the government. A congressional committee report which just listed the members of each committee filled five substantial volumes in 1955. There is danger that public policy may be twisted or directed by such committees to the advantage of particular firms or industries. Sometimes a trade association may dominate a committee to the detriment of independent producers; sometimes the large firms may dominate to the detriment of the small ones not represented.

In the midfifties, Representative Emanuel Celler of New York used his House Antitrust Subcommittee for extensive investigation of these and related problems, which have also greatly interested the Justice Department's Antitrust Division. The latter, partly in response to Celler's hearings, has set up guidelines for industry advisory committees which are designed to guard against the use of public policy for private purposes. Among the requirements it has established are breadth of representation from all segments of an industry and the chairing of meetings and setting of agenda by a government representative. But, most important, it has required that the advice of such committees be reviewed independently by the government agency receiving it. Without such checks on the committees' recommendations, the advisers from the private sector become in effect the public decision makers, and public policy becomes controlled by private policy. Scandals in stock-piling programs and in the award of rapid amortization certificates during the Korean War exemplify what can result from carelessly entrusting public business to private persons.

A more direct problem of the conflict of public and private interest revolves around the use of WOC's (without compensation employees), successors to the dollar-a-year men of World War II. The WOC is a person on private salary who is employed fulltime by the government. The rationale behind this system is that some men cannot afford to take the great loss of income involved in switching from private to public payroll, but the government cannot afford to do without their knowledge; hence they work for the government, but draw their private salaries. In wartime production agencies —the War Production Board in World War II, the National Production Authority in the Korean War—this arrangement was accepted as a necessary evil, and it was hoped that patriotic motivation would be sufficiently strong to cause the WOC's to work only for the public interest and not for the advantage of the industries from which they came.

Although the Eisenhower administration espoused the idea of separating business from government, it actually took a further step in bringing them closer together by replacing the National Production Authority at the end of the Korean War with an agency which combined residual defense production controls and Department of Commerce services to business. The Business and Defense Services Administration until 1957 had WOC's in charge of most of its twenty-odd industry divisions. The aluminum division was headed by a WOC; three assistant administrators of the agency were WOC's; and an industry advisory committee was used extensively. The result was a situation in which a committee of private representatives of aluminum firms chose a man to head the aluminum division, then gave advice to this "public" official who remained on his private payroll; and finally this advice and this man's decisions were reviewed by an assistant administrator of the agency who was also on private salary. Here a major component of a public agency had been effectively captured by private interests.

The Regulatory Straddle

Confusion of public and private purposes is notable also in the regulatory agencies, for it has been the standard observation in the past few years that the regulated tend to capture the regulators. The Interstate Commerce Commission, for example, was for many years more a protector and promoter of the railroads than their regulator. The same can be said, in lesser or greater degree at different times, of the commissions regulating power, communications, and air and motor transport. Partly this results from statutory requirements: the Civil Aeronautics Board has an impossible mandate from Congress, which directs it to promote the economic health of the airlines while at the same time regulating rates in the interests of maximum public use of air travel. In larger part it is a matter of political power. The regulated industries are well organized and in continuous contact with the regulators and with the nominally overseeing congressional committees; the consuming public is not. And partly it is a matter of procedure: the regulatory agencies, encumbered in judicial procedures, have rarely had the time to draw up public policy guides to action. The policy vacuum has been filled by the initiative of the regulated firms and the accidents of case development. Motor carriers, for example, scored gains in recent years over the railroads, despite the ICC's apparent sympathy for the latter, by having a clear policy goal of their own and making it ICC policy through a series of initiatives in filing rate schedules.

To the extent that the commissions and boards are captured by the interests they are regulating, public policy becomes not an independent assessment of the consumer's needs but simply publicly sanctioned private policy. This phenomenon has led to some breast beating among liberals, bemoaning their own failure to realize that the effective manning of a regulatory program depends on who the regulators are and which groups are exerting the most pressure on the agencies. Recent developments suggest, however, that there is a more hopeful view: if regulatory programs can become promotional, promotional programs can also provide a handle for regulation. To put it another way, what is designed as an aid to the private sector can be used to achieve public objectives.

Some examples of this phenomenon can be cited. The CAB promotes feeder airlines by direct subsidies where traffic is too light to pay its own way at approved rates. The subsidy can be used, as one report has hinted it will be used, to push mergers, desired by CAB, between strong and weak carriers even when the carriers involved are not eager to merge. Since the railroads are now living in part on government aid, they, too, may find that loan guarantees and other forms of aid can become levers for governmental intervention in managerial decisions.

When the Eisenhower administration was encountering difficulties in persuading oil companies "voluntarily" to curb their imports of crude oil in 1958, a "buy American" order issued to federal agencies was used as a regulatory device as well, by requiring that sellers of oil to government agencies prove their compliance with the voluntary import curbs as a condition of participation in sales to the agencies. With the import curbs now on a compulsory basis (at the insistence of one part of the industry and against the wishes of the Eisenhower administration), a stronger handle is available to the government. The national government lacks authority over oil and gasoline prices, but, if it considered a price boost to be unreasonable, it could threaten to enlarge the quotas for imports to force the price down by increasing supply.

Government involvement in housing holds a similar potential, as illustrated by the November, 1962, executive order forbidding racial discrimination in the sale of federally aided housing. Since almost all housing is federally aided in one way or another, the national government is thus able to implement a non-discrimination policy in a vital area through executive action linked to measures voted through Congress, with southern support, as promotion for the housing industry.

Quite apart from this bridging of the public-private distinction by turning promotional measures into regulatory instruments, the very nature of public utility regulation involves a fusion of public and private management as a halfway house between government ownership and private business. The moment government begins to regulate an industry, especially its prices and, therefore, its profits, it becomes a joint manager with the corporations regulated, responsible for their survival and concerned in all corporate decisions that affect survival. Outright government ownership would be less a violation of laissez-faire expectations, for at least then an industry is clearly public; under the regulatory commission system, firms are neither private nor public, but both.

Affected with a Public Interest

Often public-private economic relationships are subordinated to the legal profession's understanding of the economic system. One example is the legal doctrine of a public utility, as reflected in Supreme Court decisions. For many years the Court drew a rigid distinction between private businesses and those which ancient English common law had defined as being "affected with a public interest." The latter category was a narrow one, including natural monopolies and businesses which by their nature opened their doors to all comers, for example, a roadside inn. All else was private, and what was private was legally beyond the reach of regulation.

In time, however, even the law bends to the facts. In the midst of the Great Depression, a New York State milk-price control statute provided the occasion for Justice Owen D. Roberts to cast aside the received doctrine and proclaim the continuity of the public and private sectors. Said the justice, "There is no closed class or category of business affected with a public interest, and the function of the courts . . . is to determine in each case whether circumstances indicate the challenged regulation as a reasonable exertion of governmental authority or condemn it as arbitrary or discriminatory." Although there was some backing and filling in the next three years, the position Justice Roberts enunciated has established itself and thus accommodated the law to economic fact, at least in this respect. Now the questions concern the wisdom of the policy and the feasibility of achieving congressional backing where necessary, but not the constitutionality of the policy: the law no longer interposes a wall between government and the economy, between public and private.

The trend of our time is in quite another direction; it runs toward explicit recognition that what is private in form is often public in substance. The whole question of the constitutionalization of private governments is involved, and as Adolf Berle has observed, this is an area of inchoate law, but, nevertheless, of a clearly emerging pattern. An example Berle uses is the case of *Marsh v. Alabama*. It concerned a company town and the efforts of an evangelizing group to use the streets of that town to spread its message. Looking beyond the formal fact that the company owned the streets and sidewalks, the Supreme Court concentrated on the general public use made of the streets and found that, because a public function was being served, the constitutional protections of the people's rights that control governments applied to this company-owned community.

As this page was being written, sit-in cases were being heard before the Supreme Court. The question in these is whether a private restaurant is exempt from the equal protection clause because it is private or is bound to nondiscrimination because it devotes itself to a public use. Whatever the outcome in these particular cases, the eventual constitutional position seems likely to be the latter one. Although courts are generally not considered the most innovative of social institutions, and although the Supreme Court once too rigidly separated the public and private spheres, the judiciary (at least the higher courts) seems today to realize better than Congress or the political parties the inadequacies of the conventional institutional labels.

Political Competition

Now that business pays only lip service to the idea that government intervention should be avoided at all costs, individual businesses are increasingly using the political arena as an instrument in intrabusiness power struggles and are trying to influence public policies in particular industries to gain competitive advantages. Usually it is the weaker economic group which actively seeks to engage government as an ally, rather than government seeking out such groups. The groups holding original power are satisfied with the status quo and hence tend to use government less often; they can rely on direct economic power in their competition with other industrial segments.

The now classic instance of the use of political power by an economic group whose market power was low was the successful campaign of the

National Association of Retail Druggists for fair trade laws in the 1930's, resulting in the Robinson-Patman Act. Independent druggists found themselves put at a disadvantage by cut-rate chain stores and by preferential discounts the chains received from producers and wholesalers, and they had no economic leverage with which to fight back. So they turned to politics. Being small businessmen, well distributed geographically across all congressional districts, with homogeneity of interest and of semiprofessional status (most drugstore proprietors are registered pharmacists), they had a good social-economic base for the exercise of legislative power. They used this base to good advantage, and the fair trade acts passed by Congress gave them price protection and a better market position in relation to the chains.

Since in most fields retailers are small and numerous, while manufacturers are large and few, market power most often lies with the latter. There are exceptions, as immediately after World War II, when automobile manufacturers were very dependent on the dealers, who were able to use the market situation to improve the terms of their franchises. But this is not to say that the development of this market power was autonomous and independent of politics, for it grew in a specific legal environment. In his description of attempts by the National Automobile Dealers Association (NADA) to obtain legislative solutions to their grievances against manufacturers, Joseph C. Palamountain calls attention to the political and economic factors involved:

> Dealers' grievances existed because manufacturers were favored by the existing framework of law. Both the rise of large corporations and the interpretation of contracts resulted from a public policy primarily stated by the courts. Another general policy—disapproval of price fixing and other restraints of trade—limited dealers' attempts to end their grievances by joint economic actions. Thus even the initial economic problems were vitally affected—almost defined—by governmental actions made in pursuance of general policies. Yet the groups affected had virtually no part in the formation of these policies. . . .
>
> Thus far political aspects of our political economy seem to be more basic, since general governmental policies define dealers' economic conditions and confine their political reactions, but in just as many respects economic aspects appear to be more causative. When dealers did win aid from federal and state governments, it was not a simple and automatic use of political strength. Problems of organization constantly plagued the dealers. The N.A.D.A. never organized more than a small proportion of dealers, nor was it successful in producing programmatic agreement. This weakness in part reflects the economic power of the manufacturers, who prevented some dealers from joining associations, "persuaded" others not to seek certain political objectives, and placed wholesale distributors and manufacturer-controlled dealers in strategic offices in at least several state and local associations.
>
> A more important cause of weakness was diversity among dealers. . . . The economic environment not only provides the bases for political conflict, it also conditions the outcome.

Because Congressmen and Senators are often small businessmen or lawyers in middle-sized cities and have small businessmen as their major clients, congressional committees are often willing to be used as sounding boards for retailer and small-supplier grievances against the giant producers. Hearings by the Senate Antitrust Subcommittee in 1955, under the chairman at the time of Joseph C. O'Mahoney of Wyoming, are an outstanding example. Dealer after dealer went on the witness stand to give vent to his grievances against manufacturers who had given them impossible sales quotas, dumped unwanted accessories on them, told them what promotions to run and how to arrange their showrooms, and as sanction for these edicts forced on the dealers one-way contracts in which the obligations fell on the dealer and the privileges—including cancelation without cause or means of appeal—on the producer. Although the legislative result of the hearings was meager, the publicity was sufficient to bring about some changes in the relationship. The producers gave longer-term franchises, and at least some of them established review boards for dealer grievances, although some of these were so structured as to make one wonder whether they would be effective.

Inevitably, as the government's purchasing role increases, so does competition among producers for relative shares of the procurement dollar. But the competition is of a different kind from that defined by the economists; it is political competition carried out through direct lobbying in Congress, through defense producers' hiring former admirals and generals to improve their access to Pentagon decision makers, and through advertising campaigns used as indirect lobbying. In 1959, for instance, when there was a congressional dispute over the relative merits of the Bomarc and Nike missiles, the respective manufacturers engaged in a battle of full-page advertisements. Some of these advertisements listed 8,000 subcontractors, showing the spread of these over many congressional districts and implying that there would be a disastrous economic impact if the Congressmen did not appropriate sufficient funds for continued procurement of the missile that kept all these suppliers in business. Douglas Aircraft has called its military advertising "a part of our partnership with Uncle Sam's Armed Forces," and the firm discusses its advertising program each year with the services for which it is producing hardware. Sometimes the initiative for these advertisements comes from the competing services, as when the Army asked Western Electric to extol the Nike-Zeus, to compete with the Air Force's Bomarc.

The financing of this form of competition also involves a mixing of public and private components, for the advertising costs are eventually charged to the government. The extent of lobbying for the aerospace industries as a whole—in their joint competition against other possible uses of public funds and to gain better contract terms for themselves—is indicated by the growth of the Aerospace Industries Association, with an annual budget of over one and a half million dollars. Defense contractors' contributions to this trade association are charged to the government in the contract as a cost of business and then deducted from income tax because the contribution is to a nonprofit organization. Then the money is used to lobby for legislative measures favorable to the industry!

Sometimes the lobbying takes a form honored in private business, but looked upon less favorably in the public sector: entertaining on a business expense account. Representative F. Edward Hebert, chairman of a House Armed Services Subcommittee, held a revealing discussion of public-private characteristics of the aircraft industry with the chairman of the Glen L. Martin Company. Hebert suggested that such wining and dining is inappropriate in public activity, and the following exchange occurred:

BUNKER: Yes, but private industry, sir.
HEBERT: Totally a government product.
BUNKER: Yes, but private industry, sir.
HEBERT: But totally government, totally subsidized by the government, if you will.
BUNKER: I don't like the use of the word subsidized.

A standard procedure of business is to claim defense-relatedness when this suits its purposes, even though the external observer may find the connection tenuous. Thus manufacturers of electric generators protested a TVA award of a contract for generators to an English firm (at a saving of $5 million) on the ground that the government should stop such foreign purchases for the sake of national security. They did not succeed in that particular case, but they, and other producers, have obtained a buy-American act which required that foreign bids had to be at least 6 per cent below the lowest American bid before a government agency could buy abroad. TVA had required 20 per cent, and still the British bid was lower.

As mentioned at the beginning of this section, economic use of the political arena includes attempts to turn public policy directly to one's own benefit, as well as to improve one's position in relation to competitors. The tax laws and legislation for protection of workers are cases in point. The oil industry's successful defense of the depletion allowance has generated over one hundred depletion allowances of varying percentages for a great variety of extractive industries. The hour and wage laws, social security program, and unemployment compensation program are shot through with exceptions and exemptions that reflect the power of particular industries in Congress rather than any rationally defensible criteria for inclusion and exclusion. Farm workers being about the weakest bargaining group in the United States either politically or economically, farm owners and food processors have been particularly successful in obtaining exemptions from the requirements imposed on other employers to protect employees from exploitation.

A particularly good example of this political approach to competition is recounted in Cornelius P. Cotter's *Government and Private Enterprise:*

An official of a regional trade association of exempt truckers went before the committee studying the problems of the railroads to "demand regulation." Regulation of what? Here lies the brilliance of the tactic: regulation of the exempt truckers. In other words, the truckers, who have built up their businesses under the protection of the exempt clause and on the basis of vigorous bargaining for rates, would not mind enactment of legislation which entitled each of the existing truckers to a certificate of convenience and necessity as a statutory right, and limited the access of newcomers to the field. Such legislation would "stabilize" competition in the trucking of agricultural products by restricting participation in the business and by eliminating rate competition—the ICC would set rates.

But it is in the area of collective bargaining legislation that perhaps the most noticeable illustration of the political nature of the economic power struggles can be found. The old American Federation of Labor was just as adamantly opposed to "government intervention" in the bargaining process as was the National Association of Manufacturers, but, once the Wagner Act was passed, both sides abandoned laissez-faire in favor of a more realistic strategy of influencing the direction of labor legislation. In fact, the NAM overcame its general opposition to "internal" interference to such an extent that it became the major proponent of measures to extend the degree of intervention far beyond that provided by the Wagner Act. That is, the Taft-Hartley Act's prohibition of the closed shop and its permission for states to outlaw the union shop also—both originated by the NAM—constitute intervention into the substance of the bargain, whereas the earlier law had affected only the procedure of bargaining.

A Marbled Mixture

From these conceptual, legislative, judicial, and political mergings of the public and private spheres of the economy we can draw generalizations in three areas: the nature of competition, the meaning of private enterprise, and criteria for distinguishing between the private and public sectors.

The concept of competition in a politically directed economy should emphasize power rather than price. Market power on the one hand, political power on the other, and the interrelationships and reciprocal influences between these are the crucial factors in an economy where the private sector is characterized by administered prices and the decisions of the public sector vitally affect the environment of profit seeking. The skills of the political scientist and those of the economist must be fused if adequate analysis of the system and appropriate prescriptions for public policy are to be developed. As the multitudinous ramifications of public policy on the fortunes of private economic groups become more evident, legislators and administrators will need to analyze more consciously and more systematically the consequences of existing and proposed programs, to ensure not only that public actions lead to desired economic performance but also that equity and a balance of power between groups are obtained. As we become more aware of the extent of political activity by economic groups, we will need also to examine more consciously its impact on the integrity of the democratic process. In short, we cannot afford to continue the outmoded, too comfortable pattern of separating the public and private spheres in our thinking about the role of government in a "free enterprise" system.

Second, we find that private competitive enterprise is no longer either private or competitive in the traditional meaning of these words. A realistic, if slightly cynical, definition of private enterprise as it now operates might be as follows:

private enterprise is a politicoeconomic system in which each private group seeks to direct public policy to the improvement of its competitive position, share of national income, or bargaining power vis-à-vis other segments of the society. The private elements in the system lie in the insistence by business that, in return for public benefits, no limitations be placed on resultant profits or managerial discretion and that the public good is not to be planned for, but is to arise as a by-product of private planning for private purposes.

Third, what is public and what is private can no longer be defined abstractly or institutionally; the dividing lines are drawn rather from study of changing attitudes and situations. Whatever is seen to affect the public interest *de facto* becomes proper matter for public action *de jure*. The price of steel, for instance, remains a private matter so long as it does not notably upset the stability of the economy or in some other way affect the larger public beyond the producer and the immediate industrial purchaser. But once it does have some publicly noticed effect, it becomes a matter for public action.

The definitions of "private" and "public" in the economy thus become relative, not absolute, concepts. An economic decision or situation or institution is private when, and only as long as, we think of it as private. It is public when another economic group, the general public, or a government agency thinks of it as affecting some publicly held value. The distinction between a public and a private matter now depends on the answer given to the question: How does it affect the public at this time?

Dealer franchises in the automobile industry, discussed above, exemplify this way of looking at public and private interest. Institutionally and ideologically private, these became public, at least temporarily, when a legislative committee became interested in their implications regarding the power position of small business, and the politically conscious community became disturbed over the problems of arbitrary control exercised by one group of men over another.

Often public programs develop as responses to inadequacies in the private sector which have public consequences of politically significant dimensions. As Gerhard Colm and Geiger have written, "Had there not been some misuse of economic power by private enterprise, there would have been no antitrust laws. Had there not been some substandard wages, there would have been no Wage-Hour Act. Had there been no severe depression, there probably would have been no Employment Act." That is to say, when private handling of economic affairs went wrong, these affairs became public instead of private.

Once it is clear that the economy is a marbled mixture of private and public forces and institutions, and that the goal of obtaining the maximum in economic productivity with the maximum of democracy in processes and social structure requires constant, conscious deliberative action in both sectors, the leading question that emerges is the adequacy of existing institutional structure and public policies for dealing with a system far more complex than the Founding Fathers—or even most living legislators, public officials, and private managers—ever envisaged. The burden of the last part of this book, therefore, will be to show that the existing patterns are very inadequate and to put forth some propositions for reformation of the American political economy in the hope that they will be debated.

Bibliographical Note

Communications Satellite Act of 1962, 76 *Stat.* 419, P.L. 87–624; John G. Palfrey, "Atomic Energy: A New Experiment in Government-Industry Relations," *Columbia Law Review* (March, 1956); 1962 research figures in report published in *Syracuse Herald-American,* December 30, 1962; Interagency (Bell) Committee, *Report to the President on Government Contracting for Research and Development,* Office of the White House Press Secretary, April 30, 1962; Don K. Price, *Government and Science* (New York: New York University Press, 1954); House Government Operations Committee, *Replies from Executive Departments and Federal Agencies to Inquiry Regarding Use of Advisory Committees,* Part I–VII, 84th Cong., 2d Sess., 1956, Committee Prints; Samuel H. Beer, "Group Representation in Britain and the United States," in *Unofficial Government: Pressure Groups and Lobbies, Annals of the American Academy of Political and Social Science* (September, 1958); House Subcommittee on the Judiciary, *Hearings, WOC's and Government Advisory Groups,* 84th Cong., 1st Sess., 1955; Michael D. Reagan, "The Business and Defense Services Administration, 1953–57," *Western Political Quarterly* (June, 1961); Michael D. Reagan, "Serving Two Masters: Problems in the Employment of Dollar-a-Year and Without Compensation Personnel" (doctoral dissertation, Princeton University, 1959); Marver H. Bernstein, *Regulating Business by Independent Commission* (Princeton: Princeton University Press, 1955); Joseph C. Palamountain, "The Administrator's Role: Issues and Hypotheses," a paper delivered at the annual meeting of the American Political Science Association, New York, September, 1960; *Nebbia v. New York,* 291 U.S. 502 (1934); *NLRB v. Jones & Laughlin Steel Corporation,* 301 U.S. 1 (1937); *Marsh v. Alabama,* 326 U.S. 501 (1945); Joseph C. Palamountain, *The Politics of Distribution* (Cambridge: Harvard University Press, 1955); Al Toffler, "The Airpower Lobby: Salesmen in Uniform," *Nation* (November 30, 1957), and "The Airpower Lobby: Who Will Make the Missiles?", *Nation* (December 7, 1957); Cornelius P. Cotter, *Government and Private Enterprise* (New York: Holt, Rinehart, and Winston, 1960); Gerhard Colm and Theodore Geiger, *The Economy of the American People* (Washington: National Planning Association, 1958).

39 THE CONTRACT STATE

■ *H. L. Nieburg*

American society has shown considerable resilience in adapting to rapid change. When need arises, an existing institution leaps to meet it, becoming quite a different institution in the process. In recent years the industrial corporation, which "began life as a sort of legal trick to spread the ownership of industrial equipment over a lot of people,"[1] has evolved into a routine and

From H. L. Nieburg, *In the Name of Science* (Chicago: Quadrangle Books, 1966), pp. 184–199. Reprinted by permission of Quadrangle Books. © Copyright 1966 by H. L. Nieburg.

immensely powerful method of organizing large undertakings. But the relation-ship between individuals and corporations has been greatly modified by the overshadowing concentration of corporate power. Government has ceased to be merely a passive arbiter of "the rules of the game" and is forced to become an omnipresent force for balancing the competition for values and controlling the dynamics of social change.

Government has become the economy's largest buyer and consumer. The government contract, improvised, *ad hoc,* and largely unexamined, has become an increasingly important device for intervention in public affairs, not only to procure goods and services but to achieve a variety of explicit or inadvertent policy ends—allocating national resources, organizing human efforts, stimu-lating economic activity, and distributing status and power. The government contract has risen to its present prominence as a social management tool since World War II, achieving in two decades a scope and magnitude that now rival simple subsidies, tariffs, taxes, direct regulation, and positive action programs in their impact on the nature and quality of American life. This evolution has occurred quietly and gradually through a series of improvised reactions to specific problems. Its central role has been achieved without public consideration of far-reaching social and political implications. Even today there is precious little consciousness of the trend; political leaders tend to see each contract as an isolated procurement action, overlooking the general pattern. Just as federal grants-in-aid to state and local governments have (since 1933) become principal means for national integration of divided local jurisdictions, so federal contracting with private corporations is creating a new kind of economic federalism.

The implications of grants-in-aid have acquired some clarity: state taxation still takes care of traditional functions, while new and greatly expanded activi-ties devolve upon local bodies through national decision making, the states operating more and more as administrative districts for centrally established policies. Here, decision making is nationalized under the constraints of public attention and democratic politics. On the other hand, economic federalism based on contracts holds implications that are far from clear. To some degree, the forms and effects of contracting evade the forums of democracy, obscur-ing the age-old conflict between private and public interests. Mobilized to serve national policy, private contractors interpenetrate government at all levels, exploiting the public consensus of defense, space, and science to aug-ment and perpetuate their own power, inevitably confusing narrow special interests with those of the nation.

Explicit authority for the United States government to conduct its business by contract is not found in the Constitution, but has historically been accepted as a means of achieving explicitly constitutional objectives. There is ample precedent, such as the use of railroads for troop movements, or General McClellan's arrangements with the Pinkerton Detective Agency for espionage against the southern Confederacy.

What is new is the persistence and growth of government-industry contract relationships under which, in the words of David E. Bell (then director of the

Budget Bureau), "numbers of the nation's most important business corporations do the bulk of their work with the government." The Martin Company, for example, does 99 per cent of its business with the government. Bell asked: "Well, is it a private agency or is it a public agency?" Organized as a private corporation and "philosophically . . . part of the private sector," yet "it obviously has a different relationship to governmental decisions and the government's budget . . . than was the case when General Motors or U.S. Steel sold perhaps 2 or 5 per cent of their annual output to government bodies." [2] Except in time of war, the government traditionally has not been the dominant customer for any private firm. The contract state of the postwar world must be viewed as a drastic innovation full of unfamiliar portents.

Grandiose claims are heard on all sides for the "unique contribution" that the contract mechanism has made in preserving "the free-enterprise system" at a time when it could have been damaged. Atomic energy has been cited as an example of the new collaboration: "Without contracts, it would be government-owned and operated. With contracts, one person in sixteen in the industry works for government; the other fifteen work for contractors." [3] An aerospace journal cites space technology as "the fastest moving, typically free-enterprise and democratic industry yet created," achieving these values "not on salesmanship" (that is, traditional quality/cost competitiveness) but "on what is needed most—intellectual production, the research payoff." [4] Lyndon B. Johnson, while Vice-President, argued: "If we want to maintain credibility of our claim to the superiority of a free political system—and a free private enterprise system—we cannot seriously entertain the thought of precipitating now so massive a disillusionment as would follow a political default on our commitments in space exploration." [5]

The government contract has made it possible to perform new tasks deemed essential without direct additions to the size of federal government, thus preserving the alleged rights of private property and profit. But these huzzahs ignore the real ambiguity of the system that is emerging—neither "free" nor "competitive," in which the market mechanism of supply/demand (the price seeking the level which best serves over-all productivity and social needs) has been abolished for key sectors of the economy, its place taken by the process of government policy and political influence. Instead of a free enterprise system, we are moving toward a government-subsidized private-profit system.

Key to the Kingdom

Unlike older government-fostered industries, the new contractor empire operates without the yardsticks of adequate government in-house capability or a civilian market in areas where research and development has become *the* critical procurement and the crux of the system. As described in the 1962 Bell Report: The companies involved "have the strongest incentives to seek contracts for research and development work which will give them both the know-how and the preferred position to seek later follow-on production contracts." [6] Favored corporations that win R&D work thereafter exploit a number of special advantages: They may achieve sole-source or prime contractor status, which eliminates competition and dilutes all cost and performance evaluation. The open-end, cost-plus nature of the contract instrument, the lack of product specifications, official tolerance of spending overruns, all of which increase the total contract and fee (in a sense rewarding wasteful practices and unnecessary technical complication), permit violation of all rules of responsible control and make possible multiple tiers of hidden profits. The systems management or prime contractor role enables favored companies to become powerful industrial brokers using unlimited taxpayer funds and contract awards to strengthen their corporate position, cartelize the contract market, and exert political influence.

In less than a decade the area surrounding Washington, D.C., has become one of the nation's major R&D concentrations. Every large corporation has found it necessary to establish field offices in proximity to NASA, the Pentagon, and Capitol Hill. Most of these new installations emphasize public relations and sales rather than research and development. The Washington area now ranks first in the nation for scientific personnel (per 1,000 population), although the major product is company promotion and politics rather than science.

The gross figures provide an index of the economic impact: the 1966 federal budget called for $23.7 billion in new obligational authority for defense and space—$11.4 billion for Defense Department procurement of hardware and control systems, $6.7 billion for R&D, $5.26 billion for NASA (virtually all R&D), and an additional $272 million for space-related R&D conducted by the Weather Bureau, the National Science Foundation, and the Atomic Energy Commission. Over 90 per cent of this flows to the highly concentrated aerospace industry.[7] Another $3.3 billion was budgeted for other kinds of R&D, making a total of $27 billion. The 1967 budget allocated more than $30 billion to aerospace. Space, defense, and R&D together now comprise the single most substantial allocation of federal funds, towering over all other programs. In the mid-1960's, government R&D (excluding related procurement) stabilized between 2 and 3 per cent of the GNP. Cumulative missile/space spending in the decade which began in 1955 amounted to over $100 billion (Defense Department, $84 billion; NASA, $18 billion), and the remainder of the sixties will add at least an additional $125 billion.[8] Virtually every department and agency of the federal government is involved to some extent in R&D contracting, although the Defense Department and NASA account for more than 96 per cent.

The first result of this staggering outpour has been the artificial inflation of R&D costs which has enabled contractors to raid the government's own in-house resources. Officials in the lower reaches of the government bureaucracy (both civilian and military), charged with administration of contracts, find themselves dealing with private corporate officials who often were their own former bosses and continue as companions of present bosses and congressional leaders who watchdog the agencies. A contract negotiator or supervisor must deal with men who can determine his career prospects; through contacts, these industrial contractors may cause him to be passed over or transferred to a minor position in some remote bureaucratic corner, sometimes with a ceremonial drumming before a congressional committee.

The military cutbacks that characterized the Eisenhower years were accompanied by expanding military budgets, a paradox explained by the systematic substitution of private contractors to carry out historically in-house activities. This trend was heralded as a move back to "free enterprise." Government installations and factories built in World War II were sold to industry, usually at a fraction of the taxpayers' investment. Others were leased at low fees to contractors who were then given government business to make the use of these facilities profitable. In some instances government built new facilities which it leased at nominal fees. Such facilities were permitted to be used, without cost, for commercial production as well.

The splurge of mobilizing private contractors for government work occurred as a part of the unprecedented growth of the Air Force. As an offspring of the Army, the new branch lacked the substantial in-house management, engineering, and R&D capability that the Army had built into its arsenal system. The Air Force sought to leapfrog this handicap in competing for jurisdiction over new weapons systems, turning to private contractors to correct the defect. In its rapid climb during the fifties, the Air Force fostered a growing band of private companies which took over a substantial part of regular military operations, including maintaining aircraft, firing rockets, building and maintaining launching sites, organizing and directing other contractors, and making major public decisions. In the area of missilery, junior officers and enlisted men were subordinated to the role of liaison agents or mere custodians.

This had several bonus effects, enabling the Air Force to keep its military personnel levels down in conformity with Defense Department and administration policies, while building an enormous industrial and congressional constituency with a stake in maintaining large-scale funding of new weapons systems. The Air Force's success over her sister services during the Eisenhower years established the magic formula that all federal agencies soon imitated. It set in motion a rush to contract out practically everything that was not nailed to the floor; and, in the process, it decimated the government's in-house management, engineering, and R&D capability, inflated the costs of R&D through futile contests for supremacy among contractors financed by contract funds, and as a consequence reduced as well the scientific and engineering resources available to the civilian economy and to the universities.

The Army learned an important lesson in its struggle with the Air Force during the Thor-Jupiter controversy: that its extensive in-house engineering-management capability was a positive *disadvantage* in mobilizing congressional and public influence to support military missions and budgets. Private industry had provided the Air Force with a potent weapon in Congress for outflanking the Army during all the years of strategic debate over missile development and the role of infantry forces in a nuclear world. In part, the Air Force lobbying instrument of the 1950's contributed importantly to over-dependence by the nation on nuclear weaponry and massive retaliation as the primary security doctrine, while the complete range of subnuclear military capabilities was allowed to wither. This lesson was inscribed on the Army-Navy skin by the budget-paring knife of the Eisenhower administration and led to gradual weakening of the arsenal system. In the sixties all the military services and NASA sought to parade bankers, captains of industry, local business leaders, and politicians through the halls of Congress and the White House as lobbying cadres in every new engagement.

The old research triad—government, industry, university—has virtually disappeared. In its place is a whole spectrum of new arrangements, such as the so-called systems engineering and technical direction firms operated on a profit or nonprofit basis (for example, General Electric is employed by NASA to integrate and test all launch facilities and space vehicles, while Bellcomm, a subsidiary of American Telephone and Telegraph, is employed for engineering and management of all NASA operations; Aerospace Corporation plays a similar role for the Air Force). In between are the major corporations, universities drawing a majority of their research budgets from government, nonprofit institutions conducting pad-and-pencil studies of strategic and policy matters for government agencies, and government laboratories operated by industry or by universities.

Knitting the complex together is an elite group of several thousand men, predominantly industrial managers and brokers, who play a variety of interlocking roles—sitting on boards of directors, consulting for government agencies, serving on advisory committees, acting as managers on behalf of government in distributing and supervising subcontracts, moving between private corporations and temporary tours of duty in government. Private corporations have contracts to act as systems engineers and technical directors for multibillion-dollar R&D and production activities involving hundreds of other corporations. Instead of fighting "creeping socialism," private industry on an enormous scale has become the agent of a fundamentally new economic system which at once resembles traditional private enterprise and the corporate state of fascism. A mere handful of giants (such as North American Aviation, Lockheed, General Dynamics, and Thompson-Ramo-Wooldridge) holds prime contracts over more than half the total R&D and production business. In dealing with their subcontractors and suppliers, these corporations act in the role of government itself:

> These companies establish procurement organizations and methods which proximate those of the government. Thus large prime contractors will invite design competition, establish source selection bids, send out industrial survey teams, make subcontract awards on a competitive or a negotiated basis, appoint small business administrators, designate plant resident representatives, develop reporting systems to spot bottlenecks, make cost analyses of subcontractor operations, and request monthly progress and cost reports from subcontractors.[9]

They are in the position of deciding whether or not to conduct an activity themselves or contract it out, and they may use their power over a subcontractor to acquire his proprietary information, force him to sell his company to the prime, or make or break geographical areas and individual bankers, investors, and businessmen. They may themselves create "independent" subcontractors in order to conceal profits, to keep certain proprietary information from the government, or for other purposes. Generally, they can and do use their decision-making power to stabilize their own operations, expanding or contracting their subcontracts in accordance with the peaks and troughs of government business, thus protecting their economic strength at the expense of smaller and weaker companies, seeking to assure their own growth and standing among the other giant corporations by mergers, acquisitions, and investments in the flock of companies dependent on them for government largess.

The same top three hundred companies that perform 97 per cent of all federal R&D also perform 91 per cent of all private R&D. Most of the private R&D is a means of maintaining the inside track for new awards in anticipated areas of government need. Since these same companies do all or most of their business with government, the so-called private R&D is paid for by the government in the form of overhead on other contracts.[10] For example, the United States is still paying for Douglas Aircraft's investment in developing the DC-3 thirty years ago. A congressional committee noted the trend:

> At the moment a small number of giant firms in a few defense and space-related areas, with their facilities located principally in three states, and engaged almost exclusively in the application of existing engineering and physical knowledge to the creation of new products and processes, receive the overwhelming preponderance of the government's multi-billion dollar research awards. . . . Clearly, if the resulting technical discoveries are permitted to remain within these narrow confines rather than be disseminated widely through the society, a disproportionate amount of the benefits will be channeled into the hands of the few and further economic concentration will take place.[11]

Prime contractors are becoming brokers of the managerial elites that control American industry, their power limited only by self-restraint and political necessity. Congressman Carl Hebert, after a 1961 investigation, declared his amazement at "the daring of these individuals," recalling that during World War II "the brokers became so prevalent in Washington that they wore badges," and the only office space they had was "under their hats." That was twenty years ago, "and yet we find the same practice not only not halted but increasingly becoming exposed as we go along these days."[12]

Government itself continues to enhance the power of the primes by accentuating the trend toward fewer and bigger contracts. Peter Slusser, an aerospace securities specialist, noted in 1964 the increasing concentration of procurements within a hard core of big contractors. It appears, he said, that the industry may eventually be dominated by a few firms, much as the automobile industry is today. Further, there will be a concentration within the concentration. "It seems to us," he asserted, "that this concentration ratio will probably continue among the larger companies."[13] The House Select Committee on Small Business reported that while defense procurement increased by $1.1 billion in 1963, small-business awards declined by $268 million. NASA doubled its prime procurements, while the small-business share dropped from 11.7 to 8.5 per cent. The congressional Joint Economic Committee reported that a hundred companies and their subsidiaries accounted for 73.4 per cent of total federal procurement value in 1964; the number of companies receiving annual awards of more than $1 billion has been steadily narrowing. Six companies belonged to that exclusive club in 1964; their combined NASA and defense work: Boeing, $2.3 billion; North American Aviation, $1.9 billion; Lockheed, $1.4 billion; McDonnell Aircraft, $1.4 billion; General Dynamics, $1.1 billion; and General Electric, $1.03 billion. North American alone, whose vending machine business made Bobby Baker a millionaire, held 28 per cent of all NASA procurements.

Erosion of Public Control

The dominant centers of corporate power have largely usurped the government's evaluation and technical direction responsibilities. Frank Gibney, one of the early consultants to the House Space Committee, observed that "the spectacle of a private profit-making company rendering national decisions makes the old Dixon-Yates concept look as harmless as a Ford Foundation Research Project." [14] The government's Bell Report of 1962 expressed concern at the erosion of its ability to manage its own affairs and to retain control over contracting, which "raises important questions of public policy concerning the government's role and capability and potential conflicts of interest." [15] The proliferation of quasi-public corporations, both profit and nonprofit, springing from the soil of R&D spending (such as Bellcomm, Aerospace Corporation, or Comsat Corporation), symbolizes the bewildering innovations of the Contract State. Congressmen throw up their hands trying to understand their relations to these new organizations under the traditional dichotomy between private and public enterprise.

Nageeb Halaby, former head of the Federal Aviation Agency, insisted that the private airlines fund at least 25 per cent of costs of developing a supersonic transport: "I think we have a half-free enterprise industry now, and I don't want to see it any more under government control than it already is. This is going to take some risk and . . . some ingenuity in figuring out how the government helps a relatively free enterprise to remain so, at a profit." [16] The industry itself insists that the SST will be profitable in commercial service, but demurs from investing in a small share of the developmental cost, claiming that government is obliged to do the whole job in the name of national prestige. GE Board Chairman Ralph J. Cordiner worries about the future course of the American system, the secret of whose "drive and creativity" lies in maintaining "many competing points of initiative, risk, and decision." As we move into the frontiers of space, he declares, "many companies, universities, and individual citizens will become increasingly dependent on the political whims and necessities of the federal government. And if that drift continues without check, the United States may find itself becoming the very kind of society that it is struggling against." [17]

Labor joins its voice, decrying those sectors of industry that in the name of preserving free enterprise call for ever greater farming out of government responsibility:

> It is purely charlatanism to claim that the government is in any form in competition with private industry because the government researches and develops and manufactures products for its own exclusive use. . . . It is competing only with the right of private industry to make a profit at the expense of the American taxpayer. But this is competition of a different color.[18]

The arrangements of the Contract State may, in the words of Don K. Price, avoid the problems that come with the growth of bureaucracy, but "encounter them again in more subtle and difficult forms. . . . If public ownership is no guarantee of unselfishness, neither is private ownership." [19] President Eisenhower, who came to office as a believer in the American business community and with a commitment to get rid of "unfair" government competition, ended his term of office with a forceful warning that private corporations (hired for the government's work) were tending to subordinate public to private weal, using strategic positions and influence for economic and political aggrandizement at the expense of democracy and the public interest.

There is no doubt that the flow of billions of federal dollars into narrow areas of the economy tends to create a self-perpetuating coalition of vested interests. With vast public funds at hand, industries, geographical regions, labor unions, and the multitude of supporting enterprises band together with enormous man power, facilities, and Washington contacts to maintain and expand their stake. Pork-barrel politics and alignments with federal agencies and political leaders provide a powerful political machine to keep the contract flow coming.

The pattern is already in the process of filtering down to state and local governments. In the name of preserving and utilizing the "unique" systems engineering and management capability that NASA publicists claim as one of the space program's major benefits to the civilian economy, underemployed aerospace industrial teams are now pushing for contracts in such areas as urban traffic management and water conservation. Governor Pat Brown of California has led the way. The only way to approach such problems, he declared, . . . is from the systems management viewpoint. Waste management facilities will be built with or without the aerospace industry, he told a congressional committee, but the new capability holds great promise. The state has already retained Aerojet-General for preliminary studies. An aerospace trade magazine commented: "The governor's effort to put aerospace talents to work on these problems is an imaginative one. Other states and the federal government are watching the experiment with interest." [20]

If the method of work follows the pattern cut for the federal government, the aerospace firm will win a major contract by hiring some civil engineers (including some from the state agencies already responsible in the area) to write a persuasive proposal. Once the contract is awarded, the corporation will hire away from the state government, the universities, and other ongoing operations all the technical people required, paying them greatly augmented salaries for work they were already doing under the traditional arrangements.

The first product will be an integrated state plan with engineering details, specifications, and cost estimates (always optimistically low at this stage). The company will then move for a prime contract to conduct the work, performing some of it itself and subcontracting some of it to the local builders and architects who possess knowledge and experience because of work they have already done for the state on a piecemeal basis. The contractor will cut across the cleavages of state, county, and municipal jurisdiction, ensuring everyone a reasonable return while retaining for itself two tiers of profit: one from its own work, the other added to that of the subcontractors. In time the systems teams, having emasculated state and local technical resources in these fields, will by judicious use of contract money build a political machine in the state legislature—relegating to their own managerial cadre (and the investment brokers who control their corporate paper) a large share of the decision-making authority of the State of California.

Later, as the contract arrangements acquire stability, the prime contractor may begin a process of mergers and acquisitions among its subcontractors, directed at building the resources of the company and in the process eliminating competition and much of the cost yardstick. The result will be a new concentration of economic power in these areas of activity which will increasingly give the corporation sole-source status. Like the conventional political party, the corporation will have acquired the ability to allocate state resources, to dispense job and financial patronage, and to ensure profits for its investors from the tax resources of state government.

Aerojet-General completed its preliminary waste disposal study in late 1965, recommending a ten-year program to be conducted by systems management techniques at a cost of billions.

The California experiment may achieve the positive goal of building or imposing a consensus for state-wide planning and technical, rather than political, logic in solving large-scale problems. The traditional political parties have so far failed to achieve this goal. But it must be asked: Cannot social consensus and rational planning be achieved without the abdication of traditional political and governmental processes? The slower progress of traditional politics is preferable to a system that evades democratic controls and may eventually spread its grip into all areas of public policy.

In essence, the same questions may be directed at the full-blown Contract State nurtured by the federal government. Adherence of the R&D contract cult to the shibboleths of free enterprise may be a cloak to conceal the fact that the sharks are eating the little fishes and that a kind of backhanded government planning, in which they participate and from which they benefit, has come to replace free enterprise. In spite of such temporary stimulants as tax cutting and the multiplier effect of missile-space spending, the civilian economy maintains a faltering pace of growth. The aerospace industries, on the other hand, ride high on unprecedented profits and diversify their holdings, biting deep into the most succulent portions of the civilian production machine in a new wave of economic concentration. In order that their "unique capability" not be wasted, defense firms are now moving into "systems management" of Job Corps camps and national conservation programs.

The politics of corporate finance have accelerated concentration not only in the government contract market but also in the civilian market, both of which are now thoroughly interpenetrated and interlocked. The aerospace giants have built huge conglomerate empires that span both markets, and the old respectable firms are playing major roles as public contractors. Among the top hundred prime aerospace contractors are such household names as General Electric, General Motors, AT&T, Westinghouse, Chrysler, Ford, Socony-Mobil, Firestone, Philco, Goodyear, and so on. Many of the aerospace companies are mere façades and legal fictions having no individual existence, but representing entities of financial and/or political convenience. In a 1965 House Judiciary Committee report, the five largest aerospace firms were cited as flagrant examples of corporate interlock. Douglas has fifteen directors interlocked with managements of seventeen banks and financial institutions, one insurance company, and twenty-eight industrial-commercial corporations (including Cohu Electronics, Giannini Controls, and Richfield and Tidewater Oil companies). Not uncommon is the pattern by which each company holds stock in its nominal competitors (McDonnell Aircraft holds a large block in the Douglas Company "as an investment"). A study of seventy-four major industrial-commercial companies found that 1,480 officers and directors held a total of 4,428 positions. The antitrust subcommittee staff concluded that management interlocks today are as prevalent as they were in 1914 when the Clayton Act, prohibiting interlocking directorships, was passed.

Point of No Return?

The quasi-governmental mercantilist corporations' maintained in a position of monopoly power through royal franchises, were anathema to the classical liberals. Thomas Hobbes compared them to "worms in the entrails of man," and Madison in *The Federalist* dealt at length with the problems of limiting their growth. At the end of the nineteenth century Henry Adams emphasized the origin of the corporation as an agency of the state, "created for the purpose of enabling the public to realize some social or national end without involving the necessity for direct governmental administration."

During the second half of the nineteenth century the corporation proved a powerful vehicle for mobilizing and organizing productive resources to achieve rapid economic growth made possible by burgeoning technology. Its very success, the efficiencies of bigness, and the inevitable politics of corporate empire building thrust into American skies the spires of monopoly power. Since that time sectional and economic interests have shifted and changed, the social and technological landscape has vastly altered, and government has emerged as guarantor of social interests against the claims of private power. Government contracting on its present scale has added another dimension. Business and industry have always been close to the centers of political power, but never before in peacetime have they enjoyed such a broad acceptance of their role as a virtual fourth branch of government—a consensus generated by the permanent crisis of international diplomacy. Sheltered by this consensus, government has accepted responsibility to maintain the financial status of its private contractors as essential to United States defense and economic health. Cost competitiveness, the traditional safeguard against corporate power and misallocation of national resources, has been suspended by R&D contract practices.

NASA and the Pentagon use their contracting authority to broaden the productive base in one area, maintain it in another, create more capability here or there for different kinds of R&D, create competition or limit it. Under existing laws they may make special provisions for small business and depressed areas and maintain contracts for services not immediately required in order to preserve industrial skills or reserve capacity for emergency needs. All of this represents national planning. But without recognition of planning as a legitimate government responsibility, planning authority is fragmented, scattered among federal agencies and Congress, and the makeshift planning that results serves the paramount interests of the most powerful political alignments. In place of forward planning responsible to the broad national community, the nation drifts sideways, denying the legitimacy of planning, yet backhandedly planning in behalf of narrow special interests whose corridors of power are closed to public control.

The result is severe distortion in the allocation of resources to national needs. For almost three decades the nation's resources have been commanded by military needs, consolidating political and economic power behind defense priorities. What was initially sustained by emergency comes to be sustained, normalized, and institutionalized (as emergency wanes) through a cabal of vested interests. The failure of nerve on the part of these interests to redirect this magnificent machine toward a broader range of values denies the nation what may be the ultimate basis of diplomatic strength and the only means to maintain the impetus of a mature economy; namely, the fullest enjoyment by all of our people of the immense bounty of equity and well-being almost within our grasp.

The shibboleths of free enterprise perpetuate a system by which, one by one, the fruits of the civilian economy fall into the outstretched hands of the aerospace group. The so-called Great Consensus assembled by President Johnson is based on the paradox of support from great corporate giants as well as from labor and the liberals. The civilian economy and home-town industry have been systematically neglected in the vicious circle of government contracts and economic concentration, leading the small businessman, vast numbers of middle-management, white-collar workers, and professional groups to embrace the simple formulas of Goldwater conservatism, directing the anxieties generated by incipient stagnation against the targets of autocratic organized labor and government spending for welfare and foreign aid. The exploitation of the myths of free enterprise has deflected attention from the feudal baronies of economic power and the tendency of the administration to attack the symptoms of growing inequality of wealth without disturbing the steepening slope itself.

The dynamics of the Contract State require close scrutiny lest, in the name of national security and the science technology race, the use of the nation's resources does violence not only to civilian enterprise but also to the body politic. In place of sensational claims about the ability of the American system to meet the challenges of new tasks and rapid technological change, it is necessary to judge the appropriateness and adequacy of national policies that increasingly raise a question concerning the relation between government and private contractor: who is serving whom?

The R&D cult is becoming a sheltered inner society isolated from the main stream of national needs. More and more it departs from the reality principles of social accounting, insulated against realism by the nature of its contract relations with government and its political influence. The elementary principle of economics applies: whatever is made cheaper tends to grow proportionately. Massive government subsidies to R&D facilitate its expansion beyond the point of rational response to international politics; it becomes a self-perpetuating pathology, intensifying the regressive structure of the economy and making further pump-priming exertions necessary.

As the arms race slows and is sublimated in space and science, as world politics break the ice of bipolarity and return to the troublesome but more flexible patterns of pluralism, it becomes important that great nations achieve positive values. Military power, though essential, remains essentially a limited and negative tool. Economic and social equilibrium at maximum resource use may hold the key to ultimate international stability, prestige, and national power. Federal expenditures are a response to national needs and aspirations in all areas of public responsibility. The needs and aspirations are limitless, while the resources to satisfy them are relatively scarce. Many rich societies have withered because they allocated their resources in a manner that precipitated the circular pathology of inequity and instability. "Neither Rome's great engineering skills, its architectural grandeur, its great laws, nor, in the last analysis, its gross national product, could prevail against the barbarians." [21]

The problem of bringing the Contract State under democratic control is but a new phase of a continuing challenge in Western industrial societies. The legal fiction that holds economic and political institutions to be separate and distinct becomes ever less applicable as economic pluralism is swallowed up by corporate giantism. The myths of economic freedom tend to insulate the giants from social control, protecting their private-government status and threatening the political freedom of the majority. The tension between private and public decision making can be a self-correcting process when its causes are visible and understood and when public authority is not wholly captive to the pressures of narrow interest groups. The process is delicately balanced, and there are points of no return.

▪ Notes

1. Robert Colborn, editorial, *International Science and Technology* (April, 1965), p. 21.
2. *Systems Development and Management, Part I*, pp. 51–52.
3. James McCamy, *Science and Public Administration* (Birmingham: University of Alabama Press, 1960), pp. 58–59.
4. *Industrial Research* (December, 1959), pp. 8–9; cited in U.S. Congress, House, Committee on Science and Astronautics, Staff Study, *The Practical Values of Space Exploration*, 87th Cong., 1st Sess. (Washington: Government Printing Office, 1961), p. 74.
5. *Astronautics and Aeronautics, 1963*, p. 400.
6. Bell Report, printed in Appendix I, *Systems Development and Management, Part I*, p. 205.
7. U.S. Congress, House, Select Committee on Government Research, *Report, Impact of Federal Research and Development Programs, Study No. VI*, 1964, p. 55.
8. See *Aerospace Facts and Figures, 1962* (Washington: Aerospace Industries Association of America, 1963), p. 20; *U.S. Aeronautics and Space Activities, 1962*, Bureau of the Budget, cited in *Missiles and Rockets*, January 21, 1963, p. 12; see *Aviation Week*, January 21, 1963, p. 30; also *NASA Authorization for Fiscal Year 1965*, p. 56.
9. *Eleventh Report, Organization and Management of Missile Programs*, p. 49.
10. See Carl E. Barnes, "Industrial Research, Is It Outmoded?" *Business Horizons* (Summer, 1964).
11. U.S. Congress, House, Select Committee on Government Research, *Report, Contract Policies and Procedures for Research and Development, Study VII*, House Report No. 1942, Union Calendar No. 835, H. Res. 504 as amended by H. Res. 810, 88th Cong., 2d Sess. (Washington: Government Printing Office, 1964), p. 58.
12. U.S. Congress, House, Committee on Armed Services, Subcommittee for Special Investigations, *Hearings, Sole-Source Procurement, Part I*, H. Res. 78, 87th Cong., 1st Sess. (Washington: Government Printing Office, 1961), pp. 17–18.
13. Quoted in *Missiles and Rockets*, July 20, 1964, p. 15.
14. *Harper's* (January, 1960), p. 43.
15. Testimony of David E. Bell, Director, Bureau of the Budget, *Systems Development and Management, Part I*, p. 4.
16. *Panel on Science and Technology, Sixth Meeting*, p. 65.
17. Ralph J. Cordiner, "Competitive Private Enterprise in Space," in Simon Ramo, ed., *Peacetime Uses of Outer Space* (New York: McGraw-Hill, 1961), p. 222.
18. Statement by William H. Ryan, then lobbyist for the AFL-CIO, now New York Congressman, testifying, *Systems Development and Management, Part I*, p. 127.
19. Don K. Price, "The Scientific Establishment," in *Scientists and National Policy Making*, p. 39.
20. William J. Coughlin, *Missiles and Rockets*, August 2, 1965, p. 46, Governor Brown's statements are cited here as well.
21. James M. Gavin, Address to the International Bankers Association, December, 1958, quoted in *The Practical Values of Space Exploration*, p. 25.

PART FIVE

■ THE RESPONSE OF POLITICAL SCIENCE

INTRODUCTION

Professionally, political scientists engage in their quite various activities to cope not only with the problems they see in political life but also with the inadequacies they detect in one another's formulations. They seek to order phenomena they regard as disordered—their political environment as well as their common discipline. Unlike political actors directly involved in politics, their primary concern is with enlarging understanding, with comprehending and explaining the politically relevant part of reality.

The professional arena in which political scientists engage in research may itself be regarded as political. Working in it, political scientists whose interests and aspirations conflict may be seen as seeking to satisfy different intellectual and practical interests. They are aware of competing professional movements and alignments, of innumerable ways of dividing labor and integrating activities, and of a large variety of communication channels and media. They compete for foundation support, space in scholarly journals, and places on panels at professional conventions. They rank their departments as well as one another. Like any political organization, that of political science may be evaluated by asking to what extent it successfully incorporates the greatest diversity of interests. Does its output—its theories and findings—integrate the greatest manageable variety of politically relevant facts and events?

That there *is* a distinctive discipline of political science has only recently been acknowledged. This is not to say that the study of politics is new. Men

353

have responded to political predicaments by wishing to understand and control them since the dawn of political consciousness. As historians and artists, they have sought to illuminate specific events, delineating and displaying their unique features. As philosophers, they have sought to make plausible the criteria by which policies may be regarded as good or bad. And as scientists, they have recurrently sought explanations, isolating certain aspects of political behavior, inquiring under what conditions these aspects are manifest, and incorporating assorted findings in empirical theory.

It is as science that the study of politics has become organized and self-conscious in the recent past. Both the profession of political science and the methods by which politics have been studied have undergone fundamental changes during the last quarter-century. New problems have been identified as significant; quantitative techniques have been developed and applied systematically; psychological and social variables have come to be regarded as among the crucial factors for understanding political behavior; new distinctions—especially between evaluation and description—and a new idiom have been introduced. By the early 1960's it became possible to think of the new behavioral approach as established and to characterize it as a successful protest against unscientific ways of understanding political life.

The acceptance of a behavioral persuasion may usefully be interpreted in terms of a dialectic which took place in an American setting. Initially, at least in this interpretation of the development of political science, Americans had been preoccupied with constitutional government; more specifically, government under the United States Constitution. They were accordingly concerned with legally constituted political institutions, with government pure and simple. They focused on constitutional history and law. Accepting the Constitution as the centrally relevant reality, their recurrent question was how policy was made within its explicit framework. The totality of clearly visible politics was designated "the state"; to study the state in America meant to learn how effectively and how well its sovereign will was expressed and executed. The focus was on what seemed so obviously present: the formal organization of government, the federal system, the three branches of government.

Against this preoccupation with the fixed structure of government, a widespread reaction set in during the Progressive Era at the turn of the twentieth century. The traditional legalistic, formalistic way of viewing politics was challenged by scholars with pragmatic inclinations. Attuned to the equalitarian pressures of Populism, they turned to expose the less visible behavior patterns behind the façade: actual power relations, interest groups in action. Politics was to be perceived more realistically as an ongoing decision-making process.

This new realism—manifest in the works of James Bryce, Woodrow Wilson, Arthur Bentley, Charles Beard, and Charles Merriam—led to an outpouring of descriptive studies and case histories which jeopardized the traditional approach. Ultimately, the sheer volume of unrelated published work, a hyper-factualism, was to provoke a plea for order. Moreover, the emergent forces of urbanization, depression, mass movements, modern war, and totalitarian regimes remained unintegrated in any theories of political science. It seemed timely to search explicitly for a comprehensive theory, at least a common framework for analysis, and to develop stable units of measurement which political scientists might profitably use. After World War II, David Easton in particular sought to make the nontheoretical empiricism which prevailed between the 1880's and the 1930's more rigorously scientific. Employing the concept of the political system, he helped provide an escape from a parochial Americanism, encouraging subnational as well as cross-national comparisons. In the name of behavioralism and systems analysis, political science could proceed to widen its scope, become more precise in its formulations and its quest for an explicit general theory of politics.

The new approach, as Robert A. Dahl was to observe, may thus be seen as improving "our understanding of politics by seeking to explain the empirical aspects of political life by means of methods, theories, and criteria of proof that are acceptable according to the canons, conventions, and assumptions of modern empirical science." The phenomena of politics are to be described in terms of observed behavior. In the end, behavioralism will disappear as a distinctive approach because, in Dahl's words,

> it will become, and in fact already is becoming, incorporated into the main body of the discipline. The behavioral mood will not disappear, then, because it has failed. It will disappear rather because it has succeeded. As a separate, somewhat sectarian, slightly factional outlook, it will be the first victim of its own triumph.[1]

It would be mistaken to assume, of course, that beneath a triumphant behavioralism all conflict has been resolved. Doubts remain about proper objectives, approaches, research methods, and central concepts. Certainly there is nothing in political science corresponding to the concepts of length, time, and mass in classical physics. Nor is there agreement on the boundaries of the discipline, so that it remains difficult to devise an acceptable theoretical model which might unify the welter of empirical findings.

Not only does the discipline remain eclectic, but there are also stirrings which question the behavioral orientation. As behavioralists have begun to relate political phenomena to the concept of system, they are being challenged by members of the profession who insist that politically relevant factors are omitted and that these factors can be perceived only by a reformulation of the dominant form of behavioralism. Various critics have come to feel, for example, that the focus on "the political system" tends to discriminate against political change and novelty. Because the prevailing norm is system maintenance, emergent phenomena are too readily categorized as dysfunctional. The criticism is that the presently supported systems approach fails to involve man as agent, as self-directed, active, political participant. It fails to accommodate precisely those interests, needs, and values at the margin of "the political system" which differently formulated analytical models might welcome. True, the systems approach does go beyond the conventional boundaries into the fields of anthropology, sociology, and psychology. Yet all it has accepted from neighboring disciplines is methods which treat man not as actor, but as someone acted on by a system of forces.

Is it possible to design approaches sensitive to concealed phenomena—the interests of outcast groups, for example—now placed at the periphery? Can we learn to incorporate marginal interests and values in our conceptual models even though they may not be—not yet be—manifest in political life? These questions, it is recognized, are not properly answered by proposals to return to the position which the systems approach has effectively criticized and to which it is itself a response. If the older empiricism is acknowledged to have yielded all it can for a science of politics, to have provided historically important but theoretically unrelated case studies, it would seem that the problem for political science at this juncture is to formulate theoretical positions transcending both the old empiricism and the subsequent systems theory.

Moving in this direction would allow us to give recognition to interests not now in the range of vision of political scientists. It would mean doing justice to unrealized possibilities; that is, to lost causes and ideal options. Such an orientation would lead us to respect the experiences ordered by historians and artists whose ambiguous language necessarily puts into doubt what those in power deem functional and established. To welcome what is dysfunctional and unestablished would test our capacity for recognizing peripheral needs and underprivileged strata, for using new modes of analysis and new approaches. We would thus test the profession of political science precisely as we test our ideologies, our institutions, and ourselves as citizens.

■ *Note*

1. Robert A. Dahl, "The Behavioral Approach in Political Science: Epitaph for a Monument to a Successful Protest," *American Political Science Review,* LV (December, 1961), 767, 770.

40 GAMES OF SCHOLARSHIP

■ *James N. Rosenau*

I view the gathering of data and the structuring of concepts as a game one plays in order to move ever nearer to the truth. The game has its rules. These are sometimes codified and sometimes implicit, but are always operative. Usually the rules are inhibiting, and only rarely do they allow unrestrained action. The play is often dull as the opponent, elusive and stubborn, brings action to a standstill. Yet tense and exciting moments, full of the drama of forward move-

From James N. Rosenau, "Transforming the International System," *World Politics,* XVIII (April, 1966), 525–528. Reprinted by permission.

ment, do occur as the opponent gives way in the face of a break-through. And who is the opponent? He is Man, both individually and collectively, acting in unexpected and complex ways that constantly challenge the researcher's ingenuity, resist his classifications, elude his disciplined procedures, and refuse to be arrayed in simple and clear-cut patterns.

We can, it must quickly be added, play a variety of games with our subject matter. We can play the scientific game or the historical game, the game of the journalist or the game of the preacher. We can abide by strict rules of evidence, heed our consciences, or rely on informed impressions. We can derive our findings from quantitative data, from the lessons of a single case, or from the values we espouse.

Furthermore, whatever the game, we can play it in a number of different ball parks. In the world politics league, our contests with human behavior are scheduled in a few supranational parks, many national sites, some conference rooms, and occasional foreign offices. Our opponent, in other words, is Man in a variety of guises—as international organization, national society, diplomatic situation, bureaucracy, or individual decision maker.

Finally, whatever game we play and wherever we play it, we can adopt a seemingly infinite range of styles and strategies. We can subject the opponent to the rigors of realism, to the tenets of idealism, to the precepts of decision-making analysis, to the assumptions of general systems theory, and so on through all the concepts, approaches, and schools that researchers have used to guide their play.

Let us carry the analogy one step further and emphasize that while it may be possible to rank the ball parks according to their elegance, and the strategies of play according to their effectiveness, we cannot do the same with the games themselves. Baseball is not better than football or worse than golf. They are different games that appeal to different people, require different skills, and serve different interests. If a person is small and prefers to compete against himself, he plays golf; whereas football appeals to those who are large and like to engage in contact sports. So it is with the various games through which truth is acquired. Each can be played well or poorly, and each can be won or lost or stalemated; but none can be judged as inherently better or worse than any other. Each is played for different reasons and to attain different kinds of truth. The adequacy of the truth in each game is measured against the rules of that game, not against the truths achieved in other games. The assessments of world politics made by the journalist who depends on informed observation are neither more nor less accurate than those asserted by the preacher who relies on spiritual perceptions or those developed by the scholar who employs systematic analysis. These are simply three different sets of truth, derived from the play of three very different games. Likewise, the findings of the historian who uses the case method to search for meaning in a single instance of world politics are neither better nor worse than those of the political scientist who applies quantitative techniques in order to discern the patterns that emerge from a number of situations. Again these are different kinds of truth, answering different kinds of questions that stem from different kinds of scholarly interests.

While it is thus inappropriate to pass judgment on the value of the game that a scholar plays in order to acquire and interpret data, the question of how he scores against his opponent can and must be addressed. Distinguished performance in the various games of scholarship is marked by a processing of data that, within the rules of the researcher's own game, is so imaginative or persuasive as to fashion a wide intersubjective consensus among those who play the same game. A record-setting performance is achieved when a researcher's findings are so striking and so clearly a consequence of opportunities provided by the rules of his game that the scope of the resulting consensus is widened to include not only all the devotees of his game, but also a number of people who ordinarily prefer other sports. Contrariwise, low or losing scores will be recorded by researchers who either process their data in a pedestrian fashion or fail to live up to the rules of their game. Such performances are not likely to attract large crowds, and those few who do attend are likely to drift away before the play is over.

The games scholars play . . . can be reduced to two major types: the historical and the scientific.[1] The rules of the historical game are far less stringent than those of the scientific. In historical analysis the researcher may roam freely over a wide and varied expanse of data in order to tell his story. He scores well if the story is coherent and full of insight; but however high his score may be, the story is always his, and its findings never become independent of the coherence and insight with which he organizes and analyzes his materials. To be sure, the rules oblige him to indicate where he obtained each component of his story and prohibit his misrepresenting the nature of his data. Beyond this, however, he is free to draw on archival materials for one part of the story, to cite a historical example in another, to quote respected authorities in still another, and to use common knowledge, anecdotal wisdom, rigorous logic, and sustained reflection to link the various parts to each other. If the resulting composite impresses players of the historical game as yielding new comprehension about some aspect of world politics, it will assume a conspicuous place in the literature of the field.

The rules of the scientific game, on the other hand, are not nearly so flexible. The scientist must also piece together a coherent and insightful tale out of his data, but, unlike a player in any other game, he must do so in a way that renders his findings independent of himself. The distinguishing feature of the scientist's "truths" is that they must be susceptible to confirmation by independent observers. Thus the rules of his game require him to make his assumptions, concepts, and procedures sufficiently explicit to permit any researcher to arrive at the same conclusions by gathering the same data and processing them in the same way. The scientist is free to employ the views of respected authorities in developing his framework, and there is nothing to prevent his constructing hypotheses out of historical example, anecdotal wisdom, or, indeed, sheer hunch. Once he proceeds to test the hypotheses, however, the rules of the game become stringent because, if they are not followed, the findings can never be dissociated from the finder.

The rules governing the processing and the interpretation of data are equally stringent. The researcher must indicate each operation performed in the gathering of the data, specify the boundaries of the categories used to classify the data, and note each step, both conceptual and statistical, taken in discerning patterns in the data. Further, he must explicate the criteria used to interpret quantitative differences in the distributions of the data and must indicate clearly how the relationships that emerge confirm or negate his hypotheses. Adherence to both sets of rules is necessary to achieve distinction in the game of science. If the player abides by the "process" rules, but is lax in using the interpretation rules, the same data will mean different things to different observers and intersubjective consensus will not develop. Similarly, fidelity to the "interpretation" rules will not offset laxity in those pertaining to process because, obviously, different observers will produce different data that are bound to mean different things even if common criteria of interpretation are employed. . . .

■ *Note*

1. Still other types are, of course, played by journalists, politicians, citizens, preachers, and the many other actors who have occasion to discern and evaluate the international scene. Here we are concerned only with scholarly games, which are assumed to be distinguished from all other types by their goal of understanding *why* the course of events unfolds as it does. As will be seen, scholarly games can vary considerably in their rules and subordinate goals, but they do share an aspiration toward comprehension.

41 TRADITIONALISM AS GUIDE TO KNOWLEDGE

■ *Richard B. Wilson*

It will be argued . . . that political scientists can best serve the practical requirements of society as well as the intellectual and theoretical demands of the discipline by utilizing the concepts, values, and descriptive theory which are implicit in an already existing "system" of political knowledge—the "constitutional" system in its broadest sense. . . .

Among the various alternative conceptual schemes is one which has a rich tradition in American political scholarship, whose implications are largely incompatible with the methods and objectives of comprehensive empirical theory, but which has been neglected in recent years both as a source of methodological criticism and as an architectonic pattern for political thought and

From Richard B. Wilson, "System and Process: Polar Concepts for Political Research," *Western Political Quarterly*, XIV (September, 1961), 761–763. © Copyright 1961 by the University of Utah. Reprinted by permission of the University of Utah.

research. Only the bare bones of this position will be suggested here, and considerable work would be needed to spell out its configurations in a meaningful way.

The basis of a viable orientation for political research was articulated with his usual clarity by Michael Oakeshott in his inaugural lecture at the London School of Economics in 1951. "Political activity," he asserted, "springs neither from instant desires nor from general principles, but from the existing traditions of behavior. . . . And the form it takes, because it can take no other, is the amendment of existing arrangements by exploring and pursuing what is intimated in them."[1] In the American context, at least, the "existing traditions" of political behavior are expressed by the constitutional system viewed in its broadest sense: a system whose major features are spread widely through statutes, judicial decisions, administrative orders and customs and which in most cases have little relevance to the provisions of the original document. What is "intimated" in that system—to use Professor Oakeshott's phrase—is a set of ever changing concepts and principles which both describe the essential aspects of political behavior and provide guides for modification of that behavior in terms of each new continuum of public issues. These dual purpose concepts are neither hopelessly ambiguous nor exclusively value statements. They get their meaning from the slow accretion of historical experience and usage; "they compose a pattern and at the same time they intimate a sympathy for what does not fully appear."[2]

Constitutional concepts receiving the greatest attention, of course, are precisely those which current descriptive theory finds most sterile and unrewarding; separation of powers, federalism, due process of law, judicial review, and the like, are criticized as being sufficiently ambiguous to validate an infinite variety of actual behaviors, as "myths" so often bent to accommodate new situations that they lack an identifiable core, and as time-worn irrelevancies removed from the realities of politics or administration, and hence incapable of either describing or guiding the essential processes of political life. To the extent that these objections rest on the nonquantifiable character of constitutional data, they are correct but futile: enough has been said above to indicate the difficulty, if not the undesirability, of applying quantitative methods to social data. Often, however, such criticisms arise more from a misconception of the nature of constitutionalism than from methodological disagreement. The alleged ambiguity of a concept such as separation of powers stems from a seemingly persistent tendency to view it as an absolute and universal formulation, the components of which are defined in nature, or at least in the immutable traditions of Anglo-Saxon legal history. That this view soon compels disenchantment is patent: there are not and there cannot be rigid definitions of power classified according to function, nor inflexible patterns for the distribution of duties. It does not follow, however, that failure to meet an impossible ideal requires abandonment of the idea as useless or ambiguous. A careful inspection of legislative, executive, and judicial competencies at any given point in time reveals a complex, yet rather exact, configuration of power allocation; the pattern emerges *from*, it is not imposed *upon* the living stuff of governmental experience. Thus conceptualized inductively rather than deductively, the dominant characteristic of constitutional ideas is revealed as plasticity and mutation rather than ambiguity and myth.

Similarly, the contention that constitutional notions comprise a detached superstructure unrelated to the realities of politics and administration derives from a faulty notion of constitutional theory. The descriptive as distinguished from the normative function of constitutional principles is directive and hypothetical, rather than comprehensive and discrete. That is, they function as guides or standards of judgment concerning the relevance of empirical inquiry, delineating the areas and issues concerning which we require further information if the constitutional system is to realize "a sympathy" for "what is intimated" in it. To be sure, constitutional notions are not convenient descriptive summaries of political behavior within each and every government agency, political interest group, or nation-state; they do not purport to provide us with comprehensive designations of the infinite variety of behaviors and arrangements which compose political life. Neither, however, does an assertion of their primacy deny the legitimacy of exhaustively inspecting the intricacies of behavior, function, and arrangement, wherever found. Rather, constitutional notions should serve as an orienting framework for such investigation and as a "system" —if the term must be used—of empirical research.

A constitution, then, functions in two capacities, it *describes* those aspects of reality which are most intimately and significantly related to the basic ethical and moral norms of the society, and it identifies those norms. It is to be analyzed exclusively in neither positivistic nor idealistic terms—a dichotomy which has contributed much confusion and little enlightenment to discussions about the nature of law and society. In twentieth-century thought the idea of a constitutional system implies a rejection of both natural laws of human behavior, inductively derived, and natural law of human destiny, deductively derived. Hence, it focuses on the unique and the novel, affirms the centrality of process and change, and, analytically, seeks only to retard rather than to freeze and isolate in time and space the components of political life. Its ultimate methodological implications are abandonment of the quest for certainty in human knowledge and frank recognition that the great purposes of any political society—liberty, equality, rule of law, and so on, in our own case— are necessarily ambiguous, representing a distillation of the past, but only a promise for the future. Nevertheless, the ambiguity and tentativeness of these principles should not be allowed to obscure the very real distinction to be drawn between *jurisdictis* and *gubernaculum,* to borrow a felicitous phrase from McIlwain. However difficult it may be to define them adequately, "there is the problem of restriction and the problem of responsibility . . . the problem of law versus will. . . . The long and fascinating story of the balancing of *jurisdictis* and *gubernaculum* . . . should be, if we study it with an open mind, of some help in adjusting and maintaining today the delicate balance of will and law, the central practical problem of politics now as it has been in all past ages." [3]

Certainly any uniformities of economic, social, or even political behavior which can be discovered will be useful for the future shaping of constitutional concepts. But it is the elaboration and application of those concepts which must remain the *focus* of our attention as political scientists, rather than psychological and sociological data or "laws" which cannot encompass and, so far, have not comprehended the rich and varied texture of political experience.

It might in one sense be fortunate if we could rely on a simplistic yet complete systematization of data to guide us in our search for political wisdom. But then again, much that is truly creative and inventive would thereby be removed from the enterprise. Perhaps we should conclude with Lord Halifax's remark that "the struggle for knowledge has a pleasure in it, like that of wrestling with a fine woman." And, as Lindsay Rogers so thoughtfully asks in a recent essay, "Who is rash enough to suggest a method for making that wrestling a success?"[4]

▪ Notes

1. Michael Oakeshott, "Political Education," in Peter Lasslett, ed., *Philosophy, Politics and Society* (Oxford: Blackwell, 1956), p. 12.
2. *Ibid.*, pp. 12–13.
3. Charles H. McIlwain, *Constitutionalism: Ancient and Modern* (Ithaca: Cornell University Press, 1958), pp. 145–146.
4. Lindsay Rogers, "Philosophy in the Twentieth Century," in Roland Young, ed., *Approaches to the Study of Politics* (Evanston: Northwestern University Press, 1958), p. 210.

42   THE PREVAILING PARADIGM

▪ *Gabriel A. Almond*

A new paradigm is surely developing in political science. Its first formulations are crude, partial, and often pretentious. But theory formulation will undoubtedly go forward with the rapid growth of the profession and with the high capabilities and research opportunities of an increasing proportion of its members. What are some of the principal features of this emerging approach?

1. The first is a statistical approach to the universe of political systems. We no longer focus simply on the "great powers," but are concerned with sampling the total universe of man's experiments with politics, contemporary and historical, national, subnational, and international. Increasingly, we select our cases for study in order to test hypotheses about the relations between variables: environmental influences on politics, political influences on the envi-

From Gabriel A. Almond, "Political Theory and Political Science," *American Political Science Review*, IX (December, 1966), 873–878. Reprinted by permission of the author and the publisher.

ronment, and the interaction of political variables with each other. The comparative method is used more rigorously, in a self-conscious search for control, not only in cross-national comparisons but in subnational comparisons and international system comparisons as well.[1]

2. A second significant characteristic of this emerging paradigm of political science is the differentiation and specification of variables and the assumptions of probability and reflexivity in their relations. Thus, in our efforts to establish the properties of political systems, compare them with each other, and classify them into types, we explicitly separate structure from function, structure from culture, social systems from political systems, empirical properties from their normative implications. We tend to view the individual political system as a universe of interactions and make case studies of its operations according to some sampling strategy. The result is a movement away from black-and-white typecasting, toward classification based on statements of probability of process and performance patterns which enable us to compare, explain, and evaluate more precisely.[2]

3. The emerging analytical framework in contemporary political theory is the concept of system whether it is employed at the level of subnational, regional, or structural units such as communities, legislative bodies or committees, at the level of national political units, or at the level of the international political system. The principal advantage of the system concept is that it analytically differentiates the object of study from its environment and directs attention to the interaction of the system with other systems in its environment, to its own conversion characteristics, and to its maintenance and adaptive properties. In the development of the political system concept, Lasswell's seven functional categories of the decision process and Easton's demand-support-output model represent post-separation-of-powers efforts at postulating sets of categories which are logically distinct and universally applicable. The scientific approach to categorization is the modest approach of the coder, rather than that of the philosopher. There is constant revision of the code as it is used to organize data. The ease with which we can get and analyze data these days gives us a secular attitude toward our categories. They have a short and instrumental life, and we avoid becoming their prisoners as we once were of separation-of-powers concepts.

In this search for an adequate system of functional categories, one thing seems to be clear. Our analytical framework has to enable us to relate three aspects of the functioning of political systems. We need functional categories in order to describe and compare political systems at the level of their performance—as systems interacting with other systems in their domestic and international environments. We need functional categories which will enable us to describe and compare political systems according to their internal conversion processes. And finally we need functional categories in order to describe and compare political systems according to their maintenance and adaptive characteristics. Modern political theory will consist in good part of a logic which will enable us to relate changes in the performance of political systems to changes in internal process and conversion patterns and to changes in recruitment and socialization patterns. Another part of it will consist of a logic which will enable us to move from empirical relationships to normative judgments.

4. The Enlightenment theory of progress toward democracy and the rule of law is giving way to a multilinear theory of political development leading us to break through the historical and cultural parochialism of the field. Enlightenment theory began with the leviathan state and postulated as the legitimate problem of political theory that of bringing the leviathan under control through institutional and legal checks and balances and through popular processes. Modern political theory has to ask how the leviathan itself comes into existence, in order to cope with the intellectual problems of understanding the political prospects and processes of the new nations. We are beginning to break through the historical barrier of the French Revolution and the ethnic barrier of western Europe, reaching into historical and anthropological data for knowledge of the variety of political development patterns. And we are on the eve of a search for rational choice theories of political growth—an approach which may make political theory more relevant to public policy. Like the authors of the *Federalist Papers*, contemporary political theorists are inescapably confronted with the problem of how resources may be economically allocated to affect political change in preferred directions. The justification for this quest for an allocation-of-resources theory of political development is not only its relevance to central concerns of public policy but its uses as a test of the validity and power of our theories. It forces us to place our bets, set the odds, and confront straightforwardly the issue of the kind of prediction which is possible in political science.

These developments are not matters of the remote future; they are already to be observed in the thrust of the various subfields of political science. Thus, American political studies are moving out of their parochial orientation in the search for the illumination and increased rigor which can be gained through cross-national and subnational comparison.[3] We are discovering that the American political system, no matter how much we love it, is still a political system comparable to other systems and that we can perhaps love it better as we acquire the perspective and illumination which systematic and rigorous comparison makes possible. Some of the subdisciplines of political science—political parties, interest groups, public opinion and communication, bureaucracy—previously based almost entirely on American experience, are increasingly treated in system terms and in a cross-national, comparative context. As the mood of the cold war changes from obsession to concern, Soviet and Communism studies are becoming more systemic and comparative. The newest developments in international relations theory reflect the impact of system concepts and comparative methods. Political theory begins to show signs of claiming its role as the systematizer, codifier, hypothesis formulator, and ethical evaluator of the field as a whole.

It has been the great privilege of the subdiscipline of comparative politics to have acted as a catalyst in this process of professional development. Because of the existing division of labor, comparative politics dealt with European, Asian, African, and Latin American political systems. Leaving out as it did the American and Communist political systems in an empirical, though not in a theoretical, sense, it could avoid the pressures of ethnocentrism and the distortions of the cold war. And, confronted by the exotic and unstable phenomena of the new and modernizing nations, it was uniquely challenged by the problems of comparison, classification, and change and led in the search for analytical frameworks and categories suitable for coping with these intellectual problems. It is not accidental that it fell to comparative politics to be particularly active in re-establishing the relationship between the analysis of individual political systems and their classes and varieties with general political theory and that it dramatized the necessity of reforging the links between historical political theory, empirical political theory, and normative political theory. . . .

These trends toward rigor and scope, systematic exploration of the consequences for politics of social and psychological variables, and the formulation of general analytical frameworks represent a significant step into the modern world of science. And the rate of growth and professionalization of political science gives promise that the intellectual rate of growth will be correspondingly rapid. It may very well be that there is no word of counsel, of caution, which the older Turks can give to the young ones, no unexplored area or neglected problem in the field which this numerous, talented, and highly skilled generation has not already anticipated or soon will encounter and solve more effectively than those who preceded them.

It may be appropriate, however, to point out that the persisting bipolar conflict in the field between humanists and behavioralists conceals a lively polemic in both camps and perhaps particularly among the so-called behavioralists. Among the modernists neologisms burst like roman candles in the sky, and wars of epistemological legitimacy are fought. The devotees of rigor and theories of the middle range reject more speculative general theory as nonknowledge; and the devotees of general theory attack those with more limited scope as technicians, as answerers in search of questions. . . .

Confusion, even loss, of identity is inevitably associated with professional growth. And when quantitative and qualitative growth occurs at such extraordinary rates, the confusion and conflict may be multiplied. If Dahl was correct when he wrote the epitaph for a monument to a successful protest, it may be that the battle of science has been won, and this may be an appropriate moment for the victors to take a look back at their intellectual origins.

If we consider the tradition of political science and the place of political science in the university curriculum, it becomes quite clear that, while drawing heavily upon other disciplines, political science is not a science in general and not social science. However we define it, we have a limited and special responsibility for the political aspects of the social process. Our past imposes this structural restraint upon us; and the existence of anthropology, sociology, law, history, philosophy, statistics, economics, and mathematics in the community of the university confronts us with an inescapable problem of intellectual and institutional boundaries. We are not the best judges of psychological, sociological, mathematical, and statistical competence, though we are or should be the best judges of the appropriateness and usefulness of the application of these disciplines to the special field in which we have or should have the highest competence. . . .

▪ *Notes*

1. Gabriel Almond and James Coleman, *The Politics of the Developing Areas* (Princeton: Princeton University Press, 1960), Conclusion; Seymour Martin Lipset, *Political Man* (New York: Doubleday, 1960); Karl Deutsch, *The Nerves of Government* (New York: The Free Press, 1963) and "Social Mobilization and Political Development"; Bruce Russett *et al., World Handbook of Political and Social Indicators* (New Haven: Yale University Press, 1964); Arthur Banks and Robert Textor, *A Cross Polity Survey* (Cambridge: MIT Press, 1963); Richard Rosecrance, *Action and Reaction in World Politics* (Boston: Little, Brown, 1963); Heinz Eulau, "Comparative Political Analysis: A Methodological Analysis," *Midwest Journal of Political Science,* VI (November, 1962), 397–407.
2. In this connection see Robert Dahl, *Who Governs?* (New Haven: Yale University Press, 1961); Zbigniew Brzezinski and Samuel P. Huntington, *Political Power: USA/ USSR* (New York: Viking, 1965); and Almond and Coleman, *op. cit.,* Chapter I.
3. Robert Dahl, *Political Opposition in Western Democracies* (New Haven: Yale University Press, 1966); John C. Wahlke *et al., The Legislative System* (New York: John Wiley, 1962); Robert E. Agger *et al., The Rulers and the Ruled* (New York: John Wiley, 1964).

43   POLITICAL SCIENCE AS SCIENCE

▪ *Arthur S. Goldberg*

The Problem

Why does one need to go into the realm of science to make intelligible the particular segment of human experience called political? For example, how is science useful in answering the question, "Why do the British have a stable political system and the French an unstable one?" This can be made understandable on the grounds that the British people are phlegmatic, while the French are of volatile temperament. Quite as simply, one can explain the higher degree of personal civil liberties in the United States vis-à-vis the USSR by the presence of an effective separation of powers in the former and

From Arthur S. Goldberg, "Political Science as Science," in Nelson W. Polsby *et al., Politics and Social Life* (Boston: Houghton Mifflin, 1963), pp. 26–35. © Copyright 1963 by Nelson W. Polsby, Robert A. Dentler, and Paul A. Smith. Reprinted by permission of Houghton Mifflin Co.

the lack thereof in the latter. Assuming for the moment the truth of the descriptive aspects of these explanations, they certainly make the phenomena more intelligible by common sense than would a great deal of scientific jargon. They are, however, unsatisfactory in that they fail to account for a broader range of similar experiences. Thus, one is aware of what is perhaps a higher level of personal civil liberties in Great Britain than in the United States, with a less clearly defined or functioning separation of powers in the former than in the latter. One is also aware of an alleged volatile temperament among Spaniards along with the ominous stability of Franco Spain. Admittedly, these were "simple" explanations, but it would be well to keep in mind the grounds for their rejection; that is, their failure to account for a broader range of similar experiences.[1]

More complex nonscientific explanations often suffer from a different defect; that is, they cannot be rejected. They may be argued in terms of plausibility, or in terms of logical consistency, but they cannot be empirically refuted for lack of prescribed operational tests. Thus, for example, the causes of the American Civil War are a source of continuing debate. Each proposed explanation rests on an implicit theory; yet none of these is so articulated as to enable recognition of an empirical refutation of the theory when one is encountered.[2] One of the definitive characteristics of science, on the other hand, is that it seeks to explain the world in terms of testable ideas. It is thus empirical—but science is not empiricism.

The distinction between science as empirical and science as empiricism is not a trivial one. The failure to make this distinction has, I suggest, been the fundamental source of conflict between the "traditionalists" and the "behaviorists" in the study of political phenomena. The former have looked with grave misgivings upon the behaviorists' penchant for experiential data, arguing that such "pure facts" offer no meaningful explanations. The behaviorists, in turn, have argued that the theoretical abstractions of traditional political theory have failed, after centuries of speculation, to produce reliable explanations of political phenomena. Both points are well taken, as will be shown.

Facts as Theory

Consider the advice of Lord Bryce to the members of the American Political Science Association:

> I start by offering you one maxim of universal validity. Keep close to the facts. Never lose yourself in abstractions. Never fancy that a general proposition means anything more than the facts which it sums up.[3]

And further with regard to facts:

> Every political organism, every political force must be studied in and cannot be understood apart from the environment out of which it has grown and in which it plays. Not all of the facts of that environment are relevant, but till you have examined all of them, you cannot pronounce any irrelevant.[4]

Such advice is, to be sure, well intended. It seeks to ensure objectivity and comprehensiveness—to deal with "reality" on its own terms. On application, however, the advice encounters some difficulty. As David Easton has called to our attention:

> There is an infinite level of detail possible about any event. The aspect of the event selected for description as the facts about it is determined by the prior interest of the observer; the selection is made in the light of a frame of reference that fixes the order and relevance of the facts. When raised to the level of consciousness this frame of reference is what we call a theory.[5]

Thus, it is theory which provides the criteria by which the judgment of relevance is made for only certain of the myriad of details entailed in any event. But theory is even more intimately involved with facts. It provides more than criteria of relevance. Easton implies this when he says, "A fact is a peculiar ordering of reality in terms of a theoretic interest." [6]

It is theory which provides the bridge between the infinitely complex reality with which we are faced and the means through which we are aware of this reality: our senses. Take the extreme position for a moment and consider facts as the data of the senses. Facts then consist in patches of color, shapes, sounds, smells, tastes, and tactile sensations. A moment's reflection will indicate how far such data are from being objective.[7] How many people's sensory receptors react in exactly the same way to the same external stimulus? What would be the content of human communication if our minds were capable of no more than recording the data of the senses and commanding effectors to respond to these data? What, under these circumstances, would be the chance of developing any phase of man's science as we know it today, or even as it was known at the time of Ptolemy?

It seems unlikely that Lord Bryce meant for us to deal simply with the data of the senses—to examine such characteristic political phenomena as revolutions in terms of quantities and qualities of noise and flow of reddish liquid. But the moment that one moves off this extreme position one deals no longer with pure facts. Rather one deals with concepts. This is exactly the case when one examines a revolution in terms of personalities, power, culture, income distributions, and electoral processes. No criticism is here intended of the data with which we deal. Rather it is the intent to recognize such data for what they are, viz., concepts. As such, they are products of *mental postulation,* complex statements about the way we think the world is; for who has seen a personality, a power, or a culture? For that matter, how would one recognize a revolution, utilizing only the data of the senses? Without mental postulation these data would simply fail to cohere.

However, while mental postulation is thus essential for the cognition of a fact, this very process imposes a limit on the reliability of the cognition. Norwood R. Hanson comments significantly on this point: "Seeing a bird in the sky involves seeing that it will not suddenly do vertical snap rolls; and this is more than marks the retina. *We could be wrong.* But to see a bird, even momentarily, is to see it in all these connexions."[8] If one agrees that the data of the senses would fail to cohere without mental postulation, and that the cognition of facts is inextricably dependent on such postulation, Hanson's comment becomes salient. With regard to the theoretical assumptions and implications of any fact, "We could be wrong." It therefore behooves us to be aware of the postulational framework within which our cognition of facts takes place.

Consider one of the "hardest" of the few "hard data" with which political scientists deal: votes. Bryce notwithstanding, votes are taken as data by the political scientist not simply because they occur but because they are believed to have meaning. Are they measures of approval, habituation, apathy, civic obligation, distributions of philosophic preferences, or personal popularity? What is the significance of the voting process itself? Unless the political scientist either makes assumptions about these meanings of votes or seeks to test them, he falls prey, deservedly, to the charge of the traditionalist that "one cannot learn anything by counting noses."

The Theoretical Context of Causal Relationships

If the theoretical nature of facts be conceded, one is well on the way to an appreciation of the role of theory in causal relationships. For here, in addition to the theoretical aspects of the facts involved, one is concerned with a relationship between, or among, facts. Consider the example offered in Hanson of a classic causal chain: "For want of a nail a shoe was lost; for want of a shoe a horse was lost; for want of a horse a rider was lost; for want of a rider a battalion was lost; for want of a battalion a battle was lost; for want of a victory a kingdom was lost—all for the want of a nail." [9] Indeed, the events described in the "chain" succeed one another in time, and (as will be discussed shortly) this is a necessary condition in a causal relationship. However, unless one has some theory about the importance of proper shoeing for effective functioning of horses, and about the importance of military victories for the maintenance of kingdoms, this does not constitute a causal chain, but a sequential series of accidents. Scientific method specifies a set of necessary conditions for the establishment of causality. Causation is seen as established only in the case of repetitive events wherein an event, or paradigm of events x, is always followed by an event y, regardless of what events precede x.[10] While these are necessary conditions for the establishment of causality, it is here argued that they are not sufficient. What is needed in addition is a meaningful explanation relating the events (a battalion-strength force in military strategy; war and empire, and so forth). Given this additional condition, one is not forced to accept sunrise in New York as the cause of sunrise in California simply because the former is invariably followed by the latter.

In the subject matter of political science the necessary and sufficient conditions for the establishment of a causal relationship are rarely encountered. Certainly this is the case if one seeks unicausal relationships. For example, if one suspected that college education increased political interest and therefore tested the hypothesis that *all* college-educated persons had a higher level of interest on completion of a college education than when they entered college, it would be very likely to be falsified by the evidence.[11] However, if one were to posit an invariate direction to the change in the proportion of a group voting as the average level of education in the group was increased, the hypothesis might withstand considerable testing.[12] If the hypothesis withstands testing, one has an event (education of a man or group) followed by another event (increase in probability that an individual will vote or increase in proportion of group members voting) regardless of preceding events; and thus one has fulfilled some of the necessary conditions for the establishment of causality. Ignoring for the moment the problem raised by regarding a change in probability as an event, one still lacks sufficient conditions for the establishment of a causal relationship between college education and change in the probability of having a given level of political interest.[13] In the absence of a meaningful explanation relating these two events, one has only an empirical relationship which, if it withstands a great deal of testing, may, by convention, come to be regarded as an empirical law. However, it is not causal law. Only a meaningful explanation, taken together with the other requisite, can establish a causal law. Thus, for example, if there were a reliable body of theory which held that our values are affected by our learning experiences, and that college education over a given span of time affords individuals learning experiences not equally available outside of that education during that span of time, and that our level of political interest results from our values, the empirical relationship between college education and increased probability of change in party allegiance would be regarded as causal. Here, Hanson's remarks are quite relevant: "Causes certainly are connected with effects; but this is because our theories connect them, not because the world is held together by cosmic glue. The world *may* be glued together by imponderables, but that is irrelevant for understanding causal explanation."[14]

Before moving to a consideration of the nature of explanation, a word of reassurance is due the reader with respect to regarding a change in probability as an event. This tactic may appear to be designed to evade the issue; that is, the existence of an invariant relationship. If one insists on regarding the individual as the sole significant unit in political analysis, the introduction of probability certainly does evade the issue; for to know that a given individual's probability of voting Republican is 0.692 is not to know very much. However, if one is willing to regard the behavior of large numbers of people as significant units of political analysis, the knowledge that any given individual's probability of voting Republican is 0.692 is quite useful; for under certain attainable conditions it is to know that about 70 people out of every hundred in the electorate will vote Republican. It seems unlikely that political science will arrive at a position where its laws can govern the actions of individuals taken singly. However, it is perhaps reassuring to note that even the physical sciences have encountered this problem—in fact, it is a problem of that "exact science," physics. As it happens, it is impossible to predict either the direction or the velocity of the movement of any given atomic particle. Rather, one must deal with probability statements about groups of particles. Yet particle physics is regarded as quite scientific and has, in fact, been able to discern "conceptual order among puzzling data," to use Hanson's terms.[15]

The Nature of Scientific Explanations

Explanation, scientific or otherwise, is essentially an attempt to make some event understandable. There exists some disagreement among philosophers of science as to how events are made understandable. One school argues that explanation consists in showing the particular event to be subsumed under more general laws.[16] The other school holds that explanation is accomplished by showing that the unfamiliar comports with familiar experiences.[17] Obviously if the more general laws are a part of our *familiar* experience the problem is resolved. In the training of a scientist in a field with an established body of body of theory, many general laws are assimilated, and for this scientist they are a part of his experience. However, the argument of the anti-general-law-explanation school is that the true explanation consists in accounting for the more general laws, and that this is done by analogy, or in the case of mathematics by mathematical neatness.[18] Thus, the Dynamical Theory of Gases is based on an analogy with moving particles of solid matter and their impacts on each other and the walls of their container. A little thought will indicate that familiar experience traced back to fundamentals eventually reaches back to inchoate general laws, and the argument seems to be one of the chicken-egg-which-came-first type. The attempt will not be made to solve the conundrum here. However, it is necessary to understand the utility of our experiences for suggesting explanations. Thus, for example, animosities and greed have been offered as explanations for wars because experience has shown that these often lead to individual acts of violence. Whether or not an explanation is accepted depends on a number of factors, not the least of which is its ability to withstand the testing of its implications. Testing requires separate treatment and will be so handled at another point. There are criteria which are applied to scientific explanations prior to testing. The theory—and scientific explanation is here seen as a theory—must permit the phenomena to be accounted for to be deduced from it; it must also either not do damage to existing theory or, if it does damage, be able to account for the phenomena subsumed under the theories which it damages. Thus, for example, one could argue, as does David Truman, that the cohesive potential of an interest group is inversely related to the degree that its membership overlaps those of groups with conflicting interests, on the grounds that the cross pressures tend to produce apathy.[19] Such an explanation immediately recommends itself for acceptance because of its fit with existing role theory. This theory holds that the way in which an individual behaves is in large measure determined by the role which he sees himself playing, and a single individual is capable of playing a great variety of roles. However, a role theory also holds that the requirement of performing incompatible roles (such as striking railway worker loyal to his union and patriotic citizen with attendant loyalties during a war) constitutes a personality threat to which withdrawal may be a response.[20]

The Ubiquity of Theory Restated

The attempt has been made above to demonstrate the theoretical natures of fact, causality, and explanation. An awareness of the theoretical, and therefore tentative,[21] nature of the matrix in which all perception takes place is essential to an understanding of science. In the absence of such an awareness, astronomy would still have to think in terms of the earth as being at the center of a set of planets orbiting in perfect concentric circles about it. Such awareness has certainly not been lacking among political theorists. Political thinkers as far apart as Edmund Burke and John Stuart Mill were well aware, for example, that votes meant different things to different people. The empiricists' criticism (with Burke as a leading critic) is that no amount of theorizing can ascertain the meaning of votes or the causes of war or of group disintegration. It is the method of science to so combine theory and verification as to make increasingly intelligible the phenomena of experience. To the elucidation of this method this chapter now addresses itself.

The Scientific Method

At the heart of scientific method lies a system of thought. The exact nature of the system is a matter of some controversy,[22] and it is felt that a discussion of these controversies [here] would prove more confusing than beneficial. Therefore, it is preferred to proceed directly to the heart of scientific method: that is, retroduction and verification (more properly, falsifiability).

The Development of Theory

The term "retroduction" is used, not in order to move the familiar into the esoteric, but as a form of shorthand. The term derives from Pierce's transla-tion of the Greek for Aristotle's third class of inference[23] (the other two being deduction and induction). The term is here defined as an imaginative leap, a flight of fancy, taken to account for observed phenomena. Pierce makes a neat distinction among the three types of inference: "Deduction proves that some-thing *must* [logically] be; induction shows that something *actually* is operative [to the extent of observations]; . . . [retroduction] merely suggests that some-thing *may be.*" [24]

Thus, one thing the scientist does is observe certain phenomena, such as the acceleration of falling bodies, the occurrence of revolutions, the growth of totalitarian systems. He then seeks an explanatory principle beyond his obser-vations to account for them. He seeks these by the use of creative imagination. Induction will not do it, as induction—the reasoning from the specific to the general—is the specific writ large. It is descriptive, describing the universal as a replica of the observable; [25] for example, in all observed cases, an increase in educational level is associated with an increase in political participation,[26] therefore, by induction, all cases of increased education level are associated with increased political participation. It does not seek to explain why in any or all cases an increased level of education is associated with increased political participation. Nor will deduction provide explanation, except in the case of an imaginatively conceived major premise. Thus, for example, Pareto's explanation of revolutions has deductive aspects, but these are not the source of his major premise. They are (in very simplified form):

"(1) All societies are divided into ruling elites and ruled.

(2) Into each group, people of leadership ability are born.

(3) In each group, certain persons with leadership ability have a strong desire to lead." [27]

These premises were arrived at neither inductively (although experience was a guide in their selection) nor deductively. Rather they are *a way of conceiving the world to be organized,* selected in order to permit Pareto to deduce that "(*a*) Unless the elites either kill off non-elite natural leaders, or admit them to the elite ranks, such leaders will provide the leadership for revolution." Thereby he offered an explanation for revolutions. The effort has been made to distinguish retroduction from both deduction and induction in order to make it clear that explanations are arrived at by no mechanical process, but by a creative one.[28] Such a process is essentially psychological, and the question might be raised as to whether such processes are part of the formal requirements of scientific method. Morris R. Cohen, in a critique of traditional doctrine concerning deduction, has distinguished the formal logic of deduction (wherein the conclusions are contained in the premises and form no temporal series at all) from the psychological process of perceiving the logical conclusions implied by a set of premises.[29] The distinction is a fruitful one in an analysis of deduction, and one could gain some appreciation of the role of deduction in science by concentrating on its formal logic. However, at present, this is not the case with retroduction. There exists as yet no statement of its formal rules of procedure. It can be appreciated only as a psychological process. Yet its role in science is pivotal. For example, Kepler was able to use deductions from Copernican theory and the incompatibility of his own and another's (Tycho Brahe's) observations with those deductions to refute the concept of planetary orbits as circles concentric to the sun. However, no set of logical rules could have led him to the concept of the ellipticity of planetary orbits. Yet, without that concept the observations could not have been explained. If it is the role of science to explain observations in terms of a set of testable ideas, retroduction is the means by which science expands its explanatory powers. In a letter to Karl Popper, Einstein commented, "I think (like you, by the way) that theory cannot be fabricated out of results of observation, but that it can only be invented." [30]

Before moving on to the second essential feature of scientific method—that is, verification—one word of caution is due the reader. To recognize the vital role of imagination is not to ensure that it will readily or satisfactorily provide explanations. (The satisfactory nature of an explanation is its ability to withstand testing, which will be treated in the discussion of verification.) Philosophers of science occasionally leave one with this mistaken impression. Thus, for example, Northrop argues that Galileo, in attempting to account for the motion of a falling object, allowed an analysis of his initial problems to guide his imagination in terms of three relevant variables, viz., weight, distance, and time; that by testing the explanatory powers of the first two, Galileo eliminated them and was left with the third variable, time, which proved satisfactory.[31] This is deceptively simple, for, as Hanson points out, it took Galileo more than thirty years to recognize the significance of time as a variable.[32]

Verification

The satisfactory nature of a particular scientific explanation consists, as has been mentioned, in its ability to withstand testing. Essentially, this is a matter of failing in the face of suitable tests, to be proved false, as distinguished from being proved true. The class of statements which can be proved to be true is so temporally limited as to be of little use to science. These are what Popper calls *existential* statements.[33] Such statements say that something exists: for example, "There are white, Protestant, Anglo-Saxon, upper-class Americans who are extreme liberals." One could prove such a statement by finding two such individuals. Of itself, the statement when proved contributes little to an understanding of political phenomena. It may be objected that such a statement when proved does enlighten, for it invalidates the statement, "All white, Protestant, Anglo-Saxon, upper-class American are conservatives." The objection is valid, and it is the point to be made here. Note that the existential statement takes on significance only from its relation to a different type of statement—one that not only says that something exists, but one which says implicitly that something does not exist, namely, white, Protestant, Anglo-Saxon, upper-class Americans who are not conservative. Such a statement is called a *universal* statement,[34] for its purports to define the universe by excluding certain things from it. Both types of statement are "empirically decidable," to use Popper's terms, but each in only one direction. The existential can be proved by finding the existence of that which it postulates. However, it cannot be disproved, as failure to find the object in question cannot be taken as conclusive evidence that it does not exist. The universal statement, on the other hand, can be disproved by finding that which it excludes from the universe. However, it cannot be proved, as that which it excludes, while undiscovered, may yet exist and someday be discovered. Since the universal statements are so much more informative (they postulate both what exists and what does not exist, and the latter includes all possible worlds minus one), it is with these, rather than with existential statements, that science is concerned. Thus, science is concerned with statements that can be disproved rather than with those which can be proved. Popper offers as his criterion of demarcation for science, falsifiability rather than verifiability, and it is hoped that in the light of the foregoing explanation this is seen as justifiable.[35]

"I shall not require of a scientific system that it shall be capable of being singled out, once and for all, in a positive sense; but I shall require that its logical form shall be such that it can be singled out, by means of empirical tests, in a negative sense: *it must be possible for an empirical scientific system to be refuted by experience.*" [36]

There exists one crucial problem in Popper's criterion for science. There is the implication that by putting a statement into a particular logical form—the form called universal—one ensures the possibility of its empirical refutation. One should be aware that this is not necessarily the case. Consider the statement, "All human actions are predetermined." Such a statement is in universal form. One could refute it by finding a human action that was not predetermined. However, the substance of the statement is such that it is not empirically possible to refute it unless additional conditions are specified. Specifically one must be told how to recognize a nonpredetermined human action upon encountering it. Thus while the logically refutable form is a necessary condition for the possibility of empirical refutation, it is not a sufficient one. There must be specified, in addition, criteria of invalidation: that is, an empirical means of recognizing what would count as negating evidence. Whether, for every universal statement, there can be devised and implemented such criteria, which will discriminate without doing damage to the meaning of the original statement, remains a moot point. [37] However, in the absence of such criteria, evaluation of theory is limited to tests of consistency, argument by analogy, and the use of indirect and sometimes ambiguous evidence.

Problems of Criteria of Empirical Invalidation

One is specifically concerned here with criteria for empirical invalidation of a relationship among postulated concepts. There are at least two problems inherent in the generation of such criteria. There is the epistemological problem of relating the meaning of the data of sensory perception on which the empirical judgment is to be made to the meaning of the postulated concepts about which judgment is to be made. Then there is the problem of operationalization, that is, of the design and construction of empirical sensing and recording devices which can be both epistemologically justified and physically accomplished. Their significance rather than their solution is the point of the discussion which follows.

The set of epistemological problems seems comprehended by what F. S. C. Northrop calls epistemic correlation—an intellectual feat which "joins a thing known in the one way to what is in some sense the same thing known in a different way." [38] We are thus concerned with establishing a connection between such postulated concepts as, for instance, power, or ideology, or authoritarian personality, or anomie, on the one hand, and the empirical referents which are taken as indicative of their presence (and in some cases of the degree in which they are present); for example, the relationship between an individual's voting record in a legislative body and the voting record of the majority of that body has on occasion been taken as a measure of the power of that individual over that legislative body.[39] Similarly, there are indices of ideological thinking,[40] of authoritarian personality,[41] and of anomie.[42] In each case two epistemological questions are salient. First, what is the rationale by which the empirical referent is linked to the postulated concept; second, to what extent are they the "same thing" known in different ways?

Dahl's treatment of the concept of power affords an opportunity for gaining an appreciation of the import of these questions.[43] He sets out his postulated concept of power as follows: "My intuitive idea of power, then, is something like this: A has power over B to the extent that he can get B to do something that B would not otherwise do." He then specifies the properties of this concept: (1) the necessity of a time lag between the effort of A to influence B's behavior and B's behavior itself, (2) no "action at a distance," that is, the establishment of some connection between A and B, (3) a difference between the probability that B will do something (X) if A does not act to influence him and the probability that B will do X if A acts to influence him.[44] In turning to examine the empirical referent used in ranking United States Senators in terms of power over legislative voting—that is, roll-call votes—he notes that these properties do not inhere in the referent. One cannot establish by the roll call alone either that a given Senator acted to influence the voting behavior of his fellow legislator or the direction of that action if it occurred. Thus this particular referent requires additional support in the form of observers' reports and explicit assumptions to link it with the postulated concept of power. Finally, even if a link is established between the two, Dahl makes it clear that the empirical referent is something subsumed under, but less than, the postulated concept of power. Here concern shifts to the problem of operationalization, but the problem of epistemic correlation is relevant. Dahl perceives in the concept of power at least three dimensions, or variables—specifically, scope, number of respondents, and change in probabilities; that is, the areas of behavior in which A has influence over B, the number of people over whom A has influence, and the change in their probable behavior which A effects. The question then arises as to whether any scale could be devised to handle simultaneously all these dimensions and still meet the requirements of epistemic correlation; that is, have the same properties as the concept and be linked to it by a satisfactory rationale. An additional aspect of the operationalization problem should be noted. Various empirical referents are occasionally used for the same concept with nonidentical results. Here again, epistemic correlation comes to the fore. A choice among such referents for the purpose of testing theoretic implications of a concept should be made on the basis of the similarity in properties between the concept and each of the referents and the satisfactory nature of the rationale by which they can be linked.[45]

These are, of course, not the only problems in the generation and application of empirical criteria of invalidation. There are the problems of the constancy of meaning of indicators over time and environment. How satisfactory is any given SES index over a twenty-year period or cross-culturally? How does one intercalibrate two such indices developed at different points in time and within different cultures? There is the host of problems raised by the impact of sensing operations on the environment under examination. Do surveys of voting intentions affect those intentions? Does the presence of observers affect the behavior of the individuals in the groups under observation? If so, to what extent? Then there are policy and ethical problems that arise. Does the known presence of social science researchers operate unequally to the advantage of some groups? What are the ethical implications of hiding their presence or concealing their purpose? These are not trite questions, but they have been ignored in favor of focusing attention on the importance of the relationship between operationalization and epistemic correlation in order to stress again that while science is empirical it is not empiricism. It is in the failure to make this distinction that "operationism" has been wanting.[46]

Conclusion

Of the two principal intellectual tools of science, retroduction and universal, empirically falsifiable statements, traditional political theory has certainly not been lacking in the former. The complex theoretical structures of Plato, Aristotle, Aquinas, Harrington, Hobbes, Hegal, and Marx attest to no lack of imaginative abilities. What has been lacking has been the casting of theory into universal, empirically falsifiable form, and the provision of criteria of falsification. Wrestling with the problem of criteria, while perhaps not incumbent on the political philosopher, is certainly incumbent on the political scientist as scientist. This is not to say that speculative thought is to be denied the political scientist. On the contrary, the discussion of retroduction should have made clear the vital role of such thought in the construction of any scientific theory and in the discovery of any scientific "facts." Nor need the establishment of criteria of falsifiability precede the structuring of theory; that is, the explication of the logical relationship of its parts. Quite the opposite, the theory may have to be structured, by deduction, a long way to some fairly remote implications of its major premises before criteria (normally operational criteria) can be devised to test the major premises via their implications. However, to the extent that the political scientist seeks to contribute to the reliability of the body of political knowledge, he must concern himself with finding criteria for the rejection of the unreliable.

Political science is identified herein as a science, not on the basis of its achievements, but on the basis of its available aspirations. That these may prove illusory, in whole or in part, cannot be denied[47]—but that is an occupational hazard in the pursuit of knowledge.

▪ *Notes*

1. For a most enlightening treatment of common-sense explanation in general, see Karl W. Deutsch, "The Limits of Common Sense," *Psychiatry*, XXII, No. 2 (May, 1959), 105–112.
2. The difficulties entailed in attempting to refute such explanations empirically can perhaps be better appreciated after reading a collection of arguments on the Civil

War such as that available in Edwin C. Rozewenc, ed., *Slavery as a Cause of the Civil War* (Boston: Heath, 1949). One ought in this case to read with a view to making an empirically based decision among the arguments.

3. James Bryce, "Presidential Address to the Fifth Annual Meeting of the American Political Science Association," *American Political Science Review,* III, No. 3 (1909), 4.

4. *Ibid.,* p. 8.

5. David Easton, *The Political System* (New York: Knopf, 1953), p. 53.

6. *Ibid.*

7. For a systematic *reductio ad absurdum* of pure empiricism, see F. S. C. Northrop, *The Logic of the Sciences and the Humanities* (New York: Meridian, 1959), pp. 39–49.

8. Norwood Russel Hanson, *Patterns of Discovery* (Cambridge: Cambridge University Press, 1958), p. 21. Italics supplied.

9. *Ibid.,* p. 50. Hanson's discussion of the problem is quite lucid; cf. *ibid.,* p. 53.

10. Cf. Paul F. Lazarsfeld, "Interpretation of Statistical Relations as a Research Operation," in Paul F. Lazarsfeld and Morris Rosenberg, eds., *The Language of Social Research* (New York: Free Press, 1955), p. 125.

11. Cf. Bernard R. Berelson, Paul F. Lazarsfeld, and William N. McPhee, *Voting* (Chicago: University of Chicago Press, 1954), p. 25, for an indication of this.

12. *Ibid.* However, one would have to test for spurious relationships, for other variables may be operative, such as aging, the student selection process, and SES (Socio-Economic Status), to name a few possibilities.

     A word of caution is due on the difficulty of actually meeting all the criteria posited for a causal relationship. Not only are these criteria rarely fulfilled, but even when fulfilled, the tentativeness of theoretical explanation of causality, and the frequent multiplicity of variables operative, have led scientists to abjure the term "causality" in preference for "association." Cf. Stephen Toulman, *The Philosophy of Science: An Introduction* (New York: Harper and Row, 1960), pp. 119–124.

13. For a thorough discussion of empirical causal relationships, and of methods of analysis when several variables may be related, see Lazarsfeld, *op. cit.,* pp. 115–125.

14. Hanson, *op. cit.,* p. 64.

15. Cf. *ibid.,* Chapters 5 and 6. See also Northrop, *op. cit.,* Chapter 11.

16. Cf. Richard B. Braithwaite, *Scientific Explanation* (New York: Harper and Row, 1960), pp. 342–343.

17. Norman Campbell, *What Is Science?* (New York: Dover, 1952), pp. 79–86.

18. The argument for mathematical explanation founded on mathematical neatness rests on the improbability of a mathematically neat universe. Thus, if one can find a simple set of mathematical equations which account for a given phenomenon, the set of equations will be taken as explanation. Cf. Campbell, *op. cit.,* pp. 153–157.

19. David B. Truman, *The Governmental Process* (New York: Knopf, 1951), pp. 156–167.

20. Cf. Ralph Linton, *The Cultural Background of Personality* (New York: Appleton-Century-Crofts, 1945), pp. 79–82.

21. See discussion of the reliability of cognition, above.

22. For argument on the roles of inductive and deductive logic see Northrop, *op. cit.,* pp. 1–18; Karl R. Popper, *The Logic of Scientific Discovery* (New York: Basic Books, 1959), pp. 27–34; Herbert Feigl and Wilfred Sellars, eds., *Readings in Philosophical Analysis* (New York: Appleton-Century-Crofts, 1949), Chapter 5.

23. Hanson, *op. cit.,* p. 85.

24. *Ibid.*

25. Perfect induction—that is, without inductive risk—is a special case of deduction. Cf. Morris Cohen and Ernest Nagel, *An Introduction to Logic and Scientific Method* (New York: Harcourt, Brace, and World, 1934), p. 275.

26. Cf. Robert E. Lane, *Political Life* (New York: Free Press, 1959), pp. 351–352. N.B.: Professor Lane does not make the induction used in illustration here.

27. Vilfredo Pareto, *The Mind and Society* (New York: Harcourt, Brace, and World, 1935), Vol. III.

28. This effort may herein have been given a deceptively simple portrayal. The effort involved in retroduction is perhaps best illustrated in Hanson's account of Kepler's study of the orbit of Mars. Hanson, *op. cit.*, pp. 77–89. See also Arthur Koestler, *The Sleepwalkers* (New York: Macmillan, 1954), pp. 324–333.

29. Morris R. Cohen, *A Preface to Logic* (New York: Meridian, 1956), pp. 26–27.

30. Albert Einstein in Popper, *op. cit.*, p. 458.

31. Northrop, *op. cit.*, pp. 23–26.

32. Hanson, *op. cit.*, p. 68. For a recent and timely treatment of the difficulties of scientific discovery, see Koestler, *op. cit.*

33. Popper, *op. cit.*, pp. 68–70.

34. *Ibid.*

35. *Ibid.*, pp. 40–41.

36. *Ibid.* For objections to Popper's criterion, see Arthur Pap, *Elements of Analytic Philosophy* (New York: Macmillan, 1949), p. 458.

37. See discussion below.

38. Northrop, *op. cit.*, p. 119. For a thorough discussion of the concept, see *ibid.*, pp. 119–131.

39. See Robert A. Dahl, "The Concept of Power," *Behavioral Science*, II (July, 1957), 210–214.

40. Angus Campbell *et al.*, *The American Voter* (New York: John Wiley, 1960), pp. 188–215.

41. T. W. Adorno *et al.*, *The Authoritarian Personality* (New York: Harper and Row, 1950), pp. 224-279.

42. Leo Srole, "Social Dysfunction, Personality and Social Distance Attitudes," mimeographed paper read before the American Sociological Society, 1951 Annual Meeting, Chicago; quoted in Arthur Kornhauser *et al.*, *When Labor Votes* (New York: University Books, 1956), pp. 189–190. See also Robert K. Merton, *Social Theory and Social Structure* (New York: Free Press, 1957), Chapters 4 and 5.

43. Dahl, *op. cit.*, pp. 201–215.

44. Note that these assumptions rule out the alternative of A influencing B solely by way of B's expectations about A. See Herbert Simon, "Notes on the Observation and Measurement of Political Power," *Journal of Politics*, XV (1953), 500–516.

45. An example of such a problem is provided in George A. Lundberg and Pearl Friedman, "A Comparison of Three Measures of Socioeconomic Status," *Rural Sociology*, VIII (1943), 227–236. Reprinted in Lazarsfeld and Rosenberg, *op. cit.*, pp. 66–73.

46. See A. Cornelius Benjamin, *Operationism* (Springfield, Ill.: Charles C Thomas, 1955), pp. 64–91.

47. For a discussion of the operative limits on theoretical development, see Northrop's discussion of economic theory in Northrop, *op. cit.*, Chapter 3.

44 THE HISTORICAL IMAGINATION

■ *C. Wright Mills*

The productions of historians may be thought of as a great file indispensable to all social science—I believe this a true and fruitful view. History as a discipline is also sometimes considered to contain all social science—but only by a few misguided "humanists." More fundamental than either view is the idea that every social science—or better, every well-considered social study— requires a historical scope of conception and a full use of historical materials. This simple notion is the major idea for which I am arguing.

1. In our very statement of what-is-to-be-explained, we need the fuller range that can be provided only by knowledge of the historical varieties of human society. That a given question—the relations of forms of nationalism with types of militarism, for example—must often be given a different answer when it is asked of different societies and periods means that the question itself often needs to be reformulated. We need the variety provided by history in order even to ask sociological questions properly, much less to answer them. The answers or explanations we would offer are often, if not usually, in terms of comparisons. Comparisons are required in order to understand what may be the essential conditions of whatever we are trying to understand, whether forms of slavery or specific meanings of crime, types of family or peasant communities or collective farms. We must observe whatever we are interested in under a variety of circumstances. Otherwise we are limited to flat description.

To go beyond that, we must study the available range of social structures, including the historical as well as the contemporary. If we do not take into account the range, which does not, of course, mean all existing cases, our statements cannot be empirically adequate. Such regularities or relations as may obtain among several features of society cannot be clearly discerned. Historical types, in short, are a very important part of what we are studying; they are also indispensable to our explanations of it. To eliminate such mate-

From C. Wright Mills, *The Sociological Imagination* (New York: Oxford University Press, 1959), pp. 145–152, 154. © Copyright 1959 by Oxford University Press, Inc. Reprinted by permission.

rials—the record of all that man has done and become—from our studies would be like pretending to study the process of birth, but ignoring motherhood.

If we limit ourselves to one national unit of one contemporary (usually Western) society, we cannot possibly hope to catch many really fundamental differences among human types and social institutions. This general truth has one rather specific meaning for work in social science: in the cross-section moment of any one society there may often be so many common denominators of belief, value, institutional form, that no matter how detailed and precise our study, we will not find truly significant differences among the people and institutions at this one moment in this one society. In fact, the one-time-and-one-locale studies often assume or imply a homogeneity which, if true, very much needs *to be taken as a problem*. It cannot fruitfully be reduced, as it so often is in current research practice, to a problem of sampling procedure. It cannot be formulated as a problem within the terms of one moment and one locale.

Societies seem to differ with respect to the range of variation of specific phenomena within them as well as, in a more general way, with respect to their degree of social homogeneity. As Morris Ginsberg has remarked, if something we are studying "exhibits sufficient individual variations within the same society, or at the same period of time, it may be possible to establish real connections without going outside that society or period." [1] That is often true, but usually it is not so certain that it may simply be assumed; to know whether or not it is true, we must often design our studies as comparisons of social structures. To do that in an adequate way usually requires that we make use of the variety provided by history. The problem of social homogeneity—as in the modern mass society, or, in contrast, as in the traditional society—cannot even be properly stated, much less adequately solved, unless we consider in a comparative way the range of contemporary and historical societies.

The meaning, for example, of such key themes of political science as "public" and "public opinion" cannot be made clear without such work. If we do not take a fuller range into our study, we often condemn ourselves to shallow and misleading results. I do not suppose, for example, that anyone would argue with the statement that the fact of political indifference is one of the major facts of the contemporary political scene in Western societies. Yet in those studies of "the political psychology of voters" which are noncomparative and nonhistorical, we do not find even a classification of "voters" —or of "political men"—that really takes into account such indifference. In fact, the historically specific idea of such political indifference, and much less its meaning, cannot be formulated in the usual terms of such voting studies.

To say of peasants of the preindustrial world that they are "politically indifferent" does not carry the same meaning as to say the same of man in modern mass society. For one thing, the importance of political institutions to ways of life and their conditions are quite different in the two types of society. For another thing, the formal opportunity to become politically engaged differs. And for another, the expectation of political involvement raised by the entire course of bourgeois democracy in the modern West has not always been raised in the preindustrial world. To understand "political indifference," to explain it, to grasp its meaning for modern societies, requires that we consider the quite various types and conditions of indifference, and to do that we must examine historical and comparative materials.

2. Ahistorical studies usually tend to be static or very short-term studies of limited milieus. That is only to be expected, for we more readily become aware of larger structures when they are changing, and we are likely to become aware of such changes only when we broaden our view to include a suitable historical span. Our chance to understand how smaller milieus and larger structures interact, and our chance to understand the larger causes at work in these limited milieus, thus require us to deal with historical materials. Awareness of structure, in all the meanings of this central term, as well as adequate statement of the troubles and problems of limited milieus, requires that we recognize and that we practice the social sciences as historical disciplines.

Not only are our chances of becoming aware of structure increased by historical work; we cannot hope to understand any single society, even as a static affair, without the use of historical materials. The image of any society is a historically specific image. What Marx called the "principle of historical specificity" refers, first, to a guideline: any given society is to be understood in terms of the specific period in which it exists. However "period" may be defined, the institutions, the ideologies, the types of men and women prevailing in any given period, constitute something of a unique pattern. This does not mean that such a historical type cannot be compared with others, and certainly not that the pattern can be grasped only intuitively. But it does mean—and this is the second reference of the principle—that within this historical type various mechanisms of change come to some specific kind of intersection. These mechanisms, which Karl Mannheim—following John Stuart Mill—called *"principia media,"* are the very mechanisms that the social scientist, concerned with social structure, wishes to grasp.

Early social theorists tried to formulate invariant laws of society—laws that would hold of all societies, just as the abstracted procedures of physical science had led to laws that cut beneath the qualitative richness of "nature." There is, I believe, no "law" stated by any social scientist that is transhistorical, that must not be understood as having to do with the specific structure of some period. Other "laws" turn out to be empty abstractions or quite confused tautologies. The only meaning of "social laws" or even of "social regularities" is such *"principia media"* as we may discover, or if you wish, construct, for a social structure within a historically specific era. We do not know any universal principles of historical change; the mechanisms of change we do know vary with the social structure we are examining. For historical change *is* change of social structures, of the relations among their component parts. Just as there is a variety of social structures, there is a variety of principles of historical change.

3. That knowledge of the history of a society is often indispensable to its understanding becomes quite clear to any economist or political scientist or sociologist, once he leaves his advanced industrial nation to examine the institutions in some different social structure—in the Middle East, in Asia, in Africa. In the study of "his own country" he has often smuggled in the history; knowledge of it is embodied in the very conceptions with which he works. When he takes up a fuller range, when he compares, he becomes more aware of the historical as intrinsic to what he wants to understand and not merely as "general background."

In our time problems of the Western societies are almost inevitably problems of the world. It is perhaps one defining characteristic of our period that it is one in which for the first time the varieties of social worlds it contains are in serious, rapid, and obvious interplay. The study of our period must be a comparative examination of these worlds and of their interactions. Perhaps that is why what was once the anthropologist's exotic preserve has become the world's "underdeveloped countries," which economists no less than political scientists and sociologists regularly include among their objects of study. That is why some of the very best sociology being done today is work on world areas and regions.

Comparative study and historical study are very deeply involved with each other. You cannot understand the underdeveloped, the Communist, the capitalist political economies as they exist in the world today by flat, timeless comparisons. You must expand the temporal reach of your analysis. To understand and to explain the comparative facts as they lie before you today, you must know the historical phases and the historical reasons for varying rates and varying directions of development and lack of development. You must know, for example, why the colonies founded by Westerners in North America and Australia in the sixteenth and seventeenth centuries became in due course industrially flourishing capitalist societies, but those in India, Latin America, and Africa remained impoverished, peasant, and underdeveloped right up into the twentieth century.

Thus the historical viewpoint leads to the comparative study of societies: you cannot understand or explain the major phases through which any modern Western nation has passed, or the shape that it assumes today, solely in terms of its own national history. I do not mean merely that in historical reality it has interacted with the development of other societies; I mean also that the mind cannot even formulate the historical and sociological problems of this one social structure without understanding them in contrast and in comparison with other societies.

4. Even if our work is not explicitly comparative—even if we are concerned with some limited area of one national social structure—we need historical materials. Only by an act of abstraction that unnecessarily violates social reality can we try to freeze some knife-edge moment. We may, of course, construct such static glimpses or even panoramas, but we cannot conclude our work with such constructions. Knowing that what we are studying is subject to change, on the simplest of descriptive levels, we must ask: What

are the salient trends? To answer that question we must make a statement of at least "from what" and "to what."

Our statement of trends may be very short-term or of epochal length; that will, of course, depend on our purpose. But usually, in work of any scale, we find a need for trends of considerable length. Longer-term trends are usually needed if only in order to overcome historical provincialism: the assumption that the present is a sort of autonomous creation.

If we want to understand the dynamic changes in a contemporary social structure, we must try to discern its longer-run developments and in terms of them ask: What are the mechanics by which these trends have occurred, by which the structure of this society is changing? It is in questions such as these that our concern with trends comes to a climax. That climax has to do with the historical transition from one epoch to another and with what we may call the structure of an epoch.

The social scientist wishes to understand the nature of the present epoch, to outline its structure and to discern the major forces at work in it. Each epoch, when properly defined, is "an intelligible field of study" that reveals mechanics of history making peculiar to it. The role of power elites, for example, in the making of history varies according to the extent to which the institutional means of decisions are centralized.

The notion of the structure and dynamics of "the modern period," and of such essential and unique features as it may have, is central, although often unacknowledged, to the social sciences. Political scientists study the modern state; economists, modern capitalism. Sociologists—especially in their dialectic with Marxism—pose many of their problems in terms of "the characteristics of modern times," and anthropologists use their sensibilities to the modern world in their examinations of preliterate societies. Perhaps most classic problems of modern social science—of political science and economics no less than of sociology—have, in fact, had to do with one rather specific historical interpretation: the interpretation of the rise, the components, the shape, of the urban industrial societies of The Modern West—usually in contrast with The Feudal Era. . . .

But above all, the social scientist is trying to see the several major trends together—structurally, rather than as happenings in a scatter of milieus, adding up to nothing new, in fact not adding up at all. This is the aim that lends to the study of trends its relevance to the understanding of a period and which demands full and adroit use of the materials of history.

▪ *Note*

1. Morris Ginsberg, *Essays in Sociology and Social Philosophy* (London: Heinemann, 1956), II, 39.

☐ *Epilogue*

45 CHILDREN PLAYING

▪ *Learned Hand*

... And so when I hear so much impatient and irritable complaint, so much readiness to replace what we have by guardians for us all, those supermen, evoked somewhere from the clouds, whom none have seen and none are ready to name, I lapse into a dream, as it were. I see children playing on the grass; their voices are shrill and discordant as children's are; they are restive and quarrelsome; they cannot agree to any common plan; their play annoys them; it goes so poorly. And one says, let us make Jack the master; Jack knows all about it; Jack will tell us what each is to do and we shall all agree. But Jack is like all the rest; Helen is discontented with her part and Henry with his, and soon they fall again into their old state. No, the children must learn to play by themselves; there is no Jack the master. And in the end slowly and with infinite disappointment they do learn a little; they learn to forbear, to reckon with another, accept a little where they wanted much, to live and let live, to yield when they must yield; perhaps, we may hope, not to take all they can. But the condition is that they shall be willing at least to listen to one another, to get the habit of pooling their wishes. Somehow or other they must do this, if the play is to go on; maybe it will not, but there is no Jack, in or out of the box, who can come to straighten the game.

From Learned Hand, address quoted in the *Federal Bar Journal,* I (March, 1932), 40–45. Reprinted by permission.

◼ FOR FURTHER STUDY

Part One: The Norm of Politics

Aristotle. *Politics.* Oxford: Clarendon Press, 1958.

Barker, Ernest. *Reflections on Government.* New York: Oxford University Press, 1942.

Dewey, John. *The Public and Its Problems.* New York: Holt, 1927.

Kariel, Henry S. *Open Systems: Arenas for Political Action.* Itasca, Ill.: F. E. Peacock, 1969.

Mill, John Stuart. *On Liberty, Considerations on Representative Government, The Subjection of Women* (1859, 1861, 1869). New York: Oxford University Press, 1954.

Rousseau, Jean Jacques. *The Social Contract* (1762). New York: Hafner, 1947.

Tussman, Joseph. *Obligation and the Body Politic.* New York: Oxford University Press, 1960.

Part Two: Challenges to Politics

Arendt, Hannah. *The Origins of Totalitarianism.* New York: Harcourt, Brace, 1951.

Burckhardt, Jacob. *Force and Freedom* (1905). New York: Meridian, 1955.

Ellul, Jacques. *The Technological Society.* New York: Knopf, 1964.

Harrington, Michael. *The Accidental Century.* New York: Macmillan, 1965.

Heilbroner, Robert A. *The Great Ascent: The Struggle for Economic Development in Our Time.* New York: Harper and Row, 1963.

Kornhauser, William. *The Politics of Mass Society.* New York: Free Press, 1959.

Lederer, Emil. *The State of the Masses.* New York: Norton, 1940.

Lindsay, A. D. "The Industrial Revolution," in *The Modern Democratic State.* New York: Oxford University Press, 1943, pp. 167–190.

Lippmann, Walter. *Essays on the Public Philosophy.* New York: Mentor, 1956.

Mannheim, Karl. *Man and Society in an Age of Reconstruction.* New York: Harcourt, Brace, 1940.

Michels, Robert. *Political Parties* (1911). New York: Free Press, 1949.

Moore, Wilbert E. *The Impact of Industry.* Englewood Cliffs, N.J.: Prentice-Hall, 1965.

Mumford, Lewis. *The City in History: Its Origins, Its Transformation, and Its Prospects.* New York: Harcourt, Brace, and World, 1961.

Myrdal, Gunnar. *Challenge to Affluence.* New York: Pantheon, 1962.

387

Neumann, Franz. "Anxiety and Politics," in *The Democratic and the Authoritarian State.* New York: Free Press, 1957.
Ortega y Gasset, José. *The Revolt of the Masses.* New York: Norton, 1940.
Reisman, Leonard. *The Urban Process.* New York: Free Press, 1964.
Schumpeter, Joseph A. *Capitalism, Socialism and Democracy.* New York: Harper, 1942.
Tocqueville, Alexis de. *Democracy in America* (1835). New York: Knopf, 1945.
Weber, Max. "Bureaucracy" (1924) in H. H. Gerth, and C. W. Mills, eds. *From Max Weber.* New York: Oxford University Press, 1964.

Part Three: The Ideological Response

DOCTRINES

Ali, Tariq. *The New Revolutionaries: A Handbook of the International Radical Left.* New York: Morrow, 1969.
Cohen, Carl, ed. *Communism, Fascism, and Democracy.* New York: Random House, 1962.
Cooperman, David, and Walter, E. V. *Power and Civilization: Political Thought in the Twentieth Century.* New York: Crowell, 1962.
Grimes, Alan P., and Horwitz, Robert H. *Modern Political Ideologies.* New York: Oxford University Press, 1959.
Kariel, Henry S., ed. *Sources in Twentieth-Century Political Thought.* New York: Free Press, 1964.
Lynd, Staughton, ed. *Nonviolence in America: A Documentary History.* Indianapolis: Bobbs-Merrill, 1966.
Mills, C. Wright. *The Marxists.* New York: Dell, 1962.
Sigmund, Paul E., Jr., ed. *The Ideologies of the Developing Nations.* New York: Frederick A. Praeger, 1963.

ANALYSES AND INTERPRETATIONS

Apter, David E., ed. *Ideology and Discontent.* New York: Free Press, 1946.
Mannheim, Karl. *Ideology and Utopia.* New York: Harcourt, Brace, 1936.
Sargent, Lyman Tower. *Contemporary Political Ideologies.* Homewood, Ill.: Dorsey Press, 1969.
Shklar, Judith N., ed. *Political Theory and Ideology.* New York: Macmillan, 1966, Introduction.
Sutton, Francis X. *et al. The American Business Creed.* Cambridge: Harvard University Press, 1966.
Watkins, Frederick N. *The Age of Ideology.* Englewood Cliffs, N.J.: Prentice-Hall, 1964.

Part Four: The American Response

THE PUBLIC-PRIVATE COMPLEX

Bernstein, Marver. *Regulating Business by Independent Commission.* Princeton: Princeton University Press, 1955.
Coffin, Tristram. *The Armed Society.* Baltimore: Penguin, 1964.
Derthick, Martha. *The National Guard in Politics.* Cambridge: Harvard University Press, 1965.

Domhoff, G. William. *Who Rules America?* Englewood Cliffs, N.J.: Prentice-Hall, 1968.

Foss, Phillip O. *Politics and Grass.* Seattle: University of Washington Press, 1960.

Galbraith, John Kenneth. *The New Industrial State.* New York: Houghton, Mifflin, 1967.

Gilb, Corinne Lathrop. *Hidden Hierarchies: The Professions and Government.* New York: Harper and Row, 1966.

Lackoff, Sanford A., ed. *Knowledge and Power: Essays on Science and Government.* New York: Free Press, 1966.

Miller, Arthur S. "Private Governments and the Constitution," in Andrew Hacker, ed. *The Corporation Take-Over.* New York: Harper and Row, 1964, pp. 122–149.

THE INCORPORATED PUBLIC

Hacker, Andrew. "Imperium in Imperio Revisited," in Gottfried Dietze, ed. *Essays on the American Constitution.* Englewood Cliffs, N.J.: Prentice-Hall, 1964, pp. 42-58.

Harrington, Alan. *Life in the Crystal Palace.* New York: Knopf, 1959.

Jacobs, Paul. *The State of the Unions.* New York: Atheneum, 1963.

Mason, Alpheus T. "Business Organized as Power: The New Imperium in Imperio," *American Political Science Review,* XLIV (1950), 323–342.

Mills, C. Wright. *White Collar.* New York: Oxford University Press, 1951.

Whyte, William H., Jr. *The Organization Man.* New York: Simon and Schuster, 1966.

THE UNINCORPORATED PUBLIC

Harrington, Michael. *The Other America: Poverty in the United States.* New York: Macmillan, 1962.

Part Five: The Response of Political Science

Almond, Gabriel A., and Powell, G. Bingham. *Comparative Politics: A Developmental Approach.* Boston: Little, Brown, 1966.

Bailey, Stephen K. *et al. Research Frontiers in Politics and Government.* Washington, D.C.: Brookings Institution, 1955.

Charlesworth, James C., ed. *A Design for Political Science.* Philadelphia: American Academy of Political and Social Science, 1966.

Crick, Bernard. *The American Science of Politics.* Berkeley: University of California Press. 1959.

Eckstein, Harry, and Apter, David E., eds. *Comparative Politics.* New York: Free Press, 1963, pp. 3–32, 725–740.

Haas, Michael, and Kariel, Henry S., eds. *Approaches to the Study of Political Science.* San Francisco: Chandler, 1970.

Neumann, Franz. "Approaches to the Study of Power," in *The Democratic and the Authoritarian State.* New York: Free Press, 1957.

Somit, Albert, and Tanenhaus, Joseph. *The Development of American Political Science.* Boston: Allyn and Bacon, 1967.

Truman, David. "Disillusioned Regeneration: The Quest for a Discipline," *American Political Science Review,* LIX (December, 1965), 865–873.

Waldo, Dwight. *Political Science in the United States.* Paris: UNESCO, 1956.
Young, Roland, ed. *Approaches to the Study of Politics.* Evanston: Northwestern University Press, 1958.

■ INDEX

abundance, and technology, 73–74, 75, 77–78
Adams, Henry, qt., 349
Adams, John, 12, 13, 14 *n*
administrative and executive agencies: federal budget, 325–326; importance, 235; vs. labor unions, 323–324, 325; and legislative process, 237–239, 240–241; multiplicity of, 317–319; and Presidency, 235, 236, 237, 239, 240, 241–242, 244 *n;* pressure groups, 236–237, 322; vs. private government, 324–326; vs. private power, 320–322; public relations, 239–240; vs. rackets, 324, 325; separation of powers, 319–320; at state level, 263–264
Adorno, T. W., 23 *n,* 379 *n*
advertising, and mass production, 29, 32, 33
agriculture, 60, 74, 76, 96, 97, 108, 143, 174, 211, 236, 237, 238, 239, 241, 243 *n,* 264, 297; regulation of, 188
Alexander, Franz, 19, 22 *n*
alienation, 16, 66, 125; Marxist, 134; and rebellion, 142
Allport, Gordon, 7
Almond, Gabriel A., 297, 362–366
ambition, vs. emulation, 12
American Federation of Labor (AFL), 167, 179, 216, 337
American Legion, 168, 169
American Medical Association (AMA), 167, 169, 185, 188
American Revolution, 13–14
anomie, 42, 126, 375
antiurbanization, 48
Appleby, Paul, qt., 206
Arendt, Hannah, 12–14, 27
Aristotle, 7, 7 *n,* 8–10, 15, 377
arts, 12, 78, 189; performing, vs. politics, 14

autarchy, 8
authoritarianism, 68, 72
automobile, and municipal government, 274–275, 279

Bailey, Stephen K., 204–213
Barrès, Maurice, 89–91
behavioralism, 354–355, 367, 369
Bell, Daniel, 200–204, 244–247
Bell, David E., 352 *n;* qt., 340–341, 346
Bell, Gertrude, qt., 71
Bendiner, Robert, qt., 217
Berle, A. A., Jr., 182 *n,* 333; qt., 173
Bernstein, Eduard, 127
Black Muslims, 46
black power: and civil rights, 140–141; distortion of, in press, 136–137; and independent political organization, 142–143, 145; individual vs. institutionalized racism, 138–139; and integration, 140–141; integration, results of, 142; powerlessness of Negroes, 138, 139; reconstruction era, 141
Bolivar, Simon, qt., 68
Boulding, Kenneth E., 59–67, 78–84, 120
bourgeoisie, 93, 94–97, 98, 115, 281, 382; adulteration of Marxism, 109, 110–111; petty, 98, 100; vs. proletarians, 99–102, 107–108
Brinkley, David, 39
Brogan, D. W., qt., 219
Bryce, James, 22 *n,* 272, 295 *n,* 354, 368, 378 *n;* qt., 367
Bundy, McGeorge, 300, 310, 314
Burckhardt, Jacob, 28
bureaucracy, 26, 28, 34, 36, 51, 55, 56, 76, 113, 126, 145, 146, 147, 150, 159, 163, 167, 175, 200, 203, 218, 234, 237, 240, 241, 282–283, 288, 289; and government contracts, 342–343, 347; and pol-

bureaucracy (*con't*)
icy making, 302; under socialism, 130-131
Burke, Edmund, 12, 372
Burns, James MacGregor, 217
business (*see* government and business, government contracts)

Cabot, Etienne, 124
Cairo, and urbanization, 46
Campanella, Thomas, 123, 124
Canada, and Rush-Bagot Agreement, 65
capital, 98, 101, 103, 104
capitalism, 30, 31, 112, 113, 114, 115, 126, 129, 134; Chinese, 116; ethic of, 120; transition to communism, 113–114, 130, 131
Carmichael, Stokely, 136–143
Carr, E. H., 28–34
Cassirer, Ernst, qt., 136
causality, in political science, 369–371
Chamber of Commerce, U.S., 169
Chardin, Teilard de, 64
Chase, Stuart, 182 *n;* qt., 177
Chester, Colby, 121
Chicago, 11
Chile, costs of urbanization, 41
Chinese revolution, 116, 118, 119
Christianity, and class struggle, 107, 112
cities: and civilization, 60, 96; and communication, 48–49; dissident groups, 49–51; and French Revolution, 40; and nature, 53; populations of, 41–42, 75–76; social interdependence, 47; squatter communities, 43–44; *see also* government, municipal; urbanization
citizen, mature, 7; as participator, 10–12
citizenship: Greek view of, 10–12, 14; participatory democracy, 144; in U.S., 10–11
civil rights, 48, 140–141, 146
civil service, 164, 165; *see also* bureaucracy
Clapp, Charles, qt., 215
Clark, Colin, 132
class struggle, 93, 99, 100, 102, 107; and the state, 109; in U.S. politics, 210, 211–212
Cohen, Morris R., 373
Cole, G. D. H., 131
collage theatre, 3–4
collective bargaining, 337
collectivism, vs. individualism, 31–32
collectivities, vs. individualism, 200
communication, and city problems, 48–49; mass, 164
communications satellite system, 327, 346
communism: transition from capitalism, 113–114, 130, 131
communism, Chinese: dogmatism vs. empiricism, 118–119; theory vs. practice, 115–117
Communist Manifesto, 93–108; abolition of inheritance, 107; abolition of private property, 102–104, 107, 132; bourgeoisie, 93, 94–97, 98, 99–102; capital, 98, 101, 103, 104; Christianity, 107; class struggle, 93, 99, 100, 102, 107; communization of women, 106; democracy, 107, 108; education, 105, 108; family, 95, 100, 105–106; income tax, 107; labor unions, 99; production, 92, 93, 94, 95, 96, 97, 104, 107; proletarians, 93, 94, 97, 98, 99–102, 102–107, 107–108; wage labor, 101, 103, 104; *see also* Marxism
Communist Party, of China, 116
communists, 216; and proletarians, 102–107
communization of women, 106
competition, 336–337, 350
Comte, Auguste, 125
concerns, manageable, 5–7
conflict, and society, 66–67
Congress of Racial Equality (CORE), 137, 140
Congress, U.S., 13, 14, 148, 161, 162, 163, 164, 173, 174, 184, 205, 235, 246, 250, 254, 255, 327; vs. administrative and executive agencies, 235, 236, 237–239, 240–241, 317, 318, 319, 320, 322; and American democracy, 220–221; and foreign policy making, 298, 299, 301, 304, 308, 309–312, 313, 314, 315; and government-business relations, 330, 334, 335, 336, 343, 344, 345, 346, 350; House vs. Senate, 219; legislative function, 217–218; and party system, 205–207, 208, 210, 211, 212, 213; vs. parliament, 297; and the President, 222, 223, 224, 225, 229, 230, 231, 232; *see also* House of Representatives
conscientious objection, 148–149
Constitution, U.S., 8, 9, 152–155, 205, 220, 223, 224, 248, 252, 254, 256, 354; framing of, 152–155, 210; government-industry contracts, 340–341; separation of powers, 319–320
constitutions, state, 257, 259, 273, 276, 277, 293
consumer, 175–176, 331
consumer expectations, and urbanization, 45, 75, 292, 293
corporation, 200, 201; community relations, 176–177; and consumer, 175–176; employees, 172, 173–175; and foundations, 177; managements' role, 121–122; and national wealth, 120; ownership vs. management, 172–173, 283; participatory democracy, 148–149; and power structure, 159, 160, 162,

163, 164, 166; and public policies, 171–172; and public power, 177–178; and role of government, 344–345; and self-government, 119–121, 122; social responsibilities, 120; *see also* government and business; government contracts
Coser, Lewis, 122–136
Cotter, Cornelius P., qt., 336–337
crisis, 320; and decision making, 303; and political inventiveness, 151–152; and social transitions, 85–87
Crossman, R. H. S., qt., 133

Dahl, Robert A., 247–255, 356 *n*, 379 *n*; qt., 309, 355
Darwin, Charles, 31
Davis, Kingsley, qt., 43
decentralization, under socialism, 131–133
decision makers, and international system, 81–82
democracy, 8, 161, 165; bourgeois vs. proletarian, 112; as choice of alternative policies, 297–298; and Congress, 220–221; and the corporation, 120; as dehumanizing force, 27–28; vs. efficiency, 133; government-business relations, 338; government contract system, 340, 347, 348, 351; liberal, 33; Marxist, 113, 114; mass, 29–30, 31–33; at municipal level, 272, 276, 277, 278, 280, 285; national elites, 71; national unity, 69; in new states, 68–69, 70; nonvoting, 190–194, 198; in over-developed society, 36; personal leadership, 71–72; political tradition, 70–71; preconditions of success, 69–70, 72; and proletarians, 107, 108; propaganda, 29–30; at state level, 260, 263, 264, 268; and Supreme Court, 249, 252, 255; in suburbs, 293; and withering away of state, 111; *see also* electorate
democracy, participatory: in churches and professions, 147; defined, 144; and foreign policy, 148–149; functions of, 146; issues and programs, 146; national planning, 149–150; political mobilization of the poor, 144–145; in universities, 146–147, 148, 149; workers' control, 147–148
democratic character: destructiveness, 20; expectation of benevolence, 18; importance of early years of life, 15–16, 18; as multivalued, 16–18; personal vanity, 17; pursuit of power, 16; miserliness, 18; prejudice, 20–21; rectitude, 17–18; self-system, 15, 16, 18, 19–21; sexuality, 17, 19; the unconscious, 19–21
Deutsch, Karl W., qt., 7
developing society, defined, 35
De Voto, Bernard, 176
Dewey, John, 7

dictatorship, 9; of the proletariat, 111, 112, 113
Donovan, Robert, 227
Douglas, Paul, qt., 215
Dreyfus Affair, 90
Drucker, Peter, 120
Drummond, Roscoe, qt., 246
Dyckman, John W., 40–52

Easton, David, 378 *n;* qt., 368
economic determinism, 92–93, 215
education, 105, 108, 200
efficiency, vs. democracy, 133
ego, closed vs. open, 15, 17, 19; primary, 15, 20
Eisenhower, Dwight D., 222, 225, 226, 227, 228, 229, 243 *n*, 251, 312, 313, 314, 315, 324, 330, 332, 343, 344, 347
electorate: expansion of, 191–192; extent of nonvoting, 190–191; national uniform election law, 193; Negro, 192; public policy, 197–199; self-disenfranchisement, 191, 193; in the South, 192; urban vs. rural, 258–259; voters vs. nonvoters, 194–195, 370, 372, 375–376, 381
elites: old vs. new, 200; and revolution, 373; *see also* power elite
elitism, 26–27, 71, 88, 125, 126, 145, 148, 149, 150, 176, 245–246, 250, 252, 257, 344, 345
Emerson, Rupert, 68–72
empire, profitability of, 80
emulation, vs. ambition, 12
Engels, Friedrich, 30, 93–108, 111, 116, 119, 129, 133; qt., 109, 110, 124–125
ethics, and politics, 8–10
ethnic minorities, 275, 279, 280, 281, 284, 285, 288, 292–293, 294; *see also* Negro
Europe, urbanization in, 75–76
exchange system, 63, 64
expertism, and politics, 29, 130, 164, 205, 313

fair trade laws, 334–335
familism, 275, 292, 293, 294, 295
family, 95, 100, 105–106
farmers, 266, 313, 336; and power structure, 161, 163, 164, 236; *see also* agriculture
fascism, 27
federalism, and centralization, 256
Flacks, Richard, 144–150
flight from reason, 30
folk culture, 67
folk wisdom, 82, 83
foreign aid, U.S., 48
foreign policy, and participatory democracy, 148–149
foreign policy-making process: attentive publics, 297, 299, 304, 309, 315; com-

foreign policy-making process (*con't*)
munication and consensus, 302; conflict
and consensus, 296–297, 300, 301, 303,
305, 314–315; decision making, 296–
297; incremental steps, 303–304; inner-
circle decisions, 298; in international
affairs, 305–306; leaks, to press, 300–
301; politics of, 307–309; public discussion, 299; simplification of issues, 301–
303; success of, 304–305
foundations, 177
Fourier, Charles, 124, 127
France, and nationalism, 89–91
Frankfurter, Felix, 251, 255 *n*
Frankel, Charles, 28 *n;* qt., 27
freedom, 12, 13, 14, 34, 40, 122, 135,
150, 157, 166; communist, 113; in socialism, 129
French Revolution, 40, 102, 164
Frenkel-Brunswik, Else, 21
Freud, S., 31
Friedman, Wolfgang F., 182 *n;* qt., 177
Fromm, Erich, 27
future, forecasting of, 246–247

Garceau, Oliver, 170 *n;* qt., 168, 169
Geddes, Patrick, 40
Germany, 80
gerrymander, 259
ghetto, 139, 142, 143, 293
Ginsberg, Morris, 384 *n;* qt., 381
Glazer, Nathan, 37–39
Goldberg, Arthur S., 366–379
Goodman, Paul, 28, 37, 39
Gordon, Robert Aaron, 182 *n;* qt., 173
government: invisible, 163; mixed, 9;
quality of citizenship, 10–12; referee
theory, 184, 187–189; vector-sum theory, 184, 185–187; ward, 13, 47, 49
government, and business: collective bargaining, 337; consumer interests, 331;
defense-relatedness argument, 336; fair
trade laws, 334–335; housing and racial
discrimination, 332–333; intrabusiness
competition, 333–335; oil import quotas, 332; public vs. private interests,
330, 332, 337–339, 346, 350–351; regulatory agencies, 331–332; Supreme
Court rulings, 332–333; without-com-
pensation employees (WOC), 330–331
government commissions, 244–247; as
elite formulas, 245–246; and future forecasting, 246–247; types and functions,
244–245
government contract system: aerospace
industry, 341, 342, 346, 347, 348, 349,
350; Air Force, 343, 344; Army, 343–
344; atomic energy program, 327, 341;
budgets for, 342–343; communications
satellite system, 327, 346; and competition, 336–337, 350; concentration and
interlocking, 344–346, 348, 349, 350;
corporations in role of government,
344–345; dangers of, 349–351; dual
appointments, 329–331; enforcement of
public policies, 328–329, 340; erosion
of public control, 346–349; lobbying,
335–336, 342, 347; NASA, 342, 344,
346, 347, 350; prime contractors, 342,
345, 346, 348; for research and development, 328, 341–342; security
clearances, 329; staffing, 328, 342–343;
at state and local level, 347–348; sup-
ply/demand and price, 341
government, municipal: bureaucratization
of city services, 282–283, 289; and
business interests, 281, 283, 285, 286–
287; central city government, 278–282;
central city vs. suburbs, 274–277, 284–
285; Democratic vs. Republican
strength, 284–287, 288; development of,
271–273, 279; effect of automobile,
274–275, 279; ethically significant citizenship, 9, 10–11; ethnic minorities,
275, 279, 280, 281, 284, 285, 288; machine of incumbents, 287–288; mayor,
287–289; metropolitan complex, 277–
278; party machines, 272, 273, 280–282,
284, 285, 286, 287, 288; planning, 273–
274, 282; policing, 279–280; population
changes, 283–285; power elite, 281–
282, 283, 284–285; promise of, 11, 12;
relation to state, 272–273; *see also* suburbia
government, state: administrative systems,
263–264; constitutions, 257, 259, 273,
276, 277, 293; and contract system,
347–348; decentralization, 256–257;
gerrymander, 259; governors, 264, 265,
266, 267, 268–269; interest groups,
262–263; interest groups and regulatory
agencies, 265–266, 267; legislatures,
258–259, 262, 267, 269, 273; licensing
boards, 266–267; majority rule, 257–
258; multiplicity of agencies, 264–266;
multiplicity of elective offices, 263–264;
party politics, 259–262; and private
power, 256–257, 261, 262, 264; public
vs. private power, 268–269; urban vs.
rural representation, 258, 259
government, U.S.: defects, 204–207; federalism and centralization, 256; framing of Constitution, 152–155, 210;
grants-in-aid to state and local units,
340; and social problems, 163, 189–
190; stability of, 152; *see also* administrative and executive agencies
governors, state, 264, 265, 266, 267, 268–
269
Gray, Justin, 170 *n;* qt., 168
Great Britain, 29; as monarchy, 33
Greek view, of citizenship, 10–12, 14
Greer, Scott, 271–296

gross national product, 65; comparative, 58–59; and government contracts, 351; per capita, for 60 countries (table), 57–58; vs. research and development costs, 342
gross world product, 79
Guild Socialism, 128, 131, 132

Halaby, Nageeb, qt., 346
Halleck, Charles, qt., 217
Hand, Learned, 385
Hanson, Norwood R., 374, 378 *n*, 379 *n;* qt., 368–369, 370
Harlem, 46, 139, 141, 142
Harrington, Michael, 12, 27, 377
Hauser, Philip, 296 *n;* qt., 284
Hegel, G. W. F., 30, 31, 54, 109, 111, 377
Herring, Pendelton, 170 *n;* qt., 168
Hilsman, Roger, 296–316
historians, 65
history: in Marxism, 127, 129; and power structure, 156–157, 158; and social sciences, 380–384; and utopias, 123, 124, 125, 136
Hobbes, Thomas, 123, 349, 377
House of Representatives: Appropriations Committee, 216; local pressures, 218–219; Rules Committee, 216–217; traditionalism of, 214–216, 220–221
household, vs. polis, 9
housing, 12, 332–333
Howe, Irving, 122–136
human relations, in modern society, 55–56; *see also* man
Hunter, Floyd, 281, 296 *n*

id system, 19
identity, personal, in modern society, 75, 76–77
ideologies: and politics, 87–88; and power structure, 156
income tax, 107
individualism, 26, 27, 28, 29, 30, 47, 77, 150; vs. collectivism, 31–32; vs. collectivities, 200; and socialism, 128–129
industrialism, 26, 27, 35, 36, 157; and erosion of environment, 54
infancy, and democratic character, 15–16, 18
information system, and international system, 81–82
inheritance, abolition of, 107
innovation, 74, 75, 257, 289; and abundance, 77–78; and research, 77–78
integration, racial, 140–142
integrative development, 65, 67
integrative systems, 63, 64, 65, 66; and superculture, 67
intellectuals, 121, 124, 161, 165, 200, 201; communist, 115, 117, 118; in military

establishment, 202–203; as utopian rulers, 125
interest groups, 262–263, 265–266, 267
international system: benefits of, 79–80, 172; cost of, 78–79, 80; decision-making procedures, 305–306; and empires, 80; gross world product, 79; and information system, 81–82; and integrative development, 65, 67; and nuclear war, 61–62, 187, 343–344; reactivity coefficient, 81; vs. science, 82–83; and scientific revolution, 80; and stable peace, 83; and war industry, 79–80, 81

Jackson, Andrew, 222
Jacobs, Paul, 183 *n;* qt., 181
Janowitz, Morris, 23 *n;* qt., 202–203
Japan, 69; costs of war industry, 79; economic growth, 58, 60, 80; population growth, 62; urbanization, 75, 76
Jefferson, Thomas, 13–14, 14 *n*
Jessup, John K., 119–122
Johnson, Lyndon B., 341, 350
Jouvenal, Bertrand de, qt., 247
justice, 8

Kansas City, citizenship in, 11
Kariel, Henry S., 171–183, 187–188
Kempton, Murray, qt., 219–220
Kennedy, John F., 301, 302, 305, 310, 311, 312, 314, 315
Key, V. O., Jr., 213 *n*, 235–244, 263, 270 *n*, 285, 296; qt., 204, 208–209, 260–261
King, Martin Luther, 146
knowledge, perceptual vs. rational, 117–118

labor unions, 99, 167, 169, 245, 279, 322, 323, 324, 325; and corporations, 121; and government contracts, 347, 350; leadership, 160, 178–181, 188; and power structure, 161, 162, 163, 164
Laski, Harold J., 172
Lasswell, Harold D., 15–23
leadership: charismatic, 29, 145; in democracies, 71–72; of labor unions, 160, 178–181, 188; nonprofessional, 168–170; oligarchical, 166–170; political, 205, 254; presidential, 221–224, 235, 254–255; professional, 168
League of Nations, 205–206
leaks, to press, 300–301, 319
learning process, and society, 64
Le Bon, Gustave, qt., 164
legislatures, state, 258–259, 262, 267, 269, 273
legitimacy, 165, 254, 255; as power, 313; and rites, 87; and social integration, 63–64, 65, 66
leisure, under socialism, 134–135; in urban society, 75, 77, 78

Lenin, V. I., 109–115, 116, 119, 127–128, 157

licensing boards, state, 266–267

Lindblom, Charles E., 303

Lippmann, Walter, 27; qt., 220

lobbies, 163, 184, 204, 335–336, 342, 347

Locke, John, 31, 33, 54, 178

Long, Norman E., 8–12

Lubell, Samuel, 234 n; qt., 222

Lynd, Staughton, 145

McCarthy era, 312

McConnell, Grant, 183 n, 256–271

McDonald, David J., 180

McKean, Dayton D., 168, 170 n, 270 n

Madison, James, 153, 171, 349

man: and environment, 53–54; and human relations, 55–56; marginal, 77; and nature, 52–53; personality disintegration, 56; and property, 54–55

management, 172–173, 201–202

Mandelbaum, Seymour J., 47, 51 n, 52 n

Mannheim, Karl, 27, 382

Mao Tse-tung, 115–119, 313

marginal men, in modern society, 77

Marshall, John, 153

Marx, Karl, 26, 36, 54, 88, 92–93, 93–108, 112, 116, 119, 123, 124, 126, 134, 135, 141, 156, 377, 382; flight from reason, 30–31; as utopian, 125–127

Marxism, 313, 384; adulteration of, 109, 110–111; alienation, 134; and democracy, 113, 114, 166, 215; state, and class struggle, 109; transitional state, 113–114; withering away of state, 110–111, 112–113, 113–115; *see also* Communist Manifesto

Marxist-Leninist theories, 115, 116, 117, 118, 119

mass communication, 164

mass democracy, 29–30, 31–33

mass society, 162, 164

materialism, 75, 78

mayors, municipal, 287–289

mental illness, in U.S., 77

Merriam, Charles E., 22 n., 354

metropolis, 277–278; and citizenship, 11–12; *see also* cities; government, municipal; urbanization

Michel, Robert, 130, 168, 170 n, 179

middle class, 9; old and new, 163, 164, 201

military establishment, 38, 39; financial budget, 229–230, 342, 343; and foreign policy making, 298, 299, 305, 311, 312, 313; and government contracts, 343, 344, 350; intellectuals in, 202–203; and power structure, 157, 158, 159, 160, 166, 201, 351; *see also* war industry

Mill, John Stuart, 10, 372, 382

Millis, Harry A., 170 n; qt., 167

Mills, C. Wright, 34–36, 46, 52 n, 154, 155–160, 380–384

minority rights, and Supreme Court, 249–250, 250–252, 254

Minow, Newton, 39

monism, 9

Montgomery, Royal E., 170 n; qt., 167

moral sensibility, and reason, 34–35

Morgenthau, Hans J., 317–326

Morris, William, 128

Mumford, Lewis, 28, 40

Murray, Philip, qt., 180

Myrdal, Gunnar, 170 n, 261; qt., 169, 170

Nasser, G. A., qt., 71

National Aeronautics and Space Administration (NASA), 342, 344, 346, 347, 350

National Association of Manufacturers (NAM), 167, 169, 337

national defense, U.S., 38–39

nationalism, 96; in France, 89–91

nationalization, of production, 132

national uniform election law, 193

nations (*see* society)

nature: and classical culture, 52, 53; and modern city, 53; and technology, 73–74

Nazis, 34

Negro: and municipal government, 275, 279, 289; as political issue, 210–211, 212; in South, 192; and state government, 261, 268; in suburbia, 292–293, 294; and Supreme Court, 254, 255; and urbanization, 47, 50–51

Neustadt, Richard E., 221–234; qt., 315

New Left, 147, 148, 149, 150

New York, citizenship, 11; future population, 41; ward government, 49

New York Times, qt., 137–138

Nieburg, H. L., 339–352

Nietzsche, F. W., 28

nuclear war, 61–62, 187, 343–344

Nuremburg principle, 148–149

Oakeshott, Michael, 362 n; qt., 360

occupational displacement, and technology, 74–75, 77

oil import quotas, 332

oligarchy, 8, 9, 160–170

operationism, 375, 376, 377

organizational revolution, 37–39, 121

organizational society, 77

Ortega y Gasset, J., 28

overdeveloped nations, defined, 35–36

Owen, Robert, 124, 127

ownership, vs. management, of corporations, 172–173, 283

Palamountain, Joseph C., qt., 334

Pareto, Vilfredo, 373, 379 n

Paris Commune, 111, 112

parliament, vs. Congress, 297
participatory democracy, *see* democracy
party system: class conflict, 210, 211–212; defects of, 205–207; in municipal government, 284–287, 288; Negro issue, 210–211, 212; old vs. new settlers, 209–210, 211; party organization, 207–209; recent developments, 212–213; regional interests, 210, 211, 212
Pascal, Blaise, qt., 136
peace movement, 187
personal identity, in modern society, 75, 76–77
personality, and social disintegration, 56
persuasive society, 77
Petrillo, James C., qt., 179
planning: democratization of, 149–150; and government contract system, 350; municipal, 273–274, 282; under socialism, 131–133
Plato, 9, 377
pluralism, 9; referee theory, 184, 187–189; and social problems, 163, 189–190; vector-sum theory, 184, 185–187
politeuma, 8
political institutions, and crisis, 151–152
political landlordism, absentee, 11
political science: behavioralism, 354–355, 367, 369; common sense vs. science, 366–367; criteria of empirical invalidation, 375–377; historical and comparative approaches, 380–384; induction, deduction, and retroduction, 372–374, 377; operationism, 375, 376, 377; probability, 370–371; as professional discipline, 353–354; role theory, 371–372; scientific explanation, 371–372; as scholarly game, 356–359; as study of constitutional systems, 354, 359–362, 367, 369; systems approach, 355–356; theory, and causality, 369–371; theory, and facts, 367–369; verification, 374–375
politics: bureaucracy, 26; class struggle, 210, 211–212; defined, 6; economic issues, 29, 32, 33; effect of democratic revolutions, 26, 27; and ethics, 8–10; expertism, 29, 130, 164, 205, 313; under extreme threats, 25; governing elite, 26–27; Greek view of, 10–12; as group decision making, 307–309; ideal of, 5–7; and ideologies, 87–88; industrialism, 26, 27; leadership, 205, 254; mass conformity, 27; mass democracy, 29–30, 31–33; normative concept of, 6; and the poor, 144–145; and power structure, 160, 161, 313–315; propaganda, 29–30, 31–33; and reason, 28–29, 30, 31; regionalism, 210, 211, 212; at state level, 259–262; in suburbia, 293–294, 294–295; and television, 27, 47; and the

unconscious, 19–21, 31, 33; and universal reason, 30
pollution, 54, 60–61
Popper, Karl, 373, 374, 378 *n*, 379 *n;* qt., 375
population: of cities, 41–42, 75–76, 283–285; control of, 62–63; density, 41–42; suburban, 291–293
Potter, David, qt., 210
poverty, 186–187
power elite, 157, 158–160, 161, 164, 166, 172, 202–203, 313; municipal, 281–282, 283, 284–285
power structure: centralization of, 157; changes in, 200–201; corporations, 159, 160, 162, 163, 164, 166; farmers, 161, 163, 164; and history, 156–157, 158; labor unions, 161, 162, 163, 164; lobbies, 159, 163; and the military, 157, 158, 159, 160, 166; nature of, 155–156, 166; old vs. new middle class, 163, 164; party politics, 160, 161; power elite, 157, 158–160, 161, 164, 166, 172; public opinion, 164–165; pure power theory, 305–306; sources of power, 313–315; and violence, 157
Presidency, U.S., 148, 205, 206, 207, 216, 217, 219, 220, 250, 327; and administrative and executive agencies, 235, 236, 237, 239, 240, 241–242, 244 *n;* authority as executive, 224–225, 233, 317, 318, 319, 320, 325, 326; choice making, 225–227, 228; complexity of issues, 229; and Congress, 222, 223, 224, 225, 229, 230, 231, 232; constituencies, 223–224; deadlines, 227; effectuation of choices, 230, 233; and foreign policy making, 298, 301, 302, 303, 308, 310, 311, 312, 313, 314, 315; leadership, 221–224, 235, 254–255; military budget, 229–230; personal prestige, 233; power to persuade, 230–234; presentation of issues, 228–229
Price, Don K., 329, 347, 352 *n*
pricing, and government contracts, 341
prime contractors, 342, 345, 346, 348
production, 93, 94, 95, 96, 104, 107, 110, 111; overproduction, 97; vs. property relations, 92, 93, 107
productivity, and prosperity, 121, 174
Progressive Era, 354
proletarians, 10, 31, 93, 94, 98; vs. bourgeoisie, 99–102, 107–108; and communists, 102–107; as elite, 126; emancipation of, 106
propaganda, and mass democracy, 29–30, 31–33
property, private, 200, 201, 202; abolition of, 102–104, 107, 132
property relations, vs. production, 92, 93, 107

psychologists, 64; and propaganda, 29, 32, 33
psychosomatic medicine, 19, 20
public happiness, 13
public opinion, 27, 28, 33, 164–165, 175, 325
public order, 189
public policies, and private enforcement, 328–329, 340

racial segregation, in cities, 45–46
racism, individual vs. institutionalized, 138–139
radio, and social disorder, 44
Randall, Clarence B., 183 n; qt., 177
Rayburn, Sam, 217, 234 n; qt., 215
reactivity coefficient, and war industry, 81
Reagan, Michael D., 327–339
reason: flight from, 30; and moral sensibility, 34–35; and politics, 28–29, 30, 31, 32; and science, 34, 37; universal, 30
reconstruction era, 141
referee theory, of government, 184, 187–189
regionalism, in U.S. politics, 210, 211, 212
regulatory agencies, 265–266, 267, 331–332
research, and innovation, 77–78; U.S. investment in, 73
retroduction, 372–374, 377
revolution: American, 13–14; organizational, 37–39, 121; scientific, 37, 80; unsuccessful, 37
Riesman, David, 55
rites, and legitimacy, 87
role theory, 371–372
Roosevelt, Franklin D., 221, 222, 226, 237, 251, 303, 312, 318
Roosevelt, Theodore, 221, 222, 303
Rosenau, James N., 356–359
Rossiter, Clinton, qt., 222
Rousseau, J. J., 7, 30, 31
rural, vs. urban voting power, 258–259
Rush-Bagot Agreement, 65
Russett, Bruce M., 57–58

Saint-Simon, L. R., 125, 127
Schattschneider, E. E., 190–199, 213 n; qt., 207
Schechner, Richard, 3–4
Schumpeter, Joseph A., 176
Schwartz, David, 49, 52 n
science, 56, 73; vs. common sense, 366–367; vs. international system, 82–83; and rationality, 34, 37; and social problems, 39
scientific revolution, 37, 80
self-government, and the corporation, 119–121, 122
self-system, and democratic character, 15, 16, 18, 19–21

separation of powers, 319–320
sexuality, and democratic character, 17–19
Skinner, B. F., 65
Smith, Howard, 217; qt., 216
social disorder, and urbanization, 41, 42, 43, 44, 80
socialism, 31; and bureaucracy, 130–131; creeping, 344; decentralization, 131–133; and individualism, 128–129; and leisure, 134–135; nationalization, 132; planning, 131–133; social problems, 129–130; vs. utopias, 122–128, 136; and work, 134–135
social problems, and government, 163, 189–190; and socialism, 129–130
society: adjustment to change, 74–75; biological dangers, 62; and conflict, 66–67; crisis, 85–86; developmental levels, 35–36, 60; integrative development, 65, 67; integrative systems, 63–64, 65, 66; learning process, 64; marginal men, 77; mass, 162, 164; materialism, 75, 78; organizational, 77; persuasive, 77; and pollution, 54, 60–61; population growth, 62–63; rites, 87; spaceship, 60, 61, 62; urban, and personal identity, 75, 76–77
Southern Christian Leadership Conference, 146
spaceship society, 60, 61, 62
squatter communities, 43–44
Stalin, J. V., 116, 117, 119
state, 162, 163, 166; class struggle, 109; ethical sovereignty, 8–10; Greek view of, 9–10; withering away of, 110–111, 112–113, 113–115
states, new, and democracy, 68, 69, 70
Steel, Ronald, 214–221
Steffens, Lincoln, 281, 296 n
Students for a Democratic Society (SDS), 145, 146
Student Non-Violent Coordinating Committee (SNCC), 137, 140, 142, 145, 146
suburbia: and business man, 295; vs. central city, 274–277, 284–285; ethnic minorities, 292–293, 294; local politics, 294–295; political issues, 293–294; population increase, 291–292; rising consumption norms, 292, 293
Sullivan, Harry Stack, 15
superculture, vs. folk culture, 67
superego system, 19
superstition, as preceived order, 65
Supreme Court, U.S., 218, 221; affected-with-public-interest decisions, 332–333; character of Justices, 251; as defender of minority rights, 250–252; and democratic system, 249, 252, 255; on government vs. business, 332–333, as legal vs. political institution, 247–249; majority vs. minority interests, 249–250, 254; and

national policy, 253–255; and natural rights, 252–253

Sweden, 80

systems approach, in political science, 355–356

Taft, Philip, 170 *n;* qt., 167

Tawney, R. H., qt., 158

teach-ins, 148

technology, and abundance, 73–74, 77–78; and power, 158, 349

television, and politics, 27, 47

theatre, collage, 3–4

threat system, 63, 64

Thucydides, 10

timocracy, 8

Tinder, Glenn E., 52–56

Tocqueville, Alexis de., 28 *n,* 36; qt., 26–27, 214

Tolstoy, Leo, qt., 122–123

Trotsky, Leon, 135

Truman, David B., 166–170, 371, 378 *n*

Truman, Harry S., 222, 226, 227, 229, 230, 251, 304, 312, 315, 324

unconscious, the, and politics, 19–21, 31, 33

underdeveloped countries, defined, 35

Union of Soviet Socialist Republics (USSR): centralization of power, 157; gross national product, 57, 58; as a superpower, 35; vs. United States, 36

United States: governmental defects, 204–207; gross national product, 57, 59; interest payments on foreign aid loans, 48; investment in research, 73; and legitimacy, 64; mental illness in, 77; occupational displacement, 74–75, 77; as overdeveloped society, 35–36; quality of citizenship, 10–11; Rush-Bagot Agreement with Canada, 65; self-government in, 119, 121, 122; as a superpower, 35; urbanization, 75–76; urban racial segregation, 45–46; vs. USSR, 36; *see also* government, U.S.

United States Information Agency, 206

university, 28, 63, 203; and conflict, 67; and government research, 344; and participatory democracy, 146–147, 148, 149

University of California (Berkeley), participatory democracy in, 147

University of Michigan, 65

urban vs. rural voting power, 258–259

urbanization: antiurbanization, 48; consumption expectations, 45, 75; epidemic violence, 44; in Europe, Japan, and U.S., 75–76; and the Negro, 47, 50–51; overurbanization, 43–44; and personal identity, 75, 76–77; in poor countries, 43; population densities, 41–42; racial segregation, 45–46; rich vs. poor nations, 47–48; and social disorder, 41, 42, 43, 44, 80

utopias, Marxist, 125–128, 136; pre-Marxist, 123–125

Veblen, Thorstein, 36, 177

vector-sum theory, of government, 184, 185–187

Vietnam War, 148, 149, 299, 302, 303, 306, 308, 310–311, 312, 313

village, and self-government, 9

violence, and power structure, 157; and urbanization, 44

wage labor, 101, 103, 104, 112, 114

Ward, Barbara, 58–59

ward government, 13

war industry: annual growth, 81; costs of, 79, 80, 81; and power elite, 159

War on Poverty, 143, 146

Watts (Los Angeles), 46, 49, 141; population density, 42, 45

wealth, 8, 9, 200; national, and the corporation, 120; national, imbalances of, 58–59

Weber, Max, 27, 29

Wheeler, Harvey, 41, 51 *n*

Wilde, Oscar, 128

Wilson, Bob, qt., 216

Wilson, Charles E., qt., 177

Wilson, Richard B., 359–362

Wilson, Woodrow, 223, 233, 234 *n,* 297, 303, 354; qt., 214, 222

Wint, Guy, 68 *n;* qt., 72

withering away, of state, 110–111, 112–113, 113–115

Wolff, Robert Paul, 184–190

women, communization of, 106

Wood, Robert C., 73–78

work, under socialism, 134–135

Young, Stephen, qt., 219

Zimmern, A. E., 56 *n;* qt., 53